The Israeli Economy, 1995–2017

This book describes and analyzes developments in the Israeli economy from 1995 to 2017. During this period, inflation was vanquished, the deficit in the balance of payments turned into a surplus, the public debt to GDP ratio sharply decreased, and unemployment declined to an historical low. Nevertheless, the economy still suffers from many maladies: the productivity level is among the lowest in the developed world, and inequality has generally been on the rise. In the face of these threats to future growth and social cohesiveness, the question arises: has the reliance on market forces gone too far, and has the government retreated from its traditional tasks, tasks the private sector cannot (or does not) perform.

AVI BEN-BASSAT is Professor Emeritus at the Department of Economics at the Hebrew University of Jerusalem. He specializes in macroeconomics and the Israeli economy. From 1987 to 1996 he was director of the Research Department, Bank of Israel; and from 1999 to 2001 he was director general of Israel's Ministry of Finance. During the years 2003–2004, he served as president of the Israeli Economic Association.

REUBEN GRONAU is Professor Emeritus at the Department of Economics at the Hebrew University of Jerusalem. He is currently a member of the Bank of Israel's Monetary Committee. He was awarded the Jacob Mincer Award for his lifetime contribution to the field of labor economics by the Society of Labor Economics in 2008 and the Mifal Hapais "Michael Landau Award" for research on the economy of Israel in 2005.

ASAF ZUSSMAN is an Associate Professor and the William Haber Chair in the Department of Economics at the Hebrew University of Jerusalem. From 2015 to 2020, he was the director of the Maurice Falk Institute for Economic Research in Israel. His work as an applied microeconomist focuses on two topics: discrimination and bias in market and nonmarket settings and economic aspects of conflict, terrorism, and counterterrorism.

The Israeli Economy, 1995–2017

Light and Shadow in a Market Economy

Edited by

AVI BEN-BASSAT
The Hebrew University of Jerusalem
REUBEN GRONAU
The Hebrew University of Jerusalem
ASAF ZUSSMAN
The Hebrew University of Jerusalem

CAMBRIDGE
UNIVERSITY PRESS

CAMBRIDGE
UNIVERSITY PRESS

University Printing House, Cambridge CB2 8BS, United Kingdom

One Liberty Plaza, 20th Floor, New York, NY 10006, USA

477 Williamstown Road, Port Melbourne, VIC 3207, Australia

314–321, 3rd Floor, Plot 3, Splendor Forum, Jasola District Centre,
New Delhi – 110025, India

79 Anson Road, #06–04/06, Singapore 079906

Cambridge University Press is part of the University of Cambridge.

It furthers the University's mission by disseminating knowledge in the pursuit of
education, learning, and research at the highest international levels of excellence.

www.cambridge.org
Information on this title: www.cambridge.org/9781108830461
DOI: 10.1017/9781108907620

First published 2021

A catalogue record for this publication is available from the British Library.

ISBN 978-1-108-83046-1 Hardback
ISBN 978-1-108-82085-1 Paperback

Contents

Figures

Tables

Contributors

Doron Avramov
The Interdisciplinary Center Herzliya – IDC

Victor Bahar
Bank Hapoalim

Avi Ben-Bassat
The Hebrew University of Jerusalem

Dan Ben-David
Shoresh Institution for Socioeconomic Research and Tel Aviv University

Gabi Bin Nun
Ben Gurion University of the Negev

Adi Brender
Bank of Israel

Momi Dahan
The Hebrew University of Jerusalem

Efrat Dressler
The Hebrew University of Jerusalem

Zvi Eckstein
Interdisciplinary Center Herzliya – IDC

Neil Gandal
Tel Aviv University

David Genesove
The Hebrew University of Jerusalem

Reuben Gronau
The Hebrew University of Jerusalem

Moshe Hazan
Tel Aviv University and CEPR

Nitsa (Kaliner) Kasir
The Haredi Institute for Public Affairs

Ayal Kimhi
Shoresh Institution for Socioeconomic Research and The Hebrew University of Jerusalem

Esteban F. Klor
The Hebrew University of Jerusalem

Konstantin Kosenko
Bank of Israel

Nadav Kunievsky
Tel Aviv University

Tali Larom
The Interdisciplinary Center Herzliya

Doron Lavee
Tel-Hai College and Pareto Group Ltd, Israel

Leonardo Leiderman
Tel Aviv University and Bank Hapoalim

Osnat Lifshitz
The Interdisciplinary Center Herzliya

Lior Metzker
The Hebrew University of Jerusalem

Gur Ofer
The Hebrew University of Jerusalem

Sigal Ribon
Bank of Israel

Stefania Roccas Gandal
Afeka Tel Aviv Academic College of Engineering

Eytan Sheshinski
The Hebrew University of Jerusalem and The Israel Democracy Institute

Avia Spivak
Ben Gurion University of the Negev

Michel Strawczynski
The Hebrew University of Jerusalem and Bank of Israel

Shay Tsur
Bank of Israel and Tel Aviv University

Eran Yashiv
Tel Aviv University

Asaf Zussman
The Hebrew University of Jerusalem

Preface

This book is the third in a series of edited volumes on the Israeli economy initiated by the Maurice Falk Institute for Economic Research in Israel. Each was first published in Hebrew and then in English. The first volume, *The Israeli Economy: Maturing Through Crises*, edited by Yoram Ben-Porath (1986), covered the years 1973–1984. Coming at the heels of the Yom Kippur War, this period was characterized by slow growth and accelerating inflation. The second volume, *The Israeli Economy, 1985–1998: From Government Intervention to Market Economics*, edited by Avi Ben-Bassat (2002), covered a period characterized by the conquest of hyperinflation, improved macroeconomic performance, major structural reforms, mass immigration from the former Soviet Union, and a shift of resources from the government to the public sector.

The third volume follows this tradition. It analyzes the evolution of the Israeli economy from the mid-1990s to the mid-2010s, a period in which the economy has gone through a dramatic transformation. A key element in the transformation has been Israel's continued shift toward a more market-oriented economy, including notably the meteoric rise of the high-tech sector. It is time to take stock of the implications of this change.

Work on the Hebrew language volume started in the summer of 2016. The English language volume is based on the Hebrew language one. However, the chapters went through a major rewriting in order to make them more concise and accessible to a foreign audience. The volume contains eighteen chapters and an introduction, written by us, the editors. In keeping with tradition, most chapters contain both a description of major developments in the relevant subject area and an analytical section, which provides an empirical investigation of specific questions. The introduction provides a bird's-eye view of the evolution of the economy over this twenty-year period, highlighting major accomplishments and challenges.

Completing this project would not have been possible without the help of many individuals. We are indebted to Ronit Ashkenazi, the administrator of the Falk Institute, who has devoted countless hours in order to keep this multi-year project moving forward. We also want to thank the reviewers of the various chapters – Aamer Abu-Qarn, Claude Berrebi, Kobi Braude, Alex Cukierman, Alon Eizenberg, Yoav Friedmann, Daniel Gottlieb, Niron Hashai, Zvi Hercowitz, Leo Leiderman, Rafi Melnick, Efraim Sadka, Michael Sarel, Analia Schlosser, Amir Shmueli, Michel Strawczynski, Yishay Yafeh, and Noam Zussman – as well as audiences in the conferences where preliminary versions of the books were presented. Their comments and suggestions greatly improved the book. For their constructive criticism, we thank two anonymous reviewers who have read the book proposal and sample chapters. We thank Elhanan Helpman for his support and advice. For generous financial support, we thank the Bank of Israel, Bank Leumi, and an anonymous donor. Finally, we thank Phil Good and Toby Ginsberg at Cambridge University Press for their support and guidance throughout the work on this volume.

Avi Ben-Bassat
Reuben Gronau
Asaf Zussman

1 | *Lights and Shadows in the Market Economy*

AVI BEN-BASSAT, REUBEN GRONAU, AND ASAF ZUSSMAN

1.1 Introduction

This is the third in a series of volumes discussing the various aspects of the development of Israeli economy over the last four decades. The first volume, *The Israeli Economy: Maturing Through Crises*, edited by Yoram Ben-Porath (1986), discussed the aftermath of the 1973 Yom Kippur War, the slowdown in growth, and the fast inflation. It covered the period from 1973 to 1984 and stopped just before the Stabilization Program brought the hyperinflation to a stop.[1] The second volume, *The Israeli Economy, 1985–1998: From Government Intervention to Market Economics*, edited by Avi Ben-Bassat (2002a), described the economic developments following the 1985 Stabilization Program and the great influx of immigrants from the former Soviet Union in the 1990s. It analyzed the structural reforms undertaken in the commodity market and in the financial markets to make the economy more competitive, the shift of resources from the government to the private sector, the acceleration in growth, the reduced inflation, the reduction of public debt, and the increased competitiveness of Israeli companies in the international market.

This volume brings the story up to date. Like its predecessors, it is a collection of articles written by leading scholars in their fields, describing the various aspects of the Israeli economy over the period 1995–2017.

The last two decades signaled the fulfillment of many of the hopes raised in the previous books: inflation was finally vanquished, the

---

[*] We thank Nathan Hemmendinger and Stav Mushkat for excellent research assistance.
[1] Ben-Porath's book was preceded by Patinkin (1960), who covered the first decade, and Halevi and Klinov (1968), who covered the period up to the mid-1960s.

deficit in the balance of payments turned into a surplus, the ratio between public debt and GDP declined to an acceptable level, Israel turned from a debtor vis-à-vis the rest of the world to a creditor, the labor force participation rate (specifically that of males), which had been on the decline, changed direction and has risen to international standards, and the unemployment rate has declined to a historical low. Still, the economy suffers from many of the maladies mentioned by Ben-Porath and Ben-Bassat: the productivity level in most industries is among the lowest in the developed world, and up to quite recently inequality among the various socio-economic groups has been on the rise.

In the face of this threat to future growth and social cohesiveness, the question arises: has not the reliance on market forces gone too far, and has not the government retreated from its traditional tasks, tasks the private sector cannot (or does not) perform.

1.2 The Background: Demography, the Geopolitical Situation, and the Global Economy

Throughout the first fifty years of its existence, Israel's economy has been shaped by demographic and political factors. From the day of its establishment, Israel has been a country of immigration. Over the period 1948–2017, Israel's population grew elevenfold, net migration contributing one-third of this growth.[2] The Jewish population (or more accurately, the non-Arab population) grew at about the same rate, constituting about 80 percent of the population both in 1948 and in 2017.[3] Net immigration has contributed over 40 percent of this growth.[4] As Ben-Porath (1986, p. 3) observes, "Immigration drove the growth of the Jewish economy sector of Mandatory Palestine and of Israel for the fifty years or so ending in the early 1970s." But Ben-Porath's conclusion was premature. After a lull in immigration in the 1980s, it resumed in the 1990s. The new wave, which followed the collapse of the Soviet Union, increased the population of Israel by almost one-fifth, and the process of absorption shaped the economy

---

[2] Gross immigration was even higher, exceeding net immigration by a quarter.

[3] The non-Arab population consists of Jews and non-Arab Christians. The non-Arab Christians are mostly (over 80 percent) immigrants.

[4] In contrast, the growth of the Arab population is almost exclusively due to natural growth.

throughout that decade.[5] Subsequent immigration, though far from negligible (contributing about 15 percent of population growth), played, perhaps for the first time in Israel's history, only a minor role in the process of economic growth.

The second factor that has played a major role in Israel's growth process over the years and seems to have lost some of its importance in the last decade is the geopolitical environment. Ben-Bassat, discussing the period following the peace accord with Egypt in 1979, noted the effect of the "peace dividend" on the economy: the gradual reduction in the defense budget, the access to new markets barred earlier by the Arab boycott, and a stream of new foreign investment. This trend strengthened following the peace accord with Jordan in 1994 and the agreements with the Palestinians in 1993 and 1995. Still, security tensions played an important role in the years 1995–2002, culminating in the Second Intifada and the economic crisis of 2001–2003. Surprisingly, the effect of security tensions on the economy in later years has been only minor. As shown by Klor and Zussman, in Chapter 6 of this volume, in spite of a minor war (the 2006 Second Lebanon War) and three extensive operations in the Gaza Strip in 2008/2009, 2012, and 2014, operations that were accompanied by massive rocket attacks, mostly targeting southern Israel, economic activity was hardly affected.

In contrast to the decline in the sensitivity of the economy to demographic and geopolitical changes (in particular toward the second part of this period), its vulnerability to the global economic environment increased (Figure 1.1). The integration in the global economy had its price: the bursting of the dot-com financial bubble in 2000 reinforced the destructive effect of the Second Intifada to push the economy into the worst crisis it had ever suffered – a recession that lasted for over three years, GDP per capita declining by more than 5 percent.

Globalization was also associated with the second crisis the economy went through during this period. The breakdown of trade, following the global financial crisis in 2008, caused a slowdown in economic growth. The slowdown in this case was relatively brief (the decline in GDP per capita lasting for only four quarters), but the decline in the

---

[5] More than 900,000 people immigrated to Israel from the former Soviet Union over the period 1990–2001.

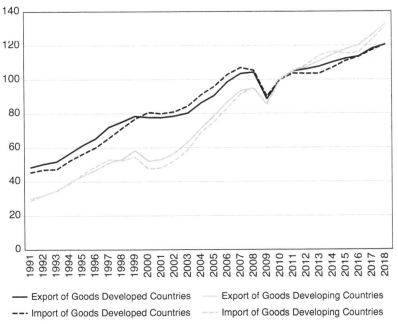

— Export of Goods Developed Countries   ···· Export of Goods Developing Countries

--- Import of Goods Developed Countries   ···· Import of Goods Developing Countries

Figure 1.1 World Trade Index, 1990–2017 (2010=100).
Sources: CPB Netherlands Bureau for Economic Policy Analysis, World Trade Monitor

growth rate of world trade slowed the growth of the Israeli economy throughout the following decade.[6]

1.3 Economic Policy

The last two decades have witnessed a continuation of the shrinkage of the public sector and the simultaneous growth of the private sector. The pace of this process, which started with the Stabilization Program, was, however, far from even. The share of the private sector in GDP, which was 69 percent in 1995, hardly changed for the next seven years (Figure 1.2). The private sector share resumed its growth following the change in fiscal policy in 2001–2003 – which was part of policy changes intended to pull the economy out of the recession – and in 2011 the share reached 74 percent. The 2003 decision to cut the public sector (referred to as the

---

[6] The average annual growth rate of world trade, which was 7 percent during the dozen years preceding the crisis, declined to 1.5 percent ever since.

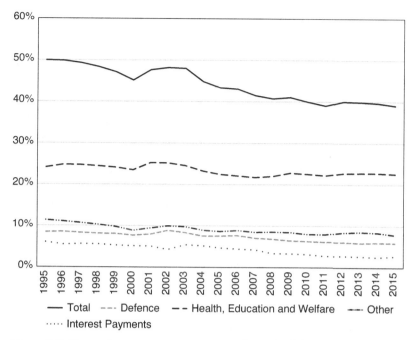

Figure 1.2 Share of government sector expenditures in GDP, 1995–2015 (%). Sources: Central Bureau of Statistics, General Government Sector Accounts 1995–2015, Publication No. 1672

"Fat Man" in a famous slogan coined by the then minister of finance, Benjamin Netanyahu) in favor of the private sector (the "Thin Man") was manifested over the period 2002–2011 both in a decline in public sector expenditures, from about 50 to 39 percent of GDP, and in a decline in public consumption, from 27 to 22 percent of GDP.[7] This trend ended in

[7] The Central Bureau of Statistics, "Public Sector Accounts 1995–2015," Publication #1672 (published 3.30.2017). The public sector consists of the central government, the local authorities, and the national institutions (the institutions established by the Zionist movement prior to 1948). The expenditures of this sector consist of public consumption, transfer payments, and public investment. The Fat Man–Thin Man slogan called for strengthening the Thin Man (the private sector) who carries on his back the Fat Man (the public sector). The slogan seems to have overlooked the large share of transfer payments in public expenditures (including the interest on the public debt). Ironically, in terms of employment, the Thin Man accounts for 70 percent while the Fat Man accounts for only 30 percent. Government fiscal policy is discussed by Adi Brender in Chapter 2 of this volume.

2011, following mass demonstrations that protested the high cost of living and housing prices, and called, in the name of "Social Justice," for a more socially balanced economic policy.

None of the public expenditure items escaped the cut: the share of defense expenditures declined from 8 percent of GDP in 1995 to 6 percent in 2015; the decline in public debt, accompanied by the fall in global interest rates following the financial crisis, reduced government interest payments from 6 percent to 3 percent of GDP; and the share of government social expenditures (education, health, and welfare) declined from 24 percent to 22.5 percent.[8] Government investment in physical capital suffered even sharper cuts, its share in GDP falling from 3.8 percent to 1.4 percent. The reduction in government investment in the country's infrastructure is particularly troubling, since it may have affected the overall level of investment – the share of private investment in GDP declining over the period from one-quarter to one-fifth. As will be shown, this decline in investment (both in human and in physical capital) had long-range implications for the growth of productivity and output during the period and will likely continue to influence these variables in years to come.

The changes in government expenditures were accompanied by changes in the government's revenue and its composition: taxes, which constituted 35 percent of GDP in the year 2000, were cut to 31 percent in 2013. Israel, which ranked above average among the OECD countries in terms of its tax burden early in the period, was below average by its end. The cut in taxes was accompanied by a sharp change in their composition: while direct taxes were sharply reduced following the 2001–2003 crisis, indirect taxes increased over the period, their share in total taxation increasing from one-third in 2000 to 40 percent in 2015. The reduction in the progressiveness of taxation, accompanied by the cut in welfare allowances, had far-reaching implications for inequality in the net income of Israeli households.

The declared motive for the tax cut was speeding up economic growth. However, as the academic literature shows, the link between the tax burden and economic growth is quite tenuous. Strawczynski, in his chapter on taxation in this book, argues that, with the exception of corporate tax, the tax cut did not contribute to economic growth. If

---

[8] Real GDP doubled over the period, so the only expenditure item that declined in absolute terms was interest payments.

there was an effect, it was indirect. According to Strawczynski's analysis, tax cuts preceded expenditure cuts throughout the period and, in this way, contributed (for good or ill) to the growth of the private sector.

The impact of the tax cut on public expenditures, following the 2001–2003 crisis, reflects the lesson learned by finance ministers that a large budget deficit impairs government credibility and may adversely affect Israel's international credit rating. Maintaining a low budget deficit has become an almost permanent feature of the government's economic policy since that crisis, and explains, at least in part, why the Israeli economy was barely affected by the 2008 global financial crisis.

The conservative budget policy had an immediate impact on the ratio between public debt and GDP and on its composition. In contrast to most developed economies, which saw an increase in their public debt following the global financial crisis, in Israel the debt/GDP ratio declined from 100 percent in 1995 to 60 percent in 2015 (Figure 1.3).

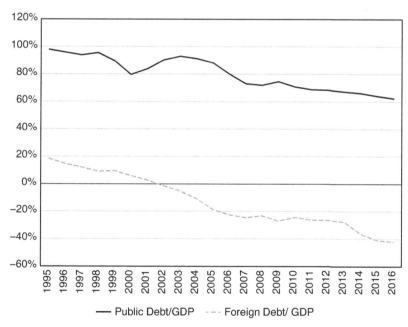

Figure 1.3 Debt to GDP ratio and share of foreign debt in GDP, 1995–2016. Sources: Central Bureau of Statistics, General Government Sector Accounts 1995–2015, Publication No. 1672

The decline was the result of three factors: the contraction of the public sector, the increased budgetary discipline, and a series of redefinitions of the national accounts.[9]

This achievement is even more noteworthy given the changes in the composition of debt: whereas early in the period, external debt constituted about a quarter of public debt, this share was cut to one-eighth in 2015. The changes in Israel's balance of payments and public debt turned the country from a debtor into a creditor. Whereas in 1995 Israel's foreign obligations exceeded its foreign assets by 17 percent of GDP, in 2015 foreign assets exceeded foreign obligations by 44 percent of GDP.

No less important for the preservation of Israel's credibility in the world financial markets was the conduct of its monetary policy. Though the Stabilization Program brought hyperinflation to an abrupt stop, it did not bring price stability. The average annual rate of inflation in the years 1990–1995 was still almost 13 percent (Figure 1.4). This rate was cut by half over the next five years and inflation even seemed to have disappeared in the years 2000–2001. But then came an outburst of inflation in 2002, with prices rising at a rate of over 5 percent, showing that inflationary forces have not been vanquished. It required a sharp rise of the monetary interest rate, and a sharp decline in demand associated with the 2002 crisis, to break the inflationary inertia and establish price stability within the government's boundaries of the inflation target. This stability has been preserved ever since.

Monetary policy faced new challenges following the global financial crisis. The economy's resilience, and specifically the stability of its financial sector, minimized the economic damage of the crisis aftershocks. Monetary policy reacted to the crisis in the financial markets by a sharp reduction in the monetary interest rate from 4.25 percent in September 2008 to 0.5 percent in April of the following year. Since then monetary policy has tried to straddle the chasm between the expansive monetary policies adopted by the USA, the European Union, and Japan and the relatively stable growth of the Israeli economy. The Bank of Israel lowered its interest rate almost to zero, intervened aggressively in the foreign exchange market to

---

[9] According to Brender, who discusses this issue in Chapter 2 of this volume, the OECD redefinition of the contribution of high-tech to GDP explains about 30 percent of the decline, while the faster rate of growth of GDP compared to that of the public debt explains only 15 percent.

Figure 1.4 Annual inflation rate, 1990–2016 (%).
Sources: Central Bureau of Statistics, Statistical Abstract of Israel no. 68, 2017, table 13.1

prevent an excessive appreciation of the shekel, and, for the first time in its history, had to combat negative inflation in a period of full employment in the years 2015–2016.[10]

1.4 Structural Reforms

1.4.1 Financial Reforms

The transformation from an economy based on government intervention to a market-based economy would not have been possible had it not been for a series of reforms in the input and goods markets that contributed to the competitiveness and the efficiency of the private sector.

In the first four decades of Israel's existence, the government dominated the capital market using a wide array of tools to achieve its targets: administrative barriers, exceptionally high liquidity requirements,

[10] Israel's monetary policy over the period is discussed by Ribon in Chapter 4 of this volume.

credit quotas, restrictions on international capital flows, and discriminatory tax and subsidy rates, in effect "nationalizing" the market. A long list of reforms was required to liberalize capital flows (Ben-Bassat, 1990, 2002b): the permission to issue corporate bonds, the suspension of the requirement imposed on the pension funds to invest in government bonds, the end of government-allocated directed credit, and the removal of all restrictions on international capital flows. As Table 1.1 shows, the reforms brought dramatic changes to almost every aspect of the capital market. Yet the financial system (banks, insurance companies, and long-term investment institutions) was still characterized by high concentration and little competition. Specifically, despite of the potential conflict of interest that existed between their various activities, the banks were involved in almost every aspect of the financial system. The government's attempts to break this oligopolistic structure have continued throughout the last two decades but have met with only limited success.

The government was more successful in reforming the main saving channel – the pension market.[11] The roots of this reform had already been planted in 1995, when the government blocked the entrance to the existing pension funds, which had operated on the basis of "defined benefits" and suffered from growing actuarial deficits. New entrants were referred to new funds that were required to operate on the basis of "defined contribution." A similar arrangement was applied in 2001 to new government employees, who were not entitled, as their predecessors had been, to a budgetary pension plan but were referred, instead, to the new "defined-contribution" funds. Finally, in 2008, the government passed the Mandatory Pension Law, which required all employers to insure their employees in a comprehensive pension plan.[12]

The various reforms significantly expanded pension coverage and increased the share of long-term savings in total savings and the share of pension assets in total financial assets. But the reforms changed not merely the size of the pension market, but also its structure. In 2003 the

---

[11] The pension market reforms are discussed in detail by Gronau and Spivak in Chapter 8 of this volume.

[12] The law was expanded in 2017 to also include the self-employed. The effect of this law is controversial. Brender (2010) argues that the new arrangements affected mainly the employees of small firms, whose employers often did not provide a pension plan. Many of these workers are low paid, and the pension requirement reduced their income at an age where they most need it.

Table 1.1 *Government involvement in the financial market, selected indicators, 1985–2016 (%)*

	1985	1987	1995	2000	2016
Reserve ratio on unindexed local currency deposits[1]	50	38	6	6	6
Provident funds' compulsory investment in government bonds	92	78	50	40	0
Pension funds' compulsory investment in government bonds	92	92	70	70	30
Share of government directed credit out of total bank credit to the public[2]	60	50	5.1	2.3	0.9
Share of government directed credit out of total mortgage credit	65	53	33	32.7	3.2
Share of private bonds in total credit to businesses[3]	4.2[4]	7.4[4]	6.2	4.3	31.5
Overdraft interest rate minus the Bank of Israel interest rate[5]	79.2	34.6	7.1	6.1	6.9
Interest rate differential between long-term credit to government and mortgages[6]	5.6	6.2	1.1	1.1	2.5
Investment abroad + investment from abroad (% of GDP)	0.4	0.6	3	15.8	13.6

Sources: Central Bureau of Statistics and Bank of Israel
Notes:
[1] Current account and deposits of up to six days.
[2] Excluding housing.
[3] Credit to businesses from the banking system, institutional intermediaries, and households.
[4] In these years the share relates only to marketable bonds.
[5] In annual nominal terms.
[6] Indexed loans, credit to government for nine years, mortgages for between five and ten years.

government, as part of a policy package aimed at pulling the economy out of the crisis, took over from the trade unions the running of the old defined-benefit funds and closed them to new membership. New members were referred to new funds that were based on the "defined-contribution" principle and were, eventually, sold to institutional investors (mostly insurance companies). The sale of the new pension funds and the sale of the provident funds by the banks (as part of the Bachar Reform in 2005) changed the shape of the industry.[13] The gradual reduction in government support of the pension funds, in the form of subsidized bonds, forced them to compete in the open market, both in terms of their annual return and in terms of their fees. Despite the reduction in government support and the fluctuations in the capital market, the funds were able to achieve an average annual real rate of return of over 5 percent over the period 2001–2015. It is too early to determine how successful were the reforms in preserving the standard of living of the retirees, but current household expenditure surveys do not indicate that households headed by old people (seventy and older) suffer from a lower standard of living than younger families.

The sale of the pension and provident funds to institutional investors increased competition in the saving market and, at the same time, made the credit market more competitive (Figure 1.5). However, it was only the large business entities (those that could issue bonds) that benefited from the better terms. The markets for credit for small businesses and households remained uncompetitive.[14] To address this problem, two policies where adopted. First, the Bank of Israel set up the Credit Rating Register (CRR), which forces banks and non-bank institutions to share the credit-record information of their clients.[15] Second, the government forced Israel's two leading banks to sell the credit card companies they owned.[16]

Finally, in 2008, after eight years of deliberations and partial solutions, the government imposed a 25 percent tax on real capital gains, interest and dividends. This equalized the tax rate on all capital income sources and facilitated a reduction in taxes on wage income.

---

[13] The Bachar Reform is discussed by Avramov, Dressler, and Metzker in Chapter 7, this volume.

[14] Small corporations cannot issue bonds and, thus, have no access to the institutional investors' credit.

[15] The CRR became operational in 2019.

[16] The sale followed recommendations of a government committee (the Strum Committee) established to consider ways to encourage competition in these markets. Among its other recommendations were the reduction of capital requirements of new banks, government support for the financing of the new banks' computer services, and the establishment of a formal deposit insurance system.

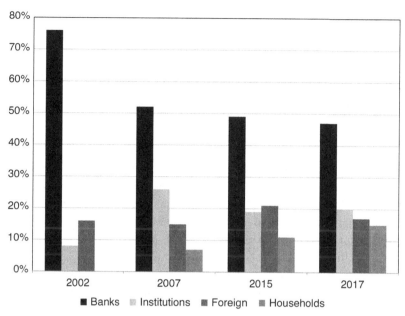

Figure 1.5 Credit to the business sector, by source, 2002–2017 (%).
Sources: Bank of Israel

1.4.2 Reforms in the Markets for Goods and Services

The period following the 1985 Stabilization Program was character-ized by major reforms in the markets for goods and services, a primary aim of which was to expose these markets to foreign competition. A cornerstone of this policy was agreements with the United States and the European Union which called for mutual tariff reductions. In the early 1990s, other steps were taken to liberalize foreign trade: discriminatory exchange rate and tax policies were eliminated and exposure to imports from new markets was increased. The liberaliza-tion resulted in an increase in the efficiency of the manufacturing industries and a shift of labor from industries in which Israel did not have comparative advantage (e.g., furniture, rubber, plastics) to indus-tries in which it did (Gabay and Robb, 2002).

Liberalization of foreign trade did, however, have its limits: a host of nontariff barriers helped maintain the semi-monopolistic power of large importers and some markets continued to be protected, a notable example being the market for agricultural goods. During the last two decades, the agricultural lobby prevented any reduction in tariffs on agricultural products, and only the mass demonstrations in 2011, which protested the high cost of living, brought about some minor changes in policy. The effects of the differential rates of liberalization are evident in the data: during the period 1997–2015, whereas the price of clothing, furniture, and home equipment (the imports of which had been liberalized) declined 22 percent, the price of food increased by 76 percent, twice the rate of increase in the Food and Agriculture Organization of the United Nations (FAO) world food price index (36 percent).

Still, the most protected sector over the whole period was the government-owned business enterprises, most notably the infrastructure monopolies in the fields of electricity, communications, water supply, public transportation, ports and airports, and the refinery industry. The low efficiency of these companies affected the economy as a whole. Following the Stabilization Program, there were few attempts to open these industries to competition, but the title of the chapter which analyzed these attempts in the previous volume on the development of the Israeli economy – "Structural Changes in the Israeli Public Utilities: The Reform that Never Was" (Gronau, 2002) – captures the essence of the story. It sums up the failure of the attempts to break up the Israel Electric Corporation (the electricity monopoly); to make the two seaports (Haifa and Ashdod) compete with each other; to privatize the two oil refineries and sell them to separate owners; and to break the monopoly power of the two major bus companies, Egged and Dan. The only case where reform was successful was the communications market, where a series of determined government ministers have managed to bring about the passing of a law that forced the communications monopoly (Bezeq) to separate its activities in the various sub-markets (domestic, international, cellular, and the sale of equipment). Bezeq preserved its monopoly power in the wired domestic network, but new entrants were allowed into the other markets. The beneficiaries of the monopoly power of the public utilities were their employees, who enjoyed excessive wages. The companies' low efficiency and the government's policy of keeping prices low resulted in them being the only "monopolies" with low (and sometimes even negative) rate of return.[17]

---

[17] The only company that exhibited adequate rates of return, Bezeq, was prevented by its employee' union from declaring dividends

The employees' unions took advantage of their political influence in the two major parties (Likud and Labor) and used the threat of shutting down essential services to block any attempt of reforms that would result in a reduction in the number of employees or a slowdown in the rate of increase of wages. On the other hand, the unions were unable to block the introduction of a new cost-based system of rate setting. The new rates reduced the cross-subsidization among the various services (e.g., international phone rates and local rates) and among various users, introduced an 'efficiency factor' in the rates of most services, and set up a multi-period rate adjustment system. Basing the rate systems on "normative" (i.e., objective) costs, the new regime resulted in some cases (e.g., the communications market) in the lowering of the relative price of the service and in other cases isolated consumers from the inefficiency of production. The last two decades saw little change in this pattern, with one modification: though the government has been unsuccessful in implementing reforms in its own monopolies, it was successful in industries that had been privatized. Thus, the reforms in electricity and the ports are still at the planning stage, but reforms have been introduced in bus transportation, air transport, and the communications industry. The bus duopoly lost half its market, the "Open Sky" agreement tripled the rate of growth of outgoing tourism, and the rates of mobile phones (the largest of the communication industry's subsectors) were slashed by more than one-half, and following the introduction of wholesalers in the internet market, internet rates were reduced.

Bezeq was able, however, to block any reform in the fixed-line phone market. Preventing the introduction of a wholesale market and blocking the adjustment of retail rates since 2008 has made this segment of the market the most lucrative part of the monopoly's business.[18] Thus, although in 2016 the number of its fixed-line subscribers was only one-quarter of the total number of subscribers of the mobile industry, Bezeq's fixed lines' profit exceeded the total profit of the mobile industry by 60 percent.

---

[18] According to the rate setting system established in 1989, Bezeq's phone rates have been reevaluated every four to five years, the rates being readjusted to eliminate any excess profit (Gronau, 2002). In this fashion rates were reexamined three times (in 1993, 1999, and 2003), with rate cuts ranging from 5.5 to 10.5 percent.

Because of its size and political situation, Israel is ultimately a small island economy. The production of public utility services is characterized by returns to scale and network economics. Given the market size, oligopoly becomes the natural form of competition. Containing oligopolistic market power calls for all the sophistication and political stamina the regulator can muster.

1.4.3 The Reform to Reduce Economy-Wide Concentration

The small island character of the Israeli economy makes concentration not merely an industry feature but an economy-wide characteristic. Conglomerates are not new to the Israeli scene. Throughout the first five decades of its existence, large conglomerates operated in the economy – the most notable one owned by the national trade union (the Histadrut). The phenomenon became a focus of public debate toward the end of the 2000s, when there was increased concern that economy-wide concentration undermines competition and efficiency. It was felt that the advantages of the economy-wide conglomerates in the dispersion of risk and in their access to low-cost capital are outweighed by the increased risk to the economy of having a small number of owners affecting macroeconomic developments and by their power to curtail competition (in particular if they also wield political power). These problems were amplified by the pyramid structure of the conglomerates' ownership, which allowed "tycoons," owning relatively little capital, to govern entire "empires" through their ownership of a relatively small company at the top of the pyramid. These problems become particularly severe when the conglomerate includes a financial institution. The ownership of a financial institution (e.g., a leading bank, or an insurance company) raises the fear of preferential treatment in the allocation of credit, the access to inside information on competitors, and discriminatory allocation of credit to block entry into industries in which the conglomerate has a stake.

Economy-wide concentration was already of concern to policymakers twenty years ago. At the time, policymakers were worried about the excessive power of the two largest banks, who owned large amounts of the equity of firms. These fears led, in 1995, to the establishment of the Brodet Committee, which recommended that no banking firm will control a non-banking firm and that the largest bank had to divest its equity stakes in at least one of the two powerful industrial conglomerates which it controlled (Blass and Yosha, 2002). When this recommendation turned into law a year later, the banks divested themselves of most of their equity holdings.[19] The sale of this equity, as well as the sale of the provident funds (following the Bachar Reform), may have solved the problem of the banks' conflict of interest but, paradoxically, served as the stepping stone for the formation of the newly founded conglomerates. A second group of conglomerates was created by the dismantling of the national trade union's conglomerate, and a third group resulted from a change in ownership of existing conglomerates.

The law was successful in reducing the level of economy-wide concentration, but this trend reversed as new business groups came into being. What made the establishment of the new conglomerates especially worrisome was the excessive leverage of their financial structure, and their increased political clout due to their ownership of leading media outlets (e.g., newspapers, TV stations).

According to a study by Kosenko and Yafeh (2010), the largest ten groups accounted for about one-third of the equity registered on the Israeli Stock Market, one of the highest rates among Western economies. According to Kosenko's estimate (in Chapter 9, this volume), the twenty largest business groups in Israel constituted 70 percent of the market value of public corporations.

The 2011 mass demonstrations brought to the fore the issue of the large conglomerates and their effect on competition and the cost of living (especially food prices).[20] The demonstrations put pressure on the Concentration Committee, which was established a year earlier, to finish its deliberations. The committee recommended to restrict the number of levels in the pyramidal structure of business groups to two, to disallow the control of real (i.e., nonfinancial) companies by large financial institutions, and to include considerations of economy-wide concentration in the government's privatization decisions. The Law for Promotion of Competition and Reduction of Concentration was passed in December 2013, but it is too early to tell what its effects will be.[21]

---

[19] It should be mentioned that at the time the government was, as a result of the 1983 banking crisis and its aftermath, the dominant shareholder of most of the Israeli banks.

[20] The business groups owned at the time the largest food chains in Israel, and the increase in markups was blamed, among other factors, for the high cost of food.

[21] High leverage and turmoil in the financial markets resulted in the collapse (or change of ownership) of five out of the fourteen leading business groups

1.5 Economic Growth: Employment, Capital, and Productivity

The main beneficiaries of the shrinkage of the public sector and the growth of the private sector were private consumption and exports of goods and services. Both increased as a share of GDP, but the latter did so much faster: while the share of private consumption increased from 52 to 56 percent, the share of exports increased from 24 to 31 percent (Figure 1.6). Exports benefited from the continued trend of globalization and reduction in trade barriers, and its rate of growth was strongly tied to the rate of growth of world trade. It was 10 percent per year in the early part of the period, slowed down to 7 percent following the dot-com crisis, and went down to 2 percent after the global financial crisis. Unsurprisingly, the slowdown in exports was the main cause of the slowdown of Israel's overall rate growth following the global crisis.

Exports changed not only in terms of volume but also in terms of composition. For the first time in its history, Israel took advantage of its abundant stock of human capital and its scientific infrastructure and turned it into an engine of growth. The share of high-tech in industrial exports increased from 37 percent in 1995 to 50 percent in 2015, while the share in industrial exports of traditional manufacturing industries declined from 39 to 19 percent (Figure 1.7). An even more dramatic shift occurred in the advanced services sectors (information and communications services and research and development services), whose share in total exports increased from zero in 1995, to almost half of exports in 2015.[22]

The slowdown in investment resulted in a reduction in the share of imports in GDP. Partly as a result of this, since 2003 Israel consistently has a surplus in the current account of the balance of payments.[23] The reversal in the current account from a deficit to a surplus and the growing inflows of foreign capital (both foreign direct investment and investment in financial assets) has had a dramatic influence on the value of the Israeli currency.

---

mentioned in the 2010 list prepared by Kosenko and Yafeh. Three additional leading groups were forced to undertake extensive capital restructuring.

[22] The shift in the structure of industry to high-tech sectors had already begun in the early 1990s, following cuts in the defense industries and the growth in the stock of human capital that resulted from the massive immigration wave from the former Soviet Union. These changes are discussed in Justman's chapter in Ben-Bassat (2002) and in Gandal, Roccas Gandal, and Kunievsky, Chapter 17, this volume.

[23] The developments in Israel's balance of payments are discussed by Leiderman and Bahar in Chapter 5 of this volume.

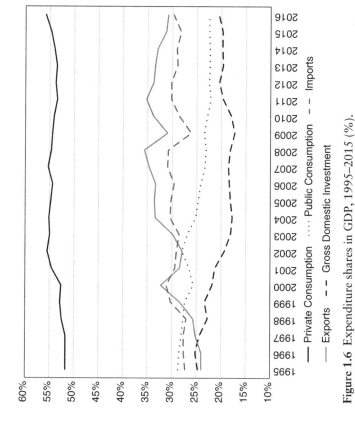

Figure 1.6 Expenditure shares in GDP, 1995–2015 (%).

Sources: Central Bureau of Statistics, Statistical Abstract of Israel no. 68, 2017, table 14.2

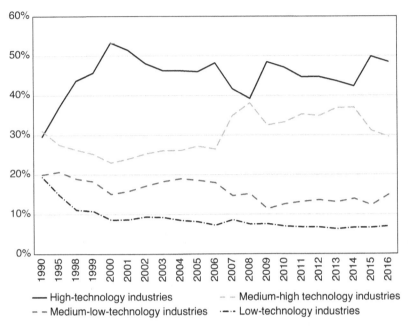

Figure 1.7 Composition of industrial exports, 1990–2016 (%).
Sources: Central Bureau of Statistics, Statistical Abstract of Israel no. 55, 2004 (table 16.7) and no. 68, 2017 (table 16.11)

The shekel, which had weakened in nominal terms against other major currencies since Israel's establishment, reversed its trend, and since 2005 the currency has been appreciating in nominal terms. The appreciation of the shekel has posed new challenges to monetary policymaking and was one of the main factors responsible for the low rates of inflation since 2013.[24]

All in all, it seems that the last two decades have been a period of almost unprecedented economic prosperity: inflation has been tamed, the perennial deficit in the current account has disappeared, the debt to GDP ratio has been reduced, Israel has turned from being a debtor vis-à-vis the rest of the world to being a creditor, and growth has become export-oriented. Naturally, we would have expected that these developments would manifest themselves in growth figures. And, indeed, the growth rate of GDP during 1995–2015 puts Israel in eighth place

---

[24] See Chapter 4 by Ribon, this volume. It is important to emphasize that, in real terms, the shekel has been appreciating since the late 1980s.

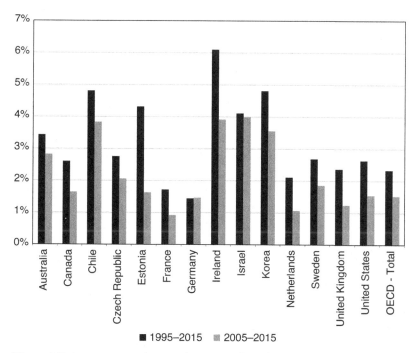

Figure 1.8 Average growth rate of output, selected countries, 1995–2015 and 2005–2015 (%).
Source: OECD

among the thirty-six members of the OECD (Figure 1.8). Thanks to exports, the rate of economic growth over this period, 4.1 percent, was faster than the rate of growth of potential output (3–3.5 percent) and much faster than the average rate of growth among OECD countries (2.3 percent).[25] This achievement has been even more notable in 2005–2015, the decade of the great recession, in which the rate of growth of output in Israel (4.0 percent), had hardly an equal among OECD countries.[26]

---

[25] The rate of growth of potential output is determined by the rates of growth of inputs (labor and capital), given the current structure of expenditures. Since the productivity of inputs is not uniform (it is higher in the production for exports than in the production for domestic uses), the share of exports in production has a large influence on the rate of growth of output.

[26] Turkey, the only OECD country with a higher growth rate during this decade, saw a marked slowdown in growth in later years.

Nevertheless, and without belittling these accomplishments, the ultimate test of an economy and an economic regime is that of the growth of per capita income. After all, it is this measure, and the rate of growth of per capita income in terms of purchasing power parity (PPP), in particular, that reflects the improvement in households' material well-being. Surprisingly, according to these criteria, the Israel's achievements in the last two decades were less than spectacular: although the rate of growth of per capita income (1.67 percent) was faster than the corresponding rate during the "lost decade" of 1973–1984 (1.08 percent), it was much slower than the rate of growth in the post-Stabilization Program period of 1984–1995 (2.39 percent). The rate of growth of per capita income in the last two decades places Israel only close to the median of the OECD countries, and so does its rate of growth in PPP terms (Figure 1.9). Not only did its ranking among OECD countries in terms of income per capita not improve, but when it is measured in PPP terms, it even deteriorated.[27] Despite the global financial crisis, which affected almost all developed countries, and the improvement in most of Israel's economic parameters (inflation, debt, balance of payment, etc.), the narrowing of the gap in standard of living between Israel and the United States and most of the European countries has been minuscule.

The difference between Israel's standing in terms of output growth and its standing in terms of the growth of per capita income lies, of course, in its population growth. Israel has been for years one of the leaders among developed countries in this parameter. Its average annual rate of population growth (2.1%) was 3.6 times higher than the OECD average. As a result, whereas the OECD population has increased over the last two decades by one-eighth, Israel's population grew by more than one half.

Israel's poor performance in terms of GDP per capita is particularly striking given its employment record. Whereas Israel's male labor force participation was almost ten percentage points below that of the OECD average in the early 2000s, by the end of the period it equaled the OECD average (Figure 1.10). This increase encompassed all population groups, Jews and Arabs, ultra-Orthodox and non-orthodox, and

---

[27] Israel's performance stands in sharp contrast to that of Ireland. Ireland's PPP-adjusted per capita income was lower than Israel's in 1995 but was almost double that of Israel in 2015.

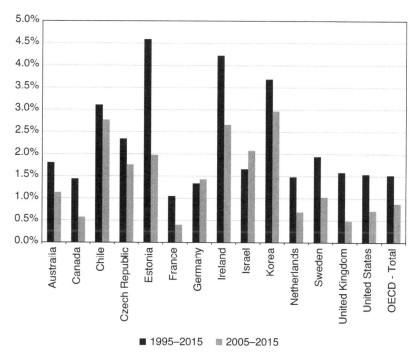

Figure 1.9 Average growth rate of PPP-adjusted per-capita output, selected countries, 1995–2015 and 2005–2015 (%).
Source: OECD

affected especially the elderly and those with low levels of education. Similarly, women's labor force participation rate, which already exceeded the OECD average at the beginning of the period, continued its rise.

The increased participation of men with little experience (and low levels of education and skills) in the labor force naturally had an adverse effect on productivity. However, the low level of productivity and its slow growth relative to other developing countries are not new phenomena. Until 1973 Israel was one of the fastest-growing countries, both in terms of per capita income and in terms of total GDP. The slowdown in growth after the Yom Kippur War was one of the main topics analyzed in Ben-Porath's book, and it remained an important issue in Ben-Bassat's book. In both volumes, it was found that a key factor behind the slowdown was the decline in productivity growth. The authors of the relevant chapters in the two books – Metzer (1986)

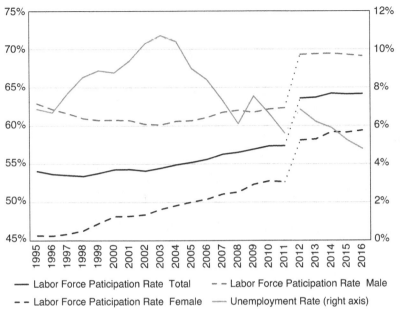

Figure 1.10 Labor force participation rate and unemployment rate, 1995–2016 (%).
Source: Central Bureau of Statistics, Labor Force Surveys

and Hercowitz (2002) – tried hard to uncover the causes of the productivity reversal. Metzer tied it to the underutilization of capital, because of inflation and the government's wasteful credit policy. Hercowitz explained the slowdown in productivity in the early 1990s as the outcome of a lag following the adoption of new technologies and equipment as part of the absorption process of the Russian immigration wave. Unfortunately, productivity has not rebounded since 1995.

In Chapter 11 (this volume), Hazan and Tsur compare levels of output per worker in Israel and in six reference countries of similar size (Austria, Denmark, Finland, Ireland, the Netherlands, and Sweden). They find that productivity in the reference states is almost 50 percent higher than in Israel. Investigating the sources of this difference, they find that it cannot be attributed to differences in the industrial structure (i.e., Israel's higher share of service industries) but rather that it is almost exclusively explained by differences in levels of physical capital inputs per employee, which are twice as high in the reference countries than in Israel. At first glance, this result is not surprising.

After all, the many years of low investment (including low rates of government investment) in Israel should have resulted in low levels of physical capital inputs per employee. Nevertheless, one could have expected that the low levels of physical inputs should have been compensated by high levels of human capital inputs per employee. After all, Israel's labor force is known to have the highest levels of formal education in the Western world!

The authors argue, however, that relying on data on formal education (i.e., the number of years of schooling) as a measure of human capital is misleading: surveys taken in the mid-2010s examining workers' skills (the PIAAC – Programme for the International Assessment of Adult Competencies – survey) show that the skill level of Israeli workers is significantly lower than that of workers in the reference countries.[28] Adjusting for these findings, Israel's "true" human-capital per-worker input is 8 to 25 percent lower than that of the reference group, reinforcing the effect of the low levels of physical capital inputs.

As mentioned above, the "productivity gap" between Israel and the OECD countries is certainly not new. Still, the investment in vocational training, job placement and on-the-job training is not only low, but even declining.[29] The Israeli government plays a major role in this trend. Its reduced involvement in these programs is only one manifestation of its declining role in the investment in human and physical infrastructure. According to Hazan and Tsur, raising the skills of the Israeli worker to the average level of skills in the reference states would narrow the output-per-worker gap from 30 to 18 percent, not counting its beneficial effect on the productivity of physical capital.

The key to raising the standard of living in Israel is, therefore, investment – in both physical and human capital. The government plays a major role in both. Israel has a much lower capital-output ratio than its reference group. This holds for the private sector capital-output ratio but is even more pronounced when it comes to the public one. The Israeli government did very little in the last two decades to

---

[28] The results for literacy and numeracy in Israel are one standard deviation lower than the average in the reference countries.

[29] According to OECD data, public spending on active labor market programs accounted for only 0.7 percent of Israel's GDP in 2015, a much lower share than a decade earlier (1 percent in 2005). The share is also much lower than in the reference group.

close this gap. Government investment in infrastructure declined during the 2000s and recovered only in the last few years, placing Israel close to the bottom of the list of developed countries in terms of the public capital-output ratio (27 percent).[30]

There is no better illustration of the adverse effects of low public investment on productivity than the investment in road infrastructure.[31] In the last two decades, investment in roads accounted, on average, for 0.7 percent of GDP. During this period, road area has increased by two-thirds (urban road area increasing by only a quarter). However, while early in the period the investment matched the growth in traffic, in the last decade it lagged behind (traffic per road surface increasing by 40 percent). Congestion, which was already a major problem in 1995 (Gronau, 1997), turned into one of the economy's most serious problems in the last decade. The cut in sales tax, the appreciation of the shekel, and the shift to more fuel-efficient car models reduced the costs associated with the use of private vehicles. Given the low initial rate of vehicle ownership, the rise in living standards and in labor force participation rates led to a 2.3- fold increase in private vehicle ownership and traffic.[32] According to the OECD report, congestion in Israel (defined as the number of vehicles per kilometer of road) is 3.5 times the OECD average. The Israeli Ministry of Finance has estimated that the annual economic costs of congestion are 35 billion shekels (about 3 percent of GDP). In spite of the millions of hours wasted daily, very little has been done to tackle this problem. The Ministry of Transport and Road Safety has for years blocked any attempt to deter the usage of private cars through congestion pricing or increased parking fees, and at the same time has done relatively little to advance public transport in the major urban centers.

The low level of investment in the last decade cannot be blamed on the level of savings. Though early in the period (1995–1999), negative public savings and the shortage of private savings necessitated foreign capital inflows to finance investment, things turned around in the early 2000s (Figure 1.11). The decline in investment and in the government budget deficit turned the deficit in the current account into

---

[30] OECD (2018).   [31] The discussion here in based on Friedmann (2018).

[32] In 1995, 45 percent of employed persons reported that they work in a different locality than the one they reside in. Two decades later this share increased to 55 percent.

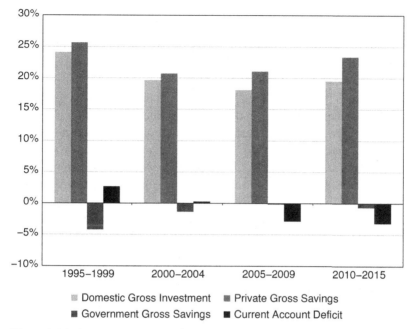

Figure 1.11 Gross investment and savings, 1995–2015 (% of output)
Sources: Central Bureau of Statistics, Statistical Abstract of Israel (table 29).

a surplus, which has continued to grow in the last five years despite the recovery in investment.[33]

Although there is no research evidence on this issue, it seems that one of the factors that contributed to the increase in household savings was the adoption of the mandatory pension law in 2008. And, indeed, since 2011 net deposits in pension savings have increased considerably, and as a result their share in overall net savings almost doubled (an increase from one-sixth to almost one-third) and so did their share in GDP (an increase from 2 to 4 percent). The liberalization of international capital flows and the foreign exchange market, and the equalization of the tax rates on foreign and domestic investment (introduced in 2003) contributed significantly to the diversification of the public's portfolio, and to the increase in the share of foreign assets.

---

[33] Government savings are defined as government revenue less government spending (public consumption and transfer payments).

From the social perspective, more worrisome than the low investment in physical capital is the low investment in human capital.
Though Israel ranks close to the top of the developed countries in
terms of human capital per worker, in their chapter on education in
this volume (Chapter 14) Ben-David and Kimhi argue that this position
is threatened by the decline in the share of resources devoted to education. One manifestation of the cut in public expenditures was the
decline in the share of government expenditures on education from
7.6 to 6.2 percent of GDP during 1995–2007, and though the government reversed this trend in 2008, the increase was only minuscule.
National education expenditures reveal a similar pattern. Although
Israel has managed to preserve its position in the center of the OECD
distribution in terms of public expenditures per student in elementary
education, it is placed along the lower spenders when it comes to public
expenditures per student in secondary education. This trend is especially worrisome given the large differences in the quality of education
across different population groups, gaps that are manifested not just in
adult skills, but already during school years. Israeli students' performance in international tests of knowledge (e.g., PISA – Programme of
International Student Assessment) is poor, and although there has been
some improvement in recent years, the Israeli average is still among the
lowest among the developed countries.

The poor performance of Israeli students in these tests is partly
explained by the gaps in performance between Jewish and Arab students. While the performance of Jewish students puts them in the
middle of the distribution, the performance of Arab students puts
them at its bottom.[34] This gap has not narrowed over time. The
Jewish–Arab gap is just one manifestation of the large disparity of
test results, whether it is tests of knowledge taken at school or tests of
skills taken in later years. This disparity, which places Israel among the
least equal in the developed world, is only partly explained by the
between-group disparity and is as large when it comes to the within-
group disparity (i.e., the disparity of skills within the Jewish

---

[34] When comparing average scores among Jews to those in other countries, it is
important to keep in mind that the ultra-Orthodox students, who make up
about one- tenth of the total, do not participate in the PISA tests, and that in
other countries, too, there are minority groups whose scores are low relative to
the rest of the population.

population). Needless to say, this dispersion in skills translates into inequality of household income.[35]

1.6 Lights and Shadows in a Market Economy

1.6.1 Economic Freedom

The reduction in the role of the government in economic activity increased the share of resources put at the disposal of the business sector. The market reforms were supposed to insure that these resources would be used efficiently. This policy, however, had its price. As noted by Brender in Chapter 2 on fiscal policy, choosing to have a "small government" means shifting more responsibility not only to the business sector but also to private households, with the government playing a regulatory role. Several such examples are discussed in the book: mandatory pension savings, private health insurance, and private education.

The increase in regulation was intended to ensure that the business sector would perform its duties properly. However, the reduction in public expenditures has resulted in many cases also in a reduction of enforcement, which was replaced by stricter licensing and more bureaucracy.

The structural reforms made a significant contribution to the efficient allocation of resources in the economy and to sustainable growth. Our discussion above of reform processes illustrates just how difficult is the reformers' task, given the opposition of powerful economic actors whose excess profits are at stake.[36] As we noted, the share of the business sector in GDP has increased in the last three decades from 59 percent just before the Stabilization Program, to 69 percent a decade later, and to 74 percent by the end of the period.[37] But these figures may

---

[35] The economics of the Arab sector in Israel is discussed by Kasir (Kaliner) and Yashiv in Chapter 16, this volume.

[36] Ben-Bassat (2011), who examined thirty-two reform attempts in Israeli financial markets, found that it took, on average, three attempts and ten years for the implementation of each of the reforms. The reforms' success and its speed of implementation depend largely on the agreement among regulators and the strength of opposition from the stakeholders.

[37] The comparison with 1984 is slightly biased because of a 1995 change in national income accounting methodology, which increased the business sector share by two percentage points.

give an oversimplified picture of the change. To evaluate this change in more detail, and place it in international perspective, we employ the Fraser Institute's Economic Freedom of the World Index.

The index is composed of both qualitative and quantitative indicators. It measures government involvement in several key areas: size of government, legal system and security of property rights, sound money, freedom of international trade, and regulation. Table 1.2 shows Israel's progress over the years. Whereas in 1985 Israel's index was one of the lowest among OECD countries, since then it has improved its relative ranking in all of the different areas, and by the end of the period Israel was able to boast an average almost equal to that of the OECD (in four out of the seven criteria it even surpassed the average).

The table emphasizes the improvements in the measurable macroeconomic indicators (fiscal policy and price stability), but no less important were the reforms in the financial market and the regulation of credit. According to the Fraser Institute, Israel still lags behind the OECD average in terms of regulation of the labor market and of businesses, and in terms of the legal system and the security of property rights.[38] Even more worrisome is the slowdown in the pace of reforms. Israel's progress was very fast in the decade following the 1985 Stabilization Program but slowed down as time passed. However, this phenomenon is not unique to Israel; and the authors of the Fraser report note that in many advanced countries there is growing skepticism about the claim that the "free market" is the solution to all economic and social problems.[39]

[38] Support for these findings can be found in the Index of Economic Freedom produced by the Heritage Foundation. The methodology used to construct the two indices is similar, but the indicators chosen in each area are not identical. Nevertheless, the rankings of Israel relative to other countries based on the two indices are very similar.

[39] The Fraser Institute is identified with libertarian positions, advocating laissez-faire capitalism and favoring business sector solutions over government solutions. It is not clear how the authors of the report relate to some of the reforms adopted in Israel in the last decade, such as the law intended to reduce economy-wide concentration or the steps taken to increase competition in the banking sector. Thus, for example, Israel's mandatory military draft law is viewed by the Institute as reducing freedom in the labor market.

Table 1.2 *Economic freedom in a comparative perspective, Israel and OECD, 1985–2015*

		1985	1990	1995	2000	2005	2010	2015
A. Size of government	Israel	2.74	3.72	3.1	4.65	5.84	6.17	6.23
	OECD	4.37	4.80	4.89	5.53	5.75	5.27	5.43
B. Sound money (price stability)	Israel	1.25	3.95	7.43	8.09	9.34	8.96	9.49
	OECD	7.55	8.58	9.10	8.98	9.28	9.39	9.45
C. Regulation	Israel	4.67	4.58	5.91	6.62	6.88	7.24	7.33
	OECD	6.99	7.37	7.43	7.73	7.69	7.55	7.73
C.1 Legal system and property rights	Israel	6.65	4.30	6.85	6.78	6.30	6.04	6.13
	OECD	7.39	7.88	8.21	7.74	7.59	7.28	7.21
C.2 Freedom to trade internationally	Israel	6.22	6.86	6.89	8.66	8.46	8.23	8.11
	OECD	7.89	8.23	8.59	8.74	7.98	7.87	8.02
C.3 Credit market regulations	Israel	1.14	3.81	5.38	6.06	7.67	9.27	9.57
	OECD	7.94	8.30	8.36	9.01	9.24	8.55	9.14
C.4 Labor market regulations	Israel	–	3.35	3.84	3.81	4.87	5.28	5.38
	OECD	4.73	5.09	5.19	5.33	6.50	6.68	6.80
C.5 Business regulations	Israel	–	–	6.60	8.13	7.20	7.12	7.20
	OECD	–	–	6.81	7.82	7.15	7.39	7.47
Total	Israel	4.04	4.48	5.91	6.84	7.30	7.32	7.47
	OECD	6.70	7.24	7.52	7.67	7.64	7.47	7.58

Source: Fraser Institute, Economic Freedom of the World

Notes: The figures for the OECD are simple averages for member countries. Countries that joined the OECD from 1985 to 2015 were included in the calculations only after the year in which they joined. The score for regulation (C) is a simple average of all the regulation subcategories (C.1 through C.5).

One of Israel's weak spots lies in the regulation of labor and businesses. Although the Fraser Institute ranks Israel close to the OECD average, the OECD experts themselves seem to disagree with this ranking. These experts regard the strictness of the regulation, the bureaucracy that characterizes government services, the lack of transparency of some of the rules, and barriers to trade and to entrepreneurship imposed by the government as some of the leading explanations for the low levels of productivity of Israeli workers.

1.6.2 Inequality in Income and in Social Services

Another manifestation of the retreat of the government from its traditional functions, and probably the largest concern associated with this process, is its effect on income distribution. The rise in inequality is not new. Dahan, who covered the topic in the Ben-Bassat (2002) volume, extends the analysis to the last two decades in this book (Chapter 12). The analysis highlights a unique pattern in Israel: while the inequality in net income (i.e., income after taxes and transfers) has been rising throughout most of the last two decades, the inequality in economic income (i.e., in gross income) had already started to decline in the early 2000s (Figure 1.12). Israel does not stand out in terms of inequality in economic income but still counts (in spite of a slight improvement recently) as one of the "leaders" among OECD countries in the inequality in net income.

There is wide agreement that the decline in economic inequality was driven in part by the increase in labor supply of those with low levels of

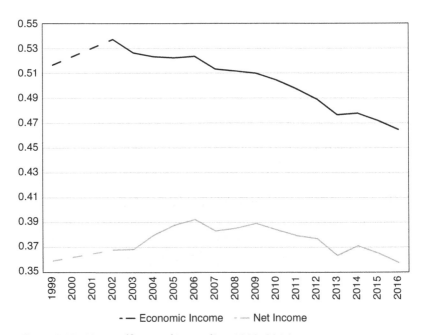

Figure 1.12 Gini coefficient of inequality, 1999–2016.
Sources: Endbeld, Gottlieb, Helker, Karady, Poverty and Social Gaps Report (table 12), The National Insurance Institute, Jerusalem, 2016

education. The more than 50 percent increase in the number of those employed belonging to the lowest five deciles has significantly increased labor income at the bottom of the income distribution. Since the 2002 recession, labor income has increased by a factor of 2.5 in the lowest quintile, but by only a factor of 1.6 in the center of the wage distribution (i.e., the fourth to sixth deciles). Explaining the increase in labor supply, Dahan emphasizes the "pull" factors – the improvement in employment prospects and the decline in unemployment, which reached a historic low by the end of the period. On the other hand, Eckstein, Larom, and Lifshitz, in Chapter 13 on labor force participation and employment patterns, emphasize the "push" factors – the cut in government allowances and transfer payments undertaken as part of the reforms of the early 2000s.

The increase in labor supply contributed to the reduction in inequality at the bottom half of the wage and income distributions but did little to reduce inequality at the top. The integration of the wave of immigrants in the labor market led to an increase in the mean wage, but this process came to an end with the 2002 recession. The mean real wage has been stagnant since then, and it was only in 2015 that it returned to its pre-recession level. The integration of low-skilled workers in the labor market reduced the average wages of workers without an academic education, while the average wages of workers with an academic education increased only slightly. According to Danieli and Kornfeld (2017), the wage increase at the tails of the distribution has been significantly faster than the increase of the median wage. Hence, while intergroup disparity (among schooling or occupational groups) has declined, there has been a rise in intragroup disparity. As shown in the chapter on education, there are significant wage gaps between graduates of research universities and graduates of colleges, and even larger wage gaps between the graduates of different academic fields. While the growth of the high-tech and the business services sectors resulted in an increase in the relative wage of graduates in computer science, mathematics, engineering, and the exact sciences, excess supply of graduates in other fields led to the over-qualification of many employees, whose wage hardly changed.

Furthermore, not only has wage inequality increased, but there has also been a decline in the share of labor income in output (Figure 1.13). The stagnation in real wages since 2002, on the one hand, and the fast growth in output following that crisis, on the other, resulted in the last

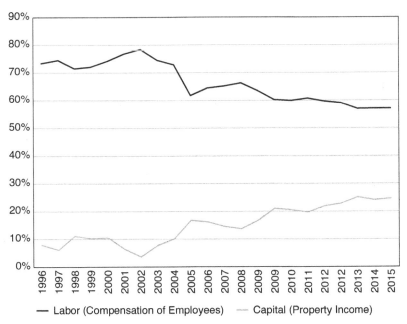

Figure 1.13 Share of labor and capital in business sector output, 1996–2015 (%).
Source: Central Bureau of Statistics, Statistical Abstracts of Israel 1996-2016 (different years) – Distribution of Income of the Business Sector

two decades (1995–2015) in a sharp decline in the labor share in business sector output (from 73 to 57 percent) and an increase in the share of capital income (from 8 to 25 percent). The decline in the size of the labor-intensive public sector amplified this trend. The rise in the share of capital income in output contributed to the increase of inequality in total income, especially in the higher deciles of the distribution.

The rise in the share of capital in output is manifested in the growth of the public's financial portfolio. The increase in this portfolio was almost twice as large as the increase in output, and significantly faster than the increase in labor income. These trends have immediate implications for the inequality in the resource distribution in the economy: while the share of the top decile in national income in 2013 was 27 percent, its share in total wealth (physical and financial) was 50 percent (Milgrom and Bar-Levav, 2015).

The increase in wage inequality and the decline in the share of labor income in total output are associated with the decline in the economic and political power of the trade unions (the Histadrut). The decline of manufacturing and the public sector resulted in a shrinkage of employment in the unionized sectors. The collapse of the Histadrut's business "empire," the takeover of its pension funds by the government, and finally the implementation of universal health insurance resulted in "mass desertion" of the unionized employees (particularly, those in mid-income scales of pay). As a result, the share of unionized labor dropped from 80 percent in the 1980s, to 45 percent in 2000, just over 30 percent in 2006, and 25 percent in 2012. The sharp decline had its bright side, the increased flexibility of the labor market, but at the same time it cast a heavy shadow on the economy as far as inequality in the distribution of income is concerned.

Tax policy has a major role in reducing inequality. The gap between the changes in Israel's gross income inequality and net income inequality is explained to a large extent by the tax and welfare payment cuts undertaken during the 2002 crisis. As mentioned, the 2002 policy may have been successful in reversing the trend in the males' labor force participation, thus reducing the gross income inequality, but it increased net inequality and deprived the government of its main weapon to combat the problem. The shift from direct taxation to indirect taxes made things even worse.

Even more serious in its long-run implications was the effect of the 2002 cut in government expenditures on human capital services, which made it harder for households to combat inequality on their own. Topping this list are the cuts in government expenditures on health and education.

The government's involvement in the market for health in the last two decades is characterized by a move in two opposite directions: starting with the "nationalization" of health services, followed by a retreat. The inequality in access to healthcare, and the financial collapse of Israel's largest health service organization (owned by the trade unions) led in 1995 to the adoption of the National Health Insurance Law. The law shifted the responsibility for funding health service organizations from the insured households (and their employers) to the government. The additional costs were financed through an increase in the social security tax (the imposition of a "health tax") and from the government's general funds.

Though the share of health services in GDP over the last two decades has not changed, the reduction in the government's share put an ever-increasing burden on households: whereas the share of public funds declined from 66 to 62 percent, the share of private funding increased from 31.5 to 36 percent.[40]

As noted by Bin Nun and Ofer on the health sector (Chapter 15, this volume), the partial adjustment of the "medical services basket," and the freeze in the healthcare system's infrastructure investment – specifically in the expansion of hospitals and their staff – have resulted in a deterioration in the quality of healthcare services (e.g., the availability of interns and hospitalization services) and increasingly forced households to rely on private health insurance plans. As a result, the share of healthcare services supplied by private providers increased from 22 to 30 percent. Though the partial privatization of the system has not affected standard indices of health outcomes (e.g., life expectancy and infant mortality), it did increase the gap in the availability of services between the center and the periphery, and given the decline in public investment in the training of medical staff, this trend may become even more severe in the future.

Expenditures on education account for the largest share, other than defense expenditures, in the government budget. As noted, the education budget was among the first to go through the 2002 cut. Noting the damage to education quality, it took the government half a decade to reverse its steps, but though the growth in its expenditures on education exceeded that of GDP, government expenditures as a share of GDP are still below the 2002 level. The government tried to overcome the wide dispersion in the education system's outcomes by adopting differential funding: schools with students from relatively weak socioeconomic background receive more generous funding than other schools. However, this attempt has been only partly successful. Gaps in funding still remain between the Jewish and the Arab school systems, and between the different school systems within the Jewish sector.[41] These gaps are broadened by the schooling expenditures of local authorities and those of households.[42]

---

[40] The decline in the government's share is due to the drop in the budgetary contribution (from 45 to 38 percent).

[41] The funding gaps between the different school systems are manifested in the allocation of instruction hours and in class size. On the complexity of implementing the differential funding, see the discussion in the Israel Democracy Institute's 2014 Hurvitz Conference on Economy and Society: www.idi.org.il/media/3835/differential_budgeting_in_education_2014.pdf.

[42] According to household expenditure surveys, expenditures on education by households in the upper half of the income distribution are three times larger than those at the bottom, while the ratio for total consumption is only two.

When adding to these factors the intergenerational transmission of human capital, i.e., the contribution of parents' education (and in particular, mother's education) to the success of their children in the schooling system, one realizes the enormous challenge facing Israeli society in its attempt to close the gaps in skills between different groups within the country, and between Israel and the rest of the developed world. Given demographic trends – and in particular the accelerated growth of the ultra-orthodox population and (to a lesser degree) that of the Arab population – it will take an extreme effort by the government to prevent a deterioration in Israel's relative standard of living in years to come.

References

In Hebrew

Brender, A. (2010). The Effect of the Retirement Savings Arrangements on Income Distribution. *Bank of Israel Economic Review*, 84, 87–123.

Danieli, O., and Cornfeld, O. (2017). Sources of Israel's Income Inequality: Processes and Policies. *The Economic Quarterly*, 61(2), 7–53.

Friedmann, Y. (2018). Private Transportation in Israel: An Analysis of Developments in the Past Two Decades. Jerusalem: Bank of Israel. [in Hebrew]

Gronau, R. (1997). Intervention and Competition in the Israeli Passenger Ground Transport Market: II. The Cost of Congestion. Falk Institute Discussion Paper No. 97.03ii.

Halevi, N., and Klinov-Malul, R. (1968). *The Economic Development of Israel*. Jerusalem: Academon Press.

Milgrom, M., and Bar-Levav, G. (2015). Inequality in Israel: How Is Wealth Distributed? Working Paper. The Institute for Structural Reforms.

In English

Ben-Bassat, A. (1990). Capital Market Reform – Objectives and Initial Results. *Bank of Israel Economic Review*, 65, 43–57.

(2002a). *The Israeli Economy, 1985–1998: From Government Intervention to Market Economics*. Cambridge, MA: MIT Press.

(2002b). The Obstacle Course to a Market Economy in Israel. In A. Ben-Bassat (ed.), *The Israeli Economy, 1985–1998: From Government Intervention to Market Economics*. Cambridge, MA: MIT Press, 1–58.

(2011). Conflicts, Interest Groups, and Politics in Structural Reforms. *Journal of Law and Economics*, 54(4), 937–952.

Ben-Porath, Y., ed. (1986). *The Israeli Economy: Maturing through Crises*. Cambridge, MA: Harvard University Press.

Blass, Asher A., and Yosha, O. (2002). Reform in the Israeli Financial System and the Flow of Funds of Publicly Traded Manufacturing Firms. In A. Ben-Bassat (ed.), *The Israeli Economy, 1985–1998: From Government Intervention to Market Economics*. Cambridge, MA: MIT Press, 189–219.

Dahan, M. (2002). The Rise of Earning Inequality. In A. Ben-Bassat (ed.), *The Israeli Economy, 1985–1998: From Government Intervention to Market Economics*, Cambridge, MA: MIT Press, 485–517.

Gabai, Y., and Rob, R. (2002). The Import-Liberalization and Abolition of Devaluation Substitutes Policy: Implications for the Israeli Economy. In A. Ben-Bassat (ed.), *The Israeli Economy, 1985–1998: From Government Intervention to Market Economics*. Cambridge, MA: MIT Press, 281–307.

Gronau, R. (2002). Structural Changes in the Israeli Public Utilities: The Reform that Never Was. In A. Ben-Bassat (ed.), *The Israeli Economy, 1985–1998: From Government Intervention to Market Economics*. Cambridge, MA: MIT Press, 309–345.

Hercowitz, Z. (2002). Capital Accumulation, Productivity, and Growth in the Israeli Economy. In A. Ben-Bassat, ed., *The Israeli Economy, 1985–1998: From Government Intervention to Market Economics*. Cambridge, MA: MIT Press, 423–444.

Justman, M. (2002). Structural Change and the Emergence of Israel's High-Tech Sector. In A. Ben-Bassat (ed.), *The Israeli Economy, 1985–1998: From Government Intervention to Market Economics*. Cambridge, MA: MIT Press, 445–483.

Kosenko, K., and Yafeh, Y. (2010). Business Groups in Israel. In A. Colpan, T. Hikino, and J. Lincoln (eds.), *Oxford Handbook of Business Groups*. Oxford: Oxford University Press, 459–485.

Metzer, Y. (1986). The Slowdown of Economic Growth: A Passing Phase or the End of the Big Spurt? In Y. Ben-Porath (ed.), *The Israeli Economy: Maturing Through Crises*. Cambridge, MA: Harvard University Press, 75–100.

OECD (2018). *OECD Economic Surveys: Israel 2018*. Paris: OECD Publishing.

Patinkin, D. (1960). *The Israeli Economy: The First Decade*. Jerusalem: The Maurice Falk Institute for Economic Research in Israel.

PART I

Government Policy and Macroeconomic Developments

2 | Fiscal Policy: The Journey Toward a Low Debt to GDP Ratio and Smaller Government

ADI BRENDER

2.1 Introduction

All the Israeli governments since 1991 have adopted a target of reducing the budget deficit with the goal of lowering the public debt to GDP ratio. According to the data available to the government toward the end of the 1990s, the debt ratio was 111 percent, a relatively high rate from an international perspective, which restricted the government's ability to cope with security events and cyclical shocks, and levied a heavy budgetary burden of interest payments. By 2017, the debt ratio had declined to about 60 percent (Figure 2.1), a level that was viewed as the long-term target for policy throughout the surveyed period. During that period, the share of public expenditure within GDP was also reduced significantly – from one of the highest among OECD countries to below the average – and similarly in the case of the tax burden.

This chapter examines which characteristics of fiscal policy contributed to the reduction in the debt ratio and the level of public expenditure and which did not, while distinguishing between the direct effect of fiscal policy management and the significant contribution of accounting revisions and various revaluation effects. This differentiation helps to explain how the debt ratio was substantially reduced even though the formal policy targets that were meant to support the reduction – namely ceilings on the deficit and on government expenditure – were raised and breached repeatedly, while the average growth rate was close to the policy assumptions made at the beginning of the period. The article also discusses the feedback between the formulation of policy targets and the behavior of the government and economic activity.

Israel's fiscal policy during the period 1998–2017 was formulated during three main episodes: (1) the wave of immigration from the USSR

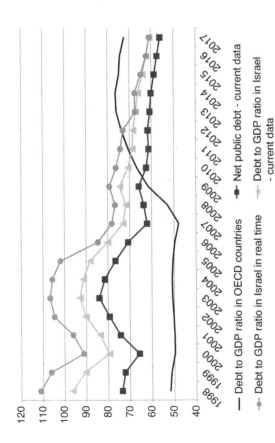

Figure 2.1 The debt to GDP ratio in Israel and the OECD, 1998–2017 (% of GDP).[a]

[a] The OECD average excludes Chile, Mexico, and Turkey due to missing data for part of the period. "Real time" data for Israel: For 1998–1999, the data published in 1999; for 2000–2005, the data published in 2005; for 2006–2010, the data published in 2010; for 2011–2017, the data published in the *Bank of Israel Annual Report* for the specific year.

Source: For OECD countries, the IMF's World Economic Outlook, as OECD data on public debt in Israel are not comparable to most OECD countries

and the expansionary policy in the early 1990s, which preceded the surveyed period; (2) the economic-financial crisis at the beginning of the 2000s and the fiscal austerity program implemented in its wake; (3) the social protest in 2011, which led to an increase in expenditure and in the deficit, primarily following the 2015 elections. The article looks at these events against the background of changes in the global economy and the important demographic and social processes in Israel that influenced policymaking.

The reduction in the share of public expenditure within GDP began in 2002–2003 and over the entire period totaled 9 percentage points, of which 7 occurred between 2002 and 2007. This decline predominantly reflected measures adopted as part of the fiscal consolidation program in 2002–2004 (which was implemented gradually until 2007)[1] but continued with low intensity until 2015 when the newly elected government changed the trend and increased public expenditure significantly. The low level of expenditure relative to GDP alongside large defense expenditure and interest payments are reflected in Israel's primary civilian expenditure being almost the lowest in the OECD.

The fiscal trends are analyzed while attempting to differentiate between cyclical effects on fiscal aggregates and the effect of policy measures. The analysis also examines specific policy measures implemented during the period with the goal of connecting the developments in the actual aggregates and policy decisions that were sometimes made well before. It is found that these decisions, whose effects were identifiable in "real time" in most cases, had a major influence on fiscal trends, including both the consolidation and the frequent changes in the government's fiscal targets. The analysis also shows that the policy focus on reducing the size of the government and the tax burden – rather than reducing the deficit – began long before the policy's results began to appear in the data. Similarly, the expansion of the structural deficit since the 2015 elections was manifested in the headline deficit only from 2018.

The analysis shows that fiscal policy was conducted in a pro-cyclical manner throughout the surveyed period, while avoiding any long-lasting deviations from a deficit level of about 3 percent of GDP. During years in which the (positive) output gap was growing, the government adopted policy measures that increased the cyclically

---

[1] See Brender (2007).

adjusted deficit in subsequent years, which was sometimes accomplished by increasing expenditure and sometimes by reducing tax rates. The opposite occurred when output gaps narrowed. Since the pro-cyclical policy was also accompanied by the frequent approval and cancelation of various government programs and changes in tax rates, it adversely affected confidence in the implementation of the government's long-term plans, in addition to the reduced ability of the business sector and households to plan their activities with any certainty.

The analysis of the impressive reduction in the debt ratio during the period shows that most of it resulted from the following factors: changes in National Accounts definitions, which retroactivity revised GDP data upward; privatization revenues and the repayment of credit that the government had provided to the public in the past; and the effect of revaluation due to the real exchange rate appreciation during the period. The dynamics of the government deficits relative to the economy's growth rates – which reflect the effects of the policy – made only a secondary contribution to this achievement, most of which occurred during the period 2003–2008.

Section 2.2 presents the considerations in setting the size of the deficit and the debt ratio. It also discusses the considerations in reducing government size and the tax burden. Section 2.3 presents the analytical relationships between the deficit, growth, and the debt ratio; it examines the background to the adoption of targets in Israel and analyzes the formulation of the fiscal rules that were chosen. Section 2.4 describes key fiscal developments during the period according to sub-periods and section 2.5 analyzes the development of the deficit and public expenditure relative to their targets and the factors leading to the reduction in the debt ratio. Section 2.6 examines the trend in government expenditure according to its components. Section 2.7 concludes and presents insights into the formulation of fiscal policy.

2.2 Deficit Targets and Government Expenditure Ceilings

2.2.1 *The Background for Setting Deficit Targets in Israel*

At the beginning of the 1990s, the government faced a number of conflicting challenges in the formulation of fiscal policy. On the one hand, it had to deal with the absorption of a massive wave of immigration from the Soviet Union and in a way that would provide them with a sufficient livelihood and enable them to integrate within the labor market and within Israeli society as quickly as possible; on the other hand, it needed to persuade the public and the markets that it is committed to reducing the budget deficit in the intermediate term in order to contain the debt ratio. This was particularly the case in view of the relatively short time that had elapsed since the financial crisis during the early 1980s and the high level of debt ratio relative to other countries.

Lacking a positive track record, the government decided to enhance its credibility by adopting a fiscal rule targeting a balanced budget in the intermediate term. This target, adopted during the discussion of the 1992 budget, was intended to clarify that despite the high deficits in the short term due to the cost of absorbing immigration, the government was committed to gradually converging to a balanced budget by 1995 and to preserving that balance subsequently. The commitment to consolidation was grounded in law, and although it reflected the specific circumstances of that period, formal long-term deficit targets have been a feature of Israel's fiscal policy ever since. Nevertheless, the rules put in place had two main flaws: First, they did not take into account the business cycle, and second they did not establish mechanisms to monitor whether the government's long-term decisions were consistent with the deficit targets and at a later stage whether they complied with the expenditure ceiling. The fact that business cycles were not accounted for reflected the desire to increase the targets' transparency, since cyclical adjustments involve nontrivial calculations and are subject to change.[2] As discussed below, the lack of cyclical adjustment led to repeated over- and undershooting of targets, to pro-cyclical policies, and to the reduced ability of the government to implement its long-term plans.

2.2.2 *Reducing Government Size and the Tax Burden*

Starting in 2005, the government adopted long-term expenditure ceilings, in order to improve compliance with the deficit targets and to reduce gradually the share of public expenditure in GDP and the tax burden. The adoption of expenditure ceilings was intended to neutralize the pro-cyclical component of government behavior, such that

---

[2] See, for example, Larch and Turini (2009) and IMF (1997).

during high-growth periods the government could increase its expenditure without missing the deficit target. The problem with such behavior is that during a slowdown the government finds it difficult to cut back its expenditures, thus leading to deviations from the deficit targets over the business cycle. The long-term expenditure ceiling – if it is adhered to – also creates certainty with regard to total public expenditure and facilitates more stable planning of government activity, without having to adapt to cyclical revisions. Therefore, the adoption of the expenditure ceiling following the Stabilization Program of 2003 was meant to ensure that the pro-cyclical dynamics that had previously undermined the achievement of the deficit targets would be constrained. Nonetheless, for long-term expenditure ceilings to generate the aforementioned advantages, they must be accompanied by a system for monitoring the costs of the government's long-term programs, to ensure that they are consistent with the expenditure ceiling. No such mechanism was in place in Israel until 2016.

The aspiration to reduce the size of the government stemmed from the recognition that the level of public expenditure in Israel (54 percent of GDP according to the data at that time) leads to a high tax burden, which is a drag on business activity. As a result, the expenditure rules reflected an intention to reduce the share of public expenditure within GDP, although they were more aggressive at the outset than in later years, when the share of public expenditure declined. Moreover, the government specifically limited expenditure growth, but not tax cuts, and thus facilitated pro-cyclical reductions in tax rates, which would make it more difficult to raise expenditure in the future.

2.2.3 *Institutional Changes to Reinforce Fiscal Compliance: The General Government and Public Entities*

The definitions and procedures that accompany the fiscal targets are essential for compliance. The more the accounting and institutional framework of the fiscal rules is limited in scope, the easier it is to circumvent them, and "shadow deficits" in various sectors of the economy – in particular in those parts of the public sector that are not directly included in the State budget – are liable to result in violations of the rules. The risk is particularly large in the case of entities that are "too big to fail": entities, which, for economic or social reasons, cannot be allowed to collapse or not to meet their obligations.

Examples of this in other countries include local authorities, financial bodies, infrastructure companies, and the health system. In the Israeli context, important institutional changes were made since the beginning of the surveyed period, which helped to restrain some of the potential threats to the government budget and supported the internalization of the remaining risks within the public sector's accounting system. In the case of the local authorities, budget transparency was increased and a tighter system for monitoring their activities was put in place (Brender, 2003). In the pension sector, new public sector employees were no longer eligible for budget-financed pensions and no new members were allowed to join occupational defined-benefit pension funds; in addition, a rescue plan was put together for existing members, which included the reduction of accumulated benefits. Independent supervisory mechanisms were created for government infrastructure companies, some of which were privatized, and the health system was subjected to the National Health Insurance Law, rigid budget constraints, and strict reporting requirements.

2.2.4 Budgeting Processes and Monitoring of Budget Implementation

Budget management in Israel is tightly controlled by the Ministry of Finance (the Accountant General and the Budget Commissionaire branches). This control is manifested in the preparation and the implementation of the budget and is based primarily on legislation and working procedures established by the Stabilization Program of 1985, following the lessons learned from the unsound budget behavior that led to that crisis (Ben-Basset and Dahan, 2006). These laws included the Budget Foundations Law and the Arrangements Law, which provide the Ministry of Finance (MOF) with a dominant status relative to other ministries in the formulation of the budget framework and its details.

During the preparation of the budget, the power of the MOF (and of the prime minister) is based on the approval of the budget framework by the government before its various expenditure lines are discussed.[3]

---

[3] In recent years, this procedure has been eroded and all of the voting in the government occurs at the same meeting. Nonetheless, the government or the Knesset never changed significantly the budget framework that was submitted by the MOF during the budget discussions.

Therefore, when the ministries' budgets are being discussed the full picture of budgetary needs is known only to the MOF, which must verify that total expenditure converges to the approved ceiling. Under these circumstances, the MOF can regulate ministries' demands and direct budgetary supplements toward its priorities. Furthermore, since the discussions with each ministry are disaggregated to dozens and sometime hundreds of lines, the Budget Commissionaire can advance or delay specific programs according to its discretion. This level of detail makes it possible to prevent ministers from promoting programs that they favor for extraneous reasons while underfunding more important programs, knowing that the government will eventually have to implement these programs in any case.

One of the main power sources of the MOF in the budget preparation process in an age of deficit targets is the responsibility for preparing the revenue forecast. An overly optimistic forecast allows the government to increase its expenditures beyond the level consistent with the deficit target, and an overly pessimistic one imposes restraint.[4] An examination of the forecasted tax revenues since the creation of the deficit target regime (Bank of Israel, 2013) shows a significant shift in the MOF forecasts since the fiscal consolidation of 2003. Thus, during the period 1993–2003, the revenue forecast was upwardly biased by about 1 percent of GDP (3 percent of tax revenues), allowing the government to systematically exceed the expenditure level consistent with the deficit targets. In contrast, since 2004, the forecasts were on average somewhat below actual revenue.

To examine the source of errors in the MOF's tax revenues forecast, we estimated a regression (see Table 2.1) in which the dependent variable is the error in the forecast of tax revenues (in percent of the original forecast) and the explanatory variables are the error in the IMF's global trade forecast for that year (and also the squared error), the deviation of the increase in the NASDAQ index from its long-term average (and the deviation squared) and the revenues from exceptional or unexpected events.[5] The regression shows that the forecast error not explained by the

[4] According to the law, the government must present a budget that is consistent with the deficit targets but is not required to meet them after the fact if revenues turn out lower than forecasted.

[5] Eran Politzer, who first carried out this analysis for the period up to 2012, provided us with the data and the estimation tools.

Table 2.1 *Factors explaining the revenue forecast error in the budget, 1992–2016**

Variable	Coefficient	Standard deviation	T-statistic	Prob.
Constant	0.042	0.010	4.008	0.001
Dummy variable for years after 2003	−0.042	0.015	−2.851	0.011
Error in IMF world trade forecast[a]	0.030	0.009	3.414	0.003
IMF forecast error, squared	0.001	0.000	2.928	0.009
Change in NASDAQ above the multiyear average[b]	−0.022	0.025	−0.872	0.395
Above change, squared	−0.109	0.054	−2.301	0.033
Anomalous and surprise one-off changes[c]	−1.811	0.791	−2.292	0.034
R^2	0.631			
Adjusted R^2	0.508			
D.W. stat.	2.107			
Observations	25			

[*] The dependent variable is the error in the tax revenue forecast as a percentage of the forecast.
[a] Based on the IMF's World Economic Outlook published before the budget forecast.
[b] The deviation from the simple average of annual changes. The results do not notably change when the variable is calculated as a deviation from the geometric mean throughout the period, or from the average change in the five years preceding the preparation of the budget.
[c] The sale of Iscar in 2006, the sale of Oil Refineries Ltd., and the banks' mutual funds in 2007 and taxes on "trapped profits" in 2013 and 2014.

aforementioned variables – none of which is under the control of the MOF – was 4.2 percent of the forecast up until 2003 and negligible following that. Hence, since 2004, the bias in the revenue forecasts disappeared and they have no longer facilitated the circumvention of the deficit targets.

In the execution stage, the budget's division into its numerous lines and the meticulous approval process for transferring funds from one line to another give the MOF significant power, since the ministries cannot deviate from the very specific budget allocations.[6] If a budget line is underutilized, the MOF can prevent the use of the freed-up budget for a different purpose, when, for example, there is a fear that the deficit ceiling will be exceeded. Furthermore, the MOF also controls the ministries' expenditure commitments for coming years ("authorization to commit"). This tight control granted to the MOF throughout the budget process is unusual among the developed countries, where there is usually a concentration of control in certain stages of the process but greater dispersion in others (Dahan and Strawczynski, 2017).

In conclusion, the structural reforms carried out in the public sector in Israel prior to and during the surveyed period significantly increased the government's ability to monitor the budget process and the "shadow risks" originating from the autonomous public entities. Thus, in addition to the tight supervision over the budget implementation by the ministries, the government created a convenient "work environment" for fiscal stability and budget reliability. The component to which the institutional restrictions did not apply was, of course, government and Knesset decisions, which have the power to change or bypass the fiscal targets.

2.3 The Relationship Between the Deficit, Growth, and the Debt to GDP Ratio

The mathematical relationship between the deficit, economic growth, and the debt ratio is described by a simple formula (all the variables are in percentage of GDP):

$$D_t = \frac{D_{t-1} + def_t}{1 + g_t} - K_t - F_t \tag{1}$$

where D_t is the public debt, def_t is the budget deficit in the current period, g is the growth rate of GDP, K_t is the government's net capital revenues from the sale of assets (privatization) and net redemption of credit (which the government provided to the pubic), and F_t is the effect of revaluation of the debt as a result of change in the relative prices of

---

[6] Each expenditure requires the approval of the ministry's comptroller, who reports to the Accountant General, and transfers between budget lines require the approval of the Budget Commissionaire's branch.

debt components, such as the exchange rate and GDP. According to the equation, the debt ratio converges in the long term to *def/g**100.

The indexation structure of the public debt is important in the calculation of def_t and g. Until the end of the 1990s, almost all of the public debt in Israel was indexed to the Consumer Price Index (CPI) or the dollar[7] and therefore it was possible to calculate the equation on the basis of a deficit that included only real interest expenses (without indexation differences on the principal) and to use the real growth of GDP; or on the basis of the nominal interest rate and to use nominal GDP growth (in the long term, the increase in the GDP deflator and the CPI – to which the public debt is indexed – is very similar).[8] During the surveyed period, the non-indexed portion of the debt grew, and since the government started to fully include interest on non-indexed debt within the budget – but not the indexation differences on the indexed debt – it became necessary to adjust the official data to fit one of the two definitions. The Bank of Israel (BOI) and the OECD report the deficit according to the "internationally accepted definition," which is analogous to using the nominal budget, and therefore we will use that definition below.

Equation 1 makes it possible to analyze the debt dynamics resulting from government decisions regarding the deficit targets, given estimates of the growth rate. Thus, for example, assuming an average real growth rate of 4 percent annually, which was the working assumption during most of the surveyed period (the actual rate was 3.9 percent), the implication of the first deficit target set by the government – a balanced budget from 1995 onward – was convergence to a debt ratio of 60 percent within sixteen years (from 111.9 percent, according to the data known in 1998).

The component of capital revenues in equation (1), K_t, is usually small. Although countries occasionally sell assets such as government companies, broadcasting frequencies or land, the scope of these sales is usually only a few percent of GDP.[9] The risk in the other direction is

---

[7] In 2000, only 11 percent of the public debt was non-indexed; about one-half of that bore a variable interest rate.

[8] Between 2000 and 2015, the GDP deflator rose at an annual average rate of 2.0 percent and the CPI by 1.9 percent.

[9] The sale of some assets is accompanied by the loss of current income from the asset, which may offset the saving in interest payments from debt reduction or even exceed it.

usually larger and is realized when governments rescue entities – usually financial institutions – that are experiencing liquidity problems or have defaulted (e.g., the bank crisis in 1983). Another risk is the provision of government credit to public entities, businesses, or disadvantaged populations, which in the end is not repaid. In Israel, a significant proportion of the increase in public debt up until 1985 resulted from such credit that was eroded by inflation. Therefore, minimizing these risks was highly important in Israel and contributed in a major way to the reduction in the debt ratio, as described below.

The component F_t is primarily determined by two factors: (1) the ratio of the CPI – to which much of the debt is indexed – to the GDP deflator; and (2) the change in the exchange rate relative to local prices. The effect of the first factor is negligible as discussed above, while the effect of the latter depends on the proportion of public debt that is denominated in foreign exchange.

2.4 Major Developments: 1998–2016

This section describes the major trends in fiscal policy that affected fiscal outcomes during the surveyed period. The description is divided into sub-periods that differ from one another in the policy stance and its outcomes. However, one should not ignore developments during the period 1991–1997 that influenced policy in subsequent years. These included the adoption of the medium-term deficit targets regime since the 1992 budget, the immediate change of these targets due to the expansionary policies adopted between 1992 and 1995, and launching several reforms that phased in gradually later on in the decade and accelerated the growth in public expenditure (Sussman and Zakai, 2000). The resulting deficits led the government to adopt a fiscal restraint program in 1996, predominantly composed of an increase in tax rates and a reduction in infrastructure investment. The deficit indeed fell significantly up until 1999, but this policy-mix was also reflected in a significant deceleration in GDP growth, in line with the findings in the literature that tax-based consolidations affect growth more adversely than expenditure-based ones (Alesina et al., 1998). These results strongly affected the design of the 2003 consolidation program discussed below.

2.4.1 1999–2003: Backing Off from Consolidation and an Economic Shock

Following the fiscal restraint during 1996–1998, the government that came into power in 1999 adopted a number of expansionary policy measures. Nevertheless, the deficit continued to decline because an unusually high growth in 2000 dramatically increased tax revenues. In response, the government marginally reduced the target for 2001, but the reduced level was still one percent of GDP above the actual deficit in 2000. In practice, the expansionary policies, deteriorating security situation, and slowing global growth pushed the deficit to well above the target in 2001 and 2002, despite adopting a comprehensive consolidation package in mid-2002.

Figure 2.2 shows that the rise in the cyclically adjusted deficit from 1999 to 2002 was similar to that in the actual deficit, indicating that the increase in the deficit mainly reflected the expansionary measures implemented in 2000 and 2001.[10] The additional increase from 2002 to 2003 was cyclical, reflecting the recession.

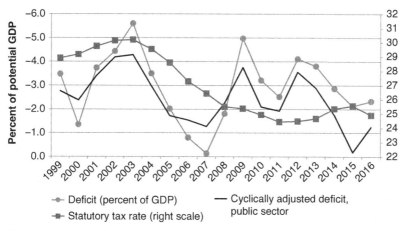

Figure 2.2 The cyclically adjusted deficit, 1999–2016

[10] The cyclically adjusted deficit is calculated by dividing government expenditure and non-tax revenue by potential GDP instead of actual GDP, and adjusting tax revenues for exceptional capital market developments, according to the BOI tax model (Brender and Navon, 2010). Potential GDP is calculated using a production function approach (Menashe and Yakhin, 2004).

2.4.2 2003–2007: *Fiscal Consolidation and Tax Reductions*

During the 2002–2003 crisis, short-term interest rates approached 12 percent and the yield on ten-year indexed government bonds approached 6 percent. Fiscal policy lacked the credibility to bridge over the recession, in view of the fiscal performance during the preceding decade. Thus, by the end of 2002, the debt ratio approached the level that prevailed during the latter half of the 1990s (according to the data available at that time) and the deficit surged. In these circumstances, it was unlikely that another program promising future reductions in the deficit would be credible. Thus, a credible and sustainable program was called for that would deal with the structural factors that had pushed public expenditure upward.

In March 2003, the government presented a fiscal adjustment program composed of cumulative expenditure cuts of 1.9 percent of GDP in 2003 and 2004 (Table 2.2). The measures included a variety of immediate reductions in public sector wages and in transfer payments, alongside structural measures that moderated the future path of public expenditure growth, and a comprehensive pension reform.[11] This focus on structural expenditure reduction reflected the lessons learned from the 1996 consolidation program and the experience in other countries that consolidations focused on reducing public expenditure are more credible and affect economic activity less adversely than tax-based ones (Alesina et al., 2015).

To accelerate the consolidation, the government adopted a second fiscal package for the period 2005–2010 during the 2004 budget discussions (Table 2.2). In addition, guidelines for budget implementation were tightened, which in light of the multitude of specific changes in ministries' budgets made as part of the adjustment packages, was reflected in substantial underutilization of the budget during 2003–2005 (about 3.5 percent of the budget on average).

The Economic Program altered the trend of fiscal aggregates. Deficits fell from an expected level of 6 percent of GDP to a balanced budget in 2007, predominantly due to the specific expenditure-cutting measures, which reduced the share of government expenditure within GDP by 4 percent of GDP. A further reduction of about 1 percent of GDP reflected the administrative measures mentioned above and the

---

[11] For a detailed discussion of the program and its medium-term effects, see Braude and Brender (2003).

Table 2.2 *Government balance forecast and the debt to GDP ratio,*
according to the 2003 fiscal plan and afterward

	2003	2004	2005	2006
		(% of GDP)[b]		
Before the plan, without adjustments[a]				
The government budget balance	−6.0	−7.0	−7.1	−7.2
Debt to GDP ratio	105.7	109.5	111.5	113.6
After the adjustments plan[a]				
The government budget balance	−5.4	−5.1	−4.4	−3.7
Debt to GDP ratio	105.0	106.9	106.4	105.0
After the 2004 budget[c]				
The government budget balance	−5.4	−4.1	−3.7	−3.2
Debt to GDP ratio	103.3	104.7	104.4	102.8
Ex-post forecast, at the beginning of 2004[d]	. . .	−3.7	−2.6	−1.7
Actual balance	−5.4	−3.7	−1.9	−0.9

[a] All the scenarios assumed that annual interest rates and growth are both 4 percent, for modeling purposes. The debt ratio in the scenario presenting the impact of the 2004 budget also reflects the effects of the debt revaluation that occurred between June 2003 and January 2004.
[b] All the figures are based on the GDP data and GDP definitions as known in 2006.
[c] The forecast is based on specific measures adopted in the plan and as part of the 2004 budget.
[d] The forecast is based on the measures adopted until the beginning of 2004 and the actual growth rates in 2004–2006.
Source: Brender (2007).

decrease in interest rates and public debt due to the unexpected improvement in the fiscal situation. A further reduction of 1.5 percent reflects the higher-than-expected GDP growth.

Alongside the reduction in expenditure, the government adopted a program that gradually reduced income taxes on individuals and corporations, which was accelerated whenever growth was better than expected. According to the statutory tax burden index (Mazar, 2014), this reduction totaled about 4 percent of GDP between 2004 and 2008 and was reflected in the cyclically adjusted deficit, declining by only 2.5 percent of GDP between 2002 and 2007 (Figure 2.2), despite the much larger contribution of the expenditure measures adopted. Nevertheless, this reduction did not significantly show up in actual revenues at first because of sharp price increases in the capital market.[12]

2.4.3 2008–2011: *The Global Financial Crisis*

The global financial crisis moderated growth rates in 2008 and 2009 and led to substantial declines in stock prices and lower interest rates, thus reducing tax revenues.[13] These developments brought to the fore the effect of the tax-reduction program, and the tax revenues to GDP ratio fell by about 4 percentage points. Since during that same period the effect of the Stabilization Program's expenditure cuts had already been realized, the deficit rose to 5 percent of GDP, a level similar to that in 2003. However, unlike past crises, the credibility achieved by implementing the 2003 Stabilization Program allowed the government to respond to the crisis in an acyclical manner, substantially mitigating the intensity of the crisis.

2.4.4 2011–2016: *The Social Protest and Policy Zigzag*

During the second half of 2011, a social protest evolved, putting forward demands for a more generous social policy ("social justice"). In response the government established a public committee (the Trajtenberg Committee) and adopted its main recommendations, primarily a gradual but substantial increase in social expenditure and a moderate increase in tax rates for high-income individuals and for corporations (Committee for Socioeconomic Change, 2011). The recommendations were presented as being fiscally balanced and consistent with the long-term expenditure ceiling. In practice, however, the main source for financing in 2012 was meant to be a major cut in the defense budget, which the government actually decided to increase for 2012 and reduce only in 2013. Moreover, the intention to finance the future increase in expenditure by means of the "regular" increase of expenditure ignored the fact that the cost of previously approved

---

[12] According to the BOI model, the price increases in the capital market contributed about 0.5 percent of GDP to tax revenues in both 2006 and 2007.

[13] According to the BOI tax model, capital market developments reduced tax revenues by 1.1 percent of GDP between 2007 and 2009.

programs already exceeded the expenditure ceiling for coming years
Bank of Israel, 2012). These decisions, accompanied by a drop in tax
revenues, led to a rapid deficit expansion during 2012 – 4.2 percent of
GDP, well above the 2 percent target.

The government elected in mid-2013 responded by raising the deficit
ceiling, and implemented a comprehensive restraint program, which
immediately raised tax rates and deferred or canceled expenditure
programs planned for 2013 and 2014. These measures, combined
with one-off tax revenues, substantially reduced the deficit in 2013.
At the same time that these budgets were approved (in a biennial
budget), the expenditure ceiling was tightened for 2015 and subsequently, even though much of the expenditure reduction in
2013–2014 reflected only a deferral of expenses. Thus, in mid-2014
there were already signs of a significant excess of planned expenditure
for 2015 and 2016 relative to the target[14] that was later manifested in
a massive breach of the ceiling in the budgets for 2015–2019.

2.5 Analysis of Fiscal Developments from a Birds-Eye View

2.5.1 *The Deficit Targets and the Actual Deficit*

Figure 2.3 shows that the governments during the surveyed period
tended to adopt ambitious deficit targets for the intermediate term
(the pale line) while gradually raising them as the target year
approached. The target was left unchanged in only a few years, usually
when growth and tax revenues were unexpectedly high. In most years
the deficit target for the budget year was set at 3 (or 2.9) percent of
GDP, and when it was set at a lower level (as in 2001, 2009, and 2012)
they were exceeded by a large margin, since they had been adopted at
the peak of a business cycle.

The anchoring of long-term deficit targets in law was meant to provide
policymaking a stable path when governments change. In Israel, there
were many such changes during the surveyed period. (Even when the
incumbent prime minister was reelected, in many cases the change in
government was accompanied by a major shift in socioeconomic policy.)
In practice, eight of the nine governments elected since 1992 have raised
the deficit targets, and the government elected in 2006 – when the deficit

---

[14] Bank of Israel (2014).

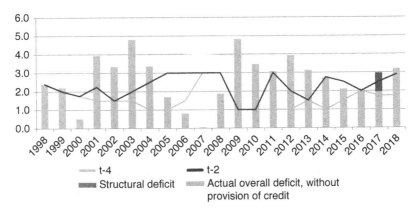

Figure 2.3 Deficit target and actual deficit, 1998–2018 (% of GDP)[a]
[a] The deficit targets for t-2 and t-4 are the targets established for each budget year, two and four years in advance, respectively. The actual deficit is the realized deficit at the end of the year t, as reported in the *Bank of Israel Annual Report* for that budget year.

was significantly below the ceiling – raised the expenditure ceiling. The changes in the deficit ceilings following an election did not reflect an exceptionally high deficit in the election year (Bank of Israel, 2005; Box 6.4), which – as in other developed countries – is not a common phenomenon in Israel.[15] Rather, it reflected the unwillingness of newly elected government to tackle immediately the commitments that the previous government accumulated during its term.

The long-term deficit targets did not therefore serve their purpose as a compass for fiscal policy. The annual deficit target was missed in most years and policy did not converge to the medium-term path that had been declared repeatedly. An advantage of medium-term targets is that they facilitate bridging over cyclical or one-off developments that change the deficit. However, Figure 2.3 reveals that policy was not accompanied by convergence of the cyclically adjusted deficit toward the medium-term targets but rather by significant policy-driven fluctuations.

One of the challenges in meeting annual deficit targets is the difficulty in forecasting tax revenues. Until 2013, the budget forecasts in Israel were based on the assumption that tax revenues (adjusted for the effect of legislative changes) would grow at the same rate as nominal GDP.

[15]   See Brender and Drazen (2005, 2008).

Although this assumption is accurate in the medium term, in the short term, tax revenues often deviate significantly because of various economic and financial variables (Brender and Navon, 2010). In addition, tax revenues' response to changes in growth rates is nonlinear, leading to erratic though temporary movements in tax revenues during periods of economic fluctuation. Furthermore, the government forecasts have assumed that legislative changes will be fully manifested in revenues immediately. However, Brender and Politzer (2018) show that legislative changes affect tax revenues only by about 70 percent of the predicted change in tax revenues, which assumes that the tax base does not change as a result of the legislative changes (the assumption that was used in budget preparation at least until 2012), and even that occurs only two years after the change (the effect during the first two years is even smaller). The focus of budget planning on short-term targets, while using a long-term elasticity to forecast revenue changes, made it difficult for policy-makers to manage policy effectively.

Table 2.3 highlights the pro-cyclicality of government policy by showing a clear connection between the changes in the cyclically adjusted deficit during the surveyed period and the lagged output gap. Since the budget is determined in the year before its implementa-tion, and because the deficit targets are not cyclically adjusted, a positive output gap during the year in which the budget is prepared influences policymakers to increase expenditure or reduce tax rates. Positive output gaps have therefore been followed by fiscal expansion in the subsequent year and vice versa. The regression coefficient implies an addition of about 0.3 percent of GDP to the cyclically adjusted deficit in the subsequent year for every one percent of output gap in the current year. An increase in the GDP deflator (which affects tax revenues) relative to the CPI (which affects the calculation of the expenditure ceiling) is also manifested in fiscal expansion during the subsequent year (when the gap is more than 0.5 percent).[16]

The government's pro-cyclical behavior illustrates the inability of policymakers to "mature" and internalize the credibility that was achieved over the years. Instead of focusing on their medium-term targets, policymakers reacted strongly to cyclical developments, trying

---

[16] Adding variables such as the deviation from the deficit target in the year in which the budget is approved or a deficit above 3 percent of GDP did not affect the coefficients. The additional variables were not statistically significant.

Table 2.3 *Indicators of the deficit's pro-cyclicality, 1998–2016**

	Coefficient	Standard deviation	T-statistic	P-value
Intercept	0.572	0.234	2.441	0.029
Preceding year's positive GDP gap	–0.379	0.107	–3.530	0.003
Election year (t–1)	–0.097	0.365	–0.265	0.795
Change in GDP deflator beyond the CPI (t–1)	0.259	0.137	1.888	0.080
Change in GDP deflator beyond the CPI (t–1) squared	–0.234	0.066	–3.539	0.003
R Square	0.648			
Adjusted R Square	0.548			
Observations	19			

* The table presents coefficients in a regression conducted on annual data in which the dependent variable is the change in the cyclically adjusted deficit, in percent, of potential GDP (increased deficits are shown with a negative sign).

to avoid too high deficits in bad times and to exploit short-term opportunities for fiscal expansion in good times.

2.5.2 *The Expenditure Ceiling*

Starting in 2005, the government added long-term expenditure ceilings to the deficit targets. These ceilings are meant to be more stable than the deficit targets, since most of the expenditures are determined according to parameters whose paths are largely known in advance, such as public sector wage agreements, expansions of health services, the number of students and the number of individuals eligible for National Insurance benefits and the size of those benefits.

Figure 2.4 presents the gap for each year between the level of expenditure approved in the budget and the level that meets the expenditure rule. It can be seen that until 2010 the approved budget was higher than the ceiling. This was due to "one-off" additions including the disengagement from Gaza from 2005 to 2008, the costs of the Second Lebanon War in 2007–2008, and the global financial crisis in 2008–2009, and persisted even after the expenditure ceiling was

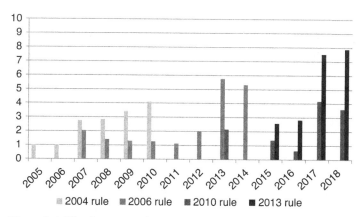

Figure 2.4 The deviation of total expenditures in the approved budget from the expenditure ceiling based on the fiscal rule[a] (% of total expenditures)

[a] The permitted expenditure based on each rule is calculated under the assumption that the rule's formula was implemented in the relevant years, and net of one-off adjustments to the level of permitted expenditures or changes in the expenditure base, including deviations from the rule of amending expenditures in respect of price deviations in the preceding budget year from the budget forecast. The budget for 2017 and 2018 was approved in December 2016.

Source: The government's budget highlights documents and author's calculations.

raised – starting from 2007. When these one-off additions ended, the expenditure ceiling was raised again, prior to the approval of the biennial budget for 2011–2012. Essentially, only in 2014 – following the 2013 economic adjustment program – was the actual budget below a long-term expenditure ceiling that was not decided on with the budget's approval (the rule had been adopted in 2010).[17] The figure shows that the expenditure ceiling set in 2013 was seriously breached in the 2015 and 2016 budgets and to an even greater extent in the subsequent budgets, and that the expenditure level in these budgets exceeded even the previous – more expansionary – rule set in 2010.

---

[17] By definition, a budget approved together with a change in the expenditure ceiling is consistent with that ceiling, including biennial budgets, as those approved since 2010.

The breach of the expenditure celling in the 2015–2019 budgets reflected the approval of long-term expenditure programs in previous years, without accounting for their consistency with the expenditure ceilings. When the time came to implement the programs, the government changed the fiscal rules in order to meet its excess commitments. This was in contrast to its behavior in the period 2003–2008, during which long-term decisions were used to reduce expenditure and led to the prolonged moderation of public expenditure growth. The government initially dealt with some of the excess expenditure by spreading the expenditure over a longer period and applying administrative barriers to project execution and accounting gimmickry rather than carrying out the required fundamental revisions. Furthermore, it anchored the excess expenditures by raising the ceiling and, later, the deficit ceiling as well. This behavior was a response to unexpectedly high tax revenues between 2013 and 2017, the very outcome that the expenditure ceiling was intended to prevent.

A comparison of the actual budget to the long-term budget forecasts published by the BOI since 2003 shows that the information needed to predict deviations from the expenditure ceiling was available to the government, implying that the deviations of long-term commitments from the expenditure path reflected conscious decisions. Thus, the two to three years forward BOI forecasts published from mid-2004 until 2007 showed that government expenditure was not expected to exceed the ceiling, reflecting the expenditure restraining measures adopted in the 2003–2004 program. Indeed, apart from the cost of the Second Lebanon War in 2006, no major budget revisions were needed during those years. Starting in 2007, the government's commitments started to exceed the expenditure ceiling for 2010 and 2011, which was reflected in the forecasts published at the beginning of 2008 (Bank of Israel, 2007). When the time came to deal with the excess commitments – in the 2011–2012 budget – the government raised the expenditure ceiling and carried out a major budget revision. This revision more or less "reset" the excess long-term commitments for 2013, but new decisions in 2011 – and in particular following the social protest – led to the accumulation of new commitments, which required a broad cut in the 2013–2014 budget. Since a significant portion of the budget commitments were only deferred and new commitments were added, the gap – as 2015 approached – was large and known about (Bank of Israel, 2013). Despite this gap, the government adopted additional expenditure programs, which led to significant expansions of the expenditure ceiling in the 2015–2016 and 2017–2018 budgets.

Apart from the technical-economic side, the repeated raising of the expenditure ceiling during the past decade indicates the government's difficulty in achieving policy targets in the areas of defense, social welfare, and the support of economic growth within the budget framework dictated by the fiscal rule. As a result, there developed a practice in which the government adopts long-term expenditure programs, but since they are not consistent with the legislated budget framework, it is forced to deviate from the rules and/or to defer or postpone some of the programs. The process in which programs are approved and then deferred or cancelled – even though this could have been predicted – is deleterious not only to the efficiency of government operations and to the credibility of the fiscal targets but also to the confidence of the public in government promises, an outcome that has negative implications for Israeli society and the economy's performance. Despite these damages and the availability of the required information, the government adopted only in 2016 a procedure that monitors whether the cost of a long-term program is consistent with the medium-term expenditure ceiling.

2.5.3 *The Decline of the Debt to GDP Ratio*

The dramatic decline of about 50 percentage points in the debt ratio since 1998 seems surprising given the conduct of fiscal policy and in particular the repeated deferrals in achieving the "yearned-for" deficit target of 1.0–1.5 percent of GDP "in another five years." Figure 2.1 presents part of the explanation of this apparent contradiction by demonstrating that the decrease in the debt ratio significantly reflected the revisions of the GDP figures and the method of their calculation by the Central Bureau of Statistics and that the decline in the ratio according to the current estimates of GDP was more moderate. Furthermore, a significant proportion of the decline in the ratio reflected the monetization of government assets (primarily the repayment of mortgages), such that the decline in the net debt ratio (deducting the debts of the public to the government) was far more moderate than the decline in the gross ratio. Notwithstanding the methodological issues in the calculation of net debt figures, it is important to mention that Israel has been an outlier among the developed countries with respect to the gap between net debt and gross debt (i.e. the government's financial assets) during the past two decades. Only the Czech Republic and Slovakia showed a decline in the ratio similar to that of Israel, while in most of the countries the gap grew substantially.[18]

Figure 2.5 presents the factors that contributed to the drop in the debt ratio. Revisions of GDP were responsible for 30 percent of the

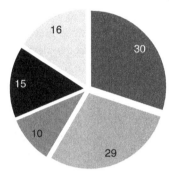

■ Change in GDP definitions
▨ Credit repayment
■ Privatizations
■ Appreciation
░ Dynamics of deficit and growth

Figure 2.5 Components of the decline in gross debt to GDP ratio[a], 1998–2016 (% of total decline)

[a] The change in GDP definitions is the change between the data for 1998, which was published in 1999, and the data published in 2016. Credit repayments' contribution was calculated as the difference between the gross and net decline in debt as defined in the new accounting definitions. The contribution of privatizations was calculated by dividing privatization proceeds in each year by the GDP of that year (using the new definitions). The appreciation's impact was calculated by multiplying the change in the exchange rate each year by the stock of foreign exchange denominated debt at the end of the previous year, and dividing by GDP of that year. The contribution of the deficit and growth dynamics was calculated as a residual, and alternatively, based on equation 1 – by the nominal definition (including indexation differentials on the principal and divided by the nominal growth in GDP).

[18] According to OECD figures, the simple average of the increase in the gap between the net and gross public debt from 1998 to 2016 was 9 percentage points (excluding Norway, where the increase was an outlier), while in Israel it *fell* by 14 percentage points.

reduction[19] and the repayment of debt by the public to the government contributed another 30 percent. The real appreciation during the period contributed about 15 percent and privatization proceeds another 10. The contribution of the ratio of the deficit to the rate of growth was responsible for only 15 percent of the decline, which is equivalent to 8 percentage points. This figure is consistent with a simulation in which the debt ratio (GDP according to the revised figures) is substituted into equation (1) along with the average growth rate in nominal GDP during the surveyed period (6 percent) and the average nominal deficit (4 percent of GDP).

Notwithstanding this breakdown, the reduction in the debt ratio made a significant contribution to reducing the risk premium on government debt. According to the coefficients in Brender and Ribon (2014), the decrease in the debt to potential GDP ratio since 2003 reduced the real 10-year interest rate by about 220 basis points and substantially lowered the yield on five-year bonds. Such a reduction, if it persists for five years, permanently reduces annual interest expenses by 0.5 percent of GDP and thus vacates significant fiscal sources, in addition to the direct contribution of the reduction in the debt.

2.6 Public Expenditure

Figure 2.6 presents public expenditure and its components during the surveyed period. First, the graph shows that policymakers were, for much of the period, working with information that is completely different from what we have today. While according to the data for 1998–2003 public expenditure constituted, on average, about 53 percent of GDP (55 percent according to international definitions), according to current figures it was only 46 percent. According to the figures available then, the level of expenditure in Israel was among the highest in the OECD, where the average was 40 percent of GDP.[20] This situation contributed to the government decision in

---

[19] The GDP figures for 1998 were revised upward by 15.3 percent in Israel and by an average of 8.4 percent in the twenty-eight countries for which data are available. These revisions reflect to a large extent reclassification of activity that was not included in GDP rather than the emergence of new activities in the economy. Accordingly, the estimated elasticity of tax revenues with respect to GDP fell in parallel to the data revisions.

[20] The figures for most of the OECD countries have not changed significantly since that period.

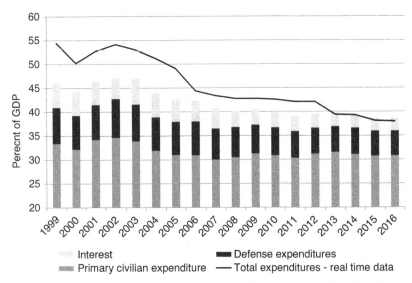

Figure 2.6 Public expenditure – amount and distribution, 1999–2016, "real time" expenditures for Israel: for 1999, the 1999 data; for 2000–2005, the 2005 data; for 2006–2010, the 2010 data; for 2011–2016, the *Bank of Israel Annual Report* for the specific year. Expenditure components are presented in percent of the updated GDP data.
Source: Central Bureau of Statistics and author's calculations

2003 that the fiscal consolidation program should be based on cuts in public expenditure.

Table 2.4 shows that, as in other countries, the reduction in transfer payments was a major component in the reduction of civilian expenditure.[21] The table also shows that most of the reduction in the share of public expenditure within GDP was used to reduce tax rates, such that the tax burden fell by about 3.5 percent of GDP, while the average deficit fell by about 1 percent of GDP. In other words, the main objective of downsizing the government was in fact the reduction in the tax burden rather than a long-term deficit reduction.

---

[21] The decrease in the "other" category primarily reflects the reduction in housing subsidies, which are essentially transfer payments.

Table 2.4 *Components of the change in the size of public expenditure and revenue, 1998–2017*

	1998–2003	2004–2009	2010–2017
Total public expenditure	**46.4**	**42.1**	**39.5**
Defense	7.5	6.6	5.4
of which: Domestic defense consumption	*5.9*	*5.3*	4.4
Interest	5.1	4.6	2.9
Primary civilian expenditure	33.8	31.0	31.2
of which: Education	*7.3*	*6.5*	6.8
Healthcare	*5.2*	*5.0*	5.3
Social security and welfare	*11.9*	*10.9*	10.9
Of which: Transfer payments to households	10.4	9.2	9.1
Other	*8.5*	7.6	7.2
Total revenues	**42.9**	**39.7**	**36.6**
of which: Taxes	33.9	32.6	30.9
Transfers from governments abroad	2.7	1.6	1.1
Other	6.3	*5.5*	4.6
Additional calculations:			
Total public expenditure net of grants	44.0	40.3	38.4
of which: Defense and interest net of grants and of revenues from property	8.2	8.4	6.5
Total revenues net of grants and revenues from property	38.5	36.9	34.8

Source: Author's calculations based on BOI data

2.7 Conclusion and Recommendations

The discussion above highlights the importance of analyzing policy-makers' behavior during the past two decades in relation to the data that was available to them at the time. The gap between the currently available information and the information they faced in real time is of a magnitude with significant implications. Thus, for example, in 2003 policymakers faced a debt ratio of 105 percent, public expenditure was 54 percent of GDP and the deficit 5.3 percent of GDP; the analogous figures available in 2016 for that year are 91, 47, and 4.3, respectively. These data also ranked Israel differently relative to the reference countries and therefore influenced the urgency and the intensity of the government's response.

Since the 1990s, fiscal policy was supposedly guided by medium-term deficit targets, and since the middle of the previous decade also by expenditure rules. Our analysis demonstrates that the government's level of compliance with the rules was not particularly high and that the legislated targets were replaced by each of the governments elected during the surveyed period. This behavior in part reflected the difficulty in combining medium-term targets with short-term ones, without accounting for the business and financial cycles. Nonetheless, the path of the cyclically adjusted deficit indicates that policymakers were not in any case obligated by the medium-term deficit targets and adopted pro-cyclical policies. Thus, when the (positive) output gap grew, the government increased expenditure or reduced tax rates in the subsequent year and vice versa. From a structural perspective, the government largely neutralized the budgetary threats originating from various public sector entities, such as the local authorities, the health system, the pension funds and government companies, as well as from the defense budget, which declined substantially relative to GDP. This is an important achievement, which has evaded many other countries, but it is also evidence that the repeated abandonment of the medium-term targets reflected policy preferences rather than unforeseen constraints.

On the expenditure side, the government experienced growing gaps between the cost of long-term programs it had adopted and the expenditure ceiling. The gaps arose due to the lack of a monitoring mechanism of the match between the cost of government decisions, which determine expenditure in subsequent years, and the expenditure ceiling. They also reflect the difficulty in achieving government targets with the limited sources permitted by the expenditure ceiling. The government responded to the gap by deferring programs and through accounting gimmickry, but in the end the deviations led to a significant and permanent increase in the expenditure ceiling for the period 2015–2019. By 2017, the share of government expenditure in GDP returned to a level similar to that at the end of the previous decade, violating the built-in goal of the expenditure rule, i.e., to reduce the weight of government expenditure within GDP over time. Only at the end of 2016 did the government adopt a mechanism to monitor the consistency of the costs of its long-term programs with the expenditure rule, even though the information required for this mechanism existed throughout the surveyed period. Since then, the government has already found a number of ways to circumvent the new monitoring system (Bank of Israel, 2018).

The fiscal adjustment program of 2003 constituted an anchor to improve fiscal management, following years of deviation from the targets set by the government. The program's design was based on the successful experience with the 1985 Stabilization Program and similar programs in other countries. The program's core was a sizable reduction in government expenditure focused on transfer payments and public sector wages. Furthermore, the program included many structural changes that were to be gradually implemented and which constituted an anchor for permanent reduction in the weight of public expenditure within GDP (of about 5 percent of potential GDP) by the end of the decade. However, the reduction was used primarily to reduce tax rates – also by about 5 percent of GDP – rather than for the long-term reduction of the deficit. Consequently, public expenditure and the tax burden in Israel – which prior to the program were among the highest in the OECD – are today among the lowest, and primary civilian expenditure is almost the lowest in the OECD, while the deficit in Israel is still very high.

Explaining why the public in Israel chose a policy of reducing the size of the public sector and the tax burden is beyond the scope of this analysis. Nonetheless, the year in which key decisions were made, i.e., 2003, may point to an important role played by the low level of public confidence in both the government and the collective activity of Israeli society. The 2003 crisis followed significant expansions of the welfare system and indications of its exploitation by some (Brender et al., 2002), combined with an increasing weight of the Arab and ultra-Orthodox sectors among recipients of government support. Moreover, Israel was dealing with a wave of terror attacks, which had begun with the events of October 2000 in the Arab sector and continued with the Defensive Shield Operation, which drew attention to the exemption of the ultra-Orthodox from military service. It is possible that this split in Israeli society, which since then has been present in public discourse, created fertile ground for adopting policies that trimmed collective activity and the size of government.

The choice of a small government shifts greater responsibility for social welfare issues and various aspects of economic activity on to the country's citizens. Thus, the government obligated all workers to save for retirement, it became involved in private health and long-term care insurance, and it began to regulate many private activities in the domain of education, all of which serve as substitutes for public expenditure. Aghion et al. (2010) claim that greater regulation is also necessary in the case of a lack of mutual trust within a society, since the public has no confidence in the discretion of the government. This policy led to both a high level of inequality and greater regulation, which is meant to ensure that the private sector carries out the tasks that the reduced public sector does not. Low public expenditure is also manifested in underfunding of the regulatory system, increasing the bureaucratic burden on business sector activity.

A breakdown of the marked decrease in the debt to GDP ratio during the period shows that deficit reduction played only a limited role. The reduction predominantly reflected three components, in relation to which Israel was an outlier relative to other developed countries: the significant upward revisions of GDP figures; the repayment of government loans provided to the public and the decision not to provide new ones; and privatization proceeds. Also contributing to the debt ratio's reduction was the continuing appreciation during the surveyed period, which eroded the ratio of the external debt to GDP. The contribution of policy derived from the ratio of the deficit to economic growth accounts for only one-sixth of the reduction and occurred almost entirely from 2003 to 2008. Despite this mix, the debt ratio's reduction contributed substantially to reducing the economy's cost of financing and supported the reduction in the weight of annual interest expenses (less interest receipts) by 1.4 percent of GDP.

The current low level of government expenditure, both in historical perspective and relative to other countries, is reflected in its limited effect on income inequality and in the low level of public services and public investment (Bank of Israel, 2016). These have a potentially large effect on the prospective economic growth and on Israeli society. Against this background, the government finds it difficult to maintain the share of public expenditure within GDP and all the more so to reduce it, as is demonstrated by budget management in recent years. In addition, there appears to be a political commitment not to increase tax rates, even though they are low by international standards. Given the high structural deficit reached towards the end of the period, and since it appears that the technical/accounting factors that worked to reduce the debt ratio since 2003 have been exhausted – the public's debt to the government has been almost completely repaid, the banks have been privatized, the government is using land sales' revenues to finance off-budget expenditure, and the external debt is only a small part of the remaining debt – maintaining the current debt ratio over time, and even more so further reducing it, is becoming increasingly challenging.

References

In Hebrew

Braude, K., and Brender, A. (2003). The Effect of the Israeli Government Liabilities on Its Deficit, 2003–2008. *Position Paper*, Bank of Israel.

Brender, A., Peled-Levi, O., and Kassir, N. (2002). Government Policy and Labor Force Participation Rates Among the Primary Working Ages: Israel and OECD Countries in the Nineties. *Bank of Israel Review*, 74, 7–61.

Brender, A., and Politzer, E. (2018). The Effect of Legislated Tax Changes on Tax Revenues in Israel. *The Economic Quarterly*, 62, 87–128.

Brender A., and Ribon, S., (2014). The Effect of Fiscal and Monetary Policies, and the Global Economy on Israeli Government Bonds' Real Yields: A Reexamination after a Decade. *Bank of Israel Review*, 88, 7–51.

Committee for Socioeconomic Change (2011). *Committee Report*.

In English

Aghion, P., Cahuc Y., and Shleifer, A. (2010). Regulations and Distrust. *Quarterly Journal of Economics*, 125(3),1015–1049.

Alesina, A., Favero C., and Giavazzi, F. (2015). The Output Effect of Fiscal Consolidation Plans. *Journal of International Economics*, 96, S19–S42.

Alesina, A., Perotti, R., and Tavares, J. (1998). The Political Economy of Fiscal Adjustments. *Brookings Papers on Economic Activity*, 1, 197–248.

Bank of Israel. *Bank of Israel Annual Report*. Various years. Jerusalem: Bank of Israel.

(2013). *Recent Economic Developments: October 2012 to March 2013*, 135, February. Jerusalem.

(2014). *Recent Economic Developments: October 2013 to March 2014*, 137, June. Jerusalem.

(2018). *Fiscal Policy in the Past Two Years and Fiscal Projection for 2019–2022*. Jerusalem: Bank of Israel Research Department, August 2018.

Ben-Bassat, A., and Dahan, M. (2006). *The Balance of Power in the Budgeting Process*. Jerusalem: Israel Democracy Institute.

Brender, A. (2003). The Effect of Fiscal Performance on Local Government Election Results in Israel: 1989–1998. *Journal of Public Economics*, 87 (9–10), 2187–2205.

(2007). If You Want to Cut, Cut, Don't Talk: The Role of Formal Targets in Israel's Fiscal Consolidation Efforts, 1985–2007. *Fiscal Policy: Current Issues and Challenges*, 348–376.

Brender, A., and Drazen, A. (2005). Political Budget Cycles in New Versus Established Democracies. *Journal of Monetary Economics*, 52(7), 1271–1295.

(2008). How Do Budget Deficits and Economic Growth Affect Reelection Prospects? Evidence from a Large Panel of Countries. *American Economic Review*, 98(5), 2203–2220.

Brender, A., and Navon, G. (2010). Predicting Government Tax Revenue and Analyzing Forecast Uncertainty. *Israel Economic Review*, 7(2), 81–111.

Dahan, M., and Strawczynski, M. (2017). *Budget Institutions and Government Effectiveness*. SSRN Mimeo.

International Monetary Fund (IMF) (1997). *World Economic Outlook*, October, Chapter 3.

Larch, M., and Turrini, A. (2009). The Cyclically-Adjusted Budget Balance in EU Fiscal Policy Making: A Love at First Sight Turned into a Mature Relationship. *European Economy-Economic Papers*, (374).

Mazar, Y. (2014). *Development of the Structural Deficit in Israel, 2000–12*. Periodic Papers 2014.101. Jerusalem: Bank of Israel Research Department.

Menashe, Y., and Yachin, Y. (2004). Mind the Gap. *Israel Economic Review*, 2(2), 79–106.

Sussman, Z., and Zakai, D. (2000). *From Promoting the Worthy to Promoting All: The Public Sector in Israel 1975–1999*. Jerusalem: Bank of Israel Research Department.

3 | *Israel's Taxation Policy*

MICHEL STRAWCZYNSKI

3.1 Introduction

This chapter analyzes Israel's taxation policy in the period 2000–2015 based on two criteria: over time and in an international perspective.

According to public finance tradition, taxes are generally viewed as a way to finance government spending. Basic fiscal policy models relate to taxes as a tool designed to maintain government's multi-period budget constraint and to prevent the creation of government debt to be financed in the future by the next generation, which is not party to decisions made at the time of preparing the budget. To prevent this undesirable pattern, government decisions regarding tax levels must constantly be examined to ensure that they are consistent with budget expenses. This chapter presents such a review and asks whether the tax cuts in the period from 2004 to 2011 are consistent with the tax smoothing framework proposed by Barro (1979).[1] Barro's model posits that taxes must reflect the permanent level of government spending plus interest payments on the debt. Previous studies[2] based on this model showed that in 2012 there was a discrepancy in the state budget between income and expenditure ("structural deficit"), reflected in a significant increase in the cyclically adjusted deficit, which caused tax rates to be increased from 2012 to 2014. According to the framework proposed in the tax smoothing model, tax rates can only be reduced in parallel to a corresponding reduction in the permanent

---

[*] I wish to thank Daniel Achdut for his excellent research assistance. I would also like to thank Efraim Sadka and the book's editors for their useful comments, and the Falk Institute for its support in this study.
[1] Existing legislation in 2011 included a deeper tax cut, based on corporate and income tax reductions to be implemented gradually until 2016. In practice, following the social unrest of summer 2011, these tax cuts were abolished.
[2] See Strawczynski (2016). Regarding data for the cyclically adjusted deficit, see analyses in the Bank of Israel Report from 2012 onwards.

expenditure. However, in Israel, the creation of a structural deficit during that period raises the question of reverse causality: did the tax reductions of the previous decade dictate the general development of fiscal policy in Israel? In other words: did tax cuts cause government spending to GDP to decline – contrary to the expectation according to the theory of tax smoothing? According to this theory, taxes may only be reduced after permanent expenditure has declined. We will answer this question using Granger's causality tests, addressing the period 1960–2014 and focusing on the sub-period in which the tax rates were reduced.

This section is followed by a study of the connection between taxes and politics. In recent years a number of studies have been conducted on the relationship between the ideology of political parties and the size of the government – a relationship reflected in tax levels. Another question we will ask in this current study is therefore: has the development of statutory tax rates in Israel been influenced by the political makeup of the parties in government, and specifically, government of a prime minister belonging to right and left blocks?

3.2 Taxation in Israel

In this section, I will examine three aspects of Israel's taxation policy in the period 2000–2015 – taxation policy over time, comparative taxation policy at the international level, and the question of whether tax levels in Israel reflect the level of permanent expenditure, a subject I will also address in the next section.

3.2.1 Taxation Policy over Time

To explain in detail the development of tax revenues, we must monitor government decisions relating to tax credits, tax withholding, tax exemptions, and the statutory tax rates, and also take into account developments in business turnover. All these significantly affect tax revenues. The last of these features is important given that the elasticity of taxes to GDP is greater than 1 – particularly during periods of economic prosperity.[3]

---

[3] See Brender and Navon (2010) and Brender and Politzer (2014).

While all the decision variables mentioned above are important for analyzing tax revenues, the most important variable – the one that provides direct confirmation of the decisions made by the Israeli government over time – is the average statutory tax rate. The statutory tax rate is the rate prescribed by law for a particular tax channel, for example: 17 percent as a basic tax rate for Value Aggregate Tax (VAT).[4] Any decisions made on this subject directly impact tax revenues as a percent of GDP, and without doubt they are the principal instrument applied by government in the budget discourse each year. I will describe the development of the average statutory tax rate in the method I developed in a previous article (Strawczynski, 2015), which addresses the statutory tax rates for the vast majority of the tax channels in Israel. Notably, although the government plans its budget at the annual level, numerous decisions are also made during the course of the year – mainly with respect to indirect taxation[5] – and it is therefore extremely important to show the picture based on quarterly data.

3.2.1.1 The Development of Statutory Taxes

Figure 3.1 shows the development of taxes as a percentage of GDP from the 1960s, in parallel with the description of the development of the average statutory tax rate (1960 = 100). The diagram shows a clear positive correlation between the average statutory tax rate trends and the development of taxes as a percentage of GDP in the long term (a relationship that we will test econometrically later on). In particular, we can see that in periods in which statutory tax rates increase, the response of taxes as a percentage of GDP is delayed, and similarly, when taxes are lowered, the response of tax as a percentage of GDP is more moderate. As we will see later on, this characteristic of taxation policy is critical for Israel's fiscal policy, perhaps because government decisions relating to statutory tax rates are not reflected in real time in revenues as a percentage of GDP, and the repercussions are felt much later, and not necessarily while the politicians who made these decisions are in office.

---

[4] As well known, in Israel there is a different statutory VAT tax rate for financial institutions.

[5] For example, the last two VAT changes – the increase from 17 percent to 18 percent and return to 17 percent – were applied at the beginning of March 2013 and the beginning of September 2015, respectively.

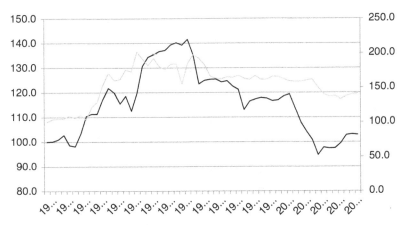

Figure 3.1 Development of taxes from the 1960s until 2015
Black line – Statutory tax rate – left axis
Gray line – income as percent of GDP – right axis

One of the examples I will analyze below is the tax reductions that began in 2004: Figure 3.1 shows that the sharp reduction in the statutory tax rate did not, in the initial years of 2004–2008, cause taxes as a percentage of GDP to decline. This is because at that time, the economy was booming as a result of exogenous causes,[6] which in turn helped increase tax revenues.[7] It was only in 2009, following the start of the global financial crisis, that taxes as a percentage of GDP dropped in line with the statutory tax rate cuts which eventually determined the long-term development.

According to the generally accepted analysis in public economics, when determining the tax rates a distinction must be made between taxes that reflect externalities and taxes aimed at financing government activity. The former are intended to bridge the market failure arising

---

[6] Regarding the positive economic cycle in the period 2004–2008, Flug and Strawczynski (2007) show that it was mainly attributable to exogenous factors – end of the Intifada and the recovery of global trade.

[7] Notable examples of tax channels that, in periods of boom, have an elasticity of more than 1 are income tax and corporate tax. In income tax, high-income individuals move up the tax ladder in periods of prosperity so that tax revenues increase more than proportionally to the rate of the increase. In corporate tax – after a prolonged period of prosperity, the companies complete the offset of losses for previous periods so that many of them move over from not paying tax to becoming taxpayers.

from the failure of economic units to take particular events into account – traffic congestion, air pollution, etc. The imposition of taxes in such instances improves allocation of the resources. Examples of taxes of this kind are taxes on vehicles, on fuel (gasoline), and to a lesser degree on cigarettes and alcohol. Obviously, most taxes are imposed to finance public products or to reallocate income, and they lead to an excess burden, while adversely affecting economic activity. Most taxes imposed by the government are included in this group – income tax, National Insurance, capital gains tax, VAT, and purchase tax. We also note (by looking at decision timing) that, in practice, taxes that reflect externalities, such as fuel tax, are often raised due to fiscal-budgetary considerations.

Over the last twenty years, we have witnessed substantial changes both in overall taxation and in the composition of taxes in Israel. Regarding overall taxation, Figure 3.1 shows that following the successful 1985 Stabilization Program, tax rates were lowered, paving the way, from 1988, for sixteen years of relative stability (with some fluctuations) in the average statutory tax rate. In 2004, a process of tax reduction began, and although the tax rates were raised again in 2012 and 2013, they remained low (approximated at 2007 rates). More recently, statutory tax rates have once again been reduced.[8]

The sharp change in policy relating to the average statutory tax rates is evident in the composition of the taxation, with most of the reduced tax channels falling under the direct taxation category. The two key taxes that were reduced over time are corporate tax and income tax for individuals. The direct taxation reform included the introduction of capital gains tax in 2004, initially at 20 percent, which was raised to 25 percent at the beginning of 2012 following the recommendations of the Trajtenberg Committee. The pie graphs in Figure 3.2, showing the amounts collected in the tax channels in 2000 and 2015, confirm significant changes, mainly in two channels – income tax (which fell from 30 to 20.4) and VAT (which rose from 24.9 to 30.1).

Although part of the change in direct taxation reflects a substitution between tax on labor and tax on capital – which was 1.2 percent in 2015 compared with zero in 2000 – the reduction in income tax was far

---

[8] On October 1, 2015, VAT was reduced from 18 to 17 percent, and corporate tax was reduced from 26.5 to 25 percent. Following the budget approved for 2017 and 2018, corporate tax was reduced to 23 percent on January 1, 2018.

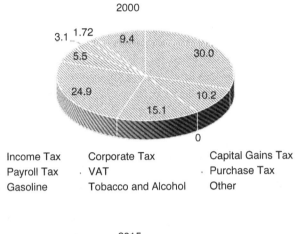

2000

Income Tax	Corporate Tax	Capital Gains Tax
Payroll Tax	VAT	Purchase Tax
Gasoline	Tobacco and Alcohol	Other

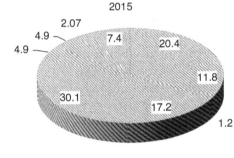

2015

Income Tax	Corporate Tax	Capital Gains Tax
Payroll Tax	VAT	Purchase Tax
Gasoline	Tobacco and Alcohol	Other

Figure 3.2 Composition of tax revenues (%), 2000 compared with 2015

beyond this substitution: in 2015 income tax accounted for 20 percent of total tax revenues, 10 points less than in 2000. A significant share of this shortfall was filled by VAT, whose share of tax revenues increased by 5 points. Another share was supplemented by an increase in the level of taxes that deal with the externalities, where the weight of fuel tax increased by 1.8 percentage points. Strawczynski (2014) shows that changes in the composition of taxation between the key tax channels are closely related to government decisions regarding statutory taxes – the reduction of income tax for individuals and reduced corporate tax on the one hand, against higher VAT and fuel tax on the other.

Another dimension analyzed in public economics is the progressivity of taxes. Owing to the difficulty of knowing what the social benefit of the public products is for individuals, and based on the desire to reallocate the tax revenues, developed countries generally apply a progressive taxation system, in which the average tax rates increase as income rises. For many years, there has been a lively debate in the literature on public economics as a result of findings by Atkinson and Stiglitz (1976), who propose that the optimum mechanism for tax collection is the use of direct taxes (nonlinear income tax) as a way of redistributing income, and proportional indirect taxation, which does not discriminate between products, thus preventing a negative effect on the allocation of resources. Numerous articles challenge this conclusion and assert that indirect taxation should also serve as an instrument for the redistribution of revenues and financing of public products. Nygard and Revesz (2015) have written many articles over time showing that the findings of Atkinson and Stiglitz do not hold and that indirect taxation plays an important role in financing government activity, as is the case all over the world.

As a result of the changes described above, Israel has become one of the countries in which the ratio of direct taxes to indirect taxes is one of the highest among the OECD countries (Figure 3.3).

To examine the changes in progressivity, we built an index of the average tax rate for the different tax channels based on data in the

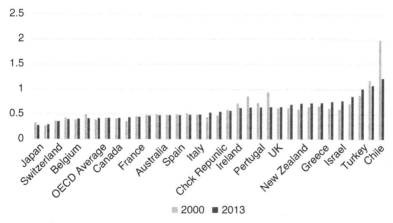

Figure 3.3 Relationship between direct taxes and indirect taxes, 2000 compared with 2013

Central Bureau of Statistics 2012 Household Expenditure Survey, and we divided them among those in which the average tax rate increases with individual income ("progressive taxes"), and those in which the tax rate decreases with income ("regressive taxes").[9] To analyze the relationship between regressive and progressive taxes, "pure" progressive or regressive taxes, namely taxes where the increase or decrease of the average tax rate was consistent along the entire curve, were defined separately from "expanded" progressive or regressive taxes, namely those in which the increase or decrease is not monotone with income, but they can be reasonably attributed to one of the groups according to their behavior over most of the curve. Based on these criteria, income tax and National Insurance payments (including health tax) were defined as pure progressive taxes, whereas VAT and purchase tax on alcohol and cigarettes were defined as pure regressive taxes.[10] According to the expanded definition, in addition to the pure progressive taxes, the progressive taxes also included tax withholding from the capital market, purchase tax, corporate tax, and tax on the purchase of private cars. The expanded definition of regressive taxes also includes excise tax on gasoline. Figure 3.4 shows the tax revenues examined from a progressive and a regressive perspective. A comparison of the pie graphs for 2000 and 2015 shows that the progressivity in the Israeli tax system declined considerably in this period: the share of progressive taxes shrank from 62 percent of all taxes revenues in 2000 to 58 percent in 2015.

To summarize this section: Taxes have been reduced sharply over the past two decades. Income tax for individuals and corporate tax were cut, at the expense of indirect taxes – mainly VAT and tax on gasoline, which increased.

3.2.1.2 The Effect of Statutory Taxes on Inequality

Studies that examine the relationship between specific taxes and inequality, beyond the direct effect described in the previous subsection, question the impact of taxes on the behavior of individuals. Regarding the effect of income tax, which could explain gross income, one of the better-known articles is that of Gruber and Saez (2002), who

---

[9] See Strawczynski and Kedar (2016).

[10] With respect to VAT, it is well known that its regressivity tapers over the individual's lifetime, although it is retained. For a comparison based on the amended taxation for lifetime incidence, see Capersen and Metcalf (1993).

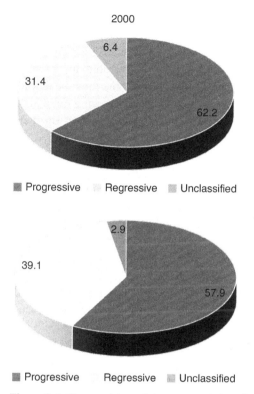

Figure 3.4 Composition of the progressivity of tax revenues (%): A. 2000 and B. 2015.
Source: Bank of Israel, Tax Revenues Administration and author's notes

show that "high income taxpayers are particularly responsive to taxation" responding in the transition from income from work to other income.

In the case of Israel, Dahan (2011) showed that in the past ten years, the upper decile increased its share of gross income steeply as the tax rates declined. However, this pattern can be attributed to a variety of factors, and it is difficult to determine what contribution was made by the reduction in direct taxation. In another article which investigated the effect of taxes on inequality, Strawczynski (2015) found that the lowering of income tax leads to greater inequality in gross income, namely – before taking taxes and transfer payments into account.

It is worth mentioning the literature linking inequality with growth, further to Zeira's study (2007). Zeira showed that in theory, there are forces at work creating a negative relationship between inequality and growth, but there are also other forces that work – through incentives – to create a positive relationship, and the final outcome must be empirical. Numerous articles show that in the long term, growing inequality could negatively affect growth, but other articles cast doubts on their economic relationship. Among the well-known articles in the theoretical and empirical fields we mention Panizza (2002), Person and Tabelini (1994), Banerjee et al. (2001), and Galor and Moav (2004). Barro (2000) examined the issue separately for wealthier and poorer countries, and he found that the negative effect of inequality is indeed stronger in less wealthy counties, and weaker but not significant in developed countries.

3.2.1.3 The Impact of Taxes on Growth

A large number of articles examine the relationship between taxes and growth. A survey of the empirical articles that discuss the impact of taxes on GDP and growth, based mainly on samples of developed countries, is summarized in an article by Strawczynski (2015). This article presents an interesting finding relating to the composition of taxes: whereas for overall taxes and for personal income tax and indirect taxes, the research shows conflicting effects on growth, with respect to corporate tax most of the studies found that the impact on growth was negative.

Research conducted in Israel also shows that the effect of the different tax channels on growth is mixed and that the negative impact of corporate tax on GDP cannot be ruled out. Few studies make a distinction between individual taxes and groups of channels; most studies separate only direct and indirect taxes (Mazar, 2013; Geva and Drucker, 2015). Contrary to previous studies and to the research of Geva and Drucker (2015), which found that direct taxes had the strongest impact on growth, Mazar (2013) found that indirect taxes actually have a stronger impact. Regarding corporate tax, Hercowitz and Lipschitz (2015) address the relationship between corporate tax and growth directly, and using simulations they show that the reduction of corporate tax explained a significant part of the growth of the economy in the period 2004–2010. Strawczynski (2015) presented a direct review of the effect of statutory taxes on growth using the technique of Romer and Romer (2010). Accordingly, while there is little evidence of the impact of changes in the statutory rates of indirect taxes and some of the direct taxes on growth, it was found that changes in the corporate tax rate have a clear impact on growth in Israel.

Strawczynski (2015) analyzed the effect of statutory taxes on growth, distinguishing between exogenous changes (decided upon by policymakers independently – unrelated to the business cycles) and endogenous changes (changes made in response to the economic cycle). Similar to findings from other parts of the world, a review of the effect of the former on growth revealed that most of the tax channels have no clear impact on growth. The only tax channel that was found to have a significant impact is corporate tax, and it is therefore important to conduct an international comparison of the rate of corporate tax,[11] for which the consideration of international competition is the most relevant.

A comparison of this kind shows that although in 2000 the corporate tax rate in Israel was 20 percent higher (6 out of 30 percentage points) than the average in the OECD countries, the current rate is much closer to the average. The importance of this closing of the gap is reinforced in view of the tax reduction which entered into force on January 1, 2016, when the rate was reduced to 25 percent (10 percent above the average – 2 out of 23 percentage points). In the wake of this reduction, Israel is approximately in the middle of the range, and following the reduction of 2018 (when the tax rate became 23 percent), it is part of the group of countries in which the tax rate is similar to or even below the average. In addition to Israel, other countries that have drastically reduced their corporate tax rate are Germany, Poland, Greece, Turkey, Ireland, Holland, Czech Republic, and Italy.

It should be emphasized that the issue of corporate firms' migration requires us to analyze the tax benefits offered in different countries. These benefits include those given when the investment is made, benefit tracks in which companies pay no tax at all or pay taxes at a reduced rate, and

---

[11] The relevant comparison is that of the effective tax – which takes into account the tax benefits, offset of losses, accelerated depreciation, etc. Oxford University publishes such a comparison (see document from the Knesset Research and Information Center from December 2016), but it is difficult to judge the quality of the estimates given that there are no common standards for reporting by different countries. For a comparison of these data, see also the report of the Tax Revenues Administration.

more. Although an analysis of the tax benefits is beyond the scope of this chapter, it should be emphasized that many companies in Israel enjoy an even lower tax rate. This is particularly the case for a Preferred Enterprise in Development Area A (domestic production + an export component of at least 25 percent) but also for plants in Class-A Development Areas.

3.3 Tax Policy and Fiscal Discipline

3.3.1 *The Tax Smoothing Model*

The generally accepted model used for analyzing fiscal policy is Barro's tax smoothing model (1979). According to this model, multi-period tax constraints may be set out as follows:

$$\sum_{i=0}^{\infty} \frac{G_{t+i}}{(1+r)^{t+i-1}} + (1+r)B_{t-1} = \sum_{i=0}^{\infty} \frac{\tau Y_{t+i}}{(1+r)^{t+i-1}} \tag{1}$$

Where G indicates the general government's total spending, B indicates debt and Y indicates GDP; r is the interest rate and τ is the (smooth) rate of tax prevalent in the economy. In other words: on the left side of the equation, we see the government's future spending discounted to the present time, plus payment of the principal and interest on the debt. On the right side, we see the way in which the government finances these expenditures – through taxes; these are equal to multiplying the (smooth) tax rate by GDP, which varies in line with projected business cycles.

If we look at the fixed flows which tracks the varying flows (for expenditure as well as for GDP – marked with upper ~) we can write the tax rate as follows:

$$\tau = \frac{\tilde{G}}{\tilde{Y}} + rB_{t-1} \tag{2}$$

This formula allows us to calculate the tax rate according to the anticipated expenditure flows, interest payments on the debt, and forecasts relating to GDP. The GDP forecast is determined according to its rate of growth over time; if we look back in time and calculate the average for a twenty-year period, we find that this rate is slightly less than 4 percent.

It is worth emphasizing that this formula does not take into account the presence of the debt reduction target defined by the government, which is currently 50 percent of GDP.[12] As demonstrated by Hercowitz and Strawczynski (2004), the increased tax rate required to reach the target is higher even than that presented in equation 2. Calculating the permanent level of spending of Israel's general government is beyond the objective of this present chapter, and I will therefore assess the validity of the tax smoothing model in two indirect ways. The first uses a co-integration model for the tax revenue equation to examine whether changes in the statutory tax rates explain the long-term developments of tax revenues in Israel. The second test, presented in section 3.3.1.1 will examine the causal relationships between the smoothed expenditure (assuming that it reflects the permanent expenditure) and the statutory tax rates.

3.3.1.1 The Tax Revenues Equation

First, I will attempt to validate the statutory tax rates by examining the development of tax revenues according to the right side of equation (1) for the period 1960–2015. Table 3.1 shows various specifications of tax revenues as a function of the statutory tax rate, GDP, and debt. According to the model, the expectation is that all these variables will correlate positively with the tax revenues. The test is important as it checks the long-term relationship: we would expect the relationship between the dependent variable (tax revenues) and the vector of the independent variables (the variable in the different regressions) to be significant. The technique known as co-integration is generally used to examine the intensity of the long-term relationship according to the proposed model which uses ADF statistics.[13]

Specification (1) in Table 3.1 is the most naïve – and its results therefore show that it does not manage to reflect a long-term relationship between the tax revenues and the vector of the independent

---

[12] According to the existing expenditure rule, introduced by the previous government when Yair Lapid served as Minister of Finance, reaching a debt target of 50 percent of GDP will enable the government to increase the real growth percentage of government spending.

[13] ADF is an acronym for Augmented Dickey-Fuller – the generally accepted test for examining a long-term connection. ADF at an appropriate level of significance reflects the presence of co-integration between the dependent variable and the independent variables. The higher the absolute value of this statistic, the greater the chance that there is a long-term relationship. The asterisks next to the ADF value confirm the level of significance in each specification.

Table 3.1 *Explanation of tax revenues in the long term (dependent variable: log of tax revenues deflated at GDP prices, period 1960–2015)*

	(1)	(2)	TSLS (3)	TSLS (4)
Constant	−3.3 (0.9)***	−3.5 (0.8)***	−6.5 (0.7)***	−4.1 (0.8)***
Log of average statutory tax	1.2 (0.3)***	1.2 (0.3)***	0.7 (0.2)***	0.5 (0.2)***
Log of global trade	0.8 (0.05)***	0.8 (0.05)***		
Log of GDP			0.9 (0.04)***	0.9 (0.04)***
Log of general government debt	0.3 (0.08)***	0.4 (0.07)***	0.2 (0.06)***	0.1 (0.05)***
Dummy for 1984		−0.4 (0.12)***		
Log for Inter-government transfers				0.04 (0.01)***
Adj. R Squared	0.98	0.98	0.99	0.99
ADF	−2.5	−3.8	−3.5	−5.2**

In equations 3 and 4, global trade is used as an auxiliary variable for GDP,
*** significant at 1 percent; ** significant at 5 percent; * significant at 10 percent.

variables. In this specification, I used global trade as an approximation for the development of GDP, given that the Israeli economy is small and open. Notably, all the variables appear in a log so that the coefficients reflect the elasticities. The coefficients for the variables are reasonable and have the correct indication, but the low value of the ADF statistic requires us to attempt to improve this specification.

In specification (2), I added a dummy variable, equal to 1 in 1984 and 0 in all the other years. As we know, 1984 was an exceptional year in which there was hyper-inflation. In this specification, although the intensity of the long-term connection increased substantially, as shown by the increase in ADF from 2.5 to 3.8, here too the relationship is not significant.

The next stage is to bring GDP into the regression – but here we must consider the presence of endogeneity between GDP and taxes, since changes in GDP are also affected by changes in taxes, and this requires us to find a variable that correlates directly with GDP but not necessarily with changes in the tax rates. To offset the effect of taxes on GDP, I used specification no. 3, in which I applied the Two Stages Least Squares (TSLS) method in global trade as an auxiliary variable for GDP. This is due to the fact that there is a significant correlation between GDP and global trade, whereas changes in the tax rates are not necessarily affected by it. The result confirms that there is a significant improvement in the long-term connection, even though the ADF variable is not significant at the level of 5 percent. Notably, the coefficients are not far from 1 and the equation therefore seems to be a reasonable approximation (although it could be improved).

The final stage is to consider the unilateral transfers that the Israeli economy receives from foreign residents. This is a significant factor on the financing side given that since the establishment of the State of Israel, the United States government has provided it with defense assistance (and in the past civilian assistance as well). The inclusion of a log for unilateral transfers in the regression significantly improves the long-term relationship: in Specification (4) it becomes significant at 5 percent. Notably, the coefficient for GDP remains close to 1 (0.94), whereas the coefficient for statutory taxes declines considerably. This seems to confirm that in the past the government has taken the unilateral transfers into account as a source of finance for its spending.

3.4 Does Government Spending Cause Tax Revenues?

As noted above, in 2004 there was an unprecedented change in the statutory tax rate: taxes decreased sharply and consistently for more than a decade. According to the tax smoothing model, a tax decrease of this kind is possible only if it is accompanied by a parallel decrease in the government's permanent expenditure: if the permanent expenditure declined, then the tax rates can be reduced immediately afterwards (or even concurrent with this decrease, if the reduction in expenditure is certain). This tax reduction might be connected with the ongoing decline in defense spending as a percentage of GDP, which in turn led to a corresponding decline in deficit and debt as a percentage of GDP; and consequently, in interest payments as a percentage of GDP. However,

in 2012–2014, the government was forced to increase taxes, implying that the previously implemented tax rate cuts were premature
and at a rate that was greater than inferred from the decline in
government spending in percentage GDP. An interesting question
must therefore be raised: in the period after 2003, was it government spending that set the tax reduction in motion, as would be
expected according to the tax smoothing model? Or perhaps the
tax reduction preceded the decline in government spending as
a percentage of GDP, and it was then forced to adapt (at least
partially) after the reduction in taxation? It is worth noting that
following the lessons learned from the stabilization plan, all of
Israel's finance ministers recognized that a high deficit cannot be
sustained over time. Consequently, any reduction in the tax rates
(which causes a reduction in tax revenues) must be accompanied
by a reduction in expenditure as a percentage of GDP, unless we
are willing to sustain a high level of government deficit.[14] To
address this question, I used Granger's causality tests. These tests
examine the probability that expenditure caused the change in the
statutory tax rate and also the probability that the change in the
tax rate caused the change in expenditure; the test therefore examines what preceded what – did the tax reduction precede the
reduction in general government spending or vice versa? In Table
3.2 I compare the causality in the entire period (1960–2015) with
the causality in the period under discussion – 2003–2015. For this
purpose I use real government spending deflated by GDP deflator;
using this deflator allows picking increases in government wages,
which is one of the important mechanisms of government spending
changes.

[14] Theoretically, it is possible for tax revenues to increase when the economy is on
the wrong side of the Laffer curve. It is possible that in the years of hyperinflation, Israel approached such a point in the context of inflation tax. But in the
context of ordinary taxes, economists are in broad agreement that such
a possibility is practically irrelevant in cases for which the statutory tax rates
are not excessively high compared to competitive countries. In fact, over time
Treasury officials in Israel quantified tax rate reductions in the budget (with the
support of economists from the academic world) as a corresponding decline in
tax revenues – consistently with the "correct side" of the Laffer curve. Brender
and Politzer (2014) show that tax revenues in Israel are indeed managed on the
correct side of the Laffer curve. Veber and Strawczynski (2019) show a similar
finding for the corporate tax rate in Israel.

The results of the Granger tests, which are shown in Table 3.2, allow us to determine that the period 2003–2015 was exceptional compared with the previous periods. The first four rows of the table report the test results relating to total expenditure. These tests were performed with two lags for the long period and one lag for the short period – due to the limited degrees of freedom. The result shows that in the entire period, taxes were triggered by government spending and not the reverse. In contrast, in the period 2003–2015, we found that, unusually, tax cuts triggered the decline in expenditure and not the reverse. This result is particularly interesting in view of the unprecedented tax cuts in this period. One plausible interpretation of this unusual result is that after taxes had been reduced, the government was left with no alternative other than to limit the increase in expenditure; otherwise it would have been forced to increase the deficit. Since increasing the deficit is a problematic issue that could lead to a downgrading of the credit rating, politicians prefer to avoid it. In fact, there is considerable evidence, even from the end of the 1990s, that all Israel's finance ministers were careful to avoid a high deficit and only did so in periods of clear exogenous shocks (such as in 2001–2003 following the Intifada and the decline in global trade, and in 2009 following the global financial crisis). The only remaining option for not increasing the deficit in percentage GDP is to reduce the rate of increase of expenditure.

The second test is based on the tax smoothing theory according to which changes in the tax rate are connected only with a decline in permanent expenditure. In the large sample, in which there are more degrees of freedom, the test was performed with longer lags: three quarters and six quarters (a year and a half). With a lag of three quarters, the smoothed expenditure triggers taxes and vice versa; in contrast, with a lag of six quarters the result obtained was similar to the one noted for total expenditure: government spending triggers taxes but not the reverse. For the shorter period, from 2003 to 2015, I obtained the same result as noted above: taxes triggered government spending rather than the reverse.

The conclusion drawn from this analysis is that whereas historically, the cause–effect factor was from government spending to taxes, in the period 2003–2015 we noticed the opposite process: first the government reduced the statutory tax rate, as a result of which, due to the

Table 3.2 *Does government spending trigger taxes or vice versa?*

Causality	F	Probability	Observations	Period	Lags
Expenditure is not the cause of the statutory tax rate	2.73991	0.075	54	1960–2015	2
The statutory tax rate is not the cause of expenditure	0.97536	0.384	54	1960–2015	2
Expenditure is not the cause of the statutory tax rate	1.76471	0.214	13	2003–2015	1
The statutory tax rate is not the cause of expenditure	6.13702	0.033	13	2003–2015	1
Smoothed expenditure is not the cause of the statutory tax rate	2.46764	0.074	53	1960–2015	3
The statutory tax rate is not the cause of the smoothed expenditure	18.2026	0.000	53	1960–2015	3
Smoothed expenditure is not the cause of the statutory tax rate	2.82945	0.023	50	1960–2015	6
The statutory tax rate is not the cause of the smoothed expenditure	1.24202	0.10	50	1960–2015	6

Table 3.2 (*cont.*)

Causality	F	Probability	Observations	Period	Lags
Smoothed expenditure is not the cause of the statutory tax rate	1.28289	0.283	13	2003–2015	1
The statutory tax rate is not the cause of the smoothed expenditure	23.4666	0.001	13	2003–2015	1

inability to increase the deficit over time, it reduced expenditure. This strategy is consistent with statements made by Benjamin Netanyahu,[15] who initiated this process as finance minister and was subsequently prime minister for several terms of office.

To conclude this section, I will mention that in 2012 a reverse trend began in Israel in which, following the social unrest of summer 2011, statutory taxes were increased. Even before the Trajtenberg Committee discussed increasing direct taxes while discontinuing the increases in indirect taxes, the prime minister decided to cancel the legislated reduction in income tax and corporate tax that were supposed to occur gradually until January 1, 2016.[16]

I also wish to mention that the increase in the tax rates have recently been halted, with two consecutive tax reductions (VAT and corporate tax in 2016 and corporate tax in 2017 and 2018) introduced by Finance Minister Moshe Kahlon. In view of the experience of the past few years

---

[15] In March 2003, Netanyahu delivered his famous speech addressing the difficulties faced by the business sector in financing the public sector in the form of a thin man who is forced to carry a fat man on his back.

[16] We recall that according to the decisions prescribed in the Economic Arrangements Law, marginal income tax should have been 39 percent at the beginning of 2016 (instead of 51 percent in 2019, after taking the surtax into account), and corporate tax should have been 18 percent (instead of 26.5 percent in 2015 and 23 percent since 2018).

and the high cyclically adjusted deficit, as shown above, it is still too early to know how long the current tax rates will remain in force.

3.5 The Connection between Politics and Taxes

A new school of thought has emerged in the literature in recent years which examines whether there is a relationship between the ideologies of political parties and fiscal policy in general, and specifically in the context of the size of the government. One of the preferred variables used in this test is taxes, given that it is generally accepted among economists that tax increases/decreases should reflect a true increase/decrease in the scope of general government spending. As we explained above, according to the tax smoothing theory, tax reductions by the government should reflect a decrease in permanent expenditure. For example, Petterson-Lidbog (2008) found that left-wing parties in Sweden's local authorities spend between 2 and 3 percent more than right-wing parties, while increasing the tax rate by a corresponding amount. Fredrikson et al. (2013) found that in different states in the United States, a Democratic governor was more likely to increase income tax than a Republican governor.

In this section I will examine whether changes in the tax rate in Israel are influenced by the governing party's affiliation with the left or right wing, or perhaps even with a centrist party. The test uses quarterly data in an effort to capture the precise timing of regime changes, which as we know are quite frequent in Israel. Changes in the statutory tax rate are recorded on the precise date on which they entered into force and the same applies to changes of government. Unfortunately, not all the parties publish their manifestos regularly,[17] and the test is therefore based on the actual changes in the statutory tax rate, which do not necessarily reflect the parties' declared opinions, as is the case in other parts of the world. We also emphasize that other factors were included in the regression that might affect the tax rates.

---

[17] Regarding the last two election campaigns, see a comparison between the parties' economic manifestos in the electronic magazine of the Van Leer Institute's Economic and Society Program, January 2013 and February 2015.

3.5.1 The Relationship Between Politics and Tax Channels for Individuals

In the first stage, we will run the following regression:

$$T = \alpha + \beta(Y) + \gamma(\text{Working\_Population}) + \delta(\text{population } 65+)$$
$$+ \varepsilon (\text{population } 15-) + \zeta(\text{immigration stock}) + \eta(Z) + \nu$$

$$(3)$$

The relevant variables that appear in regression (3) and explain government spending which is financed by taxes are: GDP (represented by Y), the working-age population (in which we would expect a negative coefficient), population in the 65+ and 15− age groups (in which we would expect a positive coefficient), the number of immigrants (assuming that the immigration process − Aliya − lasts six years, namely twenty-four quarters), and other relevant variables described below (and represented by Z); v represents the residual.

Table 3.3 reports the results of this regression. In Z, I tried variables that reflect the cause of the defense spending (expenditure of the historically rival countries − Jordan, Syria, Lebanon, and Egypt).[18] In the final outcome, these variables were not reported because they severely reduced the sample, losing degrees of freedom without any improvement in the results. The results show that in three specifications (the statutory tax rate, income tax, and VAT) out of the five, a significant long-term relationship is obtained, and the ADF reflects a significance level of 5 percent. In the other two regressions, in which the ADF coefficient is not significant, we can repeat the test to see whether there is a tendency toward a long-term relationship, using Engle and Granger's hypothesis which shows that if in the short-term regression a statistical significance is found in the coefficient of the lagged residual (Error Correction Model) − this is an adequate indication of a long-term relationship.

In Table 3.4, we report on the results of the short-term regression, which is based on the rates of change of the variables (represented by *d*log):

$$\text{dlog}(T) = \alpha + \beta(Y) + \gamma\text{dlog}(\textit{Working\_Population})$$
$$+ \delta\text{dlog}(\textit{population } 65+) + \varepsilon \, \text{dlog}(\textit{population } 15-)$$
$$+ \zeta(\textit{immigrants}) + \mu \, v_{t-1} + \eta(X) + \nu'.$$

$$(4)$$

---

[18] On this, see the analysis of Zeira and Strawczynski (2001).

Table 3.3 *Historical taxes: long-term model (in parentheses: statistic t)*

	Total – Index	Income tax – Index	Corporate tax – Index	VAT – percentage	Tobacco – percent
Constant	169.0	193.6	149.1	0.15	–3.7
	(15.8)	(14.9)	(21.8)	(–6.97)	(–4.7)
Age 15– (thousand)	–0.1	–0.2	–0.1	0.00003	0.001
	(–4.4)	(–7.7)	(–9.1)	(6.6)	(6.5)
Age 65+ (thousand)	0.4 (8.1)	0.4	0.2	0.00003	–0.001
		(7.6)	(6.4)	(3.3)	(–2.8)
Working population (thousand)	0.01	0.04	0.007	–0.0001	–0.002
	(1.95)	(5.7)	(2.2)	(–1.4)	(–6.9)
Seasonality adjusted GDP – billion (in 2010 prices)	–0.1	–0.1	–1.1	–0.002	–0.002
	(–8.7)	(–7.0)	(–1.4)	(–10.2)	(–2.0)
Stock of immigrants (thousand)	–0.8	–0.8	–0.6	0.3 (1.4)	0.5
	(–6.8)	(–6.2)	(–8.7)		(6.8)
Adj. R squared	0.87	0.87	0.94	0.82	0.35
ADF	–4.81**	–4.92**	–3.1	–4.75**	–3.2

*** Significant at 1 percent; ** significant at 5 percent; * significant at 10 percent.

Where X is the vector of the dummy variables which represent the parties in power: right, left, union of right-wing parties and centrist party. The prime minister's political allegiance determines the identity of the party in power: if the prime minister is from the Likud or the Labor Party, the variable will be given the value "right" or "left," respectively; if the prime minister is from Kadima, the variable will receive the value "centrist." Note that I left out the "left-wing union" block, implying that all the results are reported relative to it. It must also be emphasized that the regression includes the Error Correction Model (ECM), which is represented by the lagged residual, and which, as mentioned, confirms the long-term relationship. The results are reported in Table 3.4.

Table 3.4 *Does politics affect statutory taxes? (in parentheses: statistic t)**

	Dlog Total statutory taxes	Dlog Income tax	Dlog Corporate tax	Dlog VAT	Dlog Tobacco
Constant	−0.07 (0.8)	−0.01 (−0.8)	0.03 (1.97)**	−0.03 (−1.5)	−0.18 (−2.3)**
Dlog Age 15−	0.7 (1.2)	1.5 (1.5)	0.06 (0.07)	1.9 (1.4)	−0.8 (−0.2)
Dlog Age 65+	20.3 (4.5)***	1.0 (1.1)	−0.2 (−0.3)	0.004 (0.03)	20.3 (4.5)***
Dlog Working population	0.91 (1.8)*	0.04 (5.7)	0.007 (2.2)	−0.0001 (−1.4)	−0.002 (−6.9)
Dlog GDP adjusted for seasonality	−0.22 (−2.5)***	−0.3 (−1.7)*	−0.1 (−1.0)	−0.007 (−0.4)	0.9 (1.3)
Dlog stock of immigrants	−0.7^−6 (−0.9)	0.1^−8(−0.2)	−0.1^−8(−0.1)	0.9^−6 (−1.5)	0.4^5 (0.2)
Residual lag	−0.001 (−5.2)***	−0.002 (−4.5)***	−0.003 (−4.5)***	−0.2 (−5.2)***	−0.2 (−3.8)***
Right	0.006 (0.8)	0.02 (1.2)	−0.02 (−1.5)	0.02 (1.2)	−0.03 (−0.6)
Left	0.003 (0.4)	0.01 (1.0)	−0.02 (−1.6)	−0.004 (−0.3)	−0.06 (−1.0)
Right-wing union	−0.005 (−0.6)	−0.002 (−0.2)	−0.003 (−2.8)***	−0.001 (−0.08)	0.09 (1.5)
Center	−0.02 (−2.5)**	−0.02 (−1.7)*	−0.002 (−2.2)**	−0.03 (−2.1)**	0.1 (2.0)**
Adj. R squared	0.17	0.13	0.09	0.14	0.13

* The regressions were made in TSLS and they include world trade as an instrumental variable for GDP together with lags in the other variables;
*** significant at 1 percent; ** significant at 5 percent; * significant at 10 percent.

Regarding the average statutory tax rate, it was found that of the variables relating to politics, the only significant variable is "centrist"; in fact, even in a test by category of tax, we found that the centrist party lowered income tax, corporate tax, and VAT. Nevertheless, we found that it also increased the tax on tobacco, a significant result at a level of 5 percent.

Another interesting result relates to corporate tax: right-wing union parties tend to reduce corporate tax. This outcome is consistent with the expectation concerning the direction of the effect of ideologically based changes on taxes.

Israel posted an extraordinary result compared with findings for other parts of the world in that the coefficient for left-wing parties is not significant for all categories of tax, whereas in other countries it was found that left-wing parties raise taxes, particularly direct taxes (Stein and Caro, 2013; Anderson, 2016). Nevertheless, it is possible that the left parties in Israel have a broad perspective; consequently, in section 3.5.2, I will examine whether there is any significance when testing the connection between progressive and regressive taxes – instead of individual taxes.

3.5.2 *The Connection Between Politics and the Relationship Between Progressive and Regressive Taxes*

In this subsection, I will repeat the above test, this time based on the relationship between different categories of tax, some of which are progressive and some of which are regressive. Specifically, I will examine the following equation in the long term:

$$\text{Log}(T_i) - \text{Log}(T_j) = \alpha + \beta(Y) + \gamma(Working\_Population)$$
$$+ \delta(population\ 65+) + \varepsilon(population\ 15-) + \zeta(immigration\ stock)$$
$$+ \eta(Z) + \nu \tag{5}$$

Where *i* reflects progressive tax (focusing on corporate tax and income tax) and *j* reflects regressive tax (focusing on tobacco tax and VAT). Table 3.5 shows the result of the long-term regressions.

Similar to the approach I adopted in the previous section, I will use the residual of the long-term relationship (v) to examine the short-term relationship:

Table 3.5 *Long-term model for the ratio between progressive and regressive taxes (in parentheses: statistic t)*

	Income tax (i) and tobacco tax (j)	Income tax (i) and VAT (j)	Corporate tax (i) and tobacco tax (j)	Corporate tax (i) and VAT (j)
Constant	11.9 (11.3)	10.0 (52.0)	12 (11.0)	10.1 (44.7)
Age 15 – (thousand)	–0.1 (–7.1)	–0.005 (–12.5)	–0.02 (–7.3)	–0.005 (–11.0)
Age 65+ (thousand)	0.02 (3.9)	0.003 (3.3)	0.02 (3.8)	0.002 (2.5)
Working population (thousand)	0.3 (6.8)	0.6 (6.4)	0.3 (6.4)	0.3 (3.1)
GDP adjusted for seasonality – billion (in 2010 prices)	–0.1 (–3.0)	–0.8 (–3.6)	–0.2 (–2.4)	0.1 (5.2)
Stock of immigrants (thousand)	–0.7 (–6.3)	–0.009 (–4.7)	–0.07 (–6.7)	–0.01 (–5.8)
Adj. R squared	0.45	0.93	0.59	0.95
ADF	–3.1	–4.9**	–3.3	–4.1*

** Significant at 1 percent; ** significant at 5 percent; * significant at 10 percent.

$$\mathrm{dlog}(Ti) - \mathrm{dlog}(Tj) = \alpha + \beta(Y) + \gamma \mathrm{dlog}\,(Working\_Population)$$
$$+ \delta \mathrm{dlog}\,(population\ 65+)\ \varepsilon\ \mathrm{dlog}\,(population\ 15-)\ + \zeta(immigrants)$$
$$+ \mu\ v_{t-1} + \eta(X) + v' \tag{6}$$

Here too, the progressive taxes to be examined are income tax and corporate tax, and the regressive taxes are tobacco tax and VAT. The results of the test are presented in Table 3.6.

Before analyzing the results, I wish to emphasize that the lagged residuals are significant in all the regressions presented in Table 3.6, a finding that (according to Engel and Granger's hypothesis) supports the presence of a long-term relationship in all the cases that were

Table 3.6 *The relationship between politics and the ratio between progressive and regressive taxes (in parentheses: statistic t)**

	Income tax (i) and tobacco tax (j)	Income tax (i) and VAT (j)	Corporate tax (i) and tobacco tax (j)	Corporate tax (i) and VAT (j)
Constant	0.1 (1.0)	−0.04 (−0.8)	0.1 (1.1)	0.02 (0.6)
Dlog – Age 15–	9.3 (1.5)	2.7 (0.9)	8.6 (1.5)	1.8 (0.7)
Dlog – Age 65+	−18.9 (−4.3)***	−0.8 (−0.5)	−20.8 (−5.0)***	−0.4 (−0.2)
Dlog – Working population	−5.0 (−0.3)	−1.8 (−0.2)	−2.2 (−0.1)	−7.3 (−2.3)**
Dlog GDP adjusted for seasonality	−3.4 (−1.7)*	−0.2 (−0.7)	−1.2 (−1.5)	−0.1 (−0.6)
Dlog stock of immigrants	0.4 ^−7 (0.1)	−0.3^−6 (−0.3)	−0.1^−5 (−0.3)	0.9^5 (1.1)
Residual in lag	−0.1 (−2.8)***	−0.3 (−5.0)***	−0.1 (−3.2)***	−0.2 (−3.8)***
Right	0.08 (1.3)	0.03 (1.0)	0.07 (1.3)	−0.01 (−0.4)
Left	0.13 (1.9)*	0.07 (1.7)*	0.1 (1.8)*	0.01 (0.4)
Right-wing union	−0.04 (−0.6)	0.03 (1.1)	−0.06 (−0.9)	−0.004 (−0.1)
Center	−0.1 (−2.1)**	0.003 (0.2)	−0.1 (−2.6)***	0.006 (0.4)
DW	2.0	2.05	2.0	1.95
Adj. R Squared	0.06	0.09	0.13	0.07

* The regressions were made using TSLS and they include world trade as an instrumental variable for GDP together with lags in the other variables. In some cases, the serial correlation was also modified: *** significant at 1 percent; ** significant at 5 percent; * significant at 10 percent.

analyzed. As for the connection between politics and taxes, the results indicate two consistent patterns:

A. Parties at the center of the political map tend to minimize the relationship between progressive and regressive taxes, when discussing the connection between income tax and corporate tax and the tax on tobacco.

B. Left-wing parties tend to increase the relationship between progressive and regressive taxes: in income tax in relation to both VAT and tobacco tax, but in corporate tax in relation to tobacco tax only (with a significance of 10 percent). We emphasize that the last results show a lower level of significance.

These results are in the direction expected according to the findings of studies conducted in other parts of the world.

3.6 Summary and Conclusions

This chapter analyzes Israel's tax policy, with particular emphasis on the last fifteen years. During this period, unprecedented tax cuts were made with the purpose of enhancing Israel's competitive position vis-à-vis other advanced countries, after becoming a member of the OECD in 2010.

The chapter shows that following the reduction of the tax rates, taxes as a percentage of Israel's GDP are below the OECD average, and in some channels with strong international competition – such as corporate tax – Israel's tax rates are lower than those of a large group of countries. Composition of the taxes has also changed: indirect taxes account for a higher proportion of tax revenues than direct taxes, a development which reduces the progressiveness of the tax system in Israel.

Following my review and finding that the tax rates are consistent with the tax smoothing model, in which taxes are set in order to finance general government spending, I progressed to the next question: does expenditure explain taxes, or vice versa, do taxes determine the level of expenditure? Using Granger's causality tests, I showed that although from a historical perspective it is expenditure that dictates statutory tax levels, during the period 2003–2014, this relationship was reversed and a process of reducing the size of general government began which was driven by the tax cuts. From the historical perspective, the process that played out in this period was extraordinary, and it ended in the wake of the social unrest which led to the cancellation of the tax cuts that had been planned until 2016 and to a reversal of the statutory tax rate trend, as recommended by the Trajtenberg Committee. Note that in recent years, reductions of VAT and corporate tax rates have been implemented. However, the level of budget deficit in 2019 – which is higher than government target – and existing government commitments as reflected in the Numerator[19], signal that the continuity of such a process is doubtful.

Finally, I looked at findings from other parts of the world whereby tax developments are connected with decisions made by political

---

[19] The Numerator is published in a current basis by the Ministry of Finance. It shows future government commitments in the next three years and is presented to the Government in order to allow a transparent multi-year framework.

blocks, that determine the direction of the change in taxes – tax increases by left-wing parties and tax reductions by right-wing parties; I check whether these findings are valid in Israel as well. We found clear evidence that governments controlled by centrist parties lowered the rates of income tax and corporate tax. We also found that coalitions controlled by right-wing parties have a clear tendency to reduce the corporate tax rate. Regarding left-wing parties, although there were no clear findings for individual taxes, a review of the ratio between progressive and regressive taxes produced similar results to those obtained in other countries: left-wing parties tend to increase the ratio between income tax and corporate tax and tax on tobacco, and the ratio between income tax and VAT.

References

In Hebrew

Brender A., and Politzer E. (2014). *The Effect of Legislated Tax Changes on Tax Revenues in Israel*. Discussion Paper 2014.08. Jerusalem: Bank of Israel Research Department.

Geva A., and Drucker L. (2015). Growth in Israel: From a Developing Economy to a Modern Economy. *Bank of Israel Economic Review*, 88, 135–156.

Dahan, M. (2011). Inequality in Israel. Lecture for the TheMarker Conference, The College, Tel Aviv-Jaffa, September 4, 2011.

Flug, K., and Strawczynski, M. (2007). Persistent Growth and Macroeconomic Performance in Israel. *Bank of Israel Economic Review*, 80, 73–103.

Mazar, Y. (2013). The Effect of Fiscal Policy and Its Components on GDP in Israel. *Bank of Israel Economic Review*, 87, 31–68.

Strawczynski, M. (2015). *Israel's Taxation Policy in Coming Years in light of Growth and Inequality*. Policy Paper 2015.2, Aaron Center, IDC Herzliya.

―――― (2016). When Do Governments Raise Statutory Taxes in Israel? In David Gliksberg (ed.), *Collection of Papers in Honor of Prof. Aryeh Lapidot*. The Hebrew University of Jerusalem, 227–244.

Strawczynski, M., and Kedar, J. (2016). Development of the Progressivity of Statutory Taxes in Israel. In Leah Achdut, Michel Strawczynski, and Avia Spivak (eds.), *The State Budget for 2015: The Fifth Conference of the Van Leer Institute Economics and Society Program*, 61–74.

Zeira, J. (2007). *How Does Inequality Affect Growth?* Disputes in Economics Series. Publications of the Economics and Society Program, The Van Leer Jerusalem Institute.

Zeira, J., and Strawczynski, M. (2002). Reducing the Relative Size of the Government after 1985. In A. Ben-Bassat (ed.), *The Israeli Economy, 1985–1998: From Government Intervention to Market Economics.* Cambridge, MA: MIT Press. Also published in Hebrew by Am Oved, in 2001.

In English

Anderson, P. (2016). The Left and Taxation: the Impact of Electoral Systems. Paper presented at the 72nd Annual Congress of the International Institute of Public Finance (IIPF), held in Lake Tahoe, USA.

Atkinson, A. B., and Stiglitz, J. E. (1976). The Design of Tax Structure: Direct versus Indirect Taxation. *Journal of Public Economics*, 6(1–2), 55–75.

Banerjee, A., Mookherjee, D., Munshi, K., and Ray, D. (2001). Inequality, Control Rights and Rent Seeking: Sugar Cooperatives, Maharashtra. *Journal of Political Economy*, 109, 138–190.

Barro, R. J. (1979). On the Determination of Public Debt. *Journal of Political Economy*, 87, 941–971.

(2000). Inequality and Growth in a Panel of Countries. *Journal of Economic Growth*, 5, 5–32.

Blumkin, T., Margaliot, Y., and Strawczynski, M. (2016). *The Effect of Permanent Tax Cuts on Emigration from Israel.* CESIFO Working Paper No. 6095.

Blumkin, T., Sadka, E., and Shem-Tov, Y. (2014). International Tax Competition: Zero Tax Rate at the Top Re-established. *International Tax and Public Finance*, 22(5), 760–776.

Brender, A., and Navon, G. (2010). Predicting Government Tax Revenues and Analyzing Forecast Uncertainty. *Israel Economic Review*, 7(2), 81–111.

Capersen, E., and Metcalf, G. (1993). Is a Value Added Tax Progressive? Annual Versus Lifetime Incidence Measures. NBER Working Paper 4387. https://www.nber.org/papers/w4387.

Galor, O., and Moav, O. (2004). From Physical to Human Capital Accumulation: Inequality and the Process of Development. *Review of Economic Studies*, 71(4), 1001–1026.

Gomeh, C. and Strawczynski, M. (2019). Simulating corporate tax rate at Laffer Curve's peak using micro-data. Journal of Economics and Business, Forthcoming.

Gruber, J., and Saez, E. (2002). The Elasticity of Taxable Income: Evidence and Implications. *Journal of Public Economics*, 84, 1–32.

Hercowitz, Z., and Lipshitz, A. (2015). Tax Cuts and Economic Activity: Israel in the 2000s. *Israel Economic Review*, 12(2), 97–106.

Hercowitz, Z., and Strawczynski, M. (2004). The Dynamics of Public Debt When There Is a Debt/Output Guideline. *Israel Economic Review*, 2(1), 91–106.

Fredriksson, P., Wan, L., and Warren, P. (2013). Party Politics, Governors, and Economic Policy. *Southern Economic Journal*, 80(1), 106–126.

Nygard, O. E., and Revesz, S. T. (2015). Optimal Indirect Taxation and the Uniformity Debate: A Review of Theoretical Results and Empirical Contributions. Statistics. Norway Research Department, Discussion Paper No. 809.

Stein, E., and Caro, L. (2013). Ideology and Taxes. IDB Discussion Paper.

Panizza, Ugo (2002). Income Inequality and Economic Growth: Evidence from American Data. *Journal of Economic Growth*, 7, 25–41.

Persson, Torsten, and Tabellini, Guido (1994). Is Inequality Harmful for Growth? *American Economic Review*, 84, 600–621.

Pettersson-Lidbom, P. (2008). Do Parties Matter for Economic Outcomes? A Regression-Discontinuity. *Journal of the European Economic Association*, 6(5), 1037–1056.

Romer, C., and Romer, D. (2010). The Macroeconomic Effects of Tax Changes: Estimates Based on a New Measure of Fiscal Shocks. *American Economic Review*, 100, 763–801.

Strawczynski, M. (2014). Cyclicality of Statutory Tax Rates. *Israel Economic Review*, 11(1), 67–96.

4 | Inflation and Monetary Policy

SIGAL RIBON[*]

4.1 Introduction

The Israeli economy has come a long way since 1985, when the Stabilization Program was put into place to extricate it from hyperinflation, to the second decade of the twenty-first century, in which price stability prevails. The Stabilization Program succeeded in steering the economy from hyperinflation to a low double-digit inflation environment of approximately 20 percent. The attainment of price stability entailed a multiyear process, one customarily described as stepwise – a gradual slowing of the inflation rate, when opportunities presented themselves, from double digits down to near zero at the end of the period discussed.

In the early 2000s – as the Israeli economy settled into a price-stability environment fifteen years after the Stabilization Program – the main challenge for monetary policy was cementing the credibility of both the policy itself and the price stability attained. The inflation-target framework had not yet been adequately entrenched in Israel and abroad, and the exchange rate regime remained, officially, a managed float within a band. Later, from 2003 onward, after the government switched from setting calendar-bounded inflation targets to an ongoing inflation target of price stability within a 1–3 percent range, the credibility of monetary policy did establish itself and long-term inflation expectations have been around the 2 percent midpoint of the band in all years since 2005.

[*] The views expressed in this chapter are not necessarily those of the Bank of Israel. Gratitude is expressed to Daniel Levi and Chen Sakal for their assistance in preparing the data for the chapter, and to Alex Cukierman, the participants in the two Falk Institute workshops, and the editors of this book for their useful comments.

Until 2008, policy was managed in accordance with domestic business cycles, and inflation fluctuated widely around the 2 percent mark. The exchange rate regime moved to a free float when the band was officially abolished in 2005, and the Bank of Israel had not intervened in foreign currency trading since 1997. From 2004, following sharp upward and downward fluctuations, until the 2008 financial crisis, the monetary interest rate was relatively stable at around 3–5 percent. The crisis, conventionally said to have erupted with the collapse of Lehman Brothers in September 2008, changed the operating environment of monetary policy and, to a large extent, the framework of policy thinking in all countries including Israel.

Israel belongs to the group of small and open economies that did not sustain a financial or a real crisis pursuant to the events of 2008 but were affected by them through the impact of global activity on domestic activity and via the financial markets. Generally speaking, the dilemma that economies faced at this time can be described as tension between a monetary policy attuned to the state of the domestic business cycle and a policy considerate of the effect of the international financial markets and global monetary policies. Thus, even though activity in Israel was not seriously impaired when the crisis broke out, the uncertainty about the possibility of such impairment in the future made a very accommodative monetary policy an imperative at the time. The effect of very accommodative monetary policy abroad and the relatively good state of the domestic economy on the real exchange rate and through it, on activity, particularly that of the tradable sector, were given considerable weight in the management of domestic policy. Accommodation abroad and a similar policy at home, both reflected in major declines in yields to all maturities, drove the public to switch to riskier assets and, specifically, to the housing market. The need to adopt accommodative monetary policy due to activity and inflation and, in contrast, mounting risks in the assets market underscored the importance of a broad perspective, including considerations of financial stability, and led to the realization that monetary policy could be supported by means of additional, macroprudential, tools, in order to cope with the tension that had come about between the divergent goals of the policy.

In the years since the onset of the financial crisis, as significant monetary accommodation continued around the world, additional challenges to policy management have developed. In Israel, like else-where, nominal and real interest rates declined to historically low levels as the inflation environment decelerated. It is important to determine how much of the decline in (real) interest rates reflects a natural[1] decrease occasioned by expectations of a protracted growth slowdown.[2] It is also important to understand the reasons for the low inflation – those that obtain in the long term and those that reflect both the global business cycle and, in turn, the extent to which a small and open economy can conduct an independent monetary policy.

Another important debate that has evolved in recent years concerns the use of additional tools, initially called "unconventional," for policy management. In Israel, quantitative easing and negative interest rates have not been put to use; the main discussion concerns intervention in the foreign exchange market (manifested in purchases, for the time being).[3] In addition to intervening in the foreign exchange market, Israel has used forward guidance.

This chapter continues the chapters that described monetary policy and inflation in the previous reviews of the Israeli economy. The most meaningful change that occurred in Israel's economic environment relative to that of the decade starting in the second half of the 1980s, described in the book summarizing the Israeli economy in 1985–1998 (Ben-Bassat, 2001), is reflected in the main topics analyzed in the chapters of that book that discuss monetary policy and inflation.

The analysis in the three chapters of the previous book focused on the transformation of Israel's economy and its convergence to a low-inflation environment. Given that the principal role of fiscal policy was to facilitate the disinflation process, the need to maintain a stable and responsible fiscal policy was central to the analysis in those chapters. The background for the discussion of developments and policy in the current chapter, in contrast, is a stable underlying environment of monetary policy, fiscal policy, and inflation, and an acute external shock – the

---

[1] The natural rate of interest is the theoretical rate that the economy would set without price inelasticities. It may be estimated as the average of the real rate on 5Y–10Y sovereign bonds.

[2] See Larry Summers' references to "secular stagnation" in http://larrysummers .com/category/secular-stagnation.

[3] For a short time in 2009, long-term sovereign bonds were purchased in order to attenuate the slope of the yield curve. This was done alongside issuance of (one-year) T-bills (*Makam*) in order to sterilize the accommodation.

2008 financial crisis –whereas the fundamentals of the economy remained steady from the start of the research period to its end.

This substantive change in the characteristics of the monetary-policy discussion underscores how far the Israeli economy has come in respect of inflation and monetary policy since the mid-1980s Stabilization Program, and the most important policy achievement during that time – steering the economy to an environment in which the main challenge is maintaining price stability so that other important economic policy goals can be attained as well.

This chapter, in which monetary policy and inflation in Israel since the beginning of the 2000s are discussed, cannot address all issues related to policy and its management in those years. The discussion in section 4.2 of the chapter focuses on inflation and its characteristics and, particularly, the relationship between actual inflation and inflation expectations and between inflation and activity. Section 4.3 deals with the framework of monetary policy, policy tools, and transmission mechanisms, with special attention to interest rate policy and intervention in the foreign exchange market. Developments in inflation and monetary policy since 2000, with a distinction made between the period preceding the 2008 financial crisis and that following, are described in section 4.4. Section 4.5 concludes and presents some thoughts going forward.

4.2 Inflation, Inflation Expectations, and Their Connection with Activity[4]

4.2.1 Inflation

At the dawn of the twenty-first century, after the disinflation process that began with the 1985 Stabilization Program brought Israel's inflation rate down to single-digit levels, the government set, starting from 2003, an ongoing price-stability inflation target of 1–3 percent.

It is conventional to describe Israel's disinflation process in stepwise terms. Israel's first inflation target was set, in 1992, at 14–15 percent[5] for a calendar year. Subsequently, as inflation ebbed, calendar targets

---

[4] For an overview of Israel's inflation process since the early 1950s, see Cukierman and Melnick (2015).

[5] This target was set as an estimate with which the crawling band of the exchange rate could be demarcated. The transition to an inflation-target regime is conventionally said to have taken place in 1997.

for steadily falling inflation rates were set. By the beginning of the 2000s, the targets were set in a low environment – 4 percent for 1999, 3–4 percent for 2000, 2.5–3.5 percent for 2001, and 2–3 percent for 2002.[6] The setting of a long-term price-stability target in 2003 obviated the need to update the target each year. Actual inflation remained in the vicinity of price stability from the beginning of the 2000s onward but was volatile, particularly in the early years of the 2000s, staying within the bounds established in only about one-third of the period researched. In 40 percent of months, the actual annual inflation rate fell below the lower bound and in the other months, whenever there was a deviation – slightly more than one-fourth of the time – the upper bound was overshot (Figure 4.1).

Until 2008, inflation in Israel was typified by relatively acute volatility and large deviations from the target in both directions. An

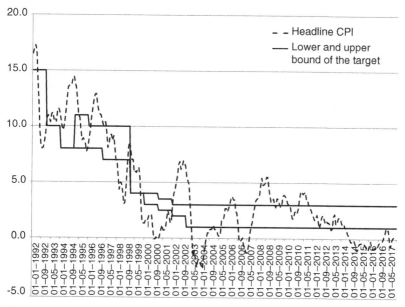

Figure 4.1 The rate of change of the overall CPI in the preceding 12 months and the inflation target, 1992–2017 (%).
Source: Central Bureau of Statistics and Bank of Israel

[6] In 1997 and 1998, the target was 7–10 percent.

important reason for this was that prices of housing services – measured by rent, and accounting for about a quarter of the Consumer Price Index (CPI) – and prices of additional goods and services (lawyers, restaurants, etc.) were denominated in dollars. Thus, the exchange rate volatility immediately found expression in these prices and in the CPI overall. From 2008 onward, after the eruption of the financial crisis in the United State, the inflation rate pursued a clear downward trend – from above the top of the target to low if not negative rates in recent years.

The contributions of the CPI components to inflation since 2000 are illustrated in Figure 4.2. Supply side factors contributed to the development of inflation during those years. These include energy prices, which are correlated with changes in global oil prices; food prices, which are also affected by global commodity prices; and telecommunication prices, which have had a moderating effect on inflation in recent

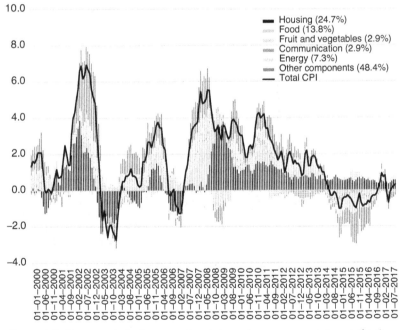

Figure 4.2 One-year inflation rate: breakdown by components' contribution, 2000–2017 (%).
Source: Based on Central Bureau of Statistics and Bank of Israel

years due to regulatory changes that stimulated competition in this market, along with technological developments.[7]

The CPI's housing component, which measures changes in rent, reflects the actual cost to renters and an imputation for owner-occupiers' expenditure on housing services. This component was markedly volatile until 2009 due to the common practice of denominating rent in US dollars along with considerable exchange rate volatility. After the dollar-denomination practice was discontinued and the quoting of rent was changed to shekels, this component became much less volatile, and its contribution to changes in the price index has been rather stable in recent years.

Since the financial crisis, the trend of inflation in Israel has resembled that of other advanced economies (Figure 4.3).[8]

The disparities between Israel and the rest of the world in the development of inflation trace to various domestic factors, particularly price changes originating in administrative changes (e.g., reducing the rate of Value Added Tax or water and electricity prices)[9] and the increase in competition and changes in consumers' behavior, including more online shopping. (For elaboration, see chapter 3 in the *Bank of Israel Annual Report* for 2016 and 2017.)

4.2.2 *Inflation Expectations*

Monetary policy under an inflation-target regime is based largely on stabilizing inflation expectations. The inflation expectations of households and firms affect their behavior and, specifically, affect firms' setting of prices and wages. This effect is described theoretically in the New Keynesian model, where firms cannot change prices (and

---

[7] A distinction should be made between the price level, which corresponds to the concept of "cost of living," and price changes, which define inflation. However, protracted changes in price level due to regulatory changes or the extent of competition in the market affect the inflation rate in the short term. For a discussion of the cost of living in Israel, see chapter 1 of the Bank of Israel Annual Report for 2014.

[8] See the analysis described in Box 3.2 of the Bank of Israel Annual Report for 2017. See also IMF WEO October 2016 and Auer et al. (2017). Mihailov et al. (2011), Mikolajun and Lodge (2016), and Forbes et al. (2017) also address the global effects on inflation and their connection with domestic activity.

[9] Although the price of electricity depends on oil prices, it is set intermittently on an administrative basis and is affected by long-term changes in oil prices, natural gas prices, and other factors.

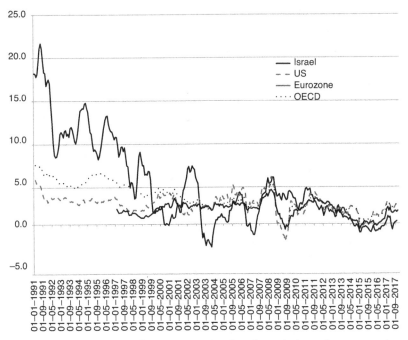

Figure 4.3 One-year inflation rate in Israel and in other countries, 2008–2017 (%).
Source: OECD data

wages) on a continuous basis and with full elasticity.[10] Within this model actual inflation is a function of producers' (suppliers') marginal cost[11] and inflation expectations. In an open economy, change in import prices (of commodities) may also be included as a factor influencing the development of inflation.[12] The decisions of savers and

[10] It is the accepted practice to assume a price-adjustment mechanism in accordance with Calvo's (1983) model, in which positive probability of a price adjustment exists in every period.

[11] The marginal cost in the New Keynesian Phillips curve may be estimated by means of the output gap or the unemployment rate, assuming that the larger the (negative) output gap is, or the higher the unemployment rate is, the milder the change in this cost will be. In the case of Israel, Elkayam et al. (2007) found that the output gap, in various measurements, has helped to predict inflation since 1992. Ribon (2004) found evidence of an effect of unit labor cost (an estimate of marginal cost) on the inflation rate.

[12] For an estimation of the Phillips curve for the Israeli economy, see Melnick and Strohsal (2016) as well as Lavi and Sussman (2007), Ribon (2004), and Box 3.2 of the *Bank of Israel Annual Report 2016*.

investors, which depend on the price of money – the expected real interest rate – also depend on inflation expectations.

It is important to examine short-term inflation expectations, which affect households' and firms' decisions, and medium- and long-term expectations, which attest to the extent to which the public has confidence in the will and ability of monetary policy to attain the inflation target and maintain it over time. Many financial and nonfinancial decisions of households and firms depend on their assessment of the extent of stability of the inflation environment over time.

Israel, given its history of high inflation, has a deep market for CPI-indexed government bonds. Thus, by considering unindexed bonds as well, one can derive the breakeven inflation rate from the market.[13]

As inflation rates converged to a low environment in the early 2000s, one-year breakeven inflation stabilized and ranged most of the time around the inflation target, with less volatility than actual inflation (Figure 4.4). Recently, however, the relation between actual and short-term breakeven inflation has strengthened, as had been the case in the late 1990s. Thus, short-term breakeven rates seem to be more "backward-looking" than before.

Cukierman and Melnick (2015) examined the β coefficient in an equation of the following type:

$$\pi_t^e = \beta \pi^T + (1 - \beta)\pi_{t-1}$$

and found that for the 2003 to mid-2014 period (the latter marking the end of their sample), breakeven rates were entrenched in the inflation-target range and were hardly affected by lagged inflation. We examined this relation across a longer period –up to the end of 2017 – by estimating a rolling regression for a four-year sub-period each time[14] and found that one-year breakeven rates were anchored firmly in the target until 2011 and much less so afterwards.

---

[13] We do not refer here to other alternative measures of inflation expectations such as professional forecasters' forecasts.

[14] Since empirical testing of the sample also reveals the existence of a constant, even though there is no theoretical justification for this, we added a constant to the estimated equation. The results of the estimation without the constant are qualitatively similar, although the coefficient of the breakeven rates is slightly smaller and more volatile across the period investigated. The constant may represent premia (liquidity, risk) included in the bond prices from which the breakeven rates were derived.

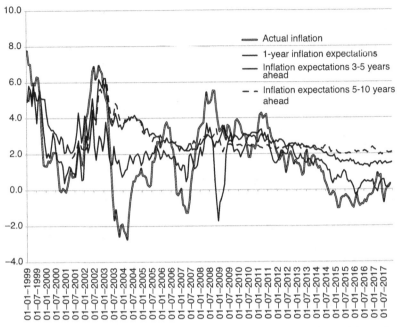

Figure 4.4 One-year inflation rate and inflation expectations derived from the capital market, 1999–2017 (%).
Source: Central Bureau of Statistics and Bank of Israel

In an earlier analysis, Elkayam and Ilek (2007) found that the hypothesis that breakeven rates (measured on the basis of the capital market) are rational, i.e., are unbiased, cannot be rejected, and that the public uses all available information to construct its expectations. Ribon and Sayag (2013), using the micro price data that the Israel Central Bureau of Statistics uses to construct the CPI – discovered that a lower inflation environment and lower one-year breakeven rates prolong the time between price adjustments, mitigate expected price changes, and reduce the proportion of prices that change each month.[15]

Breakeven inflation for longer terms reflect the probability that the public attributes to inflation's remaining within the target range set for

---

[15] Lach and Tsiddon (1996) and Eden (2001) also investigated the frequency of price adjustments in Israel and found it to be greater, in view of the relatively high inflation that prevailed during their research period. They did not relate to the effect of breakeven inflation on the frequency of price adjustments.

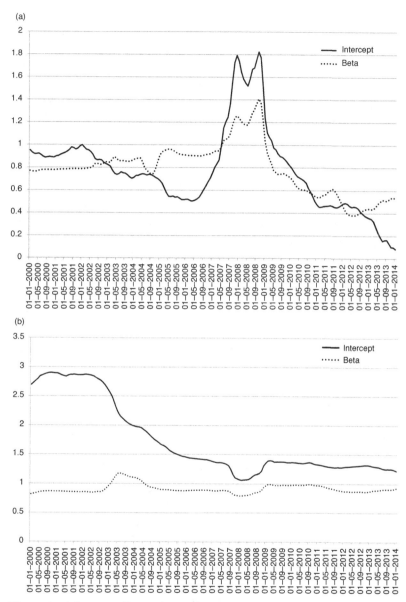

Figure 4.5 The β coefficient for the inflation target and the constant in the estimation equation for the coming year and for 5–10 years: A. 1-year expectations; B. 5–10 year expectations.

* The date on the horizontal axis in Figure 4.5 denotes the beginning month of the sample in each estimation

Source: Author's calculations

it; therefore, it indirectly reflects the public's confidence in monetary policy and its ability to attain the inflation target in the long term. Analyzing breakeven inflation expectations for five–ten years ahead, it was found that the coefficient of the inflation target has no trend around a unitary coefficient and falls into the 0.8–1.1 range (Figure 4.5). The constant stabilizes at a low level from the 2006 samples onward and reflects the convergence of long-term breakeven inflation to the midpoint of the inflation target.

4.2.3 Actual Inflation, Inflation Expectations, and Activity

We examined the relation between one-year breakeven inflation and activity as reflected by unemployment (Figure 4.6). The more break-even rates are anchored within the inflation target and the public expects monetary policy to keep inflation within the target range irrespective of the state of economic activity, the less we would expect to find correlation between activity and inflation expectations. Still, the weakening of the negative relation between unemployment and

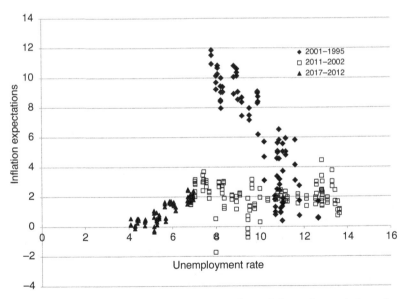

Figure 4.6 One-year inflation expectations derived from the capital market and the unemployment rate, 1995–2017 (%).
Source: Based on Central Bureau of Statistics and Bank of Israel

breakeven rates may also reflect the weakening of the relation between activity and actual inflation (the Phillips curve) in recent years.

Figure 4.6 indicates that in the 1990s and the early 2000s, before the permanent target of 1–3 percent was set, there was indeed a negative relation between unemployment and short-term breakeven rates. Afterwards, however, such a connection is hard to detect in the 2002–2011 period and in recent years, 2012–2017.

4.3 Monetary Policy Since 2000

4.3.1 Monetary Policy Goals and the Inflation Target

The goal of monetary policy is to attain the targets that the central bank has been assigned by law. According to (Section 3 of) the Bank of Israel Law, 5734–1954, in effect until 2010, the Bank's functions were to manage, regulate, and guide the currency system and to regulate and guide the credit and banking system in accordance with the government's economic policy and the provisions of the aforementioned law, so as to promote, by monetary means, (1) stability of the value of the currency in Israel and abroad and (2) high levels of production, employment, national income, and capital investment in Israel.

After the 1985 Stabilization Program, monetary policy acted to lower the annual inflation rate from 10–20 percent to the vicinity of price stability in a disinflation process, which continued throughout the 1990s and into the twenty-first century.[16] In the post-stabilization years, the exchange rate served policy as an important interim target (peg) as the Bank of Israel intervened in the foreign exchange market on a daily basis and sterilized the effect of the intervention on liquidity using monetary loans.

Israel adopted its inflation-target regime gradually.[17] It is the government that sets the price-stability range. At first, the inflation target was derived from the need to align the slope of the band with inflation differentials between Israel and its trading partners. Today, however, 1997 is conventionally marked as the starting point of the inflation-target regime. At that time, the inflation range was defined as a target

[16] For discussion of the disinflation process and its stepwise progress, see Cukierman and Melnick (2015).

[17] For a comprehensive overview of countries that operate under an inflation-target regime, see Svensson (2010) and Mishkin and Schmidt-Hebbel (2016).

on the basis of which the policy should operate, and the exchange rate band was widened considerably. Thus, the exchange rate regime moved closer to floating and the role of the exchange rate as a nominal peg diminished.[18]

From 2003 onward, the Bank of Israel has operated under a price-stability target that the government set in August 2000: 1–3 percent CPI inflation. Accordingly, the policy acted to attain the target at any point in time while allowing brief temporary deviations in either direction in order to prevent large fluctuations in the interest rate to the extent possible.[19] An inflation-target regime of this is called a "flexible inflation-target regime"[20] because it is not require / oblige attaining the target and keeping inflation within it at all points in time.

In 2010, when the new Bank of Israel Law was legislated, the Bank's goals were redefined, and maintaining price stability became the central goal (Section 3 of the law). Further in the law, where the Bank's objectives are established to include supporting other objectives of the government's economic policy – especially growth, employment, and reducing social gaps – a condition is attached: that in the Monetary Committee's opinion, "this support shall not prejudice the attainment of Price Stability over the Course of Time." The law defines "price stability over the course of time" as a situation in which the Committee, on the basis of the monetary policy that it has established, expects the inflation rate to be in the price-stability range within no more than two years.

Thus the law determined the time horizon toward which the Monetary Committee should steer its policy. The law also states that the Bank should act to support the stability and orderly activity of the financial system. To enable the Bank to strive to attain the goals set for it, the new law states explicitly (Section 5) that "To attain its objectives and discharge its functions, the Bank shall be autonomous in choosing its actions and exercising its powers." By affirming the Bank's

---

[18] On the transition from a fixed exchange rate regime to a floating regime, see Elkayam (2003). Barnea and Djivre (2004) detect a structural breakpoint in Bank of Israel policy in 1997 (in addition to the breakpoint in 1994) with the transition from an exchange rate regime to an inflation target with a floating exchange rate and unrestricted capital flows.

[19] See Bank of Israel (2007) for a report on the inflation-target regime.

[20] For references to such a regime, see Svensson (2010 and earlier studies) and the Bank of Israel Annual Report for 2006, in which a flexible inflation-target policy is discussed.

independence in using tools and taking actions to attain its goals, the law is supportive of the credibility that the public attributes to the Bank's ability to do this and, accordingly, to fulfill its purposes.

Cukierman's (2005) analysis of the extent of the Bank of Israel's independence even before the new law showed a major improvement in the actual (de-facto) Bank's independence index in the 1990s. The 2010 law also bolstered the central bank's independence by giving the price-stability target more weight than the previous version had.

In retrospect, it may be asked whether Israel's monetary policy has met its goals since the new law went into effect. Ostensibly, the parameter to examine is whether the inflation rate stayed within the designated target range, 1–3 percent, during this time. It is found that around 60 percent of the time since mid-2010 it did not (Figure 4.1). However, as stated, the essential goal of the monetary policy is to maintain long-term price stability under a flexible inflation-target regime. Thus, to assess the policy's success and credibility, it is important to examine breakeven inflation not only in the short term (one year) but in middle and long terms as well.

Table 4.1 shows that the longer and more distant the term to which breakeven inflation relates, the smaller the share of the period in which this indicator deviated from the inflation target. In particular, long-term breakeven rates have always been within the target range and, in fact, near its midpoint since 2010 if not earlier. Consequently, confidence in monetary policy has been maintained.

Table 4.1 *Proportion of months in which inflation and breakeven inflation deviated from the inflation target, 2003–2017 (%)*

	1/2003–12/ 2007	1/2003–5/ 2010	6/2010–12/ 2017
Inflation in past 12 months	70	80	61
Breakeven inflation to 1Y ahead	42	21	48
Breakeven inflation to 4Y–5Y ahead	34	47	10
Breakeven inflation to 6Y–10Y ahead	25	39	0

Source: Based on Central Bureau of Statistics and Bank of Israel

This regime, accepted in many countries, has helped to keep inflation in Israel stable for two decades but has presented policymakers, in Israel and in other developed economies, with dilemmas and difficulties in recent years due to persistent below target inflation and the difficulty of managing monetary policy in a zero-interest rate environment.[21]

4.3.2 Policy Tools and Transmission Mechanisms

To manage its monetary policy, the Bank of Israel has utilized two main tools in the past decade – the interest rate and foreign exchange market intervention. It has also operated by means of forward guidance – communicating with the public to affect its expectations of future policy.

4.3.2.1 The Bank of Israel Interest Rate

The main instrument of monetary policy in Israel and around the world, in reference to an inflation target regime, is the interest rate that the central bank sets and announces. A well-accepted way of describing a central bank's policy is to interpret its actual behavior via the "Taylor rule,"[22] according to which the interest rate that a central bank sets may be described as a function of the real long-term (natural) interest rate level and the long-term inflation rate (the inflation target) plus a response to the deviation of inflation from its target and to the output gap.[23] In Israel, this formula has been used in models that describe monetary policy and the Israeli economy (e.g., Argov et al., 2012).

Israel's interest rate decisions were made on a monthly basis until the end of 2016.[24,25] The Bank of Israel announced the interest rate that it would pay banks for their deposits with it (or would charge on loans

---

[21] The proponents of a higher inflation target include Blanchard et al. (2010) and Ball (2014). Kryvstov and Mendes (2015) argue against raising the target due to the distortions that this may cause. See also Bernanke (2016).

[22] See Taylor (1993).

[23] A central bank's behavior may also be described by presenting its utility function, as in Woodford (1999). For reference in the context of the Israeli economy, see Segal (2007).

[24] In a few cases, interest had to be reset at extraordinary times, e.g., in early October 2008 and early November 2009 in view of the global financial crisis.

[25] Since April 2017, the Bank of Israel has been making interest decisions only eight times per year. See press release, September 20, 2016: www.boi.org.il/en/New sAndPublications/PressReleases/Pages/20–9-16frequency.aspx. This brought the Bank of Israel's practice into alignment with that of central banks in other

that it gives them) and provided liquidity commensurate with demand at the interest level that it declared.

The main interest rate transmission mechanism is direct influence on demand for both private consumption and investment. Investment is also incentivized by the increase in asset prices that accompanies the lowering of the interest rate. Insofar as the change in short-term interest is manifested both in longer-term interest and in interest for households and firms, the effect on demand for credit, consumption, and invest-ment becomes increasingly powerful.[26,27] The effect of this channel on activity is relatively slow, and therefore the indirect effect of interest on prices, through its impact on activity, is even slower.

Given that Israel is a small open economy that is open to capital flows, the interest rate also has an effect via the exchange rate. The main effect of the exchange rate on prices concerns tradable goods and is usually faster than that via the direct path of activity mentioned above. Appreciation – higher prices of domestic goods, lower prices of imports, and lower local currency value of exports – is also likely to dampen domestic activity by reducing exports and boosting imports.

The third channel of possible transmission of interest rate policy is a direct effect on inflation expectations, particularly to short terms, and also, therefore, on the real interest rate. In addition, according to the New Keynesian approach, inflation expectations influence present inflation by affecting firms' pricing decisions.

In several empirical studies on the transmission mechanism in Israel,[28] it was found that the direct effect of an interest rate shock on activity is relatively meager and takes considerable time to manifest. The transmission mechanism of the exchange rate was found to be faster and more meaningful.[29]

advanced economies, e.g., the Fed, the ECB, the Bank of England, the Bank of Japan, and the Bank of Korea.

[26] Brender and Ribon (2015), examining the factors that affect real yields to various terms, find on average that monetary interest also affects medium- and long-term yields.

[27] Cohen (2017) shows that monetary policy also affects credit to firms via the "credit channel": interest changes affect firms' value, as measured in market-capitalization terms, and this, in turn, influences the supply of bank credit to firms that are identified as liquidity-limited.

[28] For example, Barnea and Djivre)2004), Azoulay and Ribon (2010), and Djivre and Yakhin (2010).

[29] A preliminary analysis, which is not presented here, shows that the links between the key variables – activity, inflation, the exchange rate, and the

4.3.2.2 Foreign Exchange Market Intervention

The Bank of Israel also conducts monetary policy by intervening in the foreign exchange market. Starting in the late 1990s, after monetary policy began to operate within the framework of an inflation target, the exchange rate was de facto floating with no central bank intervention. Only in March 2008, after more than a decade of nonintervention, did central bank intervention resume (Figure 4.7). To defend the declared interest rate, the Bank sterilized the increase in liquidity that its intervention had caused.[30]

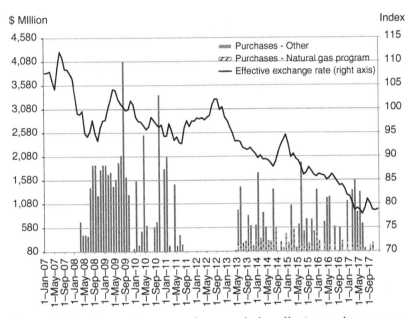

Figure 4.7 Foreign exchange purchases and the effective exchange rate, 2007–2017.
Source: Bank of Israel

policy rate –have changed over the past two decades, as a result of both structural changes and changes in the behavior of the central bank.

[30] From 2013 to the end of 2018, the Bank of Israel also bought foreign currency under a program that offset the effect of the domestic production of natural gas; the planned level of purchases in this setting was announced each year. This program was halted at the end of 2018. See also Bank of Israel, Report on the Investment of Israel's Foreign Exchange Reserves in 2016.

This intervention took place against the background of a global environment in which many countries hit by the 2008 financial crisis have been strongly accommodative since then, creating an incentive for capital flight to countries that offer more stable economic conditions and higher interest rates – particularly small and open markets such as Israel. To cope with the appreciation pressure that this has caused, many of them have reverted to intervention in their foreign exchange markets since the beginning of the crisis.[31]

At first, there were three goals for intervention: to build up the country's relatively small foreign reserves, to support the tradable sector in view of the financial crisis, and to minimize the impact of the crisis on the domestic economy. By the end of the period studied, as the monetary interest rate declined to a historical low of 0.1 percent, intervention was an additional tool of an accommodative policy that also helped to return inflation to the target range.[32]

Sorezcky (2010) examined whether the intervention manifests in an exchange rate other than the rate that would be expected when the estimation is performed without a variable that describes the intervention. He found that the main impact occurred at times when the Bank revised the nature of its intervention. More recently, Ribon (2017) found that foreign exchange purchases at a level equal to the monthly average in her research period – $830 million from September 2009 to December 2015 – contributed to nominal effective depreciation at the rate of 0.6 percent per month of intervention. Ribon's estimates shed no light on the duration and the cumulativity of this effect. Caspi et al. (2018) found that the Bank of Israel's intervention had an immediate effect on the exchange rate and that it lasted forty to sixty trading days. The three studies support signaling as an important mechanism of transmission from intervention to the exchange rate by finding that intervention, or the mere announcement of intervention, has an effect irrespective of its magnitude.

All the studies that test the impact of intervention in the foreign exchange market assume that the exchange rate regime allows the central bank to intervene. It is very difficult to estimate the effect of

[31] Ilzetzki et al. (2017), sorting the world's exchange rate regimes, particularly those of countries with inflation targets (table 2 in source), find frequent use of the limited-flexibility type.

[32] For discussion of the foreign currency market intervention, see also box in Bank of Israel, *Monetary Policy Report* for the second half of 2017.

the very existence of an intervention regime on the exchange rate, the foreign exchange market, other financial markets, and real magnitudes in the economy.

4.3.2.3 Forward Guidance

Forward guidance is another tool that the Bank of Israel, like other central banks, uses. It comes in various specifications, but the basic idea is using announcements to influence the public's expectations of the interest rate that the bank will set in the future. The Bank of Israel, like other central banks, revises its guidance policy occasionally, as specified in the section on the development of monetary policy since 2008. The effect of this policy instrument on the economy is hard to examine. Studies in this field deal mainly with understanding the short-term impact of central banks' announcements on market yields and prices of financial assets.[33] Kutai (2017), testing the impact of the Bank of Israel's use of forward guidance, found that the Bank's announcements affect yields to various durations and to different extents.

4.4 Brief Description of Monetary Developments, 2000–2017

4.4.1 *Policy Until the September 2008 Financial Crisis*

In the early 2000s, the Bank of Israel acted to solidify the credibility of the inflation-target regime. Although the inflation rate remained around the target, it was relatively volatile and strayed from the bounds of the target much of the time.

At the dawn of the new century, monetary policy operated against the background of the end of the growth period of the business cycle and the onset of slow growth, the bursting of the dot.com bubble, and the Second Intifada. As activity and inflation decelerated, monetary accommodation kicked in as the Bank of Israel lowered its interest rate from around 10 percent in early 2000 to 5.8 percent at the end of December 2001. In early 2002, the Bank made an exceptional 2 percent rate cut, to 3.8 percent. This unexpected measure induced swift depreciation that was reflected, among other things, in a spurt of inflation to around 6 percent. Concurrently, the slowdown in economic activity worsened, unemployment rose, and the public debt to GDP ratio rose

---

[33] See, for example, Filardo and Hofmann (2014) and Campbell et al. (2012).

amid uncertainty with regard to security, a slump in global activity, and fiscal accommodation in the first half of 2002. These developments, coupled with the impairment of confidence in monetary policy and an upturn in uncertainty, prompted the Bank, despite the slowing of economic activity, to raise its rate to 9.1 percent by year's end and to leave it high until the middle of 2003 (Figure 4.8).

The ongoing inflation target of 1–3 percent, set by the government in August 2000, went into effect in 2003. The changes in the monetary rate between 2003 in the middle of 2007 – mild ups and downs – reflected responses to the real activity environment, the inflation rate, and inflation expectations relative to the target, and all of these were against the backdrop of global developments, particularly changes in oil prices and fiscal policies. Overall, the interest rate in those years remained stable at around 4–5 percent in nominal terms. Short-term and longer-term real interest rates also stayed relatively steady.

The indexation of housing prices to the exchange rate lost some of its potency during the year, helping to diminish the impact of exchange

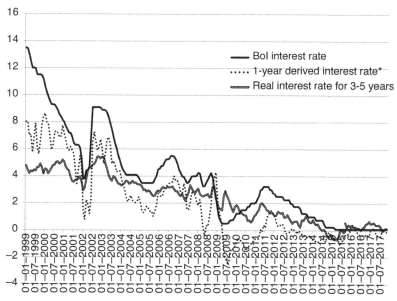

Figure 4.8 Bank of Israel interest rate and the derived real interest rate, 2000–2017 (%)

* The derived real interest rate is the Bank of Israel interest rate net of one-year inflation expectations derived from the capital market.

rate changes on inflation and mitigating inflation volatility. By the end of 2007, the share of new leases executed in USD declined to around 65 percent.[34]

The crawling band of the exchange rate was officially abolished in 2005 after considerable widening, and de facto the NIS has been allowed to float with no intervention by the Bank of Israel since 1998.[35]

From mid-2007 onward, as indications of financial crisis in the United States became apparent, the Fed began to lower the federal funds rate moderately. The Bank of Israel, in contrast, raised its rate slightly in the second half of 2007, chiefly due to domestic factors.

In March 2008, even before the crisis intensified notably in September, the Bank of Israel began to intervene in the foreign exchange market by buying foreign exchange after not having done so for more than a decade. In early March, after an abnormal change in exchange rate, the Bank purchased foreign currency and announced that it had done so "in light of the unusual movements in the shekel exchange rate in the last few days."[36] Ensuing intervention took place in amounts known in advance – initially $25 million per day and, from July 2008 to a year later, with steep appreciation in the background, $100 million per day. According to the Bank's press releases, the initial purpose of the intervention was to build up the foreign reserves to a predetermined quantitative target and in view of "the needs of the rapidly growing Israeli economy and its increasing integration into the global economy and global financial system."[37]

Overall, the Bank of Israel's policy goal between 2003 and early 2008 may be defined as adherence to the inflation target with attention to changes in real activity. The policy tool was the interest rate, which the Bank adjusted within the framework of a flexible inflation-target regime and a totally flexible exchange rate until it began to intervene in March 2008.

---

[34] The proportion fell to 19 percent by the end of 2008 and to only 3 percent in 2011.

[35] For a discussion of foreign currency market policy, see also subsection 4.3.2.2.

[36] See press release, March 13, 2008: www.boi.org.il/en/NewsAndPublications/PressReleases/Pages/080314f.aspx

[37] In its press release of March 20, 2008, the Bank announced a target of $35–40 billion. In its release of November 30, 2008, the level was adjusted to $40–44 billion.

4.4.2 Policy Since September 2008

Although the onset of the financial crisis was felt in 2007, the tipping point arrived in September 2008 with the collapse of the Lehman Brothers investment bank.[38]

Israel was not directly adversely impacted by the crisis. Its real activity environment was solid – a relatively robust growth rate, rather low unemployment by the standards of the time, a small government deficit, a downward trend in the government debt, a stable financial system, low household leverage, and a current account surplus. (See the *Bank of Israel Annual Report 2009*, particularly Section 5 of chapter1, and relevant chapters in this book.)

Policy since the crisis erupted may be divided into three main sub-periods: the onset of the crisis, typified by acute uncertainty and rapid interest rate reductions until the middle of 2009; an upward trend in monetary interest until the middle of 2011 as domestic economic activity rebounded swiftly and inflation overshot the upper bound of the target; and from then to the present, characterized by monetary accommodation coupled with near-zero interest rates, intervention in the foreign exchange market, and forward guidance.

When the global financial crisis erupted, its potential effect on Israel was accompanied by immense uncertainty. Short-term breakeven inflation rates, derived from the capital market, plunged to negative levels even though long-term breakeven inflation remained stable. Despite the onset of crisis in September, however, the actual inflation environment remained high due to continued upturns in commodity prices and the only gradual adjustment of real activity to the slowdown. The principal effect of the crisis on the Israeli economy took place in real activity – a slump in demand for Israeli exports – and in currency appreciation. The financial impact, in contrast, was limited; the uncertainty was manifested in the widening of financial spreads.

Monetary policy responded with swift interest rate decreases, from 4.25 percent in September to 1.75 percent in January 2009 and to 0.5 percent in April 2009; the last-mentioned rate was estimated then as the lowest possible effective level. The path resembled the steep cutting of interest in the United States, Europe, and other countries (Figure 4.9).

---

[38] For an extensive overview of nonconventional policies around the world since the crisis, see Borio and Zabai (2016).

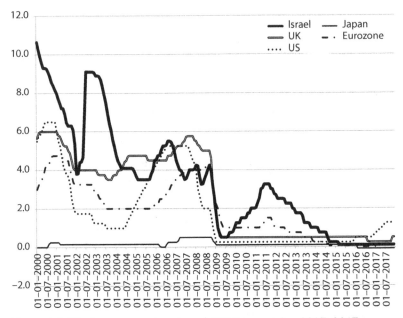

Figure 4.9 The interest rate in selected OECD countries, 2007–2017
Source: OECD and the Bank of Israel

Notwithstanding the crisis, inflation in Israel overshot the target in all of 2008 and most of 2009. Monetary policy attributed much importance to support for real activity. Owing to concern about the effect of the global crisis on the economy and the severe uncertainty that reigned at the time, monetary policy became strongly accommodative even though inflation exceeded the target.

The Bank of Israel continued to intervene in the foreign exchange market at this time.[39] After the global crisis erupted in late 2008, the Bank revised its description of the reasons for its foreign currency purchases. Now, while continuing to cite the need to build up the foreign reserves, it added references to the economic situation abroad and to its own comprehensive policy.[40]

[39] It also intervened in the secondary market, that of government bonds, in order to support the downward movement of long-term interest rates and flatten the yield curve. Doing so on the basis of a program that it had announced, it acquired NIS 18 billion in bonds by August.

[40] For a description of changes in the intervention policy, see the press releases from March 25, 2009, August 3, 2009, and August 10, 2009, and the Bank of Israel's Annual Report for 2009.

From August 2009 onward, as the concerns of the effects of the crisis on Israel waned and activity improved, monetary policy turned from accommodative to tight. The monetary rate was raised to 0.75 percent for September 2009 and to 2 percent at the end of 2010. Policy was conducted in an environment of forces acting in different directions, uncertainty about the extent of the global economy's recovery from the financial crisis, and an upturn in Europe's debt crisis. Intervention in the foreign exchange market in variable sums continued and initial macroprudential policy measures in the housing market were taken.[41] These measures are expected to make monetary accommodation easier to manage by weakening the transmission from loose money to the cost of housing credit, causing the relative price of this credit to rise.

The rate-hiking trend continued until above-target inflation and continued rapid growth pushed the rate up to 3.25 percent in the middle of 2011. That summer, social protests erupted against the cost of living generally and that of housing services particularly, leading to the establishment of the Committee for Social and Economic Change, known as the Trajtenberg Committee, as it was chaired by Professor Manuel Trajtenberg. The protests and their possible short-term effects on prices and activity made it difficult, at the time, to determine whether the activity slowdown was temporary or indicative of a trend. The slowdown in the rate of increase in home prices at that time, coupled with a downturn in the volume of transactions, proved after the fact to be a minor pause; both resumed their upward march in the ensuing years.[42]

In early 2011, the Bank of Israel acted against large short-term capital inflows that were generating appreciation pressure.[43] For this reason, along with an increase in regional risk due to the eruption of the

---

[41] Specifically, a larger capital allocation for high-leverage housing loans, reclassification of buying groups for construction and real estate instead of housing, reexamination of risk management in the credit portfolio, and a larger capital allocation for floating-interest loans.

[42] For discussion of the effects of the social protests, see the chapter on fiscal policy in this book.

[43] The steps included compulsory reporting of resident activity in foreign currency derivatives, compulsory reporting of nonresident activity in *Makams*, and compulsory liquidity for banking corporations on account of transactions in foreign currency derivatives with nonresidents. See Bank of Israel press releases, January 19 and January 20, 2011. Also, the Ministry of Finance announced the repeal of a nonresident tax exemption on investments in *Makams*.

"Arab Spring," the appreciation trend stopped and the share of non-residents in *Makam* holdings retreated from a peak of 36 percent to less than 15 percent at year's end. Accordingly, the Bank of Israel did not intervene in foreign exchange trading from August 2011 to March 2013. During that time, amid escalation of the crisis in Europe and fears of its recession-provoking impact on the Israeli economy, a decline in the inflation environment, and the acceleration of growth, a rate-cutting process ensued in September 2011 and continued until March 2015, when the monetary rate fell to its minimum of 0.1 percent and stayed there.

In 2012, the macroeconomic effects of inflation were augmented by institutional and structural factors that impacted on the CPI: regulatory changes that stimulated competition in the telecommunication market and gave telecom prices a strong downward push. Conversely, food and energy prices had an upward effect on the CPI.

The renewed increase in home prices made monetary policy harder to manage by creating tension between the main goals of the policy – maintaining price stability and supporting activity – and another goal of the central bank, macroprudential stability. To mitigate the risk created by these developments in the housing market, the Banking Supervision Department adopted additional macroprudential measures, foremost LTV limits.

In 2013, monetary policy continued to contend with mild inflation, currency appreciation, and relatively sluggish growth in view of dampened activity abroad, along with continued increase in domestic housing prices. The interest rate was reduced during the year from 1.75 percent to 1 percent, and foreign currency purchases resumed in April.

In 2014, CPI inflation continued to slow – undershooting the lower band of the target from mid-year onward and turning negative toward year's end, largely due to steep declines in oil and food prices and an upturn in price competition in the telecommunication market. Monetary policy responded by continuing to lower the rate, to 0.25 percent in September 2014 and to a minimum of 0.1 percent in March 2015, coupled with continued purchases of foreign currency. The Monetary Committee also noted that it was considering the use of additional unconventional policy tools. Although it did not make use of those, it continued to include similar wording in its interest rate decision announcements until December 2015.

Several factors prompted the Bank to leave its rate without further reduction. The real activity environment was believed to be reasonable and the low inflation rate was considered the product of exogenous effects stemming from global commodity prices along with the impact of the administrative price reductions by the government. The Bank's abstention from further interest rate cutting was also abetted by nearing an environment that would entail the use of tools that were unfamiliar in Israel, and with which other countries also had little experience, such as a negative interest rate. Apart from maintaining a near-zero interest rate, the Bank of Israel implemented forward guidance by revising the wording of the announcements that accompanied its interest rate decisions. Considerations of financial stability, for which macroprudential tools exist, acted in the same direction of caution in applying additional easing.

The persistence of low inflation despite the full employment environment and rising nominal wages is still not fully understood. Government administrative interventions do not explain all of the decline in the inflation rate during these years. Some of the explanation may have to do with the enhanced domestic competition due to a large increase in Israeli consumers' exposure to online shopping abroad.[44] In both 2016 and 2017, the Bank of Israel left its interest rate at 0.1 percent, but the Monetary Committee revised its press releases to signal future policy. The Bank also continued to purchase foreign currency as the shekel continued to appreciate in terms of its effective exchange rate.

4.4.3 Indicators of the Extent of Monetary Accommodation

In contrast to the management of monetary policy in the 1990s, when money supply served as a main indicator,[45] in an inflation-target regime, money supply is not a meaningful measure for the examination of monetary conditions in the economy. Still, it is of interest to test the effect of changes in monetary policy on the monetary aggregates.

[44] The prices of goods purchased on international sites are not included in the CPI, but they place domestic producers and merchants under pressure to reduce profit margins. The matter is also referenced in chapter 3 of the Bank of Israel Annual Reports for 2016 and 2017.

[45] Under the old Bank of Israel Law, which remained in effect until 2010, the Bank had to report whenever means of payment increased by more than 15 percent within a twelve-month period. See also Djivre and Tsiddon, in Ben-Bassat (2001).

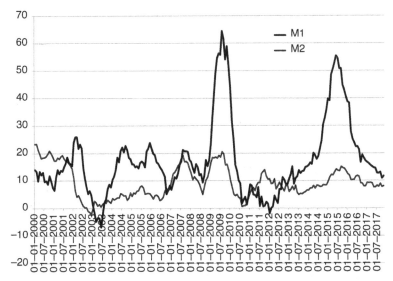

Figure 4.10 Annual rate of growth of means of payment (M1) and M2, 2000–2017 (%).
Source: Bank of Israel

The rate-cutting processes in 2008–2009 and 2011–2014 were accompanied by accelerated expansion in means of payment (the M1 aggregate – cash held by the public plus demand deposits). Nevertheless, the growth rate of the broader M2 aggregate, which includes the foregoing plus domestic-currency time deposits (up to one year), remained rather stable at around 10 percent per year or less (Figure 4.10) and was not accompanied by a faster rate of inflation.[46]

The extent of monetary accommodation is also examined by the spread between short-term interest rates, determined by monetary policy, and the far-forward interest rate, which reflects the interest rate that is expected to prevail in the long term and is affected only marginally by monetary policy.

Figure 4.11 describes the nominal forward yield for years 5–10 from today, the one-year nominal yield (which closely approximates the

---

[46] Inflation rates in other developed countries also lagged far behind the growth of money supply.

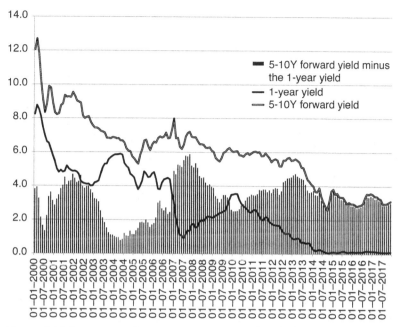

Figure 4.11 Interest rate for one year, 5–10 year forward rate, and the spread between them, 2003–2017 (%).
Source: Bank of Israel

Bank of Israel interest rate[47]), and the spread between them. It may be seen that up to 2014, and particularly from 2007 onward, when the Bank of Israel rate declined, the spread between the far-forward yield and the near-term yield widened, meaning that, according to this indicator, accommodation became stronger. In the past few years, however, even though nominal rates essentially fell to zero, their spread against long-term yields did not widen because long-term yields also declined. Although the decline in long-term nominal interest may have reflected a change in the natural long-term interest rate, it was also influenced by quantitative easing (QE) policies abroad, which had a downward effect on these rates. In other words, monetary policy acted not only on short-term yields but also on the long segment of the curve.

[47] Nominal ten-year sovereign bonds were issued only from mid-2001 onward. We chose to start the figure in 2003, when the 1–3 percent inflation target went into effect permanently.

4.5 Conclusion and Thoughts Going Forward

This chapter presented a review of monetary policy and the development of inflation since the beginning of the 2000s. The first part of the research period was typified by the end of the disinflation process and the consolidation of a price-stability environment. Developments in the second part of the period were affected mainly by the 2008 global financial crisis and its outcomes, which projected onto the Israeli economy and the frame of thought about domestic policy.

Inflation in the years since the turn of the century corresponds to a price-stability environment. In recent years, the inflation environment has been very low –below target and at times negative. Monetary policy is managed within the framework of an inflation-target regime and uses the interest rate as its primary policy tool. Intervention in the foreign exchange market has also been an important policy component, as has been forward guidance in recent years. The analysis shows that policy decisions are not derived from inflation only; activity has also figured importantly in these decisions and took on added weight at the time of the financial crisis. There is also evidence that the links between the key variables – activity, inflation, the exchange rate, and the policy rate – have changed over the past two decades.

The level of the interest rate, which remains at a historical low, presents monetary policy with a challenge in the near and medium terms. The low-interest environment limits the ability of policy to apply further easing at the present time, even if a negative shock in the future entails a sizable accommodative response. In the past decade, "unconventional" tools were central in the professional debate. Many countries used tools such as QE, negative interest, and forward guidance. Israel's policymakers chose not to set a negative interest rate because, among other reasons, the state of the economy did not warrant one. However, they made ample use of intervention (purchases) in the foreign exchange market as an additional monetary tool. The use and the effect of these tools – in Israel and elsewhere – are still not adequately understood, and research on them, including study based on the experience accumulated, is an important challenge for policymakers in the years to come.

Rapid changes in the technological environment are affecting every sphere of our lives, including monetary policy. Thus, production-function changes in industries are affecting productivity, the pricing mechanism, and our ability to measure output and its price correctly. Changes in patterns of trade and price-setting – particularly the spread of e-commerce – are affecting the structure of competition in various industries, and relations between activity and prices and among policy, prices, and inflation. Such changes, one presumes, will persist and even expand in the future.

The technological changes are also affecting our understanding of the concept of "money." Although we did not elaborate on the topic in this chapter, it is clear that means of payment as we know them today will not remain unchanged in the future. The growth of innovative electronic means of payment, possibly crowding out cash, may affect the role of the central bank in creating money and also, perhaps, its ability to control means of payment.

The developments and changes in the global environment after the 2008 financial crisis led to rethinking and discussion of the relations among macroeconomic variables – particularly activity, employment, and inflation – and between them and the financial markets. The rapid technological developments that affect these relations also pose a major challenge to central banks and other policymakers in Israel and around the world because of the need to understand them and make the requisite policy adjustments.

References

In Hebrew

Bank of Israel (2007). The Inflation Target: A Rethinking. Memorandum, August 2007. www.boi.org.il/deptdata/papers/paper13h.pdf.

Ben-Bassat, A. (2001). From Government Intervention to Market Economy: The Israeli Economy, 1985–98, Part 2: Monetary Policy and the Inflationary Process. In A. Ben-Bassat (ed.), *The Israeli Economy, 1985–1998: From Government Intervention to Market Economics*. Tel Aviv: Am Oved Publishers, 79–204.

Ben-Bassat, I. (1992). Price Indices for Tradable and Nontradable Products. *Bank of Israel Review*, 66 (January), 19–34.

Cohen, G. (2017). *A Direct Approach to Identification of the Balance Sheet Channel: An Empirical Examination in Israel*. Discussion Paper 2017.08. Jerusalem: Bank of Israel Research Department.

Elkayam, D., Regev, M., and Alashvili, Y. (2002). *Estimation of the Output Gap and Examination of its Effect on Inflation in Israel During the Last Few Years.* Monetary Studies 2005.03, Bank of Israel Monetary Department.

Orfaig (Flikier), D. (2015). *Transmission Channels from the Exchange Rate to the Consumer Price Index: The Tradable Component of the CPI by Industry.* Discussion Paper 2015.04. Jerusalem: Bank of Israel Research Department.

Ribon, S. (2009). *Core Inflation Indices for Israel.* Discussion Paper 2009.08. Jerusalem: Bank of Israel Research Department.

(2015). *Household Personal Inflation: How Does Residential Area Affect It?* Discussion Paper 2015.03. Jerusalem: Bank of Israel Research Department.

Segal, G. (2007). *An Optimal Interest Rate Rule for the Israeli Economy in the Framework of the Rational Expectations Model.* Monetary Studies 2007.05. Jerusalem: Bank of Israel Monetary Department.

Sorezky, A. (2010). *Did the Bank of Israel Affect the Exchange Rate?* Discussion Paper 2010.10. Jerusalem: Bank of Israel Research Department.

Stein, R., Nathan, D., and Gamarsani, I. (2009). Examining the Effect of Foreign Exchange Market Intervention. Internal Memorandum. Bank of Israel Research Department.

In English

Argov. E., Barnea,E., Binyamini, A., Borenstein, E., Elkayam, D., and Rozenshtrom, I. (2012). *MOISE: A DSGE Model for the Israel Economy.* Discussion Paper 2012.06. Jerusalem: Bank of Israel Research Department.

Auer, R., Borio, C., and A. Filardo (2017). The Globalization of Inflation: The Growing Importance of Global Value Chains. *CEPR Discussion Paper* 11905, March.

Azoulay E., and Ribon, S. (2010). *A Basic Structural VAR of Monetary Policy in Israel Using Monthly Frequency Data.* Discussion Paper 2010.04. Jerusalem: Bank of Israel Research Department.

Bank of Israel. *Monetary Policy Report.* Various periods. Jerusalem.

Bank of Israel. *Financial Statements.* Various years. Jerusalem.

Bank of Israel. *Bank of Israel Annual Report.* Various years. Jersualem: Bank of Israel.

(2016). *Report on the Investment of Israel's Foreign Exchange Reserves.*

Ball, L. (2014). The Case of Long-Run Inflation Target of Four Percent. *IMF Working Paper* 14/92, June.

Barnea, A., and Djivre, J. (2004). *Changes in Monetary and Exchange Rate Policies and the Transmission Mechanism in Israel, 1989.IV – 2002.I.* Discussion Paper 2004.13. Jerusalem: Bank of Israel Research Department.

Bernanke B. (2016). Modifying the Fed's Policy Framework: Does a Higher Inflation Target Beat Negative Interest Rates? September 13. *Brookings.* www.brookings.edu/blog/ben-bernanke/2016/09/13/modifying-the-feds-policy-framework-does-a-higher-inflation-target-beat-negative-interest-rates/.

Blanchard, O., Dell'Ariccia, G., and Mauro, P. (2010). Rethinking Macroeconomic Policy. *IMF Staff Position Note*, SPN/10/03.

Borio, C., and Zabai, A. (2016). Unconventional Monetary Policies: A Re-appraisal. *BIS Working Papers* No. 570.

Brender, A., and Ribon, S. (2015). *The Effect of Fiscal and Monetary Policies and the Global Economy on Real Yields of Israel Government Bonds.* Discussion Paper No. 2015.02. Jerusalem: Bank of Israel Research Department.

Calvo, G. A. (1983). Staggered Prices in a Utility-Maximizing Framework. *Journal of Monetary Economics*, 12(3), 383–398.

Campbell J., Evans, C. L., Fisher, J., and Justiniano, A. (2012). Macroeconomic Effects of Federal Reserve Forward Guidance. *Brookings Papers on Economic Activity*, 1(Spring), 1–80.

Caspi, I., Friedman, A., and Ribon, S. (2018). *The Immediate Impact of FX Intervention on the Exchange Rate and Its Persistence over Time.* Discussion Paper 2018.04. Jerusalem: Bank of Israel Research Department.

Cukierman, A. (2005). Legal, Actual and Desirable Independence: A Case Study of the Bank of Israel. *CEPR Discussion Paper* 4906.

Cukierman, A., and Melnick, R. (2015). The Conquest of Israel Inflation and Current Policy Dilemmas. In A. Offenbacher (ed.), *Maintaining Price Stability: The Bank of Israel's Sixth Decade.* Jerusalem: Bank of Israel Press, 13–62.

Djivre J., and Y. Yakhin (2010) *A Constrained Dynamic Model for Macroeconomic Projection in Israel.* Bank of Israel Discussion Paper 2010.11.

Eden, B. (2001). Inflation and Price Adjustment: An Analysis of Microdata. *Review of Economic Dynamics*, 4(3), 607–636.

Elkayam, D. (2003). *The Long Road from Adjustable Peg to Flexible Exchange Rate Regimes: The Case of Israel.* Monetary Studies 2003.04. Jerusalem: Bank of Israel.

Elkayam, D., and Ilek, A. (2007). *The Information Content of Inflationary Expectations Derived from Bond Prices in Israel.* Monetary Studies 2007.06. Jerusalem: Bank of Israel.

Filardo, A. J., and Hofmann, B. (2014). Forward Guidance at the Zero Lower Bound. *BIS Quarterly Review* (March).

Friedman, M. (1969). *The Optimal Quantity of Money*. Chicago, IL: Aldine Publishing Co.

Forbes, K., Kirkham, L., and Theodoridis, K. (2017). *A Trendy Approach to UK Inflation Dynamics*. External MPC Unit Discussion Paper No. 49, Bank of England.

Gali, J. (2015). *Monetary Policy, Inflation, and the Business Cycle: An Introduction to the New*. Keynesian Framework. Princeton, NJ: Princeton University Press.

Horvarth, R., Smidkova. K., and Zapal, J. (2012). Central Banking Voting Records and Future Policy. *International Journal of Central Banking*, 8 (4), 1–19.

International Monetary Fund (2016). Global Disinflation in an Era of Constrained Monetary Policy. Chapter 3 of IMF *World Economic Outlook*, October.

Ilzetzki E., Reinhart, C. M., and Rogoff, K. (2017). Exchange Arrangements Entering the 21st Century: Which Anchor Will Hold? NBER Working Paper No. 23134, February. www.nber.org/papers/w23134.

Kutai, A. (2017). Measuring the Effect of Forward Guidance in Small Open Economies. Unpublished memorandum.

Kryvstov, A., and Mendes, R. (2015). *The Optimal Level of the Inflation Target: A Selective Review of the Literature and Outstanding Issues*. Discussion Paper, 2015-08. Ottawa: Bank of Canada.

Lach, S., and Tsiddon, D. (1996). Staggering and Synchronization in Price Setting: Evidence from Multiproduct Firms. *American Economic Review*, 86, 1175–1196.

Lavi, Y., and Sussman, N. (2007). The Phillips Curve in Israel. *Israel Economic Review*, 5(1), 93–109.

Mihailov, A., Rumler, F., and Scharler, J. (2011). The Small Open-Economy New Keynesian Phillips Curve: Empirical Evidence and Implied Inflation Dynamics. *Open Economies Review*, 22(2), 317–337.

Melnick, R., and Strohsal, T. (2015). *From Galloping Inflation to Price Stability in Steps: Israel, 1985–2013*. SFB 649 Discussion Paper 2015-009. Freie Universitat Berlin.

  (2016). Disinflation and the Phillips Curve: Israel 1986–2015. Memorandum, August 2016.

Mikolajun, I., and Lodge, D. (2016). *Advanced Economy Inflation: The Role of Global Factors*. ECB Working Paper Series (LIFT –Task Force on Low Inflation), No. 1948.

Mishkin, F. S., and Schmidt-Hebbel, K. (2001). One Decade of Inflation Targeting in the World: What Do We Know and What Do We Need to

Know. NBER Working Paper No. 8397. www.nber.org/papers/w8397.

Primicieri, G. (2005). Time Varying Structural Vector Autoregressions and Monetary Policy, *The Review of Economic Studies*, 72(3), 821–852.

Ribon, S. (2004). *A New Phillips Curve for Israel*. Discussion Paper 2004.11. Jerusalem: Bank of Israel Research Department.

(2017). *Why the Bank of Israel Intervenes in the Foreign Exchange Market, and What Happens to the Exchange Rate*. Discussion Paper 2017.04. Jerusalem: Bank of Israel Research Department.

Ribon, S., and Sayag, D. (2013). *Price Setting Behavior in Israel: An Empirical Analysis Using Microdata*. Discussion Paper 2013.07. Jerusalem: Bank of Israel Research Department.

Ruge-Murcia, F., and Riboni, A. (2017). Collective versus Individual Decision Making: A Case Study of the Bank of Israel Law. *European Economic Review*, 93, 73–89.

Sussman, N., and Zohar, O. (2016). *Has Inflation Targeting Become Less Credible? Oil Prices, Global Aggregate Demand and Inflation Expectations During the Global Financial Crisis*. Discussion Paper 2016.13. Jerusalem: Bank of Israel Research Department.

Svensson, Lars E. O. (1997). Inflation Forecast Targeting: Implementing and Monitoring Inflation Targets. *European Economic Review*, 41, 1111–1146.

(2010). Inflation Targeting. In B. M. Friedman and M. Woodford (eds.), *Handbook of Monetary Economics*, Vol. 3B. Handbooks in Economics. San Diego, CA: North Holland, 1237–1302.

Taylor, John B. (1993). Discretion versus Policy Rules in Practice.*Carnegie-Rochester Conference Series on Public Policy*, 39: 195–214.

Woodford, Michael (1999). Optimal Monetary Policy Inertia. NBER Working Paper No. 7261. https://www.nber.org/papers/w7261.

5 | From Deficits to Surpluses: Israel's Current Account Reversal

LEONARDO LEIDERMAN AND VICTOR BAHAR

5.1 Introduction

When discussing current account reversals, the typical case considered in the literature is that of an emerging market economy that, due to adverse shocks, shifts from surpluses to deficits; see, e.g., Milesi-Ferretti and Razin (1998).[1] Things might become more complicated for such an economy if and when the foregoing developments are accompanied by a sharp reduction in foreign capital inflows. In this case, the adjustment mechanism is expected to work through nominal and real exchange rate depreciation, together with a decline in the level of economic activity as well as imports. This adjustment is often rapid and volatile, and could also feature a credit crunch, corporate failures due to currency mismatches in their balance sheets, a speculative attack on the currency, and a banking sector crisis.

Israel's current account reversal has been in the opposite direction: from deficits to surpluses. Historically, the 1960s and 1970s exhibited large deficits in the current account of the balance of payments due to the need to build the country's infrastructures and, at the same time, to put together and maintain a large and modern defense force. These processes demanded high levels of real investment, of defense imports, and of public sector spending. The main difficulty in these years was to find the foreign currency resources needed to finance the large deficit in the current account, a difficulty often termed by economists as Israel's balance of payments "problem." The main resources were donations and loans from world Jewry and from the US government. In those years, there was also a sharp discussion of the issue of Israel's "economic independence."

---

[1] The literature includes papers like Adalet and Eichengreen (2007) and de Mello et al. (2010).

138

The deficits in the current account worsened in the early 1980s, mainly due to expansionary fiscal and monetary policy, an exchange rate regime that did not match the conditions of the economy at that time, and the lack of effective supervision of the banks and the financial system. Thus, in the mid-1980s, the Israeli economy experienced a fiscal crisis together with an acceleration of inflation to a three-digit level, significant devaluations in the local currency, a banking crisis, and low credibility of the economic policies in the eyes of the public.

By mid-1985 a new stabilization plan was introduced with the aim of restoring confidence and stability to the Israeli economy. In the first years following the introduction of the Stabilization Program, the deficit in the current account declined markedly, but toward the mid-1990s, against the background of the absorption of the wave of immigration of more than 1 million people from the former Soviet Union, it returned to dimensions that could potentially damage the stability of the economy. This time, economic policy reacted quickly in order to prevent the development of a crisis. Later on, in the second half of the 1990s, there was even a gradual improvement in the current account, to the point of a shift to surpluses in 2003.

Together with this current account reversal, we saw a change in the attitude of Israeli and foreign investors vis-à-vis the Israeli currency: the confidence in the ILS (Israeli shekel) increased, the informal dollarization, or de facto indexation to the dollar, declined, and Israel's credit rating was improved. Israeli investors began to view the shekel as a stable currency, and at times even moved to hedge the currency risk of their foreign investments. In addition, foreign investors increased their investments in Israel, Israel became a net lender to the world, and the returns on net overseas assets (e.g., interest receipts, dividends, capital gains, etc.) contributed to the consolidation of surpluses in the current account.

5.2 The Current Account of the Balance of Payments

5.2.1 Theory: Two Main Approaches

The prevailing approach in theoretical and empirical analysis of the current account until the 1980s was the IS-LM model for an open economy, known in the literature as the Mundell–Fleming model. The typical framework postulated imports and exports equations that were included in a common IS-LM model. In spite of its popularity, the framework turned out to be less useful for analyzing the impact of a rise in the price of oil, like in the 1970s or the Latin American debt crisis of the 1980s.

In light of a growing dissatisfaction with the existing model, in the course of the 1990s there was a shift toward the intertemporal approach to the current account of the balance of payments; see, e.g., Obstfeld and Rogoff (1996).

Unlike the Mundell–Fleming model, which analyzes the current account in terms of import and export ad-hoc equations, the intertemporal approach focuses on analyzing the current account in terms of the gap between national saving and national investment. As is known from the national accounts, the surplus in the current account is identical to the surplus of national savings over national investment.

The intertemporal model analyzes savings and investment decisions as the result of an optimization process by the various economic agents. The approach also emphasizes the existence of a dynamic intertemporal budget constraint.

A prominent example of the implementation of the intertemporal approach is the formulation of the national saving function in the spirit of an optimization model, such as the permanent income theory of private consumption. Given an exogenous shock, as, e.g., a decline in the economy's GDP due to a decline in productivity, the predictions of the model depend, *inter alia*, on the degree of persistence of the shock. With consumption smoothing as a common result from this framework, if perceived as transitory, this shock will lead to a reduction in savings, which in turn will lead to a rise in the current account deficit. Yet, to the extent that this shock is perceived as permanent, it would result in a permanent decline in private consumption, with little impact on savings and the current account position. Along these lines, one could analyze the impact of temporary and permanent changes in fiscal policy parameters, in foreign shocks, and so on.

In this chapter, we focus empirically on both the gap between savings and investment and the behavior of exports and imports to discuss the experience of the last two decades.

5.2.2 Current Account: Key Developments

In the mid-1990s, the deficit in the current account of the balance of payments became one of the main macroeconomic risk factors of the economy. In 1994–1996, the deficit rose to a level of about 4.5 percent of GDP. The deficit was perceived as worrisome both by its size relative to the past and by international comparisons that suggested, especially after Mexico's Tequila Crisis of 1994, that when deficits get close to 5 percent of GDP, this may be a leading indicator for a balance of payments crisis in the near future. At that time, monetary policy turned to a contractionary stance with the aim of dealing with inflationary pressures. High interest rates attracted capital inflows from abroad, and the central bank intervened to attenuate the extent of real exchange rate appreciation. Yet intervention was only partial and could not avoid some degree of real exchange rate appreciation. After 1997, the current account deficit began to contract and turned into a surplus in 2003. The surplus has been maintained over the years, and in 2015–2016 it reached an average high level of 4.5 percent of GDP.

The current account consists of three parts: the goods and services trade account, the primary income account (focusing on income from labor and capital), and the secondary income account (free remittance transfers). In the period reviewed, the turnaround in the current account was mainly a result of a change in the trade account (goods and services), namely, the average annual growth rate of exports was higher than that of imports. The primary income account was responsible for part of the overall current account improvement, but the surplus in the net secondary account soon fell by three percentage points of GDP, and thus partially offset the increased surplus in the goods and services account (Table 5.1).

The gradual reduction of the current account deficit was accompanied by a real appreciation of the domestic currency during the period considered.

5.2.3 The Trade Account

The goods and services account went from a deficit of 8.1 percent of GDP in 1995 to a surplus of 3.0 percent of GDP in 2015. It was the main factor accounting for the reversal in the overall current account position (Table 5.1). The shift included both the goods account and the services account. Total exports increased during this period by an average annual volume of 5.1 percent, while total imports increased by 3.8 percent. The terms of trade (that is, the ratio of export prices to import prices) of Israel showed ups and downs during the period

Table 5.1 *The current account, percentage of GDP*

	1995 %	2000 %	2005 %	2010 %	2015 %
Exports of goods	20.3	23.1	29.3	23.1	19.0
Imports of goods	28.0	26.0	31.6	23.7	20.1
Trade in goods (net)	−7.7	−2.9	−2.3	−0.6	−1.1
Exports of services	8.3	12.1	12.5	10.2	12.3
Imports of services	8.7	9.3	10.4	7.6	8.2
Trade in services (net)	−0.4	2.8	2.2	2.5	4.1
Trade in goods and services	−8.1	−0.1	−0.1	2.0	3.0
Primary income (net)	−2.8	−6.2	−0.9	−1.8	−1.0
Secondary income (net)	6.0	4.9	4.4	3.3	3.1
Current account	−4.9	−1.4	3.3	3.5	5.1

Source: Central Bureau of Statistics

reviewed, mainly as a result of fluctuations in import prices, especially of imported energy sources. It happens that the current account surplus persisted even when energy prices were relatively high, and clearly the terms of trade were not a key factor in the shift to surpluses. However, in the last few years of the period under review, the economy has enjoyed a sharp improvement in trade conditions thanks to a decline in world energy prices.

5.2.3.1 Exports of Goods and Services

An examination of exports' growth during the period under study shows that it is not significantly different from that of world trade. Furthermore, the correlation between the two is high, and most studies have not ruled out the hypothesis that exports' elasticity in relation to world trade volume is unitary. Yet, it is important to emphasize that the composition of exports has changed significantly during these years, with the weight of the high-tech and services industries increasing over time.

An important development in the second half of the 1990s was the breakthrough of the Internet and more generally ICT around the world, and the Israeli economy was probably among the biggest winners. Foreign companies set up development and production centers in Israel, and some

Israeli startups were sold to foreign companies. Exports of high-tech goods increased by an average dollar rate of 8.7 percent per year during that time, and service exports also jumped thanks to technology and software industries as well as R&D and startup companies. The share of exports of services in total exports rose from 29 to 39 percent.

Significant changes also occurred in the geographical distribution of export destinations. In the late 1990s and early 2000s, the globalization process accelerated, China joined the World Trade Organization (December 2001), trade restrictions were reduced, and the rapid growth of emerging market economies led to a surge in demand for goods and services. For example, Israel's exports to emerging markets in Asia rose from a low of $2.5 billion in 1995 to about $17 billion in 2015. The geographical distribution of exports became more diversified, with a decline in the share of Europe and the United States. This diversification has reduced the vulnerability of the economy to negative shocks in one of the regions.

5.2.3.2 Exports of Goods and Services: Econometric Results

No doubt, long-term analysis of Israel's export trends should take into account basic factors such as productivity, changes in human capital composition, changes in government policy, and exogenous factors from the world, such as rising competition from emerging economies exports. Such an analysis is likely to require a separate discussion of the sectoral distribution of exports. These are broad issues, the discussion of which goes beyond the current framework.

We chose to focus here on a more modest question: how far past results of estimating a standard export function are valid for our updated sample. We have also expanded standard specifications by adding an explanatory variable that expresses the level of activity in the high-tech industries in the world.

The estimated export equation includes the following explanatory variables: global trade, the real exchange rate of the shekel, and the Tech Pulse Index (TPI),[2] an indicator of the world's high-tech activity. We looked at quarterly data in terms of rates of change in each quarter from the same quarter in the previous year. Running the regression using the OLS method indicated that there is a serial correlation problem, so we used the Cochrane–Orcutt method to estimate the

---

[2] The Tech Pulse index is published by the Federal Reserve Bank of San Francisco

Table 5.2 *Cochrane–Orcutt regression results*

Variable	Estimate	Standard error	P value
***q4 (World trade)	0.8983	0.1146	7.68e-14
***TPI4 (Tech Pulse Index)	0.3238	0.0637	0.0001
*fx4	–0.2744	0.0902	0.0147

*** significant at 99 CI *significant at 95 CI

regression assuming that there is first order serial correlation in the residuals. The regression results are shown in Table 5.2.

The variables:

EX4 – the real change in exports of goods and services, each quarter vis-à-vis the corresponding quarter last year;

Q4 – the real change in world trade in goods and services;

TPI4 – the change in the TECH PULSE INDEX;

FX4 – the change in the real effective exchange rate (an increase meaning a rise in exchange rate appreciation).

The regression results show that the elasticity of exports to world trade is 0.89, which is quite close to unity.

The TPI is also significant in the export estimation. The TPI helps explain the fluctuations in exports stemming from the intensity of technology, and in particular the boom in the late 1990s and the dot-com crisis in the early 2000s.

The exchange rate coefficient is negative, as we would expect: a real depreciation of 10 percent raises exports by 2.7 percent. This elasticity of exports relative to the exchange rate is similar to the elasticity estimated in previous studies.

The obvious limitation of this model is the disregard for the simultaneous relations between exports and the exchange rate. (The Israeli economy is small, and therefore does not affect global trade and the TPI.)

Another model we examined is a type of vector auto regression (VAR), in which the three variables are exports, world trade, and the exchange rate (the rates of change in each quarter relative to the previous one). The series were tested and found to be stationary. We examined IRF (impulse response functions) for each of the variables for each sample period and divided the sample period into two sub-periods: 1995–2005, 2006–2015.

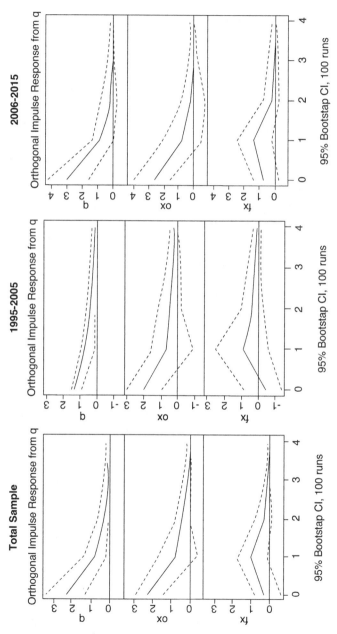

Figure 5.1 The impact of a world trade impulse on exports and exchange rate.

This sample split is due to the fact that the exchange rate regime changed in June 2005, and the shekel became a floating currency. Thus, the effects of exogenous changes, such as an increase in world trade, may be different in the two sub-period..The IRF results are shown in Figure 5.1.

The results of the IRF indicate that a positive shock in world trade raises exports in the subsequent quarter, and its effect vanishes four quarters later. The effect was found to be similar in both sub-periods. As expected, a positive shock in world trade also leads to an appreciation of the shekel in the entire sample, although in the first decade a slightly surprising result is obtained: in the first quarter following this shock, the shekel depreciated. A possible explanation for this is that during this period the exchange rate was within a currency band, so nominal appreciation in response to favorable shocks was normally attenuated via central bank intervention in the foreign exchange market (the exchange rate was close to the lower limit of the band most of the time).

Examining the effect of a positive export shock on the real exchange rate shows different results in the two subsamples. In 2006–2016, an increase in exports results in a real ILS appreciation in the subsequent quarter. In the prior ten years, a positive shock to exports leads to a less clear result. As in the previous analysis, we believe that the limits of the currency band in the first period prevented a full response of the exchange rate to exogenous events as changes in world trade or domestic export shocks.

5.2.3.3 The Startup Nation in Action: Selling Startups and the Balance of Payments

The second half of the 1990s featured a wave of startup sales to overseas investors. These deals were worth billions of dollars and therefore had a marked impact on the balance of payments. For example, in 2000, Chromatis was sold to Lucent, in return for Lucent shares worth $4.8 billion. Another example is NDS, which was sold to Cisco for $5 billion in 2012. These sales led to significant revisions in Israel's national accounts because now these had to recognize an activity with added value that previously wasn't known. The way in which these transactions should be properly recorded in the balance of payments is not a clear-cut issue: on the one hand, a purchase of an Israeli company by a foreign company can be defined as direct investment in

Israel and be included in the financial account. On the other hand, this is not a standard company. The assets of such a company are usually intangible, and in many cases, they become part of the production process of the acquiring company. In these cases, some or all of the services could be registered as exports (for example, of research and development services).

The classification has a large accounting effect on the various sections of the balance of payments. If the transaction is classified as export of services, the surplus in the current account of the balance of payments will increase. Conversely, if the transaction is classified as a sale, direct investment in Israel will increase. From an economic point of view, the classification of startups in the balance of payments has no significance, of course, and it does not affect the net debt or asset position vis-à-vis the rest of the world.

From 1998–2015, the annual contribution of startup sales to exports and the current account of the balance of payments averaged about 0.3 percent of GDP. Volatility between years was high, and in 2000, on the eve of the burst of the dot-com bubble, the contribution to the current account stood at a record 1.3 percent of GDP.

5.2.3.4 Imports of Goods and Services

The increase in imports of goods and services in 1995–2015 was more moderate than that of exports – an average increase of 3.8 percent per year, similar to the rate of GDP growth. Import growth was also lower than that of developed countries, which averaged about 5.0 percent during these years. The relatively slow increase in imports was the result of two main factors. The first is the import of oil, whose volume has increased at a very moderate rate of about 1.5 percent per year, given the shift to natural gas and streamlining energy use, as will be explained below. The second factor that explains the moderation of the growth of imports is the structure of the economy's growth: the weight of the service industries has been growing at the expense of manufacturing, especially the output of traditional sectors and the construction industry. These service industries are not capital-intensive or raw materials intensive, so imports of inputs (excluding fuels) increased by an average annual rate of only 3.6 percent. In contrast, consumer goods imports rose an annual average of 5.7 percent.

5.2.3.5 The Effect of Natural Gas and Energy Prices on the Current Account

Throughout most of its existence, Israel was dependent, almost completely, on imported energy products. In years when world energy prices were high, for example, during the oil crisis of the 1970s, the value of imports reached high levels, such as 8 percent of GDP, and this was a major component of the current account deficit.

At the beginning of the period reviewed, the Israeli economy's energy sources were mainly oil (including diesel and fuel) and coal, which were used for both electricity generation and for transportation and industrial use. Therefore, the value of energy materials imports was greatly influenced by world energy prices, and in particular the price of oil. For example, in 1998, when the world oil price got down to $10 per barrel of Brent, the value of energy imports dropped to 1.6 percent of GDP. By contrast, ten years later, in 2008, oil prices rose to $140 per barrel, and the import of energy materials rose to 6.0 percent of GDP. Energy prices therefore had a very large impact on the current account of the balance of payments.

Over the period, the intensity of energy use in production decreased significantly, as there was a rapid growth of service industries, as well as a more efficient use of energy sources and more economical vehicles and appliances.

In 1999, the first natural gas reservoir in Israel, referred to as Noa, was discovered near the Ashkelon coast by Partnership Yam-Thetis. After the initial discovery, further drilling was carried out, and in 2000 the Mary reservoir was discovered. These two reservoirs (Yam-Thetis reservoirs) contained together approximately 34 BCM of natural gas. Following the discovery of natural gas, the electricity company begun a gradual transition process of turning the energy sources from fuels to natural gas, in parallel with the gradual deployment of pipelines for natural gas distribution in Israel.

Beyond the gas sources from the Yam-Thetis reservoirs, natural gas was also imported from Egypt, which got to Israel in an extension that split from the Arab gas pipeline. Under the agreement with Egypt, signed in 2005, Israel undertook to purchase 7 BCM of gas per year for twenty years, and the gas price was set at $3 per gas unit (MMBTU). Egypt's natural gas begun flowing to Israel in February 2008 – just when energy prices in the world were very high: the price of oil in 2008 got to an average of almost $100 a barrel. The combination of Egyptian gas and a subsequent drop in world oil prices led to a decrease of about two percent of GDP in Israel's energy imports in 2009.

In early 2011, the pipeline that provided natural gas from Egypt to Israel was the subject of a terror attack, which completely halted gas supply for more than a month. About a month later, the gas supply resumed, but another explosion of the transmission pipe stopped the supply again. Even when it was renewed, the quantities supplied were lower than the contractual obligations. The gas pipeline sabotage continued until Egypt's state gas company announced, in April 2012, the cancellation of its agreement with the Israeli gas company EMG. Increased use of the Yam-Thetis reservoirs led to the virtual depletion of the stock of gas in them as early as 2011, and so it led to an increased use of expensive diesel fuel and oil for electricity generation. Energy import costs soared in 2012 to 6.2 percent of GDP.

In 2009, the Tamar reservoir was discovered off the coast of Israel, with a stock of approximately 256 BCM. Production of gas from Tamar began in April 2013, and since then natural gas consumption has grown rapidly. Natural gas has become the main source of electricity generation in the economy (about 60 percent in 2015), and the ratio of imports of energy materials to GDP fell to less than 2 percent in 2016. The fall in world oil prices during these years also contributed to a decline in the value of imports. It is estimated that the Tamar output can provide the needs of the Israeli economy for a period of two decades.

In December 2010, the Leviathan gas reservoir was discovered. The reserves in it are estimated at 540 BCM, which is more than double the reserves of the Tamar reservoir. The stock of gas in these two reservoirs and other small reservoirs discovered (Karish and Tanin) raised the possibility of exporting some of the gas output in the future. The natural gas sector has become a source of internal political controversy on a number of issues – exports versus maintaining gas reserves in the sea for future generations, the nature of gas companies' taxation, the proper use of tax receipts and royalties, the price of gas and electricity, and more. Public committees were established to determine the rate of exports (the Tsemach Committee) and taxation (the Sheshinsky Committee), and public controversies delayed the development of the reservoir by 2017.

To some extent, it can be argued that gas discoveries brought about a version of the Dutch disease. Namely, a real exchange rate appreciation that could damage other, non-energy, export industries.[3] In 2014, the law for establishing a sovereign wealth fund was enacted, according to which the proceeds from the levy on the profits of the oil companies will be transferred to a Sovereign Wealth Fund. The latter will invest these funds and transfer money to the state fund according to defined criteria.

It has also been decided that the fund will start operating in the year in which the proceeds from the levy on profits will exceed ILS 1 billion (estimated in 2020). The main purpose of the fund is to create a more equitable intergenerational distribution of natural gas incomes. It is also intended to reduce the impact of the Dutch disease on the exchange rate, since its funds will only be managed in foreign currency. The fund's income depends on the profits of the companies and the price of gas. The Bank of Israel has estimated that the total revenues for the fund are expected to reach ILS 348 billion by 2040.

The extent to which the Tamar gas discoveries contributed to the improvement in the current account of the balance of payments depends on the alternative cost of using natural gas. The use of natural gas has largely replaced the use of coal, whose price fell by about 30 percent between 2012 and 2015, and oil, whose price fell by about 50 percent. It is clear, therefore, that Israel's energy imports would have been reduced anyway, due to lower energy prices in the world.

In 2013, the Bank of Israel began acquiring foreign currency in the market to offset the effect of natural gas on the balance of payments. The calculation of the effect of natural gas on the balance of payments is in relation to the alternative prices of natural gas from Tamar, and therefore it is an estimate of the contribution of natural gas to the current account surplus (an estimate on the high side, since some of the gas receipts are returned abroad as payment for production services and overseas companies profits). As part of the policy framework for offsetting the effect of natural gas on the balance of payments, the Bank of Israel purchased $7.5 billion from 2013 to 2015, and in 2016–2017

---

[3] A notion which was used originally to describe the damage caused to the Dutch traditional export industries as a result of the big gas reservoirs found in the sea in 1959.

the acquisitions are expected to add up to $3.3 billion. As a result of the fall in energy prices, ex post the economic contribution of natural gas to the current account was not relatively high. This will of course change if and when global energy prices rise, or when natural gas exports from Israel begin.

5.2.4 Primary Income

In this account there are two main components: (a) compensation of employees, i.e., wages paid to Israelis for their work abroad (a flow that describes foreign currency inflows to Israel), or foreign workers employed in Israel (a foreign currency outflow); (b) investments income – rents, dividends, capital gains, interest, reinvested profits, etc.

At the beginning of the period under review, the primary income balance was at a deficit of 2.8 percent of GDP. The deficit rose to 6.2 percent of GDP in 2000 and then declined to stabilize at around 1 percent of GDP in 2014–2016.

The most notable changes in this account were the investments' incomes. These are volatile and dependent on financial markets, interest rates, and the like. They also depend on the volume of assets abroad of Israelis and of foreigners' in Israel, and these have changed significantly, as the surplus of assets over liabilities has grown considerably over the years. For example, the weight of receipts from overseas financial investments in total GDP has increased twofold, from 1.6 percent of GDP in 1995 to 3.0 percent of it in 2015.

5.2.5 Secondary Income (Formerly Called Unilateral Transfers)

Secondary income describes flows for which there is no compensation for a product or service, nor do they create a liability or asset as opposed to capital flows in the financial account. The component of secondary income in Israel is sizable relative to other countries, although its weight in GDP is declining: in the mid-1990s, net secondary income accounted for about 6 percent of GDP and has since declined to about 3 percent in the final years of the period reviewed.

The weight of two items has greatly diminished over the years: aid from the United States stood at 2.7 percent of GDP in the mid-1990s, falling to 1.1 percent in 2016. Compensations from Germany fell in the same period from 0.9 percent of GDP to 0.3 percent. As for US aid – at the beginning of the period it stood at about $3 billion a year, which was divided into military aid of $1.8 billion and civilian aid of $1.2 billion. Over the years, civilian aid was reduced up to its elimination in 2008, while military aid increased. An aid agreement signed with the United States in 2008 stipulates that, starting in 2009, aid will reach an average of about $3 billion per year for ten years. In addition to the amounts specified in the agreements, Israel received additional specific grants – for example, following the Iraq War in 2003, and participation in financing the "Arrow rocket" development. The increase in GDP in dollar terms has resulted in a continuing decline in the weight of US aid in domestic product. From a balance of payments perspective, most aid funds are used for military procurement in the United States, with no major impact on the current account. The question of the necessity of military assistance has often come up in the country and in the United States, as Israel is the largest recipient of aid from the US government, despite being a developed country that enjoys a large surplus in the current account of the balance of payments.

5.2.6 *Investment, Saving, and the Current Account*

It is common to analyze the current account of the balance of payments also through its mirror image – the gap between national saving and national investment. If we look at the two end points in the period reviewed – 1995 compared to 2015 – we can see in Table 5.3 that the transition from a deficit to a surplus reflected a decrease of 5.5 percentage points in the investment ratio from total income,[4] and a 3.6 percentage point increase in the savings ratio from total income. This means that, in terms of the accounting identity, the economy has saved more and invested less (as shares of total national income). The change in the investment-savings gap reflects the change in the current account of the balance of payments. An examination of the economic reasons for a decline in the investment ratio and an increase in the

---

[4] Total income is GNP at the representative exchange rate plus net transfers from abroad to individuals plus transfers from abroad to the public sector minus interest payments to abroad.

Table 5.3 *Investment, saving, and the current account percentage of total income*

	1990	1995	2015	Change in percentage point
Investments	17.7	25.1	19.6	−5.5
Savings	17.8	20.6	24.2	3.6
Private	−3.3	19.9	23.6	3.7
Public	21.1	0.7	0.6	−0.1
Current Account	0.1	-4.5	4.5	9.0

Source: Bank of Israel

savings ratio can shed additional light on the trends behind the current account reversal and their potential durability into the future.

The first half of the 1990s was the period of absorption of the immigration wave from the former Soviet Union. During this period, the weight of investment increased to a record level of about 25 percent of total national income. At the same time, the rate of public and private savings fell. The combination of large government budget deficits and current account deficits created, mainly in 1995–1996, a phenomenon known as "twin deficits." In retrospect, the major deficits in this period can be understood in terms of the great economic challenge of that time – the absorption of the massive immigration wave. The increase in investment was considered then a must, in order to adjust the capital stock, including the housing stock, to the expanded population. Under the influence of the immigrant absorption process, private and public savings rates decreased.

Things began to change in 1997. Monetary and fiscal restraint policies led to a fall in domestic demand and a marked slowdown in growth. As a result of these factors, as well as the full effects of the wave of immigration in the early 1990s, the investment rate of total economic income in the two years 1997–1998 decreased by 2.5 percentage points. At the same time, the overall savings rate rose slightly, due to a sharp reduction in the government's budget deficit.

In 2003, the economy featured a surplus in the current account for the first time since 1990. The recession in the previous two years, which originated in the Second Intifada and the burst of the dot-com bubble in the United States and its impact on the Israeli high-tech industry,

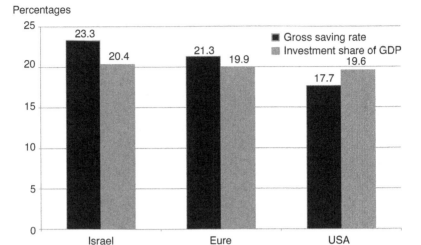

Figure 5.2 Investments and savings share in GDP, average for the years 2010–2016.
Source: OECD, Bank of Israel

continued to reduce the ratio of investment to total income. The private savings rate offset the decline in public savings. The percentage of total investment out of national income remained stable at about 20 percent by 2015. By contrast, the savings rate continued to grow, bringing the current account surplus to 5.1 percent of GDP in 2015.

Is the above savings and investment picture different from the world? We examined the average levels of investment and savings since the beginning of the current decade, a period when the current account surplus was stabilized, relative to the United States and Eurozone countries (Figure 5.2). The results show that the rate of investment in GDP in Israel is similar to that in the United States and Eurozone countries, but the savings rate in Israel is considerably higher than that of the United States and higher than the average Eurozone countries, although the variance among these countries is high.

These findings seem to contradict the widely held view that the level of investment is low relative to other developed countries, but some characteristics that may change the picture should be considered: (a) The level of investment in the comparison countries has declined following the most recent global crisis and has not recovered since. Israel has not experienced a crisis during these years, which is particularly evident in housing investments. (b) The level of GDP per capita in Israel is still lower than in the United States as well as the average of Eurozone countries, so we would expect a higher level of investment than these countries. (c) The growth rate of the Israeli population is faster and therefore requires more investment in houses and infrastructures.

If the economy does indeed suffer from sub-investment relative to other countries, the question still arises as to why this situation was generated, as there was no shortage of funding that could be used to increase investment. A possible answer lies in budgetary constraints regarding the level of government investment that is lower than desired, a situation that is reflected in poor transport infrastructure, high density in schools and hospitals, and the like. As for private investment, it may have been influenced by a high degree of uncertainty – a result of the security situation, and/or excess regulation and a multiplicity of bureaucratic processes. Investments were also possibly affected by the growth composition: high-tech was the main growth factor of the economy, and these industries do not usually require much physical capital.

The savings rate, as mentioned, is high relative to the comparison countries. According to economic theory, saving rates depend on a wide range of factors – demographic, economic, and cultural – as well as on economic policy. On the demographic factors, it is common that a high proportion of working-age people in total population positively affects the savings rate. In Israel, the share of the elderly population is lower than in the developed countries, but the proportion of children is higher, and the overall dependency ratio (non-working-age population to working-age population) is high and thus in itself does not support a high saving rate. On the economic factors, higher housing prices in Israel may create a kind of "compulsory savings": home buyers are usually faced with relatively high mortgage repayments, thus reducing their disposable income. Another argument is that the public's purchasing power following the fall in energy prices in recent years (gas discoveries and the decline in world oil prices) was not seen by the public as permanent, so the disposable income was not directed to consumption but to savings. As for policy factors, pension arrangements in Israel were changed in the twenty years reviewed. We had a move of the private sector to accrual pensions at the beginning of the period, followed by a shift of public sector employees to accrual pensions. Also, there was a gradual increase in the retirement age for men and women in 2004, and the beginning of mandatory pensions in 2008. These factors probably had a marked impact on savings rates in Israel.

5.2.7 Israel Becomes a Net Lender to the Rest of the World

While the balance of payments is expressed in terms of flows, it is also important to look at the status of the economy's assets and liabilities vis-à-vis the rest of the world. A position of a current account deficit usually creates liabilities (or decreases in assets) to the rest of the world. A country with a surplus in the current account accumulates assets (or reduces its liabilities) toward the rest of the world. The balance of assets and liabilities vis-à-vis the rest of the world is therefore affected by the balance of payments movements, but also by revaluations of these balances due to changes in asset prices and liabilities and the value of currencies. The assets and liabilities of the economy toward the rest of the world are generally classified between debt instruments, such as deposits, credit, bonds, cash, and foreign currency reserves held by the central banks, and investment instruments like shares and real estate.

In 1995, Israel had net liabilities to the rest of the world (international investment position, including all investment instruments), accounting for 27 percent of GDP. At that time, the country's net external debt (including debt instruments only) stood at 17 percent of GDP. The current account deficit began to decline during these years, but net liabilities continued to grow, reaching about 40 percent of GDP in 1999. The weight of external debt in GDP had already begun to decline during these years, against the background of the real appreciation of the shekel. The transition to surplus in the current account in the beginning of the 2000s accelerated the decline in the weight of net liabilities, until it reached a surplus in 2006. Net assets reached a level of 34 percent of GDP in 2016.

From 1995 to 2016, Israel's net assets vis-à-vis the rest of the world increased by $135 billion. Overall, the current account surplus and capital account[5] together account for about 75 percent of the increase in the balance of assets. The remainder is accounted by the revaluation of asset balances and liabilities due to price changes and exchange rates.[6]

---

[5] The capital account represents mainly capital flows related to immigrants. They are not part of the current account, nor the financial account.

[6] We disregard statistical discrepancies.

In terms of net asset composition, the most notable change was the large accumulation of foreign exchange reserves in the Bank of Israel: these increased from about $7 billion in 1995 to $98 billion at the end of 2016.

Israel is in a relatively small group of countries characterized by such a large surplus of assets on net international creditor position, with Norway, Saudi Arabia, Switzerland, Japan, Germany, and the Netherlands. These countries, as a rule, have a very high level of per capita GDP, and some of them have accumulated surplus assets thanks to exports of oil or natural gas.

5.3 The Financial Account

The balance of payments financial account describes the capital flows for which there is no compensation for a product or service, including payments for capital and labor. The movements in the financial account create an asset or liability of the economy toward the rest of the world. The main components of the financial account are direct investments, the investments in securities, other investments (deposits and credit types), and the change in the central bank's foreign currency balances.

The balance of payments financial account is largely a mirror image of the current account, so if the current account went from a deficit to surplus, then the financial account went from surplus to deficit, which means that Israel has become a net investor in the rest of the world. However, the changes in the financial account went far beyond the change in the overall balance sheet: capital flows to and from Israel changed their order of magnitude. For example, direct investment by foreign entities in Israel increased from $1.4 billion in 1995 to $11.5 billion in 2015, and investments in Israeli securities portfolios increased from $154 million to nearly $10 billion a year. These changes were the result of globalization and intensification of international capital movements, the flourishing of the local high-tech industry, an improvement of Israel's political and economic status, foreign exchange market liberalization, and economic policy.

One conclusion from the analysis is that contrary to popular opinion, which emphasizes the influence of overseas investors on financial capital flows and the exchange rate, we find that Israeli investors' weight was much greater.

5.3.1 Liberalization of Financial Markets

Like several other small open economies, liberalization processes in the financial markets in Israel began in the late 1980s, after the economy recovered from the inflationary episode of the first half of the decade and shifted toward economic stabilization. A previous liberalization attempt, in 1977, failed because of disastrous macroeconomic conditions, and the withdrawal from that liberalization attempt was rapid. In contrast to the 1977 liberalization program, a gradual reform strategy of the measures was chosen at this time. The first phase was the abolition of the restriction on long-term capital imports by Israelis. In the second stage, long-term capital export restrictions were eliminated, first on financial investments and then on direct investments by the business sector. Short-term capital flows were still limited due to concerns about financial stability.

Formal liberalization was announced in April 1998. The headline of the joint Ministry of Finance and the Bank of Israel's press release summarizes the following: "All foreign-currency restrictions on households and the business sector are abolished, except for those applicable to institutional investors and derivatives transactions of nonresidents." During this period there was tax discrimination on overseas investments and this was not eliminated. The fear of a rapid capital flight from the country also prevented the restriction from institutional investors at this time, which was completely removed only in 2003.

It should be noted that on the eve of the liberalization announcement, there were almost no restrictions on foreign residents' activities, except for restrictions on short-term investments and derivatives. Direct investments by nonresidents were not limited, including real estate investments and long-term securities investments.

The early estimates were that opening all channels would result in a marked increase in capital flows in both directions, an increase in exchange rate volatility and a growing exposure to macroeconomic shocks. Of these assessments, it can be asserted, with the benefit of hindsight, that the first was indeed fulfilled, but of course, it must be taken into account that in the background other factors also worked beyond liberalization. The assessment of the exchange rate volatility was not really met, and in the case of increasing exposure to shocks, it probably materialized in part toward the end of the period.

5.3.2 Foreign Direct Investment (FDI)

As mentioned above, there were no restrictions on direct investment by foreign entities in Israel, and yet their level was relatively low in the first half of the 1990s. In 1995, these investments stood at about 1.3 percent of GDP. Globalization was still in its infancy, and the volume of direct investment relative to GDP in Israel during this period was no different from the global average and lower than for emerging markets in Asia.

The combination of globalization progress and the rapid developments in the high-tech sector boosted direct investment in Israel to about 6 percent of GDP in 2000, on the eve of the Nasdaq bubble burst in the United States. Foreign direct investment (FDI) in Israel exhibited relatively high volatility – the result of a number of large Israeli companies' exits or sale to overseas investors. In both the 2001 episode of burst in the Nasdaq bubble and in the global financial crisis of 2009, the volume of direct investments in Israel declined. Among the most prominent foreign investments in Israel in our sample period were the establishment of a major computer chip factory in Kiryat Gat by Intel, the acquisition of Iscar by Berkshire Hattaway, and Google's acquisition of Waze.

As mentioned, liberalization in the foreign currency market also opened to Israelis the possibility of FDI outflows. The fear that Israelis would massively transfer their savings abroad did not materialize, and in most years the volume of direct investment by Israelis abroad was lower than that of foreign investment in Israel. Out of the investments abroad by Israeli entities, we find the pharmaceutical company Teva, which acquired foreign companies by sizable amounts.

5.3.3 Exchange Rate Policy, Monetary Policy, and Short-Term Capital Flows

Short-term capital flows consist mainly of investments in securities, deposits, and the undertaking of various types of credit. These movements are particularly sensitive to business cycles, risks, and economic policies. As previously indicated, most of the restrictions on capital movements were removed by 1998, when inflation was still relatively high, and the exchange rate moved along within a crawling currency band.

For the purpose of analyzing capital flows, we use the following conceptual framework. Let us define:

FA – the surplus in the financial account except the change in foreign currency reserves (i.e., a positive FA indicates net capital inflow).
CA – The current account balance.
DR – The increase in foreign exchange reserves in the central bank.

Proper balance of payments accounting ensures that, assuming away errors and omissions, the following equality is maintained:

$$FA = DR - CA$$

The period from 1995 to 2016, was divided into five sub-periods (or episodes) according to the prevailing characteristics of capital flows. As Figure 5.3 shows, net direct investment did not affect the trends of total capital flows, so in fact movements in FA mainly reflected short-term capital flows. We turn now to a discussion of each one of the episodes.

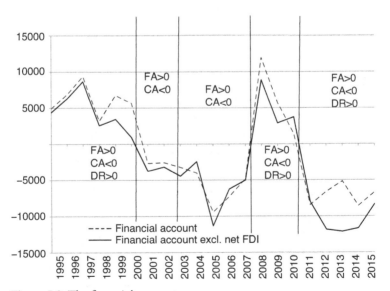

Figure 5.3 The financial account
Source: OECD, Bank of Israel

5.3.3.1 Episode 1: From the Second Half of the 1990s to 2000 – Current Account Deficit and Capital Inflows

Monetary policy in these years was intended to curb inflation. As mentioned above, restrictions on capital flows have gradually been removed, the high interest rate spreads between domestic and foreign interest rates remained high. This attracted capital inflows and the Bank of Israel was forced to defend the lower limit of the crawling currency band by purchasing foreign currency from the public. In order to sterilize the effect of the purchases on the money supply, the Bank of Israel issued an increasing number of short-term T- bills. In 1996–1997 foreign currency reserves increased as a result of the Bank of Israel's purchases to about $12 billion, i.e., more than doubled in that short period of time. Basically, this episode illustrated once again the well-known "impossible trinity" from the existing literature: a situation in which relatively free capital flows have a hard time to coexist with a semi-fixed exchange rate and a relatively autonomous domestic monetary policy. Eventually, the authorities started to increase the amplitude of the exchange rate band, thus moving toward a semi-flexible exchange rate regime. At that time, imposing restrictions on capital flows were considered, but eventually the widening of the exchange rate band made this redundant. It was expected that by expanding the width of the currency band, investors will probably see an increased degree of exchange rate risk in their activities, thus probably reducing the attractiveness of short-term speculative flows.

It turns out that most of the short-term capital inflows during this episode originated from domestic players. That is, domestic corporations found it attractive to borrow from banks in foreign currencies, at relatively low interest rates, and banks "imported" the funds for these loans from abroad. In the late 1990s, foreign currency credit reached about 35 percent of total credit in the economy. Looking at foreign investment, for example in government bonds and Treasury bills, we can see that in the second half of the 1990s, they did not exceed 1 percent of the total stock of bonds and Treasury bills. No doubt, at that time the domestic business sector took a significant degree of exchange rate risk. Most probably, the business sector assumed that the risk of sharp currency depreciation was not high at that time.

Even when considering global crisis events, such as in 1998 – when Russia defaulted on its debts, the LTCM hedge fund collapsed, and there was a sharp reduction in capital inflows to emerging market economies – most of Israel's capital inflows remained unchanged due to their high dependence on local businesses.

In summary, episode 1 was typical of many emerging economies, facing the "capital inflows problem" (analyzed by Calvo et al., 1996)). While Israel was not part of the global emerging markets crisis, the degree of vulnerability was high, mainly due to the mismatch between the currency denomination of assets and liabilities in the balance sheet of many corporates. A sharp depreciation of the shekel during this period could have caused many business entities to fail to meet their foreign currency debt repayments, with negative implications for the soundness of the banking system.

5.3.3.2 Episode 2: Recession and a Rise in Country Risk

In 2001, the financial stability of the economy deteriorated as a result of a combination of two events: the burst of the Nasdaq bubble and a sharp deterioration of the security situation in Israel. The recession led to a rapid increase in the government's budget deficit and in public debt, together with a marked depreciation of the shekel. The credibility of economic policy weakened during this period, and households and business entities diverted some of their investments abroad. The central bank did not intervene in the foreign exchange market, but responded through monetary policy. The sharp depreciation of the ILS during this period changed the exchange rate risk perceptions of economic agents, who gradually reduced their exposure to foreign currencies.

5.3.3.3 Episode 3: Current Account Surplus and an Increase in Overseas Financial Investments

In the second half of the first decade of the 2000s, international financial market integration processes accelerated. Institutional investors began diverting a growing portion of their financial investments abroad, a phenomenon perceived by many as indicating that at least some of the home bias[7] had been reduced. The leap was in 2005: Investments in securities abroad reached $8 billion (in terms of flow), compared with about $3 billion in the previous two years.

The central bank's interest rate during this period was similar to the Fed funds rate, and in part of the period it was even lower. At the same time,

---

[7] Home bias describes the tendency of investors to prefer their local markets, which are more familiar.

the yield curve in Israel was steep, so foreign investors showed interest in investing in shekel bonds, but actual inflows were relatively low.

5.3.3.4 Episode 4: Global Crisis, Major Foreign Exchange Purchases of the Bank of Israel

The global financial crisis of 2008 posed a new challenge for policy-makers – how to deal with foreign currency inflows that did not necessarily reflect a surplus in the current account. These capital movements were, partly at least, the result of an increased resilience of the Israeli economy – including the banking and financial systems – to the world's turmoil. Against this background, the Bank of Israel returned to foreign currency purchases, for the first time since 1997, with a view to moderating the real appreciation of the shekel, at least in the short term. In March 2008, the Bank of Israel announced a plan to increase foreign exchange reserves to $35–40 billion through a $25 million purchase per day.

Although Israeli investments in foreign securities portfolios continued during this period, this time, due to the continued strengthening of the shekel, institutional investors chose not to significantly increase their exposure to foreign currency through currency hedging operations, made through foreign and domestic banks. Buying overseas securities while hedging the currency is equivalent to taking foreign currency credit for the purpose of acquiring overseas securities, which means import of capital in parallel with capital exports, and therefore should not affect the exchange rate. The side effect of the hedging operation was large purchases of T-bills by foreign banks. (In the exchange swaps, the foreign bank gives foreign currency and receives ILS, the foreign bank buys T-bills with the ILS he received. At the end of the transaction, the foreign bank sells the T-bills and converts the ILS back to foreign currency at a predetermined exchange rate.) In 2011, foreign investors held more than one-third of the T-bills balance. It is difficult to know which part of the T-bills acquisitions was part of the foreign exchange swaps transactions carried out by foreigners and what part was their real exposure to the ILS. It is reasonable to believe that most T-bills purchases were part of currency swap transactions, meaning that foreign banks did not expose themselves to the ILS but, rather, took advantage of the local need for foreign currency liquidity (high basis swap spreads[8]).

---

[8] Intuitively it can be explained by the interest rate on the USD in the local market, which is higher than the interest rate on the USD in the United States.

This spread gives foreign banks the possibility of low-risk profit (in this case – the risk of the issuer of the T-bills). In July 2011, the Bank of Israel abolished the tax exemption for nonresidents for their investments in short-term debt instruments and also imposed a liquidity requirement on swap transactions. As a result, foreign holdings in T-bills gradually diminished. Therefore, it can be estimated that most foreign purchases of T-bills during this period were not for "speculative" purposes.

5.3.3.5 Episode 5: Increase of Current Account Surplus and Capital Outflows: The Bank of Israel Continues to Purchase Foreign Currency

Over the period, the surplus in the current account of the balance of payments increased as a result of a decrease in the cost of energy imports. Institutional investors channeled a growing portion of their overseas savings but continued to partially hedge the currency so that their foreign exchange exposure remained fairly stable. The appreciation pressures on the ILS intensified and the central bank continued to increase its foreign currency reserves and lowered its policy rate to almost zero.

5.4 Conclusions and the Outlook Ahead

Against the backdrop of sound macroeconomic policies in the last two decades, the ongoing improvement in the current account of the balance of payments has contributed to strengthening the economy and reducing its vulnerability to shocks. Even during periods of major geopolitical stress and/or external crises, we have seen no massive outflow of foreign currency or speculative attacks on the ILS.

Among the key findings from this research are:

• The current account reversal, from deficits to surpluses, in the period reviewed was the result of global factors, such as the accelerated growth of world trade and in particular the global boom of high-tech industries, along with local factors, including a shift to a more disciplined and sustainable macroeconomic policy.
• The consolidation of the surplus in the current account occurred alongside a real appreciation of the shekel for much of the period under study.

- In terms of national savings and investment, the improvement in the current account reflected a decrease in the investment rate and an increase in the savings rate out of total economic income. Internationally, Israel's relatively high savings rate stands out, while the investment rate is similar to that of developed countries.
- The fall in world energy prices and the production of natural gas from the Tamar reservoir had a significant impact on the large current account surpluses starting in 2013. Among these two factors, the effect of lower energy prices was the dominant one.
- At variance with other country cases, domestic Israeli investors had a crucial role in determining the strength and direction of short-term capital flows recorded in the financial account. The direction of these capital flows has changed over the years, starting with tight domestic monetary policy and capital inflows via domestic borrowing in foreign currencies, and on to a situation of private sector capital outflows, mainly by institutional investors in the second half of the first decade of the 2000s.
- Of the various episodes in the financial account in the last two decades, only in the second half of the 1990s (episode 1) did we witness a clear case of the "hot money" phenomenon, including intensive activity of carry trade players, in the backdrop of a high domestic–foreign interest rate differential.
- Over time, institutional investors increased their exposure to overseas investments, and the extent of hedging their positions against currency risks fluctuates quite frequently. Accordingly, these fluctuations have become key factors in determining the exchange rate dynamics of the ILS, especially in the short run.

Is Israel's shift to a current account surplus country a permanent phenomenon? Here we offer a few insights on this challenging question:

- National saving: Saving rates depend largely on institutional, economic, and cultural factors that do not change very quickly. Moreover, changes in the pension system in Israel continue to support a high savings rate. The retirement age of women in Israel is still low compared to the rest of the world, and its gradual rise can contribute even more to the savings rate. Several studies abroad have shown that the saving rate tends to rise in countries where income distribution is more equitable. Accordingly, a policy that would work toward a more equitable distribution of income could also increase the saving rate. The Israeli sovereign wealth fund that is expected to emerge in the coming years creates a kind of forced savings on the government, preventing the use of these funds to finance current spending.

- National investment: The trends here are less clear. On the one hand, the trend in the world in recent years has been the decline in the weight of investment in GDP, especially in developed countries, where productivity has fallen. Some believe that this trend is unlikely to change anytime soon (e.g., according to Larry Summers' "secular stagnation hypothesis"). However, in Israel there is no doubt that the low level of infrastructures, especially transportation, requires an increase in their investment in the future.

- Natural gas: The outlook here is positive in that sooner or later Israel is expected to be an exporter of natural gas. Furthermore, the dependence on imports of oil, and hence on world oil prices, can be expected to diminish over time.

- International investment position: A large surplus of assets over liabilities supports the continued improvement in the national income level, especially if and when world interest rates will start to rise.

- Technological advantage: The technology industries have made a big contribution to consolidating the surplus in the current account. Having said that, Israel's world status of a "startup nation" will continue to be challenged by other countries.

In conclusion, Israel's so-called balance of payments "problem" became much less of a problem in the period under study. World developments, domestic policies, and natural gas discoveries have all worked toward a transition from current account deficits to surpluses. Looking ahead, there is of course no guarantee that current account surpluses will be a permanent feature of the economy. Yet, from a medium- and long-term perspective, Israel's economic fundamentals are consistent with a continuation of the current surpluses. Having said this, if for some reason or another, the economy goes into a prolonged period of current account deficits and the current currency appreciation pressures are replaced by depreciation pressures, as long as macroeconomic policies are sound and the sovereign risk is kept at low and reasonable levels, there should be no major difficulties in financing such deficits.

References

In Hebrew

Bank of Israel (1995–2016). *Bank of Israel Annual Reports for the Years 1995–2016.* Jerusalem: Bank of Israel.

Central Bureau of Statistics (2017). *Statistical Abstract of Israel 2017.* No. 68. Jerusalem: CBS.

Ozer, B., Reis, S., and Sofer, Y. (2005). Liberalization of the Financial Account in Israel. Working Paper, Bank of Israel.

In English

Adalet, M., and Eichengreen, B. (2007). Current Account Reversals: Always a Problem? In Richard H. Clarida (ed.), *Current Account Balances: Sustainability and Adjustment.* Chicago, IL: University of Chicago Press for the NBER, 205–246.

Calvo, Guillermo A., Leiderman, L., and Reinhart, C. (1996). Inflows of Capital to Developing Countries in the 1990s. *Journal of Economic Perspectives*, 10(2), 123–139.

de Mello, L., Padoan, P., and Rousova, L. (2010). *Are Global Imbalances Sustainable?: Shedding Further Light on the Causes of Current Account Reversals.* Paris: OECD Publishing.

Federal Reserve Bank of San-Francisco. On the 'Tech Pulse' Index. www .frbsf.org/economic-research/indicators-data/tech-pulse/.

Lane Philip. R., and G. M. Milesi-Ferreti (2017). International Financial Integration in the Aftermath of the Global Financial Crisis. *IMF Working Papers* 17/115, International Monetary Fund.

Milesi-Ferretti, G. M., and Razin, A. (1998). Sharp Reduction in Current Account Deficits: An Empirical Investigation. *European Economic Review*, 42, 897–908.

(2000). Current Account Reversals and Currency Crises, Empirical Regularities. In P. Krugman (ed.), *Currency Crises.* Chicago, IL: University of Chicago Press, 285–323.

Obstfeld, M., and Rogoff, K. (1996). *Foundations of International Macroeconomics.* Cambridge, MA: MIT Press.

Summers, L. (2016). The Age of Secular Stagnation: What It Is and What to Do About It. *Foreign Affairs*, February 2016. https://www.foreignaffairs.com /articles/united-states/2016-02-15/age-secular-stagnation.

6 | Defense and the Economy, 1990–2016

ESTEBAN F. KLOR AND ASAF ZUSSMAN

This chapter examines the link between defense and the economy in Israel during the period 1990–2016. Since grave security threats have faced the State of Israel since its establishment, it is hardly surprising that Israeli economists have also devoted considerable attention to this topic.[1]

In the first of a series of books on the Israeli economy published by the Maurice Falk Institute for Economic Research in Israel (Ben-Porath, 1986), a chapter was devoted to the issue of defense and the economy. The chapter, written by Eitan Berglas (1986), focused on the economic burden of defense during the period 1950–1980. The simplest and most direct measure of this burden is defense expenditure as a share of GNP.

Figure 6.1 extends the series shown by Berglas (1986) and displays the development of defense expenditure (consumption) as a share of GNP from 1950 to 2015. Several interesting conclusions can be drawn from the figure. The period that preceded the Six Day War (1967) was characterized by a gradual, though relatively moderate, rise in the defense burden, from 6 percent in 1952 to 10 percent in 1966. The Six Day War was a turning point: the defense burden surged to 17 percent in 1967 and continued to rise during the War of Attrition period (1969–1970). Another sharp jump, of nearly 10 percentage points, occurred in the wake of the Yom Kippur War (1973). During

* Esteban F. Klor and Asaf Zussman are professors in the Department of Economics at the Hebrew University of Jerusalem. The authors are grateful to Avi Ben-Bassat, Claude Berrebi, Reuben Gronau, Rafi Melnick, and participants in conferences where drafts of this chapter were presented for their helpful comments and suggestions. They are also grateful to Nathaniel Sarfati for his excellent research assistance.

[1] Lifshitz (2003), who provides an overview of the development of defense economics as a subdiscipline in economics, provides a comprehensive treatment of defense-economy issues in the Israeli context and summarizes the relevant academic literature.

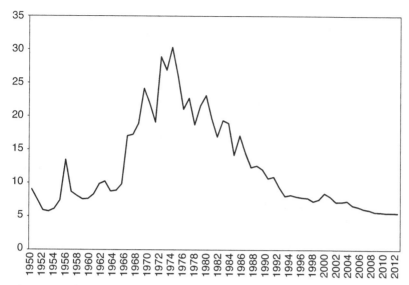

Figure 6.1 Share of defense consumption in GNP, 1990–2015 (%).
Source: Central Bureau of Statistics (2017)

the years immediately following the war, defense consumption peaked
at slightly over 30 percent of GNP. Since the mid-1970s, the defense
burden has declined steadily. In 2015, the last year for which data were
available at the time of writing, it amounted to 5.5 percent of GNP, the
lowest level since the founding of the state.[2]

It is commonly believed that the decline in the defense burden since
the late 1970s can be attributed to processes that substantially reduced
the severity of the security threats faced by Israel. A turning point in this
regard was the 1979 peace agreement with Egypt. From Israel's perspective, the agreement not only eliminated the chance of another war
with a country that until then was Israel's most important enemy but
also greatly reduced the likelihood of war with other Arab countries.
Other developments that were expected to decrease the threat to Israel

---

[2] It is worth noting that despite the steep and continued decline in Israel's defense
burden, it is still high compared with that of other countries. According to data
from the Stockholm International Peace Research Institute, Israel ranked seventh
of 148 nations in 2015 for reported military expenditure as a share of output. The
Israeli figure was 5.6 percent, while the median share among all countries was 1.5
percent. A more relevant reference group for Israel is the OECD and here Israel
ranked first. Greece ranked second in the OECD with a share of 2.5 percent. (The
median share was 1.2 percent.)

included the 1993 Oslo Accords between Israel and the Palestinians, the 1994 peace treaty with Jordan, the fall of the Saddam Hussein regime in Iraq in 2003, and the Syrian civil war that began in 2011. This period has also featured a number of negative developments – including the emergence of the Iranian nuclear threat and the threat posed by fundamentalist Islam – but, taken as a whole, it seems that the strategic environment facing Israel in recent years is much less menacing than the corresponding environment four decades earlier.

The present chapter is concerned with the link between defense and the economy in Israel since the 1990s. From among the wide variety of topics that we could have addressed, we chose to examine in depth one important and interesting aspect of the defense–economy link: the impact of security-related shocks on the Israeli economy during the period 1990–2016. This period encompassed a number of significant events and processes – including the Oslo Accords, the Second Intifada, the disengagement from Gaza, the Second Lebanon War, and the military operations in Gaza, which were accompanied by massive rocket attacks on Israeli territory. We provide an asset market perspective on the impact of these shocks to the Israeli economy. Specifically, our analysis compares the impact of security shocks with that of domestic-political and economic shocks. Within the first category, we distinguish between security events directly related to the Israeli-Palestinian conflict, and other security events that took place in the Middle East.

The chapter has three main sections. In section 6.3, we discuss turning points in major Tel Aviv Stock Exchange (TASE) indices and in the shekel–dollar and shekel–euro exchange rates during the period 1990–2016. This analysis is based on a method for identifying turning points in asset markets that was developed by Zussman et al. (2008).

Analyzing historical turning points via asset market data has several advantages over other methodologies, such as historical analysis and surveys. First, at any given point in time, asset markets reflect investor perceptions toward future developments; by contrast, the attitudes of experts (such as historians) are influenced retrospectively by processes that could not have been accurately predicted, i.e., they constitute hindsight. Second, investors are supposed to carefully consider all present and future developments, since mistakes could potentially entail financial loss, and it is therefore reasonable to assume that they are not influenced (at least not consciously) by their political outlooks.

By contrast, other sources of information, such as surveys, may be affected by their participants' political views. Third, asset markets' reactions to security and political events take into account a broad range of factors that influence the economy.

Our analysis yields a number of interesting findings. In the analysis of the Tel Aviv stock market, we find that both during the period January 1990 to May 2005, examined by Zussman et al. (2008), and from the end of that period until 2016, the number of turning points attributable to political shocks is similar to the number of turning points attributable to economic shocks. However, two major differences can be seen between the two periods: First, the share of turning points related to the Israeli-Palestinian conflict among all of the turning points attributed to political shocks fell dramatically between the two periods. Second, the share of turning points stemming from external economic shocks – cases of "contagion" – among all of the turning points attributed to economic shocks rose substantially.[3]

Our analysis of the foreign exchange market also points to significant differences between the two periods. In the earlier period, most of the turning points were attributed to events related to the Israeli-Palestinian conflict, while none of the turning points in the later period were attributed to this conflict. We also find that the share of the turning points stemming from external economic shocks rose dramatically between the two periods.

One possible argument against our use of asset market data to identify historical turning points is that it reflects a very narrow, even biased, view of the impact of security shocks on the Israeli economy. For example, it is conceivable that the Israeli-Palestinian conflict, even if it has not influenced asset markets since mid-2005, has nevertheless significantly affected real activity in the economy.

Section 6.4 addresses this methodological criticism. In this section, we examine the behavior of several real economic variables across time, the first and most important being the Bank of Israel's Composite State-of-the-Economy Index. Another important variable is the unemployment rate. Our analysis suggests that the behavior of these two variables is consistent with the results of the asset market analysis. Thus we find, for example, that the Second Intifada, which erupted in late 2000, was

---

[3] In international macroeconomics, the term "contagion" refers to the spread of market changes or disturbances from one regional market to others.

accompanied by a dramatic economic slowdown and a sharp rise in unemployment. By contrast, the three big military campaigns waged in Gaza since 2008 had very little economic impact, if any. However, it should be emphasized that the impact of security events is not necessarily uniform across sectors. One sector that is particularly sensitive to security events is tourism, and indeed, our analysis of data on tourism bears this out.

In section 6.5, we offer a possible explanation for the fact that, since the mid-2000s, the Israeli–Palestinian conflict ceased to affect asset markets. We argue that after the signing of the Oslo Accords in the early-mid 1990s, and despite the strong and violent opposition sparked by the Accords, a large proportion of the Israeli public anticipated that the conflict with the Palestinians would be resolved within the foreseeable future. The failure of the Camp David Summit in the summer of 2000, and the Second Intifada's eruption that autumn, constituted a turning point. These events undermined expectations of a potential end to the conflict and caused the view that there is no negotiating "partner" on the Palestinian side to become deeply entrenched within the Israeli public. These attitudes were reinforced during the years following the end of the Second Intifada, due to Hamas's takeover of the Gaza Strip in 2007, the rocket attacks on Israel from Gaza, and the failed rounds of negotiations between Israel and the Palestinians.

We test our hypothesis against data from the Peace Index, a monthly survey initiated by the Tami Steinmetz Center for Peace Research at Tel Aviv University in the early 1990s. Our analysis shows that the Second Intifada sparked a turnaround in public attitudes toward the Oslo Accords. Before the Second Intifada, support for the Accords and faith that they would bring peace were fairly widespread among Israelis, while immediately after the Intifada broke out, support for the Accords dropped precipitously, and confidence that they would lead to peace declined even more sharply. From the time the Second Intifada erupted until 2008 – the year when the Institute ceased asking questions about the Oslo Accords – only a sixth of the Israeli population believed that the Accords would bring about an end to the conflict with the Palestinians. A similar pattern can be seen in answers to questions about negotiations with the Palestinian Authority from the period 2001–2016. Throughout this period, the share of those who supported negotiations with the Palestinian Authority was substantially higher than the share of those who believed that negotiations would bring peace. The data show that, since 2001, less than a third of the Israeli public believes that negotiations with the Palestinians will lead to a resolution of the conflict.

Thus, our findings suggest that Israelis do not believe peace can be achieved in the foreseeable future, and that they factor the possibility of additional rounds of violence into their expectations. These expectations would seem to explain the lack of asset market response when rounds of violence do occur.

6.1 Related Literature

This chapter contributes to an extensive literature studying how violent conflict affects economic variables generally, and financial asset prices specifically. Some studies examine the impact of civil wars. For example, Willard et al. (1996) examined how developments in the American Civil War affected the greenback, a currency whose value fluctuated relative to gold, while Guidolin and La Ferrara (2007) showed how developments in the Angolan Civil War affected the values of stocks of companies involved in diamond mining in that country. Other papers have investigated terrorism's impact on real economic activity and on financial markets. Perhaps the most well-known of these studies is by Abadie and Gardeazabal (2003), who examined the economic effects of the terrorist campaign waged by ETA in Spain's Basque Country.

A number of papers have studied terrorism's impact on the Israeli economy. For example, Fielding (2003a) found that Palestinian terrorist activity from the late 1980s to the late 1990s had a negative effect on investment in Israel, and Fielding (2003b) showed that terrorism during this period negatively affected the savings rate in Israel. A study by Eckstein and Tsiddon (2004) found that the first three years of the Second Intifada caused a 10 percent decrease in Israel's GDP per capita.

Other studies focused on financial markets. Eldor and Melnick (2004) found that Palestinian terrorism during the years 1990–2003 negatively affected prices in the stock and foreign exchange markets in Israel; in a follow-up study, Eldor and Melnick (2010) showed that terrorism's impact on stock prices is mediated by media coverage of terrorist attacks. Berrebi and Klor (2010) demonstrated that terrorism's effects on stock prices are sector-dependent: stock prices in most sectors are negatively influenced by terrorism, but those of

defense-related companies show a positive impact. A study by
Zussman and Zussman (2006) assessed, through the prism of
stock prices, the effectiveness of the "targeted assassination" policy
that Israel adopted during the Second Intifada against members of
Palestinian terrorist organizations. Their analysis showed that the
targeted assassination of leaders in the terrorist organizations' military wings had a positive effect (i.e., investors perceived the measure
as effective), while the assassination of leaders in the organizations'
political wings had a negative impact.

What sets the present study apart from earlier research on terrorism
and its effect on Israel's economy and asset markets is our finding that
the negative impact of security incidents on these markets weakened
greatly over the past decade. As noted above, one potential explanation
for this desensitization of the markets is that public expectations
already take into account the likelihood of additional rounds of
violence.

6.2 Empirical Methodology

The analysis in this chapter is based on an econometric methodology
for locating turning points in asset markets that was developed by
Zussman et al. (2008). We present below a brief description of that
methodology, which is fully described in Zussman et al. (2008).

The methodology we employ assumes that the dates of turning
points in asset markets are unknown. This assumption is diametric-
ally opposed to the underlying premise of the event-study methodology – the most popular approach used in the finance literature to
estimate the effect of events on asset prices. In an event study
approach, the researcher first defines events of a certain type (e.g.,
terrorist attacks) that could potentially affect asset prices. The dates
when these events occurred are known to the investigator, and she
uses them to determine whether the events in question actually
affected asset prices. Our approach reverses this order: first an algo-
rithm statistically identifies dates that constitute turning points in
asset markets, and then we try to understand which events could
have generated these turning points. The conclusions arrived at in the
second stage are, of course, subjective, but experience suggests that,
in the vast majority of cases, they arise naturally from the historical
record.

It is important to note that the turning points we identify are not necessarily identical to the major economic or political events of the relevant period, as currently perceived by experts or by the general public. A number of factors could account for this lack of correspondence. First, in accordance with prevailing asset price theory, our method can identify only the impact of unexpected events; important but anticipated events will not be identified as turning points. Second, our analysis reflects the impact of events on the perceptions of asset market participants at the time they took place; events that today seem highly significant might have appeared unimportant in the past, and vice versa.

Having made these clarifications, we can now proceed to discuss our methodology. According to prevailing asset price theory, let us assume that the (log) of the price of a certain asset behaves as a random walk with a trend. This means that the change in the asset's price is unanticipated: today's forecast for tomorrow's price is today's price plus the effect of the trend. The trend can be thought of as reflecting long-term inflation or a similar factor. Alternatively, we can say that we assume that the return on the asset between two consecutive dates – the difference between the log of the price on a given day and the log of the price on the previous day – is a fixed value plus an unanticipated component. This component is identically and independently distributed and has an expected value of zero.

Unexpected news on a given date may affect the price of the asset and cause a structural break (or turning point). This turning point can be expressed in one of the two following ways, or both simultaneously: (1) an upward or a downward shift in the price of the asset; (2) an upward or a downward shift in the slope of the trend line. For example: let us assume that new information comes to the market on a certain date and causes a sudden and unanticipated rise in the asset price. News reaching the market later on may: reinforce the effect of the original information (rise in the slope of the trend line); be uninformative (no change in the slope of the trend line); or gradually weaken the original information's impact (decline in the slope of the trend line). By allowing both a shift in the asset price and a shift in the slope of the trend line, we avoid limiting the model to only one type of an "economic turning point."

Because we are interested in finding many potential turning points in the same time series, none of which necessarily has a permanent impact, we use a rolling-windows methodology. A "window" is a period of a certain length, such as sixty trading days. The "rolling" of the window refers to the window being moved each time by one day, beginning with the first day of the relevant period, e.g., the start of 1990, to its end, mid-2016. For each window we then test whether there is a break point in the middle of the window. In this way we identify all of the turning point dates.[4] It must be emphasized, again, that the methodology does not assume the effect of a turning point will persist forever. Rather, our assumption is that the impact continues at least until the end of the window. This assumption allows us to locate turning points that are not only statistically significant but are also economically important, even if their impact does not persist until the end of the period in question.

6.3 Turning Points in Financial Markets

In this section we identify and classify turning points in the stock and foreign exchange markets in Israel. Our stock market analysis focuses on the three major TASE indices during the period from January 1990 to May 2016. We will compare the results with those obtained by Zussman et al. (2008), who covered the period from 1988 to May 2005. In the foreign exchange market, we will identify turning points in the shekel–dollar and shekel–euro exchange rates. This analysis covers the period from January 2000 to May 2016. Our analysis of the foreign exchange market starts only in 2000 since in the 1990s the exchange rate was not determined by market forces; rather, it was heavily managed by the Bank of Israel. By contrast, during the period analyzed herein, the Bank of Israel allowed the exchange rate to move more freely, though it sometimes intervened by buying or selling foreign currency. The analysis of the foreign exchange market in Zussman et al. (2008) also started in January 2000 and ended in May 2005. It should be noted that the choice of May 2005 as the dividing point between the two sub-periods follows from the fact that this was the last month analyzed by Zussman et al. (2008); however, the division also has a more fundamental justification, in that the Second Intifada is widely considered to have ended around mid-2005.

---

[4] Because the distribution of the test statistic values in the present context is not standard, we estimate critical values via Monte Carlo simulation.

6.3.1 The Stock Market

We identify turning points in daily data for three Tel Aviv Stock Exchange aggregate indices: (1) the General Shares Index, which reflects the prices of all stocks traded on the TASE; (2) the TA-100 Index, reflecting the prices of the hundred most highly capitalized companies; (3) the TA-25 Index, which tracks the prices of the twenty-five most highly capitalized companies. For the first of these indices, the search was conducted for the period from January 2, 1990 to May 31, 2016. The TA-25 Index was created on January 3, 1992, so the identification of turning points for this index (and for the TA-100) starts on this date. For all of the series, we make use of windows of five different lengths: 60, 120, 240, 360, and 480 trading days. Thus, the length of the windows we use ranges from three to twenty-four months. The data on the indices were obtained from the Bank of Israel.

Figure 6.2 displays the three indices' values for the relevant periods. The three indices exhibit a continuous upward trend, but with great volatility, and one can discern four significant protracted declines. The first started in late 2000 and ended in 2003, and was related to the Second Intifada. The second downturn, an especially sharp one, took

Figure 6.2 Major Tel Aviv Stock Exchange indices, 1990–2016.
Source: Bank of Israel

place in 2008 and was related to the global financial crisis that had started in the United States. The third decline, also a dramatic one, occurred in 2011 and was associated with the debt crisis in Europe. The fourth decline started in mid-2015 and continued until the end of the period examined here. This decline appears to have been triggered by global developments, including a slowdown in Chinese growth.

Table 6.1 summarizes the findings of our turning points analysis. Column 1 reports the turning point date, while Column 2 provides our explanation for the turning point's occurrence. Column 3 classifies the explanations provided in terms of five categories: (1) the Israeli–Palestinian conflict; (2) political shocks in the Middle East; (3) domestic politics; (4) domestic economic shock; (5) external economic shock (we regard all cases in this category as instances of "contagion," that is, as manifestations of the spread of economic shocks from other countries to Israel). The following columns report, for each window length (60, 120, 240, 360, and 480 trading days) and each stock index (TASE General, TA-100, TA-25) the direction of the effect manifested at the turning point: In these columns the plus (+) sign indicates that the relevant index increased in value on that day, while the minus (–) sign indicates that the relevant index decreased in value. All of the turning points reported are statistically significant at a level of at least 10 percent.

The results presented in Table 6.1 are based on analysis conducted for the entire period, that is, from 1990 to 2016 for the TASE General Shares Index and from 1992 to 2016 for the other stock indices. However, we will be distinguishing in our presentation between the turning points found in the period investigated by Zussman et al. (2008), that is, from January 1988 (TASE General) or January 1992 (the other indices) to May 2005, and those found in the period from June 2005 to May 2016. The distinction enables us to illustrate the differences between the periods in the types of events that generated turning points.[5]

A detailed description of the turning points up to May 2005 is provided by Zussman et al. (2008). We will, therefore, discuss here

---

[5] There is almost perfect overlap between the turning points found by Zussman et al. (2008) in the period from January 1990 to May 2005, and those found for this period by the present study. Such an outcome is not trivial, as relative to the period covered by Zussman et al. (2008), the average return and its variance changed during the period ending in 2016.

Table 6.1 *Turning points in the Tel Aviv Stock Exchange, 1990–2016*

Date	Possible explanation	Type of event	60 days			120 days			240 days			360 days			480 days		
			General	100	25	General	100	25	General	100	25	General	100	25	General	100	25
August 19, 1990	Iraq invades Kuwait	Political shocks in the Middle East							−			−			−		
January 22, 1991	Frist Gulf War breaks out	Political shocks in the Middle East	+					+								−		
August 19, 1991	Contagion	External economic shock	−					−			−							
June 24, 1992	Rabin elected Prime Minister	Domestic politics	+			+	+		+								
June 19, 1993	Oslo Accords	Israeli–Palestinian conflict			−				+					−			−
August 21, 1994	Capital tax plan presented	Domestic economic shock	−					−			−			−			−
January 31, 1995	Capital tax plan cancelled	Domestic economic shock				+		+									
November 5, 1995	Rabin assassinated	Domestic politics	−														
May 30, 1996	Netanyahu elected Prime Minister	Domestic politics	−		−												
July 16, 1996	Contagion	External economic shock	−					−			−			−		−	
October 28, 1997	Contagion	External economic shock	−					−			−			−		−	
August 9, 1998	Bank of Israel lowers interest rate	Domestic economic shock						−	+	+							
April 16, 2000	Contagion	External economic shock	−					−			−			−			
October 12, 2000	Second Intifada breaks out	Israeli–Palestinian conflict						−			−			−		−	
September 24, 2001	9/11 terrorist attacks in US	External economic shock	+													−		

Table 6.1 (cont.)

Date	Possible explanation	Type of event	60 days General	100	25	120 days General	100	25	240 days General	100	25	360 days General	100	25	480 days General	100	25
December 23, 2001	Bank of Israel lowers interest rate	Domestic economic shock							+	+	+	+	+				
May 25, 2003	Government adopts "Road Map"	Israeli–Palestinian conflict							+	+	+	+	+	+	+	+	+
August 7, 2005	Netanyahu resigns as Finance Minister	Domestic politics			–			–	–			–	–	–	–	–	–
January 5, 2006	Prime Minister Sharon suffers stroke	Domestic politics			–	–	–		–								
July 13, 2006	Second Lebanon War breaks out	Political shocks in the Middle East							–	–		–					
July 29, 2007	External economic shock	Contagion							–					–			
September 21, 2008	External economic shock	Contagion							+	+		+	+	+	+	+	
November 23, 2008	External economic shock	Contagion													–		
January 30, 2011	Revolution in Egypt	Political shocks in the Middle East	–			–			–	–	–	–	–	–	–		–
August 7, 2011	External economic shock	Contagion				–			–	–	–	–	–		–		
August 27, 2013	Chemical attack in Syria	Political shocks in the Middle East						–									
October 12, 2014	External economic shock	Contagion	–		–												
April 12, 2015	Struggle over Perrigo acquisition	Domestic economic shock			+									–			
August 23, 2015	External economic shock	Contagion										–	–	–	–	–	–
Total points			9	6	5	12	7	6	15	12	9	10	7	7	8	8	8

Source: Bank of Israel and authors' calculations

only those tuning points located during the later period – from June 2005 to May 2016. Our discussion is organized in terms of the type of explanation offered for each, rather than chronologically.

Political Shocks in the Middle East. We located three turning points related directly to political shocks in the Middle East:

A. *July 13, 2006 (outbreak of the Second Lebanon War) – downturn*: The war erupted after a Hezbollah force attacked (on July 12) an IDF patrol within Israeli territory, near the Lebanese border fence. Three servicemen were killed in the attack, two were abducted, and three were critically injured. Israel responded to the incident with a massive offensive, first from the air and then via ground units, which fought the Hezbollah forces in Southern Lebanon. The war lasted thirty-four days, during which Hezbollah launched 4,000 rockets and mortars at northern Israeli localities and army bases. The rocket barrages caused the residents of northern Israeli localities to leave en masse and disrupted the country's economic activity. The war ended with a ceasefire agreement on August 14, 2006.[6]

B. *January 30, 2011 (revolution in Egypt) – downturn*: On January 25, 2011 street demonstrations and mass protest activities broke out against President Hosni Mubarak and his regime. These events were part of a wave of uprisings in the Arab world that came to be known as "the Arab Spring." In the wake of these demonstrations, Mubarak resigned on February 11, handing the reins of government over to the military. When trading started on Sunday, January 30, the TA-25 Index dropped by 2.3 percent, due, apparently, to the major escalation of events at the end of the previous week. When trading closed for the day, the index had dropped by 3.8 percent, relative to the end of the previous trading day. According to a report in the newspaper *Globes*, the stock indices declined on January 30 due to concerns that the events in Egypt would spread to other Middle Eastern countries and increase instability in the region.

C. *August 27, 2013 (chemical attack in Syria) – downturn*: In March 2011, civil war erupted in Syria, as part of the Arab Spring events. The confrontation was between forces loyal to the Ba'athist government headed by Bashar al-Assad and those seeking to oust

---

[6] For a detailed review of the events of this war, see Harel and Issacharoff (2008).

Assad. On August 21, 2013 a series of apparent chemical attacks were carried out in areas under rebel control. These attacks were estimated to have caused the deaths of over a thousand people. The offensive took place nearly a year after US President Barak Obama's August 2012 warning that the use of chemical weapons in the Syrian Civil War would constitute the crossing of a red line, leading to American military intervention. At a press conference held on August 26, 2013, US Secretary of State John Kerry affirmed that an "unforgivable" chemical attack had taken place on August 21, and that the Obama administration believed that the Syrian government was responsible for the attack. This announcement fueled fears within the financial markets of prolonged intervention by the United States and its allies in the Syrian Civil War.

Domestic Politics. We located two turning points related to domestic political shocks:

A. *August 7, 2005 (Netanyahu resigns as Minister of Finance) – downturn*: Netanyahu's resignation from the government expressed his opposition to the disengagement from the Gaza Strip that was being promoted by Prime Minister Ariel Sharon. Netanyahu announced his resignation an hour before trading closed for the day. During that hour, the value of the TA-100 dropped by 4 percent. This strong reaction appears to have been driven by concerns about increased political instability, and cessation of the economic reforms spearheaded by Netanyahu.

B. *January 5, 2006 (Prime Minister Sharon suffers a stroke) – downturn*: On the evening of January 4, 2006, Sharon suffered a massive stroke and lost consciousness. His powers as prime minister were immediately transferred to Acting Prime Minister Ehud Olmert. On January 5, the TA-25 and TA-100 indices fell by 4 percent due to investor fears of political, diplomatic, and economic instability.

Domestic Economic Shock. We located one turning point directly resulting from a domestic economic shock:

A. *April 12, 2015 (struggle over Perrigo acquisition) – upturn*: On Wednesday, April 8, Mylan, a major pharmaceuticals firm, made a takeover bid for the drug company Perrigo, whose stocks were traded on the Tel Aviv Stock Exchange and in the United States.

The offer reflected a 25 percent premium on the stock's value at that time and was made after Tel Aviv trading hours had ended. Because of the Passover holiday, the TASE could react to the news only on Sunday, April 12. On that day, the closing of the arbitrage gap, along with the fact that Perrigo then accounted for 10 percent of the TA-25, caused a sharp rise in the TA-25 and the other indices (*Globes*, April 12, 2015).

External Economic Shock. In six cases, the most likely explanation for the turning point was a shock originating in the international financial markets. These were instances of "contagion." The Israeli stock market is closely linked to markets abroad, especially to those of the United States. Many Israeli companies, especially those in the high-tech industry, are traded both in Israel and the United States, particularly on NASDAQ. A look at the Israeli press (*Globes*) and leading international papers (the *Financial Times* and the *New York Times*) testifies to major changes in foreign stock exchanges around the dates we identified.

A. *July 29, 2007 – downturn*: This turning point, which occurred on a Sunday, originated in sharp declines in the US stock markets. During the trading week that ended on Friday, July 27, the S&P 500 Index dropped by 5 percent. That week witnessed the sharpest drops in five years in stock markets in the United States. The declines were due to fears of an economic slowdown and problems in the American housing and credit markets (*New York Times*, July 28, 2007).

B. *September 21, 2008 – upturn*: On Friday, September 19, the US government and the Federal Reserve Board announced an emergency plan in response to the prevailing economic crisis, with 700 billion dollars being made available to US banks. The financial markets rose dramatically in response to this announcement. For example, the S&P 500 climbed by 4 percent (*New York Times*, September 20, 2008). The TASE reacted to these developments with an upturn as trading opened on Sunday, September 21.

C. *November 23, 2008 – downturn*: This turning point occurred against the background of the global financial crisis and investor fears of a prolonged economic depression. In the United States, the trading week that ended on Friday, November 21 was highly volatile, with the Dow Jones Industrial Average falling to its lowest level since early 2003 (*New York Times*, November 20, 2008). The TASE reacted to these developments with a decline as trading opened on Sunday.

D. *August 7, 2011 – downturn*: This turning point was sparked by signs of a slowdown in the US economy and a worsening of the European debt crisis. During the trading week that ended on Friday, August 5, the S&P 500 dropped by 7 percent, the steepest weekly decline since November 2008. Moreover, on Friday evening, after trading closed on the stock exchanges in the United States, Standard and Poor, for the first time in history, downgraded the credit rating of US treasury bonds from AAA to AA+ (*New York Times*, August 8, 2011). As a result, the TA-25 Index fell on Sunday, August 7 by 7 percent, its most dramatic daily downturn since 2000.

E. *October 12, 2014 – downturn*: This turning point was related to fears of a global economic slowdown. These fears manifested in a sharp decline in oil and financial market prices. The S&P 500 fell by 3.1 percent during the trading week that ended on Friday, October 10. The Israeli stock exchange, which had been closed since the previous Tuesday due to a religious holiday, reacted to these downturns on Sunday October 12 with a more than 2 percent decline in the TA-100 Index (*Globes*, October 12, 2014).

F. *August 23, 2015 – downturn*: Signs of a major economic downturn in China generated turmoil in the global financial markets. The Dow Jones Industrial Average and the S&P 500 Index declined by over 3 percent on Friday, August 21. The TASE reacted to these downturns on Sunday, when the TASE-25 fell by over 4 percent (*Financial Times*, August 22, 2015 and *Globes*, August 24, 2015).

Table 6.2 summarizes the turning points in the Tel Aviv Stock Exchange by event type, comparing the two periods. In Part A of the table we see that in the first period all the five categories we defined are represented. This means that the various types of political shocks, as well as domestic and external economic shocks, all had a major impact on the TASE. In Part B of the table we find that half of the turning points were attributable to political shocks, while the rest stemmed from economic shocks. Part C shows that 38 percent (three of eight) of the political shocks were connected with the Israeli–Palestinian

Table 6.2 *Summary of turning points in the Tel Aviv Stock Exchange by type of event, 1990–2016*

Part	Type of event	January 1990 – May 2005	June 2005 – May 2016
A	Israeli–Palestinian conflict	3	0
	Political shocks in the Middle East	2	3
	Domestic politics	3	2
	Domestic economic shock	4	1
	External economic shock	5	6
	Total	17	12
B	Politics	8	5
	Economics	9	7
C	Israeli–Palestinian conflict out of all political shocks	3/8	0/5
	External economic shock out of all economic shocks	5/9	6/7

Source: Bank of Israel and authors' calculations

conflict. The table also shows that five of the nine economic shocks (56 percent) originated in the international financial markets.

The picture obtained for the second period, the one starting in June 2005, is as follows: Relative to the first period, the distribution of turning points between political and economic shocks remained almost unchanged (Part B of the table). However, Part C of the table shows two noticeable differences between the periods. One difference is that, in the second period, there is no longer any representation of events related to the Israeli–Palestinian conflict; all of the political shocks have to do with other conflicts in the Middle East, or with Israeli domestic politics. The other difference is that nearly all of the economic shocks (6 out of 7) originate in the international financial markets.

6.3.2 *The Foreign Exchange Market*

We identify turning points in the foreign exchange market using daily data for the shekel–dollar and shekel–euro exchange rates. In both cases, our search spans the period from January 3, 2000 to May 31, 2016. As with the stock market, for each of the series we make use of windows of the following lengths: 60, 120, 240, 360, and 480 trading days. The exchange rate data were obtained from the Bank of Israel.

Figure 6.3 displays the exchange rates for the period in question. The shekel weakened significantly against the dollar from early 2000 to mid-2002, when the exchange rate reached nearly five shekels to the dollar. The shekel also declined substantially from early 2000 against the euro, but this decline continued until the end of 2004, when the exchange rate reached nearly six shekels per euro. In the later period, the one we focus on, the shekel generally strengthened, with great volatility, against both currencies. From June 1, 2005 to May 31, 2016, the shekel strengthened by 15 percent against the dollar and by 26 percent against the euro.

Table 6.3 displays the results of our analysis of turning points in the foreign exchange market. As in Table 6.1, the first column in Table 6.3 reports the date of the turning point, while the second column displays the explanation that we offer for the turning point. The third column sorts the proposed explanations into five different categories: (1) the Israeli–Palestinian conflict; (2) political shocks in the Middle East; (3) domestic politics; (4) domestic economic shocks; (5) external economic shocks.

Figure 6.3 Shekel–dollar and shekel–euro exchange rates, 1990–2016.
Source: Bank of Israel

Table 6.3 *Turning points in the foreign exchange market, 2000–2016*

Date	Possible explanation	Type of event	60 days		120 days		240 days		360 days		480 days	
			Dollar	Euro	Dollar	Euro	Dollar	Euro	Dollar	Euro	Dollar	Euro
October 12, 2000	Start of Second Intifada	Israeli–Palestinian conflict			+		+					
April 2, 2002	Escalation of violence	Israeli–Palestinian conflict			+		+		+		+	
May 23, 2003	Government adopts the "road map"	Israeli–Palestinian conflict			−		−		−		−	
May 10, 2004	Escalation of violence	Israeli–Palestinian conflict	+									
January 3, 2005	Contagion	External economic shock			+		+					
March 24, 2008	Bank of Israel lowers interest rate	Domestic economic shock			+		+		+		+	
August 4, 2009	Bank of Israel buys foreign currency	Domestic economic shock	+	+	+	+	+	+	+	+	+	+
May 11, 2010	Contagion	External economic shock				−		−				
January 13, 2011	Contagion	External economic shock				+		+		+		+
May 14, 2013	Bank of Israel lowers interest rate	Domestic economic shock	+		+	+	+	+	+		+	+
February 24, 2015	Bank of Israel lowers interest rate	Domestic economic shock			+	+	+	+	+	+	+	+
March 24, 2015	Bank of Israel unexpectedly refrains from lowering the interest rate	Domestic economic shock							−		−	
December 4, 2015	Contagion	External economic shock		+								
Total points			3	2	8	5	8	5	6	3	6	4

Source: Bank of Israel and authors' calculations

The following columns report the direction of the effect manifested at the turning point. In these columns, the plus (+) sign denotes a weakening of the shekel, while the minus (–) sign denotes the shekel's strengthening. All of the turning points reported are statistically significant at a level of at least 10 percent. As in Table 6.1, we will distinguish between the turning points that were found in the period studied by Zussman et al. (2008), that is, from January 2000 to May 2005, and those that were found for the period from June 2005 to May 2016. The separation enables us to illustrate the differences between the periods in terms of the types of events that caused the turning points.

A detailed description of the turning points during the period ending in May 2005 can be found in Zussman et al. (2008); we will, therefore, discuss in depth here only those turning points identified between June 2005 and May 2016. We describe the turning points in terms of the type of explanation proposed for each point, rather than chronologically.

Domestic Economic Shock. We identified five turning points related to domestic economic shocks:[7]

A. *March 24, 2008 (Bank of Israel lowers the interest rate) – weakening of the shekel*: The weakening reflected the expectation that on the evening of March 24 the Bank of Israel would announce a significant lowering of the interest rate. These expectations were driven by, among other things, a lowering of the interest rate in the United States by 0.75 percentage points in the previous week. The Bank of Israel in fact announced a reduction of the interest rate by 0.5 percentage points, to 3.25 percent. That day the shekel weakened by 3.5 percent against both the dollar and the euro.

B. *August 4, 2009 (Bank of Israel buys foreign currency) – weakening of the shekel*: This weakening came in the wake of a massive Bank of Israel intervention in the foreign exchange market. According to the newspaper *Globes*, during the trading week, the Bank of Israel

---

[7] It is important to emphasize a fundamental difference between turning points identified in the foreign exchange market that are attributed to domestic economic shocks, and other types of turning points. All turning points of the former type stemmed from Bank of Israel interest decisions, and from the Bank's intervention in the foreign exchange market. These actions are endogenous, that is, they reflect the Bank of Israel's reaction to developments in the state of the economy. By contrast, the other turning points reflect shocks that are exogenous to the state of the Israeli economy.

purchased more than a billion and a half dollars. On August 4 alone the shekel declined by over 3 percent against the dollar and the euro.

C. *May 14, 2013 (Bank of Israel lowers the interest rate) – weakening of the shekel*: On this date, in a surprise move, the Bank of Israel lowered the interest rate by a quarter of a percentage point (from 1.75 percent to 1.5 percent) and announced that it would be purchasing 2.1 billion dollars by the end of the year. As a result, the shekel weakened on May 15 by 2 percent against the dollar and the euro.

D. *February 24, 2015 (Bank of Israel lowers the interest rate) – weakening of the shekel*: On this date, the Bank of Israel unexpectedly lowered the interest rate by 0.15 percentage points, to 0.1 percent, the lowest interest rate ever recorded in Israel up to that time. As a result, the shekel weakened on February 24 by over 2 percent against the dollar and the euro.

E. *March 24, 2015 (Bank of Israel unexpectedly refrains from lowering the interest rate) – strengthening of the shekel*: On March 23, the Bank of Israel unexpectedly announced that it would not be lowering the interest rate, which would remain at 0.1 percent, and that it would avoid quantitative easing. The following day, the shekel strengthened by over 2 percent against the dollar and by over 1 percent against the euro.

External Economic Shock. We identified three turning points resulting from external economic shocks, i.e., instances of "contagion":

A. *May 11, 2010 – strengthening of the shekel*: This turning point was linked to the developing debt crisis in Europe. On May 9, the European finance ministers announced a comprehensive 750 billion euro aid package, to ensure financial stability across the continent. The following days were characterized by uncertainty and great volatility in the global financial markets. For example, on May 10 the dollar weakened against the euro by 2.4 percent, while the next day it strengthened against the euro by 2.5 percent (*Globes*, May 11, 2010).

B. *January 13, 2011 – weakening of the shekel*: This turning point appears to be linked to a statement by the president of the European Central Bank (ECB) on January 13, according to which the ECB would be raising the interest rate as a means of contending with the development of inflationary pressure. That day and the next, the euro strengthened against the dollar, cumulatively, by over 3 percent (*Financial Times*, January 14, 2011).

C. *December 4, 2015 – weakening of the shekel*: On this date, the president of the ECB announced that the interest rate would be lowered by 0.1 percentage points, and that the bond purchase program would be extended. This announcement disappointed the markets, which had expected more extreme monetary expansionary measures. As a result, the euro strengthened against the dollar that day by over 3 percent (*Financial Times*, December 4, 2015).

Table 6.4 summarizes the turning points in the foreign exchange market by type of event and compares the two periods. Part A of the table shows that, during the first period, four out of five of the turning points were related to the Israeli–Palestinian conflict, while the fifth was an instance of contagion. By contrast, in the second period all eight turning points were attributable to economic shocks – three cases of "contagion" and five cases of Bank of Israel actions (taken in response

Table 6.4 *Summary of turning points in the foreign exchange market by type of event, 1990–2016*

Part	Type of event	Jan 1990 – May 2005	June 2005 – May 2016
A	Israeli–Palestinian conflict	4	0
	Political shocks in the Middle East	0	0
	Domestic politics	0	0
	Domestic economic shock	0	5
	External economic shock	1	3
	Total	5	8
B	Politics	4	0
	Economics	1	8
C	Israeli–Palestinian conflict out of all political shocks	4/4	0/0
	External economic shock out of all economic shocks	1/1	3/8

Source: Bank of Israel and authors' calculations

to various developments, some of them external). Ultimately, the analyses presented in Tables 6.2 and 6.4 indicate that, in contrast to the first period, the Israeli–Palestinian conflict had no impact on the financial markets (the stock market and the foreign exchange market) during the period from June 2005 to May 2016.

6.4 Real Effects of the Israeli–Palestinian Conflict

A potential criticism of the previous section's analysis is that the Israeli–Palestinian conflict, though it may not have affected the financial markets since mid-2005, nevertheless has had a major impact on real economic activity. The present section examines the behavior of several real variables, with a view toward addressing this criticism.

The first and most important variable is the Composite State-of-the-Economy Index – a synthetic indicator that allows a real-time assessment of the development of real economic activity. It is calculated by the Bank of Israel's Research Department once a month, on the basis of ten indicators: the industrial production index; the trade revenue index; the services revenue index; consumer goods imports; imports of manufacturing inputs; goods exports; services exports; the number of employee posts in the private sector; the job vacancy rate; and the number of building starts.

Figure 6.4 displays the monthly rate of change in the Composite State-of-the-Economy Index from January 1998 (the first month for which the index is available) to May 2016, highlighting major defense-related events. In the early part of the period, the index rose at a fast rate, reaching a peak of more than 1 percent per month in early 2000. Then growth of the index declined dramatically and became negative, reaching a low of –0.6 percent per month in June 2001. The turning point in the spring of 2000 is likely related to the bursting of the dot-com bubble in the United States, which occurred at that time. The eruption of the Second Intifada at the end of September 2000 almost certainly contributed to the slowdown in growth and then to the fall in the index. This claim is consistent with the results reported by Eckstein and Tsiddon (2004) and the *Bank of Israel Annual Report 2003* (2004).

Based on the Composite Index, real activity continued to contract until the spring of 2002. The reversal from contraction to growth was likely driven (or at least aided) by Operation Defensive Shield, which

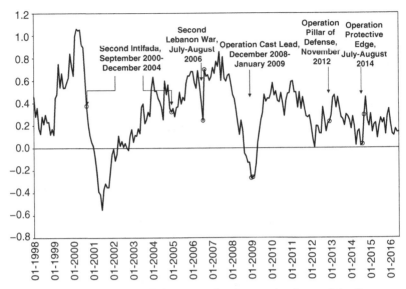

Figure 6.4 Monthly rate of change in the Composite State-of-the-Economy index, 1998–2016 (%).
Source: Bank of Israel

started in late March 2002 and brought about a sharp decline in the number of Israeli fatalities from terrorism. Positive growth continued to characterize the Composite Index until July 2008, though the growth rate slowed substantially toward the end of 2007. Interestingly, in mid-2006 there was a steep but temporary drop in the Composite Index growth rate. This drop started in May 2006, two months before the Second Lebanon War broke out. Bank of Israel analysis indicates that the fighting in the north caused only a temporary and relatively small downturn in economic activity – thanks to the country's strong economic situation prior to the military conflagration (see the *Bank of Israel Annual Report 2006* [2007]).

From August 2008 to March 2009, the Composite Index's rate of change was negative, meaning that real economic activity contracted. This contraction was probably due to the global financial crisis, which is generally thought to have started in September 2008. The growth rate reached a low of –0.3 percent in December 2008, before Operation Cast Lead, the first of the relevant period's large-scale armed conflicts in Gaza. The operation started on December 27 and continued for three weeks. The figure suggests that the operation had little or even no effect at all on real activity. (It is interesting that this military event is not mentioned at all in the *Bank of Israel Annual Report 2009* [2010].)

The Composite Index rose steadily from April 2009 to the final month of the period under investigation, May 2016, though its rate of increase fluctuated widely. It is clear that neither of the military operations in Gaza that occurred during the period, Operation Pillar of Defense in November 2012 or Operation Protective Edge in July–August 2014, had a significant impact on the Composite Index's rate of change.

The effect of defense-related shocks on real economic activity should manifest itself in another key economic indicator – the unemployment rate. Examining the development of the unemployment rate (for individuals of prime working age) yields an almost mirror image of the development of the Composite Index. Specifically, the unemployment rate rose sharply after the dot-com bubble burst and the Second Intifada broke out (the average unemployment rate in the year preceding the bursting of the bubble was 9.3 percent; at the height of the Intifada it reached a level of 11.6 percent). In contrast, the Second Lebanon War in 2006 and the big military operations in Gaza in 2008–2009, 2012, and 2014 had very little impact on the unemployment rate.

The picture obtained from analysis of aggregate data on real economic activity is thus similar to that obtained from analysis of asset markets. Both show that since the mid-2000s, the Israeli–Palestinian conflict has had no significant impact on economic activity.

However, this finding does not necessarily suggest that security shocks have had no effect at all on any of the economic sectors since the mid-2000s. An extensive body of research has demonstrated that the tourism industry is strongly affected by security threats, and Israel is no exception.[8] This is evident in data on the number of bed-nights of local and foreign tourists in Israeli hotels. The data show that the Second Intifada dealt a crippling and persistent blow to tourism: the number of bed-nights declined from September 2000 to March 2003 by over 50 percent. At the end of the Intifada, the number of bed-nights

---

[8] An early study on this topic is that of Enders et al. (1992), who found that terrorism had exerted a negative impact on tourism in Greece, Italy, and Austria. The Israeli case is analyzed in Fleischer and Buccola (2002) and Eckstein and Tsiddon (2004).

stood at only 75 percent of their pre-Intifada level. The three Gaza operations also had a negative, though relatively limited, impact on the number of bed-nights. For example, the period surrounding Operation Protective Edge in the winter of 2008–2009 saw a 10 percent decline in the number of bed-nights. The period surrounding Operation Protective Edge in the summer of 2014 saw an even more precipitous decline in tourism: the number of bed-nights fell by 21 percent.

6.5 Why Did the Israeli–Palestinian Conflict Stop Affecting the Markets?

In this section we will propose and examine a possible explanation for our main finding that, from the mid-2000s, the Israeli–Palestinian conflict ceased to affect financial markets in Israel. We claim that this finding is likely related to changing public expectations about the conflict being resolved by peaceful means in the foreseeable future.

The Oslo Accords, which were signed in the mid-1990s, constituted a turning point in the Israeli–Palestinian conflict. They represented an effort to resolve all the core conflict issues as part of a permanent arrangement. A central component of the Accords was the principle of land for peace: Israel would gradually withdraw from a major portion of the territories over which it had gained control in the Six Day War, and in return, the Palestinian national movement would abandon its armed struggle and recognize Israel's right to exist in peace.

The first Oslo agreement, signed in September 1993, generated strong opposition that manifested in extreme acts of violence, including the assassination of Prime Minister Rabin in November 1995. During the latter half of the 1990s, Israel and the Palestinian Authority remained formally committed to the Oslo Accords, but progress on implementing them slowed. An unsuccessful attempt to wrest the peace process from stagnation took place at the Camp David summit of July 2000. The Second Intifada broke out in late September 2000. Violence escalated until mid-2002 and then gradually died down. Since the end of the Intifada (around mid-2005), several other attempts have been made to further the diplomatic process between Israel and the Palestinians, but none of these efforts has yielded substantial progress.

Our contention is that, in the 1990s, following the Oslo Accords, a large proportion of the Israeli public expected that the conflict with the Palestinians would be resolved peacefully in the foreseeable future. The failure of Camp David and the outbreak of the Second Intifada were turning points. These events undermined expectations of an end to the conflict and implanted the idea that there was no negotiating "partner" on the Palestinian side. A number of developments caused these attitudes to become entrenched during the years after the Second Intifada. These included Hamas's takeover of the Gaza Strip following Israel's 2005 withdrawal from it, massive rocket attacks from the Gaza Strip on Israeli territory, and failed rounds of negotiations between Israel and the Palestinians. Thus, since the mid-2000 the Israeli public seems to have adopted the view that Israeli–Palestinian relations will continue to be characterized by sporadic rounds of violence.

To test this hypothesis, we use data from the Peace Index survey conducted by the Tami Steinmetz Center for Peace Research in Tel Aviv University. The survey has been carried out continuously since 1994, with about 500 Jewish participants each month.

Our focus is on the answers to four of the survey questions.[9] Two of the questions relate to the Oslo Accords. The first question is: "What is your stand on the agreements signed in Oslo by Israel and the PLO?" The six response options are: "Very much in favor," "Quite in favor," "So so ... somewhere in the middle," "Quite opposed," "Greatly opposed," and "Don't know / no opinion." This question was included in the surveys from June 1994 to July 2008. The second question is, "Do you believe, or not believe, that the Oslo Accords between Israel and the PLO will lead to peace between Israel and the Palestinians in the coming years?" The six possible answers to this question are: "Strongly believe," "Quite believe," "So so ... somewhere in the middle," "Hardly believe," "Do not believe at all," "Don't know / no opinion." This question was included in the surveys from March 1995 to July 2008. The other two questions appeared in the surveys only from mid-2001. They are almost identical to the questions about the Oslo Accords, with the main differences being that they ask about "peace negotiations" rather than the "Oslo Accords" and that the "So so" option is not available.

Figure 6.5 shows the development over time of the percentage of Oslo Accords supporters ("very much in favor" or "quite in favor") and the percentage of those who believe that the Accords will lead to

---

[9] See Gould and Klor (2010) for a similar use of surveys to analyze the effects of security shocks on Israeli citizens' political opinions.

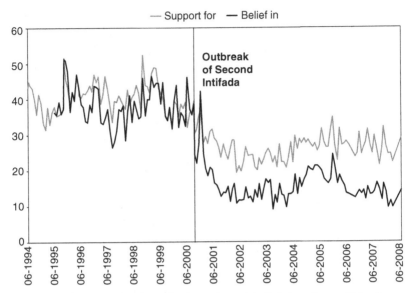

Figure 6.5 Support for the Oslo Accords and belief that they will lead to a resolution of the conflict, 1994–2008 (%).
Source: Tami Steinmetz Center for Peace Research, Tel Aviv University

peace between Israel and the Palestinians ("strongly believe" or "quite believe"). The figure clearly shows that the period can be divided into two parts: before and after the start of the Second Intifada. In the first period, both support for the Oslo Accords and the belief that the Accords would lead to peace were quite prevalent positions within the Israeli public: the mean values for the two series were 38 percent and 40 percent, respectively. The Intifada caused a sharp downturn in support for the Oslo Accords: the mean value for support during the second period was only 26 percent. The decline in belief that the Accords will bring peace with the Palestinians was even more dramatic: the mean value of this variable during the second period was just 16 percent. Another interesting finding is that, although violence levels dropped dramatically from mid-2002 onwards, the gap between the two series remained the same until 2008. For our purposes, the most important point is that, from the outbreak of the Second Intifada to 2008, only a sixth of the Israeli population believed that the Oslo Accords would lead to an end of the conflict with the Palestinians.

A possible problem with the Oslo Accords questions is that support for the Accords is associated with a specific political camp, sparking concerns of bias in the responses to those questions. This problem led the Steinmetz Center researchers, in 2001, to start asking the two alternative questions mentioned above, which are still being asked today. Figure 6.6 shows the development of support for negotiations with the Palestinians and of the belief that negotiations will lead to resolution of the conflict. Two main patterns can be seen in the figure. First, both support for negotiations and the belief that the negotiations will lead to resolution of the conflict are high in comparison with the corresponding questions relating to the Oslo Accords. From 2001 to 2016 the level of support for negotiations was, on average, 65 percent. The percentage of those who believed that negotiations will result in resolution of the conflict amounted, on average, to 31 percent. Second, the gap between belief and support is very large (34 percentage points, on average, across the relevant period) and appears stable over time. For our purposes, what is most important is that less than a third of

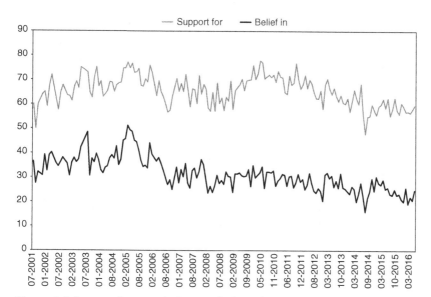

Figure 6.6 Support for negotiations with the Palestinians and belief that they will lead to a resolution of the conflict, 2001–2016 (%).
Source: Tami Steinmetz Center for Peace Research, Tel Aviv University

the public believes that negotiations with the Palestinians will lead to a resolution of the conflict.

The analysis thus yields findings which are consistent with our hypothesis regarding the factors behind the desensitization of asset markets to defense-related shocks – namely, that the Israeli public does not believe that peace is possible in the foreseeable future, and incorporates in its expectations the likelihood of further rounds of violence.

That said, it is important to note that there are alternative explanations for the reduced sensitivity of financial markets (and, more generally, the Israeli economy) to defense-related shocks. Although we cannot determine the importance of these explanations relative to the one we have focused on thus far, it is worth mentioning them. One alternative explanation is that the intensity of the security shocks declined between the two periods. One might, for instance, argue that the Second Intifada, which caused the deaths of nearly a thousand Israelis and lasted for several years, cannot be regarded as a security shock of the same order as the past decade's rocket attacks from the Gaza Strip – attacks that caused a much lower number of Israeli fatalities and were over in a matter of weeks.[10] The other alternative explanation for the asset markets' reduced sensitivity to security shocks is the continued improvement in Israel's macroeconomic environment. This improvement is manifested in, among other things, a lower ratio of government debt to GDP, a shift in the current account from deficit to surplus, a dramatic expansion in foreign currency reserves, and maintenance of low levels of inflation. The improved macroeconomic environment has enabled the Israeli economy to more easily cope with various exogenous shocks, which in turn was reflected in the mild response of asset markets to these shocks.

6.6 Conclusion

Economists have long been interested in the link between defense and the economy. Because the State of Israel has faced particularly grave security threats since its establishment, we should not be surprised that

---

[10] It should be noted that the economic implications of the rocket threat have also varied over time. See Elster et al. (2017, 2019) who study the housing market effects of rocket attacks against Israel and the introduction of the Iron Dome missile defense system.

Israeli economists have also displayed considerable interest in the defense–economy link. Taking a broad view, we can say that security issues are much less important today than they were in the past. This can be seen in the sharp and almost monotonic decline in the defense burden since mid-1970s. The decline can be attributed, first and foremost, to processes that have reduced the gravity of the threats facing Israel. Nevertheless, the threats have not disappeared, and it is, therefore, important to know how the economy copes with defense-related shocks.

In this chapter we have analyzed the impact of defense-related shocks on the Israeli economy during the period 1990–2016. Our analysis focused on the perspective of participants in the stock and foreign exchange markets, and employed a methodology that allows one to identify turning points in asset market data. The main finding of our analysis is that the share of turning points related to the Israeli–Palestinian conflict, out of all turning points in asset markets, declined during the years 2005–2016, relative to 1990–2005. Two "optimistic" explanations for this finding are that the defense-related shocks became less severe between the two periods, and that the macroeconomic environment improved. A more "pessimistic" explanation for our finding is that, since the Second Intifada, Israelis are less inclined to believe that peace with the Palestinians is possible in the foreseeable future and have come to expect further rounds of violence. Separating between these explanations is worthy of further study.

References

In Hebrew

Bank of Israel (2004). *Bank of Israel Annual Report 2003*. Jerusalem: Bank of Israel.

Bank of Israel (2007). *Bank of Israel Annual Report 2006*. Jerusalem: Bank of Israel.

Bank of Israel (2010). *Bank of Israel Annual Report 2009*. Jerusalem: Bank of Israel.

Central Bureau of Statistics (2017). *Defense Expenditure in Israel, 1950–2015*, Jerusalem: Central Bureau of Statistics.

In English

Abadie, A., and Gardeazabal, J. (2003). The Economic Costs of Conflict: A Case Study of the Basque Country. *American Economic Review*, 93(1), 113–132.

Ben-Porath, Y., ed. (1986). *The Israeli Economy: Maturing Through the Crises.* Cambridge, MA: Harvard University Press.

Berglas, E. (1986). Defense and the Economy. In Y. Ben-Porath (ed.), *The Israeli Economy: Maturing Through the Crises.* Cambridge, MA: Harvard University Press, 173–191.

Berrebi, C., and Klor, E. F. (2010). The Impact of Terrorism on the Defence Industry. *Economica*, 77(307), 518–543.

Eckstein, Z., and Tsiddon, D. (2004). Macroeconomic Consequences of Terror: Theory and the Case of Israel. *Journal of Monetary Economics*, 51(5), 971–1002.

Eldor, R., and Melnick, R. (2004). Financial Markets and Terrorism. *European Journal of Political Economy*, 20(2), 367–386.

(2010). Small Investment and Large Returns: Terrorism, Media and the Economy. *European Economic Review*, 54(8), 963–973.

Elster, Yael, Zussman, A., and Zussman, N. (2017). Rockets: The Housing Market Effects of a Credible Terrorist Threat. *Journal of Urban Economics*, 99, 136–147.

Elster, Yael, Zussman, A., and Zussman, N. (2019). Effective Counter-Terrorism: Rockets, *Iron Dome* and the Israeli Housing Market. *Journal of Policy Analysis and Management*, 38(2), 237–308.

Enders, W., Sandler, T., and Parise, G. F. (1992). An Econometric Analysis of the Impact of Terrorism on Tourism. *Kyklos*, 45(4), 531–554.

Fielding, D. (2003a). Modelling Political Instability and Economic Performance: Israeli Investment During the Intifada. *Economica*, 70 (277), 159–186.

(2003b). Counting the Cost of the Intifada: Consumption, Saving and Political Instability in Israel. *Public Choice*, 116(3/4), 297–312.

Fleischer, A., and Buccola, S. (2002). War, Terror and Tourism in Israel: Demand and Supply Factors. *Applied Economics*, 34(11), 1335–1343.

Gould, E. D., and Klor, E. F. (2010). Does Terrorism Work? *Quarterly Journal of Economics*, 125(4), 1459–1510.

Guidolin, M., and La Ferrara, E. (2007). Diamonds Are Forever, Wars Are Not: Is Conflict Bad for Private Firms? *American Economic Review*, 97 (5), 1978–1993.

Harel, Amos, and Issacharoff, A. (2008). *34 Days: Israel, Hezbollah, and the War in Lebanon.* New York, NY: Palgrave Macmillan.

Lifshitz, Y. (2003). *The Economics of Producing Defense: Illustrated by the Israeli Case*. Boston, MA: Kluwer Academic Publishers.

Willard, K. L., Guinnane, T. W., and Rosen, H. S. (1996). Turning Points in the Civil War: Views from the Greenback Market. *American Economic Review*, 86(4), 1001–1018.

Zussman, A., and Zussman, N. (2006). Assassinations: Evaluating the Effectiveness of an Israeli Counterterrorism Policy Using Stock Market Data. *Journal of Economic Perspectives*, 20(2), 193–206.

Zussman, A., Zussman, N., and Nielsen, M.Ø. (2008). Asset Market Perspectives on the Israeli–Palestinian Conflict. *Economica*, 75(297), 84–115.

PART II

Reforms and Their Effects

7 | Developments in the Israeli Capital Market, 1995–2017

Toward an Efficient Financial Intermediation

DORON AVRAMOV, EFRAT DRESSLER,
AND LIOR METZKER

7.1 Introduction

Between 1995 and 2017, there were significant developments in the Israeli economy in general and in the local capital market in particular. These developments were a result of the change in the dominant macroeconomic paradigms, which began with the 1985 Stabilization Program. Once the economy stabilized, policymakers determined the GDP of the business sector growth to be a key target. During the period reviewed, the trend of reducing government involvement in the economy and opening it up to the world continued. The structural reforms carried out were intended to reduce centralization, increase competition, and optimize the capital market to improve the allocation of resources in the economy.

With the goal of reducing centralization in the economy and reducing the power of the banks, the Brodet Committee (1995) recommended that control of real corporations by banks should be prohibited, and that the total holdings that a bank is allowed to have in these corporations should be limited. The structural reforms in pension funds and the implementation of the Bachar Committee's recommendations (2004) have contributed to reducing the government's involvement in the capital market and to a change in its players' map. The transfer of the management of provident funds and mutual funds from the banks to non-bank financial institutions reduced the banks' conflict of interest and enabled the development of non-bank credit. The banks have changed from being "universal" players, operating in most areas of the capital market, to only being providers of

* We thank Avi Ben-Bassat and Yishay Yafeh for their helpful ideas and comments.

classic banking services. The increase in the number of financial institutions managing long-term savings has contributed to improved competition in financial intermediation, which until then was characterized by extreme centralization. Alongside the treatment of centralization in financial intermediation, centralization was also dealt with in the ownership structure and control of all the companies in the economy.

During this period, global trends in the domestic capital market intensified – a continuation of the liberalization measures in capital movements in foreign currency, which occurred on the eve of the period under review.[1] In addition, an overall dramatic change in the tax system was made: among other things, the income from financial assets was taxed, and the tax discrimination that existed until then in almost every dimension was eliminated, as was the tax discrimination between foreign and domestic assets. In the past fifteen years, the share of foreign assets in total assets has grown from zero to about 24 percent. The development of the Exchange-Traded Fund (ETF) sector has contributed to making investments in foreign assets accessible to the public, both directly and through institutional investors. Adoption of international accounting principles (IFRS) and recognition of domestic prospectuses by overseas securities authorities made global capital markets accessible to Israeli companies for the purpose of raising foreign funding, and enabled foreign companies to raise funding in the domestic economy.

Along with the increase in the global exposure of the institutional investors' portfolio, the volume of credit to the business sector through both private and public offers of nongovernment bonds has also increased. The volume of bonds issued by nonfinancial companies relative to the GDP rose sharply.[2] Following the global financial crisis and the large number of debt settlements in the Israeli economy, nongovernment bonds were subject to tight regulation. In particular, the status of the bondholders in relation to other lenders was addressed.

Along with an increase in the number of companies whose bonds are traded, the number of public companies whose shares are traded on the stock market has decreased – as part of a global trend, but also in accordance with Israel's Anti- Concentration Law[3] (2013) requirement

[1] Liberalization measures in foreign currency capital movements occurred in the years 1989–1997. See Gottlieb and Blejer (2002).

[2] Sasi-Brodesky (2017).

[3] Formally "A Law for Promotion of Competition and Reduction of Concentration."

to reduce layers in Israeli business groups organized in a pyramidal holding structure. This requirement has led many companies to change from being publicly traded companies to private companies. The decline in the number of public companies, along with other factors, led to a decline in the volume of trading on the Tel Aviv Stock Exchange (TASE). The TASE plays an important role as the center of the capital market and as a tool for the effective allocation of resources in the Israel economy, and therefore a reform in its activities was required.

The financial intermediation reforms were mainly aimed at improving competition in the credit market for the business sector. The major beneficiaries of the improvement are the large companies, which can issue bonds or borrow from financial institutions. By contrast, competition in banking services for retail customers remains very low, but progress has also been made in this area.

Another effect of world events on the domestic market is evident with regard to corporate governance. The Goshen Committee drafted a corporate governance code similar to that customary in OECD countries, with a focus on self-dealing transactions. The Hamdani Committee imposed on institutional investors the role of gatekeepers in corporate governance by requiring them to participate in voting, working to make the voting process more accessible, and essentially strengthening minority shareholders by increasing the majority requirement for interested party transactions from one-third to a majority of minority votes.

The article is organized as follows: section 7.2 details the main structural reforms in the period reviewed; section 7.3 reviews the issues of corporate governance in the Israeli market, characterized by a centralized ownership structure, and the significant changes in corporate governance in recent years; section 7.4 presents the effects of the structural reforms on the development of non-bank credit, the implications of the debt arrangements on raising capital in the business sector and the regulation of the field of nongovernment bonds; section 7.5 lists new reforms that have been discussed recently – some of which have already been enacted but have not yet been implemented; section 7.6 summarizes.

7.2 Structural Reforms and Their Impact on the Capital Market

During the period reviewed in this chapter, a number of significant structural reforms were implemented in the Israeli capital market: the reform based on the recommendations of the Brodet Committee, which started the process of separating financial and nonfinancial holdings (a process that was also addressed by the Centralization Committee some fifteen years later); the reform in the taxation of income from financial instruments, which eliminated the discrimination in taxation between various financial assets; the pension reforms, which reduced government involvement in the capital market by transferring the management of new pension funds from the government and the Histadrut to the financial institutions, and reducing the government debt component in the public's assets. The Bachar Reform, which focused on the concentration on financial intermediation, and especially on reducing the power of the banks, strengthening the non-bank financial institutions and developing non-bank credit; the reform in economics centralization, which dealt with the separation of ownership and control between real and financial entities and the dismantling of the pyramid ownership structure.[4] We will focus on the pension reforms and Bachar Reform.

7.2.1 Pension Funds

The two major pension reforms, in 1995 and 2003, were aimed at reducing the actuarial deficits of the Histadrut-owned pension funds, reducing government involvement in the capital market, controlling government spending following the stabilization plan, transferring the responsibility for long-term savings from the government to the individual, and weakening the power of the Histadrut.

The 1995 reform was intended to stop the growth of actuarial deficits in the pension funds.[5] On the eve of the reform, pension funds in Israel were defined benefit funds (DB). As part of the agreement between the government and the Histadrut, which had owned the pension funds, it was decided to close the existing pension funds (hereinafter: the old funds) to new members, and instead, "new" pension funds (with inferior conditions) were established for the absorption of new members. The new funds are defined contribution funds (DC) – they have an actuarial balance at the fund level, which is

---

[4] For detailed information on the Centralization Committee, see Kosenko, Chapter 9, this volume.
[5] Spivak (2002).

achieved through a coordination mechanism between the amount of all pension payments and all of the insured persons' contributions, and includes a government safety net – meaning a mutual insurance component, which is not included in pure DC plans.[6] Two years later, the government guarantees were abolished, and the new funds changed to a pure DC system, where each insured person had his or her own personal accrual. The government, on the other hand, remains a guarantor of the rights insured in the old funds.

The new pension funds that were established were owned by the Histadrut and managed by the old pension funds. At the same time, the insurance companies were allowed to set up new pension funds, but most of the new policyholders joined the new funds that belonged to the old funds. In 1999, as part of a collective agreement between the government and the Histadrut, the budgetary (unfunded) pensions were closed to new employees, who were directed to the new pension funds.

The investment rate of the new pension funds in designated government bonds was limited to 70 percent, while in the old pension funds it was at least 93 percent, and in practice was 95 percent. These bonds are issued by the government and are designated for pension funds and insurance companies. They are not traded, linked to the Consumer Price Index (CPI) and have a relatively high and risk-free yield. The disadvantages of high rates of investment in designated bonds are the weighting on the state budget – as these bonds are an expensive government debt – and the reduction of financial institutions' available resources that can be directed to the private sector.

Following the global economic crisis of 2001–2002 (the "dot.com bubble"), the economy entered a recession. The Israeli Economy Recovery Law, 2003, included a legislative arrangement for pension funds. Owing to irregularities in the management of the old pension funds, actuarial deficits, which amounted to some NIS 110 billion, and the lack of a recovery plan, the funds were taken away from the Histadrut and nationalized, and a special director was appointed on behalf of the Treasury.[7] Subsequently, an actuarial balancing plan was formulated for the funds, which included converting them into defined contribution (DC) funds at the fund level. The immediate actuarial balance was achieved by deteriorating the members' rights, by raising the pension age, increasing the insureds' contributions, and charging

---

[6] Achdut and Spivak (2010).   [7] Yosef and Spivak (2003).

the pensioners for management fees on their pension payments. At the same time, government assistance of NIS 78 billion was promised, which, after negotiations with the Histadrut, was increased to NIS 85 billion, spread over thirty-five years. Another NIS 1 billion cash flow to the old pension funds resulted from the sale of the new pension funds, which they owned to private entities. Within a short time, four new pension funds were sold to the Menorah, Migdal, Clal, and Excellence (the Phoenix) insurance companies.

The sale of the new pension funds caused a stir in the pension sector. This was reflected in additional purchases of new pension funds by the Harel and Migdal insurance companies. At the same time, other non-bank financial institutions applied to operate pension funds, and the first, which was approved in 2004, was the new pension fund Halman-Aldubi.

The reform also reduced the government's involvement in the capital market, by reducing the pension fund's investment rate in bonds to a level of under 30 percent, gradually, according to their redemption date. The real interest rate on the bonds decreased and is now 4.8 percent. The old pension funds were still required to invest 50 percent of all their assets in negotiable government bonds.

In summary, the reform in the pension sector in 2003 resulted in the entry of non-bank financial institutions, especially insurance companies, into the capital market. In doing so, it contributed to a reduction in the centralization of the financial system and gave decision-making powers to a larger number of bodies. Furthermore, the reduction in the demand for designated bonds, by reducing the minimum investment rate, redirected credit resources to the business sector and reduced government financing costs. In July 2017, the volume of assets in the new pension funds amounted to some NIS 313 billion, compared with some NIS 7.5 billion in January 2001. The increase in the volume of managed funds accelerated in 2008, following the imposition of a pension contribution requirement for all salaried employees in the economy. Another diversion of power for the benefit of the institutional bodies at the banks' expense stemmed from the Bachar Reform, in 2005.

7.2.2 Bachar Committee

7.2.2.1 Background
In April 2004, the Bachar Committee was appointed to discuss ways to reduce the centralization and conflicts of interest of the banking system

in the Israeli capital market, and, as a result – to develop the non-bank credit market. The role of financial intermediation is to connect the savings units, that is, the public, to the investment units – the real market. The intermediation entities include banks, insurance companies, mutual funds, long-term savings (provident funds,[8] pension funds, and life insurance plans), private equity funds, etc. The centralization of the economy was characterized on two levels: the centralization of financial intermediation, which was almost entirely controlled by the banks, and the centralization of the banking system, most of which was concentrated in the two largest banks – Hapoalim and Leumi. The Committee dealt with the first issue: the financial intermediation was controlled by the "universal" banks – those that operated in most areas of the capital market – which provided credit to the business and mortgage sector for the households, and provided financial intermediation services through mutual funds and provident funds, while at the same time managing those funds. The banks had almost unlimited control over provident fund activity, which was a major part of pension savings, as the new pension funds were still in their early stages. They also served as underwriters in issuances and as buyers through the funds they managed. This was a clear conflict of interest between the banks and the saving public (Ber et al., 2001). This situation is not typical of developed capital markets in other countries around the world, where many financial intermediaries operate alongside the banking intermediary. A market structure with many intermediaries encourages competition, reduces intermediation gaps, and streamlines business and public sector activity in the economy.

On the eve of the Bachar Reform, the situation in Israel was unique in a global perspective, where non-bank credit was almost nonexistent – unlike in many developed countries, where a vibrant non-bank credit market operates. This dominance of the banks was achieved, as aforementioned, as a result of their complete control of financial intermediation. Moreover, the banking system was almost exclusively controlled by two large groups – the Bank Hapoalim Group and the Bank Leumi Group.

In a reality that combines high centralization and the financial intermediaries' conflicts of interest, a vicious circle is created, which works

---

[8] By the term "provident funds," we mean provident funds and training funds, unless explicitly stated otherwise.

to preserve the existing situation and to delay the development of an efficient and competitive capital market. The deep-rooted conflict of interest in banks in Israel has led to the obvious conclusion that a bank's investment advisors cannot simultaneously serve the client seeking the optimal investment, and the bank's interests. Therefore, according to the Committee's recommendations, a competitive and efficient capital market must be supported by decentralization of ownership and management of the existing investment funds, development of non-bank credit markets, exposure of households to investment not offered by banks, and facilitation of mobility between the banks.

7.2.2.2 Main Recommendations

The banks were forced to sell the provident funds and mutual funds that they owned, within a period of three and four years, respectively. Their activities were limited so that a bank was not permitted to act as underwriter for a company that borrowed from it (above a certain amount of debt) and was not permitted to sell the proposed security to a Nostro account or to a portfolio management company connected to it. Banks were allowed to offer investment advice, but with a separation between marketing and advising: a bank will not receive compensation from the owner of a financial or pension product.

Restrictions were set on the control of provident funds and mutual funds after they were sold by the banks, in order to prevent the concentration passing to other sectors in the capital market, to increase the freedom of choice of fund members and the degree of competition in the market, thereby reducing the potential for conflict of interest.

The conclusions of the Bachar Committee regarding public savings management in the mutual funds and the provident funds by the banks are identical to the conclusions of the National Commission by Justice Bejski, which investigated the bank stocks crisis and submitted its conclusions in 1986. The National Commission's recommendations at that time included personal recommendations against the officeholders involved in regulating the bank shares, and structural changes concerning the separation of the banks from the mutual funds and the provident funds, due to conflicts of interest to which the bank officials were subject. These structural changes were not implemented. Instead, "Chinese walls" were gradually set up to reduce the potential for conflicts of interest, but the effectiveness of these walls was never seriously tested. Relying only on "Chinese walls" missed the main point, which is the need to create a competitive financial market structure.[9] The transfer of control over the banks to the government worked in favor of their receiving lenient treatment. Only after the introduction of the Stabilization Program, with the change in the macroeconomic perspective to a concept of reducing government involvement in the economy and opening it to the world, and after the State had sold most of the bank shares it owned, was the Bachar Committee established.

7.2.2.3 Implications

The banks were the main opponents of the reform, but in practice, within a few months they succeeded in selling most of the large mutual funds and provident funds to insurance companies and foreign investment funds. When selling the managing entities, the banks received high prices, which greatly increased their financial strength and profitability and enabled them to distribute large dividends.

We will examine the implications of the Bachar Reform in terms of management fees and the performance of provident funds against the risk aversion or risk appetite of their managers regarding the various groups of controlling shareholders – banks, insurance companies, private financial entities, and those without a controlling corporation. We will also compare the concentration of local credit provided to the public directly by the banks to that provided through long-term savings.

Opponents of the reform feared that the transfer of the provident funds from the banks would result in an increase in management fees. Figure 7.1 depicts the development of management fees in the years 1999–2017, with distribution by the controlling group and the group's share in the total assets, as well as the average management fees in all the funds. Prior to the Bachar Reform, management fees charged by banks were, on average, lower than those charged by the insurance companies and the private financial entities. However, the lowest management fees were collected by the provident funds that didn't have a controlling corporation. Since most of the provident fund assets were owned by the banks, the average management fees for all provident funds are close to the banks' management fees. The transfer of the fund management from the banks to the purchasing entities began in late 2005 and ended in the first half of 2008. It can

[9] Klein (2003).

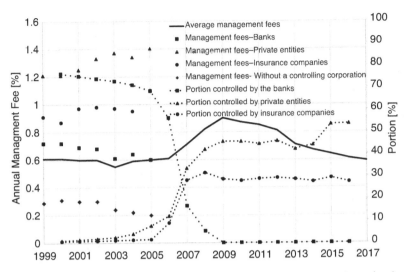

Figure 7.1 Management fees and rates of control in provident funds. Distribution by controlling entities, 1999–2017 (%).
Source: Capital Market, Insurance and Savings Unit of the Ministry of Finance, and processing by the authors.

be seen that with the transfer of control of the provident funds, the average management fees rose until 2009, but since then they have dropped and returned to their level before the reform. Much of the reduction in management fees is the result of regulatory intervention, which took effect from 2013.[10]

We will examine the performance of the training funds and provident funds and personal compensation funds according to the type of entity that controls them – banks, insurance companies, or private financial entities. The sample includes the flexible investment funds open to the general population – i.e., without investment constraints – that operated continuously from the beginning of 1999 to the end of 2005. Performance will be assessed based on three indices – the average yield, the standard deviation, and the Sharp Ratio (SR).[11] The database is the monthly yield minus the management fees, as they appear on the Gemel-Net website of the Ministry of Finance's Capital Markets,

---

[10] Schwartz (2012).

[11] $SR = \frac{E(R_p - R_f)}{\sqrt{var(R_p - R_f)}}$: R_p – monthly yield of the portfolio and R_f – risk-free interest rate.

Insurance and Savings Unit,[12] and the risk-free monthly interest rates for calculating the SR were estimated from yields of three-month government bonds.[13] We note that from 1999 to 2005, – the risk-free interest rate ranged from 13.3 percent to 3.4 percent, averaging 7.1 percent in annual terms. Finally, we used the indices to examine the performance of the training funds and the provident funds according to the controlling group. We also calculated the standard deviation of the SR for each of the groups separately. A summary of the results in annual terms for the training funds is presented in Table 7.1a. Most of the advanced study funds were controlled by the banks, and their yields were inferior to their counterparts, which were controlled by the insurance companies and the private financial entities, both in absolute terms and after controlling for risk, as reflected in the SR. The private financial institutions have performed well, but the difference within these group entities is the greatest. Similar results were obtained regarding the provident funds and the personal compensation funds, as shown in Table 7.1b.

We will now examine the implications of the Bachar Reform on the concentration of bank credit and the development of non-bank credit. We will examine the distribution of local credit to the public at three different points in time: in 2004, before the Bachar Reform, and in 2010 and 2016 – after implementation of the reform. In 2004, bank credit accounted for about 90 percent of the credit available to the public, and in addition, banks held another 6 percent of the credit available to the public through their dominant control of provident funds and mutual funds. Non-bank credit amounted to only about 4 percent. After the Bachar Reform, the bank credit stabilized at about 74 percent of total domestic credit to the public, and non-bank credit stabilized at about 26 percent. In Table 7.2, we present the concentration of bank credit at the three aforementioned points in time, according to several indices: the HHI (Herfindahl–Hirschman Index), CR3, and CR5 (Concentration Ratio). The last two indices show the market share of the three and five largest entities, respectively.

As can be seen, the concentration in the banking sector is very high, and it has even grown over the years as a result of mergers, especially of the

---

[12] http://gemelnet.cma.gov.il/views/dafmakdim.aspx.
[13] Bank of Israel website: www.boi.org.il/he/DataAndStatistics/Pages/SeriesSearc hBySubject.aspx?Level=3&sId=41.

Table 7.1 Examination of performance of advanced study funds and provident funds by type of controlling entity, 1999–2005 (in annual terms)

A. *Advanced study funds*

Controlling entity	Yield (%)	Standard Deviation (%)	SR	STD(SR)	Number of funds in sample	Proportional share of assets in sample (%)
Banks	8.50	4.60	0.31	0.13	13	87
Private entities	10.00	5.60	0.54	0.21	7	8
Insurance companies	9.40	5.60	0.41	0.08	3	5

B. *Provident funds*

Banks	8.90	5.40	0.33	0.14	36	90
Private entities	9.80	5.00	0.5	0.26	18	6
Insurance companies	9.20	5.50	0.36	0.13	9	4
Risk-free interest	7.10					

[*] In the flexible investment funds open to the general population.

mortgage banks and the regular banks – for example, Mizrahi Bank with Bank Tefahot and Bank Adanim. The three largest banks now control some 70 percent of the bank credit, and the five largest banks – some 90 percent of it. A further examination of the impact of the Bachar Reform on the non-bank credit market is described in section 7.4.1, which discusses the development of the debt in the economy for its various channels.

Another result of the Bachar Reform is the entry of players into the financial intermediation market. At the end of 2016, there were ten financial entities managing new pension funds and dozens of provident fund management entities. There are also nineteen mutual fund managers[14] and twenty active underwriters, three of which are foreign

[14] ISA Report (2016).

Table 7.2 *Bank credit concentration*

Year	2004	2010	2016
Bank credit to the public (business and household) – NIS millions	530,984	706,583	885,570
Number of banks	21	17	12
Bank credit concentration – HHI	0.20	0.20	0.20
Bank credit concentration – CR3	0.70	0.68	0.73
Bank credit concentration – CR5	0.83	0.89	0.90

Source: Bank of Israel data, annual information on the banking system, for various years and authors' processing.

Table 7.3 *Concentration of long-term savings*

Year	2004	2010	2016
Provident funds – HHI	0.13	0.06	0.06
Provident funds – CR3	0.59	0.35	0.34
Provident funds – CR5	0.82	0.48	0.46
New pension funds – HHI	0.32	0.26	0.2
New pension funds – CR3	0.87	0.81	0.76
New pension funds – CR5	0.95	0.97	0.95
Life insurance – HHI	0.23	0.23	0.17
Life insurance – CR3	0.75	0.74	0.61
Life insurance – CR5	0.97	0.94	0.90

Source: Financial statements of the Capital Market, Insurance and Savings Unit of the Ministry of Finance for various years and authors' processing.

underwriters. This trend is reflected in the drop in the long-term savings concentration index,[15] especially that of the provident funds, in the years after the reform (Table 7.3). The new pension funds and life insurance have seen a slight decrease in concentration, but this area is still largely controlled by five entities.

[15] The provident fund HHI is calculated based on the managed assets. The HHI of life insurance and pension funds is calculated on the basis of premiums.

The removal of provident funds dealing with long-term savings from the banks has weakened their power, but the transfer of these savings to the institutional bodies has exacerbated the problem of concentration: currently, the six largest financial groups manage about 70 percent of the total long-term savings. Almost all financial institutions are controlled by stakeholders, and some of their controlling stakeholders also have control in nonfinancial corporations. In order to create a competitive environment in the credit market and efficient resource allocation at the economy level, the Committee for the Reduction of Centralization and the Promotion of Competition convened and discussed, among other things, the separation of control in financial and nonfinancial entities.

7.3 Corporate Governance in Israel

The ownership structure typical of Israeli public companies is centralized. Most companies, which have a single controlling shareholder or a group of controlling shareholders, hold an average of 60–70 percent of the company's capital stock and voting rights. In such a centralized structure the main conflict in corporate governance, known as the "Principal-Agent Problem," is not between the shareholders of the company and its managers, as in a decentralized ownership structure, but between the company's controlling shareholders and the minority shareholders.

The main problem with the centralized ownership structure of a public company is the potential impairment of its functioning in a way that causes it to deviate from the goal of maximizing value for its shareholders. The deviation is caused by the imbalance between the company's controlling shareholder and the minority shareholders: the controlling shareholder may be interested in expropriating value – for example, by making transactions with interested parties that do not bring economic benefit to the company. Furthermore, the controlling shareholder appoints most of the members of the board of directors, and in particular, the CEO. In this situation, there is concern that the CEO will be at the command of the controlling shareholder and will not manage the company in the best possible way for all its shareholders.[16]

---

[16] Villalonga and Amit (2009) claim that this conflict exists in the United States as well, in spite of its diversified ownership structure.

The conflict of interest issues between controlling shareholders and minority shareholders adversely affect the entire financial system. This imbalance can result in an inefficient allocation of resources, avoidance by potential investors, and, as a result, the depletion of the domestic capital market through the severe impairment of its functioning and credibility, thereby damaging the entire economy.

Another negative consequence of the concentrated holdings structure is that the dominance of the controlling shareholder leaves no room for the activism of the other shareholders: the chance of other shareholders winning a large share of the profits in the company after its recovery is slim. Therefore, the activist activities of hedge funds or venture capital funds are avoided.

The main tools for solving corporate governance problems are divided into three circles of responsibility: the (internal) Management Circle – the supervision is carried out by the board of directors and its committees, especially the audit committee. The Shareholder Circle – through the voting mechanism, either by voting at shareholders' meeting (Voice) or by the sale of shares (Exit). The Outer Circle is an enforcement entity such as a court, which specializes in corporate and securities law. Below we will discuss the functioning of each of the three corporate governance circles in Israel.

The changes in the capital market discussed in the above sections have led to the strengthening of non-bank financial institutions and the diversion of savings from the government channel to the private sector. Of course, this move has led to an increase in corporate governance conflicts of interest. In the period reviewed, a series of actions was taken in Israel to reduce these conflicts of interest. The opening of the economy to the world, and in particular Israel's joining the OECD, has contributed to some of the changes.

During the period reviewed in this book, three public committees have dealt with corporate governance: The Goshen Committee (December 2006) recommended a Corporate Governance Code for the Israeli capital market. The Hamdani Committee (January 2008) focused on ways to ensure that institutional investors, which usually hold the majority of minority shares and have the professional capacity and duty to fulfill their responsibilities as gatekeepers of the capital market, will actually do so. The conclusions of the two committees were implemented in Amendment 16 to the Companies Law. This amendment makes it difficult to approve transactions with controlling shareholders and has increased the required level of supervision of the board of directors and the minority shareholders regarding these transactions.

The Centralization Committee has dealt with the pyramid structure, which has a high potential for profit tunneling and conflicts of interest between controlling shareholders and minority shareholders. Its conclusions were implemented in the Centralization Law, which is an international precedent for regulatory intervention in restricting ownership and control of a pyramid structure.

The actions taken contributed to improved corporate governance, as measured by the Corporate Governance Index developed by Oded Cohen (2017). Index components include the qualifications of the members of the board of directors and its committees, the ability of the members of the board to act independently of the company's controlling shareholder and/or its officers, and the private benefits of control for the controlling shareholder. The index score increased from 0.41 in 2007 to 0.63 in 2014.

7.3.1 Three Circles of Responsibility

7.3.1.1 Management Circle: Board of Directors

In Israel, the supervisory tool through the board of directors suffers from problems that characterize the local market: it is small, centralized, and its social circles are limited. Therefore, a limited number of directors serve on the boards of many companies. This fact casts a shadow over the possibility that they will be completely independent of the management or of the companies' controlling shareholders. Since the latter control a relatively large number of companies, and the directors themselves are driven, among other things, by their desire to be appointed to the boards of directors of additional companies, this motive impairs their ability to function independently as a supervisory entity over the performance of the CEO. Owing to the lack of activism on the part of institutional shareholders, most of those who propose the appointment of directors, including external directors, are the controlling shareholders or management.

In recent years, a number of changes have been introduced to improve the control arm of the board of directors, through enhancing the board's professionalism and independence. Improved professionalism is reflected in the economics and accounting knowledge required.

The independence of the board of directors is improved by the amendment that made the appointment and the extension of the term of external directors possible without the support of the controlling shareholders. The Remuneration Committee of the board, as well as the Audit Committee must be mainly composed of independent directors.

In June 2016, for the first time, an external director appointment was initiated by an institutional investor: this move received support from the consulting company, Entropy, and there have been other such appointments since then.

The possibility of "screen lifting" and multiple personal claims against directors for making decisions that are not in the best interests of the company or its shareholders are a deterrent against negligent performance, or fulfillment of the director's role not in good faith. Such a lawsuit is currently pending against the directors of IDB Corp, claiming that they approved the transaction for the purchase of Ma'ariv without discussing the transaction's profitability in any way, thereby allegedly causing harm to minority shareholders.

7.3.1.2 Shareholder Circle: Owners

After taking over the management of most of the public's funds in Israel, following the implementation of the pension reform and the Bachar Reform, the institutions became the main players in the local capital market. Their role in such a centralized ownership environment is critical, and they are seen as the "gatekeepers of the capital market." They are therefore expected to represent minority shareholders and protect their rights – for example, by opposing self-dealing transactions with controlling shareholders in companies where there is a fear of value expropriation that may harm minority shareholders.

But such a protection is only possible subject to regulatory intervention, since without such intervention the controlling shareholders will be able to pass any decision they see fit. This regulatory intervention is expressed by a special majority requirement in voting on issues where there is a fear of a conflict of interest. Amendment 16 has raised the special majority required on various issues that might be a source of value expropriation by controlling shareholders or by directly influenced by them: self-dealing transactions, controlling shareholders or their relatives' compensation, waivers of their duty as officers, insurance and indemnity to directors who are controlling shareholders, mergers or acquisitions of companies, consolidation of the roles of CEO and chairman of the board, and the election of external directors.

The regulator's hope is that balanced votes, which are free of extraneous interests and are in accordance with a well-defined voting policy, can prevent transactions that are not in the best interests of all shareholders. Management that wants to avoid refusal and an opposing vote by the major shareholders will act in advance to reach an agreement with them on the terms of the transaction, or refrain from bringing such transactions to a shareholders' meeting. In doing so, the voting power of institutional shareholders can improve the state of the company and its shareholders and the relationship between them, while improving corporate governance.

The importance of the voting mechanism in the eyes of the regulator as a monitoring and supervisory tool to be used by institutional investors is also reflected in its demand of the institutional investors' investment committee to determine, review, and update the voting policy at the general assemblies and to require the institutional investor to vote accordingly. The reliance on institutional investors' votes might raise some problems that we discuss below along with their solutions.

Monitoring through voting by the institutional investors requires an investment of resources in analyzing management proposals, examining each proposal, formulating a position, etc. There is a discrepancy between the beneficiaries of the public product – all the shareholders of the company – and those bearing the cost of the product – the institutional investors, which do not necessarily want to provide this product.[17] The regulator dealt with this problem by imposing an obligation to vote on the institutional investors in those issues where a special majority is required. It was determined that the vote must be for or against without the possibility of abstention, except in cases of conflict of interest of the fund manager. The rules have been applied in the regulation of all institutional investors: mutual fund managers and managing bodies of long-term savings. The voting obligation also applies to non-stock securities holders, primarily at bondholders' meetings.

The problem of relying on oversight by institutional investors' voting is a problem of conflict of interest, which is inherent in their activity: on the one hand, the role of the institutional investor is to represent the

---

[17]   Bebchuk et al. (2017).

savers whose money it manages, and is therefore obliged to look after their interests; on the other hand, the institutional body can have business relationships with the company it is supposed to oversee, or with related parties. Because the Israeli market is characterized by centralized ownership by a few controlling shareholders of many companies, conflicts of interest are central.

Conflicts of interest can affect the voting of institutional investors, thereby impairing the quality of shareholders' monitoring. Hamdani and Yafeh (2013) show that the voting of institutional investors is influenced by conflicts of interest. The phenomenon is not unique to Israel: Davis and Kim (2007), Ashraf et al. (2009), and Cvijanovic et al. (2016), for example, show that fund managers' additional business relationships with companies that are part of their portfolio influence their voting.

The regulator have dealt with the potential for conflicts of interest by requiring institutional investors to publish voting policies and test procedures for the purpose of formulating management's position on special transactions, such as self-dealing transactions, and reporting on the actual vote. The obligation to report on the voting and the results of the vote was imposed on the companies themselves.

Proxy advisory firms' recommendations are a possible relief for both the obligation to participate in shareholder voting and the conflict of interest problem between institutional investors and their savers clients. This recommendation market has created a kind of "natural monopoly": it is controlled by one dominant company – Entropy Group – whose market share is close to 80 percent.

A specific example of the Principle-Agent Problem in corporate governance in Israel is the remuneration of the managers. The salaries of senior executives in Israel are perceived to be too high (compared to the other earners in the same company), as incompatible with performance and as determined in a nontransparent procedure, which serves the company's controlling shareholders (who "buy" the managers' loyalty by giving them high salaries). To overcome some of these problems, the Companies Law was amended[18] to include the appointment of a remuneration committee, which must establish a remuneration policy for the company. The remuneration policy (and any senior management compensation agreement) must receive the approval

---

[18] Amendment 20, in effect as of December 2012.

of a shareholders' meeting by a special majority – a majority of minority shareholders, with one reservation: the vote is not binding: the board of directors has the right to approve remuneration policy and salaries, even if shareholders have expressed their opposition (Say on Pay). The approach on which the "Say on Pay" idea is based offers an alternative to the voting procedure of investors – Exit: a procedure in which shareholders are entitled to sell their holdings in the company if they are dissatisfied with its conduct.

We speculate here on a unique problem of relying on supervision through institutional investors' votes – the nonuse of the Exit option: Israeli investors tend not to sell significant holdings; nor do they punish companies for mismanagement, mainly because of growing net accumulation of assets under management (see Figure 7.2), reduction in public companies traded in the local stock exchange, and a tendency for home bias in institutional investors' investment policy. In the domestic market, there are examples of remuneration policy approval despite the opposition of minority shareholders that were not followed by any sells by the institutional shareholders, or even followed by additional acquisitions.

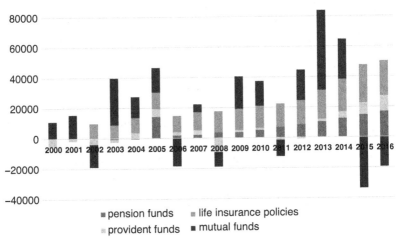

Figure 7.2 Net accumulation of managed funds in institutional investors, 2000–2016 (NIS millions).
Source: Financial statements of the Bank of Israel, annual financial statements of the Capital Market, Insurance and Savings Authority and processing by the authors.

7.3.1.3 Outer Circle: Economics Court of Law

A third measure in the corporate governance toolbox is retrospective regulation, in the form of an Economics Court of Law. Such a court serves as a professional body with expertise in corporate and securities law, similar to such a court in the state of Delaware in the United States. Its purpose is to improve criminal enforcement in its field, to shorten the length of proceedings, and to create the infrastructure for consistent and professional judgment in this field. This is in addition to reducing legal uncertainty in the capital market and strengthening proper norms of conduct among all players. This is a significant milestone in the development and upgrading of the Israeli capital market.

The Economics Court of Law was established in December 2010 as a professional department in the Tel Aviv District Court. It is considered one of the most professional and efficient departments in the judicial system. The judgments given there were precedents, which changed the rules in the business world. The following are some examples: In July 2012, for the first time in Israel, imprisonment was ruled for a defendant convicted of the use of insider information. Ephraim Kadets, VP of Elspec Engineering, was sent to prison. Another ruling provided unprecedented compensation from the controlling shareholders to minority shareholders in the "Koor" affair and the sale of Makhteshim Agan shares to ChemChina. This ruling made the use of an independent committee by the board of directors the standard in self dealing transactions with controlling shareholders.

7.4 Development of Debt and Capital Raising in the Economy

The structural reforms in pensions and the implementation of the recommendations of the Bachar Committee have led to profound changes in the economy. The purpose of the reforms was to create an efficient and competitive capital market as is customary in developed countries. In the aftermath, the power and freedom of action of non-bank financial institutions increased at the expense of the banks. A significant increase in the volume of assets managed by the financial institutions was due to the reduction in the government deficit and in government involvement in the capital market, and from the high growth rates of the economy and the mandatory pension

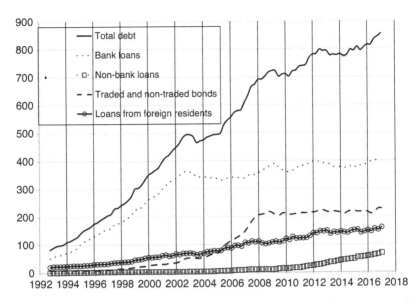

Figure 7.3 Development of debt in the business sector and its sources of financing through bond issues and loans, 1992–2016 (NIS billions, current prices).
Source: Bank of Israel data and processing by the authors

contributions for all employees since 2008. At the end of July 2017, the volume of funds managed by the non-bank financial institutions was about NIS 1.7 trillion. As a result, non-bank credit increased significantly.

The business sector is currently a major growth engine in the Israeli economy. It is therefore interesting to see how the structural reforms have affected the development of debt in this sector (Figure 7.3) and, at the same time, the capital-raising channels of the private sector (business and financial – Figure 7.4). Figure 7.4 also shows the government's net debt raising, that is, the public issuances minus redemptions. Sources of financing are increasing, while the government's net capital raising is small or even negative. To complete the picture, we will also examine the development of the non-bank financial institutions' credit (Figure 7.5) and the development of the debt to the banks (Figure 7.6). Some of the figures contain information beyond the period reviewed – 1995–2017.

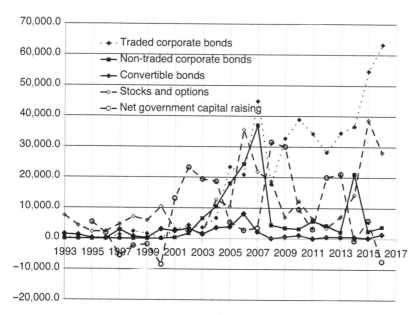

Figure 7.4 Capital raising in the private sector by types of securities and net capital raising by the government,* 1993–2016 (NIS millions, current prices).
* Issuances minus redemptions
Source: Capital raising data from the TASE and processing by the authors

The additional information, pre-1995 period, serves as an additional test indication for the period before the structural changes. We will divide the period under review into three parts.

The first period is until 2003 – the period of the "universal" and dominant banks. Until the pension reform and the Bachar Reform, most of the business sector's credit was from the banks – bank loans or corporate bonds held by the bank-owned funds. At the end of 2003, the credit supplied by the banks (which also included their provident funds) was more than 70 percent of the total credit to the business sector. The share of bonds was less than 10 percent of the total business sector credit. Most of the capital raising was through stocks and options. Much of the credit supplied by the institutional investors was directed to the government's designated bonds, because of investment restrictions imposed on them. The obligation to invest in government bonds, which first affected provident funds, was gradually eased

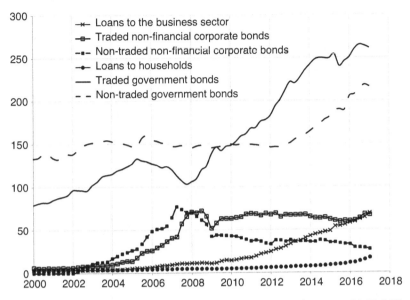

Figure 7.5 Development of the financial institutions' credit, 2000–2017 (NIS billions, current prices).
Source: Bank of Israel data and processing by the authors

between 1987 and 2001. In 2001–2003, capital raising was low, following the bursting of the dot.com bubble and the recession that ensued.

The second period, 2004–2008, is characterized by the consequences of the pension reform, the Bachar Reform, and the rise in the financial markets. A decline in the supply of designated bonds and a reduction in the budget deficit, which the government sector enjoyed during this period, increased the sources of financing available for the business sector, and the economy enjoyed high growth rates. Capital raising in the private sector has grown significantly across all its channels: bonds, convertible bonds, stocks, and bonds designated to the institutional investors.

Bonds designated to the institutional investors can be either regular or convertible. They are issued without a prospectus so the public is not permitted to invest in them. In 2001, the TASE began providing clearing services for those bonds. In May 2004, the "Retsef Mosadiim" System

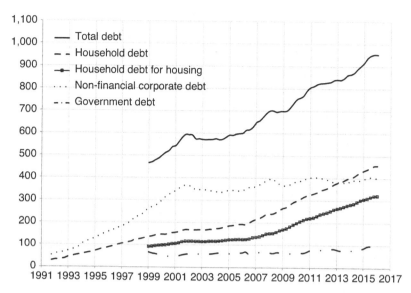

Figure 7.6 Development of debt to the banks, 1992–2016 (NIS billions, current prices).
Source: Bank of Israel data and processing by the authors

(professional services for institutional investors) was launched and enabled continuous trading in those bonds, hence increasing their liquidity and the flexibility of investing. This system is common practice around the world, as it helps to develop the non-bank credit market.

Despite the increase in credit directed to the business sector, the share of banks in the increase in credit was not significant, because the business sector went from borrowing bank credit to raising capital through bonds. At the end of 2008, bank credit was about 54 percent of total credit to the business sector, compared with about 70 percent at the end of 2003. The increase in the volume of assets managed by institutional investors led to an increase in their share in the bond market, and by the end of 2008 they held about 60 percent of the traded bond market and the vast majority of nontraded bonds. The banks increased their assets at that time through loans to households, mostly for housing purposes. The end of the period is characterized by the global financial crisis, which began in late 2008.

The third period, 2009–2017, is characterized by the consequences of the global financial crisis. Following the crisis, many companies found it difficult to meet their obligations and applied for debt arrangements. The crisis had a serious impact on investors' confidence in nongovernment bonds. In order to protect the public savings in the future, the Hodak Committee was established for setting the reference parameters for institutional entities providing investment credit through the purchase of nongovernment bonds. The Committee submitted its conclusions in 2010. They only dealt with conditions and restrictions on investments in corporate bonds, and did not discuss alternative investment channels.

Adoption of the Committee's conclusions led to a change in the credit mix provided by the institutional investors to the business sector: most of the financing sources for the business sector during this period were in the form of loans. At the end of 2016, the total credit provided by the non-bank financial institutions to the business sector in private loans was greater than their holdings in traded corporate bonds. The share of capital raising through nontraded bonds has declined over the period, as have the holdings of institutional investors in such bonds. The year 2014 was exceptional in the raising of nontraded bonds, but most of the debt raised in this channel, some NIS 13 billion, was from foreign institutional bodies. From 2015 to 2016, the business sector saw a recovery in raising debt by traded bonds.

Another change was the increase of holdings government designated bonds by the institutional investors, starting in 2012. The reason for this change is the decrease in interest rates in the economy, which led to a decline in the yields of the "regular" government bonds. In fact, the government designated bonds have become more attractive than in the past, because of their relatively high real yield. In July 2017, the assets of the old and new pension funds that were invested in those bonds accounted for some 58.4 percent and 26.4 percent, respectively, of their total assets.

The banks continued to increase the credit they supplied to households, mainly for housing purposes, while credit to the business sector has hardly changed. The Basel II regulations, which were implemented in 2009, caused banks to reduce the loans they supplied to the business sector, thereby giving non-bank financial institutions an additional standing in the credit market. The share of bank credit to the business sector in total credit declined from a high of over 70 percent in 2003 to about 47 percent at the end of 2016. This provides evidence to the continuing reduction in the power of the banks, at least in the business sector.

7.5 Reforms in the Implementation Process

7.5.1 *The Committee for Increasing Competition in Common Banking and Financial Services (Strum Committee)*

Over many years, attempts were made to develop competition in banking services for the retail sector – households and small- and medium-sized businesses. The lack of sufficient competition in the banking system is reflected in a large number of international indices with low operational efficiency and high centralization scores. As a result, customers in the retail sector pay high prices for banking services – high fees and a high interest margin compared to the business sector, where competition is higher. Previous committees focused on enforcement efforts: increasing transparency and proper disclosure, supervising banking service prices, reducing information gaps, facilitating mobility between banks and more. None of these efforts materially changed competition in the sector, which suffers from significant information gaps between service providers and consumers and between suppliers and potential competitors, as well as high entry barriers and a highly centralized structure (in fact, an oligopoly), stemming in part from the advantage of size and the complexity of financial products.

Therefore, the Strum Committee saw a need for structural change and the introduction of new competitors, outside the banks, who would provide these same services and exert competitive pressure, which would lead to a reduction in prices. The first and most available competitor, is the credit card companies. The committee recommended that they be removed from bank ownership and compete with the banks for the provision of credit to retail customers – since the infrastructure for providing such credit and customer information is already available to these companies. A list of regulatory relief for the entry of new banks was published by the Banking Supervision Department. Other potential competitors for providing credit to retail customers are the institutional investors. The implications of the reform are not yet clear, as its implementation has not yet been completed.

A supplementary measure to the Strum Reform in reaching the goal of increasing competition in the retail credit market is the Credit Data Law. The law is based on a comprehensive arrangement of credit data in a central database, operated by the Bank of Israel, as well as the possibility of sharing this data among the credit-providing bodies. The sources of information for the database will be the banks, which hold the bulk of the information about the credit customers. This gives them a significant competitive advantage and hinders competition in this market. Information will also be provided by public bodies – the Official Receiver, the Execution Offices, the law courts, Israel Electric Corporation, etc. Financial institutions can choose whether or not to join the database, on the condition of reciprocity: in order to obtain data, they must provide the data in their possession.

The novelty of the law is a change in the perception of the credit customers: a broad picture of the credit customer instead of only negative indications that were provided in the past. Each customer will be given a credit rating, which will determine their credit terms. This platform will also help to reduce the amount of credit in the gray market, which exceeds 4 percent of private credit.[19]

7.5.2 Stock Exchange Activity Reform

The Committee for Improving TASE Trading Efficiency and Liquidity was established in early 2013, following a slump in the TASE trading volume of stocks and derivatives (Figure 7.7). The Committee was established with the understanding of the great importance of the TASE as the center of the capital market and its recognition as a key tool for the efficient distribution of resources in the economy and for establishing financial tools that enable high-level risk management.[20]

The Committee recommended a series of operations required by the TASE itself – for example, making it accessible to a variety of companies in the economy, including the medium- and small-size companies. Collaboration is also required from other entities; including regulators – the Securities Authority, the Capital Market Authority, and the Bank of Israel – in easing the regulatory burden on the companies, while protecting the investors. Companies listed on the TASE are required to improve parameters such as corporate governance,

---

[19] According to the Report on the Description and Analysis of the Non-bank Loan Market, submitted to the Economics Committee on July 12, 2015.
[20] According to the Committee's report.

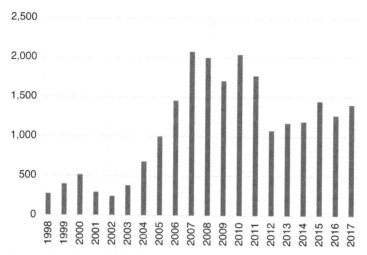

Figure 7.7 Average daily turnover in stocks and convertible securities, 1998–2017 (NIS millions, current prices).
Source: the TASE, the Annual Review, for various years, and processing by the authors

transparency, and increasing the amount of the company's float. Government support is also needed in creating a stable business environment and minimizing uncertainty.

The main recommendation for immediate action is the change in ownership of the TASE from a partnership to a for-profit corporation. Such a measure in other countries has improved important stock market parameters, such as transparency and corporate governance, attractiveness, efficiency, marketability, and accessibility of capital and cooperation with other exchanges around the world. Another recommendation referred to the establishment of a central repository of stocks for lending, which will enable short-selling positions.

The Securities Authority has been working to implement these recommendations in recent years and has taken a number of market deregulation measures, such as reducing disclosure requirements from small- and medium-sized companies, and the requirement for them to publish semi-annual reports instead of quarterly reports. The Securities Authority has also prepared a proposal for the establishment of a stock exchange for small companies.

7.6 Summary

During the period reviewed in this article, 1995–2017, many changes occurred in the Israeli capital market. The structural reforms that characterized this period were a continuation of the change in the macroeconomic perception – a change that began with the Stabilization Program in 1985. On the eve of the stabilization plan, the economy was suffering from three major problems – high inflation, considerable government involvement in the economy in general and in the capital market in particular, and centralization of financial intermediation, which was controlled by a small number of banks. The public sector's share of the GNP was about 75 percent, a rate unmatched in developed countries. With the Stabilization Program, the concept of significantly reducing the weighting of the public sector in the GNP gained support, thus reducing government involvement in the financial markets, increasing competition, and opening up the economy to the world.

At the end of 2016, the weighting of the public sector was only about 38 percent of the GNP. The resources in the economy were diverted from the government to the private sector, and the business sector became a major growth engine. With pension reform came a decrease in long-term savings invested in designated bonds. This reform and the Bachar Reform strengthened the financial institutions at the expense of the banks and increased competition in financial intermediation and in the development of non-bank credit.

In the long-term view, there is a continued reduction in the strength of the banks in the Israeli economy. The share of bank credit in the business sector's financing sources – which was about 63 percent in 1992, and peaked at over 70 percent in 2003 – declined to only about 47 percent at the end of 2016, and since then, the institutional investors have been providing about 21 percent of business sector credit. The strengthening trend of institutional investors is likely to continue, especially in view of the increase in long-term savings, the considerable growth in the economy, and the growth rate of the population, which is one of the highest in the Western world.

In addition to reducing the centralization of financial intermediation, the industry-wide centralization typical of the Israeli economy has also been reduced. The Centralization Law refers to the largest business groups in the economy, each operating in many industries. These groups are characterized by cross-ownership of real and financial corporations and have a pyramid control structure. This structure allows the controlling shareholder to leverage his equity, which could cause a conflict of interest with minority shareholders. The Centralization Law limits the pyramid's control structure to two layers, prohibits cross-ownership of real and financial corporations, and even requires treatment by the regulator in order to increase competition.

With the global development on the subject of corporate governance, similar rules have been adopted in Israel, with the changes required in view of the concentrated ownership structure in public companies. Regulatory developments include legislative changes and improvement of control tools across all three corporate governance circles of responsibility: the Management Circle – the board of directors; the Shareholder Circle – the owners, especially the institutional investors; and the Outer Circle – the Economics Court. The legislator expects the institutional investors, which represent the general public, in their ownership of the public companies, to be the gatekeepers in the conflict that characterizes the Israeli market, between controlling shareholders and minority shareholders.

The TASE is also addressing the concentrated ownership structure, by setting a minimum threshold for public ownership in companies listed for trade, in order to include these in the leading stock market indices. As a result, the controlling shareholders began to sell their stock to the general public on a considerable scale. This is a welcome trend: it has the potential to increase liquidity, to improve visibility, to incentivize activists (hedge funds and private equity funds) to operate in the local capital market, thereby improving public companies' management and raising interest in the stock market among both domestic and foreign investors.

Opening the economy to the world has increased public exposure to foreign assets. In the past fifteen years, the share of foreign assets in total assets managed by institutional investors has grown from zero to about 25 percent. In our opinion, the optimal rate of exposure to foreign assets should be examined.

The efficient functioning of financial markets ensures optimal channeling of resources to uses, which is an essential prerequisite for economic growth. This function should be examined continuously, identifying failures, and updating the rules of the game in order to steer the markets to worthy destinations.

References

Achdut, L., and Spivak, A. (2010). *The Pension System in Israel After 15 Years of Reforms*. Publications of the Economics and Society Program 8, The Van Leer Jerusalem Institute. www.vanleer.org.il/en/publication/pension-system-israel-after-15-years-reforms. [In Hebrew]

Ashraf, R., Jayaramen, N., and Ryan, Jr., H., and Harley, E. (2009). Conflicts of Interest and Mutual Fund Proxy Voting: Evidence from Shareholder Proposals on Executive Compensation. Unpublished manuscript, Georgia Tech University.

Bank of Israel. *Bank of Israel Annual Report: Statistical Appendix*. Various years. Jerusalem: Bank of Israel.

Bebchuk, L. A., Cohen, A., and Hirst, S. (2017). The Agency Problems of Institutional Investors. *Journal of Economic Perspectives*, 31(3), 89–102.

Ben-Bassat A. (2002) The Obstacle Course to a Market Economy in Israel. In A. Ben-Bassat (ed.), *The Israeli Economy, 1985–1998: From Government Intervention to Market Economics*. Cambridge, MA: MIT Press, 1–60.

Ber H., Yafeh, Y., and Yosha, O. (2001). Conflict of Interest in Universal Banking: Bank Lending, Stock Underwriting and Fund Management. *Journal of Monetary Economics*, 47, 189–218.

Capital Market, Insurance and Savings Authority, Regulation and Legislation - Investment Management. [In Hebrew]

Capital Market, Insurance and Savings Authority, Regulation codex, Chapter 5, part 1. [In Hebrew]

Cohen, O. (2017). Measuring Corporate Governance Quality in Concentrated Ownership Firms. Working paper.

Cvijanovic, D., Dasgupta, A., and Zachariadis, K. E. (2016). Ties that Bind: How Business Connections Affect Mutual Fund Activism. *Journal of Finance*, 71(6), 2933–2966.

Davis, G. F., and Kim, E. H. (2007). Business Ties and Proxy Voting by Mutual Funds. *Journal of Financial Economics*, 85(2), 552–570.

Gottlieb D., and Blejer, M. I. (2002) Liberalization in the Capital Account of the Balance of Payments. In A. Ben-Bassat (ed.), *The Israeli Economy, 1985–1998: From Government Intervention to Market Economics*. Cambridge, MA: MIT Press, 243–280.

Hamdani, A., and Yafeh, Y. (2013). Institutional Investors as Minority Shareholders. *Review of Finance*, 17(2), 691–725.

Klein D. (2003). 1983 Israel Bank Stock Crisis on the Background of the Macro-Economic Management Concepts and the Changes in the Capital Markets:

Then and Today. Bank of Israel. https://en.wikipedia.org/wiki/1983_Israel_
bank_stock_crisis.[In Hebrew]

Sasi-Brodesky, A. (2017). *Recovery Rates in the Israeli Corporate Bond
Market 2008–2015*. Discussion Paper 2017.07. Jerusalem: Bank of
Israel Research Department.

Schwartz E. (2012). The Change in the Provident Funds Management Fees
Delivered to the Pension Sub-committee in the Finance Committee. The
Knesset, Research and Information Center, Budget Supervision
Division, Jerusalem. [Hebrew]

Spivak A. (2002). The Pension Funds Reform. In A. Ben-Bassat (ed.), *From
Government Intervention to Market Economies: The Israeli Market
1985–1998*. Cambridge, MA: MIT Press,257–290.

The Capital Market Reform (Bachar Committee). (2004). *Final Report*. [In
Hebrew]

The Committee for Examining the Aspects of Banks' Holdings in Real
Corporations (the Brodet Committee). (1995). *Final Report*. [In
Hebrew]

The Committee for Examining the Measures Required to Increase the
Involvement of Institutional Bodies in the Israeli Capital Market (the
Hamdani Committee). (2018). *Final Report*. [In Hebrew]

The Committee for the Examination of the Corporate Governance Code in
Israel (the Goshen Committee). (2006). Final Report. [In Hebrew]

The Committee for the Examination of the Debt Arrangements in Israel.
(2014). *Final Report*. [In Hebrew]

The Committee for Increasing Competition in Common Banking and
Financial Services (the Strum Committee). (2016). *Final Report*. [In
Hebrew]

The Competitiveness Committee. (2012). *Final Report*. [In Hebrew]

The Israeli Securities Authority. *Annual Report*. Various years. [In Hebrew]

Villalonga, B., and Amit, R. (2009). How Are U.S. Family Firms Controlled?
The Review of Financial Studies, 22(8), 3047–3091.

Yosef R., and Spivak A. (2008). *The New Pension World: After the Big Bang
of 2003*. Publications of the Economics and Society Program 5.
Jerusalem: The Van Leer Jerusalem Institute. (Hebrew)

8 | The Reforms in the Israeli Pension System, 1995–2015

REUBEN GRONAU AND AVIA SPIVAK

8.1 Introduction

Pension saving stands at the center of four major issues, all of which are crucial to the development of the economy and to society's welfare:

(1) Saving for retirement is apparently the main form of household saving and thus determines the quantity of the economy's total savings and its potential for growth.
(2) At least part of household income in retirement is financed by taxes, i.e., on a Pay as You Go basis, and therefore government payments to these households is the main channel for intergenerational transfers.
(3) The business entities that manage pension savings control a substantial share of the capital flows in the economy. Their conduct and efficiency and the regulations that apply to them determine to a large extent the efficiency of the capital market and the patterns of investment in the economy.
(4) Retirement from the labor market naturally leads to a decline in current income. Retirement arrangements have a significant impact on the labor supply of older people and the inequality in income distribution.

The past two decades have been marked by radical changes in the structure of pension saving and the entities involved in managing pension savings, changes that have affected each of the four aforementioned issues. These are closely related to demographic developments, both in the population and in the labor market, and to the institutional changes that have taken place in the pension sector itself.

Demographic Trends and Changes in the Labor Market. The upward trend in education and income, changes in lifestyle and dietary practices

238

and improvements in sanitation and the medical system have led to an increase of 4.6 years in life expectancy in Israel during the past two decades. Between 1995 and 2015, men's life expectancy rose from 75.5 to 80.1 years and that of women from 79.5 to 84.1 years. Consequently, the share of the population aged 65+ has risen from 9.5 to 11.1 percent.[1]

The increase in education, the changes in taxation and transfer payments, and the low unemployment rate have led to the deferral of retirement and in turn to the postponement of the statutory age of retirement. A new law introduced in 2004 set the retirement age at 67 for men (an increase of two years), while that for women was set at 62. Further attempts over the years to raise the mandatory retirement age and close the gender gap have so far been unsuccessful. As a result, by the end of the period the average actual retirement age exceeded the statutory age, with labor force participation of the elderly almost doubling, from 13 to 22 percent (Figure 8.1).

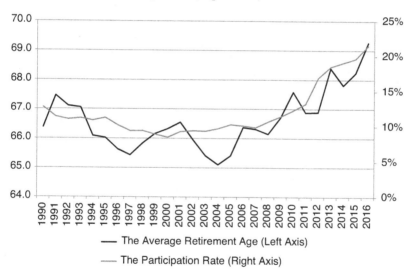

Figure 8.1 The average retirement age and labor force participation rate of the 65+ age group, 1990–2016.
Source: Effective retirement age – OECD data; participation data – Central Bureau of Statistics (CBS), *Statistical Abstract of Israel*, 2016.

---

[1] Part of the increase can be attributed to the change in the structure of the Manpower Survey, which led to a sharp increase in participation rates in 2011–2012.

Nonetheless, the deferral of retirement did not keep up with the increase in life expectancy. By the end of the period, men were expected to live for twelve years beyond their retirement and women for eighteen years, which is about 50 percent longer than at the beginning of the 1990s (Figure 8.2). Ensuring a decent standard of living for retirees is the main challenge facing the Israeli pension system.

The Institutional Setting. The government has always played a central role in pension savings, for a number of reasons: market failures; the importance of intergenerational transfers in savings decisions; the role of the government as the regulator of the business entities that manage pension savings; the large proportion of government debt held by the pension funds; and finally, the government's desire to reduce social inequality.

Economic theory attributes consumers with an unrealistic degree of knowledge about their future income and preferences (the composition of their household, state of health, etc.). According to these assumptions, consumers are able to calculate an optimal consumption path over their lifetime based on future income stream, future preferences, and future interest rates. In this model, consumers attempt to reduce the consumption shocks originating from fluctuations in income and to bridge the gap between income and desired level of consumption by saving. According to this model, when the income of consumers is low – when they are young

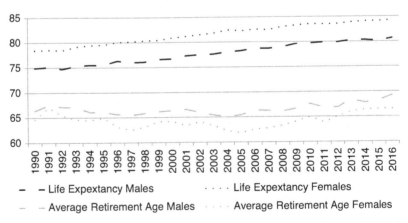

Figure 8.2 Life expectancy and effective retirement age by gender, 1990–2016. Source: Effective retirement age – OECD data; participation data – CBS, Statistical Abstract of Israel, 2016.

and during their retirement years – savings are negative, while during working years (ages 35–65), their savings are positive.

Empirical research, however, indicates that this is a simplistic picture and that the correlation between consumption and current income is much stronger than the model predicts. As a result, many households may find themselves without sufficient resources during the retirement years, since their savings during the "affluent" years are not sufficient to maintain consumption in the "lean" years. This is particularly common when retirement lasts longer than expected and when household income during the working years is too low to sustain sufficient saving. A number of studies show that a large proportion of households are hardly concerned about providing for their old age,[2] and others indicate that most individuals do not understand the pension system and do not act to ensure an adequate pension for old age. Pensions is a complex subject and requires a level of financial literacy that most people lack.[3] At the same time, the reforms of the past twenty years have shifted the risks related to pension savings from the pension funds to the savers. These risks include, *inter alia*, longevity risks, failed investments, general market risks, excessive management fees, etc., and the saver cannot always trust the advice of professional consultants, who are often motivated by their own interests. As a result, the pension market is a classic example of market failure, which calls for government intervention in order to avoid deprivation in old age.

The first tier of protection provided by the government to the retirement age population is the old age and survivors pension of the National Insurance Institute (NII), which are often accompanied by an income supplement. These add up to about one-quarter of the average wage, and income supplements can increase this to 27–35 percent. These

---

[2] According to the Socioeconomic Survey of the CBS for 2002, over 40 percent of those in the 40–65 age group "did not devote any thought to the years after retirement," and about 20 percent had devoted only "some thought" to the subject (www.cbs.gov.il/en/subjects/Pages/Social-Survey.aspx).

[3] Mitchell and Lusardi (2007) used the Health and Retirement Survey (HRS) to examine economic/financial knowledge among the 55+ age group and found that most of the respondents lacked any basic knowledge in these subjects. Similar findings were found by researchers in Israel. In the United States, it was observed that some workers are not prepared to fill in a form in order to benefit from a pension contribution from their employer, even though this did not involve any cost on their part (Benartzi and Thaler, 2004). Many in Israel draw their severance pay not realizing that by doing so they reduce their pension savings (Carmel, 2018).

payments are not based on employee and employer contributions, but rather depend only on the number of years that the individual contributed to the NII (i.e., his years of employment). Thus, the social security contribution is essentially a tax, and the old age NII pension payments constitute one of the main channels of intergenerational transfers.

During the period 1995–2015, the number of recipients of old age and survivors' pensions grew by over 60 percent, and given the growth in the average wage this led to a doubling of real expenditure. However, given the decline of the share of wages within GDP, the share of NII old age pensions in GDP remained virtually unchanged, at close to 2.5 percent for most of the period (Figure 8.3).

Most governments view social security benefits as only the first tier of income in old age, where the second consists of occupational pensions, which is the responsibility of the individual. Thus, this tier is based on the employee's own savings and is managed by the pension funds and the insurance companies. Although pension saving is a decision supposedly made by the household, the government plays a major role in this domain, given that it is the largest employer in the economy, that it determines the rules for the division of pension contributions between employers and employees, and that it serves as a "last resort" when pension saving channels fail to operate as intended.

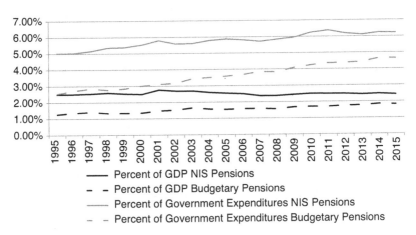

Figure 8.3 The share of NII old age pensions and government budgetary pensions within GDP and within total government expenditure, 1995–2015 (%).
Source: Bank of Israel, Components of Transfer Payments 1995-2015

As in other developed countries, the public sector in Israel has always been the largest employer in the economy. In order to attract skilled manpower and in the spirit of social welfare that has characterized government policy during the first three decades of the State, public sector employees used to enjoy budgetary pensions, where the cost of saving was borne completely by the State. According to the pension arrangements prevailing in the economy during that period, every year of employment raised pension eligibility by 2 percent of the worker's final salary; however, there were many groups in the economy who enjoyed even more favorable pension terms (including the defense sector and the military, elected public officials, judges and others).[4] Similar arrangements applied also to government corporations and other entities supported by the government.

These pension payments were financed out of current taxes, and as in the case of the first tier of old age benefits, they constituted an intergenerational transfer. The increase in the size of the public sector and higher life expectancy increased the share of the budgetary pensions within total government expenditure and within GDP. During the period 1995–2015, budgetary pensions tripled (in fixed prices), their share within government expenditure increased from 2.5 percent to 4.7 percent, and their share in GDP increased from 1.3 to 1.8 percent (Figure 8.3). Together with the expenditure on old age social security benefits, the maintenance of the elderly's standard of living has become the largest item within total intergenerational transfers, accounting for almost 11 percent of government expenditure in 2015.[5] By 2012, one-half of the elderly (aged 65+) had some pension coverage, and one-third of them had a budgetary pension (CBS, 2012).[6]

The government budgetary pension served as the basis for other pension arrangements in the economy and most notably the pension arrangements in entities owned by the Histadrut (the national trade union). The Histadrut pension funds, which for a long time dominated

---

[4] Over the years, there were also changes in the definition of the pension base, namely the worker's wage in his final year of employment and his average wage during the previous three years. It was not uncommon that the worker would be promoted before his retirement in order to increase his pension. In addition, the determining salary was revised according to increases in the government's salary pay scales.

[5] In comparison, the share of interest payments on government debt – the second largest channel of intergenerational transfer – fell from 12 to 7 percent during the period 1995–2015.

[6] See the CBS's Social Survey (www.cbs.gov.il/en/subjects/Pages/Social-Survey.aspx).

the pension market, operated on a defined benefit principle, according to which the pension benefits are guaranteed, while the fund's income depended on the employee and employer contributions and the returns on the fund's investments. According to the standard benefit formula, after thirty-five years of employment the pensioner is entitled to 70 percent of his insured wage (i.e., 2 percent per year), the employer's contribution was set at 12 percent of the wage and that of the employee at 5.5 percent, and the returns on the fund's investments were subsidized by means of earmarked indexed bonds, which were issued by the government and which paid preferential rates (5.5–6 percent). These arrangements were financially viable as long as the insured population was young, but as the population aged, the percentage of beneficiaries increased as did the length of retirement, and in addition, there was an erosion of returns as a result of failed investments.[7]

In 1995, the government closed these funds (the "old funds") to new participants, claiming they faced actuarial deficits, with newcomers being referred to "new funds" that were run on the basis of defined contributions. In the case of these funds, the benefits are not defined, and the saver is entitled only to the fruits of his savings. Subsidies to the new funds were also significantly reduced. The new regulations closed – at least in part – the gap between the pension funds and other long-term saving channels (life insurance and provident funds).

The 1995 reforms marked a watershed in pension savings in Israel. The structural changes during the subsequent two decades, the expansion of the second tier as a result of the Mandatory Pension Law of 2008,[8] and the reduction in government subsidies were part of this process. The impact of these reforms on the pension savings market, on the capital market, and on saving in the economy will be at the center of the discussion in this chapter. An equally important goal of the reforms was to ensure an adequate standard of living for the older generation. We will examine whether and to what extent the reforms succeeded in

[7] Another factor that contributed to the collapse of the Histadrut funds was ironically the competition between them, which was manifested in the acceptance of older workers without revising the pension formula. The events that led to the collapse of defined benefit funds are described in Avia Spivak's "The Pension Fund Reform" (2001).

[8] In fact, this is not a law but rather an extension of the collective agreement for comprehensive pension insurance for all employees, which was issued as a directive by the Minister of Industry, Commerce and Employment at the end of 2007 and which went into effect on January 1, 2008.

achieving this goal. Finally, the last two decades have been marked by increasing inequality in the economy. We will examine the extent to which the older generation was affected by this trend.

8.2 Institutional Changes in the Pension Funds During the Past Two Decades[9]

The structural reforms of the pension funds during the past two decades had five main elements: (1) the completion of the shift from defined benefit pensions to defined contribution pensions and the transfer of state employees (and related public sector entities) from a budgetary pension to a funded defined contribution pension; (2) a drastic reduction in government support in the form of earmarked bonds, as a result of which the pension funds increased their investments in the free capital market; (3) a change in the ownership structure of long-term savings channels; (4) the homogenization of tax benefits for all saving channels, thus concentrating tax benefits in long-term retirement saving and pension annuities rather than lump-sum payouts on retirement; and (5) the adoption of mandatory pensions for all employees (and later for the self-employed as well).

The 1995 reform did not allow new members to join the "old" pension funds, which may have slowed the growth of their actuarial deficit, but did not solve the deficit problem itself. According to the Ministry of Finance, the funds' deficit at the end of 1992 was equal to about 30 percent of the value of their assets (NIS 34 billion or more), and even if this estimate was deliberately overestimated (as claimed by the Histadrut), it created a problem of major proportions.

The need to solve the actuarial deficit problem led to a series of drastic reforms in pension arrangements, as part of the economic reforms aimed at solving the economic crisis in 2002–2004.

Under the new arrangements, which were ratified by legislation in 2003, all eight old pension funds were nationalized and transferred to the management of a liquidator. In order to cover the deficit, even partially, the old pension funds were forced to sell the new funds. Furthermore, employees insured by the old funds were required to raise their annual contributions by 3 percentage points, an amount divided equally between the employee and the employer; pensioners

---

[9] This section is largely based on Ahdut and Spivak (2010).

were charged a management fee of 1.75 percent; and the government raised the retirement age to 67 for men and 62 for women. These measures were designed to reduce the actuarial deficit. The government undertook to cover the balance of the actuarial deficit, estimated to be NIS 80 billion, and announced that if a further actuarial deficit appears, the members' benefits would be reduced accordingly.

Equally important for pension savings was the collective agreement of 1999. It stipulated that new government employees (and new employees in related government entities) would be transferred from a budgetary pension to an accrual pension, and in 2001 all government employees were transferred to the new pension funds.

The final closing of the old pension funds was accompanied by a reform of earmarked bonds and the subsidization of long-term savings by the government. As early as 1995, the government reduced the interest rate on earmarked bonds from 5.5 to 4.8 percent (both linked to the Consumer Price Index, CPI); however, a more drastic measure was adopted in 2003 when the quota of earmarked bonds sold to the pension funds was cut from 93 percent of their total assets to only 30 percent. This completed a long process that began in the early 1990s when similar rules were applied to life insurance plans. These measures significantly reduced the government's role as an active player in the capital market, while simultaneously transforming pension savings into a major factor in this market. Two years later, in 2005, the decentralization of the capital market was accelerated when the government implemented the recommendations of the Bachar Committee, which required the banks to sell their provident funds and exit the pension market.

Another reform of the long-term savings market was carried out in 2008. Its purpose was to remove the distortions in choosing between savings channels by equalizing the tax benefits between the pension funds, the life insurance companies, and the provident funds. Furthermore, the new tax regulations cancelled the tax benefits for provident funds in which the payout on retirement was in the form of a lump-sum payment and required that payout be in the form of a lifetime annuity. Another step in this direction was taken in 2012, when insurance companies – out for fear for their financial stability – were prohibited from guaranteeing a fixed annuity coefficient for the lifetime of a recipient.

The most important structural reform of this period was the aforementioned Mandatory Pension Law of 2008, which requires all employers to enroll their employees in a pension plan. The employee chooses the channel (pension fund, life insurance, or provident fund) and the entity to manage his funds. The employer contributes 12 percent of the employee's base salary and the employee 5.5 percent. The mandatory pension arrangement is limited to the base salary and up to the average wage in the economy and does not apply to other salary components such as bonuses, reimbursement of travel expenses, car allowances, and overtime. As a result, the mandatory pension contribution for highly paid employees (and government employees), who are the main recipients of the additional salary components, is less than 17.5 percent of their salary. In 2017, the regulations were expanded to also include the self-employed (albeit with lower contribution rates), and the total contribution to an employee's pension was raised by another percentage point (divided equally between the employee and the employer). Legally, the employee is free to choose the manager of his pension savings; however, in practice and in view of the limited financial knowledge of many employees and the employer's large share of the pension contribution, the employer (sometimes together with the employees' union) plays an important role in the choice of manager.

8.3 Trends in Pension Savings: The Macroeconomic Perspective

The transition from defined benefits to defined contributions, the restoration of the old funds' financial stability, the cancelation of budgetary pensions for state employees, and the mandatory pension rules were all intended to remove the threat to future generations of having to carry the burden of supporting the elderly. The question we consider in this section is whether the reforms led to increased total saving or that pension savings increased at the expense of other forms of savings?

Figure 8.4 depicts the share of net deposits (less withdrawals) in the pension saving channels (pension funds, provident funds, and life insurance) within net total private savings, and their share of private disposable income in 2001 and thereafter.[10]

---

[10] Data of the Commissioner for the Capital Market in the Ministry of Finance for deposits in provident funds starting from 2001.

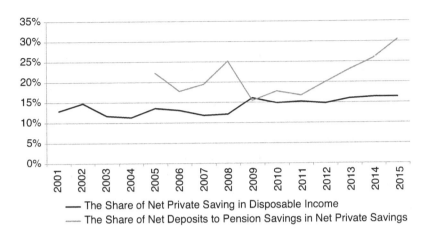

— The Share of Net Private Saving in Disposable Income
— The Share of Net Deposits to Pension Savings in Net Private Savings

Figure 8.4 The share of net private saving within iisposable income and the share of net deposits of pension savings within net private savings, 2001–2015 (%).
Source: Deposits in pension savings – data of the Supervisor of the Capital Authority, Ministry of Finance, Reports for 2012 (p. 55) and 2017 (p. 6); Gross Private Savings – CBS data

Estimates by the Central Bureau of Statistics (CBS) indicate that the average rate of net saving increased over the period by about 40 percent, from 12.6 percent in 2001–2008 to 15.7 percent in 2009–2015. It is, however, unclear whether the jump in 2008–2009 is related to the global crisis, to a measurement error, or to a change in the measurement method. Whatever the case, according to Figure 8.4, the source of the increase in saving was not pension saving, and in fact net deposits declined from 2008 to 2009, and during 2008–2011 they essentially remained unchanged. It is only in 2011 that deposits began to grow, and from that point onward grew rapidly, with their share in net savings almost doubling (from one-sixth to 30 percent) and their share of GDP increasing from 2 to 4 percent.

8.4 The Changes in the Pension Sector

The increase in the share of retirement saving was accompanied by a significant change in its composition, with the new pension funds increasing their share at the expense of the old funds and the provident funds (Figure 8.5). The transfer of the provident funds from the banks

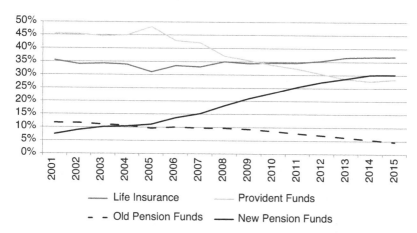

Figure 8.5 The shares of pension funds, provident funds, and insurance companies within deposits, 2001–2015 (%)
Source: Data of the Supervisor of the Capital Authority, Ministry of Finance, Reports for 2012 (p. 55) and 2017 (p. 6)

to institutional investors and the cancellation of some of the tax benefits they enjoyed accelerated this trend. Interestingly, these shifts did not affect the market share of the insurance companies, which were protected by barriers to mobility and promotion by the insurance agents. Differences in withdrawal rates reinforced these trends.[11]

The past two decades have been characterized by an increase in the value of financial assets held by the public, from 1.67 times GDP at the beginning of the period to almost three times GDP at the end. The accumulation of pension assets shows a similar trend. Thus, while at the beginning of the period pension assets were equal to about 60 percent of GDP, by the end they almost equaled GDP (about NIS 1.1 trillion) and have become (together with housing capital) the leading asset in the public's portfolio. The differential share of net deposits and, to a lesser degree, the differential rates of return are reflected in the changing shares of the long-term saving vehicles within these assets (Figure 8.6).

[11] In 2015, total withdrawals were about one-half the size of total deposits on average. However, this varied among the different savings channels. Thus, withdrawals were only about one-sixth of deposits in the new pension funds, about two-thirds of deposits in the provident funds, and almost 3.5 times deposits in the old funds.

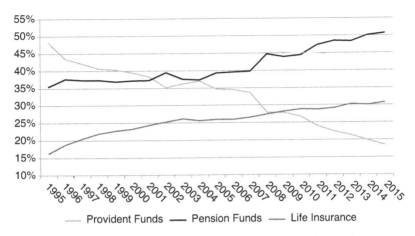

Figure 8.6 The share of pension funds, provident funds, and insurance companies within long-term assets, 1995–2015 (%)
Source: CBS, Financial Assets Held by the Public, Statistical Abstract of Israel, 1998–2015

During the past twenty years, the provident funds have lost their status as the preferred long-term saving vehicle. Whereas at the beginning of the period they controlled more than half of total pension assets, at the end they accounted for only about one-fifth. They were replaced by the pension funds, whose assets grew 4.6-fold, from one-third to one-half of pension saving assets. The new pension funds grew three times faster than the old funds; nonetheless, in 2015 the old funds still held about 60 percent of total pension fund assets, i.e., almost 1.5 times the assets held by the new funds.[12]

The decline in the share of the old funds within total pension assets had far-reaching implications for the government's degree of involvement in this market. Thus, earmarked government bonds fell from one-third of long-term saving assets in 2003 to one-fifth in 2015, and in terms of GDP from one-quarter to one-fifth. The decline in inflation also contributed to this trend by leading to a shift in investment from

---

[12] The distribution of pension fund assets between the new and the old funds is based on the data of the Capital Market Authority in the Ministry of Finance, less the accounting revision carried out on the assets of the old funds in 2009. The Capital Market Authority began reporting the distribution of assets only in 2003.

earmarked bonds (and other types of indexed bonds) to the open market.

Nonetheless, and in spite of their declining share of total long-term assets, earmarked bonds continued to affect the choice of saving channels due to their short-run effect in reducing the volatility of the pension funds' rates of return, as compared to the provident funds (which did not have the option of investing in earmarked bonds).

The increase in competition was driven not only by the decline in government support, but also by the change in the structure of ownership among both pension funds and provident funds. Following the Bachar Reform in 2006, the banks no longer played a role in the long-term saving market and were replaced by institutional investors and insurance companies. As a result, and although the industry is still over-concentrated, the share of the different operators in the market is far from stable, and the concentration indices have been dropping over time.[13]

One of the main vehicles for competition in the industry is the rate of return on investment (ROI). The almost complete withdrawal of government support exposed the industry to the price volatility of the capital market (the prices of shares, corporate bonds, and in recent years also government bonds). Figure 8.7 depicts the average real rates of return of the various long-term savings channels and illustrates the high level of volatility in rates of return due to the economic crises of 2002 and 2008 and the decline in share prices in 2011, as well as the rapid recoveries that followed. Thus, for example, following a drop of one-fifth in the average value of assets in 2008, prices recovered by one-quarter in the following year.[14] A similar pattern can be seen in the case of the other two crises as well. This volatility led to a series of proposals to adopt measures to reduce the volatility in the assets of savers who are close to retirement, according to the Chilean model, by increasing the share of earmarked bonds as the saver approaches retirement.

---

[13] According to the report of the Commission of the Capital Market for 2015, the Herfindahl Index for the concentration of the new pension funds was 0.2 in that year and the index for the insurance companies was 0.17.

[14] The drop in share and corporate bond prices in 2008 led to a call for the Ministry of Finance to create a safety net for pension savings. The Ministry of Finance rejected the idea and instead assisted the banks in establishing private investment funds in order to increase the supply of credit for recycling debt, as part of the rescheduling arrangements with bond owners.

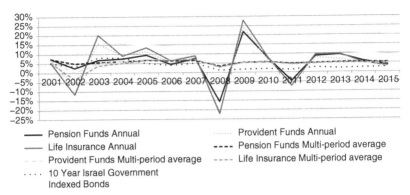

Figure 8.7 The annual and multi-period average real rate of return of the pension funds, provident funds, and life insurance, 2001–2015 (%).
Source: Reports of the Supervisor of the Capital Market Authority at the Ministry of Finance for 2010, 2011, 2016, and 2017, and calculations of the authors.

Figure 8.7 also shows the average long-term rate of return for each of the three savings channels on a deposit made in 2001. In 2015, the rate of return was close to 5 percent for all three channels (it was higher for pension funds and slightly lower for provident funds). It could be claimed that this is insufficient compensation for the volatility in the annual rate of return, but it should be recalled that pension savings are for the long term, and this average rate of return is still 1.5 percent higher than the yield on ten-year indexed government bonds.

An equally important vehicle for competition is management fees. These consist of two parts: the fee charged at the time of deposit (which reduces the amount going into savings) and the fee charged each period as a percentage of the accumulated savings (which reduces the rate of return). In contrast to the rates of return, which are not under the control of the funds' operators, management fees are determined in direct negotiations between the operator and his customers. Over the years, the bargaining power of savers, who in the case of employees are represented by their employers, has increased (and especially in the case of large employers), resulting in a decline of management fees among all the savings channels.

The competition between funds and the interventions by the Capital Market Division in the Ministry of Finance led to a reduction of about one-quarter or more in the average management fees of the new pension funds during the period 2007–2015 and somewhat less in the case of the insurance companies.[15] Nonetheless, the decline in management fees due to competition was much slower than the growth rate of deposits and accumulation in the various saving channels, and as a result the fund operators' total revenue increased. According to our estimate, the insurance companies' revenue from management fees grew by one-half during the period 2007–2015, while that of the new pension funds doubled (Figure 8.8).

Finally, the reduced role of earmarked bonds and the changes in the capital market are reflected in the composition of the pension investment portfolio (Figure 8.9). Although pension savings are long term, most pension investments are short term. The decline in the share of government bonds, as a result of the reduction in earmarked bonds, was accompanied by an increase in the share of investment in corporate bonds and to a lesser degree in shares. The global financial crisis dampened the appetite for both of these investment channels. Thus, the share of corporate bonds, which constituted almost one-quarter of the portfolio in 2007, declined to one-tenth in 2015, and the share of Israeli shares declined from 12 to 7 percent. They were replaced by

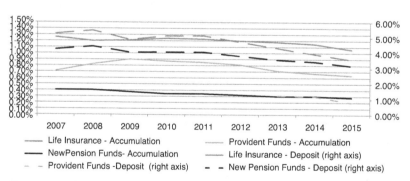

Figure 8.8 The average management fees on deposits and accumulations of pension funds, provident funds, and life insurance, 2007–2015 (%).
Source: Annual Report of the Supervisor of the Capital Authority at the Ministry of Finance, 2015

[15] The active involvement of insurance agents in the marketing process of life insurance and the lack of mobility of their customers helped to maintain the high fees in this channel.

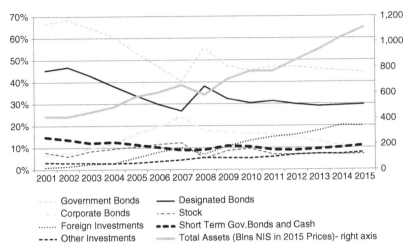

Figure 8.9 The composition of the pension investment portfolio, 2001–2015 (%). Source: Bank of Israel, Assets Portfolio of the Institutional Investors by Securities 2001–2015.

direct loans (which are included in "other assets") and by investments abroad, which doubled following the crisis (from one-tenth to one-fifth of the portfolio). The growth of financial investment abroad from NIS 4 billion in 2001 to NIS 270 billion in 2015 turned the pension saving operators into major players in the foreign exchange market.

8.5 Pension Saving: The Microeconomic Perspective

The economic model of retirement saving assumes a far-sighted consumer who maximizes a multi-period consumption function, subject to a multi-period budget constraint. The budget constraint states that the present value of the consumption stream equals that of the income stream or alternatively that the present value of consumption during the retirement years equals the present value of pre-retirement savings, such that:

$$\sum_{1}^{M} S_t/(1+r)^t = \sum_{M+1}^{N} C_t/(1+r)^t \tag{1}$$

where $S_t = Y_t - C_t$ is saving, C_t is consumption in period t, Y_t is labor income in period t, N is expected lifetime, M is the number of years in which the consumer earns labor income, and r is the discount rate.[16] The model assumes that consumers know their future income stream, the date of their retirement, life expectancy, and future interest rates. Given the uncertainty relating to each of these variables, there is a reasonable concern that consumers' saving decisions will deviate from their optimal path. This concern is reinforced by the public's limited expertise in pension matters (Lusardi and Mitchell, 2007) and behavior that often reflects myopia (Kotlikoff, 1987) or even inconsistency (hyperbolic preferences in the spirit of Laibson [1997]). In either case, government involvement is required if there is a desire to prevent the elderly from becoming a burden on society because of incorrect pension saving decisions. It can be claimed that the Mandatory Pension Law of 2008 is paternalistic, but research by Spivak et al. (2017) shows that most of the public supports it and would prefer that retirement savings be managed by someone else.

The success of the Mandatory Pension Law can be measured by the proportion of employees with pension coverage. According to Capital Market Branch data, following the introduction of the law (in the years 2007–2009) the proportion increased by one-half (from 35 percent to almost 50 percent) and increased over the following two years by another 10 percent.[17] Brender (2011) reports similar findings based on Tax Authority data. According to his data, prior to the law (in 2007) almost 40 percent of the employees aged 22+ did not make any pension contribution; this proportion had declined by one-half one year later and reached a level of 15 percent by 2012.

The CBS Socioeconomic Survey, which covers the entire population, including non-employees, reports a similar trend. According to these data, the rate of coverage among the 20+ age group increased from 53 percent in 2002 to 64 percent in 2012, with most of the newcomers

---

[16] The model ignores the altruistic component in consumers' utility function, i.e., the inheritance motive.

[17] The data of the Capital Market Branch in the Ministry of Finance does not include employees benefiting from a budgetary pension, while it does include fund members with more than one saving channel. Furthermore, some of those reported are already pensioners and not part of the employee population.

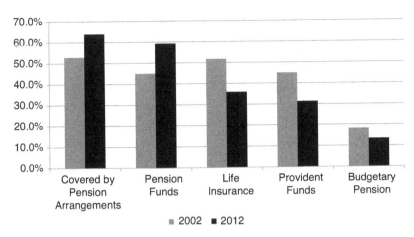

Figure 8.10 The rate of pension coverage in the different pension channels, 2002 vs. 2012.
Source: CBS, Socioeconomic Surveys 2002, 2012

joining the new pension funds and the other pension channels losing ground (Figure 8.10).[18]

A large proportion of pension savers used more than one type of long-term saving channel, and as a result the various channels add up to more than 100 percent. Thus, in 2002 each pension saver had, on average, 1.6 pension plans, which had declined to 1.4 by 2012.[19] The growth in the number of new savers in the pension market – who use only one channel – almost certainly contributed to this decline.

Though in terms of participation it appears that the mandatory pension reform was successful, it is not clear that it increased the welfare of the new participants. Brender (2010, 2011, and 2015) points out that this success was not enjoyed equally by all segments of the population and that low-income earners may have even been harmed by the reform. This group earns less than the income tax threshold and hence does not enjoy the pension tax benefits, and furthermore the increase in their future retirement income may be offset by a reduction

---

[18] The survey includes questions relating to pension saving only once every ten years.
[19] Double coverage is especially common among those eligible for a budgetary pension who take advantage of the tax benefits by obtaining an additional pension plan.

in the guaranteed income supplement. In this case, the forced pension savings distort their disposable income profile, reducing the income stream when it is most needed, i.e., during the household's expansion period, while increasing the stream in retirement, during the household's period of contraction.

The replacement ratio is defined as the ratio of an individual's retirement income to his wage prior to retirement. The mandatory pension reform was intended to ensure a minimal level of this ratio, so that a retiree would maintain the standard of living he was used to prior to his retirement. Brender claims that this ratio in the case of low-income earners is too high.

The Replacement Ratio and the Saving Formula. The replacement ratio plays a key role in the literature on pension saving. It determines the actuarial balance of the defined benefit plans and the success of defined contribution plans.

By rearranging equation (1), we can describe the accumulated value of pension savings at the time of retirement:[20]

$$A_M = \Sigma S_t(1+r)^t = \alpha W_0{}^*[(1+r)^M - (1+g)^M]/(r-g) = \mu W_0, \tag{2}$$

where α is the percentage of the wage contributed to pension savings, g is the annual rate of wage growth, r is the rate of return on the fund's investments, and μ is the ratio of the accumulated value of the pension fund on retirement to the initial wage. The present value of the consumption flow during the retirement period discounted to the year of retirement is:

$$C_M = (c/r)^*[1 - (1+r)^{-(N-M)}] = (1/\rho)\, c, \tag{3}$$

where N is life expectancy, ρ is the Capital Recovery Factor (CRF), and c is annual consumption during retirement. Let B_M denote the present value of other income received by the pensioner during retirement (family support and national insurance payments):

---

[20] A_M is the sum of a geometric series whose first term is αW_0, where the common term is of the form $A_t = (1+r)^*A_{t-1} + (1+g)^* \alpha W_{t-1}$, which represents the return on the accumulated savings and the annual deposit, respectively.

$$B_M = (b/r)^*[1 - (1 + r)^{-(N-M)}] = (1/\rho)\,b, \tag{4}$$

where b is the annual retirement receipts. The budget constraint then becomes:

$$C_M = A_M + B_M \tag{5}$$

or

$$c = \rho\mu W_0 + b \tag{6}$$

In this formulation, $\rho\mu$ is the replacement ratio of the pension benefit relative to the initial wage, and $\theta = \rho\mu/(1+g)^M$ is the replacement ratio relative to the wage prior to retirement.

It is easy to see that the replacement ratio increases with the rate of return on investment r and with the number of working years M and declines with the length of the retirement period (N–M). The value of savings, A_M, increases with the rate of wage growth, though at a slower rate, and as a result the replacement ratio declines with g.

Assuming an average rate of return of $r = 4\%$ and an annual wage growth of $g = 2\%$, that the saver starts making pension contributions at the age of 35 and retires at 65 (i.e., M = 30), that he contributes $\alpha = 17.5\%$ of his wage to his pension savings each year, and that he has a life expectancy of 75 (i.e., N = 40), the replacement value (with respect to the wage at age 65) is 85 percent. It is usually assumed that a replacement ratio of 70 percent is sufficient for a saver to maintain the standard of living he enjoyed prior to retirement. Given that our assumptions are quite similar to those underlying the pension law, the law achieves this objective. Alternatively, had the defined benefit funds not accepted members beyond the age of 35, had they required contributions of 17.5 percent of wages and had they invested wisely (given the subsidized bonds they were allocated), they could have easily achieved a replacement ratio of 70 percent without incurring a deficit.

It can be shown that a rate of return of $r = 3\%$ suffices to achieve a replacement ratio of 70 percent, and each additional percentage point in the rate of return leads to a 23 percent increase in the replacement ratio.

Crucial variables that influence the replacement ratio include the number of working years and life expectancy. Thus, an individual who starts to save at the age of 25 rather than 35 will increase his replacement ratio by one-half, and his replacement ratio will increase even if his life expectancy on retirement is fifteen years, rather than ten. In contrast, a longer life expectancy will significantly lower the pension of an individual who did not start saving at a young age or someone who retires too early, two factors that lead to the relatively low pension income of women. Another crucial variable is the definition of the wage for pension purposes. In collective wage negotiations in Israel, there is a tendency to raise wage components that are not part of the "pension base" (e.g., car allowances and overtime) by a higher rate than other components. As a result, the pension base is often only 70–80 percent of the total wage (Spivak and Tsemach, 2017), and as a result the pension contribution is only 13.75 percent (0.75*0.175) of the total wage, resulting (given our assumptions) in a replacement ratio of only 60 percent.

This parametrization also demonstrates the limitations of the replacement ratio as a measure of standard of living. Thus, a saver whose wage grows by 3 percent rather than 2 percent will enjoy a replacement ratio of only 70 percent (rather than 83 percent), though his annual pension income is going to be higher by one-fifth.

The current pension system took shape gradually over a period of twenty-years. As a result, it is difficult at this stage to determine how the institutional changes that took place during that period affected the replacement ratio. To do so would require panel data that would make it possible to track the development of wages before and after retirement. Unfortunately, the CBS started its long-term panel survey only in 2012, and it will take a number of years before anything can be learned from it with regard to pensions. In the absence of detailed panel data, we compared the cross-section data of the Household Expenditure Survey for the period 1998–2015. We focused on the average household income and consumption before and after retirement, comparing households whose head is in the 50–60 age group with those whose head is in the 70+ age group.

The sample period was characterized by an increase in labor force participation. The increased supply of labor among married women resulted in an increase in the average number of earners in a household from 1.6 in 1998 to 2.1 in 2015 in the 50–60 age group and from 0.22 to 0.49 in the 70+ age group. In other words, if at the beginning of the period there was an earner in only one out of every five households in the 70+ age group, at the end of the period, there was an earner in one out of every two households, as a result of the deferral of retirement.[21] The growth in labor supply is reflected in the share of labor income within the total income of the older group, which rose during the period by 2.6-fold, from less than one-fifth to 30 percent, which is much faster than the increase in the share of labor income of the younger group (Figure 8.11).[22]

Nonetheless, the two main income sources of this age group remain their pension income and NII benefits. As a result of the growth in employment rates, the increase in pension contributions, and the expansion of pension coverage, income from pensions and provident funds grew by 80 percent, to about one-third of an elderly household's money income. Since NII benefits grew only half as fast, their share declined from 40 to 30 percent.[23]

During the period 1998–2015, the gross money income of the older group grew three times faster than that of the younger group (75 percent vs. 24 percent), and their net income grew twice as fast (Figure 8.12).[24]

Nonetheless, the overall income gap between the older and the younger groups, though declining over time, is still substantial. In 2015, the average gross income of the older group was only one-half of that of the younger group, and their net income was only 60 percent. These replacement ratios are definitely lower than the standard level.

However, it appears that the replacement ratio in Figure 8.12 overstates the decline in the standard of living associated with retirement, for both technical and conceptual reasons. The "true" replacement ratio should reflect the difference between the income of today's 70+ old age group and their income twenty years ago (when they were 50 years old).

---

[21] Since the groups are defined according to the age of the head of the household, the earner need not necessarily be a septuagenarian. Nonetheless, the figure is consistent with the Manpower Survey, which indicates that in 2015 one out of every five individuals in the 65+ age group was working.

[22] The number of workers in the 70+ age group who were sampled in the survey is, however, quite small (only about ninety observations in 2015), and the precision of the estimate of their labor income is quite low.

[23] Nonetheless, it is worth mentioning that the 40 percent increase in the NII old-age benefits equals the rate of increase in total gross money income and is much greater than the increase in other NII benefits.

[24] Given their low labor income, the elderly did not benefit from the income tax cuts introduced during this period.

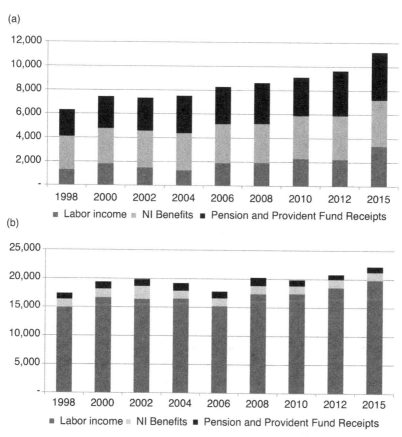

Figure 8.11 Gross income from labor, NII benefits, and pensions of households (in 2015 prices), 1998–2015: A. 70+ age group; B. 50–60 age group
Source: CBS, Household Expenditure Survey 1998–2015, and calculations by the authors.

Hence, the measured ratio is understated by the younger group's wage growth over the last twenty years. Since the real wage rose during the period 1995–2015 by 23 percent, the average net income of the 70+ age group is three-quarters of their income when they were 50–60 years old (rather than 60 percent).

The second reservation is conceptual and relates to the use of household income as a measure of standard of living, ignoring the changes in the household size as its members grow older. The average household size in the 70+ age group is only half that of the 50–60 age group (1.8 vs. 3.5).

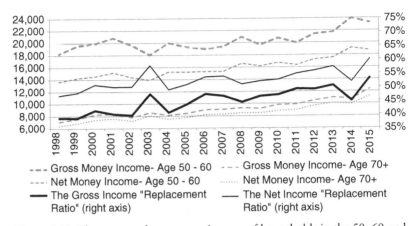

Figure 8.12 The gross and net money income of households in the 50–60 and 70+ age groups and their replacement ratios, 1998–2015.
Source: CBS, Household Expenditure Survey, 1998–2015, and calculations by the authors

After correcting for this, the difference in net income per adult equivalent (AE) between a family whose head is aged 70+ and one whose head is in the 50–60 age group was 20 percent in 1998 and only 7 percent by 2015. As Figure 8.13 shows, the differences are even smaller if consumption per adult equivalent is used as the measure of standard of living.

These results are supported by the CBS Socioeconomic Survey, which shows that satisfaction with one's economic situation increases with age and improves over time and that by 2015 more than two-thirds of the older group were satisfied (or very satisfied) with their economic situation.

8.6 Pension Saving and Income Inequality

The reduction in government expenditure during the last two decades, and in particular the sharp cutback in transfer payments, has been accompanied by a steep rise in inequality, which positioned Israel as one of the least egalitarian economies in the Western world.[25] The elderly, who are the most dependent on transfer payments, are naturally among the most

---

[25] See the detailed discussion by Momi Dahan in Chapter 12, this volume.

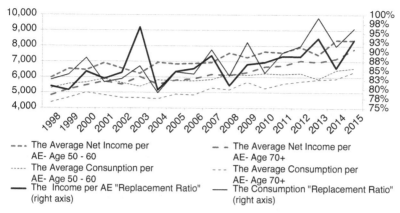

Figure 8.13 The net income and consumption per adult equivalent (AE) of households in the 50–60 and 70+ age groups and their replacement ratios, 1998–2015.
Source: CBS, Household Expenditure Survey, 1998–2015, and calculations by the authors

affected by these cutbacks, and the question arises as to what extent the pension reforms have mitigated the effect on income inequality.

The Household Expenditure Survey, as of 2007, includes a direct question on pension saving.[26] Figure 8.14 describes the share of households (below retirement age) that reported positive pension contributions in 2007 and in 2015. The graph confirms Brender's finding of a major shift in pension coverage following the introduction of the Mandatory Pension Law. This shift encompassed all income levels but is particularly noticeable in the second to fourth deciles, in which the share of savers increased by 30–35 percent. By the end of the period, in all but the three lowest deciles, the share exceeded 80 percent. Part of the explanation of the low proportion among the lower deciles is their weak labor force attachment; but given the low proportion of households that report labor income, it appears that part of the problem is also the low compliance with the Mandatory Pension Law in this group.

To what extent are the elderly subject to poverty? To answer this question, the households were sorted according to quintiles of net income per adult equivalent. The results, reported in Figure 8.15, are

---

[26] Owing to underreporting of income, the surveys cannot be used to measure savings.

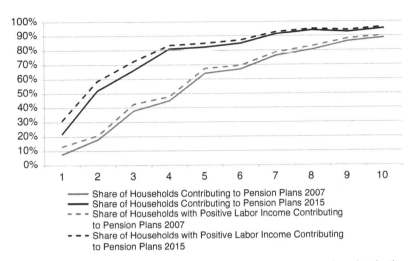

Share of Households Contributing to Pension Plans 2007
Share of Households Contributing to Pension Plans 2015
Share of Households with Positive Labor Income Contributing to Pension Plans 2007
Share of Households with Positive Labor Income Contributing to Pension Plans 2015

Figure 8.14 The share of households contributing to pension plans by decile, 2007, 2015 (%).
Source: CBS, Household Expenditure Survey 2007, 2015, and calculations by the authors.

somewhat surprising, in that the elderly's distribution of income (standardized for family size) is similar to the distribution for the rest of the population, with two exceptions – they are underrepresented in the lowest quintile, and overrepresented in the second quintile. During the period 1998–2015, on average, only one out of six households aged 70+ had income levels that placed them in the lower quintile; and, on the other hand, their share in the second quintile exceeded 20 percent throughout the period. The underrepresentation of the elderly in the lowest quintile is partly explained by their small household size, but perhaps also by the fact that the poor have a shorter life expectancy and hence may not reach old age.[27]

The breakdown of money income by its source (NII benefits, labor income, and pension payments) underlines the small role pension payments have played in the lower income quintiles during the last two

---

[27] According to Gottlieb et al. (2018), the expected life expectancy of an individual born in 1930 who belongs to the lowest quintile is 1.5 years less than that of an individual in the second quintile and 4.4 years less than that of an individual in the highest quintile.

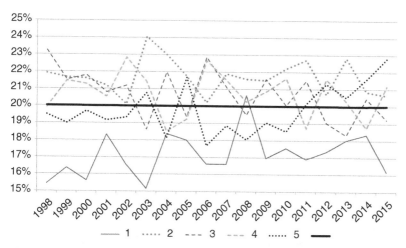

Figure 8.15 The composition of households in the 70+ age group by quintile according to net income per adult equivalent, 1998–2015 (%).
Source: CBS, Household Expenditure Survey, 1998–2015, and calculations by the authors

decades (Figure 8.16).[28] Thus, although pension payments have doubled for the three lowest quintiles, they still only constituted a small fraction of their money income in 2015, and thus the elderly still largely relied on NII benefits, which account for 90 percent of the lowest quintile's income and two-thirds of the second quintile's income. It is only in the third quintile that pension income starts to play a significant role (accounting, in 2015, for a little over a quarter of total income), but even in this group NII benefits still accounted for 70 percent of total income. In contrast, pension income is the main source of income for the two upper quintiles. Ironically, the increase in labor income in these quintiles resulted in a decline in the share of pension income within total income. The increase in labor income in the upper quintiles also appears to be the source for the widening gap between the upper and lower quintiles.

---

[28] For purposes of comparison, we used an identical income scale for each pair of quintiles in Figure 8.16. The income composition of the fourth quintile is presented twice, once to allow its comparison with the third quintile, and again to allow its comparison to the highest quintile. The quintiles relate to the distribution of net income per adult equivalent for the total household population.

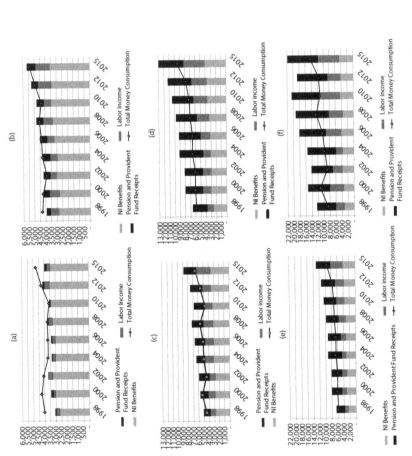

Figure 8.16 The composition of households' gross money income in the 70+ age group by quintile, 1998–2015 (in 2015 prices): a. first quintile, b. second quintile, c. third quintile, d. fourth quintile, e. fourth quintile, f. fifth quintile.

Source: CBS, Household Expenditure Survey, 1998–2015, and calculations by the authors

The government plays a major role in determining the income distribution of the elderly. On the one hand, it sets the rates of NII benefits, which is the main source of income for the lower quintiles; on the other hand, and as shown above, it still plays a major role in the pension market and hence has an impact on the income of the upper quintiles. The government involvement in the pension market takes the form of tax credits on pension contributions, reduced tax rates on the capital gains earned on pension savings, and indirect support through the allocation of subsidized earmarked bonds.[29] This complex system developed over a long period, during which pension contributions were voluntary. In view of the impact of this system on income inequality, the question arises as to whether this heavy support of long-term savings is still necessary, since pension contributions are now required by law.

Abramson and Sarel (2015) argue that pension support is the most expensive income support program implemented by the government. According to their estimate, the cost of the tax breaks totaled NIS 13.9 billion in 2015, to which must be added another NIS 3 billion for the subsidy implicit in the earmarked bonds. The value of these tax breaks rises progressively with income. Thus, the pension tax benefits enjoyed by a taxpayer in the fifth decile are twice those in the second decile, and in turn are only 30 percent of those in the highest decile. According to the authors' simulation, the present value of the lifetime benefits in the highest decile is NIS 1.5 million. The complexity of the tax rules, which requires expert advice in order to make optimal decisions, increases the probability that it is mostly high-income earners who are the beneficiaries of the tax breaks.

8.7 Summary and Conclusions

This survey described the reforms in the pension market during the last two decades and their impact on household welfare and the economy as a whole. During this period, the pension market went through a complete transformation: pension funds were switched from being defined benefits to defined contribution; budgetary pensions were

---

[29] The tax breaks include a partial income tax exemption on contributions by the employer and the employee to pension saving, a full exemption on capital gains earned on pension savings, and a partial exemption on pension payouts.

discontinued; the contribution to pension saving became mandatory; and a complete overhaul of the ownership structure led to increased specialization and competition. Competition, in turn, led to a reduction in management fees and more importantly to an increase in the average long-term real rate of return to 5 percent, which is 1.5 percentage points higher than the yield on long-term government bonds. This is a significant achievement given the series of stock market crises during the period and the government reduction in support in the form of subsidized earmarked bonds. The reduced reliance on the government facilitated the development of a competitive capital market.[30]

It is too early to tell whether the new pension arrangements will provide retirees with the standard of living they were used to before retirement. What can be said is that the Mandatory Pension Law and the increase in labor force participation resulted in an increase in the proportion of households with pension coverage. Long-term saving has become the dominant component of total saving, and pension assets have become the largest component in a household's financial portfolio.

A comparison based on the Household Expenditure Survey for the period 1998–2015 shows that in 2015 the net income per adult equivalent (the most common measure of standard of living) in the 70+ age group was almost identical to that in the 50–60 age group. It appears that the elderly have adjusted their supply of labor and their saving behavior to a longer life expectancy, such that their income has grown at three times the rate of the younger group (75 percent vs. 25 percent). It is often assumed that pension income should equal 70 percent of the retiree's pre-retirement wage, in order for him to maintain his pre-retirement standard of living. However, this prescription overlooks the dramatic changes that have taken place over the last twenty years in the number of earners in a household and the differences in household size (an elderly household is only half the size of a household in the younger group), and ignores other sources of income (particularly NII benefits).

In 2015, NII benefits still constituted one-third of the average money income of households in the 70+ group, which is almost equal to the share of labor income and that of pension income. There are, however,

---

[30] The development of the capital market is discussed in detail by Abramov, Dressler and Metzker (Chapter 7, this volume).

major differences in the composition of income between the various quintiles of the elderly household distribution. Whereas in the lower three quintiles, NII benefits constitute the largest source of income (and the lowest quintile is almost totally dependent on this source of income), the upper two quintiles rely mostly on pension income, with NII benefits constituting less than one-third of income.

The growth in income inequality has become a major concern during the past two decades; it is considered a byproduct of the government's reduced involvement in the economy. It appears, however, that at this stage the elderly have escaped the sharp cutbacks in transfer payments, such that the incidence of poverty among the elderly is lower than among the rest of the population (partly due to their small household size). Of greater concern is the implicit cost of the higher pension contributions of the upper quintiles. Abramson and Sarel (2015) estimated the annual loss in taxes as a result of the favorable pension regulations at about NIS 14 billion, which equals about half of the annual cost of the NII old-age benefits. Given the implication for income inequality, and given that pension contributions are no longer voluntary, this money could be better used to offset some of the cuts in the government's healthcare budget.[31]

In conclusion, the main threat facing the elderly's standard of living is demographic trends. The share of the 65+ age group in the population in 2035 is forecasted to increase by 50 percent over what it was two decades ago (13.7 vs. 9.5 percent). Thus, within two decades one out of every eight Israelis will be above the official retirement age, with the dependency ratio between the 65+ and 25–64 age groups increasing from one-quarter to one-third. Although the forecasts for other Western countries are worse than that for Israel, the differential rates of population growth between the various socioeconomic groups in Israeli society (the ultra-Orthodox, the Arabs, and the Jewish non-ultra-Orthodox sector) and their differences in productivity will have dire consequences for the economy's growth rate, the rate of return on investment, and intergenerational transfers.[32] Although it appears that

---

[31] In Chapter 15 (this volume), Ben Nun and Ofer discuss the changes in the Israeli health system over the last two decades.

[32] See Poterba (2014) for further discussion of the macroeconomic implications of the aging of the population in the West. The effects of demographic changes on the Israeli economy are discussed in Chapter 13 on the labor market by Eckstein, Larom, and Lifshitz, in Chapter 14 on the economics of education by Ben-David and Kimhi, and in Chapter 11 on economic growth and labor productivity by Hazan and Tsur.

the elderly's economic situation has not worsened during the last two decades, it is doubtful whether the authors of this chapter twenty years from now will reach a similar conclusion.

Bibliography

Abramson, S., and Sarel, M. (2015). Pension Savings Tax Benefits. Position paper, Kohelet Forum. [Hebrew]

Ahdut, L., and Spivak, A. (2010). The Pension System in Israel After Fifteen Years of Reform. Policy Research 8, Economy and Society, Publications of the Economics and Society Program 8, The Van Leer Jerusalem Institute. www.vanleer.org.il/en/publication/pension-system-israel-after-15-years-reforms [In Hebrew]

Benartzi, S., and Thaler, R. (1995). Myopic Loss Aversion and the Equity Premium Puzzle. *The Quarterly Journal of Economics*, 110, 73–92.

Brender, A. (2010). The Effect of the Retirement Savings Arrangement on Income Distribution. *Israel Economic Review* (December), 87–123. [Hebrew]

(2011). Effects of Mandatory Pension on Wages. *Economic Quarterly*, 91–120. [Hebrew]

(2015). *The Welfare and Labor Market Effects of Mandatory Pension Savings: Evidence from the Israeli Case.* Bank of Israel, Research Department. www.bancaditalia.it/pubblicazioni/altri-atti-convegni/2015-beyond-austerity/Brender.pdf?language_id=1.

Carmel, E. (2018). Towards a Dual Process Conception of the Selective Influence of Financial Literacy on Economic Behavior. Doctoral dissertation, retrieved from the National Library of Israel (ULI No. 021746810).

Dahan, M. (2003). Mandatory Pension: Estimation of Additional Designated Bonds. *Economic Quarterly*, 511–528. [Hebrew]

Gottlieb, D., Sheshinski, E., Pinto, O., Zaken, H., Cohen, R., Heilbron, G., and Shmeltzer, M. (2018). Pension Savings After Retirement. Israel Democracy Institute. [Hebrew]

Kotlikoff, L., and Wise, D. (1987). The Incentive Effects of Private Pension Plans. In Z. Bodie, J. B. Shoven, D. A. Wise (eds.), *Issues in Pension Economics.* Chicago: University of Chicago Press, 283–336.

Laibson, D. (1997). Golden Eggs and Hyperbolic Discounting. *Quarterly Journal of Economics*, 62, 443–477.

Lusardi, A., and Mitchell, O. (2007). Baby Boomer Retirement Security: The Roles of Planning, Financial Literacy, and Housing Wealth. *Journal of Monetary Economics, 54*, 205–224.

Poterba, J. (2014). Retirement Security in an Aging Population. *American Economic Review*, 104(5), 1–30.

Spivak, A. (2001). The Pension Fund Reform. In A. Ben-Bassat (ed.), *From Government Intervention to a Market Economy: The Israeli Economy 1985–1998*. Tel Aviv: Am Oved, 257–290. [Hebrew]

Spivak, A., and Tsemach, S. (2017). *Mandatory Pension in Israel and the Effect of Pension Inequality: The Risks in the New Pension System*. Policy Research 22, Economics and Society Program, Van Leer Jerusalem Institute. [Hebrew]

Spivak, A., Tsemach, S., and Carmel, E. (2017). *The Mandatory Pension Reform: Its Characteristics and Success*. Economics and Society Program, The Van Leer Jerusalem Institute.

Aggregate Concentration in Israel, 1995–2015

KONSTANTIN KOSENKO

9.1 Introduction

One of the main challenges in examining aggregate concentration arises from the lack of a transparent, agreed-upon definition of this concept in the economic literature – aside from the intuitive statement that it relates to the ability of a few individuals and/or business entities to control and direct significant portions of aggregate activity. This results in a methodological deficiency and makes the analysis of the phenomenon's characteristics and its implications for economic activity very difficult. Nevertheless, "aggregate concentration" is an integral part of the daily discussion of macroeconomics and political economics on various levels – growth and cost of living, resource allocation and inequality, rent-seeking, antitrust issues, financial stability, etc. Although in many cases the discussion of the topic is not purely scientific, the existence of this concept in the public sphere is essential from both the conceptual and the ethical perspective. This is due to its significance in defining and identifying potential market failures and focal points of economic inefficiencies at the aggregate level and identifying tools to address them. However, it is also because of its importance for understanding the role of ordinary citizens in a system in which a significant portion of economic (and even political and social) power is concentrated in the hands of a few individuals or entities.

* The work on this chapter was highly challenging because of the lack of a conceptual framework for analyzing the topic and the need for unique data. I would like to thank all those who contributed to this work, especially Noam Michelson, Tal Sido, Jonathan Sidi, Amit Gilboa, Ayelet Muenster, Eran Yaakov, Noam Modai, Aida Faur, and Yishay Yafeh. I would also like to thank the editors, the economists of the Bank of Israel's Research Department, and the participants of the interim forum of the Falk Institute for their useful remarks.

This chapter analyzes the structure of the Israeli economy in terms of ownership over means of production and the interactions between them and the various economic units operating in the economy. The focus is on the development of aggregate concentration in Israel in the past few decades and the impact of the government's policies on that development. Most of the chapter is a factual description of the changes in the three key components of market concentration – concentration of production, industrial concentration, and concentration of corporate control (means of production) – as well as an analysis of the trends and reasons for the manner in which they evolved.

9.2 Aggregate Concentration: The Analytical Framework

Before reviewing the main trends in aggregate concentration in Israel, I outline the key characteristics of the phenomenon and present a conceptual framework for discussion.

First, it should be noted that the *concept of aggregate concentration is an economy-wide measure*, which refers to the impact (power) of a business entity or a defined group of business entities (firms) at the market level, and to a much lesser extent –to the power of any such entity's impact on the industry in which it operates. The difference is evident even at the very basic stage of evaluating the degree of concentration. Thus, an analysis of the impact of Israel's 200 largest companies (Figure 9.1) shows that in 2003–2015, their share of the total turnover,[1] excluding holding and investment companies,[2] averaged 45 percent. Since the remaining turnover is accounted for by about 300,000 other businesses, the result demonstrates an indisputably high level of aggregate concentration.[3] In contrast, the C4 Index – used to measure industrial concentration, the market share of the four largest

---

[1] The data are from the CBS's "Businesses/Dealers and turnover by VAT, by economic industry table (2011 classification)." The data are for 2003 to 2015 (NIS million, at current prices, excluding diamonds).

[2] Weighting the turnover of holding and investment companies creates a double counting problem, as the assets of these intermediaries largely consist of the liabilities of the enterprises to which they have lent or in which they have invested, with those liabilities in turn having been used to fund the assets of those enterprises.

[3] As a comparison, note the US market in the 1930s. The weight of the 200 largest nonfinancial companies during that period was about 50 percent (see Kandel et al., 2013).

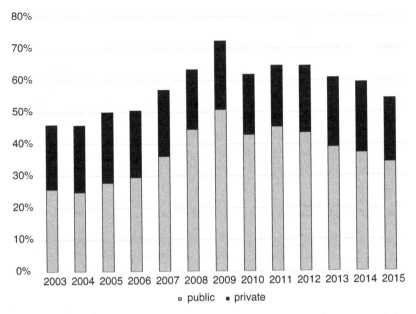

Figure 9.1 The share of the 200 largest companies in the total turnover of the business sector, 2003–2015 (%).
1. According to the turnover. Excluding holding and investment companies.
Source: Based on data of D&B Israel and the Central Bureau of Statistics

companies in the turnover of the major industries (e.g., agriculture, manufacturing, construction, commerce, transportation, telecommunications, etc.) – was relatively high only in the manufacturing and in the electricity and water industries, at 34 and 69 percent, respectively. In the other major industries (according to the Israel Central Bureau of Statistics' (CBS hereafter) two-digit classification), no exceptional levels of industrial concentration were recorded.

However, the differences between the approaches are not confined to the question of the economic entity's absolute size and market boundaries. By its very definition, an economy represents a broad group of markets, products, and strategies of various entities operating in it, and the business reality provides conclusive proof for that: Many companies, especially large ones, span various products, industries, and markets. As a result, their level of (product) diversification, i.e., the share of their business activity in the various sectors, and the level of integration (synergy) between these sectors are essential to the analysis of market concentration.[4] In addition, beyond examining the firms' share of the GDP, aggregate concentration is about corporate ownership and control. Such control, like the diversification of the firms' business activity, is not confined to any one industry and is often reflected in the concentration of capital (physical or industrial) and its relation to financial capital and the formation of business groups – groups under a single, administrative control operating in different industries. As a result, when examining aggregate concentration, it is also essential to address concentration in terms of asset (means of production) ownership.[5]

Second, aggregate concentration cannot be defined in terms of competition, nor examined using classic concentration measures. This may be partially explained by the essence of industry classification, the nature of the economic unit being examined (for example, a product, a firm, or a business group), and questions about the firm's boundaries and ownership of means of production.[6] Another explanation is the incongruity between the (theoretical) model of perfect competition – which helps to understand economic processes – and viewing the model as the norm to which economic policies should aspire. According to multiple empirical findings, no economy has perfect competition, and the conditions under which perfect competition maximizes profit are almost impossible to attain. In addition, firms vary in size, and in practice, in many (both advanced and developing) economies, a few "sustainable" mega-corporations control significant shares of the output, demand, and even employment. In a sense, these corporations form a kind of monopolistic (oligopolistic or even monopsonistic)

---

[4] A certain industry may be defined as concentrated (from an antitrust aspect) but may not be central for production from a market standpoint, and therefore its concentration has a limited impact on the aggregate concentration. However, a business entity (conglomerate or business group) may operate in multiple markets, which also have strong synergies through the production (input–output) function. In this case, the effect of that entity on aggregate concentration is much greater than that of a single concentrated industry.

[5] Thus, for example, if some of the 200 largest companies are jointly held, their aggregate concentration is underestimated.

[6] The following two examples illustrate this argument: (1) Dismantling a firm into two enterprises ostensibly reduces the industrial concentration statistically, but market concentration remains unaffected. (2) If the economy (i.e., a significant portion of the total market activity) is held by a mere 200 large companies, the level of aggregate concentration is very high. However, if the firms are almost equally active in each of the economic sectors, the level of concentration in these sectors may be lower than the threshold that raises concerns about anticompetitive behavior.

core around which a (more or less) competitive sector, consisting of SMEs (small and medium enterprises), operates. Thus, since we are interested in the economy's structure rather than in analyzing competition in specific industries and/or in diagnosing monopolies, oligopolies, or monopsonies, the fundamental issue behind the discussion of aggregate concentration is different: an analysis of the economic structure reflects, primarily, the level of market's efficiency, and therefore, its productivity, profitability, and economic stability.

Third, it should also be noted that there is no practical way to define the "right" or "reasonable" level of aggregate concentration to which anyone can refer. As opposed to classical indices used to evaluate concentration (such as the Herfindahl–Hirschman Index)[7] – the index for measuring absolute aggregate concentration is less informative and is neither intuitive nor easy to interpret.[8] Nevertheless, using the relevant data, and based on the findings indicating a clear economic correlation between aggregate concentration and a market's level of efficiency,[9] it is possible to draw from the changes in the aggregate concentration index conclusions regarding an improvement or deterioration in the allocation of resources, the efficiency of using the means of production, and changes in the productivity level of a domestic economy.

9.3 A Brief History of Concentration in Israel

For many years, there were debates in Israel regarding the desired pattern of development for attaining optimal resource allocation. Some supported government ownership and a model of a central planner; others – employee ownership of the market; still others advocated a free market model as the optimum the market should converge to, viewing competition as a panacea for any distortion, a goal of economic policy, and even a supreme value. The debates were not merely about economic perceptions: the development of market concentration

---

[7] According to the US Department of Justice, the concentration levels in an industry – which are measured according to the Herfindahl–Hirschman Index – are defined as follows: 0–0.15 – low concentration; 0.10–0.25 – moderate/medium concentration; over 0.25 – high concentration.

[8] Thus, for example, according to the Herfindahl–Hirschman Index for measuring aggregate concentration (calculated based on companies' turnover), market concentration in Israel in 2012 is 0.0008.

[9] See Gabaix (2011), Giovanni et al. (2014), and Acemoglu (2012),

in Israel and of the economic structure were highly influenced by policymakers' ideological perceptions. As a result, over the years, competition in Israel was often perceived as unwanted, even negative, conduct. In accordance with the geopolitical situation and prevailing ideology, the government had immense power both due to its extensive control of the actual market activity – reflected in the direction of capital movements, involvement in the financial market, foreign trade, etc. – and due to its unlimited ability to intervene in business decisions. The policy became reflected in highly concentrated market activity.

From a historical perspective, the roots of market concentration in Israel date back to the British Mandate period. During that time, most economic activity was concentrated in the hands of a few national institutions (later inherited by the Government of Israel) and the "Histadrut" (General Organization of Workers in Israel), and a small private sector, with a limited scope of activity. The objectives of the national institutions were not business-oriented, but rather were to establish a national infrastructure and find employment solutions for Jewish workers (Gronau, 2011). Therefore, business groups owned by the government and by the Histadrut spread across a wide range of industries, creating "centers of gravity" and connections between industrial and financial capital through joint ownership of enterprises and financial institutions.[10] The transition from a concentrated market to a market economy, privatization and dismantling the assets of the workers' economy caused the business activity's center of gravity to shift to the private sector (Aharoni, 1976; Maman, 2002). However, in addition to significant changes in the Israeli economy in recent decades (due to the absorption of a large wave of immigration, financial and security crises, etc.), several structural reforms and changes in the business elites (Aharoni, 2007), the government has retained its significant influence over economic activity. The many areas in Israel's economy continuing to be defined as vital or regulated[11] reflect direct or

---

[10] Since the groups' business activity was not profit-driven, the synergy between the companies in each group was limited.

[11] According to the Israel Antitrust Authority, the number of entities defined as concentration factors (pursuant to the Minimizing Market Centralization and Promoting Economic Competition Law) is 3,020 (1,830 of which are local). These are present in most industries in Israel, mainly in the commerce, real estate, banking and insurance industries.

potential intervention by the establishment and its ability to define both the desired structure of the market (industries) and rules of the game in any given moment or situation.

The increased regulation that characterized the business environment in the past decade may reflect the public's lack of trust in the efficiency of the free market and the functioning of the market mechanisms (Aghion et al., 2010).[12] This is against the background of the high level of concentration (control) that characterized the private sector in recent decades. Thus, in addition to the ideological change, the transition to a market economy in Israel in the 1990s was characterized, in fact, by increased power concentrations in the private sector in the hands of a few individuals (families) and diversified pyramidal business groups (Maman, 2008; Kosenko and Yafeh, 2010; Kosenko, 2012). In the mid-2000s, Israel had become, in terms of corporate control, one of the most concentrated countries in the West and was close, in that respect, to emerging economies.[13] These groups had easy access to the means of production and to credit markets; they were characterized by wide distribution (and geographic dispersion) of activity, and their interactions were reflected in a complex network of social connections (interlocking boards of directors) and in multi-market contacts. It was found that twenty groups controlled approximately 70 percent of the market capitalization and around 40 percent of the total market turnover.[14] However, the profitability of their affiliates was not higher than that of other, stand-alone firms; their growth rates and market performance, as well as their R&D investments, were low, but they embodied extensive risk (Kosenko, 2008). Against this backdrop, the business groups' activity raised concerns of anticompetitive behavior, of compromising consumer welfare, and of inefficiency in allocation of market resources as well as increased market exposure to shocks. These concerns led to the enactment of the Concentration Law (2013) and to a gradual dismantling of the business groups to simplify the ownership structure in the economy.

---

[12] Over the past few years, Israel's "doing business" scores have gradually decreased, yet another indication of a worsening of the business environment in Israel.

[13] See an interim report published by the Committee for Increasing Competition in the Economy.

[14] According to State Revenue data, Department of the Chief Economist, Ministry of Finance.

This reform was unique to Israel, since it was launched in a period of an economic boom, as opposed to several other markets (such as the United States, Japan, and Korea), which experienced similar processes during crisis periods (Kandel et al., 2013).

Owing to the market size, the consequences of the structural changes, and prevailing ideology, concentration became one of the main characteristics of the Israeli economy over the years (Aharoni, 2007; Ben-Bassat, 2002). It was not confined to the economy alone. There seems to have been, and may still be, significant overlap between centers of economic and political power in Israel. The social culture and system of incentives, which developed in the Israeli market over the years, encouraged the firms' owners' deep knowledge of the structure of the establishment, as well as personal ties with policymakers. Large companies, business groups, and their owners enjoyed significant advantage in this sense. The ownership structure in Israel, as it has evolved in the past few decades, allowed a small group of families to become entrenched in their positions[15] and to control most of the economic activity in the market without bearing the full economic cost of the control position (Hamdani, 2009). As the companies under their ownership developed and grew, so did their political (economic) clout and negotiation power. As a result, and as a direct manifestation of the "regulatory capture" phenomenon (Sigler, 1971), not only did the large firms (or business groups) active in the market throughout history become dependent on the government – the regulatory and legislative authorities were influenced by these firms, becoming largely dependent on them. So it comes as no surprise that many Israelis see a gap between their perception of their desired impact over economic processes and functioning of the free market mechanisms and their actual impact; between the conscious need to participate in economic and political decisions and the consequences of their voting; between the faith in their ability to evaluate the government and impact its quality and their actual impact. It is therefore not surprising that in the Israeli reality, when the political playing field is impacted by a disproportionate distribution of the economic power, the aggregate concentration phenomenon has assumed a significant antidemocratic character.[16]

---

[15] For a further discussion of economic entrenchment, see Morck et al. (2005).
[16] See Schechter (2012).

The prevailing ideology, the political concentration, the social structure, and rent-seeking issues are not discussed in this chapter. The chapter focuses on the Israeli market structure and the economic conduct of business entities (firms and business groups) in the past decades. Given the historical background and market origins, the relevant questions, for our purpose, are therefore: *Which structure developed in the past decades? What are the economy's centers of power (at both the industry and the corporate levels)? How was the market concentration impacted by developments in these centers of power?* In the next few sections, I will present the basic model and empiric analysis of the market concentration components, the interactions between them, and their main trends.

9.4 Basic Model for Evaluating Aggregate Concentration

Research on market concentration traditionally focuses on two levels: Literature focusing on *aggregate/market concentration* discusses at length the question of the impact of the (100 or 200) largest companies on aggregate activity. Studies on this subject evaluate the impact of large companies by calculating their share of total assets (or turnover, revenue, etc.) and/or in the total employment in the economy (for a comprehensive overview, see Berle and Means, 1932; White, 1981, 2002; White and Yang, 2017; and Aharoni, 1976, and Rowley et al., 1988 for Israel).

In contrast, numerous studies focus on *industrial concentration* – on the dominance of leading companies in specific (geographic) markets or industries, on their level of competitiveness, and on the existence of a monopolistic market (or on identifying the characteristic of such a market). The extent and intensity of the companies' control over a given market are measured using classic concentration indices, such as the Herfindahl–Hirschman Index, the Entropy Index, and the C3 and C4 indices, which indicate the percentage share of activity (share) of the three and four largest companies in a given industry, respectively.

Over the years, these topics have led to independent research tracks, and at least on a theoretical level, not enough effort has been put into mapping a clear connection between them, despite the growing efforts to find such both in regulatory practice and in public discourse in Israel and abroad (Gal and Cheng, 2016). To address the challenge, I present the relatively simple analytical framework, the aim of which is to serve as a necessary tool for analyzing aggregate concentration in Israel and the factors affecting it.[17]

First,[18] let there be N independent, standalone firms, operating in an economy, which comprises K different industries (markets). I define V_i as the size of firm i, which is measured by the turnover, sales, added value, or total assets, and V_{ij} as the size of firm i in industry j.[19] It is thus possible to present the economy's aggregate size V of the market as the total (amount) of the assets of all its firms or as a total activity at the industry level:

$$V = \sum_{i=1}^{N} V_i = \sum_{i=1}^{N}\sum_{j=1}^{K} V_{ij} \tag{1}$$

And the size of industry j as:

$$V_j = \sum_{i=1}^{N} V_{ij} \tag{2}$$

Second, to simplify the discussion, I use the Herfindahl–Hirschman Index to examine the concentration at both the aggregate and the industry levels.[20] Hence the level of the *aggregate concentration* is:

$$H_{A(Aggregate)} = \sum_{i=1}^{n} \frac{V_i^2}{V^2} \tag{3}$$

And the level of *industrial concentration* (for industry j) is:

$$H_j = \sum_{i=1}^{n} \frac{V_{ij}^2}{V_j^2} \tag{4}$$

To find a correlation between H_A and H_j, I define an indicator for activity diversification for firm i[21]

---

[17] In this context, please see "Methodology for Examining Aggregate Concentration," The Antitrust Authority, January 2017, Preliminary Draft.

[18] The model is based on Clarke and Davies (1983).

[19] V_{ij} Is equal to 0 in cases where a firm is inactive in industry j.

[20] This index is chosen for convenience purposes only. The use of additional indices (Entropy, for example) would not have compromised the quality of the analysis or the basic conclusions.

[21] For $K > 1$. If a firm is active in one industry, its industrial diversification is, by definition, equal to 0.

$$D_i = 1 - \sum_{j=1}^{K} \frac{V_{ij}^2}{V_i^2} \tag{5}$$

Therefore, and by placing equation (5) in equation (3), if follows that:

$$H_A = (1 - D)^{-1} \sum_{j=1}^{K} w_j H_j \tag{6}$$

If:

$$D = \frac{\sum_{i=1}^{N} D_i V_i^2}{\sum_{i=1}^{N} V_i^2} = \sum_{i=1}^{N} w_i D_i;$$

$$w_i = \frac{V_i^2}{\sum_{i=1}^{N} V_i^2};$$

$$w_j = \frac{V_j^2}{V^2};$$

The components of equation (6) show that aggregate concentration is a weighted average of the concentration indicators in each economic sector, multiplied by a factor, which depends positively on D – an aggregate index of diversification.[22] Thus, if all the firms in the market completely specialized ($D = 0$), the aggregate concentration is equal exactly to the weighted average of the industry concentration indicators.[23]

In day-to-day reality, however, many firms are active in more than one market (industry). Therefore, their level of diversification, as well as the economy's aggregate diversification, is significantly different from zero.[24] However, the expansion of a firm's activity and its entry

---

[22] The diversification measure presented here is widely addressed in the literature (Berry, 1975). This measure ranges from 0 (full specialization by the firm) to $K-1/K$ if the firm is equally active in K markets.

[23] This result is a known decomposition of the H Index (Cowell, 1977).

[24] To illustrate this point based on the population of reporting companies –private and public – in the economy: It was found that 32 percent of these companies stated in their business description that they were active in two or more of the main economic sectors (according to the CBS classification). In addition, approximately 27 percent of the reporting companies were defined as holding and investment companies (Bank of Israel, 2013).

into a new industry increases its diversification (D_i) only when the new venture is on significant scale. According to the above equation, it appears that the measure for the economy's diversification, at the aggregate level, is a weighted average of the diversification indices at the firm level across all industries. It is therefore easy to see that the large firms have a higher weight in the aggregate diversification index,[25] and therefore, a more significant impact on aggregate concentration.[26] In this context, the weight of the largest firms in the economy increases in two cases: (a) as a result of the business's (organic) growth, which may also be associated with the use of monopolistic power, and (b) as a result of growth through M&As and increase of the joint ownership, through formation of business groups, for example.[27]

The simplicity of the basic model is appealing, but for a more correct and accurate evaluation of the market's aggregate diversification level, and the resulting calculation of its concentration level, its outcomes will not suffice. An examination of the diversification at the firm level must consider the economic link between the various segments that constitute its activity, based on the level of connectivity between the industries in which the firm operates and the centrality (importance) of these industries to the market's productivity function (Fan and Lang, 2000). The solution for calculating the diversification at the firm and market level and of the aggregate concentration lies in the weighting of the shares of the firms' lines of activity (and of the industries) according to the centrality of these in the production function. Therefore, I define CS_j as the "centrality score" of industry j in the economy's production

---

[25] We can present a segmentation of the aggregate diversification according to the economic size (weight) of the firms, in the following manner:

$$D = (\sum_{i=1}^{200} V_i^2 D_i + \sum_{i=201}^{N} V_i^2 D_i)/\sum_{i=1}^{N} V_i^2 = W_{200} D_{200} + W_{rest} D_{rest}$$

Thus, the weight of the 200 largest companies in the Israeli economy is equal to: $W_{200} = \sum_{i=1}^{200} V_i^2 / \sum_{i=1}^{N} V_i^2$ According to Clark and Davies (1983), the weight of the diversification of Britain's 120 largest industrial companies is 0.986 when calculating the total aggregate diversification.

[26] The significance of large companies in terms of the market power is supported by the empirical literature (Axtell, 2001; Gabaix, 2011; Wagner, 2012; Acemoglu et al., 2014).

[27] In this case, an assumption regarding the number N of the independent firms, as in the basic model, is violated.

function.[28] Using the terms of the basic model, the use of the centrality score of industry j leads to two main extensions:

a. The level of diversification at the firm level is given by:

$$D_i = 1 - \sum_{j=1}^{K} \frac{V_{ij}^2}{V_i^2} \, CS_j \ \text{(for K>1)}$$

b. The weight of industry j is : $w_j = \dfrac{V_j^2}{V^2} CS_j$

Decomposition of the aggregate concentration index, as presented in equation (6), given such adjustments, provides a wider perspective on the role of industrial concentration and the level of aggregate diversification, and their contribution to aggregate concentration: First, it is possible to see that the aggregate concentration in the market positively depends on the industrial concentration level. Second, the extent of the correlation between the industrial concentration and the aggregate concentration depends on the industry's centrality score in the market's production function (CS); third, the aggregate concentration is positively associated with the level of diversification of the large companies (or the business groups).

Based on the analytical framework and according to the decomposition presented in the above model, I review, in the following sections, the developmental dynamics of each of the main aggregate concentration components in Israel in recent decades. For the purpose of the empirical examination, I use three unique data sources: (a) data from the Israel Tax Authority (for 2008–2013), to calculate the concentration indices at the industry level; (b) turnover/revenues data from D&B Israel (Dun and Bradstreet Israel) (for 2003–2015), to examine the developments in the size and weight of the market's largest companies; and (c) ownership data on firms operating in Israel (for 1995–2015), from the

---

[28] This centrality is calculated by weighting the centrality of industry j in the production network $B_j^{v_{kj}}$ (Bonacich, 1987), according to the level of vertical integration between industry k and industry j (for more information, see Fan and Lang, 2000 and Acemoglu et al., 2009).

Companies Registry database, to identify and define the structure of corporate control.[29]

9.5 An Empirical Examination of the Aggregate Concentration Dynamics in Israel

Aggregate concentration, according to the abovementioned model, is derived from a combination of two main interfaces – the system of interactions between the means of production in the market[30] and the ownership over them. For the purpose of discussion, I assume that the production function of any market, including that of the Israeli market, can be presented by a Cobb–Douglas function decomposed into the intermediate inputs required for final production (Acemoglu et al., 2010, 2012). This manner of presentation assumes that the market is a production network defined by interactions (demand and supply of the intermediate inputs) between the economic sectors and determined by the strength of these as reflected in the input–output direct coefficients matrix (input–output tables, CBS, 2013). Economic analysis based on input–output (IO) matrices is useful for examining the market's level of exposure and its ability to sustain various shocks as well as for examining its concentration and efficiency levels (Long and Ploser, 1983; Horvath, 1998; Conley and Dupor, 2003; Gabaix, 2011; Acemoglu, 2012; Carvalho, 2014). One of the immediate conclusions from this manner of presentation is that a market may be defined as concentrated due to a highly dense production function, which may result from a small number of central inputs (industries) in production, from production technology and from the market's wealth – natural or other resources –determining the advantage, specialization, and quality of production. The basic argument of this chapter is that a dense production function is exogenous and is not dependent on the level of concentration or on the ownership of means of production used by various firms. In contrast, the density of the production function is relevant to measuring the centrality of the economic sectors, thus providing a necessary input for the discussion of aggregate concentration.

---

[29] According to the method of analyzing the ownership/control map of (public) companies in Israel (Aminadav et al., 2011). For the application, see Kosenko (2008), Kosenko and Yafeh (2010).

[30] The aggregate production function has two levels: the production level and the distribution level. The model's implicit assumption is that companies have no specialization except in the production or distribution of the final product.

9.5.1 Production Concentration (Density of the Production Function): Connectivity and Centrality of the Main Economic Sectors

The level of production concentration in the economy is examined within the analytical framework of "network analysis" (Ballester et al., 2006; Carvalho, 2008, 2014), using the IO matrices (see Leontief, 1986), and centrality indices calculated according to the Bonacich (1987) method.[31] Figure 9.2 presents the means of production network in Israel (based on intermediate inputs) at two points in time –1995 and 2006.[32] Each node in this chart presents a major economic sector according to the (CBS, 1993) classification of sixty-one (3-digit) economic sectors. The descriptive statistics – i.e., the main parameters describing the characteristics of the production network at different points in time – indicate that between 1995 and 2006, the production network in Israel became highly interconnected. This was manifested in an increase in the number of cross-industry connections from 2,402 to 3,181, as well as in increased density: The density index, which is calculated as the number of actual connections out of the total potential connections in the production network, was up by almost 20 percent between the two points in time. In addition to an increase in the network's connectivity and density (which is also reflected in a decrease of the length parameter, i.e., the average economic distance between the main economic sectors), according to the network's clustering coefficient (CC), the industries' level of aggregation increased too. That is, in addition to multiple new connections between economic sectors and an increase in the level of density, several key power centers – industries and industry clusters – which have significant impact on the level of production and on the volatility (stability) of

---

[31] The centrality indices (of the impact of players in the network) according to the method proposed in this chapter are an alternative to the connectivity indices under the Hirschman-Rasmussen (1956, 1958) approach.

[32] These are the only two input–output matrices available in Israel: for 1995 and 2006. The input–output matrix for 2006 was published in 2011. It is therefore the "most recent evidence" of the state of the economy in terms of its production connections in the past decade. The input–output matrices featured two different versions of industry classification made by the CBS in 1993 and 2011. To maintain consistency, I aggregated all the original sixty-five industries and separated them into sixty-one economic sectors.

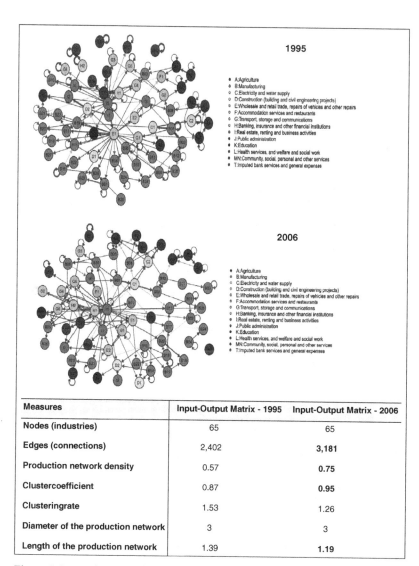

Measures	Input-Output Matrix - 1995	Input-Output Matrix - 2006
Nodes (industries)	65	65
Edges (connections)	2,402	3,181
Production network density	0.57	0.75
Clustercoefficient	0.87	0.95
Clusteringrate	1.53	1.26
Diameter of the production network	3	3
Length of the production network	1.39	1.19

Figure 9.2 Israel's means of production network (input–output matrix), 1995 and 2006

The figure shows the (intermediate) production means network out of the input-output matrices of the Central Bureau of Statistics at two points in time: 1995 and 2006. The table includes statistical data for the network's characteristics, specifically: the number of industries in the production network (nodes) the number of direct connections between the industries (edges), the network's density (a measure of the actual connectivity between various industries), a measure of the network's level of aggregation (cluster coefficient). Each node in the figure represents an industry according to an input-output matrix (65 industries). The color of the industry is according to the main economic sectors defined by the CBS (14 sectors). The arrows point in the direction in which the production means are supplied from each industry to other industries and to itself.

(a)

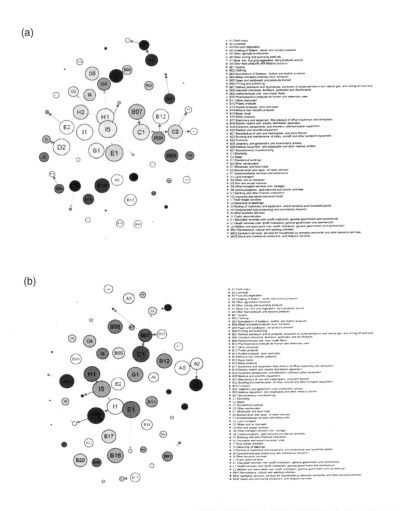

(b)

Figure 9.3 Industry centrality index, 1995 and 2006

The figure presents a weighted centrality score for each of the 61 industries in 1995 (A) and in 2006 (B), respectively. The arrows point in the direction in which the intermediate means of production of each industry is supplied to other industries. Their color expresses the intensity of the direct coefficients out of the input-output matrix. Each node represents the industry according to its IO classification; its size - the centrality score; its color - the power of the industry in the IO network (according to the Bonacich Index, with positive beta). The darker the circle, the more central the industry is in the production network.

the production in the economy were created in the Israeli production network between 1995 and 2006.

Figure 9.3 presents, from an additional perspective, the power of economic sectors in the input–output network and its dynamics over time, according to the level of centrality of the economic sectors in the production network (Katz, 1953; Bonacich, 1987).

A high centrality score means that the industry is a significant supplier of intermediate inputs to (numerous) other industries, so that if it undergoes shocks (whether positive or negative – such as a decrease in the global price of petroleum, decrease in production due to geopolitical events, technological improvements, shocks to exports, prices and idiosyncratic industrial shocks), it may have a significant impact on other parts of the production network. Following the findings presented in Figure 9.2 and Figure 9.3, it can be seen that, while the level of aggregation of Israel's production network increased between the two points in time, the centrality of several industries, e.g., refined petroleum and its products, extraction of crude petroleum and natural gas, and mining of coal industry (B7); wholesale and retail trade (E1); other business services (I5); banking and other financial institutions (H1); real estate activities (I1) and computerized data processing and research (I4) rose too. It seems that, in addition to the development of natural resources, this trend reflected the technological changes in the market's production function and its reliance on the service sector as a leading growth engine in recent decades. Owing to the changes in the level of density of the production network in Israel and increasing centrality of the said industries, the question is whether the level of concentration in these industries has also increased.

9.5.2 Industrial Concentration in the Israeli Economy, 2008–2013

To analyze the aggregate concentration under the model specifications, I examine the level of concentration of the industries, specifically the dynamics within the main industries, as defined in the analysis of the density of the economy's production function. The index chosen for calculating the industrial concentration is the Herfindahl–Hirschman Index, which was applied to sixty-one industries. Figure 9.4 illustrates the development of the concentration level in Israel by economic sector.

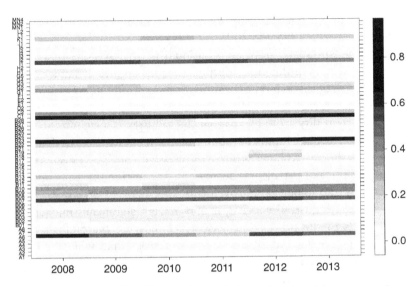

Figure 9.4 The Herfindahl–Hirschman Index of industrial concentration, 2008–2013.

The figure presents the Herfindahl–Hirschman Index (HHI) (of industrial concentration) according to the turnover of each of the 61 main industries, classified according to the input–output matrix (Appendix A). The level of concentration is measured according to the scale on the right-hand side, which corresponds to the distribution range of the Herfindahl–Hirschman Index, on a scale of 0 to 1. (The darker the color, the higher the concentration score.) The concentration levels in a given industry, which are measured according to the HHI, are divided into three ranges: 0–0.15 – low concentration; 0.10–0.25 – moderate/medium concentration; over 0.25 – high concentration.

Source: Based on Israel Tax Authority data

Figure 9.4 indicates that when examining a relatively short time frame (five years), the level of industrial concentration, measured by the HHI, is, on average, relatively moderate and stable (the average HHI score was 0.12 and the median was 0.05). Industries in which the rate of change in the HHI score during the relevant period was positive and relatively high (over 30 percent) were: fruit and vegetables; other food products and tobacco products; cars and equipment; furniture; land transport; basic metals, and public administration. In contrast, the concentration level in telecommunications; banking and other financial institutions; other chemicals; and wood and wood products declined. The intensity of the concentration and interpretation of the test results are sensitive to the choice of industry classification level (market or industry boundaries) (Hausman et al., 1992). However, under the 61-industries classification (3 digits), it should be noted that the most prominent industries characterized by an especially high level of concentration include: electricity (C1); manufacture of cars and motorcycles and parts thereof; and other transport equipment (B22–23); refined petroleum and its products (B7); petrochemicals and pharmaceutical products (B9–10); other mining and quarrying products (A6). In general, and based on the analysis of the firms' turnover data, it may be said that the level of industrial concentration of a large number of industries in Israel is moderate or high. The weight in GDP of the industries, in which the industrial concentration is above average or above the median, is 22 and 35 percent, respectively.

Figure 9.5 summarizes the concentration and centrality indices for 2013. According to this figure, there is no significant correlation between the centrality level of economic sectors and their concentration.[33] Indeed, the high centrality of the electricity; water (government-owned monopolies); refined petroleum and its products; petrochemicals, and synthetic fibers in the economy's production function is also characterized by high industrial concentration. In contrast, many industries that are not defined as central according to their weight in the economy's production function are also characterized by high levels of industrial concentration. These include pharmaceutical products; other mining and quarrying products; building and maintenance of ships, aircraft and other transport equipment;[34] and others.

9.5.3 Concentration of Control in Israel (1995–2015)

9.5.3.1 Business Groups

To complete the picture of aggregate concentration in accordance with the theoretical framework, it is necessary to address the level of diversification

---

[33] In terms of correlation between industrial concentration and an industry's weight in the final product (output) and private consumption, it appears that there is no significant linear correlation between the weight of the industry in the total market turnover (or total private consumption) and its level of concentration. Thus, there is no concern for statistical bias in weighting industrial concentration using the aggregate concentration index in Israel.

[34] Especially Israel Aerospace Industries and Israel Shipyards.

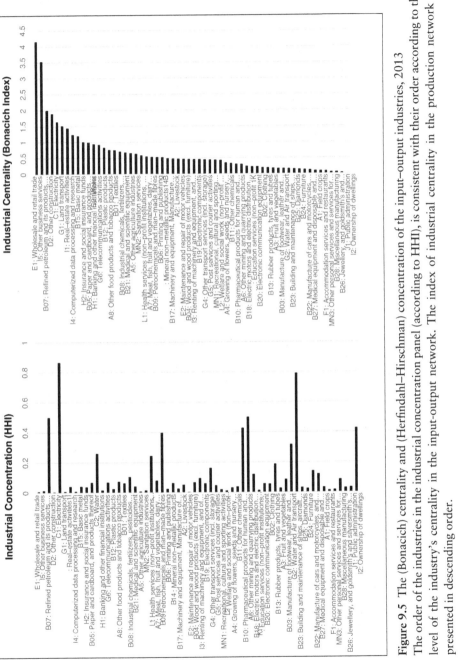

Figure 9.5 The (Bonacich) centrality and (Herfindahl–Hirschman) concentration of the input–output industries, 2013 The order of the industries in the industrial concentration panel (according to HHI), is consistent with their order according to the level of the industry's centrality in the production network. The index of industrial centrality in the input-output network is presented in descending order.

and ownership of economic units (firms) composing the country's economy. Owing to the limitations of the data, it is possible to examine the aggregate diversification in the Israeli economy only on two main levels – the level of the business groups and the level of the large companies.[35]

Following the evidence from the literature on ownership structure in Israel (Maman, 2002, 2006; Kosenko, 2008; Hamdani, 2009; Kosenko and Yafeh, 2010), control in the Israeli market in the past decades was concentrated in the hands of a few business group owners – clusters of companies (private and public) under single administrative control – which operated in the private sector. In fact, the existence of business groups in the past few decades brought about a change in the position of the relative legal entity when discussing a firm's boundaries, its diversification, and the level of industrial integration among the business units composing these groups. The business groups had significant presence in terms of market share, and for many years, enjoyed access to government and financial institutions in seeking political clout or credit sources, and were involved in directing the activity in key segments of the domestic economy. These complex ownership structures were dynamic, and their composition changed over time due to acquisition (and taking control over) new companies and aligning their activity to suit the group's needs. According to Kosenko (2012), the development pattern of Israeli business groups over time was consistent with the diversification strategy of business conglomerates. In other words, the activity of these groups spanned numerous market sectors, among which vertical integration was low or negligible. The diversification strategy of the groups included acquiring companies from various areas of activity, especially the acquisition of financial institutions and media outlets, which are known to have significant impact on shaping public opinion. Owing to their wide diversification, the activities of Israeli business groups led to multi-industry contacts (Figure 9.8) and even raised concerns regarding tacit collusion and mutual forbearance (Bernheim and Whinstone, 1990; Parker and Roller, 1997; Gimeno and Woo, 1999; and Greve, 2008), and, as a result, potential harm to the efficient functioning of

---

[35] Under an optimal scenario, we would calculate the level of diversification at the firm level according to its assembly lines. In other words, we would have liked to calculate the industry asset portfolio at the firm level and/or at the business group level. Such decomposing is possible only at the level of the data of the CBS, which serve for calculating the value added by industry. Unfortunately, these data are highly sensitive and were not made available to us.

various economic sectors. However, it was actually concern for the harm
to investors' welfare and to public savings, the joint interface of ownership
of financial and nonfinancial assets, and fears of pyramidal business
groups becoming too big or too complex to fail[36] that led to the establishment of a government committee and to the enactment of the
Concentration Law in Israel.[37] The new law was mainly concerned with
decreasing the complexity of business groups (leveling the pyramidal
structures) and separating financial assets from nonfinancial ones.
Figures 9.6 and 9.7 illustrate the evolutionary dynamics of business groups
in Israel. Figure 9.6 shows the development of the number of business
groups (which include two or more public companies) and the percentage
of public companies affiliated with them out of the total number of public
companies in the economy.

According to these figures, one may conclude that the trend in the
development of the groups in Israel in the past two decades was not
constant: After reaching a peak (sixty-five groups) at the beginning of
the decade, there was a clear decline in their number (down to forty
groups) and the number of companies affiliated with them. This
occurred in tandem with the Concentration Committee and the
Concentration Law, which were pushed along the tailwind of the social
protests in the summer of 2011, and during the economic boom – as
opposed to other periods, when a positive correlation between the
number of business groups (and their market shares) and the business
cycle phase was observed.

Figure 9.7 further emphasizes the significance of the trend. The
number of the largest business groups in Israel (companies with at
least three affiliated companies) declined in the past few years from
about thirty to less than twenty, and the weight of the companies
affiliated with them, which is measured by their market capitalization
relative to the total market capitalization of all public companies in
Israel, was down from approximately 70 percent at the beginning of the
decade to a mere 23 percent in 2015. At the same time, in view of
actions taken by the group owners in order to meet the requirements of
the new law[38] (which included, *inter alia*, purchase offers, mergers,

---

[36] See chapter 4 in the *Bank of Israel Annual Report 2009*.
[37] The Promotion of Competition and Reduction of Concentration Law,
      5773–2013.
[38] Out of forty-seven groups with pyramidal structures that were required to meet
      the criterion of simplifying their complex ownership structure, thirty-seven

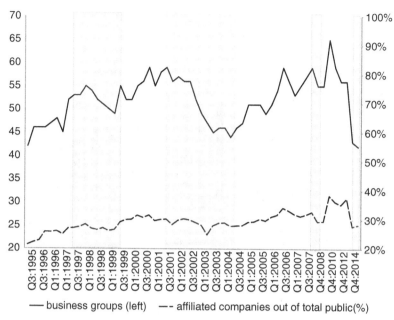

Figure 9.6 Number of business groups (two or more affiliated public companies) and the percentage of companies affiliated with them, 1995–2014 The figure shows the number of business groups (defined as having two or more publicly traded affiliates), and the percentage of affiliated publicly traded companies out of total number of public companies in the economy; the grey areas represent periods of decline in the business cycle (Djivre and Yakhin, 2011).

sales to third parties as well as creditor arrangements and delisting of companies), and influenced by economic shocks which plagued the groups in recent years, the number of pyramidal (ownership) levels declined from 2.5 to 1.9 on average. Significant progress was also made on the issue of separating the ownership of financial assets from ownership of nonfinancial assets. An examination of the diversification level of Israel's business groups shows that the level of vertical integration increased, so that their actual diversification declined. Regarding multi-market contacts of business groups in Israel, as shown in

complied. In addition, according to Tel Aviv Stock Exchange data, in 2013–2017, forty-six companies affiliated with pyramidal groups were delisted.

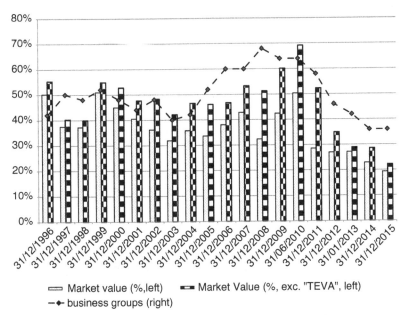

Legend:
- ▭ Market value (%, left)
- ▬ Market Value (%, exc. "TEVA", left)
- ◆ business groups (right)

Figure 9.7 Number and market capitalization of the largest business groups (three or more affiliated public companies), 1996–2015
Note. The figure shows the number of the largest business groups (with at least three affiliated companies) and the weight of the public companies affiliated with them (with the aggregate market capitalization of all public companies in Israel).

Figure 9.8,[39] the number of Israel's largest business groups in 2013 was indeed the same as in 2003 (which marks the beginning of the large-group trend in the economy – IDB, Africa Israel, Delek Israel, etc.). However, the number of contacts in the various economic sectors in which the groups operate declined significantly – from twenty-six to twenty. Nevertheless, the activity (and contacts) of the groups in the central industries, e.g., trade, finance, refined petroleum and its products, and construction and real estate continued. All in all, even though according to the absolute figures, the business groups phenomenon in Israel has not disappeared altogether, there is no doubt that it has significantly declined and that its economic importance has diminished in recent years.

[39] I would like to emphasize that the comparison in the figure took into account the economic sector classification of the private companies (rather than only of the publicly traded ones) affiliated with business groups.

2003	Fruit and vegetables	Meat, fish, fruit and vegetables, dairy products and oil	Textiles	Paper and cardboard, and products there of	Refined petroleum and its products, extraction of crude petroleum and natural gas, and mining of hard coal	Industrial chemicals, fertilizers, pesticides and disinfectants	Petrochemicals and man-made fibres	Rubber products, tyres and tubes	Mineral non-metallic products	Basic metal	Machinery and equipment, Manufacture of office machinery and computers	Electric motors and electric distribution apparatus	Electronic components, and electronic communication equipment	Other construction	Wholesale and retail trade	Accommodation services and restaurants	Water and Air transport	Other transport services including storage	Communications, post services and courier activities	Banking and other financial institutions	Insurance and social insurance funds	Real-estate activities	Renting of machinery and equipment, and of personal and household goods	Computerized data processing and research	Other business services	Education services non-profit institutions, general government and commercial
BG1																				*		*				
BG2													*		*		*		*	*		*				
BG3															*					*		*		*		
BG4		*	*												*											
BG5											*									*						
BG6																				*				*		*
BG7															*								*	*		
BG8																		*						*	*	
BG9			*					*														*				
BG10							*							*						*					*	
BG11																				*		*		*		
BG12												*		*	*					*		*				
BG13	*			*		*								*	*			*	*	*	*	*		*		
BG14															*					*						
BG15																*				*		*			*	
BG16				*																*						
BG17																				*			*			
BG18		*			*									*						*						
BG19									*					*		*				*						
BG20					*				*	*										*		*				
Contacts	1	1	2	2	2	1	1	1	2	1	1	1	1	5	7	2	1	2	2	16	1	9	2	6	3	1

2013	Fruit and vegetables	Other food products and tobacco products	Paper and cardboard, and products thereof	Printing and publishing	Refined petroleum and its products, extraction of crude petroleum and natural gas, and mining of hard coal	Petrochemicals and man-made fibres	Electronic components, and electronic communication equipment	Medical and scientific equipment	Building and maintenance of ships, aircraft and other transport equipment	Medical equipment and disposable and other medical articles	Other construction	Wholesale and retail trade	Accommodation services and restaurants	Communications, post services and courier activities	Banking and other financial institutions	Insurance and social insurance funds	Real-estate activities	Renting of machinery and equipment, and of personal and household goods	Computerized data processing and research	Other business services
BG1			*					*				*			*		*		*	
BG2												*			*		*		*	
BG3										*		*								
BG4																		*	*	
BG5							*								*					
BG6								*					*							
BG7					*	*					*	*			*		*			*
BG8		*										*								
BG9	*				*			*			*	*		*	*	*	*			
BG10					*										*		*			
BG11											*	*			*					
BG12														*	*					*
BG13					*										*		*			
BG14											*				*		*			
BG15															*		*			
BG16									*			*			*					*
BG17						*									*					*
BG18												*			*		*			
BG19											*	*			*		*			
BG20												*					*			
BG21				*							*	*			*	*			*	
Contacts	1	1	1	1	4	2	1	3	1	1	6	12	1	2	16	2	11	1	4	4

Figure 9.8 Multi-market contacts, the largest business groups (with at least three affiliated public companies) in 2003 and 2013
The tables show "contacts" between business groups in various economic sectors. For each business group (BG), its area of activity is shown (according to the industrial classification of the private and public companies affiliated with it). The sum of the contacts, i.e., the number of business groups active in each industry, appears at the bottom row of each table. The industry classification is according to sixty-five input-output industries.

9.5.3.2 The Israeli Economy's Largest Companies

The decentralization of business groups' ownership in the Israeli economy and the trend of their declining weight and level of diversification in the past decade lead to the conclusion that the Israeli economy is gradually converging to a business environment that is characteristic of other advanced economies. In such an environment, the main centers of power are a few standalone companies, which have a material and growing impact on the economy's level of activity, on diversification, on stability, and on resource allocation, and as a result on the level of concentration in specific industries and the economy as a whole (Grullon, et al. 2017). An examination of the impact of Israel's 200 largest companies based on their turnover data for 2003–2015 (from D&B Israel's database) shows that their composition has remained relatively stable over the years. In other words, the Israeli economy has a restricted, fixed "club" of mega-corporations, which have been active for a long time. The weight of these companies in the economy's total turnover (Figure 9.1) ranges from 55 to 45 percent, on average, with and without the turnover of the holding and investment companies, respectively, and the weight of the "200 largest" public companies is slightly higher than that of the private companies. An examination of the distribution of the economic size of the "200 largest" companies indicates a distinct/significant right tail. The average size of a company in the "200" list is approximately NIS 4.5 billion, with the maximum size being NIS 72.5 billion, and the mean size, NIS 2 billion. This finding supports the assumption regarding a Zipf distribution in corporate assets (Axtell, 2001), i.e., the empirical evaluation of a "granular hypothesis" (Gabaix, 2011) shows that the Israeli economy has a small number of mega-corporations and high aggregate concentration. In addition, as of the end of 2015, only 35 of the largest companies in the economy are affiliated with large business groups, compared to 105 in 2003 and 125 in 2010. The weight of the affiliated large companies in the total turnover of the largest companies was up from 28 percent in 2003 to 39 percent in 2010, and then down to a mere 14 percent in late 2015.

Looking forward, both theoretical studies and empirical findings around the world and in Israel point to the growing economic impact of the largest companies. The business integration (in commerce) and the globalization processes further boost the power of these corporations (Di Giovanni and Levchenko, 2012). Similarly, the consolidation among the various industries – which is derived from the M&A strategy of the largest companies – may result in a thick tail distribution of the firms operating in the market, according to their economic size. These structural developments increase the level of aggregate concentration and, as a result, production volatility, rendering the business cycle more vulnerable to idiosyncratic shocks.[40] It should also be noted that, at the same time, the boundaries of the firm in the modern business environment are ever evolving so that production in the economy is distributed among various focal points – internal and external (outsourcing). The activity undergoes fragmentation, both in and among firms' boundaries, and between the various industry sectors. This development increases the distribution of business activity, creating yet another channel of shock transmission from the individual company level to the economy as a whole (Franko and Phillipon, 2007).

9.6 Summary

A clear conclusion emerging from analyzing the aggregate concentration in Israel is that its level was relatively high even during the early days of the State. It increased over time as a result of both an increase in the level of concentration in most industry sectors – as a result of mergers and acquisitions of firms by business groups or by large companies – and government policy. A close examination of the developments in the main components of market concentration in Israel in recent decades indicates that the level of industrial concentration in Israel remained high but stable. This happened at the same time as technological changes and adjustments in the economy's production function took place, accompanied by an increase in the centrality of various industries and in the density of the production network (function). The process translated into the creation of a few "central" industries and industrial clusters with significant impact on the economy's productivity level fluctuations, and occurred in parallel with a significant change in the economy's ownership

---

[40] Empirical research on this topic shows that shocks incurred by the economy's largest companies explain anywhere from one-third to two-thirds of the market volatility (of the aggregate output [Gabaix, 2011; Foerster et al., 2011]).

map, in view of a decline in the number and market share of business groups. This development manifested in a simplification of the ownership structure as well as in a decline in the level of aggregate diversification.

In this chapter, I do not conduct any statistical test to evaluate the impact of these changes on the efficiency and nature of resource allocation in the economy. Based on the data presented here, it can be stated with a great degree of certainty that the level of concentration in various industry sectors in Israel is high, reflected in the economy's oligopolistic structure, and that there is a high level of diversification at the firm level. This picture is more evident when taking into account the interrelations between the various industries and joint ownership of firms. However, it can be also said that the aggregate concentration in Israel has decreased in recent years, largely because of the decline in the level of aggregate diversification. This development should, at least theoretically, improve resource allocation efficiency. At the same time, against the background of the decentralization of ownership and declining importance of business groups in the Israeli economy, it seems that mega-corporations have become the key focal point of power. Much as in other advanced economies, these corporations have a significant, increasing impact on the level of aggregate diversification and activity, and hence on the present and future level of aggregate concentration.

References

Acemoglu, D., Johnson, S., and Mitton, T. (2009). Determinants of Vertical Integration: Finance, Contracts and Regulation. *Journal of Finance*, 63 (3), 1251–1290.

Acemoglu, D., Ozdaglar, A., and Tahbaz-Salehi, A. (2010). Cascades in Networks and Aggregate Volatility. NBER Working Paper No. 16516. www.nber.org/papers/w16516.

Acemoglu, D., Carvalho, V. M., Ozdaglar, A., and Tahbaz-Salehi, A. (2012). The Network Origins of Aggregate Fluctuations. *Econometrica*, 80, 1977–2016.

(2017). Microeconomic Origins of Macroeconomic Tail Risks. *American Economic Review*, 107(1), 55–108.

Aghion, P., Algan, Y., Cahuc, P., and Shleifer, A. (2010). Regulation and Distrust. *Quarterly Journal of Economics*, 125, 1015–1049.

Aharoni, Y. (1976). *Structure and Performance of the Israeli Economy*. Tel Aviv: Cherikover.

(2007). New Business Elites. In E. Ben-Rafael & Y. Sternberg (eds.), *New Elites in Israel*. Jerusalem: Bialik Institute., 80–113. [In Hebrew]

Aminadav G., Bachrach, Y., Kosenko, K., Rosenschein, J., and Wilf, Y. (2011). Rebuilding the Great Pyramids: A Method for Identifying Control Relations in Complex Ownership Structures. Working Paper, The Hebrew University in Jerusalem. SSRN: https://ssrn.com /abstract=1903941.

Axtell, R. L. (2001). Zipf Distribution of U.S. Firm Size. *Science*, 293, 1818–1820.

Ballester, C., Calvo-Armengol, A., and Zenou, Y. (2006). Who's Who in Networks. Wanted: The Key Player. *Econometrica*, 74, 1403–1417.

Ben-Basset A. (2002). *The Israeli Economy, 1985–1998: From Government Intervention to Market Economics*. Cambridge, MA: MIT Press.

Berle, A. A., and Means, G. C. (1932). *The Modern Corporation and Private Property*. New York, NY: Macmillan Press.

Bernheim, B. D., and Whinston, M. D. (1990). Multimarket Contact and Collusive Behavior. *RAND Journal of Economics*, 21: 1–26.

Berry, C. H. (1975). *Corporate Growth and Diversification*. Princeton, NJ: Princeton University Press.

Bonacich, P. B. (1987). Power and Centrality: A Family of Measures. *American Journal of Sociology*, 92(5), 1170–1182.

Carvalho, V. M. (2008). Aggregate Fluctuations and the Network Structure of Inter-sectoral Trade. Working Paper, CREI.

(2014). From Micro to Macro via Production Networks. *Journal of Economic Perspectives*, 28, 23–48.

Cheng, T., and Gal, M. S. (2016). Aggregate Concentration: An Empirical Study of Competition Law Solutions. *Journal of Antitrust Enforcement*, 282.

Clarke, R., and Davies, S. W. (1983). Aggregate Concentration, Market Concentration and Diversification. *Economic Journal*, 93, 182–192.

Conley, T. G., and Dupor, B. (2003). A Spatial Analysis of Sectoral Complementarity. *Journal of Political Economy*, 111(2), 311–352.

Cowell, F. A. (1977). *Measuring Inequality*. Oxford: Oxford University Press.

Di Giovanni, J., and Levchenko, A. A. (2012). Country Size, International Trade, and Aggregate Fluctuations in Granular Economies. *Journal of Political Economy* 120(6), 1083–1132.

Di Giovanni, J., Levchenko, A. A., and Mejean, I. (2014). Firms, Destinations, and Aggregate Fluctuations. *Econometrica*, 82, 1303–1340.

Djivre, Y., and Yakhin, Y. (2011). Business Cycles in Israel, 1987–2010: The Facts. The Maurice Falk Institute for Economic Research in Israel, the Hebrew University, Working Paper No. 11.02.

Fan, J., and Lang, L. (2000). The Measurement of Relatedness: An Application to Corporate Diversification. *Journal of Business*, 73(4), 629–660.

Foerster A. T., Sarte, Pierre-Daniel, G., and Watson, M. W. (2011) "Sectoral Versus Aggregate Shocks: A Structural Factor Analysis of Industrial Production. *Journal of Political Economy*, 119, 1, 1–38.

Fortuna, G., Yaniv, Y., and Freeman, D. (2014). Fortuna, G., Neev, Y., and Friman, D. (2014). *Analyzing Teva Corporate Contribution to Israel Economy*. Haifa: Samuel Neaman Institute, 2014. https://www.neaman.org.il/EN/Analyzing-Teva-corp-contribution-Israel-Economy.

Franco, F., and Philippon, T. (2007). Firms and Aggregate Dynamics. *The Review of Economics and Statistics*, 89(4), 587–600.

Gabaix, X. (2011). The Granular Origins of Aggregate Fluctuations. *Econometrica*, 79(3), 733–772.

Gimeno, J., and Woo, C. Y. (1999). Multimarket Contact, Economies of Scope, and Firm Performance. *Academy of Management Journal*, 42, 239–259.

Greve, H. R. (2008). Multimarket Contact and Sales Growth: Evidence from Insurance. *Strategic Management Journal*, 29, 229–249.

Gronau, R. (2011). The Israeli Economy: Are Too Few Controlling Too Much? Panel on concentration at the Israeli Presidential Conference, Jerusalem. [In Hebrew]

Grullon, G., Larkin, Y., and Michaely, R. (2017). Are U.S. Industries Becoming More Concentrated? SSRN: https://ssrn.com/abstract=2612047.

Hamdani, A. (2009). *Concentrated Ownership and Business Groups in Israel: A Legal Analysis*. Policy Paper No. 78. Jerusalem: The Israel Democracy Institute.

Hausman, J. A., Leonard, G. K., and Zona, J. D. (1992). A Proposed Method for Analyzing Competition Among Differentiated Products. *Antitrust Law Journal*, 60, 889–900.

Hirschman, A. O. (1958). *The Strategy of Economic Development*. New York: Yale University Press.

Horvath, M. (1998). Cyclicality and Sectoral Linkages: Aggregate Fluctuations from Independent Sectoral Shocks. *Review of Economic Dynamics*, 1(4), 781–808.

Kandel E., Kosenko, K., Morck, R., and Yafeh, Y. (2013). The Great Pyramids of America: A Revised History of US Business NBER Working Paper No. 19691. www.nber.org/papers/w19691.

Katz, L. (1953). A New Status Index Derived from Sociometric Analysis. *Psychometrica*, 18, 39–43.

Khanna, T., and Yafeh, Y. (2007). Business Groups in Emerging Markets: Paragons or Parasites? *Journal of Economic Literature*, 45(2), 331–372.

Kosenko, K. (2008). Evolution of Business Groups in Israel: Their Impact at the Level of the Firm and the Economy. *Israel Economic Review*, 5(2), 55–93.

(2012). The Nature of Organizational Hybrids: Exploring the Evolutionary Dynamics of Business Groups. Unpublished manuscript. SSRN: https://ssrn.com/abstract=2287530.

Kosenko, K., and Yafeh, Y. (2010). Business Groups in Israel. In A. M. Colpan, T. Hikino, and J. R. Lincoln (eds.), *The Oxford Handbook of Business Groups*. Oxford: Oxford Press University, 459–485.

Leontief, W. W. (1986). *Input-Output Economics*. 2nd edn. New York, NY: Oxford University Press.

Long, J. B., Jr., and Plosser, Ch. I. (1983). Real Business Cycles. *Journal of Political Economy*, 91(1), 39–69.

Maman, D. (2002). The Emergence of Business Groups: Israel and South Korea Compare. *Organization Studies*, 23, 737–758.

(2006). Diffusion and Translation: Business Groups in the New Israeli Corporate Law. *Sociological Perspectives*, 49(1), 115–135.

Morck, R., Wolfenzon, D., and Yeung, B. (2005). Corporate Governance, Economic Entrenchment, and Growth. *Journal of Economic Literature*, 43(3), 655–720.

National Resources Committee (1939). *The Structure of the American Economy*. Washington, DC: US Government Print Office.

Parker, P. M., and Röller, L.-H. (1997). Collusive Conduct in Duopolies: Multimarket Contact and Cross-ownership in the Mobile Telephone Industry. *RAND Journal of Economics*, 28(2), 304–322.

Rasmussen, P. N. (1956). *Studies in Inter-sectorial Relations*. Amsterdam: North Holland P.C.

Rosenstein-Rodan, P. (1943). Problems of Industrialization of Eastern and Southeastern Europe. *Economic Journal*, 53, 202–211.

Rowley, R., Bichler, S., and Nitzan, J. (1988). Some Aspects of Aggregate Concentration in the Israeli Economy, 1964-1986. *Working Papers*. Department of Economics, McGill University, No. 7/88.

Schechter, A. (2012). *Rothschild: Chronicle of a Protest*. Tel Aviv: Hakibbutz Hameuchad Publishing House. [In Hebrew]

Stigler, G. (1971). The Theory of Economic Regulation. *Bell Journal of Economics and Management Science*, 2(1), 3–21.

Wagner, J. (2012). The German Manufacturing Sector is a Granular Economy. *Applied Economics Letters*, 19(17), 1663–1665.

White, L. J. (1981). What Has Been Happening to Aggregate Concentration in the United States? *Journal of Industrial Economics*, 29, 223–230.

(2002). Trends in Aggregate Concentration in the United States, *Journal of Economic Perspectives*, 16(Fall), 137–160.

White, L. J., and Yang, J. (2017). What Has been Happening to Aggregate Concentration in the U.S. Economy in the 21st Century? Working Paper.

Appendix 9.A Index of Economic Sectors

Industry code	Industry
A1	Field crops
A2	Livestock
A3	Fruit and vegetables
A4	Growing of flowers, seeds, and nursery products
A5	Other agriculture industries
A6	Other mining and quarrying products
A7	Meat, fish, fruit and vegetables, dairy products, and oil
A8	Other food products and tobacco products
B01	Textiles
B02	Clothing
B03	Manufacture of footwear, leather, and leather products
B04	Wood and wood products (excl. furniture)
B05	Paper and cardboard, and products thereof
B06	Printing and publishing
B07	Refined petroleum and its products, extraction of crude petroleum and natural gas, and mining of hard coal
B08	Industrial chemicals, fertilizers, pesticides, and disinfectants
B09	Petrochemicals and synthetic fibers
B10	Pharmaceutical products for human and veterinary uses
B11	Other chemicals
B12	Plastic products
B13	Rubber products, tyres, and tubes
B14	Mineral non-metallic products
B15	Basic metal
B17	Metal products
B18	Machinery and equipment, manufacture of office machinery and computers

(cont.)

Industry code	Industry
B19	Electric motors and electric distribution apparatus
B20	Electronic components and electronic communication equipment
B21	Medical and scientific equipment
B22	Manufacture of cars and motorcycles, and parts thereof
B23	Building and maintenance of ships, aircraft, and other transport equipment
B24	Furniture
B25	Diamonds
B26	Jewellery, and goldsmith's and silversmith's articles
B27	Medical equipment and disposable and other medical articles
B28	Miscellaneous manufacturing
C1	Electricity
C2	Water
D2	Other construction
E1	Wholesale and retail trade
E2	Maintenance and repair of motor vehicles
F1	Accommodation services and restaurants
G1	Land transport
G2	Water and air transport
G4	Port and airport services
G5	Other transport services (incl. storage)
G6	Post services and courier activities, telecommunications activities
H1	Banking and other financial institutions
H2	Insurance and social insurance funds
I1	Real-estate activities
I2	Ownership of dwellings
I3	Renting of machinery and equipment, and of personal and household goods
I4	Computerized data processing and research
I5	Other business services
J1	Public administration
K1	Education services (nonprofit institutions, general government and commercial)
L1	Health services (nonprofit institutions, general government and commercial)

(***cont.***)

Industry code	Industry
L2	Welfare and social work (nonprofit institutions, general government and commercial)
MN1	Recreational, cultural, and sporting activities
MN2	Sanitation services; other personal services and services for households by domestic personnel
MN3	Social and comm unity institutions, and religious services

10 | *Taxation of Natural Resources*

EYTAN SHESHINSKI

10.1 Introduction

The discussion of the taxation of natural resources in this chapter will focus primarily on natural gas, oil, and minerals (such as potash). The taxation of natural resources constitutes a major source of revenue for many governments, in both developed and undeveloped countries. For example, it accounts for 80 percent and upward of the government's revenues in Middle East countries (the Gulf states, Iraq, and Iran) and 35 percent of government revenues in Equatorial Guinea, Brunei, and Botswana come from minerals, while the figure for Bolivia, Congo, Indonesia, and Russia is about 25 percent (according to IMF reports). The level of revenues is somewhat lower though still significant in a number of OECD countries, such as Australia, Canada, Norway, and Britain. The taxation of natural resources is therefore an important issue in many countries.

The taxation of revenue from natural resources takes various forms, including royalties, taxation of excess profit (rent), and production by companies under government ownership, including companies in which the State partners with private capital. This taxation is, of course, in addition to corporate income tax, which is imposed on all companies in the economy.

A comprehensive survey of the taxation of natural resources can be found in *The Taxation of Petroleum and Minerals: Principles, Problems and Practice (2010)*. The analysis that follows will focus on royalties and taxation of excess profit (rent), in view of their widespread use. There is a clear conceptual distinction between these two types of taxation, in that the base for the taxation of rent is profits (revenue less costs), while that for the calculation of royalties is revenue (or quantity), with no consideration of costs. This is not an unambiguous distinction, as it may appear at first glance, since the definition of rent sometimes does not include all costs (see below) and the definition of royalties sometimes includes part of the costs (Boadway and Keen, 2010).

The final section of the chapter will deal with the uses of government revenue from natural resources and specifically will relate to the following two questions: (a) Should these revenues be used to finance the current budget or should they be saved for future generations which have a justified "claim" on the ownership of these resources? and (b) To what extent do the revenues from natural resources lead to rent-seeking, corruption, and impaired governance, as a result of the fact that with respect to natural resources the government is not dependent on the activity of the rest of the economy.

Natural resources constitute an example – almost the only one of its type – of tax revenues that do not create distortions in economic activity, since the supply of natural resources is fixed and cannot be moved to other countries. This is the reason that the profit from natural resources can be defined as economic rent, namely income that is not affected by demand and supply considerations, or in economic terms, income that has no marginal effects.

Another important aspect of revenue from natural resources is the long time period until production, starting from the exploration stage (locating the natural resources), continuing with the drilling stage and the building of production facilities (rigs and accompanying facilities in the case of offshore resources), and ending with the production and marketing stage. The long lead time introduces the issue of uncertainty (primarily during the stage of exploration but also subsequently), in view of the high volatility in the markets for natural gas, oil, and minerals. The taxation regime must take this uncertainty into account, which sometime means recognizing losses (from unsuccessful exploration) and the imputation of interest during the period between the investment and the generation of revenue. These factors need to be considered when defining the tax base, which will determine the level of economic rent; otherwise – and in contrast to the definition of rent – private companies, which invest their capital in natural resources, may decide to invest elsewhere.

10.2 Legal Aspects of Natural Resource Ownership

In all countries, except for the United States, the legal ownership of natural resources is in the hands of the state. Private ownership of land does not include natural resources found underneath it. Various laws determine the rules according to which the state compensates owners of private land in order to produce revenue from the natural resources located on the land. The United States is an exception in that a private owner of land on which a natural resource is discovered is also the owner of that natural resource. Offshore natural resources come under the Law of the Sea Treaty of 1982, a UN treaty that defines three types of maritime zones:

a. Territorial waters: the zone up to 12 miles from the coastal baselines, which is under the full sovereignty of the coastal state.
b. Contiguous Zone: the area of up to 24 miles from the baselines, over which the country has partial ownership. It has the right to grant exclusive rights to produce revenue from the natural resources in this zone.
c. Exclusive Economic Zone: this area can range up to 200 miles from the baselines, when the baselines of the countries on the other side of the sea are more than 400 miles away from the country's baselines. In this zone, the country has sovereign rights over exploration and exploitation of natural resources.
d. Continental Shelf**: The definition of the continental shelf applies up to a certain depth but not more than 350 miles from the baselines. The country has exclusive sovereign rights over the exploration and exploitation of natural resources also in this zone.

In the case of Israel, the definitions are relevant in the case of Cyprus (which is located more than 200 miles from Israel). Israel signed an agreement with Cyprus in 2010 defining the Exclusive Economic Zones between the two, and it also declared the economic demarcation line between Israel and Lebanon, which is disputed by Lebanon. The UN, which is responsible for the demarcation line, apparently supports the position adopted by Israel. It is possible therefore to conclude that there is no significant problem in international law with respect to the gas fields located in Israel's territory (primarily Tamar and Leviathan).

10.3 Background: The Gas Discoveries in Israel

Large natural gas fields were recently discovered in Israel's economic waters in the Mediterranean, and it is reasonable to assume that there are additional fields of unknown size to be discovered. The exploration for oil and gas on dry land in Israel has not had much success (in 1955 the Heletz field produced 17 million barrels of oil and was then closed). The exploration situation began to change in 1999 when a number of offshore gas fields were discovered: Mari B opposite Ashkelon with about 30 BCM (billions of cubic meters); Tamar which is about 90 kilometers from Haifa and which contains about 250 BCM; and Leviathan which was discovered in 2010 and which contains about 550 BCM, more than twice the size of Tamar. The total size of the other proven fields, such as Karish and Tanin which are near Tamar, is about 100 BCM (this estimate was recently doubled). Therefore, Israel has total proven fields of about 1,000 BCM. According to the American Geological Institute, the reserves in the Eastern Mediterranean basin are about 3,400 BCM, and it is estimated that two-thirds of that is in Israel's territory. There have also been significant discoveries in Egypt and Cyprus of about 1,000 BCM and about 500 BCM, respectively. The strategic significance of these discoveries will be discussed below.

10.4 Regulation of the Sector's Activity

Private Israeli and international companies are carrying out the exploration activities and the development of Israel's gas fields, which are regulated by the Petroleum Law of 1952. Private entities in this domain possess three types of rights: pre-permits, licenses, and leases. The permit is given for a period of eighteen months and allows the permit holder to carry out surveys. A license is given for three additional years and allows the holder to carry out tests and seismic surveys, and provides him with the exclusive right to carry out test drillings. When a commercial field is discovered, the license holder receives a special lease for the production of natural gas or oil in the area defined by the license. The leasing period is thirty years with the possibility of a twenty-year extension.

10.5 The Fiscal Framework Prior to 2011

The Petroleum Law (paragraph 32) establishes an obligation to pay royalties on the production of oil (or gas) at the rate of 12.5 percent of the market value of the oil (or gas) at the wellhead. The law allows the deduction of costs of transporting the natural resources from the wellhead to the point of sale. With respect to natural gas, there is a lack of clarity in the law with respect to the expenses that can be deducted, and therefore it was decided that 70 percent of the cost of building the rig and the transmission pipeline would be recognized. Additional tax breaks were provided, the main one being the depletion allowance. As in the case of the depreciation of fixed assets for production, the depletion allowance is a deduction for the decrease in the stock of the natural resource and for which a deduction of up to 27.5 percent of gross annual income was permitted. As pointed out by the Sheshinski Committee (see below), the result of the deduction was that none of the gas fields (in comparison to commercial companies in other industries) paid any tax on the exploitation of a natural resource owned by the public. The first recommendation of the Sheshinski Committee was to cancel the depletion allowance.

A tax regime based on royalties does not distinguish between fields according to level of profitability, and more importantly the taxation of royalties is *regressive*. In other words, the revenues of the government as a percentage of the profit decreases as profit increases, a clearly undesirable characteristic. A comparison of the fiscal regimes applied to natural resources was carried out according to Government Take (GT), an indicator of the State's revenues from all of the fiscal instruments, i.e., corporate income tax, royalties, a designated profit tax, etc., relative to profit.

Figure 10.1 presents GT for a wide variety of countries with oil and gas activity. As of 2010, when the Sheshinski Committee was established, GT in Israel was the lowest among all the countries.

The global average of the GT index is estimated to be between 67 and 72 percent and, as mentioned, Israel had the lowest GT during that period, which ranged from 24 to 31 percent. It is worth noting that in the case of the United States, unlike the other countries, a significant component of the payment to the government is made on the granting of a concession (known as the signature bonus), which brings the GT up to 70 percent or even higher. The question has often arisen as to which countries Israel should be compared to, and it has been claimed that the developed countries within the OECD should be the benchmark for this purpose (see Table 10.1).

Table 10.1 shows that the average GT in the OECD ranges from 55–58 percent. In countries with 650 BCM or more – the relevant benchmark for Israel – the GT ranges from 61–65 percent. Therefore, prior to Sheshinski Law I, Israel was clearly an outlier, with the public receiving the lowest share of natural gas profits among comparable countries.

Table 10.1 *Government Take in the*
OECD countries (%)

	Government take
75–77	Norway
62–66	Holland
62–64	Denmark
60–63	Canada
56–58	Australia
45–50	Britain
47–50	US (not including signature bonus)

Source: Ministry of Finance (2011)

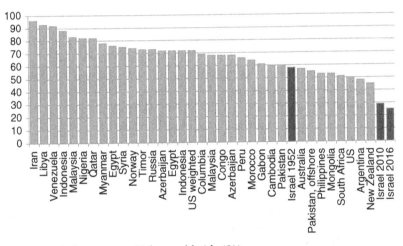

Figure 10.1 Government Take worldwide (%).
Source: *Oil and Gas Journal*, April 18, 2005.

10.6 Sheshinski Law I

10.6.1 Sheshinski Committee I

In 2010, the Minister of Finance appointed the Committee to Examine Fiscal Policy regarding Oil and Gas in Israel (Sheshinski Committee I). The Committee worked for eighteenth months during which it was presented with economic and legal briefs, and in 2011 it published its final report – Conclusions of the Committee to Examine Fiscal Policy regarding Oil and Gas in Israel. In 2011, the government adopted its conclusions. An outcome of the Committee's activity was the text of a law (which became known as Sheshinski Law I) that would replace most parts of the 1952 Oil and Gas Law. The core of the law was the adoption of a designated progressive levy on oil and gas profits. The law left the rate of royalties unchanged at 12.5 percent, despite the disincentive effects of royalties – which are based on income – on the volume of production, the pace of production, and the number of companies. The positive elements of royalties are the stability in amount collected, the early timing of collection, and the difficulty in exploiting accounting manipulations, since such manipulations are for the most part related to costs (timing, inflation of costs, etc.). (The depletion allowance was, as mentioned, cancelled immediately.) The mix of royalties and an excess profit tax was considered to be optimal by the Committee and the IMF supported this conclusion (see the appendix to the Committee's report).

An efficient fiscal regime is based on taxing economic rent, i.e., excess profits, which reflects the non-costing of the natural resource which is granted by concession to a private company. Economic rent is defined as the profit beyond the norm in the industry, which is defined (and measured according to the CAPM – the Capital Asset Pricing Model) as the profit threshold that would induce a developer – whose investments are optimally diversified – to invest in the industry. The most important parameter in this context is the correlation between revenues in the industry and those in the market as a whole, since that is the measure of investment risk (known as the β-coefficient in the literature).

There are a number of mechanisms that can be used to impose a tax on rent (including the method of tenders and the signature bonus, which is used in the United States), such as rate of return (RoR) or the R-factor mechanism, which was found to be suited to conditions in Israel. According to this method, the levy is imposed only after the investment in exploration, development, and construction has been fully returned, with an additional return to compensate for the risk of the developer and the necessary financing costs. As a result, the levy will not be collected during the initial years of production, but rather only after the cost of the investment has been recouped. The rate of the levy is relatively low at the start and rises with the level of profitability.

According to this method, projects with relatively low levels of profitability do not pay the maximum rate and perhaps do not pay the levy at all. Since this is a tax on profits whose rate varies with level of profitability, it has built-in flexibility, since changes and revisions will not be required as a result of changing economic conditions, such as a shift in the price of the product.

A levy on excess profit of the R-factor type is calculated on a cash basis, or in other words, revenues and costs for which there is cash flow in the current year. Thus, for example, investments are fully depreciated in the year of execution, rather than over a number of years. The index of the levy reflects the ratio of the accumulated revenue flow to the investment carried out to establish the project, measured on a cash basis, along with a risk coefficient for the risk implicit in exploration costs and the recognition of standard costs incurred during the period of construction.

The precise equation is as follows:

$$R_t = \frac{\sum_{i=T_2}^{t}(income_i - opex_i - royalties_i - I_i^{other}) - \sum_{i=T_2}^{t-1}(levy_i)}{2 * I^{exploration} + \sum_{j=T_1}^{T_2}(I_j^{developement})(1 + r_j^{norm})^{T_2-j}}$$

R_t – levy index for period t
T_0 – year of project start
T_1 – year of discovery
T_2 – year of production start
$opex$ – operating expenses
$levy$ – levy on oil and gas profits
$I^{exploration}$ – exploration costs until the discovery
$I^{development}$ – development and construction costs
I^{other} – investment during production
R^{norm} – normal interest rate

The investment in exploration, development, and construction, which is usually prior to commercial production from the field, appears in the denominator of the index. The investment carried out during production is weighted in the numerator. In order to also encourage investment that will increase the efficiency of production from already-producing fields, that investment is depreciated over the period from

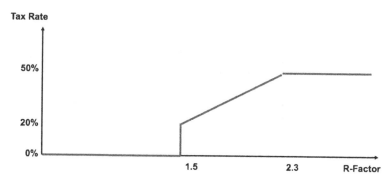

Figure 10.2 Tax rate and R-factor.
Source: Ministry of Finance (2011)

the base of the levy and from the levy index immediately in the year of the investment, rather than over a number of years, according to a rate of depreciation, just as capital investment is treated in the Income Tax Ordinance. In view of the aforementioned, the denominator of the levy index is "locked," i.e., not subject to change after the initial investment in exploration, development, and construction is completed.

The rate of the levy rises linearly, from a minimum of 20 percent to a maximum of 50 percent. Figure 10.2 graphically presents the rates of the levy as set by the Committee.

The levy formula is as follows:

Value of R-factor index	Rate of levy (H)
R<1.5	H=0%
1.5<R<2.3	H=20%+(R-1.5)/0.8*30%
R>2.3	H=50%

10.6.2 Summary of the Economic Effects of Sheshinski Law I: The Fiscal Mix

Figure 10.3 shows the correlation between level of profitability and the rate of taxation of profits for the two fiscal instruments: royalties and

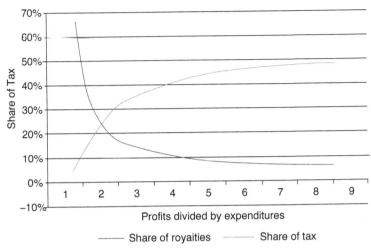

Figure 10.3 The association between tax and royalties' share in revenue and revenue, expenditure ratio.
Source: Ministry of Finance (2011)

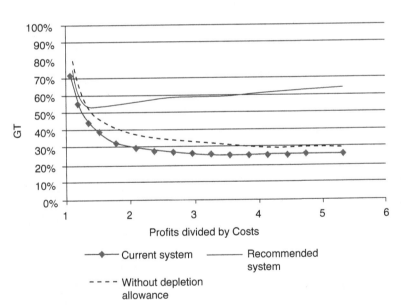

Figure 10.4 The influence of the fiscal system on GT.
Source: Ministry of Finance (2011)

a levy on excess profits. The graph clearly shows the contrast between the regressivity of royalties and the progressivity of the levy. Since the levy postpones the receipt of revenues by the government, royalties at a low rate constitute a balancing instrument that promises revenues to the State already at the start of production.

Figure 10.4 contrasts the regressivity of the fiscal system prior to 2011 with its progressivity after 2011.

10.7 Sheshinski Law II

10.7.1 Sheshinski Committee II

Another committee was created in 2013 to examine the taxation of other natural resources (known as Sheshinski Committee II). The Committee found that the situation of other natural resources was similar to that of oil and gas prior to Sheshinski Committee I, namely a regressive fiscal framework based only on royalties which generates higher rates of profit than those normally observed in other industries.

As in the case of oil and gas, it was found that the GT for other natural resources exploited by private entities was much lower than in many other countries. The recommendations of Sheshinski Committee II, which were published in 2014, included a levy similar to the one imposed in the oil and gas industry. The Knesset accepted the Committee's recommendations in full (Sheshinski Law II). The Committee primarily discussed quarry products for which the rate of royalties ranged from 2 to 10 percent of the value of the product. The Committee recommended a uniform rate of royalties (5 percent) and that royalties would not be the main component of the tax regime.

As in the case of the law imposed on the oil and gas sector, it was decided to impose an excess profit tax on the profits from Dead Sea minerals, and in particular potash, bromine, and magnesium, as well as phosphates. Table 10.2 presents the tax rates based on the calculations of regular profit rates that are applicable in this industry. The tax base is the company's operating profit, as it appears in the profit and loss statement, less financing costs in the amount of 5 percent of the company's working capital and less an amount to reflect the yield on the

Table 10.2 *Tax rate on calculated profit*

Annual return[1]	Tax on excess profit[2]
R<14%	$0\% = T_0$
14%≤R<20%	$25\% = T^1$
R≥20%	$42\% = T^2$

[1] R = annual operating profit after modifications for tax purposes and after the return on working capital, but before the deduction of the return on the remaining cost of the fixed assets divided by the remaining depreciated cost of the fixed assets in the books.
[2] T = tax rate.

depreciated cost of the fixed assets used in the production of the quarry product and its sale.

It should be mentioned that in contrast to the oil and gas industry which is relatively new, Dead Sea production started sixty or more years ago and involved a major amount of investment in fixed assets. Therefore, the Committee concluded that a fairly high return should be allowed in this industry.

10.7.2 Tax Boundaries on Natural Resources

The subject of products based on Dead Sea resources brought up a problem with broader implications. Thus, some natural resources, such as bromine, are used as an input in production, where the raw bromine is added to other inputs. Thus, a natural resource levy is meant to be imposed on the raw bromine inputs and therefore the question arises of how to value this input. (Most of the bromine is "sold" by the potash company to the bromine company, but the two companies have the same ownership and therefore a problem of transfer pricing arises, in the absence of an objective index for the price of raw bromine.) The law created a mechanism to determine rules for the allocation of costs between the various sectors and resources.

There was no excess profit tax imposed on quarry products, since the industry is highly concentrated (two companies supply about 80 percent of the total quantity) and competition needed to be dealt with first. As a result, royalties of only 5 percent are currently imposed on the industry.

10.7.3 *Summary of the Economic Effects of Sheshinski Law II: The Fiscal Mix*

As in the case of Sheshinski Law I, Sheshinski Law II for the taxation of natural resources being exploited by private entities was enacted in 2014. Until that time, royalties of 2 to 5 percent were imposed on the various quarry products. The Committee decided to impose a uniform royalty rate of 5 percent on all quarry products. A special excess profit tax was imposed on all the products produced by the Israel Corporation from the Dead Sea and its environs (potash, bromine, magnesium and phosphates). Although the tax was similar to that imposed on oil and gas, there were several important differences. The cash flow model applied to oil and gas – a new industry without a long history of investment in fixed assets – had to be modified, primarily in the case of the Dead Sea Works, which has been producing potash for a number of decades and had made additional investments in order to produce the potash. It was therefore decided to deduct an amount that would represent a return of 14 percent on the remaining cost of the fixed assets used in production. Thus, it was ensured that the tax is imposed only on excess profit. Using the CAPM in order to ensure a fair return, it was decided to introduce the tax brackets which appear in Table 10.2. As mentioned, the tax on each resource was calculated separately. The goal, among others, was to overcome the above-mentioned problem of transfer pricing. The most profitable quarry product is potash as can be seen in Figure 10.5.

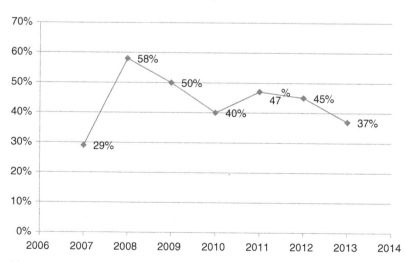

Figure 10.5 Potash operating profit, 2007–2013 (%)

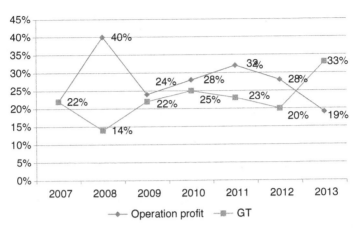

Figure 10.6 The GT rate, 2007–2013

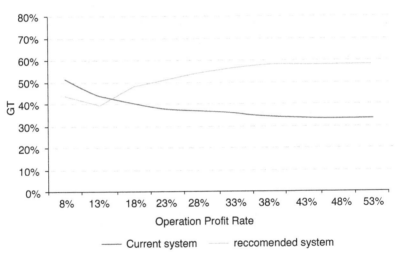

Figure 10.7 The influence of the suggested model on GT

Figure 10.6 shows that prior to Sheshinski Law II GT was also low and the average during the previous seven years was only 23 percent.

As reflected in Figure 10.7, it is expected that after Sheshinski Law II goes into effect GT will rise to about 60 percent, the average rate in the OECD countries.

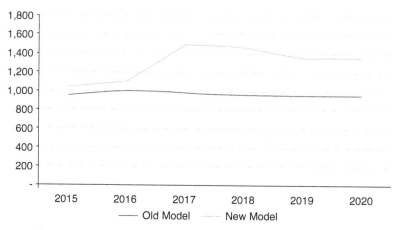

Figure 10.8 The influence of the suggested model on state income (NIS millions)

Figure 10.8 presents the expected effect of the model on government revenues, which are expected to grow by about NIS 400 million annually.

10.8 The End of the Concession Period for Dead Sea Production

The concession for producing Dead Sea quarry products will expire in 2030. At that time, the State, in accordance with paragraph 24 of the Dead Sea Works Assets Law, must pay the value of the tangible assets to the company if the concession is awarded to a different company. The uncertainty surrounding the end of the concession period is a recognized phenomenon in other domains (such as build-operate-transfer [BOT] for toll roads in South America) and already today constitutes a disincentive to invest. Years prior to the end of the concession, the Sheshinski Committee recommended the creation of a committee that would examine the possibilities for the concession to be awarded in 2030. Such a committee was indeed established and it is currently holding discussions. It is worth mentioning that if there is a tender to choose the next concessionaire, the Israel Corporation will have first right of refusal and therefore there is little chance of a multi-participant open tender.

10.9 Israel's Wealth Fund

It is worthwhile at this point to mention a paradox known as the resource curse, in which countries rich in natural resources, such as oil and gas, grow at a *slower* rate than countries with limited natural resources. Figure 10.9 shows the negative relationship between the rate of growth in GNP and the share of natural resources production in GNP. This is generally explained by the fact that natural resources do not have to be manufactured and therefore there is no incentive for economic efficiency. In other words, when state revenues are largely disconnected from economic activity, the government has no incentive to increase the efficiency of the system.

Furthermore, the existence of natural resources leads to corruption due to rent-seeking. The fact that the resources are exhaustible and are subject to high price volatility forces a rational government to "smooth" its structural expenditure according to the flow of revenue from the natural resources. Figure 10.10 clearly shows the difference in

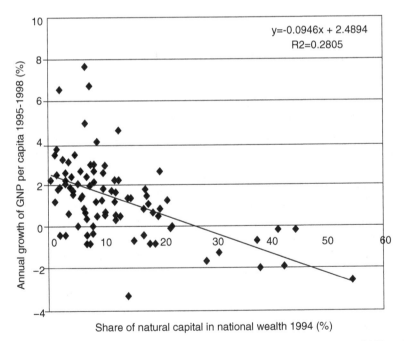

Figure 10.9 The relationship between annual growth in per capita GNP and the share of natural resources production in GNP

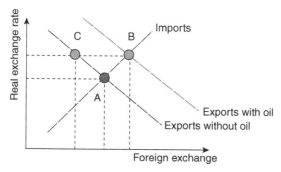

Figure 10.10 The relationship between foreign currency and the local currency in the case of exports with oil and exports without oil.
Source: Humphreys et al. (2007)

behavior between governments with strong governance and those with weak governance.

Humphreys et al. (2007) bring out (ch. 8) that in countries with strong checks and balances, government consumption bears little relationship to oil sales volatility. However, there is a strong effect in countries with worse governing systems. The elasticity of the change in government consumption with respect to the change in oil sale is 0.92 in countries with few checks and balances, meaning that for a doubling of oil sales, government consumption in such countries increases on average by 9.2 percent. This implies, they state, "a high rate of pass-through of oil revenue changes."

Another phenomenon attributed to natural resources is known among economists as the Dutch Disease. Following the discovery of oil fields in the North Sea, the export of oil from Holland and Norway led to an inflow of dollars into those countries and as a result the appreciation of their currencies. The appreciation in turn harmed the traditional export industries and led to a general slowdown in the economies of these countries.

In order to overcome the resource curse and the Dutch Disease, a number of countries have established a Natural Resource Fund (NRF) into which the receipts from the export of natural resources are deposited. These funds are invested abroad in order to "smooth" the revenues from the funds over a long period. There are currently about ten NRFs (the largest are those of Norway and Qatar, each of which has a value of about $1 trillion).

As part of Sheshinski Law I, Israel established a wealth fund in which the receipts from the special levy on oil and gas are deposited. When Sheshinski Law II went into effect, the receipts from the levy on the Dead Sea Works were also deposited there. The central bank will manage the investment of the fund (as in the case of Norway). The managers of the fund will define its goals, although the law specifies that the targets of investment are to be long-term projects in education and special defense expenditures related to the protection of the gas fields. The fund will begin receiving revenue in 2019. The law states that during the first five years of its existence the fund will transfer 3 percent of its assets each year (on the assumption that that will be its rate of return) and in subsequent years according to the decision of the fund's managers. Figure 10.11 presents the expected annual revenues to be deposited into the Wealth Fund during the period 2018–40.

Figure 10.12 presents the expected returns on the assets in the Wealth Fund during the period 2019–2040. Although the revenues from the natural resources in Israel do not approach those in Norway (about 2 percent of GNP later on in the decade), decision-makers should hold a comprehensive discussion of how the fund will be used. Thus, for example, the fund could be spent on a worthwhile long-term goal, such as the strengthening and expansion of the pension and long-term care systems in Israel.

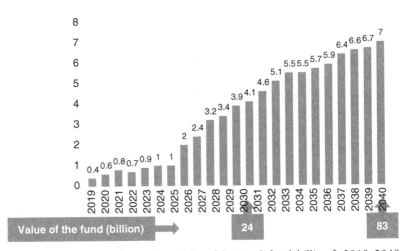

Figure 10.11 Expected annual royalties of the Israeli fund, billion $, 2018–2040

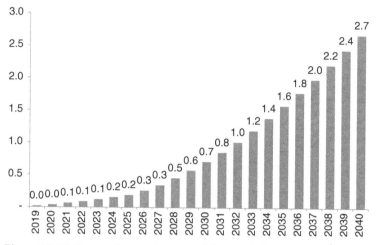

Figure 10.12 Expected annual return of the Israeli fund, Billion $, 2018–2040

References

Boadway, R., and M. Keen. (2015). Rent Taxes and Royalties in Designing Fiscal Regimes for Nonrenewable Resources. In R. Halvorsen and D. Layton (eds.), *Handbook on the Economics of Natural Resources.* Cheltenham: Edwin Elgar, 97–139.

Dead Sea Concession Law, 5721. 1961. [Hebrew]

Humphreys, M., Sachs, J. D., and Stiglitz, J. E., eds. (2007). *Escaping the Resource Curse.* New York: Columbia University Press.

Ministry of Finance (2011). *Conclusions of the Committee to Examine Fiscal Policy regarding Oil and Gas Resources in Israel.* Jerusalem. [Hebrew]

(2014). *Conclusions of the Committee to Examine Fiscal Policy on the Share of the State in Exchange for the Exploitation of National Natural Resources by Private Entities.* Jerusalem. [Hebrew]

PART III

Investment in Human Capital, Productivity, and Inequality

11 | *Why Is Labor Productivity in Israel So Low?*[*]

MOSHE HAZAN AND SHAY TSUR

11.1 Introduction

This chapter reviews the development of output in Israel between 1995 and 2014. Its main goal is to understand why gaps in output per capita and output per worker, "labor productivity," have not narrowed over the past twenty years and have remained substantial, relative to developed economies. The empirical approach is to compare Israel to a set of countries that Israel could resemble, namely small, open, developed economies. Based on this criterion and data availability, we chose Austria, Denmark, the Netherlands, Finland, and Sweden. Henceforth we refer to these countries as the "comparison group."

Below we begin with the main developments over the relevant period. In section 11.2 we review the data. We begin with the development of output per capita and output per worker in Israel relative to the United States and the comparison group. We then look at the inputs, namely, the labor force, years of schooling of the adult population, and investment in physical capital. Finally we review the development of total factor productivity. Section 11.3 presents the development accounting exercise. The main innovation is the use of the Survey of Adult Skills, "PIAAC," to measure human capital, in addition to years of schooling. Our findings show that while Israel is perceived as a high human-capital country, even relative to other developed economies, it has large disadvantages in terms of literacy and numeracy skills. This implies that when we estimate human capital including these skills, gaps in accumulated factors explain 76 percent of the gap in output per worker, while total factor productivity (henceforth: TFP) explains the

[*] We thank Eyal Argov, Avi Ben Bassat, Reuben Gronau, Zvi Hercowitz, and Asaf Zussman for helpful comments and Ehud Cohen and Inbaal Maayan for excellent research assistance.

remaining 24 percent.[1] This is against a split of 60–40, when only years of schooling are used as input into the human capital production function. In section 11.4 we estimate physical capital per worker at the industry level for both Israel and the comparison group. We show that industrial composition cannot explain any of the large gap in physical capital per worker. When we distinguish between equipment and machinery and nonresidential buildings, we find that the stock of equipment in Israel is about 50 percent of that of the comparison group, while the stock of nonresidential buildings is about 60 percent of that of the comparison group. In section 11.5 we estimate human capital per worker at the industry level for both Israel and the comparison group. The main finding in the section is that the industrial composition contributes 4 percent to the stock of human capital. That is, had the industrial composition of Israel been the same as in the comparison group, the stock of human capital in Israel would have been 4 percent lower. In section 11.6 we extend our sample to include all OECD countries for which we can estimate physical capital and human capital per worker at the industry level. We end up with thirteen countries. We show that there is a strong positive correlation between physical capital and human capital per worker. Our estimates suggest that if Israel closes its gap in numeracy skills, it will lead to an increase of its physical capital per worker by nearly 9 percent and will close about one-fifth of the gap in output per worker, relative to the comparison group.

11.1.1 Main Events During the Reviewed Period

Several events that took place either just before 1995 or during the period 1995–2014 have had profound effects on the development of output per worker. These include (i) the mass migration from the former Soviet Union (henceforth: FSU) to Israel, (ii) the unilateral reduction in trade barriers vis-à-vis developing countries, (iii) the large expansion of higher education in the form of public colleges, and (iv) the process of reducing the size of the public sector.

---

[1] These results are obtained when we use only numeracy, rather than numeracy and literacy skills. Since Israel's achievements in literacy and numeracy, relative to to the comparison group are remarkably similar, the results are very almost identical when using both skills. For brevity we do not present them in the paper.

During the 1990s, about 1 million immigrants arrived in Israel from the FSU. On the eve of this large migration inflow, the Israeli population was about 4.8 million. The absorption of this flow of migrants required large investments in infrastructure, in housing, and in the stock of productive capital that substantially contributed to the growth process in the 1990s. Additionally, the migrants came with high human capital. About 60 percent of the adult migrants had an academic education, and a quarter of them had advanced degrees. Nevertheless, some of this education was useless in Israel. Paserman (2013) found that initially the immigrants were employed in unskilled jobs and occupations, and only after a few years did some of them settle into technological occupations and begin to contribute to labor productivity. Overall, however, Paserman concluded that immigration from the FSU had little effect on labor productivity in Israel.

Another important development that took place during the 1990s was the unilateral reduction in trade barriers vis-à-vis developing countries. As Gabai and Rob (2002) wrote, only during these years did free trade policy gain the support of the political leadership in Israel. This process dramatically increased the exposure of Israel to international trade and contributed to large increases in imports that competed with local traditional, low-productivity industries. This led to a decline in employment in traditional industries, and many of the workers in these industries found themselves in low-paid jobs in trade and services. Brand and Regev (2015b) found that this process contributed to the polarization in output per worker between trade and services industries with low labor productivity and tradeable sectors with high productivity. Nevertheless, Brand and Regev (2015a) showed that the process also led to an increase in labor productivity in traditional sectors that had to cope with international competition and focus in more intensive human capital products for which they had comparative advantage.

The 1990s saw a large expansion of public colleges which were established in response to the growing size of the population and governmental effort to increase the supply of higher education, on the one hand, and keep the quality of the universities, especially of the elite ones, on the other hand (Volansky, 2005). The fraction of students enrolled in these colleges as a share of total students in the higher education system grew from 12 percent in 1995 to 50 percent by 2014. At the late stages of this process, the fraction of individuals who receive at least a bachelor's degree out of the population aged

25–34 was close to 50 percent, similar to the fraction of those obtaining matriculation certificate ("Bagrut"). The large expansion of colleges triggered research on whether the returns to a college degree is similar to that of a university degree. Achdut et al. (2018) showed that the annual wage of graduates of universities was 10 to 20 percent higher than the wage of public college graduates. Consistent with that, Lipiner et al. (2019) showed that among people with a bachelor's degree, those who are most likely to be employed in jobs but are educated beyond what is necessary for their job are graduates of public colleges. In summary, while the expansion of colleges contributed to the increase in the proportion of the population with an academic degree, the rate at which the quality of human capital increased is not entirely clear These question marks highlight the importance of measuring human capital not only by average years of schooling but also by measures of the quality of education. We elaborate on that in section 11.3.

Starting in 2002, the government began a process of reducing the size of the public sector. This policy renewed the passage of the process that had started in the 1980s as part of the Stabilization Program (Strawczynski and Zeira, 2002). This policy included a drastic reduction in direct taxes, on the one hand, and a reduction in defense expenditure, interest rate payments, and in government transfers on the other hand (Dahan and Hazan, 2014). In addition to the immediate need to reduce the governmental deficit, the declared objective of the policy was to foster the private sector of the economy and increase the participation rates among segments of the population that rely on transfers. Flug and Strawczynski (2007) found that about one-third of the transition to growth in 2004 can be attributed to changes in economic policy, such as the tax cuts. Using a calibrated representative model, Hercowitz and Lifschitz (2015) found that the tax cuts contributed significantly to the increase in labor force participation and output growth. However, using administrative data, Igdalov et al. (2017) found that tax cuts had little effect on labor force participation. An alternative explanation is that labor supply has been increasing in the intensive, rather than the extensive margin, though this hypothesis has not received serious attention. In section 11.2 we elaborate on the growth in labor force participation rates (henceforth: LFPR).

11.2 Overview of the Data

11.2.1 *Output per Worker and Output per Capita*

Israel's GDP per capita in 2014 was $31,250 (in 2011 Dollars). This is compared to $51,600 in the United States and $44,900 in the comparison group. On relative terms, Israel's GDP per capita was 60 percent that of the United States and 70 percent that of the comparison group. The gap in GDP per capita reflects the gap in GDP per worker, given the similarity in employment rates in 2014 among Israel, the United States, and the comparison group. Figure 11.1 displays the dynamics of output per capita and output per worker in Israel, relative to the United States and to the comparison group over the period 1995–2014. The figure shows that Israel has not closed any of the gaps over these two decades, though the dynamics have not been monotone. The decline in the early period is mainly due to the decline in GDP per worker, relative to the comparison group and the United States, while the later increase is due to an increase in employment rates. Our main conclusion is that over

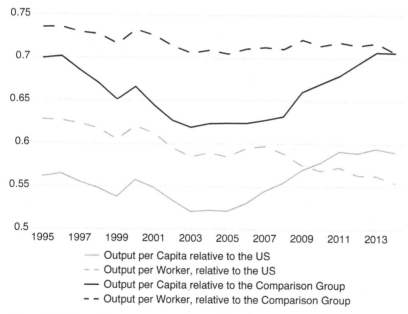

Figure 11.1 Israel's output per capita and output per worker relative to the United States and to the comparison group

these two decades, Israel has not been able to close the gap in terms of income per capita and that gaps in output per worker have mildly increased.

11.2.2 The Labor Force

The labor force has increased at an annual rate of 2.5 percent, faster than the growth of the population aged 15 and above or of prime working age, 25–64, which were 2.1 percent and 2.2 percent, respectively. With the end of the large inflow of immigrants from the FSU in the early 2000s, the growth rate of the working age population subsided, but the growth rate of the labor force declined only slightly due to an acceleration in labor force participation rates (Figure 11.2). Between 1995 and 2003, participation rates increased by 1.8 percentage points, whereas during the period 2003–2011, it increased by 2.9 percentage points.[2] The increase in LFPR is not unique to these two decades and reflects a long process of increasing female LFPR, similar to a worldwide trend, whereby women's participation rates became similar to men's (Goldin, 2006; Blau and Kahn, 2013). The acceleration during the 2000s reflects the cessation of the decline of men's participation rates accompanied with a secular acceleration in women's LFPR. This is not trivial, since the typical dynamics of female LFPR is an S-shape: When LFPR are low, they increase very slowly but at an accelerating rate. However, at a relatively high rate, the growth rate of LFPR decelerates till it stays relatively constant (Hazan and Maoz, 2002; Fernandez, 2013). There are, potentially, three factors that can account for this: the rise in the level of education, the cut in welfare payments, and the rise in the mandatory age of retirement for both men and women.[3]

---

[2] In 2012, the Central Bureau of Statistics changed its Labor Survey and increased its frequency from quarterly to monthly. Additionally, the definition of participation in the labor force has changed, with the main change being a switch from "civilian workforce" to "workforce," which includes military service. Therefore, one should be very cautious about interpreting changes in labor force participation for the periods up to 2011 and from 2012. For more information, seewww.cbs.gov.il/he/publications/doclib/2019/lfs17_1746/intro4 a_e.pdf.

[3] Hercowitz and Lifschitz (2015) suggest an alternative view, arguing that the increase in LFPR is the outcome of a process of cuts to the marginal tax on labor, which occurred between 2003 and 2012.

Percent

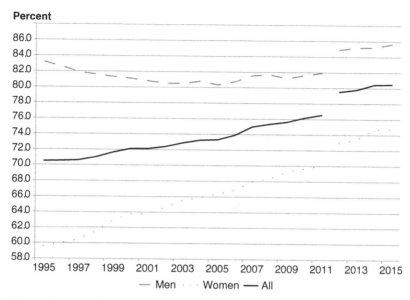

Figure 11.2 Israel's labor force participation, ages 25–64

The rise in the level of education is a secular phenomenon Argov (2016) that was temporarily intensified during the 1990s, perhaps as a result of the expansion of public colleges and the absorption of the inflow of immigrants from the FSU. Since LFPR increase with the level of education, one can attribute at least part of the rise in LFPR, especially that of women, to the rise in average years of schooling. However, there is no evidence that the rise in the level of education caused a rise in LFPR during the 2000s (Bank of Israel Report, 2017).

As part of the government policy to cut welfare payments since 2003, the cut in child allowances was very pronounced. Theoretically, such cuts to government transfers can have large effects on the LFPR of both men and women during the child-bearing years. Mazar and Reingewertz (2018) found that this cut has contributed 4.3 percentage points and 2.8 percentage points to the LFPR of women and men with four or five children, respectively, compared to women and men with two or three children.

Finally, in 2004, the mandatory retirement rate increased by two years for both men and women. This should have had a positive effect on the LFPR of the older population. Indeed, the *Bank of Israel Annual*

Report (2017) found that men aged 60–64 contributed 0.9 percentage points (out of a total increase of 1 percentage point for men aged 25–64) to male LFPR between 2003 and 2011, whereas LFPR among this age group dropped in the earlier period, 1995–2003. For women, the rise in LFPR among the age group 60–64 contributed 1.2 percentage points out of a total of 3.8 percentage points for women aged 25–64. In the earlier period, 1995–2003, the age group 60–64 contributed only 0.5 percentage points to the rise of women's LFPR.

Although some of these are only descriptive statistics, as a whole they suggest that government policy in the form of welfare payment cuts, and especially in raising the mandatory retirement age positively contributed to the increase in LFPR. Either way, the rise in LFPR closed the gap in LFPR between Israel, on the one hand, and the United States and the comparison group on the other hand. This happened, despite the very low LFPR among two subgroups that are not very small – ultra-Orthodox men and Arab women. Thus, the rise in LFPR allowed Israel to increase its relative income per capita to its 1995 level, while at the same time output per worker fell. These are likely to be interdependent, as the marginal workers presumably have low market skills, thus contributing less than the average worker. The next two subsections discuss the dynamics of education and investment in fixed assets that are of great importance to the determination of output per worker.

11.2.3 The Evolution of Average Years of Schooling

The long-run secular rise in the average years of schooling of the adult population (ages 25–64) has continued during the period 1995 and 2014 (see Figure 11.3).[4] Over this time period, however, the rate of growth in years of schooling has been decelerating. In the early 1990s, the growth rate of the average years of schooling had been affected in part by the inflow of immigration from the FSU, who were more educated than the native population in Israel (Cohen-Goldner et al., 2015), and in part by the expansion of the public colleges in Israel, which allowed more high-school graduates access to higher education (Volansky, 2005). As the expansion of public

---

[4] We use average years of schooling from Argov (2016). He adjusts the estimates on various dimensions, among them a downward correction to the average years of schooling of ultra-Orthodox yeshiva students.

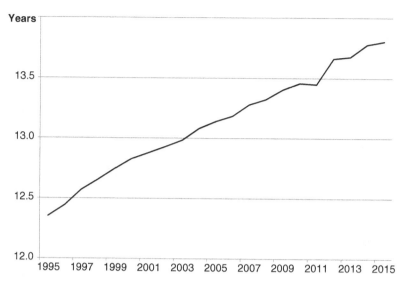

Figure 11.3 Israel's average years of schooling, ages 25–64

colleges subsided over time, it stopped contributing to the growth of education. Finally, throughout this time period the exit of older cohorts, who are characterized by low levels of education, and the entrance of younger cohorts have been an additional force behind the increase in average years of schooling among the population aged 25–64.

11.2.4 *Investment in Fixed Assets*

Investment in fixed assets as a share of total gross domestic product (henceforth: GDP) was especially high in the mid-1990s as part of an adjustment process of the stock of physical capital to the inflow of immigrants from the FSU (see Figure 11.4). Investment then declined until the mid-2000s. The mild rise in recent years reflects "one-time" investments which are related to the discovery of natural gas in the Mediterranean. In the mid-2000s, the investment rate stabilized at about 18 percent, about 2 percentage points below the comparison group. This gap has remained intact in recent years, despite the increased rate in Israel and the economic crisis in the European Union.

The relatively low investment rate is due to the low investment rates of the private sector as well as the public sector. As we elaborate in

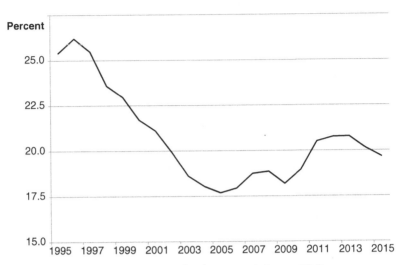

Figure 11.4 Israel's investment in fixed assets, relative to GDP

section 11.4, the accumulation of physical capital per worker is much lower than in the comparison group in almost all industries. In addition, public investment conducted by the government is lower than in the past and in international perspectives. Indeed, the level of net public capital per capita in Israel is much lower compared to the comparison group (Eckstein and Lifschitz, 2017).

11.2.5 Total Factor Productivity

The tradition in the field of economic growth is to decompose growth into the growth arising from the accumulation of factors of production and an unexplained growth that is attributed to total factor productivity (Solow, 1957; Kendrick, 1961). Gaaton was the pioneer in this field in Israel with the publication of his book *Economic Productivity in Israel* in 1971 (Gaaton, 1971). Hercowitz (2002) examined the evolution of TFP in Israel and concluded that between 1975 and 1989, GDP increased by 60 percent, the stock of physical capital and labor increased by 30 percent, and TFP increased by 23 percent. In contrast, between 1989 and 1997, TFP was constant as both GDP and physical capital and labor increased by 60 percent. Hercowitz attributed the stagnation in TFP to the absorption of immigrants from the FSU. Whereas during the period explored by Hercowitz, Israel was mostly affected by local developments, such as the historical peace agreement with Egypt, the hyperinflation followed by the stabilization, and the large inflow of migrants from the FSU, between 1995 and 2014, the developments in Israel were mostly related to development in the global economy (with the exception, perhaps, of the temporary effect of the Second Intifada). Indeed, during the period 1995 and 2014, average annual growth of GDP per capita was 1.6 percent, similar to the average among the comparison group.[5]

A decomposition of the growth in Israel between 1995 and 2014 is consistent with the statement that developments in Israel go hand in hand with development in the global economy. During this period, factors of production per worker have increased by about 15 percent, while TFP has increased by 8 percent. In the comparison group the equivalent numbers are 16 percent and 11 percent, respectively.[6] Since the evolution of both factors of production and TFP has been very similar over this period, our analysis below focuses on the gap in output per worker as of 2014. Such an analysis enables us to use the PIAAC, which encompasses both Israel and the comparison group. As we show below, this survey sheds new light on the sources of the gap between Israel and the comparison group.

11.3 Development Accounting

11.3.1 Theoretical Framework

Development accounting is a useful tool to understand differences in output per worker in a given point in time. It assumes a production function, calibrates its parameters, and uses measures of its inputs and output to decompose observed differences in output into differences in measured factors of production and unobserved differences in total factor productivity.[7]

---

[5] The increasing importance of exports to growth in Israel during the 1995–2014 period is consistent with the increased correlation between the growth in Israel and worldwide economic developments. Leiderman and Bahar (Chapter 5, this volume) show that the elasticity of exports with respect to world trade is close to unity.

[6] Author's calculation using data from the Penn World Tables (Feenstra et al., 2015).

[7] See Klenow and Rodriguez-Clare (1997) and Hall and Jones (1999) for early applications of this methodology, and Caselli (2005) for a survey of this literature.

Let the aggregate production function be:

$$Y_i = A_i K_i^\alpha (L_i h_i)^{1-\alpha},$$ (11.1)

where Y_i is total output, K_i is the aggregate stock of physical capital, L_i is total number of workers, h_i is the average human capital per worker, and A_i is TFP). i is an index for countries and $\alpha \in (0, 1)$ is the elasticity of output with respect to physical capital. Divide equation (11.1) by L_i to get:

$$y_i = A_i k_i^\alpha h_i^{1-\alpha} \equiv A_i X_i,$$ (11.2)

where y_i and k_i are output and physical capital per worker, respectively, and $X_i \equiv k_i^\alpha h_i^{1-\alpha}$ is the composite inputs per worker. Let us now assume only two countries, Israel, denoted by IL and the comparison group denoted by C. Using equation (11.2) we can write:

$$\frac{y_{IL}}{y_C} = \frac{A_{IL} k_{IL}^\alpha h_{IL}^{1-\alpha}}{A_C k_C^\alpha h_C^{1-\alpha}} = \frac{A_{IL} X_{IL}}{A_C X_C}$$ (11.3)

Equation (11.3) decomposes the ratio of output per worker to differences in TFP and differences in accumulated factors of production. In our empirical implementation we use equation (11.3) to calculate the contribution of the relative TFP, $\frac{A_{IL}}{A_C}$, and the contribution of the relative factors of production, $\frac{X_{IL}}{X_C}$, to the relative output per worker.

11.3.2 Empirical Implementation

11.3.2.1 The Elasticity of Capital with respect to Output, Output per Worker, and the Stock of Physical Capital per Worker

To apply equation (11.3) to the data, we need information on output per worker, human capital per worker, and physical capital per worker and an estimate on the elasticity of physical capital with respect to output. For the latter, we assume $\alpha = 0.42$.[8,9] Data on output and

---

[8] Under the assumption of perfect competition, $1 - \alpha$ is also the share of labor in national income. Over the period 1990–2014, the share of labor in national income has declined in most countries (Karabarbounis and Neiman, 2014). The value of 0.42 is based on the average labor share in the OECD in 2016.

[9] Caselli and Feyrer (2007) showed that the share of national income that is accrued to reproducible capital varies greatly across countries, mostly due to agricultural land and urban land. Nevertheless, reproducible capital share across Israel and the comparison countries are very similar.

Table 11.1 *Data for development accounting: Israel and the comparison country*

	Output per worker (1)	Physical capital per worker (2)	Human capital per worker 1 (3)	Human capital per worker 2 (4)	Human capital per worker 3 (5)
Israel	63,162	196,844	3.582	3.314	0.925
Comp. group	90,550	398,559	3.139	3.207	1.022
Ratio	0.698	0.494	1.141	1.027	0.905

Notes: Data on output per worker and physical capital per worker are in 2011 US dollars. "Human capital per worker 1" uses only years of schooling, "Human capital per worker 2" uses years of schooling, and numeracy skills, and "Human capital per worker 3" uses numeracy skills.

physical capital per worker, adjusted for purchasing power parity (henceforth: PPP), and number of workers are taken from the Penn World Table (henceforth: PWT) (Feenstra et al., 2015).[10]

Table 11.1 shows the data for Israel and the comparison group. The comparison group is measured as a weighted average of the six countries, where the weight is the relative employment of each country. As can be seen from the table, output per capita in Israel is 69.8 percent of the output per capita in the comparison group. Israel's physical capital per worker is only about one-half that of the comparison group.

11.3.2.2 Human Capital per Worker Based on Schooling

Since Hall and Jones (1999), it is standard to measure human capital per worker by:

$$h_i = e^{rs_i} \tag{11.4}$$

where s_i is average years of schooling and r is the returns to schooling. In contrast to its inferiority in physical capital, the average number of years of schooling in Israel exceeds the average numbers years of

---

[10] We use Penn World Table V9.0. We use the variables "cgdpo" for total output, "rkna" for aggregate physical capital, and "emp" for the number of workers.

schooling in the comparison group by about a year and a half.[11] Moreover, average years of schooling in Israel is higher than in any of the countries underlying the comparison country. The smallest gap is between Israel and Ireland – about one-half a year – and the largest gap is between Israel and Austria – nearly three years of schooling. The accepted estimates for the returns to schooling, r, is in the range of 7–13 percent (Hall and Jones, 1999). Hanushek et al. (2015a) conducted a development accounting exercise across states in the United States. They assume that $r = 0.1$. We follow them and assume that the return to a year of schooling is 10 percent.[12] Column (1) in Table 11.1 shows that under this assumption, the human capital per worker in Israel is larger by 14.1 percent compared to the comparison group.

11.3.2.3 Human Capital per Worker Based on Schooling and Skills

The literature that followed Klenow and Rodriguez-Clare (1997) and Hall and Jones (1999) has tried to improve the measurement of human capital in an attempt to increase the variance in output per worker that is accounted for by accumulated factor of production. Caselli (2005) summarizes this literature. The motivation for these attempts comes from the presumption that the quality of schooling varies across countries and therefore taking into account only differences in the quantity of schooling is not accounting for other dimensions, such as quality.

Starting in 2011–2012, the OECD has conducted a survey of adult skills, called the Programme for the International Assessment of Adult Competencies, or "PIAAC," with the goal of measuring the key cognitive and workplace skills needed for adult individuals to participate in society and in the workforce. The survey measures three main skills: literacy, numeracy, and problem solving in technology-rich environments. The main advantage of this survey is that it provides comparable data across OECD countries regarding the skills of adult individuals. Round 1 of the first cycle of PIAAC was conducted in 2011–2012 and included all the countries in our comparison group. Israel participated in Round 2 of the first cycle, in the years 2014–2015. In Israel about 9,000 individuals were assigned to the survey and about 6,000 were tested. The test was conducted in Hebrew, Arabic, and Russian.

---

[11] Years of schooling for all countries have been calculated based on PIAAC variable "Education – Highest qualification – Level" (B_Q01a).

[12] Frish (2007) estimated the casual effect of schooling on wages and found that the returns to schooling in Israel are about 9 percent.

Hanushek et al. (2015a) conducted a development accounting exercise across states in the United States. They proposed an extended form of (11.4) to estimate human capital and used micro data on skills in the USA to calibrate it. Specifically, they assumed that:

$$h_i = e^{rs_i + wT_i}, \tag{11.5}$$

where T_i is a measure of skills and w is the returns to skills. Notice that T could be a vector containing all three skills measured in PIAAC. To calibrate (11.5), we need estimates for the vector w. Hanushek et al. (2015b) used micro data from PIAAC for twenty-three countries to estimate the returns to skills. For each country, Hanushek et al. (2015b) standardize each skill to have mean zero and standard deviation of one and regressed log wages on this Z-score in a similar fashion to Mincerian wage regression. We follow Hanushek et al. (2015a) and use years of schooling and numeracy skills. We parameterize this specification by assuming that the return to a year of schooling is 10 percent and the return for each standard deviation in numeracy is 17.8 percent.[13] We also considered an alternative specification where we use both numeracy and literacy in addition to schooling. Quantitatively, this specification yields very similar results because the gap in the numeracy and literacy tests between Israel and the comparison country is very similar. We therefore do not report based on this specification for brevity. Finally, there are good reasons to believe that estimates of human capital based on measured skills (quality) are more desirable than those based on years of schooling (quantity). Hanushek and Kimko (2000) conducted a "horse race" between years of schooling and test scores in affected growth rates. They found that the former declines sharply and loses its statistical significance when the latter is added to the regressions. Hence, we also calibrate a version of (11.5) where we assume that only numeracy skills affect human capital. We use the same return to a standard deviation, namely that $w = 0.178$.

The achievement of the Israeli population in PIAAC is substantially lower than what the average years of schooling in Israel would predict. In numeracy and literacy the average score was 251 and 255, respectively. The average across all OECD countries is 266 and 269,

---

[13] Setting the return to each standard deviation in numeracy to 0.178 is based on table 2 of Hanushek et al. (2015b).

respectively, with a standard deviation of 12.3 and 10.3, respectively.[14] Note, however, that the returns estimated in Hanushek et al. (2015b) is per standard deviation in the micro data for each country. The latter is much higher than the standard deviation across countries. Averaging the standard deviation in the micro data across all OECD countries, we find that the standard deviation in numeracy is 47 (and 47 in literacy as well). This implies that the Z-score for Israel is −0.44 and −0.39 standard deviations in numeracy and in literacy, respectively. The countries underlying the comparison group, in contrast, are all above the OECD average, with the exception of Ireland.[15] In numeracy the smallest gap is between Israel and Ireland and is equal to 0.1 standard deviation and the largest gap is between Israel and Finland and is equal to 0.66 standard deviation. In literacy the smallest gap is 0.26 (vis-à-vis Ireland) and the largest is equal to 0.70 (vis-à-vis Finland). Hanushek et al. (2015a) report similar gaps across US states.[16]

The large disadvantages that the adult population in Israel has in terms of skills offset the advantage Israel has in years of schooling, such that human capital is fairly similar between Israel and the comparison group. Column (4) in Table 11.1 shows the estimates of human capital per worker when schooling and numeracy skills are used to calibrate equation (11.5). Under this specification, the human capital in Israel is larger by only 2.7 percent of the comparison group. Finally, when the specification of equation (11.5) includes only numeracy skills the human capital in Israel is equal to 90.5 percent of the comparison group.

11.3.3 Results

11.3.3.1 Human Capital per Worker Based Only on Schooling
Assuming that human capital is solely determined by schooling (column 3 in Table 11.1), we calculate the ratio between the contribution of accumulated factors of production in Israel and the comparison

[14] We omitted Turkey and Chile because although these countries are in the OECD, they are much less developed than other member countries.
[15] The average score in numeracy and literacy are 275 and 269 in Austria, 280 and 275 in Belgium, 285 and 271 in Denmark, 282 and 288 in Finland, 256 and 267 in Ireland, 280 and 284 in the Netherlands, and 279 and 279 in Sweden.
[16] The gap between the state with the highest skills, Minnesota, and the state with the lowest skills, Mississippi is 0.87 standard deviations.

group and find that it is equal to 0.8. Using this ratio and equation (11.3), we find that TFP in Israel, relative to that in the comparison group, is equal to 0.87. This implies that accumulated factors of production contribute 60 percent to the gap in output per worker, while the gap in TFP contributes the remaining 40 percent.[17]

11.3.3.2 Human Capital per Worker Based on Schooling and Skills

An alternative to the case where only schooling determines human capital is to assume that human capital is determined by both schooling and numeracy skills (column 4 in Table 11.1). Under this calibration of the human capital production function, we recalculate the ratio between the contribution of accumulated factors of production in Israel and the comparison group. We find that it equals 0.76. This is smaller by 4 percentage points, relative to the case where human capital is determined solely by years of schooling. Again, using and equation (11.3) we find that TFP in Israel, relative to that in the comparison group, is now equal to 0.92. In terms of the contribution of accumulated factor of production contribute to the gap in output per worker vs the contribution of TFP, we now find that accumulated factors of production contribute 76 percent while TFP contributes the remaining 24 percent.

11.3.3.3 Human Capital per Worker Based only on Skills

Finally, we assume that human capital is solely determined by numeracy skills (column 5 in Table 11.1). We recalculate the ratio between the contribution of accumulated factors of production in Israel and the comparison group. We find that it is equal to 0.70. This is smaller by an additional 6 percentage points, relative to the case where human capital is determined by both years of schooling and numeracy skills. Once again, using equation (11.3), we find that TFP in Israel, relative to that in the comparison group, is now equal to 0.92. This implies that accumulated factors of production contribute 76 percent to the gap in output per worker, while TFP contributes the remaining 24 percent.[18]

---

[17] The contribution of accumulated factor is given by $\frac{1-0.8}{(1-0.8)+(1-0.87)} \approx 0.6$.

[18] More precisely, accumulated factors of production contribute 97 percent while TFP contributes the remaining 3 percent.

11.4 Physical Capital per Worker at the Industry Level

In the previous section, where we conducted a development accounting exercise, we saw that the physical capital per worker in Israel is substantially lower than that of the comparison group. Specifically, according to the PWT, the physical capital per worker in Israel, adjusted for PPP, is slightly below 50 percent that of the comparison group.

In this section we address two hypotheses as to why this ratio is so low. First, we examine the industrial composition of the Israeli economy. If Israel specializes in industries that have low capital intensity, then the main question to be asked is why Israel chose to specialize in these sectors: is it because of Israel's lack of physical capital, or is it due to other factors. One reason for that could be related to Israel's chronic balance of payments deficits, which lasted for decades until the early 2000s (see Leiderman and Bahar, Chapter 7, this volume). In that case, history dependency can explain such specialization. Second, the low level of physical capital per worker could be driven by differences between structures and equipment. For example, if Israel is more densely populated, it could be the case that Israel is lagging behind in physical capital per worker mostly or entirely because of structural disadvantage. To address these questions, we estimate physical capital per worker by industry for both Israel and the comparison group.

11.4.1 Methodology

The estimation of physical capital per worker uses the perpetual inventory method. According to this method, the stock of physical capital in industry j, in country c, in period $t +1$, $K_{jc,t+1}$, depends on the stock of physical capital in period t in that industry country, $K_{jc,t}$, and on investment in period t, $I_{jc,t}$:

$$K_{jc,t+1} = (1 - \delta_j)K_{jc,t} + I_{jc,t}. \tag{11.6}$$

Here δ_j is the depreciation rate in industry j. Using equation (11.6) recursively we can write:

$$K_{jc,t+1} = (1 - \delta_j)^{t+1}K_{jc,0} + \sum_{i=0}^{t} (1 - \delta_j)^{t-i}I_{jc,i}. \tag{11.7}$$

To estimate physical capital using (11.7), one needs data on investment at the industry level, as well as data on depreciation rates by industry. In addition, one needs data on $K_{jc,0}$.[19]

Inklaar and Timmer (2013) offer a method for estimating $K_{jc,0}$. The idea is to assume that in $t = 0$, each or industry is in steady-state of the neoclassical growth model. Thus:

$$K_{jc,0} = \frac{I_{jc,0}}{g + \delta} \tag{11.8}$$

where g is the growth rate of investment. Thus, using equations (11.7) and (11.8) we can estimate physical capital at the industry level in each country in each year. As in Inklaar and Timmer (2013), we assume that $g = 0.02$, consistent with output growth of 2 percent and the assumption that, in the steady-state, investment grows at the same rate as output. Finally, we need to parameterize δ_j. Again, following Inklaar and Timmer (2013) we assume that depreciation on structures is 2 percent. Inklaar and Timmer (2013) divided equipment into five categories, with annual depreciation rates that are in the range of 12.6–31.5 percent. We choose an annual depreciation rate of 15 percent for equipment. Under these two values, we estimate that 77 percent of the capital stock is structure and the remaining 23 percent is equipment. In turn, this implies that the average depreciation rate is 5 percent, similar to Inklaar and Timmer (2013).

11.4.2 Data

Data on investment and employment at the industry level for the countries underlying the comparison group are available from Eurostat for the years 1995–2014. The investment data are in 2010 Euros. Similar data for Israel were obtain from the Israeli Central Bureau of Statistics and the Bank of Israel.[20]

---

[19] Notice that the importance of $K_{jc,0}$ diminishes as one uses data further back in time. Nevertheless, since depreciation on structures is fairly low, even if we had data on investment going back to 1950, still 28 percent of structure capital would be in use in 2014 with an annual depreciation rate of 2 percent. Moreover, our data only begins in 1995, thus $K_{jc,0}$ plays an important role.

[20] Data on investment in Israel are in 2010 constant NIS. We converted them to Euro prices using the average exchange rate between the NIS and the Euro in 2010.

11.4.3 Results

Figure 11.5 shows physical capital per worker by industry in Israel relative to the comparison group. As can be vividly seen from the figure, it varies greatly across industries, ranging from 0.105 in public services to 2 in textiles, apparel, and leather. While some of these estimates are very small, perhaps unrealistically, the average across all industries is 52.4 percent. Interestingly, the gap between our (aggregate) estimate and that of the PWT is fairly close, standing at 3 percentage points.[21]

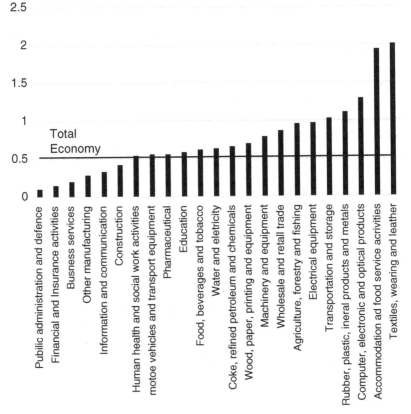

Figure 11.5 Israel's physical capital per worker at the industry level relative to the comparison group

---

[21] we used investment in constant NIS and converted them to Euro using the average exchange rate in 2010, so that our estimates are unadjusted to PPP.

The Contribution of Industrial Composition to Gaps in Physical Capital per Worker. To evaluate the contribution of industrial composition to gaps in physical capital per worker, we compute the hypothetical physical capital per worker that Israel would have had if its industrial composition had been as in the comparison group. This is measured in terms of relative employment. Formally, the hypothetical capital per worker is computed as:

$$k_{IL}^b = \sum_j \omega_{jC} k_{j,IL} \qquad (11.9)$$

where ω_{jC} is the fraction of workers employed in industry j in the comparison group and $\sum_j \omega_{jC} = 1$. If Israel's industrial composition explained the whole gap between Israel and the comparison country, we would expect no gap between Israel and the comparison group in each industry. Figure 11.6 shows the fraction of workers employed in industry j in Israel and the comparison group. As the figure makes clear, there are relatively small differences in the industrial composition

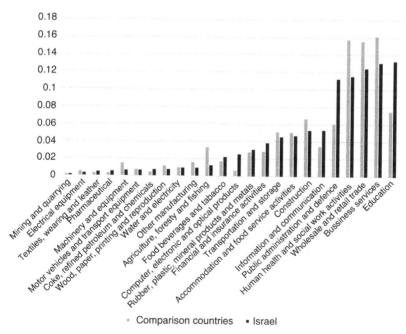

Figure 11.6 The distribution of employment by industries: Israel and the comparison group

between Israel and the comparison country. Consistent with that, computing the hypothetical capital per worker using (11.9) yields capital per worker that is larger than the actual capital per worker in Israel by less than 2 percent.

Structure versus Equipment and Machinery. Our second hypothesis is that Israel's disadvantage is mainly in structures. As we noted above, structures constitute about 77 percent of the physical capital stock and equipment constitutes the remaining 23 percent. In the comparison group, the division is 80 percent structures and 20 percent equipment. We find that the stock of structures in Israel is only 50.8 percent relative to the comparison group, while the stock of equipment is about 60.8 percent, relative to the comparison group. This finding in consistent with the hypothesis that the cost of building in Israel is higher than in the comparison group. While we do not investigate this issue in more depth, we think this deserves further research in the future.

Our overall assessment is that the composition of the industrial composition in Israel is relatively unimportant to understand why Israel's capital per worker is only about one-half that of the comparison group.

11.5 Human Capital per Worker at the Industry Level

As discussed in Section 11.3 Israel leads the comparison group in terms of formal schooling while lagging behind in terms of cognitive skills. Figure 11.7 shows human capital per worker at the industry level, relative to the comparison group. It varies from about 0.8 in construction to more than 1.2 in textile, wearing, and leather. Below we answer the question what is the contribution of the industrial composition of Israel to its human capital. We evaluate this question the same way we did when asking the hypothetical question what would have been Israel's physical capital per worker, had the industrial composition of Israel been that of the comparison country. Formally, the hypothetical capital per worker is computed as:

$$h_{IL}^h = \sum_j \omega_{jC} h_{j,IL} \tag{11.10}$$

where ω_{jC} is as defined above in section 11.4. If Israel's industrial composition explained the whole gap between Israel and the

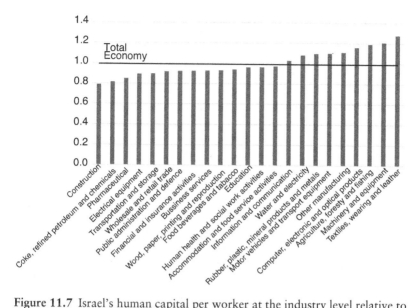

Figure 11.7 Israel's human capital per worker at the industry level relative to the comparison group.

Human capital is based on (11.5)withr = 0.1 for each year of schooling and w = 0.178 per one standard deviation in numeracy skill.

comparison country, we would expect no gap between Israel and the comparison country in each industry. We find that the industrial composition contributes 4 percent to the stock of human capital. That is, had the industrial composition of Israel been the same as in the comparison group, the stock of human capital in Israel would have been 4 percent lower. Again we conclude that the industrial composition of Israel is relatively unimportant in explaining difference in average human capital, relative to the comparison group.

11.6 Physical and Human Capital per Worker at the Industry Level

There is a theoretical justification to assume that there is a positive relationship between the stock of physical capital per worker and the average human capital per worker. Acemoglu (2003) argues that the development of new technologies responds to the quality of the workforce. Thus, when the stock of human capital increases, new technologies are developed. Krusell et al. (2000) estimated the elasticity of substitution between physical capital and unskilled workers and between physical capital and skilled workers. They found that while the former is 1.67, the latter is 0.67.[22] Zeira (1998) shows that adoption of technologies depends on the price of labor relative to capital. The higher the price of labor, the larger the incentive for firms to invest in capital that embodied labor-saving technology.

In our development accounting exercise, we assume that the aggregate production function is Cobb–Douglas. If we assume that this holds true also at the industry level, we get:

$$\frac{\partial y}{\partial k} = \alpha A \left(\frac{h}{k} \right)^{i-\alpha} \tag{11.11}$$

The left-hand side (henceforth: LHS) of equation (11.11) is the marginal product of physical capital per worker. Under the assumption that it is determined by the real interest rate, and that the real interest rate is exogenously given to a small open economy, the LHS is constant. Taking logs of (11.11) and manipulating, we obtain a linear relationship between the log of physical capital per worker and the log of human capital per worker, with a coefficient of one on the log of human capital per worker.

Below we examine this hypothesis. Specifically, we estimate the relationship between the log of physical capital per worker and the log of human capital per worker at the industry level across countries. To this end, we estimated physical capital and human capital per worker at the industry level for all countries for which we have investment level at the industry level in Eurostat and data on numeracy skills at the industry level in PIAAC. In total, we have data for thirteen countries.[23] The goal of this analysis is to examine if Israel's disadvantage in the skills of the adult population, also negatively affect the accumulation of physical capital.

Table 11.2 shows summary statistics of the data. There are two salient features in the data. First, there is large variation in physical capital per worker across industries. Second, structures represent the lion share of capital.

---

[22] There is a large literature on the elasticity of substitution between capital and labor. Even though this literature has not reached a consensus, most research finds an elasticity smaller than 1. For a review of this literature, see Chirinko (2008).

[23] These are Austria, Cyprus, the Czech Republic, Denmark, Finland, France, Greece, Ireland, Israel, Italy, the Netherlands, Slovakia, and Sweden.

Table 11.2 *Summary statistics*

Variable	Observations	Mean	Standard deviation	Minimum	Maximum
Physical capital per worker	260	198.72	319.02	8.43	3,255.55
Structures per worker	260	153.91	282.32	1.61	2,996.09
Machinery per worker	260	44.81	63.08	1.22	555.57
Log physical capital per worker	260	4.72	1.00	2.13	8.09
Log structures per worker	260	4.34	1.11	0.48	8.02
Log machinery per worker	260	3.22	1.09	0.20	6.32
Human capital per worker	260	3.66	0.68	1.74	5.82
Log human capital per worker	260	1.28	0.19	0.55	1.76

Notes: Physical capital, structures, and equipment per worker are measured in thousands of 2010 Euros. Human capital per worker is parameterized under the assumption that both schooling and numeracy skills contribute to human capital.

Figure 11.8 shows a scatter plot of the log of physical capital per worker and human capital per worker across thirteen countries and twenty-three industries.[24] The figure shows that there is a positive relationship between the log of physical and the log of human capital per worker. Additionally, we see that the dispersion of observations for Israel is not different from the dispersion for the other countries in the data.

[24] Human capital per worker is based on (11.5) with $r = 0.1$ for each to year of schooling and $w = 0.178$ per one standard deviation in numeracy skill.

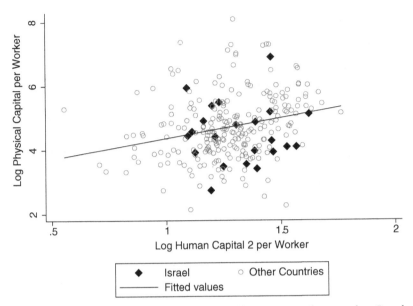

Figure 11.8 The stock of physical capital and human capital per worker: Israel and 12 OECD countries

Despite this clear relationship, it is better to examine the relationship using regressions to account for country and industry characteristics. For example, it could be the case that industries with more physical capital per worker employ workers with lower human capital per worker, but that more productive countries have higher physical and human capital. If this is the case, then country fixed effects would weaken, or even eliminate the relationship shown in the figure. Likewise, it could be the case that within industries there is small variation in physical capital because they use similar technologies. Again, if this is the case, then industry fixed effects would weaken or eliminate the relationship altogether.

Hence we estimate regression of the form:

$$\log k_{ic} = \alpha + \beta \log h_{ic} + \delta_c + \delta_i + \epsilon_{ic}, \tag{11.12}$$

where k_{ic} and h_{ic} are physical and human capital per worker in country c in industry i, δ_c and δ_i are country and industry fixed effects, and ϵ_{ic} is a random error. As we described above, given our Cobb–Douglas production function specification, we expect to find $\beta = 1$. We note that although our purpose is to document a relationship between physical and human capital per worker and not a casual relationship between the two, there are at least two reasons why we choose to put physical capital as the dependent variable in (11.12). First, human capital is determined in a process that usually takes longer than physical capital. It is the result of formal schooling, starting at a young age, going through high school, and sometimes college, and continues with on the job training, and so on. We measure human capital as a weighted average over workers at different ages, and so this average changes relatively slowly. In contrast, physical capital can be adjusted at a faster pace, especially in industries where technological progress is important. A second reason for our choice is that for the most part, human capital is determined by the public education system, whereas most of the physical capital is determined by the private sector. Thus, if one wants to take a causal interpretation of (11.12), then the government should improve the average human capital through its public education system, if it wants to contribute to fostering investment in physical capital by the private sector.

Table 11.3 presents the results of estimating (11.12). The table has three panels, where each corresponds to a different specification of the human capital production function. In Panel A, human capital is based on (11.12) with $r = 0.1$ for each to year of schooling. In Panel B, human capital is based on (11.5) with $r = 0.1$ for each to year of schooling, and $w = 0.178$ per one standard deviation in numeracy skill. Finally, in Panel C, human capital is based on (11.5), but only numeracy skills are rewarded: $r = 0$ and $w = 0.178$ per one standard deviation in numeracy skill.

In each panel there are three "blocks" of regressions: in columns (1)–(3) the dependent variable is the total physical capital per worker, whereas in columns (4)–(9) we breakdown the total physical capital per worker into two components: physical capital per worker in the form of structures (columns 4–6) and physical capital per worker in the form of equipment and machinery per worker (columns 7–9).

In column (1) we present estimates of β without controlling for fixed effects. The estimates range between 1.278 and 2.659, and are all statistically significant. When we add both country and industry fixed effects, the estimates are very close to 1 and are highly statistically significant in Panels A and B. In column (2) we add country fixed effects. The point estimates in Panels A and B increase due to this inclusion but remain statistically significant, while the one in Panel

Table 11.3 *The relationship between physical capital and human capital per worker*

	Log capital per worker			Log structures per worker			Log machinery per worker		
	(1)	(2)	(3)	(4)	(5)	(6)	(7)	(8)	(9)
Panel A: Human capital based solely on years of schooling									
Log HC1	1.**	2.019**	1.081***	1.943***	2.512***	1.635***	0.254	0.385	0.844
	(0.583)	(0.757)	(0.379)	(0.684)	(0.847)	(0.538)	(0.682)	(0.849)	(0.633)
R2	0.048	0.175	0.772	0.059	0.165	0.680	0.001	0.186	0.775
Panel B: Human capital based on years of schooling & numeracy skills									
Log HC2	1.278**	1.424**	0.836***	1.460**	1.670**	1.225***	0.631	0.548	0.782
	(0.453)	(0.616)	(0.264)	(0.525)	(0.695)	(0.373)	(0.500)	(0.652)	(0.477)
R2	0.061	0.172	0.772	0.065	0.153	0.680	0.012	0.192	0.777
Panel C: Human capital based solely on numeracy skills									
Log HC3	2.659**	2.384	1.017	2.640**	2.314	1.337	2.851**	2.232	1.450*
	(1.121)	(1.657)	(0.713)	(1.238)	(1.766)	(0.931)	(1.170)	(1.711)	(0.840)
R2	0.046	0.140	0.768	0.037	0.108	0.671	0.045	0.203	0.775
Common to all panels									
Country FE	No	Yes	Yes	No	Yes	Yes	No	Yes	Yes
Industry FE	No	No	Yes	No	No	Yes	No	Yes	Yes
Obs.	260	260	260	260	260	260	260	260	260

Notes: The dependent variable in columns (1)–(3) is the log of physical capital per worker, the dependent variable in columns (4)–(6) is the log of structures per worker, and the dependent variable in columns (7)–(9) is the log of equipment and machinery per worker. The main regressor in Panel A, Log HC1, is the log of human capital per worker, where human capital is based on (11.4) with $r = 0.1$ for each year of schooling. The main regressor in Panel B, Log HC2, is the log of human capital per worker, where human capital is based on (11.5) with $r = 0.1$ for each to year of schooling and $w = 0.178$ per one standard deviation in numeracy skill. The main regressor in Panel C, Log HC3, is the log of human capital per worker, where human capital is based on (11.5) but only numeracy skills are rewarded: $r = 0$ and $w = 0.178$ per one standard deviation in numeracy skill. Standard errors, clustered at the country–industry level. Observations are at the country–industry level. Standard errors, clustered at the industry level are in parentheses. * $p < 0.10$, ** $p < 0.05$, *** $p < 0.01$.

C remains relatively stable but loses its statistical significance. Finally, in column (3), we add industry fixed effects. The estimates in all panels decrease, getting fairly close to 1, and are statistically significant in Panels A and B. Looking at the goodness of fit, the R^2, across columns (1)–(3), we see that it increases substantially between columns (2) and (3), suggesting that much of the variation in the data is due to variation across industries rather than across countries.

The breakdown of physical capital to its two components in columns (4)–(9) reveal an interesting pattern. While in Panels A and B the positive correlation between physical capital and human capital is due to a positive correlation between structures and human capital, in Panel C the positive correlation is mostly due to a positive correlation between equipment and machinery and human capital per worker. Our prior was that human capital would be more correlated with this type of physical capital than with structures. We interpret this result as consistent with the literature that emphasizes the superiority of quality of schooling over the quantity of schooling in relation to output growth (see Hanushek and Kimko, 2000).

We can use the estimates presented in Table 11.3 to examine by how much output per worker would have increased had the gap in numeracy skills between Israel and the comparison group been closed. The gap in numeracy skills equals 0.56 standard deviations. With a return of 17.8 percent to one standard deviation, the direct effect on Israel's human capital is an increase of 10.4 percent. Such an increase, in turn, would increase the stock of physical capital per worker. Taking the estimate of 0.836 (column 3 in Panel B), this implies that the stock of physical capital would increase by 8.7 percent. Together, these direct and indirect effects would increase output per capita by 9.7 percent, or 6.75 percentage points. Given that the gap in output per capita is 30.5 percentage points, closing the gap in numeracy skills can account for about 22 percent of the gap in output per worker.

11.7 Concluding Remarks

We analyzed differences in labor productivity between Israel and a group of small OECD countries. We assumed a more general human capital production function and calibrated it using PIAAC surveys, which examine the literacy and numeracy skills of the adult population in OECD countries. Whereas Israel has more years of schooling, its population has lower measured skills. Using a development accounting exercise, we show that once literacy and numeracy skills are taken into account, differences in accumulated factors explain more than three-quarters of the gap. This is against a split of 60–40 between accumulated factors and total factor productivity, when these skills are ignored. We also estimated physical capital per worker and human capital per worker at the industry level. We show that differences in the industrial composition between Israel and the comparison group can explain very little of the gap in physical capital per worker or in human capital per worker. When we distinguish between structures and equipment and machinery in physical capital per worker, we do see that Israel's disadvantage is larger in structures, although this finding cannot explain why physical capital is generally so low in Israel. Finally, using panel data on thirteen OECD countries, we estimate the relationship between physical and human capital. A causal interpretation of our estimates implies that closing the gap in skills – an increase in human capital per worker of 10.4 percent – will indirectly close 18 percent of the gap in physical capital and 22 percent of the gap in output per worker

References

In Hebrew

Achdut, L., Gutman, E., Lipiner, I., Maayan, I., and Zussman, N. (2018). *The Wage Premium on Higher Education: Universities and Colleges.* Discussion Paper 2018.11. Jerusalem: Bank of Israel Research Department.

Argov, E. (2016). *The Development of Education in Israel and its Contribution to LongTerm Growth.* Discussion Paper 2016.15. Jerusalem: Bank of Israel Research Department.

Eckstein, Z., and Lifschitz, A. (2017). *Growth Strategy 2017.* Aaron Institute for Economic Policy, Policy Paper 2017.02.

Flug, K., and Strawczynski, M. (2007). *Persistent Growth Episodes and Macroeconomic Policy Performance in Israel.* Discussion Paper 2007.08. Jerusalem: Bank of Israel Research Department.

Frish, R. (2007). *The Causal Effect of Education on Earnings in Israel.* Discussion Paper 2007.03. Jerusalem: Bank of Israel Research Department.

Igdalov, S., Frish, R., and Zussman, N. (2017). *The Wage Response to a Reduction in Income Tax Rates: The 2003–2009 Tax Reform in Israel.* Discussion Paper 2017.14. Jerusalem: Bank of Israel Research Department.

Lipiner, I., Rosenfeld, D., and Zussman, N. (2019). *Over-education and Mismatch Between Occupation and Major Subject Among University and College Graduates.* Discussion Paper 2019.12. Jerusalem: Bank of Israel Research Department.

Mazar, Y, , and Reingewertz, Y. (2018). *The Effect of Child Allowances on Labor Supply: Evidence from Israel.* Discussion Paper 2018.07. Jerusalem: Bank of Israel Research Department.

Volansky, A. (2005). *Higher Education Policy in Israel 1952–2004.* Tel Aviv: Hakibbutz Hameuchad.

In English

Acemoglu, D. (2003). Patterns of Skill Premia. *The Review of Economic Studies*, 70(2), 199–230.

Bank of Israel (2017). *Bank of Israel Annual Report 2016.* Jerusalem: Bank of Israel.

Blau, F. D., and Kahn, L. M. (2013). Female Labor Supply: Why Is the United States Falling Behind? *American Economic Review*, 103(3), 251–256.

Brand, G., and Regev, E. (2015a). Causes of the Widening Productivity Gaps Between Israel and the OECD: A Multiyear Industry-Level Comparison. In A. Weiss and D. Chernichovsky (eds.), *State of the Nation Report: Society, Economy and Policy in Israel.* Jerusalem: Taub Center, 231–287.

(2015b). The Dual Labor Market: Trends in Productivity, Wages and Human Capital in the Economy. In A. Weiss and D. Chernichovsky (eds.), *State of the Nation Report: Society, Economy and Policy in Israel.* Jerusalem: Taub Center, 185–230.

Caselli, F. (2005). Accounting for Cross-Country Income Differences. In P. Aghion and Steven N. Durlauf (eds.), *Handbook of Economic Growth*, Vol. 1A. Amsterdam: Elsevier, 679–741.

Caselli, F., and Feyrer, J. (2007). The Marginal Product of Capital. *The Quarterly Journal of Economics*, 122(2), 535–568.

Chirinko, R. S. 2008. [sigma]: The Long and Short of It. *Journal of Macroeconomics*, 30(2), 671–686.

Cohen-Goldner, S., Eckstein, Z., and Weiss, Y. (2015). The Immigration from the Former Soviet Union to Israel. In C. Dustmann (ed.),

Migration: Economic Change, Social Challenge. Oxford: Oxford University Press, 10–32.

Dahan, M., and Hazan, M. (2014). Priorities in the Government Budget. *Israel Economic Review*, 11(1), 1–33.

Feenstra, R. C., Inklaar, R., and Timmer, M. P. (2015). The Next Generation of the Penn World Table. *American Economic Review*, 105(10), 3150–3182.

Fernández, R. (2013). Cultural Change as Learning: The Evolution of Female Labor Force Participation over a Century. *American Economic Review*, 103(1), 472–500.

Gaaton, Arie Ludwig. (1971). *Economic Productivity in Israel*. New York: Praeger.

Gabai, Y., and Rob, R. (2002). The Import-Liberalization and the Abolition of Devaluation Substitutes Policy: Implications for the Israeli Economy. In A. Ben- Bassat (ed.), *The Israeli Economy, 1985–1998: From Government Intervention to Market Economics.* Cambridge, MA: MIT Press, 281–308.

Goldin, C. (2006). The Quiet Revolution That Transformed Women's Employment, Education, and Family. *American Economic Review*, 96(2), 1–21.

Hall, R. E., and Jones, C. I. (1999). Why Do Some Countries Produce So Much More Output per Worker than Others? *The Quarterly Journal of Economics*, 114(1), 83–116.

Hanushek, E. A., and Kimko, D. D. (2000). Schooling, Labor-Force Quality, and the Growth of Nations. *American Economic Review*, 90(5), 1184–1208.

Hanushek, E. A., Ruhose, J., and Woessmann, L. (2015a). Knowledge Capital and Aggregate Income Differences: Development Accounting for U.S. States. NBER Working Paper No. 21295. https://www.nber.org/papers/w21295.pdf.

Hanushek, E. A., Schwerdt, G., Wiederhold, S., and Woessmann, L. (2015b). Returns to Skills Around the World: Evidence from PIAAC. *European Economic Review*, 73(January), 103–130.

Hazan, M., and Maoz, Y. D. (2002). Women's Labor Force Participation and the Dynamics of Tradition. *Economics Letters*, 75(2), 193–198.

Hercowitz, Z. (2002). Capital Accumulation, Productivity, and Growth in the Israeli Economy. In A. Ben-Bassat (ed.), *The Israeli Economy, 1985–1998: From Government Intervention to Market Economics.* Cambridge, MA: MIT Press, 423–444

Hercowitz, Z., and Lifschitz, A. (2015). Tax Cuts and Economic Activity: Israel in the 2000s. *Israel Economic Review*, 12(2), 97–125.

Inklaar, R., and Timmer, M. P. (2013). *Capital, Labor and TFP in PWT8.0.* Groningen Growth and Development Centre, University of Groningen.

Karabarbounis, L., and Neiman, B. 2014. The Global Decline of the Labor Share. *The Quarterly Journal of Economics*, 129(1), 61–103.

Kendrick, J. W. 1961. *Productivity Trends in the United States.* Princeton, NJ: Princeton University Press.

Klenow, P., and Rodriguez-Clare, A. (1997). The Neoclassical Revival in Growth Economics: Has It Gone Too Far? In Ben S. Bernanke and Julio Rotemberg (eds.), *NBER Macroeconomics Annual 1997, Volume 12.* Cambridge, MA: MIT Press, 73–114.

Krusell, P., Ohanian, L. E., Rios-Rull, J.-V., and Violante, G. L. (2000). Capital-Skill Complementarity and Inequality: A Macroeconomic Analysis. *Econometrica*, 68(5), 1029–1054.

Paserman, D. M. (2013). Do High-Skill Immigrants Raise Productivity? Evidence from Israeli Manufacturing Firms. *IZA Journal of Migration*, 2(6).

Solow, R. M. (1957). Technical Change and the Aggregate Production Function. *The Review of Economics and Statistics*, 39(3), 312–320.

Strawczynski, M., and Zeira, J. (2002). Reducing the Relative Size of Government in Israel After 1985. In A. Ben-Bassat (ed.), *The Israeli Economy, 1985–1998: From Government Intervention to Market Economics.* Cambridge, MA: MIT Press, 61–84.

Zeira, J. (1998). Workers, Machines, and Economic Growth. *The Quarterly Journal Economics*, 113(4), 1091–1117

12 | Income Inequality in Israel: A Distinctive Evolution

MOMI DAHAN

12.1 Introduction

Following a widening of the economic gap over the last thirty years, Israel today has one of the highest levels of disposable income inequality among the developed countries (Figure 12.1). In contrast, market income inequality has shown an inverted U-shape evolution, which peaked in 2002. As a result of this distinctive path, the Gini coefficient of market income in Israel is now below the OECD average (Figure 12.2). These developments raise a few related questions: What factors account for the rise in disposable income inequality over time? Why is disposable income inequality higher in Israel as compared with most developed countries? What explains the rise and fall in market income inequality? What are the explanations for the relatively low market income inequality in Israel? This research focuses on describing the evolution of various measures of income inequality since 1990 because Dahan (2002) covered previous years at length. In addition, the mass immigration from the former Soviet Union to Israel – which potentially had a significant effect on income inequality – started in 1990. Naturally, this is a relatively short period of time in which to identify causal relations. Instead, this chapter offers indicative evidence that accounts for the evolution of income inequality in Israel.

The vast interest in income inequality reflects its important consequences on our society and the economy worldwide. Excessive inequality might indicate economic inefficiency and slow down long-term economic growth. The possible negative effect of income inequality on economic growth is the result of barriers, such as credit constraints in financing adequate human capital, that prevent certain social groups from exercising their full economic potential (Galor and Zeira, 1993; Dahan and Tsiddon, 1998). It could be also due to the restricted

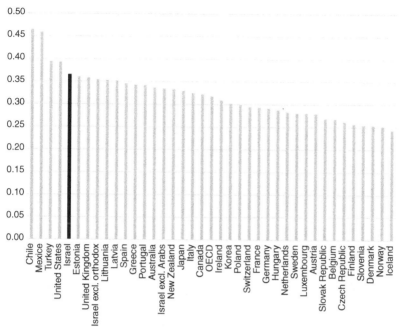

Figure 12.1 Net income inequality in OECD countries
(Gini for 2013 or last available year)

economic opportunities that minorities may face in the labor market. In such a case, the damage is even greater due to the social costs associated with the grievances that those groups feel. Perotti (1996) presents evidence that inequality results in political and social instability, which hurt economic growth. In fact, the social burden of income inequality is massive, even if it does not have any effect on economic growth. Extreme inequality might imply that a group of individuals may lack the essential means to preserve their human dignity. Moderate economic gaps may also be crucial for gaining the trust of disadvantaged groups in the political system and consequently for a thriving democracy. Excessive inequality might be translated into unequal political participation that may even further exacerbate income inequality if public policy is affected more by the preferences of those who participate in political activities such as voting.[1] The risk of income inequality being too wide

---

[1] Hill and Leighley (1992) show that welfare policy is less generous in states with low levels of voter turnout among disadvantaged groups.

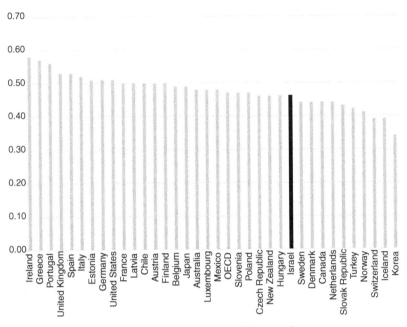

Figure 12.2 Market income inequality in OECD countries
(Gini for 2013 or last available year)

for democracy is much greater if public policy is dictated by those at the top. In recent years, international institutions such the OECD and IMF have emphasized the danger of social groups that suffer from widening income inequality supporting candidates and political parties that favor barriers to international flows of goods, capital, and labor that would hurt economic growth (OECD, 2015a; Dabla-Norris et al., 2015).[2]

Because of its potential implications on quality of life, the rising inequality in many developed countries has created extensive research efforts to document and explain the evolution of income inequality since the end of the nineteenth century. The selective survey of scholarly works presented here is intended to uncover the main factors behind the rise of income inequality, which may help to explain its evolution in Israel, although it is by no means exhaustive.

[2] Alesina and Rodrik (1994) have suggested a somewhat similar mechanism whereby higher income inequality leads to greater political support by the decisive voter for higher redistribution, which harms economic growth. However, Perotti (1996) did not find empirical backing for that hypothesis.

There is abundant research on the economic factors that explain the rise in income inequality in the United States and other developed countries. Skill-biased technological change (SBTC) was one of the first hypotheses offered to explain the widening of income inequality. According to this hypothesis, the computer revolution has been associated with an expansion of demand for goods that are produced by a large share of high-skilled labor, together with stable or even declining demand for products that are made by low-skilled labor-intensive technology (Bound and Johnson, 1992; Juhn et al., 1993; Berman et al., 1994).[3] Dahan (2002) presents evidence for Israel that is consistent with the SBTC hypothesis.

A change in labor market institutions, such as the strength of labor unions, minimum wage, and performance pay for top managers, is another prominent suggestion offered by scholars for the widening economic gaps. Card and his associates have shown that wage differentials between high- and low-skill workers (mainly men) have increased as a result of a declining share of workers being covered by union contracts (Card and DiNardo, 2002; Card et al., 2004), with the erosion of minimum wages especially hurting the wages earned by women (DiNardo et al., 1996). Kristal and Cohen (2007) lend empirical support for the connection between labor market institutions and income inequality in Israel.

Surprisingly, globalization has not been a popular factor among economists who are interested in exploring the rise in inequality. Ostensibly, larger trade between countries should generate more wage inequality between workers in developed countries and smaller wage differentials in developing countries. However, inequality has increased in both developed and developing countries. Nevertheless, some scholars attribute part of the widening income inequality to globalization (Miller, 2001; Feenstra and Henson, 2003).

The exploration of rising inequality has gained momentum following an impressive research project that documented the evolution of the share of the top 10 percent – which covers a two-digit number of both developed and developing countries – since the nineteenth century (Piketty and Saez, 2003).[4] This research endeavor offers a historical

---

[3] In series of more recent works, Autor and his colleagues present a modified SBTC that shows a polarization of earning distribution (see, for example, Autor et al., 2008).

[4] Unfortunately, this research project does not include Israel.

perspective on the super-rich that was missing in previous works, which allows for existing hypotheses to be examined and for new ones to be raised (Atkinson et al., 2011).

Piketty and Saez have uncovered a significant rise in the share of the top decile in the United States since the late 1970s, which has reached a level that was observed at the end of the nineteenth century. That rise, which has also occurred in the United Kingdom and Canada, mainly represents an increasing share of the super-rich. In contrast, the share of the top 1 percent has been stable or increased moderately in other developed countries such as Germany, France, and Japan. The differing evolution of the share of the very rich has generated doubts regarding the previous causes of widening inequality. Seemingly, the structure of economic growth should have worked in similar fashions in both the United States and Germany, but the benefits of growth were shared differently in different developed countries. Following these findings, the explanations that emphasize country-specific changes in labor market institutions became more convincing. In addition, the rise of the share of the super-rich has partially shifted the focus to the role of tax policy and performance pay contracts (Atkinson et al., 2011).

The role of government has been almost entirely missing from the discussion of widening income inequality. The absence of government may reflect the focus on earnings rather than income inequality that is created in the labor market. Piketty and Saez (2003) were the first to introduce the degree of tax progressivity by presenting evidence on the similar timing of a noticeable reduction in top marginal income tax rates and increasing income inequality.

A battery of hypotheses has emerged from the short survey above regarding the evolution of income inequality in Israel within the last few decades. In addition, several Israeli-specific factors, like its unique employment expansion, absorption of mass immigration, and redistribution policy, will be examined. In the next section, the evolution of income inequality in Israel over time will be presented with emphasis on the last twenty-five years. Market income inequality follows an inverted-U shape during this period, and today, Israel is ranked below the OECD average (Figure 12.3). In contrast, disposable income inequality has gone down only moderately in the last few years after a sharp rise since 1990, and now Israel's Gini index of net income is at the top of the developed countries. Section 11.3 offers a comparative analysis that addresses why disposable income inequality in Israel is

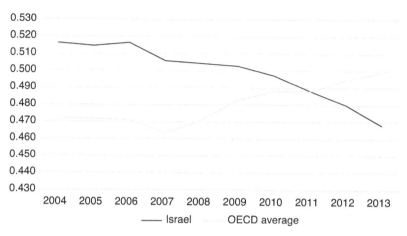

Figure 12.3 Market income inequality in Israel and OECD countries

one of the highest in the OECD by exploring preferences, restricted opportunities, labor market conditions, and the extent of redistribution. The last section discusses the main findings.

12.2 Evolution of Income Inequality in Israel

In this chapter, we focus on the last twenty-five years for three reasons. First, the data on income inequality for this time period is relatively more comparable. Second, a previous article covered the inequality dynamics in the preceding period extensively (Dahan, 2002). Last, the mass immigration from the former Soviet Union that started in 1990 – which increased the Israeli population by 15 percent in a short time period – had a potential impact on inequality developing. The next section will examine the explanatory power of a list of factors that have been suggested throughout the years to explain the dynamics of inequality in Israel. The predicted impact of these proposed factors on market income inequality is different from their expected effect on net income inequality in terms of magnitude and direction. I will examine the relationship between each factor and the two measures of market and disposable income inequality (rather than one at a time), which provides a stricter empirical test. In addition, simple OLS (ordinary least squares) regressions will be employed to test the significance of the correlations between a battery of potential candidates and market income inequality. Obviously, the OLS coefficients are seen as complementary evidence for understanding the dynamics of the inequality but do not represent causal effects.

12.2.1 Market Income Inequality[5]

Household market income inequality was on the rise from the late 1970s and accelerated following the influx of mass immigration at the start of 1990s. Inequality reached a record in 2002 with a Gini coefficient of 0.54, which is close to levels observed in Latin American countries (Table 12.1). The rise in income inequality was accompanied by an increase in the unemployment rate, and following previous findings, one may suggest that the co-evolution of the two represents a relationship between unemployment and income inequality. Dahan (1996) found that unemployment is a key factor in understanding the dynamics of income inequality in Israel.

As a result of the global slowdown and the Second Intifada (Palestinian uprising) in 2001, unemployment – which had already been relatively high in 1997 – soared, reaching a rate of 11 percent of the labor force in 2003. The rise in unemployment had a direct effect on market income inequality through a growing number of households being left without labor income (Table 12.2). The upsurge in market income inequality has been greater than that of net income inequality thanks to the social safety net, which provides income support and unemployment benefits to households without market income. The differential evolution of these two measures of income inequality is consistent with the assertion that employment indeed plays a central role in explaining the market income inequality between 1997 and 2003.

In 2004, unemployment changed course and started an almost steady downward trend to a low level (5 percent) that has not been seen since the mid-1980s. Unemployment went down as a result of the improved security following the succession of terrorist attacks in Israeli streets. The Great Recession, which started in 2007 in many developed countries, had only minor and short-lived impacts on economic activity in Israel. The labor market became more attractive in the last decade for nonparticipants following the fall in unemployment; as a result, labor

---

[5] Market income includes labor and capital income.

Table 12.1 *Income inequality, 1979–2015 (equivalence-adjusted Gini coefficient for market, gross, and net consumption)*

	Gini for:				Share of total net income in:		
	Market income	Gross income	Net income	Consumption	Bottom quintile (%)	3–9 deciles (%)	Top decile (%)
1979	0.432	0.366	0.318	0.320	..	..	..
1980	0.434	0.369	0.324		25.2	6.8	68.0
1981	0.439	0.372	0.319	..	24.6	6.8	68.6
1982	0.444	0.367	0.312	..	24.3	7.1	68.6
1983	0.439	0.360	0.301	..	..	..	..
1984	0.472	0.398	0.327	..	..	..	..
1985	0.468	0.372	0.312	..	24.9	7.0	68.1
1986	..	..	..	0.328	..	..	..
1987	..	..	..	..	24.6	7.0	68.4
1988	0.457	0.370	0.322	..	24.6	6.7	68.7
1989	0.474	0.378	0.325	..	25.4	6.8	67.8
1990	0.480	0.376	0.326	..	25.1	6.5	68.4
1991	0.490	0.377	0.327	..	25.4	6.6	68.0
1992	0.498	0.393	0.339	0.321	26.1	6.3	67.6
1993	0.494	0.383	0.329	..	25.4	6.5	68.1
1994	0.502	0.399	0.344	..	26.8	6.2	67.0
1995	0.497	0.397	0.337	..	26.1	6.6	67.3

Table 12.1 (*cont.*)

	Gini for:				Share of total net income in:			
	Market income	Gross income	Net income	Consumption	Bottom quintile (%)	3–9 deciles (%)	Top decile (%)
1996	0.496	0.387	0.329	..	25.7	6.8	67.5
1997	0.505	0.395	0.333	..	26.0	6.7	67.3
1997	0.509	0.414	0.353	0.3345	26.0	6.7	67.3
1998	0.512	0.413	0.352	0.3442	26.0	6.8	67.2
1999 [1]	0.517	0.421	0.359	0.3429	26.5	6.7	66.8
2000[1]	0.509	0.411	0.350	0.3443	25.6	6.8	67.6
2001[1]	0.528	0.420	0.357	0.3310	26.2	6.6	67.2
2002[1]	0.537	0.431	0.368	0.3340	26.6	6.1	67.3
2003	0.527	0.424	0.369	0.3356	26.3	6.0	67.7
2004	0.523	0.430	0.380	0.3454	26.6	5.5	67.9
2005	0.526	0.434	0.388	0.3431	27.4	5.4	67.2
2006	0.524	0.438	0.392	0.3464	28.0	5.3	66.7
2007	0.513	0.432	0.383	0.3443	27.2	5.4	67.4
2008	0.519	0.433	0.385	0.3380	27.3	5.4	67.3
2009	0.510	0.429	0.389	0.3507	27.4	5.2	67.4
2010	0.505	0.426	0.384	0.3429	27.1	5.2	67.7
2011	0.497	0.418	0.379	0.3404	26.5	5.4	68.1

2012[2]	0.489	0.417	0.377	0.3320	27.0	5.4	67.6
2013[2]	0.478	0.410	0.363	0.3436	26.3	5.5	68.2
2014[2]	0.477	0.413	0.371	0.3318	27.4	5.3	67.3
2015[2]	0.472	0.407	0.366	0.3361	26.6	5.2	68.2

Source: Central Bureau of Statistics and author's calculations.

[1] Does not include East Jerusalem's population.

[2] Does not include Bedouin population. Since 1997, income data have come from two surveys: a labor force survey and a household expenditures survey.

Table 12.2 Descriptive statistics (according to income survey)

	Share of population (% households)			Share of households with 0 market income (%)			No. of children per household		
	Excl. Arabs and Orthodox	Arabs	Orthodox	Excl. Arabs and Orthodox	Arabs	Orthodox	Excl. Arabs and Orthodox	Arabs	Orthodox
1990	85.0	8.6	6.4	25.5	33.1	38.4	1.3	3.0	2.9
1991	85.0	8.3	6.7	24.2	32.7	39.6	1.3	2.8	2.8
1992	84.9	8.8	6.3	24.1	30.9	38.0	1.2	2.8	2.9
1993	84.2	8.9	6.9	24.3	33.4	36.8	1.2	2.6	2.9
1994	84.5	9.0	6.5	22.2	30.4	36.6	1.2	2.6	3.0
1995	77.9	16.4	5.7	22.0	25.6	42.6	1.1	2.5	3.0
1996	77.6	16.8	5.7	23.5	28.0	33.1	1.1	2.4	2.8
1997	77.5	17.1	5.4	23.0	27.8	42.5	1.1	2.2	2.8
1997	76.9	18.0	5.2	11.2	15.0	27.9	1.1	2.2	2.8
1998	76.2	18.4	5.4	11.6	16.6	25.7	1.0	2.4	2.7
1999	76.2	18.9	4.9	9.8	15.4	26.7	1.0	2.4	2.7
2000	78.5	16.6	4.9	9.7	17.2	26.6	1.0	2.3	2.8
2001	77.0	17.3	5.7	10.5	20.8	33.1	1.0	2.5	2.7
2002	75.7	19.0	5.4	10.9	22.9	30.0	1.0	2.5	2.7
2003	74.7	19.2	6.1	10.5	20.3	30.8	1.0	2.5	2.8

2004	75.4	18.9	5.8	10.4	18.1	31.9	1.0	2.4	2.7
2005	74.4	19.6	6.0	10.1	21.9	28.5	0.9	2.4	2.7
2006	73.1	19.8	7.1	9.4	21.6	22.9	0.9	2.4	2.6
2007	73.1	19.7	7.2	8.4	18.7	20.0	0.9	2.3	2.6
2008	73.4	19.8	6.7	8.5	16.7	22.8	0.9	2.3	2.8
2009	72.8	19.9	7.3	8.5	18.3	19.7	0.9	2.2	2.8
2010	73.3	20.2	6.6	8.2	18.1	18.2	0.9	2.1	2.7
2011	72.5	20.5	7.0	8.1	17.3	15.3	0.9	2.2	2.7
2012	74.5	18.7	6.8	5.5	16.1	12.9	0.9	2.1	2.9
2013	74.4	18.5	7.1	5.4	12.7	11.7	0.9	2.2	2.9
2014	75.2	18.3	6.5	5.4	12.0	11.6	0.9	2.0	2.9
2015	73.9	18.5	7.6	5.1	10.4	14.1	0.9	2.0	2.9

Source: Central Bureau of Statistics and author's calculations

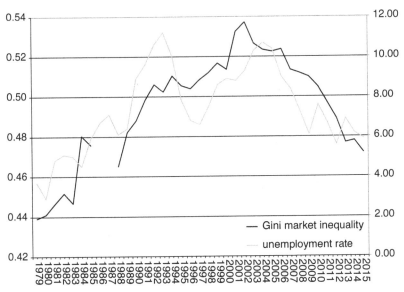

Figure 12.4 Market income inequality and unemployment

force participation increased noticeably.[6] As expected, the drop in unemployment after 2003 had the same effect, but this time to lower market income inequality. The Gini coefficient for market income inequality went down from its peak level of 0.54 in 2002 to 0.47 in 2015, which is similar to the level documented in 1989, before the wave of mass immigration to Israel. Figure 12.4 illustrates the close association between unemployment and market income inequality during the entire period under investigation. The decrease in unemployment was accompanied by a lower number of households without market income and lower market income inequality (Table 12.2). Cornfeld and Danieli (2015) also noted the positive correlation between the share of households with zero market income and market income inequality.

Table 12.3 displays OLS regression results that cover the years 1979–2015 and show that unemployment plays a key role in understanding the evolution of market income inequality. The dependent variable is the Gini coefficient for market income inequality, and the list

---

[6] Dahan (2006) found a close relationship between unemployment and labor force participation in Israel.

Table 12.3 *The correlates of inequality in market income, 1979–2015*

	(1)	(2)	(3)	(4)	(5)	(6)	(7)	(8)
Unemployment	1.02***	1.06***	0.80***	0.60***	1.03***	0.83***	0.68***	0.86***
	(0.184)	(0.232)	(0.153)	(0.197)	(0.145)	(0.094)	(0.113)	(0.090)
Welfare state generosity index		0.465						
		(0.473)						
Direct statutory tax rate index			−0.074***					
			(0.012)					
Minimum wage/ average wage				25.021**				
				(10.660)				
Participation rate					0.245***			
					(0.081)			
Arab coverage rate in income survey						0.324***		
						(0.031)		
Share of immigrant workers							0.825***	
							(0.150)	

Table 12.3 (*cont.*)

	(1)	(2)	(3)	(4)	(5)	(6)	(7)	(8)
Technical change in income/labor force survey								3.219*** (0.488)
Constant	41.470*** (1.403)	43.539*** (2.298)	50.173*** (2.057)	34.190*** (5.167)	28.018*** (4.048)	38.197*** (0.694)	37.298*** (1.130)	40.909*** (0.771)
Adjusted R²	0.495	0.426	0.724	0.265	0.606	0.855	0.744	0.791
No. of observations	35	34	35	28	35	32	35	35

* Variable equaled 1 in 1997–2015.

of explanatory variables represents various hypotheses that scholars suggested as driving income inequality dynamics in Israel. Owing to the limited number of observations (34 years), only one control variable is included in addition to unemployment rate. As seen in Table 12.3, the coefficient of unemployment is consistently positive and significant in all regressions, regardless of the other explanatory variable that is included. This finding also remains the same when the covered period is shortened to 1990–2015 or 1997–2015 (the author can provide the results). In contrast, the coefficient of labor force participation – which is surprisingly positive and significant – is sensitive to the chosen time period. This coefficient becomes negative and significant for the years 1997–2015. These results suggest that the evolution of inequality is more sensitive to changes in unemployment than to employment.

The mass immigration from the former Soviet Union is an additional key factor that may account for the inverted U-shape of market income inequality. The wave of immigration that started at the end of the 1980s immediately increased the supply of unskilled labor, despite their high level of education. In the first five years of the 1990s 600,000 Jewish immigrants arrived (equal to 13 percent of the Israeli population in 1989), which dropped to 350,000 and 180,000 in the next two five-year windows, respectively. The number of Jewish immigrants at the start of the millennium came back to the levels seen prior to 1989. The combination of the dramatic expansion of labor supply in a short period of time together with a lack of Hebrew skills had compelled many of these new immigrants to look for jobs that were not necessarily compatible with their skills and occupations, which exerted downward pressure on wages for unskilled positions. Even without sophisticated simulation, one may speculate that in the first few years, the wave of mass immigration contributed to widening wage and income inequality. In subsequent years, as more and more immigrants searched for and found jobs that matched their high human capital, it worked to reduce income inequality. This is in line with Kuznet's hypothesis of inverted U-shape inequality.

The evolution of immigrant workers in the Israeli economy is also consistent with the dynamics of income inequality. In the mid-1990s, the increasing number of mainly unskilled immigrant workers exerted downward pressure on wages for low-skilled Israeli workers. Such a development would be expected to increase the wage differential between skilled and unskilled Israeli workers and contribute to market income inequality among households. The rising unemployment as well as the fear of a large influx of seemingly temporary non-Jewish immigrant workers that would eventually stay in Israel led decision-makers to restrain their numbers. Since 2003, the share of immigrant workers in the labor force has gone down by 5 percentage points relative to its peak level (Bank of Israel, 2015). Table 12.3 shows that the coefficient of immigrant workers is positive (raising inequality) and significant after controlling for unemployment rate. This result is in line with Gottlieb (2002), who found that immigrant workers act to increase income inequality.

Over the years, several other explanations were offered for the rising inequality in Israel, such as skill-biased technological change (Dahan, 2002), globalization (Ben-David, 2003), institutional changes in the labor market that hurt low-skilled workers (Kristal et al., 2007; Endeweld and Heller, 2014; Corenfeld and Danieli, 2015) and an aging population (Blaich, 2016). However, while these hypotheses are all consistent with rising inequality, they cannot not explain the inverted U-shape that market income inequality has followed in the last twenty-five years.

No evidence indicates a reversal in the economic growth structure that harmed high-skilled workers or a U-turn in globalization that would justify the fall in inequality within the last decade. While Autor et al. (2008) suggest that polarization is a better description of the labor market, they proposed this hypothesis to account for rising rather than declining income inequality. Nonetheless, the SBTC might explain the rise and fall of inequality. SBTC first drives up the wage differential and income inequality but also generates the conditions for closing the wage gap by incentivizing investment in human capital. However, it takes time to see such an effect. Dahan (2016) suggested this mechanism to explain the considerable narrowing in the ethnic gap between Askenazim and Mizrahim in the last twenty years after a long period of the gap being relatively stable.

Kristal et al. (2007) attributed Israel's rising income inequality to the weakening labor unions, as materialized by the dramatic reduction in coverage from 79 percent in 1981 to 43 percent in 2003 and the decentralization of wage bargaining. However, the recent trend of declining market income inequality is not associated with a rise in labor union coverage or the centralization of wage bargaining. In fact, Kristal et al. (2015) show that the share of workers who are covered by centralized wage bargaining continues to fall: the coverage rate decreased from 56 percent in 2000 to 50 percent in 2012.

The minimum wage regulation is an additional institutional device that may affect the status of low-skilled workers. There are conflicting findings regarding the impact of minimum wage on employment and wages and, as a result, on income inequality. While Drucker and Epshtain (2016) show a negative effect of minimum wage on employment, Endeweld and Heller (2014) found that the level of minimum wage reduced the likelihood of being poor. Between 2003 and 2015, the minimum wage fluctuated around the same ratio relative to the average wage, which is in contrast with the downward trend in market income inequality. The OLS regressions in Table 12.3 show the lack of relations between minimum wage and inequality. The coefficient of minimum wage is positive, but its significance depends on the chosen period. Nevertheless, the minimum wage may still affect inequality depending on the enforcement efforts. However, no significant changes have been documented in compliance with minimum wage, according to Endeweld et al. (2013).

12.2.2 The Effect of Redistribution

Governments employ a battery of policy devices to reduce economic gaps, with taxes and transfers playing pivotal roles in redistribution based on their large shares in the budget. While factors like SBTC and labor union coverage affect market and disposable income inequality in the same direction, redistribution through transfers may impact these two measures of inequality in opposite ways. In addition, direct taxes, such as income tax and social security contributions, are expected to generate a larger rather than smaller effect on net income inequality as compared to market income inequality, unlike the factors discussed above.

Assessing the effects of redistribution by comparing income inequality before and after taxes and transfers is likely to cause a bias in judging the effectiveness of redistribution. To estimate the effectiveness of redistribution, a simulation of the income distribution without government intervention (a counterfactual distribution) should be developed because both taxes and transfers change the incentive to work. However, such a simulation is very complicated; therefore, both international and national institutions tend to regularly offer measures of the observed distribution (rather than the counterfactual distribution) of income before taxes and transfers. While this chapter does not provide such a simulation, I discuss below the predicted impact of taxes and transfers on income inequality while taking into account their potential changes to the incentive to work.

Lowering the marginal income tax rate for high-income individuals (or reducing the progressivity of the tax system) is expected to increase market income inequality, to the extent that it creates an incentive to work more. The impact of reduced income tax rate on net income inequality is even larger because of its mechanical effect on net income. Thus, individuals at the top benefit from higher wage rates (incentive effect) and higher after-tax earnings (mechanical effect).[7]

While the direct tax rate was stable between the start of the 1990s and 2003 (Strawczynski 2014), income inequality rose in that same time period, which suggests that taxes did not play a leading role. The multi-year program to reduce income tax rates on both individuals and corporations that the government incepted in 2003 was expected to expand market income inequality by affecting the incentive of highly skilled individuals to work more. In practice, market income inequality has gone down during most of the period since then. Moreover, the combination of declining market income inequality and rising net income inequality observed in 2003–2007 is not in line with the theoretical prediction outlined above. Following the social protest in the summer of 2011 and the Trajtenberg Committee, the reduction of income tax stopped and the tax rate has even risen slightly in the last five years, which is consistent with declining market inequality. Thus, it seems that the evolution of market income inequality has not been affected substantially by the income tax rate. In addition, OLS regressions show that income tax has a negative and significant coefficient, as expected, but its significance does not survive if the examined period is limited to the period 1997–2015.

Unlike income tax, transfer payments seem to help explain the evolution of income inequality, especially after 2003. A cut in income assistance to disadvantaged groups is expected to attract nonparticipants to join the labor market and increase the supply of labor from the

---

[7] This analysis assumes that the demand for labor is elastic enough to accommodate a rise in wage rates.

current low earners. As a result, such a cut should reduce market income inequality according to their labor supply elasticity, but the effect on net income inequality is unclear. The expected additional labor income might be higher or lower than the reduced government transfers. The combined effect is more likely to widen net income inequality in the short run due to relatively low labor supply elasticity (individuals may hesitate to join the labor force immediately due to a considerable cost, especially for parents). Net income inequality may also rise in the long run if a large share of welfare recipients is characterized by very low earning capacity.

The strong rise in income inequality between 1990 and 2003 has not been accompanied by a clear trend in the generosity of welfare payments. Thus, redistribution policy did not play a role in that time period. The considerable cuts in welfare programs – such as for income support and child allowances – that were part of a large economic program in 2003 are consistent with the differential evolution of market and net income inequality after 2003. The rise in labor force participation among individuals with low levels of education following cuts in welfare benefits and declining market income inequality is in line with the theoretical prediction. Yet, net income inequality continues to increase despite the higher labor participation, as would be expected if cuts in welfare benefits have a greater effect than the additional income from work. In the last few years, welfare benefits have remained around the same new low level, while net income has become less concentrated. Table 12.3 shows that the partial correlation between market income inequality and welfare generosity index is insignificant, which could be driven by the relatively small variation of that index.

12.2.1.1 The Change in Redistribution Policy

The economic program of 2003 not only included considerable cuts in welfare benefits but also changed the nature of social assistance. The allowances provided by Israeli Social Security, which is a key pillar of the Israeli welfare state, became de facto more universal. The degree of universal social assistance is estimated here using the actual (Gini) correlation between a household's rank on a net income scale and the size of welfare benefits received by that particular household from social security. No correlation implies pure universality of social assistance, a positive correlation represents regressive redistribution and a negative association reflects a progressive welfare policy. Such a definition does not require detailed analysis of each of the many social assistance programs. Moreover, social assistance might be universal on paper but very progressive in practice, as in the case of child allowance (due to the negative correlation between income and family size).

Table 12.4 shows that the correlation coefficient of social security benefits went down substantially in the last twenty-five years and approached zero in 2015. The total benefits, which cover other public benefits, have changed their sign and become even slightly positive. Thus, welfare policy currently plays a lesser role in reducing income inequality, not only because of the lesser generosity but also because fewer welfare benefits are channeled to low-income households.

12.3 Income Inequality in Israel from a Comparative Perspective

Israel, together with the United States, is at the top of developed countries in terms of net income inequality (Figure 12.1). This high ranking came after a considerable rise in poverty and net income inequality in Israel. In contrast, Israel is below the OECD average in terms of market income inequality, following a substantial reduction in the last decade (Figure 12.3).

How can we explain the wide net income inequality in Israel together with its relatively low level of market income inequality as compared to other developed countries? Four differences between Israel and other developed countries that may contribute to disparities in inequality will be examined. First, Orthodox Jews and Arabs are characterized by a combination of very low participation in the labor force (among Orthodox men and Arab women) and a high number of children (Orthodox households), which reflect their cultural preferences. Second, the high inequality may be caused by restricted opportunities due to formal and informal discrimination against particular social groups. Third, the difference in income inequality might be the result of disparities between Israel and other OECD countries in the phases of the business cycle, differences in the structure of economic growth, and variations in the degree of globalization. Last, the inequality differential between Israel and other developed nations might reflect differences in the extent of government intervention in education, health, and particularly the generosity of income assistance to disadvantaged

Table 12.4 *Redistribution policy and inequality, 1979–2015*

	Gini index[a]	Direct tax rate[b]	Gini correlation coefficient for direct taxes[c]	Share of transfer payments[b]	Gini correlation coefficient for transfer payments[c]	Share of social security benefits[b]	Gini correlation coefficient for social security benefits[c]	Share of non-social security aid (public and private)[b]	Gini correlation coefficient for non-social security aid[c]
1980	0.324	31.1	0.874	15.9	0.065	11.2	..	4.7	0.469
1981	0.318	31.6	0.883	16.2	0.070	11.4	..	4.9	0.492
1982	0.314	30.4	0.891	16.4	-0.073	12.7	..	3.6	0.337
1983	..	..	..	..	..	..	..	..	..
1984	..	..	..	..	..	..	..	..	..
1985	0.320	30.3	0.878	16.7	-0.113	12.7	-0.315	4.0	0.314
1986	..	..	..	..	..	..	..	..	..
1987	0.319	23.6	0.895	16.5	-0.067	12.5	-0.232	4.0	0.286
1988	0.322	22.9	0.902	16.6	-0.069	12.4	-0.229	4.2	0.266
1989	0.327	24.5	0.903	17.3	-0.080	13.2	-0.214	4.1	0.218
1990	0.329	21.1	0.900	17.7	-0.096	13.2	-0.189	4.5	0.110
1991	0.330	19.4	0.904	18.2	-0.115	12.5	-0.218	5.7	0.082
1992	0.343	20.6	0.910	20.1	0.033	12.6	-0.204	4.7	0.162
1993	0.330	20.5	0.903	21.6	0.008	14.5	-0.234	4.4	0.154
1994	0.346	21.8	0.909	17.5	-0.142	13.5	-0.262	4.1	0.136
1995	0.337	25.0	0.915	18.2	-0.121	14.3	-0.269	3.9	0.238
1996	0.330	25.0	0.909	19.2	-0.112	14.9	-0.265	4.3	0.230
1997	0.336	26.6	0.915	19.1	-0.146	15.2	-0.270	3.9	0.189
1997	0.356	29.2	0.910	19.0	-0.056	14.7	-0.233	4.3	0.320
1998	0.354	28.7	0.911	19.3	-0.080	14.9	-0.224	4.4	0.210

Table 12.4 (*cont.*)

	Gini index	Direct tax rate	Gini correlation coefficient for direct taxes	Share of transfer payments	Gini correlation coefficient for transfer payments	Share of social security benefits	Gini correlation coefficient for social security benefits	Share of non-social security aid (public and private)	Gini correlation coefficient for non-social security aid
1999	0.358	29.6	0.917	17.9	-0.058	13.6	-0.234	4.3	0.301
2000	0.349	30.3	0.914	17.7	-0.114	13.6	-0.239	4.1	0.235
2001	0.357	30.3	0.907	19.1	-0.105	14.9	-0.232	4.2	0.221
2002	0.368	30.6	0.909	19.7	-0.035	15.2	-0.176	4.5	0.289
2003	0.368	26.9	0.903	18.3	-0.073	14.1	-0.163	3.7	0.148
2004	0.380	25.5	0.914	16.9	-0.037	12.8	-0.134	3.6	0.175
2005	0.388	23.9	0.919	16.3	-0.004	11.9	-0.130	3.7	0.221
2006	0.392	22.7	0.918	16.1	0.034	11.5	-0.109	4.6	0.273
2007	0.383	23.8	0.921	15.2	0.016	11.0	-0.107	4.3	0.236
2008	0.385	21.8	0.926	14.8	0.008	10.8	-0.090	4.0	0.195
2009	0.389	19.7	0.926	15.6	0.057	11.3	-0.043	4.3	0.232
2010	0.384	19.9	0.925	15.0	0.029	11.3	-0.055	3.7	0.203
2011	0.379	18.6	0.921	15.2	0.031	11.3	-0.059	3.8	0.211
2012[a]	0.377	19.9	0.921	14.6	0.074	10.6	-0.028	4.0	0.230
2013[a]	0.363	21.3	0.918	13.5	0.066	9.6	-0.032	3.8	0.227
2014[a]	0.371	21.2	0.914	13.4	0.088	9.3	-0.015	4.0	0.238
2015[a]	0.366	21.2	0.912	13.1	0.053	9.5	0.001	3.6	0.140

Source: Central Bureau of Statistics and author's calculations.

[a] Gini index for net income (standard person) in the total population.

[b] In net income for a standard person.

[c] The income data from 1997 onward are based on two surveys: a labor force survey and a household expenditures survey. The income data from 2012 onward are based on a household expenditure survey alone.

individuals. While the first three factors all affect both market and net income inequality in the same direction, only the last factor may drive these two measures of inequality in opposite ways.

12.3.1 Preference Disparities

Monetary income serves as a proxy for welfare level based on their close correlation, as observed in Israel (Zussman and Romanov 2005) and in other developed countries. The modern welfare state rests on that positive connection between life satisfaction and monetary income, which implies that households with low income should be considered for assistance. However, the aid from most welfare programs is limited to individuals who make their best effort and yet end up with low or zero income. Orthodox Jews and Arabs are two social groups in Israel that are characterized by unique preferences that may challenge both the linkage between income and satisfaction levels and the implicit welfare state contract.

12.1.1.1 Orthodox Jews

The unique preferences of Orthodox Jews (around 7 percent of the total population) consists of three characteristics: (i) men devote a noticeable portion of their time to religion, which implies significantly lower labor force participation; (ii) religious studies do not prepare them for a modern labor market; and (iii) Orthodox Jewish families have a higher number of children (double the average). As expected, their income per capita is very low, which is directly related to their distinctive preferences. Yet, this low level of income does not imply low levels of happiness/satisfaction. Standard economic models suggest that a household with a lower level of income may still enjoy the same level of utility as a household with higher income because of their higher number of leisure hours (which are dedicated to religion studies). Zussman and Romanov (2005) show that the reported satisfaction of Orthodox Jews is higher than that of other Jews even with the same incomes.

These findings suggest that the low incomes among Orthodox Jews reflect their preferences rather than factors that are outside of their control. No other developed society consists of such a distinctive social group as the Orthodox Jews, which might justify a modification in measuring income inequality for Israel to better represent welfare inequality. A social survey from 2003 provides supporting evidence for that conclusion based on the following question: "Have you considered yourself poor ever since you were 15 years of age?" The perceived poverty rate among Orthodox Jews was slightly lower than that of the rest of the population, based on the answers to that question. This is in contrast to the standard measure of monetary poverty among Orthodox Jews, which is three times as prevalent as among other Jewish households.

How should such unique preferences be corrected? Computing an income inequality measure that excludes Orthodox Jews could account for their distinctive preferences, but such a simulation also ignores general equilibrium effects. The Gini coefficient for net income is lower by one percentage point when Orthodox Jews are excluded. This calculation suggests that factors other than Orthodox Jews' preferences are responsible for the high ranking of Israel. Note that Orthodox Jews' unique preferences should affect the market income inequality measure even more than net income inequality (due to the welfare state), yet Israel's position is below the OECD average by this measure.

12.1.1.2 The Arabs

Should income inequality also be corrected for the unique preferences of the Arab citizens of Israel, who make up about 20 percent of the population, to be more comparable to other developed countries? The answer to this question depends on the main cause for the low monetary incomes of these citizens. Two factors repeatedly emerge in the public discourse as candidates to explain the low income per capita among Arab citizens in Israel. According to the first suggestion, the high poverty rate of Arab households – around three times that of Jewish households – is the result of their cultural preferences, which translate into very low labor force participation among Arab women. The restricted economic opportunities for Arabs, such as unequal allocation of public education and infrastructure as well as discrimination in the labor market, are frequently raised as the second reason for their low incomes. While the first factor might justify contemplating a modification to measures of inequality, it would be a grave mistake to employ such a modification if their low income is mainly driven by restricted opportunities.

To estimate the relative importance of the two factors, one may compute the poverty rate for Arabs and (non-Orthodox) Jews with the same characteristics, such as in the numbers of earners and children, to isolate the effect of restricted opportunities. Flug and Kasir (2003) and Dahan et al. (2007) have done such estimations and have shown that the poverty of Arabs is three times higher than that of Jewish households after controlling for a list of characteristics. These findings seem to suggest that restricted opportunities play a central role in explaining the low incomes of Arabs.

In light of this conclusion, the justification for correcting the Israeli income inequality measures is less grounded. In fact, excluding Arabs when calculating income inequality in Israel would make the measure less rather than more representative of welfare inequality. Calculating a Gini coefficient that excludes Arab citizens, however, may serve to estimate the potential contribution (upper bound) of easing restricted economic opportunities for reducing income inequality. Note that such a calculation would ignore general equilibrium effects.

Coming back to the general question of why Israel has one of the widest economic gaps, we should be aware that restricted opportunities are expected to have a greater impact on market income inequality than on net income inequality, as has just been discussed. Thus, we cannot "blame" the Arabs for the high ranking of Israel in net income inequality; given that market inequality in Israel is below the OECD average, we should search for other reasons.

12.3.2 Differences in Redistribution Policy

Redistribution policy has been missing from the list of factors as a potential source of rising income inequality in most leading economic journals up until the late 1990s. One plausible reason for this is the focus on market income inequality. Piketty and Saez were the first to introduce the government as a factor, but that was limited to income taxes. In recent years, the OECD have devoted more attention to the declining role of government intervention, in the form of redistributing resources from rich to poor households, as a potential cause of rising inequality. In a recent publication, the OECD concluded that part of the rising inequality in the developed world should be attributed to the decreasing extent of redistribution (OECD 2015b).

The differences in redistribution policy may explain the cross-country variation in income inequality. The government could affect economic gaps using a variety of policy tools, with some impacting earning capacity and others directly influencing real income, such as taxes, in-kind and in-cash benefits and subsidies. Total public education and health expenditures in Israel, which represent the size of resources aimed at improving earning capacity, are below the OECD average when taking into account the number of beneficiaries (Dahan and Hazan, 2014). Thus, Israel spends less on resources that are supposed to reduce pre-redistribution income inequality.

One noticeable difference between Israel and other OECD countries is the generosity of the welfare state, as measured by the share of the social safety net relative to GDP. In 2014, the OECD countries spent 22 percent of their GDP on social programs, on average, as compared to only 14 percent of GDP in Israel (Dahan, 2017).

Tax rates and the composition of the tax collection are potential candidates to explain why net income inequality in Israel is one of the highest in the OECD. The overall tax rate in 2014 in Israel was lower than in many developed countries (Dahan, 2017). In addition, direct taxes, which tend to be progressive, are lower in Israel than the OECD average, while indirect taxes, which tend to be regressive, are higher in Israel as compared to in other developed countries. Moreover, the degree of progressivity follows a continuous fall, as measured by the share of direct to indirect taxes. Reduced direct taxes are expected to contribute to larger gaps in net income and to wider market income inequality, to the extent that lower income taxes induce a higher labor supply.

The low resources that are channeled to disadvantaged individuals, together with low direct taxes, seem to be the central reason why Israel has one of the highest levels of net income inequality. The difference between market and net income inequality, which is affected by redistribution policy, is one of the lowest in the developed countries (Table 12.5). Looking at Table 12.6 – which displays inequality measures by age group – provides extra evidence for this conclusion. Market income inequality among people between the ages of 18 and 65 in Israel is close to the OECD average, but net income inequality is considerably higher. Market income inequality among elderly people (above 65) in Israel is lower than the OECD average, but income inequality becomes much wider after taking direct taxes and transfer payments into account (Table 12.6).

Table 12.5 *Market and net income inequality in the OECD countries*

| | | Gini index | | |
	Year	Market income	Net income	Gini index difference
Ireland	2013	0.58	0.31	0.27
Finland	2014	0.50	0.26	0.24
Greece	2013	0.57	0.34	0.23
Belgium	2013	0.49	0.27	0.23
Austria	2013	0.50	0.28	0.22
Germany	2013	0.51	0.29	0.22
Portugal	2013	0.56	0.34	0.21
Slovenia	2013	0.47	0.26	0.21
France	2013	0.50	0.29	0.21
Luxembourg	2013	0.48	0.28	0.20
Czech Republic	2013	0.46	0.26	0.20
Italy	2013	0.52	0.33	0.19
Denmark	2013	0.44	0.25	0.19
Spain	2013	0.53	0.35	0.18
UK	2013	0.53	0.36	0.17
Hungary	2014	0.46	0.29	0.17
Poland	2013	0.47	0.30	0.17
Sweden	2013	0.44	0.28	0.16
Slovakia	2013	0.43	0.27	0.16
Norway	2013	0.41	0.25	0.16
Japan	2012	0.49	0.33	0.16
Netherlands	2014	0.44	0.28	0.16
Estonia	2013	0.51	0.36	0.15
Latvia	2013	0.50	0.35	0.15
Australia	2014	0.48	0.34	0.15
Iceland	2013	0.39	0.24	0.14
New Zealand	2012	0.46	0.33	0.13
Canada	2013	0.44	0.32	0.12
USA	2014	0.51	0.39	0.11
Switzerland	2013	0.39	0.30	0.09
Israel	2014	0.46	0.37	0.09
Korea	2014	0.34	0.30	0.04
Chile	2013	0.50	0.47	0.03
Turkey	2013	0.42	0.39	0.03
Mexico	2014	0.48	0.46	0.02

Source: OECD Stat.

Table 12.6 *Inequality by age group in the OECD countries*

	Market income inequality (Gini coefficient)		Net income inequality (Gini coefficient)		Difference	
	18–65	66 and above	18–65	66 and above	18–65	66 and above
Austria	0.426	0.874	0.281	0.275	0.145	0.599
Belgium	0.427	0.913	0.266	0.228	0.161	0.685
Canada	0.411	0.537	0.325	0.276	0.086	0.261
Chile	0.492	0.512	0.467	0.428	0.025	0.084
Czech Republic	0.387	0.863	0.259	0.19	0.128	0.673
Denmark	0.401	0.64	0.255	0.225	0.146	0.415
Estonia	0.45	0.829	0.357	0.269	0.093	0.560
Finland	0.422	0.873	0.262	0.251	0.160	0.622
France	0.445	0.801	0.294	0.297	0.151	0.504
Germany	0.419	0.752	0.299	0.26	0.120	0.492
Greece	0.512	0.89	0.353	0.271	0.159	0.619
Iceland	0.337	0.712	0.246	0.227	0.091	0.485
Ireland	0.533	0.852	0.316	0.282	0.217	0.570
Israel	0.424	0.617	0.341	0.397	0.083	0.220
Italy	0.445	0.813	0.329	0.297	0.116	0.516
South Korea	0.305	0.523	0.28	0.422	0.025	0.101
Latvia	0.433	0.773	0.345	0.308	0.088	0.465
Luxembourg	0.428	0.876	0.28	0.253	0.148	0.623
Netherlands	0.396	0.537	0.284	0.229	0.112	0.308
Norway	0.377	0.591	0.262	0.218	0.115	0.373
Poland	0.423	0.789	0.304	0.253	0.119	0.536
Portugal	0.496	0.866	0.345	0.323	0.151	0.543
Slovakia	0.372	0.771	0.27	0.197	0.102	0.574
Slovenia	0.417	0.809	0.255	0.258	0.162	0.551
Spain	0.479	0.756	0.352	0.29	0.127	0.466
Sweden	0.383	0.62	0.281	0.271	0.102	0.349
Switzerland	0.34	0.553	0.287	0.309	0.053	0.244
Turkey	0.403	0.486	0.382	0.384	0.021	0.102
UK	0.471	0.63	0.353	0.322	0.118	0.308
USA	0.478	0.682	0.392	0.406	0.086	0.276
OECD Average	**0.424**	**0.725**	**0.311**	**0.287**	**0.114**	**0.437**

Source: OECD Stat.
The data refer to the last year available in the OECD Database.
* Data are missing for Australia, Hungary, Japan, Mexico, and New Zealand.

Developed countries like Israel and the United States, which are characterized by less generous welfare states and low direct taxes, tend to exhibit high (net) income inequality. Battisti and Zeira (2016) show that the size of public expenditures plays a key role in explaining the cross-country variation in the differences between market and net income inequality. They found that countries with high shares (percent of GDP) of public spending are more likely to have low income inequality. The negative elasticity of public expenditures is 0.4 with regard to the Gini coefficient of disposable income inequality.

12.4 Conclusion

Net income inequality has risen considerably since the mid-1980s, and as a result, Israel has one of the widest economic gaps in the developed world. In contrast, market income inequality – which reached a record level in 2002 – went down significantly; thanks to that development, Israel's is below the OECD average.

In the last twenty years, several explanations have been raised to account for the rise in income inequality, such as SBTC, globalization, and institutional changes in the labor market. While these explanations are consistent with the rise in market income inequality up to the year 2002, they are not in line with the fall documented in the subsequent years. Thus, other important factors are responsible for the drop in market income inequality.

This chapter identifies three central factors that are consistent with the inverted U-shape of market income inequality: unemployment, mass immigration, and immigrant workers. The evolution of economic gaps very closely followed the rise and fall in unemployment during the examined period. The inverted U-shape in inequality is in line with the dynamics of the effective human capital following the massive wave of immigration from the former Soviet Union that started in the late 1980s. The lack of native language skills (Hebrew) exacerbated the expected immediate fall in human capital of most of the immigrants upon arrival. In the subsequent years, the effective human capital of these immigrants gradually converged to a higher level, pulling down income inequality between native Israelis and immigrants. The dynamics of immigrant workers, who are mainly unskilled, also followed a rise and fall during the investigated period and contributed to the pattern that has been observed in market income inequality. These three forces seem to have overcome the possible widening effect on income inequality that other factors had, like the multi-year reduction of direct taxes in 2003.

The fall in market income inequality should have also appeared in net income inequality, but the reduction in direct taxes and the dramatic cuts in welfare benefits prevented that from happening. It seems that the reduction in income assistance to disadvantaged households, such as in income support and child allowances, was substantial in increasing inequality, which more than offset the contracting effect of the three factors discussed above. The economic program of 2003 and the subsequent policy steps not only reduced the generosity of welfare benefits but also were less targeted toward more vulnerable households. The negative correlation between welfare benefits and the position of welfare recipients in the income ladder diminished and approached zero in 2015.

The dramatic welfare cuts and the reduction in taxes generated a policy reaction that became clearer after the large social protest that erupted in the summer of 2011. The expression of that reaction has been a series of inequality-reducing policy tools, some of which were initiated before the large social protest and the others afterward. These policy tools include lowering the starting age of mandatory education from 5 to 3, halting the reduction of income taxes, devoting more funds to enforcing workers' rights, raising the minimum wage, introducing and expanding the earned income tax credit, mandatory pension saving, eliminating the "welfare to work" program (known as the "Wisconsin Program"), and more recently, introducing child savings accounts. Some of these policy devices seem to have contributed to the declining net income inequality in the last few years. However, it is apparent that the new policy changes channel more resources to the working poor without altering the existing less generous assistance to non-working poor.

The low resources to welfare recipients and income taxes seem to be the central reasons for why net income inequality in Israel is so high. The difference between market and net income in Israel – which appears to be affected by redistribution policy – is one of the lowest in the developed world. Low expenditures on social protection could be consistent with low market income inequality and high net income inequality if the labor supply is sensitive to welfare benefits.

The distribution of net income in Israel relative to those in other developed countries shows a lower share for the bottom income quintile as well as a higher share for the top income decile; however, the differences in the shares of the bottom quintile are more pronounced. These characteristics indicate that both low direct taxes and low welfare benefits are behind the high net income inequality in Israel, although the role of low-income assistance is more important.

Other things being equal, the market income inequality in Israel should be higher than that of other developed countries due to the unique social structure of Israel, which includes two culturally distinct groups (Arabs and Orthodox Jews) with low labor force participation and large families. However, market income inequality in Israel is lower rather than higher than the OECD average. Therefore, these two social groups are not responsible for the high inequality in net income, and other explanations are needed, such as redistribution policy.

Countries may use various strategies to address economic inequality. A country may prefer to rely more on raising earning capacities by investing more in education and training, friendly policies toward low-wage workers (such as minimum wage, generous earned income tax credit), or by providing more generous income assistance to low-income households. This chapter shows that Israel has chosen neither of the two options.

References

Alesina, A., and Rodrik, D. (1994). Distributive Politics and Economic Growth. *The Quarterly Journal of Economics*, 109(2), 465–490.

Atkinson, A. B., Piketty, T., and Saez, E. (2011). Top Incomes in the Long Run of History. *Journal of Economic Literature*, 49(1), 3–71.

Autor, D. H., Katz, L. F., and Kearney, M. S. (2008). Trends in US Wage Inequality: Revising the Revisionists. *The Review of Economics and Statistics*, 90(2), 300–323.

Bank of Israel (2015). *Annual Report: Statistical Appendix.*

Battisti, M., and Zeira, J. (2016). The Effects of Fiscal Redistribution. In K. Basu and J. Stiglitz (eds.), *Inequality and Growth: Patterns and Policy. Vol. I:* Concepts and Analysis. London: Palgrave Macmillan UK, 201–224.

Ben-David, D. (2003). The Socio-Economic Paths for Israel. *Economic Quarterly*, March, 27–46. [Hebrew]

Berman, E., Bound, J., and Griliches, Z. (1994). Changes in the Demand for Skilled Labor within US Manufacturing: Evidence from the Annual Survey of Manufactures. *The Quarterly Journal of Economics*, 109(2), 367–397.

Blaich, Haim (2016). Poverty and Inequality in Israel in International Comparison. In *State of the Nation Report*. Jerusalem: Taub Center, 254–309.

Bound J., and George, J. (1992). Changes in the Structure of Wages in the 1980s: An E valuation of alternative explanations. *American Economic Review*, 82(3), 371–392.

Card, D., Lemieux, T., and Riddell, W. C. (2004). Unions and Wage Inequality. *Journal of Labor Research*, 25(4), 519.

Card, D., and DiNardo, J. E. (2002). Skill-Biased Technological Change and Rising Wage Inequality: Some Problems and Puzzles. *Journal of Labor Economics*, 20(4), 733–783.

Cornfeld, O., and Danieli, O. (2015). The Origins of Income Inequality in Israel: Trends and Policy. *Israel Economic Review*, 12(2), 51–95.

Dahan, M. (1996). The Effect of Macroeconomics Variables on Income Distribution in Israel. *Bank of Israel Economic Review*, 69, 19–43.

(1998). *The Ultra-Orthodox Jews and Municipal Authority. Part 1: The Budgetary Effect of Jerusalem Demographic Composition.* The Jerusalem Institute for Israel Studies. [Hebrew]

(2002). The Rise of Earning Inequality. In A. Ben-Bassat (ed.), *The Israeli Economy, 1985–1998: From Government Intervention to Market Economics.* Cambridge, MA: MIT Press, 485–517.

(2007). Why Has Labor-Force Participation Rate of Israeli Men Fallen? *Israel Economic Review*, 5(2), 95–128.

(2016). How Successful Was the Melting Pot in the Economic Field?, *Israel Economic Review*, 14(1), 1–51.

(2017). Income Inequality in Israel: A Distinctive Evolution. CESifo Working Paper Series No. 6542. SSRN: https://ssrn.com/abstract=3005193.

Dahan, M. et al. (2007). *Why Is Poverty Widespread in Israel? The 14th Caesarea Forum*, June 2006. Jerusalem: The Israel Democracy Institute.

Dahan, M., and Hazan, M. (2014). Priorities in the Government Budget. *Israel Economic Review*, 11(1), 1–33.

Dahan, M., and Tsiddon, D. (1998). Demographic Transition, Income Distribution, and Economic Growth. *Journal of Economic Growth*, 3 (1), 29–52.

Dabla-Norris, M. Era, et al. (2015). *Causes and Consequences of Income Inequality: A Global Perspective.* Staff Discussion Notes No. 15/13. International Monetary Fund.

DiNardo, J., Fortin, N. M., and Lemieux, T. (1996). Labor Market Institutions and the Distribution of Wages, 1973–1992: A Semiparametric Approach. *Econometrica*, 64(5), 1001–1044.

Drucker, L., and Epshtain, O. (2016). Minimum Wage Effects on Employment and Wages in Israel, February. Unpublished manuscript. [Hebrew]

Endeweld, M., and Heller O. (2014). Wages, the Minimum Wage and Their Contribution to Reducing Poverty: Israel in an International Comparison. Working Paper 119, December. National Insurance Institute, Jerusalem. [Hebrew]

Endeweld, M., Gottlieb, D. , and Heller O. (2013). Updating Findings on the Minimum Wage Noncompliance in Comparative Perspective. Policy Paper, July, National Insurance Institute, Jerusalem. [Hebrew]

Feenstra, R. C., and Gordon, H. H. (2003). Global Production Sharing and Rising Inequality: A Survey of Trade and Wages. In E. Kwan Choi and James Harrigan (eds.), *Handbook of International Trade*. Oxford: Basil Blackwell, 146–185.

Flug, K., and Kasir, N. (2003). Poverty and Employment, and the Gulf Between Them. *Israel Economic Review*, 1(1), 55–80.

Galor, O., and Zeira, J. (1993). Income Distribution and Macroeconomics. *The Review of Economic Studies*, 60(1), 35–52.

Ginor, F. (1983). *Socio-Economic Disparities in Israel*. Tel Aviv: Am Oved Publishers. [Hebrew]

Gottlieb, D. (2000). The Effect of Immigrant Workers on Employment, Wage and Inequality: 1995–2000. *Economic Quarterly*, December, 694–736. [Hebrew]

   (2002). The Influence of Non-Israeli Workers on Israeli Employment, Wages and Inequality: 1995—2000. *Economic Quarterly*, 694–736. [Hebrew]

Hill, K. Q., and Leighley, J. E. (1992). The Policy Consequences of Class Bias in State Electorates. *American Journal of Political Science*, 351–365.

Juhn, C., Murphy, K. M., and Pierce, B. (1993). Wage Inequality and the Rise in Returns to Skill. *Journal of Political Economy*, 101(3), 410–442.

Kristal, T., and Cohen, Y. (2007). Decentralization of Collective Agreements and Rising Wage Inequality in Israel. *Industrial Relations: A Journal of Economy and Society*, 46(3), 613–635.

Kristal, T., Mundlak, G., Haberfeld, Y., and Yinon, C. (2015). Union Density in Israel 2006–2012: Bifurcation of the Industrial Relations System. *Labor, Society and Law*, 20, 9–35. [Hebrew]

Milgrom, M., and Bar-Levav, G. (2015). Inequality in Israel: The Distribution of Wealth. The Institute for Structural Reforms. Unpublished manuscript. [Hebrew]

Miller, T. C. (2001). Impact of Globalization on US Wage Inequality: Implications for Policy. *The North American Journal of Economics and Finance*, 12(3), 219–242.

OECD (2015a). *Income Inequality: The Gap Between Rich and Poor*. Paris: OECD Publishing.

(2015b). *In It Together: Why Less Inequality Benefits All*. Paris: OECD Publishing.

Perotti, R. (1996). Growth, Income Distribution, and Democracy: What the Data Say. *Journal of Economic Growth*, 1(2), 149–187.

Piketty, T., and Saez, E. (2003). Income Inequality in the United States, 1913–1998. *The Quarterly Journal of Economics*, 118(1), 1–41.

Strawczynski, M. (2014). Cyclicality of Statutory Tax Rates. *Israel Economic Review*, 11(1), 67–96.

Zussman, N., and Romanov, D. (2005). Happiness of Nations: Israelis' Satisfaction with their Lives. *Bank of Israel Review*, 76, 105–138. [Hebrew]

13 | *The Israeli Labor Market, 1995–2015*

ZVI ECKSTEIN, TALI LAROM, AND OSNAT
LIFSHITZ

13.1 Introduction

In Israel, the employment rate in the main working-age bracket, 25–64, climbed from 66.8 percent in 2002 to 77.6 percent in 2016. This dramatic increase followed more than a decade of falling employment rates. It was in 2003 that the trend changed; the employment rate among men began to rise, reaching 81.4 percent in 2016, and among women the rate rose from 56.5 percent in 1995 to 72 percent in 2016. By segmenting the upturn in employment, we find that the most significant increases in employment rates took place among Arab men, ultra-Orthodox women, older workers (55–64), and the poorly educated.

The increase in employment in Israel stands out particularly against the backdrop of trends elsewhere during that time. American and OECD employment rates plummeted in the aftermath of the 2008 economic crisis, and the slow recovery from it, and have not yet returned to their pre-crisis levels. Israel, in contrast, was hardly affected by the crisis and boasts a very high employment rate today, both relative to its own past and in comparison with other countries. The overall employment rate in Israel, 76.6 percent, exceeds that of the USA (73.9 percent) and the OECD average (73 percent). Today, there is no employment gap between Israel, the USA, and the OECD countries among men (aged 25–64). Among women (aged 25–64) the Israeli rate is 7.8 percentage points higher than that of the OECD average and 4.5 percent higher than the USA.

The increase in employment has of course been paralleled by growth in labor income among all types of households and in the share of labor wage out of total income, even as hourly wages hardly changed.

In this chapter, we attempt to answer one main question: What brought about the change of trend and the massive increase in employment rates among Israel's various population groups from

2002 onward? And why was this growth in employment, while typical of all segments of the population, tilted in the direction of groups of low earning ability? To answer, we estimate employment and wage equations using data from the Israeli labor force, income, and expenditure surveys conducted by the Israeli Central Bureau of Statistics. To examine changes in the coefficients over time, the model equations were estimated for the 2001–2015 period, en bloc and for each year separately. To separate changes in characteristics from changes in returns, we deconstructed the variance into different cross-sections – levels of education, age, and household structure and size – and conducted a separate analysis for the two special population groups: Arabs and ultra-Orthodox. The purpose of this deconstruction is to determine whether the increase in employment originated in demographic changes or in changes in returns that modified incentives.

Analysis of the models' estimates and the deconstruction shows that most of the demographic changes not only failed to abet the increase in employment but actually lowered employment rates. The only exception is an increase in individuals' levels of education, which contributed about 20 percent to the upturn in the employment rate of men and 40 percent of the increase in that of women. Population aging affected employment rates adversely even though raising the pension retirement age triggered a sizable increase in employment among older workers. Changes in household structure and size also affected employment negatively. The proportional growth of the ultra-Orthodox and Arab population groups also made a negative contribution to the total employment rate, even though the employment rates of both groups rose dramatically. Therefore, demographic changes in the aggregate cannot explain the increase in employment during the years in question.

We continue by testing another hypothesis: The increase in employment was triggered by changes in the wage return to education and experience. The results of our estimation show that the return to education was static during the research period at all levels of schooling other than master's degree and up, in which the return increased. The upturn in employment, however, focused specifically on the poorly educated population, as noted above. Examination of the return on experience also showed no major changes over time. Changes in household profile coefficients on the basis of affiliation with the Arab and ultra-Orthodox populations were tested and also proved unable to explain the increase in employment.

Next, we tested the hypothesis that it was policy changes, particularly far-reaching revisions of benefit and tax policies in 2002 and 2003, that turned the trend around and allowed employment to grow. The period at issue did see dramatic policy changes in these fields: In July 2002, the criteria for unemployment benefits were toughened as part of an economic emergency program and the qualifying period for these benefits was extended from six months to one year. In 2003, unemployment compensation was cut back, its maximum payout term was shortened, and its eligibility terms were toughened. These legislative changes triggered a steep decrease in the population of persons eligible for unemployment benefits, reduced payouts of these benefits, and held payoff to a shorter term than before.

Concurrently, in 2003, the income support benefit was reduced and its terms of eligibility were revised. The same year, child allowances were slashed and the dependency of the benefit level on the number of children was revised. In this legislative change, the rising scale of per-child benefits commensurate with the number of children in the household was replaced with a lump sum per child, severely reducing benefits for large families.[1]

The income tax reform that began in 2002 expanded in 2004. The reform, focusing entirely on those of low and median income, raised the tax threshold considerably by about 33 percent and gave a full income tax exemption to some 300,000 working people who had previously been tax-liable. Also in 2004, the statutory retirement age was raised from 65 to 67 for men and from 60 to 62 for women.

From 2005 onward, welfare-to-work programs for income support recipients were piloted. In studies that evaluated the trial programs, it was found that they had a positive effect on employment and labor income and induced cutbacks on welfare payments to those participating. However, they did not affect hourly wages or total income.[2] As for the programs' effect on total employment, it should be borne in mind that they were trial programs that were activated for a small part of the

---

[1] The reduction of child benefits had an adverse effect on productivity (Cohen et al., 2013).

[2] For elaboration on the outcomes of the trial programs see Myers–JDC–Brookdale (2008, 2010) and Schlosser and Shanan (2016).

relevant population; therefore, their impact on total employment was marginal.

Since 2008, too, low-wage working people have qualified for an Earned Income Tax Credit ("labor grant"), on a trial basis at first and, since 2012, countrywide. The level of the grant is determined in accordance with income, household situation, and number of children. Most recipients are working people who have children up to age 18, with a higher sum for those eligible who have three children or more, and working people aged 55+ and over who have no children. In 2014, the grant was paid to 255,000 persons, about 6 percent of all employees countrywide, at an annual average level of NIS 3,400. Although it boosted recipients' earnings in 2012 by only about 3 percent of labor income, it has made a meaningful contribution to large and low-income households, which are also the program's main benefactees (Bank of Israel, 2015; Strawczynski et al., 2015).

The policy changes described above focused on low-income workers, low-education individuals, and large families, those among whom the most meaningful increases in employment occurred. To support the hypothesis that these policy changes explain this outcome, we calculated the change in the share of benefits out of total income and the change in the share of tax out of labor income among households of various types, and examined the correlation between these changes and the increase in employment. We found that the greater the decline in benefits in a given type of household, the stronger was the increase in that type's employment rate. Lowering the tax burden also helped to increase employment, although the effects of this change were smaller than those of the reduction in benefits and were spread more evenly among the different types of households.

In addition, the sample period was typified by a change of policy toward foreign workers, causing these workers' numbers to fall steeply from 15 percent of total business-sector employment in 2002 to 11 percent in 2015 and stimulating demand for poorly skilled workers. Concurrently, the minimum wage was raised from 45 percent of the national median in 1995 to 60 percent, expanding these workers' labor supply.

We conclude that most of the increase in the employment rates trace to the policy measures described above. The only demographic change that abetted employment was the increase in education, which, too, is attributable to a policy change – specifically, the opening of degree-awarding colleges in the early 1990s under an amendment to the Council for Higher Education Law. This conclusion leads to a direct policy recommendation: to sustain the upward movement of employment rates, sustain the current policy measures.

Importantly, these policy measures raised the employment rates of the various groups without adversely affecting their income. Even as employment increased and relatively weak population groups joined the labor market, labor income rose in all deciles and among all population groups. Equalized total gross income also grew and disposable (net) income climbed as well, at rates of 33–47 percent. This demonstrates that even though labor income and benefits are mutually substitutable, the positive effect of employment on households' disposable income exceeded the adverse effect of the lowering of benefits. It is important to stress, however, that disposable income increased more quickly among non-Orthodox Jewish households than among Arab and ultra-Orthodox households. Therefore, the disparities between these groups widened, as did net inequality. This outcome was abetted by two important and typical factors that these groups share: lower employment and wage levels, and higher birth rates.

13.2 Cross-Country Comparison

Israel's employment rate has risen by nearly 10 percent since the beginning of this century. This dramatic increase, following several years of falling employment, stands out particularly in view of trends elsewhere at this time. Thus, in the OECD countries, the group of "benchmark countries,"[3] and the USA, employment rates plummeted in the aftermath of the 2008 economic crisis and the slow recovery that followed and have not yet returned to their pre-crisis levels. In contrast, Israel was hardly affected by the crisis, and its current employment rate is very high both relative to its past and by cross-country comparison. Employment in Israel's main working-age group (25–64) rose from 66.8 percent in 2002 to 76.6 percent in 2016, surpassing that of the

---

[3] A group of developed OECD countries that resemble Israel in size, level of openness to international trade, and human capital as the basis for growth, but that have larger per capita GDP and lower poverty rates than Israel's; therefore, we chose this group as a peer (or target) for Israel. The group comprises Sweden, Denmark, the Netherlands, Austria, Switzerland, Finland, and Ireland.

USA and the OECD countries (73.9 percent and 73 percent, respectively) albeit slightly below the benchmark group (78 percent).[4,5]

Among men in the main working-age group, the employment rate fell from 80.7 percent in 1995 to 74.3 percent in 2002, and afterwards rose almost uninterruptedly to 81.4 percent in 2016. (The disparity relative to the OECD countries, 7.6 percentage points in 2002, was almost totally closed and the difference relative to the USA, even larger in the early 2000s, turned around in Israel's favor.) Among women in the same age group, the change was even more dramatic: their employment increased throughout this period, from 56.5 percent in 1995 to 72 percent in 2016. Until 2004, the employment level and its rate of increase resembled those of the OECD countries, whereas in the USA women's employment was higher and steady. From 2004 onward, women's employment accelerated briskly in Israel but continued to rise mildly in the OECD countries (apart from a slight decrease in the aftermath of the 2008 crisis) and fell in the USA as an outcome of the crisis, with no substantial recovery since then. Consequently, women's employment in Israel today exceeds that of the OECD countries and in the USA by 7.8 and 4.5 percentage points, respectively. Furthermore, whereas in Israel, as in the world at large, women's employment rates fall short of men's, the gender gap has been narrowing more quickly in Israel than in the OECD countries and the USA, standing at the time of writing at 9.4 percentage points as against 17.9 and 13.3, respectively.

The picture in labor force participation is similar. After a lengthy decrease in men's participation rates, the participation rate began to rise perceptibly in the early 2000s; today, men's participation rate is slightly higher in Israel than in the USA and is approaching that of the benchmark and OECD countries. The participation rate of women, which had risen moderately at rates similar to those in the OECD countries, spurted ahead in 2004. Today, it far surpasses corresponding rates in the USA and the OECD countries and is verging on that of the benchmark countries.

---

[4] The total employment rate among those aged 15 and over shows a similar increase, from 53.2 in 2002 to a record 61.1 percent in 2016.

[5] The years 2003–2004 were typified by economic growth that was powered by the exit from a recession in 2002. However, since the recession had little effect on employment, which oscillated at around 68 percent before the crisis (Figure 13.1), the recovery from the recession cannot explain the dramatic increase in employment.

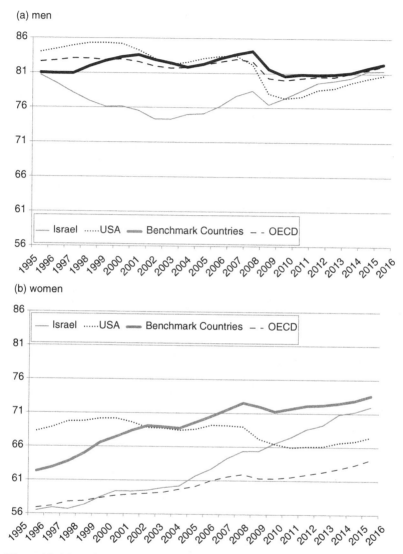

(a) men

(b) women

Figure 13.1 Employment rate, ages 25–64: A. Men; B. Women

We complete the tableau by observing unemployment rates during this time. In the early 2000s, unemployment in Israel spiked powerfully, in contrast to the benchmark countries and the USA, but has made a strong retreat since the middle of that decade. Since the effect of the 2008 crisis was relatively mild in Israel, the country's unemployment rate today,

4 percent, is far below that of the benchmark and OECD countries and approximates that of the USA.

The participation rate does not reflect the dramatic changes in the labor market and the sometimes endogenous disengagement of unemployment from nonparticipation; therefore, the analysis going forward will focus on employment rates.[6]

13.3 Employment- and Wage-Equation Estimates

In this section we estimate the employment and wage equations, reduced-form equations derived from the model that describes households' employment decisions.[7]

13.3.1 Employment Equation

Here we use a linear probability model (LPM) to estimate individuals' employment decisions.[8] The explanatory variables are individuals' education, experience, and household structure.[9] The model is estimated on the basis of 2001–2015 data[10] en bloc and for each year separately; it allows us to examine potential parameter changes over time. We also add dummy variables for Arabs and ultra-Orthodox Jews to the model equations.

In the reduced-form LPM, the dependent variable receives the value of *D=1* if the individual is employed and 0 otherwise. The employment equation obtained is:

$$D_t^j = \alpha_{0j} + \alpha_{1j}education_t + \alpha_{2j}age_t + \alpha_{3j}family\_structure_t$$
$$+ \alpha_{4j}population\_group_t + \varepsilon_{jt}^D \ for \ j = f, m \tag{1}$$

---

[6] Analysis of the change in weekly hours worked over time shows no change among women and only a very mild decrease among men. Therefore, we focus on the employment rate (extensive margin) and not on hours worked.

[7] For the model and the mathematical development of equations (1) and (2), see Eckstein et al. (2018), Appendix C.

[8] By using this model, we are able to compare the coefficients over time. A logit model for employment yielded coefficients of the same directionality as well as similar forecasts.

[9] Lacking direct data on individuals' work experience, we use age as a proxy.

[10] Education data based on the highest diploma earned are not available for 1995–2000.

where *education* represents the individual's education. We assume five possible education levels: up to secondary with no matriculation certificate; matriculation certificate; partial-academic (practical engineering, technician), baccalaureate degree; and master's degree and up. *Age* is composed of a dummy variable for the age groups. *Family structure* comprises nine dummy variables: household with one person and no children; 1–2 children, and 3+ children, where single-person households headed by women are separated from those headed by men, along with the three other possibilities: couple with no children, with 1–2 children and 3+ children. *Population_group* is composed of two dummy variables, one for Arabs and one for ultra-Orthodox Jews.[11]

We also estimated equation (1) for each population group separately. Individuals' level of education has a strong effect on their employment choices, among the population at large and in each constituent group. The equation, however, does not allow for a distinction between the effect of the increase in demand for educated persons and the increase in supply of such persons. We return to this matter in our analysis of the wage equation. The effect of age on employment varies among the groups: It becomes negative earlier in the Arab population than among the non-Orthodox Jewish population, among both women and men. Among the ultra-Orthodox population, a stronger mix of the age and cohort effect is evident: all age coefficients are positive for men and negative for women and represent the change in intergenerational employment trends in this society.

Households that have two potential breadwinners typically have much higher employment rates than do single-person households, and their employment rates decline monotonically with the number of children for women and rise with the number of children for men. Single-person households, in contrast, whether headed by women or by men, are typified by lower employment rates and a negative effect of number of children on employment. The model for the entire population shows that when all the aforementioned demographic traits are controlled for, Arabs and ultra-Orthodox Jews typically have lower employment rates, with a stronger negative effect on ultra-Orthodox men and on Arab women.

---

[11] A household is defined as ultra-Orthodox if the last place of study of one of its members is a yeshiva.

13.3.2 Wage Equation

A standard Mincer equation is used to describe personal wage:

$$lnw_t^j = \omega_{0j} + \omega_{1j}education_t + \omega_{2j}age_t + \omega_{3j}population\_group_t$$
$$+ \varepsilon_{jt}^W \ for \ j = f, m \tag{2}$$

with the explanatory variables defined as in the employment equation.

We estimated the wage equations with a Heckman correction for selection. Matriculation raises women's wages by 28 percent (for men: 12 percent) relative to non-matriculation, nonacademic post-secondary education raises wages by 36 percent among women (20 percent among men), a baccalaureate degree by 70 percent (52 percent), and a master's degree by 88 percent (63 percent). Interestingly, wage return on education is much higher for women than for men (in a model that makes no correction for selection, return on education is identical for women and men at all education levels other than the lowest). Wages are typically rather low in people's first years in the labor market (age 25–34) but rise vigorously with age among men, whereas among women wages climb as far as the 45–54 age group and decline among those aged 55–64. Wages of Arab women are 39 percent (Arab men 23 percent) lower than those of non-Orthodox Jewish women with similar characteristics. Ultra-Orthodox men's wages exceed those of non-Orthodox Jewish men of the same education attainment and age by 15 percent (as against 5 percent in the model that is not correct for selection), whereas ultra-Orthodox women receive the same wage as non-Orthodox Jewish women (as against 8 percent in favor of ultra-Orthodox women in the uncorrected model). This is an especially surprising outcome because ultra-Orthodox education is thought to be of lower quality than that of the Jewish population at large.

13.3.3 Employment Equations Parsed by Years

We estimated the employment and wage equations for each year separately. This allows us to estimate the change in employment that originates in (a) demographic changes that are included in the explanatory variables and (b) changes in the parameters that reflect changes in policy and technology (assuming that individuals' preferences remain relatively constant). For example, changes in the constant of the employment equation reflect policy changes unless a large increase occurred in the constant of the wage equation.[12]

Figure 13.2, juxtaposing the constant of the employment equation with the employment rate, shows that the change in the constant follows the same trend as the change in the employment rate for both men and women. In the LPM model, the change in the constant reflects the estimate of change in the employment rate that is independent of the explanatory variables and does not originate in demographic changes (since the model controls for changes in education, age, household composition, and population composition). Therefore, the figure shows that the increase in employment stems largely from exogenous factors (policy changes) and not from demographic changes. In the next section, we obtain further support for this outcome by decomposing the increase in employment into demographic groups.

13.4 The Effect of Demographic Changes on Employment

The effect of demographic changes on employment is parsed to include changes in level of education and age structure, population groups (non-Orthodox Jews, Arabs, and ultra-Orthodox), and household structure (couples and singles with and without children). We present the effect of each of these variables on employment along with their total impact.

13.4.1 Education

The population's level of education has risen perceptibly in the past twenty years, to no small extent due to Amendment 10 to the Council for Higher Education Law, which made it possible to open degree-granting colleges in Israel (the law extended the number of institutions that are allowed to give a bachelor's degree from six to thirty-one). Figure 13.3 presents the distribution of education and employment at each education level. The figure illustrates the monotonic decrease in the share of individuals not entitled to a matriculation certificate along with the rising share of those with an academic education. The proportion of men with education up to secondary without matriculation fell

---

[12] The results of the regression show that the change in the wage-equation constants for men and women has been very small over the years.

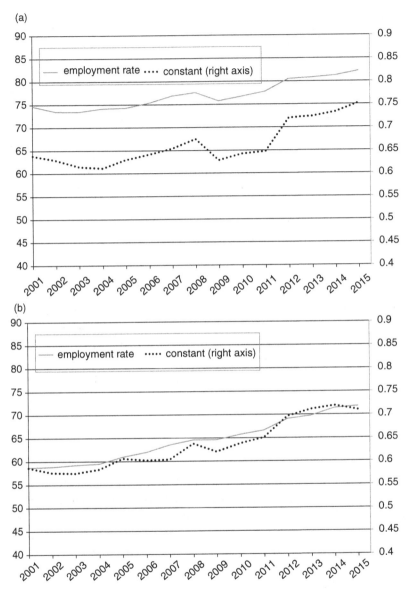

Figure 13.2 Employment rate and the constant of the LPM employment equation: A. Men; B. Women

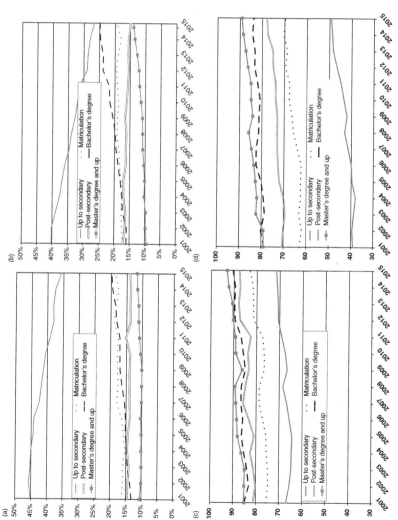

Figure 13.3 Distribution of education and employment rate by education, ages 25–64: A. Men – distribution; B. Women – distribution; C. Men – employment; D. Women – employment

from 45.7 percent in 2002 to 35.7 percent in 2015, whereas the proportion of men with baccalaureate degrees climbed from 13.7 percent to 19.9 percent. Among women, the share who had secondary education without matriculation fell from 40.2 percent in 2002 to 26.7 percent in 2015, while that of recipients of baccalaureate degrees climbed from 16 percent to 24.9 percent in the respective years. Furthermore, working-age women were better educated than working-age men in 2015: fewer had secondary schooling, with or without matriculation (46.2 percent of women as against 54.5 percent of men), and more had post-secondary and academic education.

The increase in the population's level of education helped to push employment up, of course, but, as Figure 13.3 shows, employment increased considerably in 2002–2015 at every level of schooling, among both men and women. It is commonly argued that the population of new participants in the labor market in recent years is typified by poor education and skills. This, however, is only partly so: The increase in employment stands out among matriculated men, from 74.8 percent in 2002 to 83.1 percent in 2015 (an increase of 11 percent), but is also evident among the other groups (up 9 percent). The clearly visible positive relation between education and employment persisted throughout the research period; among men, the employment disparity between the highest group (master's degree and up) and the lowest (up to secondary, no matriculation) was 21.5 percentage points in 2015.

Women's employment was lower than men's at all education levels and conspicuously so among women with up to secondary education and no matriculation: 22.2 percentage points lower than among men with the same level of schooling. (About one-third of these women are Arab.) This group also enjoyed the largest increase in employment, from 39.5 percent in 2002 to 49.4 percent in 2015 (a 25 percent boost). In the other groups, however, women's employment grew much like men's (by 5 percent for holders of baccalaureate degrees and 12 percent for all the others), leaving a large gap between the highest group and the lowest (39.8 percentage points in 2015).

Concurrent with the increase in employment, changes occurred in the distribution of employed persons' occupations and branches. The share of skilled workers among men (in manufacturing, construction, and other) fell from 37 percent in 1995 to 28 percent in 2011, whereas that of those in academic occupations, liberal professions, and technical and managerial vocations climbed from 30 percent to 38 percent. The distribution by economic branches[13] shows contraction in the share of men employed in manufacturing, from 27 percent in 1995 to 19 percent in 2011, whereas the share of those employed in business and financial services climbed from 12 percent to 19 percent. Among women, the changes were smaller but similar, giving further expression to the increase in the population's level of education and, particularly, to the upturn in the share of those with academic diploma.

Deconstructing the increase in employment in 2002–2015, we find that the most conspicuous constituent group, in all education categories, was that with secondary education, with or without matriculation.[14] As stated, the share of the less-employed groups contracted during this time; therefore, even if the employment rate at each level of education had remained at its 2002 level, total employment would have risen, but by much less: to 75.1 percent for men and 64.1 percent for women, 7.5 percentage points lower for both sexes than the actual 2015 level. In other words, the increase in education contributed *some 20 percent to the increase in men's employment and 40 percent to the growth of women's employment*; the rest originates in employment growth within each education group. Much of the disparity between the predicted employment rates and actual employment in the foregoing scenario, 30 percent for men and 35 percent for women, traces to the increase in employment of persons with up to secondary schooling and no matriculation. This group contributes much more to the increase in employment than do the other groups.

To complete the analysis of the effect of education, we return to the wage regression in section 13.3 and ask whether changes in the wages of the various education groups, and in the return on education, may explain this phenomenon. Large wage disparities among the education levels are evident; wage increased during the review period only among those with academic schooling. The return on education obtained by

---

[13] The classification of occupations and economic branches changed in 2012; therefore, to allow for consistent longitudinal comparison, we relate here to the 1995–2011 period only.

[14] For the deconstruction, we calculated the employment rates that would be obtained if the share of persons employed in each group remained at its 2002 level, and then calculated the employment that would be obtained had the rate risen to its 2015 level in only one of the groups. In both cases, the total employment rate was weighted by the size of each group in the total population aged 25–64 in 2015.

estimating the wage equation for each year separately is constant at all levels of schooling except at master's level and above; thus, it cannot explain the increase in employment among persons with secondary education (with or without matriculation). Also, the constant in the wage equation did not change over the years, giving further indication that gross wage was not a meaningful precipitant of employment changes during that time.

13.4.2 Age Groups

The average age of the population in Israel, like that in most OECD countries, is gradually rising. The share of the 25–34 age group is contracting and that of the 55–64 bracket has been moving up, accounting for about one-fifth of the main working-age population in 2015.

It was also in the 55–64 age group, the group that had the lowest employment rates, that the most substantial increase in employment took place: from 60.9 percent in 2002 to 73.8 percent in 2015 among men and from 38.6 percent to 60 percent among women (Figure 13.4). The increase in older workers' employment rates originates, among other things, in the raising of the mandatory retirement age from 65 to 67 for men and from 60 to 62 for women, implemented gradually from 2004 onward. In addition to the direct effect of this change on employment, it probably also affected the decisions of workers in younger age groups to delay their retirement. Among men, differences in employment rates in the other age groups are also evident: those aged 35–44 worked more than people both younger than them and older than them, whereas the employment rates of women in the 25–54 range showed no variance among subgroups.

The change in the population's age composition not only fails to explain the increase in employment but actually *lowers* the total employment rate. Had the employment rate in every age group stayed at its 2002 level, the change in age composition would have reduced the employment rate of men (women) by 0.6 (1.0) of a percentage point.

13.4.3 Population Groups

According to one of the most widely expressed arguments in the analysis of Israel's labor market, the increase in employment in recent years originates

(a)

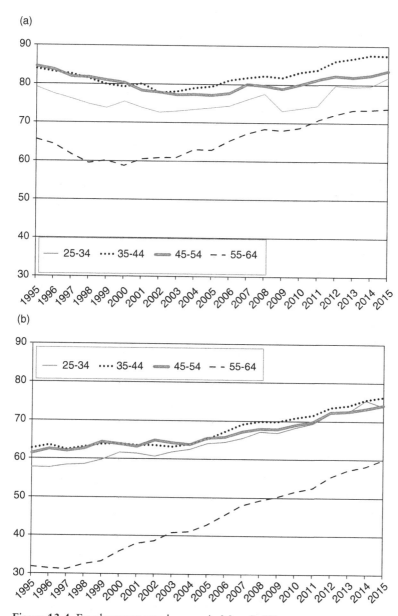

(b)

Figure 13.4 Employment rate by age: A. Men; B. Women

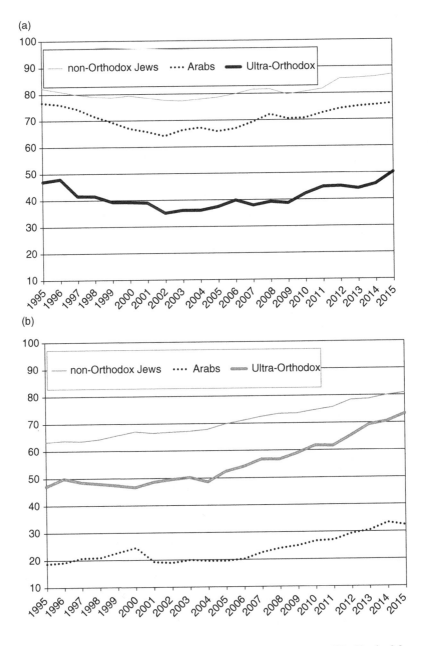

Figure 13.5 Employment rate by population group, ages 25–64: A. Men;
B. Women

in greater integration of Arab men and ultra-Orthodox women into the labor market. This claim fails to tell the whole story by far. It is true that the employment rate of these two groups has gone up, as has their share in the population (ultra-Orthodox men: from 4.4 percent among all men aged 25–65 in 2002 to 7.4 percent in 2015, and Arab men: from 16.6 percent to 18.2 percent), but this is still low relative to the rest of the population. The employment rate of Arab men of main working age has indeed risen powerfully, from 64.2 percent in 2002 to 76.1 percent in 2015 (Figure 13.6) after falling for several years, but it remains far below that of non-Orthodox Jewish men, among whom, too, the employment rate has risen: from 77.6 percent in 2002 to 87 percent in 2015. Although ultra-Orthodox men's employment rates remain much lower, the pace of increase in their employment was the fastest: from 35.1 percent in 2002 to 50.2 percent in 2015, an increase of more than 40 percent. The impact of this growth was amplified by the strong increase in their share of the population during these years.

Among women, it is undisputed that the major influx of ultra-Orthodox women into the labor market – from 49.5 percent employed in 2002 to 73.2 percent in 2015 – an increase of nearly 50 percent (Figure 13.5) – is one of the most substantive changes that the labor market has experienced. Also noteworthy is the fact that unlike the other groups (and most of the Western world), employment of women far outpaces that of men in the ultra-Orthodox sector. Employment of non-Orthodox women, however, also increased during this time, from 18.9 percent to 32.3 percent among Arab women and from 67 percent to 80.9 percent among all other women. In relative terms, it should be noted that the growth rate was steepest among Arab women, who have the lowest employment level: an upturn of 71 percent between 2002 and 2015. This may be attributed, among other factors, to their having fewer and fewer children, given the inverse relation that exists between number of children and employment, as described below.

Deconstructing the increase in employment in 2002–2015, we find that the entry of Arab men and ultra-Orthodox women is not the main, let alone the only, source of the rising employment rate. Since the share of the less-employed groups has gone up, had the employment rate of each of the population groups remained at its 2002 level, total employment would have *fallen* to 72 percent among men and 57.3 percent among women. Furthermore, had only ultra-Orthodox women's employment risen and Arab and non-Orthodox Jewish women maintained their 2002 employment rates, the share of employed women would have remained at its 2002 level of 58.9 percent; and had only the employment rate of Arab men risen, the employment level of men would have gone up by only 0.7 percentage point (and not by 8.8 percentage points, as actually happened).

Finally, we ask whether it was changes in wage returns among different groups that prompted employment in these groups to increase. Hourly wage among Arabs and ultra-Orthodox did not grow in 2002 (among Arabs it fell slightly). Furthermore, the wage gaps between the groups did not close during the period; they even became more negative among the Arab population. Thus, one cannot argue that it was the narrowing of wage gaps that caused these groups to join the labor force more intensively.

13.4.4 Household Structure

Marital status and the number of children are important characteristics that affect decisions on employment, leisure, and home production (mainly childcare). Given the different sizes and extents of change among the groups, here we analyze ultra-Orthodox, Arabs, and non-Orthodox Jews separately. Nearly all ultra-Orthodox households are composed of couples and more than half have three or more children (Table 13.1); these patterns hardly changed during the research period. Only 16 percent of Arab households are single-person and the number of children among couples has been trending downward (the share of couples with three or more children fell from 45 percent in 2002 to 37 percent in 2015), whereas among non-Orthodox Jews 30 percent of households are single-person and the number of children hardly increased during the research period.

Table 13.1 yields one main conclusion: As Arab women joined the labor force, they had fewer children. Their decline in fertility may have been a precipitant of the upturn in employment but is probably also a result of the increase. Employment rate of ultra-Orthodox women, in contrast, increased without a major decrease in household size.

As stated, employment decisions in households are a function of both spouses' characteristics, preferences, and opportunities. Therefore, it is important to present and analyze employment at the level of the entire household as well as at that of the individual only. For this purpose, we examined the employment of the head of household and his or her

Table 13.1 *Distribution of household composition by population group, head of household aged 25–64 (%)*

	2002			2015		
	Non-Orthodox Jews	Arabs	Ultra-Orthodox	Non-Orthodox Jews	Arabs	Ultra-Orthodox
Couple, no children	22.7	9.8	13.3	24.9	12.3	13.2
Couple, 1–2 children	32.9	26.7	23.4	28.7	32.5	22.7
Couple, 3+ children	13.4	45.1	57.1	15.3	36.6	55.8
Single-person households, man, no children	12.3	7.8	3.7	12.2	6.6	3.3
Single-person households, man, with children	1	1.6	0.4	0.7	2.2	0.6
Single-person households, woman, no children	11.9	5.7	1.3	9.7	5.2	1.5
Single-person households, woman, 1–2 children	4.9	1.1	0.3	4.5	1.8	0.5
Single-person households, woman, 3+ children	0.9	1.8	0.3	0.9	2	0.6

spouse and defined the total employment of the household thus: for a single-person household, 0 if the person is not working and 1 if working; for a household composed of a couple, 0 if neither spouse is working, 0.5 if one is working, and 1 if both are working. This analysis shows that employment increased in all household types and did so most meaningfully among households composed of single women with three children or more and couples with three children or more.

A more detailed analysis of employment patterns among couples shows that the share of working couples increased from 52.3 percent in 2002 to 65.8 percent in 2015, whereas that of couples in which only the male partner works fell to 20.1 percent and that of couples in which only the female partner works declined to 9.1 percent. (The complementary group, couples in which neither spouse works, also contracted.) The switch to two breadwinners took place in all groups, but at different scopes and paces. In more than half of Arab households, still only the male partner works, whereas in roughly one-third of ultra-Orthodox households the wife is the sole breadwinner.

Much like the demographic changes described in the previous two sections, changes in household structure do not explain the increase in employment. Had the employment of each of the household types remained at its 2002 level, total employment would have *fallen* by 2.2 percentage point; this is due mainly to the rising share of couples with three or more children (among whom employment is relatively low) and the falling proportion of couples with one or two children (those with the highest employment rates). Thus, in this aspect of household structure, too, the entire increase in employment originates in change within each group.

In sum, the demographic changes in age composition, household composition, and population composition are affecting aggregate employment rates adversely, whereas changes in education composition explain 20 percent of the increase in men's employment and 40 percent of women's. Changes in the wage return to the exogenous variables also fail to explain the upturn in employment and, particularly, the increase in employment among low-earning-ability groups.

13.5 Wage and Income Trends

Amid the dramatic increase in employment, hourly and monthly wages largely stagnated between 2002 and 2015 (Figure 13.6). These

(a)

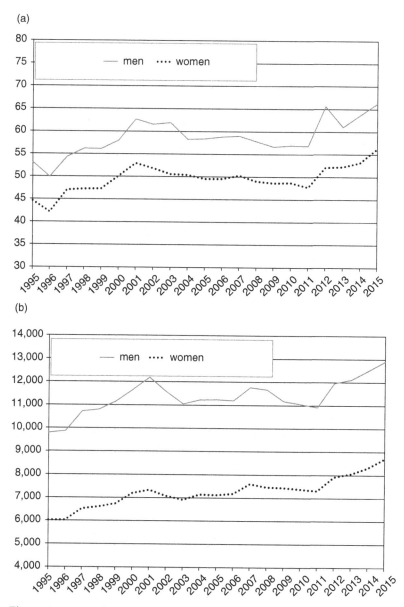

(b)

Figure 13.6 Hourly and monthly wage, ages 25–64 (2015 NIS): A. Hourly wage; B. Monthly wage

moments actually fell slightly until 2011 and only then began to rise among the non-Orthodox Jewish group only. The mild decrease in mean wage is attributable to the fact, described above, that many of those newly joining the labor market are relatively poorly schooled, advanced in years, or affiliated with lower-wage population groups.

The increase in employment-induced upturns in the proportion of households that have labor income and in the share of labor income out of gross household income, from 71.6 percent in 2002 to 78.1 percent in 2015.[15] The ascending share of labor income among ultra-Orthodox and Arab households, to 62 percent and 75 percent, respectively, is particularly salient. Furthermore, in all population sectors, equalized labor income increased among households that had labor income even though those newly joining the labor force come from relatively weak population groups, at rates of 5 percent, 17 percent, and 28 percent among ultra-Orthodox, Arab, and non-Orthodox Jewish households, respectively. Concurrently, the share of social insurance benefits in gross household income has been falling.

Analysis of the changes in various kinds of household income and among the different groups and types (Table 13.2) yields three main conclusions. First, labor income[16] increased in all households' types and all population groups, and most conspicuously among households that boosted their employment strongly (particularly couples with three or more children). Second, the across-the-board increase in household gross income shows that even though labor income and benefit income are substitutable and an upturn in household employment often triggers the loss of income support benefits, the overall effect of the increase in employment on household income has been perceptibly favorable. Third, the upturn in (net) disposable income shows that the heightened employment was accompanied by an improvement in households' measured standard of living (even though the loss of leisure, the increase in spending related to holding a job, the nonfinancial utilities of going to work, and the intergenerational effect are disregarded here). The gap between the rise in net income and that

---

[15] Total gross income is income from all sources including labor, welfare benefits, capital gains, and institutional and personal support. Disposable income (net) is gross income less income tax, social security provisions, and national health tax.

[16] Calculated in this table as average labor income for all households, meaning that households that have no labor income are weighted at zero.

in gross income reflects the lowering of income tax rates during this time (see below).

However, it is also important to emphasize the persistent disparities in income levels and growth rates among the population groups. Although the labor income of ultra-Orthodox and Arab households has risen slightly faster than that of non-Orthodox Jewish households, it remains far behind. In 2015, equalized labor income of ultra-Orthodox and Arab households was about one-third that of non-Orthodox Jewish household. Equalized disposable income, in contrast, advanced more swiftly among non-Orthodox Jewish households, by 47 percent as against 33 percent and 35 percent among ultra-Orthodox and Arab households; therefore, the disparities between them widened.[17] According to 2015 data, equalized disposable income in ultra-Orthodox and Arab households is only 41 percent of that among non-Orthodox Jewish households (NIS 3,000 as against NIS 6,900). Two main factors abetted the slower growth rates and the widening of disparities between these two groups: lower employment and wage, and higher birth rates.

In the last row in Table 13.2, the change in labor income is shown to have been greater among the Arab and ultra-Orthodox populations, allowing inequality in labor income to narrow. The change in disposable income, however, was smaller among these population groups due to the slashing of welfare benefits, causing net inequality to widen.

13.6 Policy Changes

As we saw in section 13.4, neither demographic changes (composition of education, age, and household structure) nor the increase in employment among Arab or ultra-Orthodox population can explain the dramatic upturn in employment rates. Changes in the returns to education and experience also fail to explain it. In addition, as shown, the growth in employment was particularly appreciable among poorly educated persons and households with children. The alternative explanation proposed in this section addresses itself to policy measures that revised the set of incentives to join the labor force, specifically the cutback in income support and child benefits and the lowering of income tax rates.

---

[17] For discussion of disparities and poverty in Israel, see Eckstein and Larom (2016), Dahan (2017), and Chapter 12 by Dahan, this volume.

Table 13.2 *Total changes in income by population group and household composition, 2002–2015, head of household aged 25–64 (%)*

	Change in labor income			Change in gross income			Change in disposable income		
	Non-Orthodox Jews	Arabs	Ultra-Orthodox	Non-Orthodox Jews	Arabs	Ultra-Orthodox	Non-Orthodox Jews	Arabs	Ultra-Orthodox
Couple, no children	45	22	12	41	19	11	51	27	18
Couple, 1–2 children	23	27	52	23	23	38	38	33	51
Couple, 3+ children	53	41	68	49	18	32	59	25	35
Single-person households, man, no children	30	20		37	17		50	28	
Single-person households, woman, no children	36	31		37	23		46	27	
Single-person households, man, with children	75			44			48		
All households	36	38	43	35	27	26	47	35	33

Shadowed cells are not presented due to small number of observations.

These changes, which according to the economic model provided a positive incentive to employment, were more meaningful for the poorly educated and for households with children, who derived a larger share of total household income from income support and child allowances, than for others.

13.6.1 Transfer Payments and Taxes

At the beginning of the 2000s, the government initiated far-reaching changes in the welfare-payment and taxation system: income support and child benefits were lowered, and income tax structure and tax brackets were adjusted. These changes were mirrored in actual remittances to and by households (Figure 13.7): The average monthly income support benefit per household fell by 19 percent between 2002 and 2015; the average monthly child benefit per household dropped by 47 percent during this period;[18] and the mean share of compulsory payments (income tax, social insurance, and national health tax) in household labor income dropped from 24 percent in 2002 to 18 percent in 2015.

The steep and protracted decrease in the proportion of households receiving income support, from 7.2 percent in 2002 to 2.7 percent in 2015, is not only an outcome of the increase in employment but also the main reason for the upturn. The toughening of eligibility terms for this benefit, coupled with the severe reduction in benefit levels in the early 2000s, incentivized households to join the labor market by decimating their welfare-benefit income. The income tax reduction acted in the same direction and encouraged low-wage individuals to take on jobs. Presumably, the process was also helped along by the implementation of proactive policy programs in the labor market starting in the second half of the 2000s and addressed to low-employment groups, particularly one-stop shops for the ultra-Orthodox and Arab populations, negative income tax, and welfare-to-work programs.

To reinforce the argument that changes in benefits figured importantly in the upturn in employment, we juxtaposed the change in

---

[18] The benefit for a household with up to three children was essentially unchanged, whereas that for a household with four children declined by 26 percent, for a household with five children by 34 percent, and for a household with six children by 39 percent.

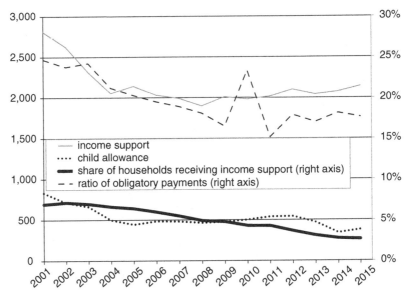

Figure 13.7 Income support, child allowance, and obligatory payments, head of household aged 25–64

employment with the change in the share of benefits and the levels of child allowance for the various types of households.

Table 13.3 shows how clearly the rate of decrease in benefits is related to the pace of the upturn in employment among the various households' types. The falling share of benefits in income is monotonic and steep in relation to the number of children and so, accordingly, is the increase in employment rates among families with children. The decline in the share of benefits was steepest among ultra-Orthodox couples; accordingly, this population achieved the fastest rate of growth in employment.

13.6.2 Additional Policy Changes

Another policy change that may have affected employment generally, and that of poorly skilled workers particularly, concerns the treatment of foreign and Palestinian workers. From 2002 onward, the share of non-Israeli workers in the business sector fell considerably, from more than 16 percent at its peak in 1999 to 12 percent or less in 2004 and

Table 13.3 Changes in employment, ratio of benefits, and level of child allowance by population group and household composition, 2002–2015, head of household aged 25–64 (%)

	Non-Orthodox Jews			Arabs			Ultra-Orthodox		
	Employment	Ratio of benefits	Child allowance	Employment	Ratio of benefits	Child allowance	Employment	Ratio of Benefits	Child Allowance
Couple, no children	13	−34	0	40	−46	0	39	−43	0
Couple, 1 child	10	−31	0	14	−47	0	22	−14	0
Couple, 2 children	13	−35	0	21	−19	0	56	−33	0
Couple, 3 children	15	−55	−6	28	−23	−6	33	−55	−6
Couple, 4 children	22	−74	−26	35	−56	−26	49	−59	−26
Couple, 5+ children	50	−64	−34 to −48	24	−60	−34 to −48	45	−61	−34 to −48
Single-person households, man, with children	16	−38							

Table 13.3 (*cont.*)

	Non-Orthodox Jews		Arabs			Ultra-Orthodox		
	Employment	Ratio of benefits Child allowance	Employment	Ratio of benefits	Child allowance	Employment	Ratio of Benefits	Child Allowance
Single-person households, woman, no children	18	−30						
Single-person households, woman, with children	26	−56						

steady since then. Given the substitution effect between foreign workers and poorly skilled Israeli workers, cutting back on the supply of the former had a favorable effect on demand for the latter (Cohen Goldner, 2019).

As government policy reduced the number of non-Israeli workers, the minimum wage was raised from 44 percent of the median hourly wage at the beginning of the period to 60 percent at its end. According to economic theory, an increase in the minimum wage may itself depress demand for poorly skilled workers. When the minimum wage rises at a time when such labor is in short supply (due to a cutback in the foreign-worker population), however, its effect on employment may be different. Furthermore, the minimum wage is not fully enforced.

In sum, after refuting the hypotheses that trace the increase in employment to demographic or wage-structure changes generally, and to wage return to education in particular, we find the definitive precipitants of the growth in employment in the policy measures that were taken, particularly the lowering of welfare benefits. The fact that employment rates have continued to rise in the past five years as well, after the welfare cuts were partly rescinded, proves that the other policy measures and proactive tools in the labor market also had meaningful effects on the growth of employment and the increase in labor income among low-income households. These results reinforce the economic argument that the continuation of active policies that encourage individuals and households to increase labor supply and earning ability will have a strong effect on their well-being, economic growth, and the country's economic and social resilience.

13.7 Summary and Conclusions

Two main processes have typified the Israeli labor market since the turn of the present century: a major increase in employment and upward movement of wage income. The employment rate in the main working-age bracket, 25–64, climbed from 66.8 percent in 2002 to 76.6 percent in 2016, surpassing the American and OECD averages. One reason for the closing of this gap is the still-ongoing slump in employment in these comparison countries due to the 2008 crisis, as against the negligible effect of the crisis on employment in Israel. The upturn in employment in Israel is an across-the-board phenomenon that spans sectors, education levels, and age groups. Employment among men aged 25–64 began to rise in 2002 after several years of decline and came to 81.4 percent in 2016. The percent of working women remains lower than that of men, but the growth trend in employment has been faster and ongoing among women, their rate rising to 72 percent in 2016.

Contrary to the conventional wisdom, joining the labor market among Arab men (of whom 76 percent were employed in 2015) and ultra-Orthodox women (73 percent) – however meaningful and rapid it has been – is neither the only source of the powerful upturn in employment nor even the main one. Analysis of the increase in 2002–2015 shows that most of it, 68 percent among men and 73 percent among women, originates in the upturn in employment of non-Orthodox Jews. Even though employment has risen in all groups, intergroup disparities remain visible, particularly the low employment rates of ultra-Orthodox men (50 percent) and Arab women (32 percent).

Conventional wisdom also has it that the newly employed are poorly schooled. This, too, is true only in part. Yes, the increase in employment was fastest among those with secondary schooling, with or without matriculation, but the employment of people with post-secondary and academic education slanted upward as well. The disparities among levels of education remained large, particularly between the employment rate of those with matriculation and those lacking it (11.5 percentage points among men and 20.4 among women). Education levels rose considerably during the research period, particularly in the share of those with baccalaureate degrees, for reasons including the opening of degree-awarding colleges. The upturn in education is one of the most important factors behind the growth of employment, accounting for 20 percent of the total increase among men and 40 percent among women.

In another noteworthy and material process, the share of employed persons aged 55–64 escalated considerably along with growth in their share of the population. Thus, 74 percent of men and 60 percent of women in this age group were employed in 2015, as against 61 percent and 39 percent in 2002. This change is traceable, among other factors, to the raising of the statutory retirement age, which also influenced younger workers to delay their retirement. It is likely that changes in the system of social benefits, particularly the toughening of eligibility terms for disability benefits, also played a role in this.

Another important factor of influence on employment rates is household situation, since decisions on apportioning time between work away from home and leisure/at-home work (foremost childcare) are made by both spouses and are dependencies, *inter alia*, of the utility gained from the quantity and quality of children and the expenses associated with raising them. The data show that the entry of Arab women to the labor market was accompanied by a decrease in their number of children; thus, the share of Arab households composed of couples with three children or more fell from 45 percent in 2002 to 37 percent in 2015. The reduction in fertility is not only a precipitant of the increase in employment but also, probably, an outcome of this increase. In contrast to Arabs, ultra-Orthodox women stepped up their employment considerably without seriously cutting back on household size. This special phenomenon entails further research. Another fact to take into account is that ultra-Orthodox women out-earn ultra-Orthodox men. Therefore, they should be allowed to acquire labor-market-suitable human capital and credentials on the widest possible scale and at the highest possible level. Among non-Orthodox Jewish households, no major changes took place except for a mild decrease in the marriage rate.

The increase in men's and women's employment also finds expression in household employment patterns. The share of two-breadwinner couples increased from 52 percent in 2002 to 66 percent in 2015; in contrast, the proportion of single-breadwinner or zero-breadwinner couple-based households dropped. This transition of households from one breadwinner to two is shared by couples with and without children and is particularly conspicuous among households with three children or more. It is important to analyze employment rates at the household level because labor income is divided among all members of the household, and it is equalized income that comes into play in analyzing the incidence of poverty and inequality.

Concurrent with the increase in employment and despite the enlistment of relatively weak population groups in the labor force, gross labor income also moved ahead among all deciles and all populations. Equalized total gross income headed upward as well, indicating that the total effect of the upturn in employment on household income was positive despite the substitutability of labor income and benefit income. Furthermore, equalized disposable (net) income increased by 33–47 percent, meaning that the growth of employment was accompanied by an improvement in households' standard of living. Importantly, however, the increase was faster among non-Orthodox

Jewish households than among ultra-Orthodox and Arab households, meaning that the disparities and net inequality among the groups grew. Two main factors contributed to this: lower employment and wages and higher birth rates among ultra-Orthodox and Arabs than among the others.

The share of labor income in total gross household income rose considerably, particularly among ultra-Orthodox and Arab households (by 62 percent and 75 percent in 2015, respectively), whereas the proportion of welfare benefits contracted and the rate of households receiving income support plummeted from 7.2 percent in 2002 to 2.7 percent in 2015. These changes are not only outcomes of the increase in employment but also the main reason for it. The toughening of eligibility terms and the sweeping cutbacks in income support and in child allowances changed the structure of incentives in the labor market and encouraged households, who saw their welfare payments fall, to join the labor market. The income tax cut acted in the same direction, that is, by encouraging low-wage individuals to accept jobs.

In sum, several main factors abetted the increase in employment: (a) an upturn in education levels, accounting for 20 percent of the total growth of employment among men and 40 percent of that among women; (b) the raising of the statutory retirement age, bringing on a major increase in employment among members of the 55–64 age group; (c) the reduction of income support and child benefits and the toughening of eligibility terms, incentivizing households to join the labor force by shrinking their benefit income; and the income tax cuts, which gave the well-educated and members of pre-retirement age groups, in particular, an additional incentive.

13.7.1 Predictions, Future Challenges, and Policy Recommendations

The aggregate picture of Israel's labor market today is quite auspicious: high employment rates, low unemployment, and rising hourly wages. This tableau, however, is composed of groups that are very different from each other and that, when one examines them in detail, reveal the challenges that Israel is facing. The Arab population, 20 percent of the country's total demographic today, is expected to grow to as much as 23 percent forty years ahead, by which time the ultra-Orthodox population is expected to grow from 10 percent to 20 percent. Thus, these two groups will account for half of the total population. Therefore, it is important to ensure continued increases in these groups' employment rates until they match those of the non-Orthodox Jewish population. In this chapter, we showed that the policy measures implemented were highly successful in raising employment rates generally and those of these groups particularly. Therefore, we recommend the continued implementation of a pro-employment policy and an attempt to expand it. The labor grant (negative income tax) should be increased, welfare-to-work programs should remain in effect and made compulsory for benefit recipients who meet an employment test and elective for all others, and these programs should focus on the Arab and the ultra-Orthodox populations. By sustaining such policies, it may be possible to continue the upward movement of these groups' employment rates and total employment or, at least, to allow total employment to remain at its current high level.

Amid the upturn in employment, the hourly wages of Arabs, ultra-Orthodox, and those lacking academic schooling, showed no increase whatsoever during the research period. This trend, which protrudes against the background of the increase in the wages of non-Orthodox Jews and of those with academic education, widened the gaps – large to begin with – and intensified inequality. To raise these workers' wages, their productivity has to be improved. Therefore, we recommend the development and use of tools that will enhance human capital generally and that of the sub-median population particularly, foremost by means of technological and vocational higher education. Enhancing these workers' skills will not only boost their income but will also mitigate poverty and promote economic growth at large.

References

In Hebrew

Cohen Goldner, S. (2019).*The Effect of Foreign Workers on Employment and Wages of Israeli Workers*. Herzliya: Aaron Institute for Economic Policy.

Eckstein, Z., and Larom, T. (2016). *Poverty in Israel: Reasons and Labor Market Policy*. Herzliya: Aaron Institute for Economic Policy.

Eckstein, Z., Lifshitz, O., and Larom, T. (2018). *The Labor Market as an Engine for Growth and Poverty Reduction*. Herzliya: Aaron Institute for Economic Policy.

Myers–JDC–Brookdale Institute and the National Insurance Institute (2008). *Evaluation Study of Mehalev: Summary Report.* Jerusalem.

Myers–JDC–Brookdale Institute and the National Insurance Institute (2010). *Findings from the Evaluation of the Lights to Employment Program: Final Report.* Jerusalem: Myers–JDC–Brookdale Institute and the National Insurance Institute.

Schlosser, A., and Shanan, Y. (2016). *The "Employment Circles" Program: Interim Report.* Tel Aviv: The Foerder Institute for Economic Research.

Strawczynski, M. et al. (2015). *The Labor Grant (EITC): Follow-up Report of the Research Team up to Eligibility Year 2012.* Jerusalem: National Insurance Institute, Israel Tax Authority, Bank of Israel, and Myers–JDC–BrookdaleInstitute.

In English

Bank of Israel (2015). *Recent Economic Developments 140: April–September 2015.* Jerusalem: Bank of Israel.

Cohen, A., Dehejia, R. H., and Romanov, D. (2013). Do Financial Incentives Affect Fertility? *Review of Economic and Statistics,* 95(1), 1–20.

Dahan, M. (2017). *Income Inequality in Israel: A Distinctive Evolution.* Munich: CESifo Group.

14 | Economics of Education in Israel

Inputs, Outputs, and Performance

DAN BEN-DAVID AND AYAL KIMHI

14.1 Introduction

Israel's education system is, in many respects, an enigma. On one hand, it is home to some of the world's best universities, and it is one of the world leaders in average years of schooling and the share of the population with academic degrees. On the other hand, its primary and secondary school children are doing very poorly on international exams in core fields of study such as reading, mathematics and science. This enigma carries over to the labor market. On one hand, Israel's high-tech sector is a world leader, and large numbers of Israelis can be found in any high-tech concentration, such as Silicon Valley. On the other hand, many of the country's working-age adults do not have the skills necessary to function in a modern labor market. Israel's average labor productivity is not only low, it has been falling further and further behind the most developed countries for decades.

One of the primary roles of a public education system is to provide equal opportunities and overcome parental lack of education, which severely constrain their children's prospects of upward economic mobility. Chetty et al. (2011) suggest that differences in school quality perpetuate income inequality and estimate that an elimination of qualitative differences among American schools would reduce the intergenerational correlation of income by about a third.[1]

The Israeli education system does not seem to perform well on this task. The additional funding that it provides schools in poorer communities is minimal (Blass, 2015). Achievement gaps in the international exams are the highest among developed countries. Not surprisingly,

---

[1] According to the OECD (2017), Israel is one of the leading countries in terms of people with academic degrees whose parents do not have academic degrees, indicating intergenerational mobility, at least with respect to the quantity of education.

Israel is one of the most unequal developed countries, and the share of its population below the poverty line is the highest in the developed world (Ben-David, 2017).

What underlies the Israeli education system's failure? Is it lack of funding, poor physical infrastructure, inadequate teachers – or is it the system as a whole that is not using its resources productively? This chapter sheds some light on these questions. It includes a review of existing studies and an empirical investigation of selected issues using macro and micro data.

Section 14.2 analyzes quantitative education measures and their labor market impact. Section 14.3 examines the quality of education in Israel and its economic impact. Section 14.4 examines educational inputs in Israel in comparison to other countries. Section 14.5 highlights the importance of curriculum and field of study to labor market achievements. Section 14.6 examines the country's higher education system, while section 14.7 concludes.

14.2 Education Quantity and Israel's Labor Market

On the face of it, Israel's prime working-age population is one of the most educated on the planet.[2] With 13.4 years of schooling per person between the ages of 35 and 54, the country is ranked third among OECD countries. In terms of academic education, Israel is ranked fourth in the OECD, with 31.6 percent of the prime working-age population having an academic degree (Ben-David, 2017).

Israel's shift in educational attainment over the years has been dramatic. Figure 14.1 displays the distribution of the country's prime working-age population by years of schooling. Haredim (ultra-Orthodox Jews) are listed separately in Figure 14.1 and are not divided by years of schooling.[3] In 1970, 60 percent of Israel's prime working-age non-

---

[2] The standard definition of prime working age as the 25–54 age group is inadequate for Israel. Compulsory military service forces many Israelis to delay their entry into higher education, thus pushing back graduation and full entry into the labor market until much later than is common in other countries. Consequently, the prime working-age population considered here is the 35–54 age group.

[3] Nearly all Haredi men study a core curriculum for no more than eight years – and even then, it is partial, excluding science, English, and other core material. After that, they continue with Torah studies for many years, sometimes decades. Consequently, they are listed in the data as having 16+ years of education, even

Haredi population had no more than eight years of schooling. This share fell precipitously, to under 10 percent, by 2015. The share of persons with 16+ years of schooling has risen steadily over the decades, from just over 5 percent in 1970 to its current level exceeding 35 percent.[4]

As Israel's economy has grown, it has shifted away from productive sectors using labor with little to no education, such as agriculture and textiles, toward services and hi-tech sectors requiring higher levels of education and skills. As a result, labor demand patterns have changed substantially (Ben-David, 2017). While there was almost no difference in 1970s employment rates between the various education groups,

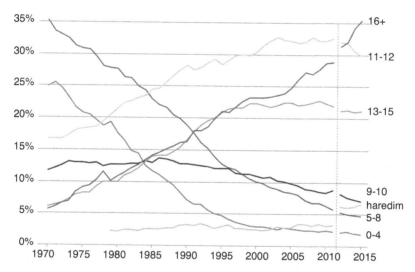

Figure 14.1 Education groups, by years of schooling as share of total 35–54 year-old population, 1970–2015.*

* As of 2012, the Central Bureau of Statistics changed the estimation methodology in labor force surveys. Data by school years in 1970–1978 includes Haredim. Since 1979, it excludes Haredim.
Source: Ben-David (2017)

though this clearly designates something entirely different from what it does for the remainder of the population. Until 1978, it was not possible to identify Haredim in Labor Force Surveys, so in the early years they are not included separately in the figure. This is the reason for the drop in the fraction of 16+ years of schooling in 1979.

[4] This trend is due, among other things, to the expansion of academic opportunities through non-research colleges since 1990.

a substantial gap has developed between them over the decades. Although the share of men with 16+ years of schooling has risen sharply during this span, demand for them has risen as well, with employment rates in 2015 over 90 percent, roughly where they were in 1970. For all other education groups, the lower the level of education, the greater the fall in male employment rates.

While a gap has always existed between employment rates of the various education groups among females, this gap has widened over the decades. Kimhi (2012) showed that the primary source of the vastly increased female employment rates was a rising number of women moving up the education ladder into successively higher education groups characterized by higher employment rates. Eckstein, Larom, and Lifshitz (Chapter 13, this volume) found that 40 percent of the rise in female employment between 2002 and 2015 can be attributed to the expansion of their educational attainment (versus 20 percent of the increase for males).

Higher levels of education also lead to higher wages. Ben-David and Kimhi (2017) found that hourly wages of full-time prime working-age employees rise strongly with the level of education. Ben-David (2017) showed that the hourly wage gap between full-time prime working-age employees with at least thirteen years of schooling and those with twelve years of schooling at most has increased from approximately 60 percent between 1999 and 2007 to 95 percent in 2015.

To summarize, employment gaps and wage gaps in Israel are closely linked to gaps in educational attainment, and these gaps have been widening over time. A national education policy aimed at enhancing educational attainment among less educated and poorer population groups could yield some major socioeconomic improvements. However, as will be shown below, it is not the quantity of education that matters most.

14.3 Education Quality and Its Economic Impact

Israel is uniquely placed among the family of nations to highlight why an emphasis on the quantity of education is insufficient. It ostensibly has one of the most educated societies among the OECD countries (as measured by the number of school years per person or the share of individuals with academic degrees). But its labor productivity is not only below most OECD countries, it has been steadily falling further and further behind the average labor productivity of the G7 countries since the 1970s (Ben-David, 2017).

Hanushek and Woessmann (2015) show that while there is a slight positive relationship between the average number of school years in a country and its average annual growth rates, there is a much stronger positive relationship between the quality of a country's education (as measured by its students' achievements in math, science, and reading) and its rate of economic growth.

Differences in quality mean that a year of schooling in one country is not necessarily equivalent to a year of schooling in another country. Gauging the quality of education in Israel is not as accurate as it could, or should, be. On the one hand, the country assesses high school students with matriculation exams. These exams have been given for decades but have never been calibrated over time, rendering useless all intertemporal comparisons. The final matriculation grades also include a local school component – with no attempt at calibration across schools. Subsequently, matriculation exams are of little use in providing comparable benchmarks that could have been utilized for measuring the quality of secondary education in Israel.

International exams, such as PISA (Programme for International Student Assessment), TIMSS (Trends in International Mathematics and Science Study), and others used by Hanushek and Woessmann (2015) in their study, provide another route for gauging educational quality. These exams are calibrated on a per exam basis to a mean of 500. This mean remains 500 regardless of the year or the number of countries participating in the exam. Hence, any improvements or declines in achievements are relative to the mean and do not necessarily denote actual progress or deterioration over time. Nonetheless, it is still possible to gauge Israel's relative position vis-à-vis other countries and whether this position has improved or declined.

As shown by Ben-David (2017), despite the steady improvements – relative to the means – in the achievements of Israeli pupils over the last decade, their mean scores have been mostly below the OECD average of 500. In particular, the average achievements in math, science, and reading in the 2015 PISA exam place Israeli children below the children of all but one of the twenty-five relevant developed countries – and even this is an overestimate of the Israeli average. Haredi boys do not study the material covered in these exams and do not participate in the exams. Moreover, Israel's Arabic- speaking children obtained an average score below many developing countries and the majority of predominantly Muslim countries.

Not only are Israel's average achievement levels below nearly all developed countries, education gaps between its children are by far the highest, and have been the highest in the developed world for many years.[5] With so substantial a disparity in what constitutes the jumping board into the labor market, it should come as no surprise that subsequent income gaps are high as well (Ben-David, 2017).

The achievement gaps appear in other measures as well. Despite a marked increase in the number of both Hebrew-speaking and Arabic-speaking students passing the matriculation exams, the percentage point gap between the two populations did not change between 1987 and 2016. While the Israeli data do not provide a very accurate gauge of the Haredi 18-year-old cohort over time, the high Haredi birth rates ensure that an ever-increasing share of the Hebrew speakers are Haredim who do not study the core curriculum beyond eighth grade – and do not even take the matriculation exam, let alone pass it. Consequently, the percentage point gap between non-Haredi Hebrew speakers and Arabic speakers has actually increased over the past three decades.

The failure of Israel's education system in reducing gaps – in comparison with other developed countries – is highlighted in Figure 14.2, which compares the PISA math achievements of pupils according to their mothers' education. All comparisons are made to the scores of children whose mothers matriculated from high school. In the ten countries with the highest PISA scores in 2015, children whose mothers did not have any formal education scored 6 percent below those whose mothers' matriculated from high school. At the other end of the education spectrum, children whose mothers had an academic degree attained scores that were 6 percent above those of children with mothers who matriculated from high school.

The impact of maternal education on the scores of Israeli pupils was considerably greater than the maternal impact in the ten leading countries. Pupils with mothers who did not study beyond primary schools received math grades that were 20 percent below the grades of pupils whose mothers' matriculated from high school. When mothers

---

[5] These gaps would have probably been even higher had all of the Haredi children taken the exam.

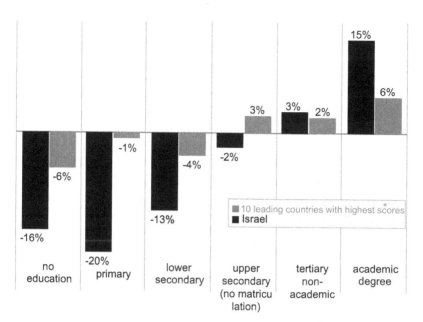

Figure 14.2 Gaps in math grades relative to pupils whose mother matriculated from high school (% gaps, by maternal education level).
[*] Ten leading countries: Canada, Estonia, Finland, Hong Kong, Japan, Korea, Netherlands, Singapore, Switzerland, Taiwan
Source: Gruber (2017)

completed no more than lower secondary school, the gap among their children fell to 13 percent. Pupils with academically educated mothers attained scores that were 15 percent higher than those with mothers who only matriculated.

While the international exams provide a relative measuring stick for comparing Israel to other countries, they do not yield any information on the absolute level of knowledge that Israeli children possess in core subjects, or whether this level has risen or fallen over time. The only exam administered in Israel providing such an indication is the Meitsav exam – and only since 2008. The average score of 500 in 2008 serves as the baseline score for all other years. Since then, scores have improved in each exam (Ben- David, 2017).

While the Meitsav exams are calibrated over time, the scores are index numbers that provide no information as to how much of the material pupils actually know. Figure 14.3 shows the percentage of correct responses in the various exams administered in 2016. Both the fifth and eighth grade pupils answered correctly on only two-thirds of the questions in the English exam. The percent correct in math was even lower (61 percent) in fifth grade and in eighth grade (56 percent). Even lower is the average score of 50 percent in science and technology.

Returning to the international exams, a comparison of the weakest pupils in each developed country – that is, a comparison of the bottom five percentiles – indicates that Israel's weakest pupils are the weakest of the weakest in the developed world (Ben-David, 2017). These children are the most likely candidates for a life of poverty, since the sub-par skills that they are being provided reduce their chances of overcoming such a negative head start in the future. Israeli pupils in the top five percentiles are ranked below the top pupils in eighteen of these twenty-five countries, an omen reflecting the country's future ability to retain

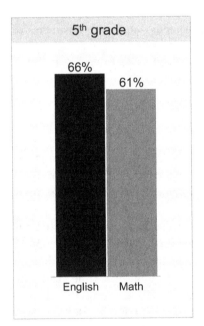
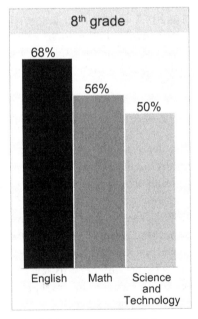

Figure 14.3 Percentage of correct responses in Meitsav exams, 2016.*
* Not including Haredi boys.
Source: Ben-David (2017)

its qualitative edge in fields that keep its economy in the developed world.

The OECD defines six levels of achievement in math, science, and reading. Pupils with a level 1 or below score are considered inadequately prepared for future labor markets. Thirty percent of Israel's pupils are at or below level 1 on average in the three exams, tying Israel with the Slovak Republic for the greatest share of unprepared children in the developed world (Ben-David, 2017). Had all of the Haredi children participated in the exam, Israel would probably own last place all by itself. The OECD also measures the problem-solving skills of children. Thirty-nine percent of Israeli children are at or below level 1, considered unable to plan ahead or set subgoals. This is double the German and American shares, and over five times the Japanese share (Ben- David, 2017).

The PIAAC (Programme for the International Assessment of Adult Competencies) survey of adult skills, conducted in Israel in 2016, provides an opportunity to examine skills of the existing labor force. Adult skills in Israel are not better, from an international perspective, than those of Israeli pupils in the international exams. Israeli workers were ranked last among OECD countries in reading skills and second to last in quantitative and problem-solving skills. The skill inequality in Israel is ranked second from top (Bank of Israel, 2016). The examination of worker skills by industry indicates that low-skilled workers tend to concentrate in low-productivity industries. Hazan and Tsur (Chapter 11, this volume) show that the gap in adult skills between Israel and other developed countries explains a significant part of the labor productivity gap between the countries.

The quality of education in primary schools greatly influences the quality of secondary school education that a pupil can attain – which in turn affects subsequent academic choices. In fact, there exist large discrepancies in quality among academic institutions. Figure 14.4 shows how much of an impact academic choices can have on wages – particularly in the high-wage fields. In disciplines where graduates tend to enter the private business sector, as opposed to public sector positions, students who attended the research universities tended to earn considerably more than students graduating from the non-research colleges. Not only do employees with degrees in computer science earn considerably more than those with degrees in engineering, wage gaps are also affected by the quality of the

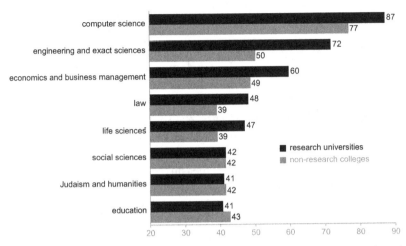

Figure 14.4 Average hourly wages by academic discipline for salaried employees, comparison of university and college graduates, 2008.
* excluding medicine
Source: Ben-David and Kimhi (2017)

higher education institution. Similarly, Achdut et al. (2017) found a wage advantage of at least 10 percent for university graduates over college graduates, after controlling for field of study, psychometric score, math skills, and various socioeconomic indicators. Thus, what a person studies, the level, and where make a great difference with regard to wages.

To summarize, Israeli pupils do poorly in both domestic and international exams, and the achievement gaps among them are substantial. These gaps carry over into adult skills and into academic education, and are subsequently reflected in high wage inequality.

14.4 Educational Inputs and Pupil Achievements in Israel

As shown above, quantitative measures suggest that Israel's population is highly educated. But qualitatively, Israeli pupils and adults alike are at, or near, the bottom of the developed world. Is this problem due primarily to a lack of education system resources necessary for quality teaching, or are these resources used ineffectively?

14.4.1 Education Expenditures

National education expenditure, as a percent of GDP, rose throughout the 1970s and fell during the early 1980s, until stabilizing in the mid-1980s (Ben-David, 2017). During a brief period in the 1990s, education received a major injection of funds, though these were allowed to dissipate over the subsequent decade. In recent years, the national education expenditure received a renewed budgetary infusion. Following major comprehensive wage agreements in 2009, national education expenditures rose by 57 perrcent in just four years in the primary schools and by 62 percent in the secondary schools. In addition, pre-primary school expenditures per pupil increased by 69 percent in 2013, following the 2011 social protests.

Israel's national education expenditure, as a share of GDP, is second among OECD countries (Ben-David, 2017). Its public education expenditure places the country in fourth place. While such comparisons are accurate and common, they can also be misleading – particularly in a country with a relatively young population such as Israel. The share of primary and secondary school pupils in Israel is higher than in most OECD countries. Thus, the relevant measure for examining Israel's education expenditures over time and in comparison to other countries is expenditure per pupil. However, simple comparisons of expenditure per pupil are insufficient and can also be misleading. Salaries constitute the vast majority of all education expenditures, and salaries are highly correlated with living standards. Thus, education expenditures per pupil in Israel that are higher than in a developing country do not mean that Israel is spending extravagantly. To make education expenditures per pupil comparable across countries, there is a need to normalize them by GDP per capita. This kind of discounting is also identical, mathematically, to the need to normalize the share of education expenditures out of GDP by the share of pupils in the population.

Examining public education expenditures per pupil normalized by GDP per capita, Ben-David (2017) shows that Israel is situated close to the center of the OECD rankings in primary school expenditures, and third from the bottom in secondary schools.

The bottom line is that in international comparisons, educational funding per pupil in Israel, at least in primary schools, seems to be sufficient, so lack of funding cannot be the main reason for the low achievements of Israeli pupils. However, the increase in school funding over the past few years was mostly to raise teacher salaries. While raising teacher salaries may in the long run attract better teachers and lead to higher pupil achievements, it has yet to be shown to be effective in the short run. This raises the question of whether teachers are paid according to what is expected from them, and whether teacher wages are sufficient to attract competent teachers.

14.4.2 Teachers' Salaries and Qualifications

On the face of it, teachers' monthly salaries in Israel range from 14 percent below the OECD average in lower secondary schools to 16 percent less in primary schools to 28 percent less in upper secondary schools (Figure 14.5). However, Israeli teachers work substantially fewer hours than in other developed countries. A comparison of total statutory working hours by Israeli teachers and the average for their OECD counterparts indicates that Israelis work 23 percent fewer hours in primary school, 30 percent fewer in lower secondary schools, and 48 percent fewer in upper secondary schools. As a result, teachers' hourly wages in Israel are higher than the OECD average (Figure 14.5). Israeli primary school teachers earn 9 percent more per hour while teachers in lower secondary schools make almost a quarter more per hour. In upper secondary schools, the gap rises to over a third more per hour for Israeli teachers.

These differences do not take into account the fact that Israeli incomes, in general, are lower than OECD incomes. When the salaries per hour are discounted by GDP per hour of work to control for differences in living standards, the gaps between what Israeli teachers earn per hour and the OECD average rises to 44 percent in primary schools, 62 percent in lower secondary schools, and 76 percent more in high school (Figure 14.5).

One might expect that the relatively high hourly wages of teachers in Israel should attract such talented and qualified individuals into the teaching profession. However, this does not seem to be the case for the majority of teachers in Israel – possibly because the standard monthly teaching schedule is so light (compared to other countries) that it yields relatively low monthly salaries that act as a negative counterbalance. Ben-David (2017) shows that over three-quarters of Israel's first-year education students study in teaching colleges with average psychometric scores (serving a similar purpose as American SATs) below 61 percent of all persons taking the exam. Another 15 percent of the first-year

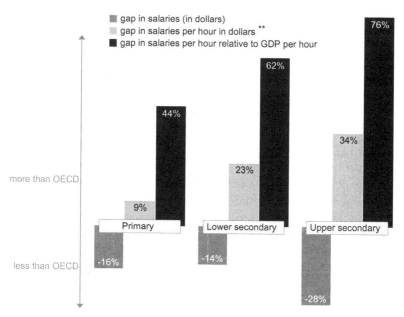

Figure 14.5 Gaps in teachers' salaries:* percentage difference between Israel and OECD average, 2014.

* Annual average salaries (including bonuses and allowances) of 25–64 year-old teachers in public institutions using purchasing power parities.
** Salaries per statutory hour worked.
Source: Ben-David (2017)

education students are taught in general non-research colleges and their average psychometric score is below that of three-quarters of all test-takers. Just 6 percent of all first-year education students study in research universities, and their average psychometric score is below the average for all university students. When a vast majority of a country's teachers do not have the personal qualifications to get accepted into a research university, how can it be expected that they will have the ability to enable their pupils to reach those levels?[6]

---

[6] Not all first-year education students end up working as teachers, though it is not clear whether those who do not join the teaching profession are from the upper part or from the lower part of the quality distribution.

14.4.3 Instruction Hours

An often-cited reason for low pupil achievements is an insufficient amount of time devoted to the study of basic material. However, the average number of school days per year in Israel is the highest among the OECD countries (Ben-David, 2017).

A comparison of all OECD countries with data on the number of instruction hours per year in core subjects and data on achievements in the recent PISA 2015 exam provides a vivid indication that the number of instruction hours do not explain Israel's low achievements (Figure 14.6). In all but one of the twenty OECD countries that provide fewer instruction hours than Israel, the pupils achieved higher scores. In general, OECD countries provide 21 percent fewer hours than Israel in reading, writing, and literature while attaining 3 percent higher reading scores. They provide 28 percent fewer math instruction hours while achieving grades that are 4 percent higher than Israel's. In the natural sciences, the average number of instruction hours in the OECD countries is 29 percent lower than in Israel, while scores are 6 percent higher.

In summation, Israeli pupils receive more instruction time yet attain lower achievements than pupils in nearly all of the OECD countries. This raises the question about what occurs within the classroom during those instruction hours.

14.4.4 Class Size and Discipline

While empirical evidence may be inconclusive with regard to the impact of class size on education outcomes, there is no doubt that Israel's classrooms are – on average – very congested. The forty children per class maximum is not a rarity in the country. There are 26.7 pupils in an average Israeli primary school class, compared to just 20.9 pupils in an average OECD classroom (Ben-David, 2017). The numbers are even higher in lower secondary schools, with 28.1 pupils per class in Israel versus 22.9 in the OECD. However, the number of pupils per full-time equivalent teacher in Israeli primary schools is nearly identical to the OECD average. In secondary schools, the number of pupils per teacher in Israel (11.2) is actually lower than the OECD average (13.4). In other words, there is no lack of teachers in Israel, and hence, this is not the reason for the large classes.

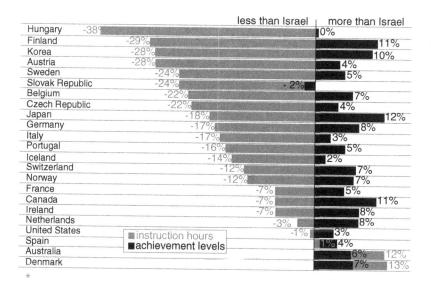

Figure 14.6 Instruction hours and achievement, 2015,*23 OECD countries relative to Israel.

* Cumulative number of compulsory instruction hours in primary and lower secondary schools. and average achievement levels in math, science, and reading in PISA 2015.
Source: Dan Ben-David (2017)

There is a question about what is transpiring within the Israeli classroom during these teaching hours. This may be affected by another factor that may be related to class size, though not necessarily so: class discipline. Gruber (2017) focused on discipline in the classroom from both a subjective perspective (how pupils view themselves) and an objective perspective (using quantifiable measures to proxy for discipline) and examined its impact on PISA grades. He found a sizable gap between how Israeli pupils perceive themselves and how they actually behave. A higher share of Israeli pupils disagreed with the subjective statement that "Pupils don't listen to what the teacher says" than was the case in the ten countries with the highest PISA math scores. For a more objective instrument for discipline, Gruber (2017) used absences and unapproved tardy class attendance. The share of Israeli pupils arriving late (without permission) to class was nearly double the

OECD average. Almost three-quarters of the pupils in the top ten countries were never tardy at all in the two weeks prior to the exam, compared to less than half of the pupils in Israel.

Using the objective discipline index, Gruber (2017) found that discipline has a major impact on scores. After controlling for a number of other determinants such as parental education, instruction hours, class size, country, and so on, Gruber estimated the addition to PISA scores as a result of increasing the class objective discipline index by one unit (Figure 14.7). These increments range from 9 to 15 additional points in classes with no more than thirty pupils. However, in classes with 31 to 35 pupils, a one unit improvement in the objective discipline index was found to improve PISA math scores by 25 points. When there are 36 to 40 pupils per class, the improvement in achievements equals 42 points. In the largest classes, with 41 to 50 pupils, scores rise by 53 points for each increase of one unit in the objective discipline index.

The interaction between class size and discipline provides additional insight to Israel's low achievements when compared to other developed countries. The country's classes tend to be more congested, while its children are among the least disciplined in the developed world. This rather combustible combination yields a less than conducive learning environment – a situation that is exacerbated when taking into account the general quality of Israel's teachers.

14.4.5 Distributional Issues

The meager achievements of the Arabic-speaking students in the international exams, and the strong correlation between mother's education and child achievements, highlight the failure of the Israeli education system to provide equal opportunities to pupils. Israel's education system is divided into four separate "streams": secular Jewish, religious Jewish, ultra-Orthodox Jewish, and Arab. These "streams" differ not only in curriculum but also in funding. This structure can constitute a relatively convenient avenue for providing extra funding to weak socioeconomic population groups, though the system has not taken full advantage of this opportunity. On one hand, the ***State generously funds private schools, including the ultra-Orthodox schools, with little influence over their curriculum.

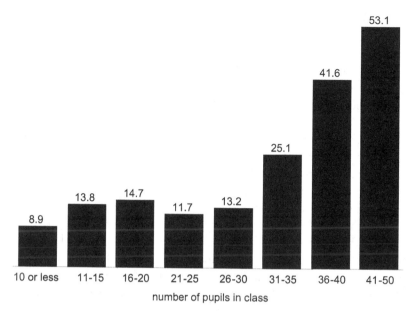

Figure 14.7 Impact of discipline on score, by class size:[*] addition to score as a result of increasing the class objective discipline index by one unit.
[*] Addition to score after controlling for country, parental education (of the pupil and of the class average), hours of mathematics, private lessons, class size, and individual discipline.
Source: Gruber (2017)

On the other hand, Arab schools do not receive sufficient funding to substantially narrow the achievement gap between them and the Jewish schools.

Klinov (2010) examined the resources allocated to primary and lower secondary schools in Israel between 2003 and 2008, and reported that the allocation of resources within the non-Haredi Jewish sector was quite progressive, while preferential funding for Arab and Haredi schools was insufficient. Blass (2015) found that the amounts allocated to preferential funding were too small to have significant impact, and that they were biased towards sectors with political power rather than to sectors with the most urgent needs. Moreover, economically strong municipalities increase the education budget from their own sources.

The Ministry of Education uses a school-level socioeconomic index to determine the extent of preferential funding to schools with pupils from low socioeconomic backgrounds.[7] An examination of per-pupil educational expenditures by quintile of the school index in Figure 14.8 shows that in most cases, schools with lower levels on the socioeconomic index receive preferential funding. However, the preferential funding is much more pronounced in Jewish schools than in Arab schools. For example, in secondary Arab schools there does not appear to be any effective preferential funding at all, while in secondary Jewish schools the expenditures per student in the lowest socioeconomic quintile are 50 percent higher than in the highest quintile. Moreover, comparing Jewish and Arab schools in the same socioeconomic quintile reveals that, with only one exception, Jewish schools enjoy higher funding than Arab schools. That is because the criteria for allocation of the differential portion of the education budget are not based solely on socioeconomic criteria. Rather, they include special funding for Jewish studies, other special funding for Jewish religious schools, extra funding for immigrants (who are all in Jewish schools), and other funding regulations that discriminate in favor of Jewish schools.

14.5 The Importance of the High School Curriculum and Academic Fields of Study

The sharp decline in the number of high school students taking the math matriculation exam at the highest level (five units) in the years leading up to 2012 motivated a Kimhi and Horovitz (2015) study on the impact of high school math levels on future hourly wages at the age of 29.[8] They found that those who took the math matriculation exam at the lowest level, three units, attained subsequent wages that were 19 percent higher than those who did not take the math matriculation exam. Those who took the exam at the intermediate level, four units,

---

[7] The school index is an average of the pupils' indices. A pupil index is a function of parents' education (40%), per-capita household income (20%), residing in the geographic periphery (20%), and the status of immigrating from a poor country (20%).

[8] Their data included some 14,000 people born in 1979, took the matriculation exams in 1997, and reported their labor market situation in the 2008 census of population.

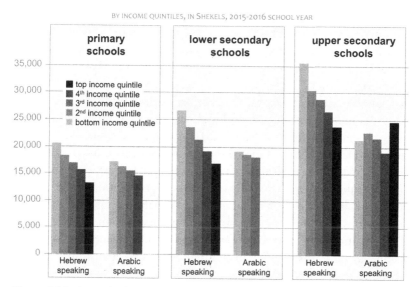

Figure 14.8 Annual education expenditures per student by income quintiles, in shekels, 2015–2016 school year.
* The numbers reported by the Ministry of Education and displayed here reflect most – but not all – of the public funds spent on education in Israel.
Data: Education Ministry

had 36 percent higher wages, while those who took the exam at the highest level, five units, had 60 percent higher wages.

The study of mathematics in high school acts as a gateway to further knowledge accumulation in other fields dependent on math – and as a necessary condition for acceptance to top academic departments in the country's best research universities. This, in turn, helps university graduates find jobs in high-paying occupations such as engineering and computer programming. Using an estimated wage equation as a function of the level of high school math as well as grades in math and other high school subjects, the existence of an academic degree and academic area of study (where relevant), economic branch and occupation, and socioeconomic background, Kimhi and Horovitz (2015) simulated a number of scenarios showing how a shift from four units of math to five units would increase subsequent hourly wages (Figure 14.9). These wage increases were divided into their direct and indirect (via field of academic studies) impact. The simulations showed that the wage increase is substantially higher for women than for men in each of the various scenarios. This is mostly due to the indirect effect. In other words, a higher level of math matriculation is more important as a key to subsequent high-level academic studies for women than for men.

Of course, math is not the only matriculation field that is important for labor market outcomes. In Israel, a declining trend of studying STEM courses at the highest levels in high school has been documented since the mid-1990s (Ben-David, 2017). Using the same data, Kimhi and Ben-David (2017) estimated the log-wage equation as a function of the level of study in each and every matriculation field (with the number of units ranging from 0 to 5), as well as the matriculation grade in each of the fields, academic field of study differentiated into colleges and universities, occupation, industry, and socioeconomic background. The equation was corrected for selectivity into wage employment, using marital status, number of children, home ownership, and number of rooms as identifying variables.

In all but a few instances, raising the level of study in a given high school field does not have a statistically significant effect on subsequent wages. Raising the level of math matriculation by one unit has

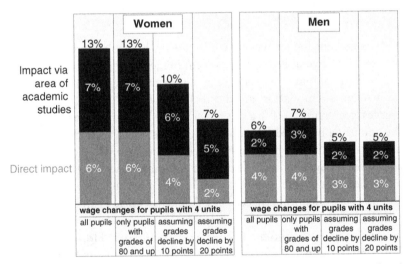

Figure 14.9 Wage impact of shift from 4 units to 5 units of math: Simulated increase in salaried employees' hourly wages.
Source: Kimhi and Horovitz (2015)

a statistically significant direct hourly wage effect of almost 7 percent for females and almost 9 percent for males. No other matriculation field has a statistically significant effect for both males and females. Other fields with positive effects on male wages are biology and Hebrew. Altogether, this confirms that the level of math is the leading and most consistent determinant of future wages among all matriculation fields.

As discussed earlier, wage gaps among people who studied different academic disciplines can be quite high. Kimhi and Ben-David (2017) show that computer science and exact sciences are the two leading academic fields for both males and females. After controlling for other covariates, males who studied computer science in a research university earned 63 percent more per hour of work than those with no higher education, while those who studied computer science in a college earned 52 percent more. Males with a degree in exact sciences from a research university earned 32 percent more, while those who studied exact sciences in college did not enjoy a statistically significant wage premium. In the case of females, the leading field is also computer science with a 68 percent hourly wage premium for graduates from research universities and 60 percent for college graduates, over those with no higher education. This is followed by exact sciences with wage premiums of 54 percent (university) and 28 percent (college) and economics/business with wage premiums of 47 percent (university) and 29 percent (college). These results are in line with the earlier findings of Shwed and Shavit (2006), Achdut et al. (2017), and others.

It turns out that academic field of study seems to be more important for future wages than levels of matriculation exams. But this may be misleading, because studying the leading academic fields in research universities is limited to candidates who took the relevant matriculation exams at the highest levels. Therefore, the overall importance of the level of math matriculation is above and beyond its direct effect on wages as expressed by the regression coefficients. In turn, the field of academic studies contributes to future wages indirectly by channeling the graduates into more remunerative occupations such as managerial, academic, and technical positions. Ben- David and Kimhi (2017) showed that, compared to unskilled workers, managerial occupations yield a wage premium of 30 percent and 33 percent for females and males, respectively. Academic occupations yield a wage premium of 22 percent and 26 percent for females and males, respectively, while technical occupations yield a wage premium of 20 percent and 18 percent for females and males, respectively. And this can again be tracked back to levels of matriculation fields.

The fact that so few pupils choose to take STEM matriculation exams at the higher levels is due, at least in part, to the inadequate preparation that these pupils received at lower levels of the education systems, as reflected in the low achievements of the Israeli pupils in the international exams. In this respect, the aggressive promotion of studying math at the highest level by the Ministry of Education in recent years perhaps had impressive immediate results, as reflected by the sharp increase in the number of pupils taking math at the highest level, but did not address the root causes of the problem.

14.6 Higher Education

In the 1990s, Israel began filling in the gap between high school and the country's top-tier research universities by establishing non-research colleges. These were initially intended to focus just on the provision of undergraduate degrees, though many have since begun to offer graduate degrees as well.

The colleges enabled the number of students per capita in Israel to take off. Initially, colleges acted as a complement to the universities, with enrollment in the universities (as a share of Israeli population) rising by 23 percent between 1990 and 2000, while the overall number of students in academia rose by 68 percent (Ben-David, 2017). The share of students per capita in the research universities then plateaued through the mid-2000s while the overall number of students per capita continues its steep climb. From this point, the colleges began to capture all of the incremental part of the population choosing to attain a higher education.

Between 2004 and 2012, the number of students per capita choosing to study in the research universities fell by 13 percent while the overall number attending institutions of higher education continued to rise. Since 2012, the share of students in Israel's population has begun to fall. In light of the fact that the share of prime working-age adults with an academic degree in the country is the fourth highest among the OECD countries (Ben-David, 2017), it is possible that Israel may have reached a saturation point in terms of the quantity of academic education demanded.

The de-emphasis of qualitative academic institutions in the nation's budgetary priorities began far before the founding of non-research colleges in the 1990s. As shown by Ben-David (2017), from 1948 to 1973, the country's population increased fourfold, while the number of senior faculty positions increased 37-fold. Though faced with tremendous economic hardships after its independence, Israel nonetheless found the wherewithal to build research universities. By 1973, there were seven such universities in the country and the share of senior faculty positions per capita had risen over ninefold.

The mid-1970s marked a turnaround in national priorities that also left its mark on the universities. Though the country's population has risen by over 3.5 times since 1973, and though Israel is much wealthier today – with a GDP per capita 107 percent greater in 2016 than it was in 1973 – the number of university senior faculty per capita has fallen to just 40 percent of what it was in 1973. Even when the public non-research colleges are included, the share of total senior faculty in Israel's population is considerably below the 1973 heights, and it is declining.

A reflection of the shift in priorities is evident in the national higher education expenditures per student, which fell steadily for decades, dropping by 60 percent from 1979 through 2009 (Ben-David, 2017). Part of this reduction was certainly warranted by the large growth in undergraduate students attending the colleges. The cost of providing education to such students in these institutions is considerably less than the cost of educating students – particularly, graduate students – in full-fledged research universities. However, as noted above, this decline also reflects a national pivot away from the state-of-the-art institutions. There has been a small change in direction since 2010, but whether this change will persist remains to be seen.

Consequently, Israel's public expenditure per student in tertiary education is one of the lowest among the OECD countries (Ben-David, 2017). In and of itself, this does not imply a lower-quality higher education system. However, a low public expenditure per student implies a higher out-of-pocket cost for students. In fact, the share of household expenditures out of total tertiary expenditures in Israel places the country in the top third of the OECD.

The higher education expansion since the early 1990s was expected to shift the focus of the universities toward a greater emphasis on graduate study. As Israel has grown and the demand for workers with greater skills and higher education has risen, this change has indeed occurred. While the number of academic degrees awarded by Israel's research universities rose by 31 percent between 1999 and 2014, the number of graduate degrees has increased by 85 percent.

Today's graduate students form the primary pool of the country's future sources of research and innovation – which are the keys to economic growth. The higher the degree, the more personal the guidance needed from senior academic faculty members. Though this surge in the share of graduate students at the universities has transpired, there was no comparable increase in the number of senior faculty to teach and train the next generation. In fact, the opposite has occurred. In 1999, there was one senior faculty member for every 7.2 graduate students. By 2014, this fell to one senior faculty member per 10.6 graduate students in the research universities.

The resultant impact of these changes does not bode well for the quality of graduate research. While many graduate students do not opt for research tracks, there has been a major increase in those who do. There are fewer mentors to provide the necessary personal guidance so important for students at these levels. Consequently, either the amount of time devoted to advising each student has fallen, or there has been a decline in the time spent by Israel's leading researchers on their own research – or a combination of both outcomes.

The primary role of academia, other than educating students, is to push the research envelope forward. Just how good are Israel's academic institutions in this regard? The total number of publications, even if discounted by country size, are mere indicators of quantity. What actually counts is quality. One measure of quality could be the number of papers, or pages, published in top journals. While this can be considered an important measure at or near the time of publication – and top-tier journals can certainly increase awareness for a paper, signaling its potential gravity to others within academia – the ultimate determinant of a paper's research impact is the number of times that subsequent studies cite it as a stepping stone for their findings.

Using Web of Science data on citations and publications since 1975, it is possible to gauge the quality of Israel's academic research in relation to other countries. This study limited its focus to all countries that are currently members of the OECD and to five-year intervals since 1975. Since the number of researchers and papers has increased considerably over the years, there is little intrinsic value to be gained from examining how the average number of citations per article has changed over time. Hence, the analysis that follows focuses on a cross-country comparative analysis rather than on the examination of absolute changes over time.

Citation customs vary from discipline to discipline, as does the average number of articles published during a career and the average number of coauthors. Making a relatively strong – and potentially inaccurate – assumption that the distribution of disciplines is relatively similar across countries and over time, Figure 14.10 compares Israel to the OECD average as well as to the average for the G7 countries and to the United States.

The gaps between Israel and the other countries were quite large in 1975. The number of citations of academic papers from Israeli universities was almost a third more than the OECD average, 16 percent more than the G7 average, but 28 percent less than papers originating in the United States. One of the interesting outcomes depicted in the figure is the steady convergence process that has taken place between Israel and

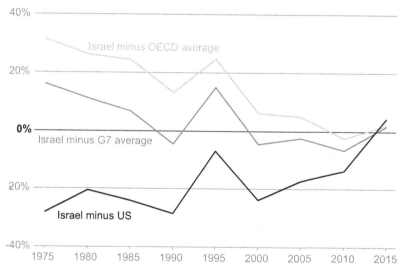

Figure 14.10 Average citations per publication, *Percentage differences between Israel and OECD, G7, and the United States.
* Observations at five-year intervals. Citations exclude self-citations.
Source: Ben-David (2017)

each of the three groups – and between each of the groups with each other. By 2015, all of the gaps had nearly disappeared entirely.

Focusing on three specific disciplines – engineering, physics, and computer science – helps pare down the noise that exists in the general comparison above. Since the idea is to gain some insight with regard to the relative quality of each country's cutting-edge research, the noise at the national level is further reduced here by concentrating only on the top five institutions in each of these fields in each country.

The Leiden Ranking, based exclusively on bibliographic data from the Web of Science database, was used to determine the top universities in each field and country. The number of publications per university refers to articles published by its faculty members.[9] Since the goal is to determine a country's most important academic institutions in the chosen fields, the size of an institution also matters.

Some universities in a few of the countries attained high rankings on the basis of just a few publications. Hence, the median number of publications was used to reduce the presence of small outlier institutions. Any university ranked among the top five that did not produce at least the median number of publications was removed and the next university in the ranking was included instead. In cases with multiple universities at the same ranking, the university with the highest number of publications was chosen.

The findings show that in all three disciplines there has been a substantial convergence in top-tier academic research across the developed world in general, and between Israel and the other countries in particular. There still remains a gap between the top American universities – which reflect the top of the top – and the leading Israeli universities. But the fact that this gap has substantially declined over the years is a good indication of the direction that academic research in Israel is headed.

The ability of Israel's universities to remain centers of excellence depends on their ability to attract and retain the top researchers. It also depends on their ability to train future generations of students at the highest levels. In the final analysis, all of the above depends on the quality of the primary and secondary education funnel into higher education.

---

[9] Fractional counting was used to designate the share of a university's authors out of a paper's total. For instance, if a publication's authors include five individuals, with two of these coming from the same university, that university will receive two-fifths of the credit for the article.

14.7 Conclusion

A superficial examination of Israel's society would appear to indicate that the country has one of the most educated populations in the world. The economic data provides a major warning light that something may be amiss in such a simplistic assessment. Israel's productivity levels are below those of most developed countries and have been falling further and further behind (in relative terms) the G7 countries for decades (Ben-David, 2017). In addition, Israel's income inequality and poverty rates are among the highest in the developed world.

The amalgamation of low productivity levels and high poverty rates suggests that Israel provides a textbook case highlighting the importance of education quality, as opposed to quantity. Despite some improvements in the quality of primary and secondary education, Israel's pupils receive a failing grade in some core subjects and barely attain above a 60 percent correct response rate in other subjects. In international exams, Israel consistently scores below almost all developed countries. Haredi boys, who do not even study the material, do not participate in either the domestic or the international exams. Had this group – which is not only large (nearly one-fifth of all the children) but by far the fastest growing in Israel – participated in the exams, the national results would have been even lower.

Hanushek and Woessmann (2015) provide a glimpse of the potential economic impact resulting from an improvement in the quality of math education at the lower end of the spectrum. They estimate the rise in a country's GDP if it instituted education reform targeted only at raising the scores of pupils below level 2 in the PISA 2012 exam. Their simulation assumes that it takes fifteen years to complete the education reform, and that it would take four decades until the only workers remaining are those who studied in the reformed system, and they calculate the present value of the increment to GDP over an eighty-year life expectancy span of a person born in 2015.

The main beneficiaries of such hypothetical reform will be countries whom today have the highest share of children with low scores – chief among them is Israel. Thus, while the leading countries can expect a present value of an increment ranging from "just" half as much more to a doubling of GDP, the authors calculate that the addition to Israel's GDP will be three times its current GDP, or 3,462 billion shekels in 2015 terms. The 2015 Education Ministry budget of

51 billion shekels provides a bit of perspective as to the enormity of the economic transformation that Israel could undergo.

Such an education reform would reverse the multi decade rise in the labor productivity gap between the G7 countries and Israel, shown by Ben-David (2017). The increment to the growth rate of GDP per capita in Israel could reach 0.45 percent annually, much more than in any G7 country. Even if the Hanushek–Woessmann projections are considerably off-mark and the benefits that accrue will be only half the estimated amounts, this would still be an outcome that would entirely change Israel's standard of living and its rate of growth. One should bear in mind that a reform that can raise the score of the lowest achievers should do wonders for all the rest of the pupils not even included in the Hanushek–Woessmann simulations.

The common thread tying together all of the above is that the necessary resources appear to be available for providing a good primary and secondary education in Israel. The key issue is not a lack of resources but a major inefficiency in nearly all aspects of education provision (see also Klinov, 2010). Throwing money and instruction hours at the problem is not a cure. Only a serious, comprehensive, education reform can overcome some of the underlying inequalities that pupils bring with them to class.

It should be noted that what have been referred to as educational reforms in recent years did not lead to anything more than major hikes in teachers' wages. While raising teachers' wages is an important step in and of itself for drawing better teachers into the system, that does not constitute a structural reform. First, the wage agreements were heavily biased toward experienced teachers, providing little incentive for young people with attractive alternatives to join the profession.[10] Second, the extra hours mandated by the new wage agreements stipulating that teachers have to stay in school to complete their off-class duties simply replaced the time that they devoted to these duties – perhaps more efficiently – at home. Finally, actual structural reform needs to include many additional changes needed for raising the quality of education in Israeli schools. Some of the other changes in the education system introduced over the past decade and a half – extending and

---

[10]   The wage agreement signed with secondary school teachers in December 2017 tried to correct this bias and reduce the salary gaps between experienced and beginning teachers.

improving the measurement of pupil achievements and teacher effectiveness, establishing the Avney Rosha Institute for training school principals and supervisors, initiating an academization of teaching colleges, reducing class sizes, promoting the study of math and English at higher levels, and favoring schools in localities with low socioeconomic status – were introduced in an ad-hoc manner rather than as parts of a comprehensive long-term strategy. No attempt has been made to significantly upgrade the core curriculum, nor to enforce it for all Israel's children, and there has been major change in the way future teachers are chosen and trained.

In academic education, what students study – and where – has a major impact on their subsequent career paths. Average hourly wages in some disciplines can be considerably higher than in other disciplines, with considerable wage gaps within the higher-paying disciplines on the basis of the academic institution where the degrees were attained. While Israel has opened up a large number of non-research colleges to fill in the gap between high school and its cutting-edge research universities, it has not established a single research university since the 1970s, though its population and standards of living have more than doubled. The number of senior faculty in the research universities, as a share of the population, has fallen by more than half since the mid-1970s.

Qualitatively, Israel's research universities are a part of a larger convergence trend within the developed world. The gap in the number of citations per academic article between Israel and the OECD average, between Israel and the G7 average, and between Israel and the United States has been nearly eliminated over the past four decades. A comparison of Israel's leading universities and America's leaders in a number of designated disciplines also indicates a substantial reduction in the gap over the past several decades.

The situation described in this study does not appear to be sustainable over the long run. If the primary and secondary school feeders into Israel's academic system continue to remain at, or near, the bottom of the developed world, it is hard to see how the country will be able to retain its top-tier research universities. From a wider perspective, the socioeconomic cost of providing such a poor education weighs down productivity and constrains future growth while at the same time increasing future welfare needs to care for a large and potentially growing segment of society lacking the qualitative tools needed for contending in a modern competitive economy. What has always been a fairly extensive brain drain out of Israel may turn into a mass exodus if the country continues falling further and further behind while needing to amass greater and greater financial resources to cover the costs of those left behind (Ben-David, 2019).

With the economic burden increasingly falling on fewer and fewer shoulders in a country situated in the most dangerous region on the planet, the provision of a considerably better education to those less fortunate is not altruism. It is self-preservation.

References

In Hebrew

Achdut, L., Zussman, N., and Mayan, I. (2017). The Returns to Studying in Universities versus Colleges in Terms of Wages and Labor Market Qualifications. Paper presented at the "Labor Market Qualifications" Conference, Research Department, Bank of Israel, June 11, 2017.

Bank of Israel (2016). Basic Skills of Workers in Israel and Industrial Productivity. In *Fiscal Survey and Selected Research Analyses*. Jerusalem: Bank of Israel, 29–36.

In English

Ben-David, D. (2017). *The Shoresh Handbook: Education and Its Impact in Israel, 2017–2018*. Cochav Yair: The Shoresh Institution for Socioeconomic Research.

(2019). *Leaving the Promised Land: A Look at Israel's Emigration Challenge*. Cochav Yair: The Shoresh Institution for Socioeconomic Research.

Ben-David, D., and Kimhi, A. (2017). *An Overview of Israel's Education System and Its Impact*. Cochav Yair: The Shoresh Institution for Socioeconomic Research.

Blass, N. (2015). Inequality in the Education System: Who Opposes It and Who Benefits from It? In D. Chernichovsky and A. Weiss (eds.), *State of the Nation Report: Society, Economy and Policy 2015*. Jerusalem: Taub Center for Social Policy Research, 497–539.

Chetty, R., Friedman, J. M., and Rockoff, J. E. (2011). *The Long-Term Impact of Teachers: Teacher Value-Added and Student Outcomes in Adulthood*. NBER Working Paper No. 17699. https://www.nber.org/papers/w17699.

Gruber, N. (2017). *Why Israel Does Poorly in the PISA Exams: Perceptions versus Reality.* Cochav Yair: The Shoresh Institution for Socioeconomic Research.

Hanushek, E. A., and Woessmann, L. (2015). *Universal Basic Skills: What Countries Stand to Gain.* Paris: OECD Publishing. http://dx.doi.org/10 .1787/9789264234833-en.

Kimhi, A. (2012). Labor Market Trends: Employment Rate and Wage Disparities. In D. Ben-David (ed.), *State of the Nation Report: Society, Economy and Policy 2011–2012.* Jerusalem: Taub Center for Social Policy Research, 123–160.

Kimhi, A., and Horovitz, A. (2015). *Impact of the Level of High School Math on Israeli Pupils' Academic and Career Outcomes.* Policy Paper No. 2015.01. Jerusalem: Taub Center for Social Policy Research.

Klinov, R. (2010). *Financing Primary and Lower Secondary Schools 2003–2008.* Discussion Paper A10.01. Jerusalem: The Maurice Falk Institute for Economic Research in Israel.

Shwed, U., and Shavit, Y. (2006). Occupational and Economic Attainments of College and University Graduates in Israel. *European Sociological Review,* 22, 431–442.

15 | *Economic Aspects of the Healthcare System in Israel*

GABI BIN NUN AND GUR OFER

15.1 Introduction

The healthcare system is composed of a number of institutions and organizations whose purpose is to improve the population's level of health and to reduce health disparities between population groups, while at the same time maintaining the quality of health services and the public's level of satisfaction with them and improving the functioning of the system.

The Israeli healthcare system, has over the years been characterized by a multiplicity of players, with respect to both financing healthcare services and supplying them. With respect to the latter, there are four groups of service providers:

a. *The Ministry of Health* is directly involved in the provision of hospitalization services and other healthcare services (such as mother and child health centers). In addition, it has overall responsibility for health planning, supervision, legislation, and policymaking. The ministerial responsibility for the system as a whole, together with government ownership of a large proportion of the general hospitals,[1] remains one of the central problems of the healthcare system.

b. *Four non-profit public health funds*, which directly provide numerous health services, both in the hospitals and in the community. Starting from the passage of the National Health Insurance Law in 1995, the health funds have also been responsible for providing the basket of health services specified in the law.

---

[1] With the establishment of the State of Israel, the Ministry of Health became responsible for operating the military hospitals that had existed during the Mandate period. This was primarily in order to deal with the health problems among the immigrants that arrived in massive waves in the 1950s.

c. *Other public institutions*. Not-for-profit organizations (such as the Hadassah hospitals and others).

These three providers provide about 70 percent of all healthcare services (Central Bureau of Statistics, 2016).

d. *For-profit institutions*, including private hospitals, dental services, private diagnostic and care services, etc.

In this chapter, we will examine the changes and main economic trends in Israel's healthcare system during the last twenty years (1995–2015) and will focus on the National Health Insurance Law and its effect. We will also look at the contribution of government involvement to improving the efficiency of the system and to preserving its built-in solidarity, as well as the methods adopted by the government to balance the tension between the two.

15.2 Twenty Years Since the National Health Insurance Law

Prior to the National Health Insurance Law implementation,[2] there were four public health funds that insured about 96 percent of the population. The health funds combine the provision of services with health insurance based on the principle of solidarity. Two of the health funds were connected to national labor unions which in turn were identified with political parties. The health insurance premiums ("member taxes" or the "uniform tax") were based primarily on wages and were collected directly by the health funds or by the national labor unions they were connected to. The member taxes were regressive, primarily due to a relatively low wage ceiling to which the tax applied, and in addition its collection was inefficient and sometimes discriminatory. The collection of the health insurance premiums by the health funds created a direct connection between a health fund's level of income and that of its members, and as a result also an inverse relationship with the health needs of its members. Prior to the passing of the law, a health fund could condition the acceptance of new members on medical examinations and could impose various restrictions on the acceptance or eligibility of elderly and sick members. Furthermore, switching between health funds was restricted by connecting membership

---

[2] See also Bin Nun and Ofer (2011).

Table 15.1 *The distribution of members between the health funds according to age and income prior to the passage of the National Health Insurance Law (1994)*

Health funds	Members aged 65+ as a percentage of total membership	Average income (average index of income = 1.0)
Clalit	13.1	0.9
Leumit	7.3	0.9
Maccabi	4.9	1.2
Meuhedet	4.2	1.0

Source: Bin Nun et al. (2010)

in a labor union or a place of work to membership in a health fund. This made it possible to direct better-off and healthier individuals to the Maccabi and Meuhedet health funds and to leave individuals with higher risk and lower income to the Clalit and Leumit health funds (Table 15.1).

The phenomenon of cream skimming for members, on the basis of both income and age, became increasingly pervasive in the late 1980s and constituted the main motivation for the National Health Insurance Law.

Twenty years after the enactment of the low, we will examine the effect of the law by comparing the healthcare system, according to the six basic principles it was based on.

15.2.1 Compulsory Health Insurance

Prior to the National Health Insurance Law, the system was characterized by voluntary health insurance arrangements implemented by the health funds. Although the insurance coverage was high (96 percent of the population), insurance was not compulsory. When the National Health Insurance Law came into effect in January 1995, health insurance became compulsory for every resident. This was a manifestation of the government's position that viewed health and health services as a basic right for all. The application of this principle brought about 250,000 individuals (about 4 percent of the population at that time) into the health insurance system and without any major impact on the level of national health expenditure.

15.2.2 Definition of the Basket of Services

Prior to the law, each health fund determined its own basket of services. The health funds did not have a clear, transparent or uniform definition of the basket. The eligibility for the basket of services was dependent on the payment of the membership tax, and each health fund could impose additional conditions on eligibility for the basket, such as a waiting period for new members, age, medical situation, etc.

The law replaced the health funds' arrangements for providing the basket of services and the conditions of eligibility to receive it and anchored the rights of health fund members in law. It also defined a uniform basket of services for all the health funds, to which every resident would be unconditionally eligible. A health fund had to provide the services in the basket at a "reasonable level of quality within a reasonable amount of time and within a reasonable distance."

15.2.3 Freedom of Choice

The law obligates all of the health funds to accept every resident without condition and it guarantees the right to switch from one health fund to another. While in the past each health fund could cherry-pick its members, now each individual could freely choose a health fund, without meeting any conditions. This principle was intended to encourage competition between the health funds in quality of service, to encourage efficiency and to reduce "cream skimming," which was prevalent prior to the law.

The flow of members between the health funds has been relatively insignificant over the years (1.5 percent per year on average), even though the law made the process much easier (including the ability to switch by mail or on the Internet). However, the very existence of the right to switch from one fund to another, even if it is not widely utilized, constitutes a continual threat to each health fund and provides an important incentive for them to maintain a reasonable level of service and to compete for members without explicit cherry-picking. The absolute freedom to choose a health fund and the allocation of resources among them on the basis of the relative risk of their members were meant to ensure this competition, while at the same time reducing the market failures that characterize the health insurance sector

15.2.4 *Collection of Health Insurance Premiums*

Prior to the National Health Insurance Law, health premiums were collected by each health fund or by the labor union it was connected to. As a result, part of the membership payments to a health fund that was connected to a labor union were used for the labor union's activities. When the law went into effect, the collection of membership payments became the responsibility of the National Insurance Institute. This improved both the base for collection and its efficiency and as a result the revenue from the health tax grew, without any change in the average rate of taxation. This change also improved the horizontal equality of the tax rates, delinked the income of the members from the revenue of the health funds and significantly weakened the connection between the health funds on the one hand and the political parties and labor unions on the other. In addition to the health tax, the law preserved the already existing "parallel tax" – which was paid by employers and whose revenues were earmarked for health. These two sources of revenue were meant to eventually finance the cost of the law, without the need for support from the State budget. However, this effort was unsuccessful due to the cancelation in 1996 of the "parallel tax."

15.2.5 *Allocation of Resources to the Health Funds*

Prior to the law, insurance premiums were paid directly to the health funds and constituted about one-half of their revenues. This arrangement led to a link between the health fund's financial situation and the income of its members, which was one of the main motives for the health fund's selective behavior. The law delinked a health fund's revenue from the income of its members by instituting the collection of the tax by the National Insurance Institute and the allocation of funding to the health funds on the basis of each fund's weighted share of the total number of insured. The law's weighting formula determines a different relative weight for each age group, which reflects differences in the expected consumption of health services between the age groups.

Over the years, the number of age groups included in the formula has been increased, and greater weight has been given to the elderly, among other changes.[3]

---

[3] In 2010, two variables were added to the risk coefficients in the allocation formula: gender and the geographic periphery.

15.2.6 *The Responsibility of the State in Financing the Law*

Since the health funds came into existence, they have received funding from the state budget, whether that support was planned ahead of time or whether it was provided to cover deficits after the fact. During those years, the support of the State for the health funds was based on the State's budget considerations, and to a great extent political considerations as well. As a result, the State's support for the health funds was characterized by wide fluctuations and uncertainty, which had an impact on the financial stability of the healthcare system.[4]

The National Health Insurance Law sought to ensure stable sources of financing (most of which are defined and earmarked) for the healthcare system in the long term. The law defined the "cost of the basket," which was a standard amount to be provided to the health funds for the provision of the basket of services. This principle is meant to ensure a stable and predictable level of financing in the long term. The definition of the "cost of the basket" is also meant to set a ceiling on expenditure, which is a kind of budget constraint that the health funds are to remain within and any expenditure beyond that will not be financed by the State.

The implementation of this principle remains a source of disagreement until today. The law only specified a partial linkage to changes in prices and recommended revising the cost based on demographic changes (although it did not specify the rate). Neither did it specify a mechanism for adopting new drugs and technologies. This partial system for updating the cost of the basket was one of the main factors behind the erosion of public funding provided by the law in real terms. This is partly responsible for the fact that the proportion of national health expenditure within GDP has not changed during the last twenty years and that Israel is an outlier according to this measure relative to other countries.

15.3 The Trend in National Health Expenditure[5]

The economic activity of the healthcare services is measured and published each year, since 1962, by the Central Bureau of Statistics (CBS).

---

[4] The State's budgeting rules for the healthcare system prior to the National Health Insurance Law are accurately described by the report of the State Investigation Committee to Examine the Functioning and Efficiency of the Healthcare System (Netanyahu Committee, 1990) as an "opaque financing and budget tool."

[5] All of the data on the trend in national health expenditure are taken from publications of the Central Bureau of Statistics. These figures are sometimes

These data make it possible to track and analyze the main trends and changes over the years in total expenditure, the entities that implement that expenditure, the sources of its funding, and other characteristics. The data also make it possible to carry out a comparison between Israel and other countries based on uniform definitions.

15.3.1 Total National Health Expenditure

The current national health expenditure (2016) constitutes 7.2 percent of GDP. This level has remained stable during the last two decades and is identical to the level that prevailed prior to the National Health Insurance Law. A comparison to the OECD countries shows that current national health expenditure in Israel is two percentage points lower than the OECD average (9 percent versus 7.2 percent; see Figure 15.1).

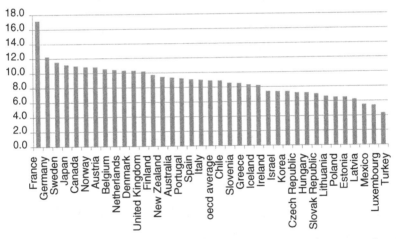

Figure 15.1 Current expenditure on health, as a percentage of GDP: Israel and the OECD countries, 2016.
Source: OECD (2017). Data for 2016 or the most recent year for which data is available.

revised retroactively. The national health expenditure data for the OECD countries is based on OECD publications.

The enactment of the law in 1995 was accompanied by serious concerns that the growth in national health expenditure would accelerate.

An analysis of the data on trends in national health expenditure show that the concerns proved to be baseless. During the decade that preceded the legislation (1985 to 1994), national health expenditure rose by about 1 percent of GDP, from 6.1 percent to about 7.5 percent, while during the twenty years subsequent to the enactment of the law it remained basically unchanged (at about 7 percent of GDP, with minor fluctuations over the years).

The stability in health expenditure in Israel since the enactment of the law is in contrast to the situation in most of the Western world (see Table 15.2). In the OECD countries, the average current national health expenditure as a percentage of GDP rose from 7 percent in 1995 to 9 percent in 2016, as opposed to the aforementioned stability of this rate in Israel. One reason for this is the erosion of funding sources provided by the National Health Insurance Law. Other reasons are apparently related to the neglect and lack of growth in the healthcare system's two main infrastructures, namely hospital beds and manpower. The supervision of total manpower and the level of salaries in the public system, as well as the tight control over investment in the physical infrastructure of hospital beds and expensive technological equipment, have contributed to the stability in national health expenditure.[6]

15.3.2 National Health Expenditure According to Provider

An analysis of national health expenditure according to provider shows that the share of public providers (the Ministry of Health, the health funds, and other non-profit public institutions, including the municipalities) has declined, while the share of business entities in providing health services has increased. In the 1990s, the share of the public sector in the provision of services was about 80 percent of total national health expenditure as opposed to 70 percent in 2015. At the same time, the weight of the private sector in national health expenditure rose from about 20 percent to about 30 percent.

---

[6] The addition of hospital beds and the acquisition of expensive technological equipment require an operating license from the State. It is worth mentioning that the rate of investment within national health expenditure in Israel during the last decade was about 3 percent, among the lowest in the OECD.

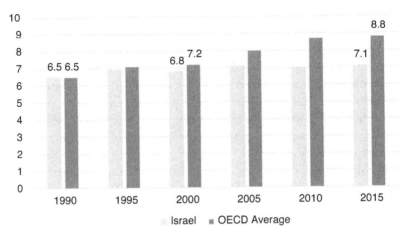

Figure 15.2 Current expenditure on health, % of GDP: Israel and the OECD average 1990–2015.
Source: OECD (2017)

Over the years, government policy has been characterized by efforts to encourage private sector involvement in the healthcare system, both in the provision of services and in their funding. This policy can be seen in the provision of licenses to operate private hospitals and in the system of economic incentives that has created a preference for the private sector (funded by private insurance) over the public sector. During the last three years, there have been signs of a change in government policy and a number of measures are being adopted in order to strengthen the public healthcare providers.

15.3.3 The Changes in the Healthcare System's Sources of Funding

The national health expenditure is funded by three groups of sources:

(a) The state budget (including the National Insurance Institute);
(b) Health insurance premiums paid by the worker (the health tax) and the parallel tax paid by the employer (up until 1996), which will be defined as a public funding source of the healthcare system;
(c) Payments for private health insurance policies (supplementary health insurance and private health insurance) and payments for

Table 15.2 *Trends in national health expenditure, 1990–2015*

	Israel					
	1990	1995	2000	2005	2010	2015
National health expenditure as a percentage of GDP	6.9	7.9	7.2	7.4	7.4	7.5
Current national health expenditure as a percentage of GDP	6.3	7.0	6.9	7.1	7.	7.3
Per capita national health expenditure in $ppp prices	980	1,370	1,700	1,770	2,030	2,710
The proportion of private financing in national health expenditure (in percent)	29.2	31.5	35.6	37.1	36.6	36.1
The proportion of for-profit producers (private provision within national healthcare expenditure)	20	22	24	25	28	30
	OECD average					
	1990	1995	2000	2005	2010	2015
Current national health expenditure as a percentage of GDP	6.3	7.0	7.4	8.3	9.0	9.2
Per capita national health expenditure in $ppp prices	1,050	1,350	1,790	2,470	3,230	3,850
The proportion of private financing in national health expenditure (in percent)	9	28	29	29	27	28

Source: Central Bureau of Statistics (2016a); Annual Abstract 2017; OECD (2017)

household consumption of services ("out-of-pocket expenses"),[7] which will be defined as a private source of funding for the health-care system.

---

[7] There is a fourth source of funding labeled as "other," which includes deficits or surpluses and financing from unknown sources. Over the years, this source has constituted 1–2 percent of the healthcare system's funding sources.

Table 15.3 *Financing of national health expenditure, 1990–2015 (%)*

	1990	1995	2000	2005	2010	2015
Financing from the state budget (including the parallel tax)	46.5	44.6	37.2	35.9	36.4	38.0
Membership fees / health tax payments	18.5	21.3	25.1	24.9	25.2	24.3
Total public financing	65.0	65.9	62.3	60.8	61.6	62.3
Total private financing	29.2	31.5	35.6	37.1	36.6	36.1
Other	5.8	2.6	2.1	2.1	1.8	1.6
Total	100	100	100	100	100	100

Source: Central Bureau of Statistics (2016a)

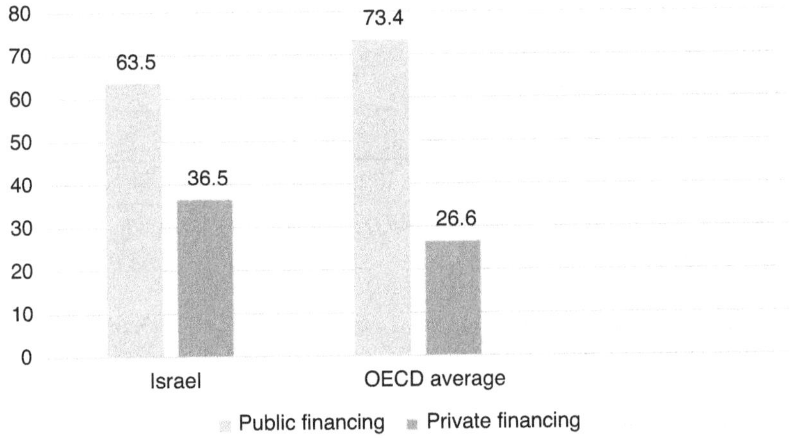

Figure 15.3 Government and compulsory health insurance schemes, percentage of current expenditure on health, 2015.
Source: Central Bureau of Statistics (2016a); OECD (2017)

An analysis of the healthcare system's sources of financing over time shows a downward trend in the share of total public sources of financing (participation of the State and health insurance premiums)- from 66 percent to 62 percent in that same period. As mentioned, the average proportion of public financing in the OECD countries has been stable at around 72 percent, about 10 percentage points higher than in Israel (Figure 15.3).

The level of private financing during that period rose from 31.5 percent to about 36.1 percent, one of the highest levels in the OECD countries (Israel is ranked sixth).

The main explanation for the decline in the share of the government in the healthcare system is related to macroeconomic policy and primarily the cut in public expenditures in general. This policy has led to a reduction in expenditure on the three main social components of the budget: education, healthcare and transfer payments.

In recent decades, private financing became an alternative source to public financing, which had a major impact on the egalitarian character of the healthcare system. Thus, the expansion of private financing strengthens the link between the use of healthcare services and an individual's ability to pay (whether directly or through private insurance) and thus reduced the availability of services to the less well-off.

15.4 Compensation and Allocation Mechanisms in the Healthcare System

The provision of services and insurance in the healthcare system is characterized by a large number of significant market failures. The lack of information among consumers, and primarily the asymmetry between them and the suppliers, results in the phenomenon of "supply creating demand," which first became evident in the excess activity in various areas of service provision. The gaps in information also limit the consumer's ability to evaluate the quality of services that he is acquiring and facilitates high prices or low quality, without any change in demand (quality failures). Similar information failures prevail in the health insurance market and most commonly involve the phenomena of cherry-picking by the insurance companies and over-insurance.

Against the background of these and other market failures, government intervention is common in the healthcare system (including licensing requirements for the main inputs into the system, setting the level of prices and numerous supervisory mechanisms).

The setting of the level of funding guaranteed to the health funds in the law ("cost of the basket") is meant to achieve long-term financial stability, and the rules for compensation between the health funds and the hospitals have ensured a security net for the health funds, which protects them against a spike in hospitalization costs and overuse of hospitalization services. However, numerous problems with these mechanisms have come to light: the competition over quality of service has led to aggressive marketing activities by the health funds; the development of duplicate services in the community by the various health funds has led to additional costs to the system, and lower availability and quality of public services.[8] The competition between the health funds over the limited number of specialists has led to the inflation of their salaries, and the development of private insurance has created incentives for the health funds and the physicians to shift patients from the public to the private system. This has led to both reduced efficiency and reduced equality in the system. Also, the law's attempt to ensure an appropriate and predictable level of funding for the health funds in the long term was shown to be wishful thinking, primarily due to the only partial mechanism for the updating of funding.

In the next section, we will examine the mechanisms for compensation and allocation that were included in the law and their effect on the efficiency and equality of the system.

15.4.1 *The Mechanism for Updating the Cost of the Basket*

The law states that the cost of the basket of services (the "cost of the basket") is to be updated annually according to changes in prices and in the size of the population. The updates are meant to maintain the real value of the funding specified in the law so as to ensure the quality and availability of the basket of services.

The updating of prices is implemented according to price coefficients that are described in the law (the Cost of Health Index); however, these coefficients only partially reflect price increases in the healthcare system's inputs.

The revision of the demographic dimension of the cost of the basket is meant to capture the aging of the population and population growth. In practice, this revision has been implemented through triannual agreements between the Ministry of Health and the Ministry of Finance, but they only partially compensate for demographic change

---

[8] The negative aspects of this competition are still prevalent today, particularly in the Periphery and in the Arab and ultra-Orthodox sectors, despite the measures implemented by the State over the years to limit them.

(about two-thirds of it). Starting from 2014, the demographic update fully compensated for population growth (2 percent every year) but still did not take into account the aging of the population.

The cumulative effect of only partial updating during the twenty-one years that the law has been in force has reached about 21 percent in the cost of the basket.[9] These shortfalls were partly exploited to support demands for greater efficiency in the system and in part were compensated for by stabilization agreements signed by the government from time to time with the health funds. However, the support did not reduce the accumulated gap in funding provided for by the law. This shortfall was, as mentioned, manifested in the repeated annual deficits of the health funds (and other parts of the system) and in the erosion of quality in the basket of services and its availability.

The lack of consensus with respect to the appropriate updating mechanism has been a decisive factor in the creation of large deficits in the system since the law came into effect. Some of the deficits over the years have been absorbed by the health funds by increasing efficiency, while other deficits have been covered by the expansion of other sources of funding, such as increased co-payments and larger premiums for the supplementary insurance plans.

15.4.2 *The Mechanism for Expansion of the Basket: The Addition of Drugs and Technologies and New Types of Services*

Many of the technological innovations in diagnosis and care lead to increases in the cost of the healthcare system. Up until 1998, there was no addition to the cost of the basket in order to finance this phenomenon. Starting from that year – approved an average annual addition of about 1 percent of the cost of the basket for technological

The decision on how the additional budget will be used each year is in the hands of the Basket Committee, which was established in 1998 and is composed of representatives of the government, the health funds, and the public, among others, who represent all of the components of

---

[9] The cumulative gap between the rise in the Index of Health Inputs and the compensation for the actual increase in prices (according to the Cost of Health Index) stood at about 11 percent. The gap between the demographic compensation and the actual growth in the population (without a correction for the aging of the population) was 12 percent.

the healthcare system. In the process to decide on the inclusion of new drugs and technologies, the Basket Committee takes into account ethical, clinical, and social considerations, as well as cost–benefit calculations. The addition of a drug or technology to the basket is, as mentioned, accompanied by a parallel addition of funding for the cost of the basket determined ahead of time based on the forecast of prices and quantities for the drugs or technologies that were approved.

The process of adopting new technologies and drugs is not unique to Israel. Indeed, most of the OECD countries use economic evaluations in order to support decisions to adopt new technologies. A number of countries have in place an annual updating process, within the framework of a predetermined budget (as in Israel), while others adopt new technologies on a continuous basis where the decision-making is based on the threshold approach.

15.4.3 The Mechanism for the Allocation of Funding Among the Health Funds: The Capitation Formula

The allocation formula is used to divide up the funding specified by the law[10] ("the cost of the basket") among the health funds according to the needs of their members and thus to create a more efficient and just division of resources and to reduce the incentives to "cream skimming' of healthy and wealthy members. The weights of the formula were based on the relative weights for nine age groups. Every change in the allocation formula changes the division between the health funds, but not the total funding available to them. Owing to differences in age distributions between the health funds, the adoption of this method in 1995 led to a significant increase in the funding of the Clalit and Leumit health funds and a reduction in that of the Maccabi and Meuhedet health funds.

The allocation according to the healthcare needs of the health fund members (even if only based on the age variable) is fairer and more

---

[10] About 95 percent of the funding provided by the law is divided according to the allocation formula being discussed. The rest of the funding is divided on the basis of each health fund's number of members who suffer from one of five serious illnesses. The age weights in the capitation formula reflect the distribution of expenditure according to age for the basket of services included in the law. It is also worth mentioning that these weights do not reflect the distribution of national health expenditure by age.

egalitarian than allocation according to the income of health fund members, which was the practice prior to the enactment of the law. Such an allocation is also more efficient, since it reduces the incentives to "cream skimming' members and results in the health funds bearing the main part of the population's insurance risk.

Over the years, a number of changes have been made in the risk adjustors included in the formula. In June 2005, the weights of the age groups in the allocation formula were updated and two age groups were added.

In 2010, a gender variable and a coefficient for the periphery were added to the allocation formula.

In 2015, the allocation formula was updated following the transfer of responsibility for mental health services to the health funds. A similar adjustment was made in the allocation formula when insurance responsibility for the victims of work accidents and road accidents was transferred to the four health funds.

15.4.4 Payment Arrangements Between the Hospitals and the Health Funds

There are a large variety of payment arrangements between the insurers and the service providers in the current healthcare system. These arrangements have wide-ranging effects on the level of service usage, the variety of the services and their location, the quality of the service, the degree of satisfaction among patients, the incentives for efficiency, etc.

This section of the chapter will focus on the acquisition of general hospitalization services, since this component of expenditure constitutes about one-quarter of national health expenditure and about 40 percent of the total expenditure of the health funds (as of 2015).[11]

As part of the economic relations between buyers and sellers of general hospitalization services, the health funds seek to minimize their expenditure on the acquisition of services from the hospitals, while the hospitals seek to increase their revenue from the health

---

[11] Four health funds currently account for over 80 percent of the general hospitalization expenditure. The rest is financed by the National Insurance Institute, the government ministries and other purchasers of services. The discussion in this section will concentrate only on the acquisition of general hospitalization services by the health funds.

funds. Against the background of this built-in conflict of interest (which has become more intense as budget pressure has increased in the system), claims have been made by both sides during the years being surveyed. Thus, the health funds have claimed that the hospitals exploit their control over demand and are creating excess usage ("supplier-induced demand") as a means of increasing their revenue. In contrast, the hospitals have claimed that the health funds are exploiting the payment arrangements in order to shift and cherry-pick patients.

There are currently a large variety of methods by which the hospitals in the Israeli healthcare system are compensated by the health funds. The main ones include: a uniform price for a hospitalization day; differential pricing (procedure-related group – PRG); a revenue ceiling (for each hospital with respect to each health fund – a cap system); and global acquisition contracts. We will briefly present each of these methods of compensation and the pros and cons of each.[12]

(1) *Payment on the basis of an average hospitalization day.* Compensation on the basis of hospitalization days (Per dime) is one of the most common methods of compensation in healthcare systems worldwide (primarily due to the availability of data).

From 1977 onward, and to some extent until today, the method of compensation between the general hospitals and the purchasers of services (the health funds) has been based on a uniform average price for a hospitalization day for the entire general hospital system. The main advantages of this method of compensation is the ease of calculation and implementation. Despite these advantages, criticism of the method continues to be voiced until today. The main criticism is focused on the "average" nature of the rate, since a uniform average rate does not capture differences in expenditure resulting from the size of the hospital, the type of departments, the types of patients, or the level of teaching and research activity.

Over the years, a number of changes and updates have been made to this method of compensation, primarily ones which included differentiation of the uniform average price of a hospitalization day into prices according to department, However, the change has not provided a solution to another problem in the hospitalization day method – lack of incentive to carry out expensive procedures, since

---

[12] See also the chapter "Methods of Payment and Compensation in the Healthcare System," in Bin Nun et al. (2010).

the payment for them (the duration of the hospital stay multiplied by the price of a hospitalization day) does not cover the costs of treatment. This was the main reason for the creation of long queues for expensive medical procedures in the early 1990s and one of the solutions was a shift to differential compensation method.

(2) *Payment according to Procedure Related Groups (PRG).* In 1990, fifteen groups of activity were chosen whose duration of hospitalization did not reflect their complexity and their cost of care (brain surgery, open heart surgery, joint replacement, bone marrow transplants, etc.) and each was assigned a predetermined rate. The health funds compensated the hospitals for these procedures on the basis of number of treatments multiplied by the differential price for each medical procedure, regardless of the duration of the patient's hospitalization. The list of differential rates was expanded over the years and now includes 200 different procedures.

The PRG method creates an incentive for the hospitals to increase the scope of compensated-for procedures (in this way preventing the creation of queues) and reduces the average hospital stay. However, the method has a number of disadvantages: There is a need for continual monitoring of both the pricing of procedures and technological developments that change the basis for calculation. Furthermore, the incentive to increase the volume of activity under this system may indeed shorten queues, but at the same time it can encourage differentiated activities that are not medically necessary in order to increase the hospital's revenue.

(3) *Compensation on the basis of "Capping."* Prior to the enactment of the National Health Insurance Law, a financial rehabilitation agreement was signed between the government and the Clalit Health Fund, according to which the purchase of hospitalization services from general government hospitals would not be compensated beyond a predetermined cap.

When the law went into effect, the compensation system was expanded to all of the health funds and all of the hospitals, but with one major change: compensation of services beyond the cap would only be partial. The capping system was meant to control the growth in the expenditure on general hospitalization, thus weakening the incentive under the previous system for a hospital to increase its scope of activity, with the goal of reducing the health funds' level of expenditure and the hospitals' revenues.

The implementation of the arrangement from 1995 until today has been subject to criticism with respect to both the annual update of the caps for each hospital opposite each health fund and the rate of reduction of compensation for expenditure beyond the caps. A further criticism was related to the ability of the health funds to shift patients to hospitals that had already arrived at the caps in order to maximize the reduction in compensation from the health fund. Currently, there are three levels of reduction in compensation for consumption beyond the cap, as well as a minimal threshold of service consumption (95 percent of the cap) which each health fund must purchase from each hospital.

(4) *Contractual payment arrangements.* During the years in which the payment arrangement between the health funds and the hospitals was based on fee-for-service, the health funds claimed that the system encourages the hospitals to increase the quantity of services – on the basis of which the payment is calculated beyond what is medically necessary. As a result, there began to develop a global system of compensation that was meant to reduce the hospital's incentive to increase its volume of activity. According to this system, the health fund was committed to a fixed annual payment to the hospital for an agreed-upon volume of services, regardless of the actual usage. The system is now part of the healthcare system regulations, and such a compensation agreement exists between each health fund and each hospital.

The advantages of the global payment system are primarily at the level of the overall system: control over the level of hospitalization expenditure. The main disadvantages of the system are related to the fact that the hospitals do not receive compensation for an addition to their activity beyond that agreed upon in the global arrangement, which is liable to create queues. Indeed, the currently long queues in the Israeli healthcare system are attributed to, among other things, this compensation arrangement.

There are no "correct" compensation systems which can serve as the infrastructure for the acquisition of general hospitalization services. The systems based on payment for service (according to hospitalization days or differential pricing) tend to increase the volume of compensated-for activity (a positive outcome when queues exist, but a negative one in situations of excess activity). Under the global payment systems, there is greater control over the level of expenditure, but a lack of incentives to expand activity or to improve quality. It appears that, from time to time, the methods of compensation need to be modified according to the utilization of services (the length of queues), changes in the process for producing services (the ratio between fixed and variable costs), and various changes in the behavior of service providers and insurers.

15.5 The System's Inputs and Outputs

15.5.1 Inputs

The general hospital beds and manpower (Physicians and Nurses) are the main component in the input of the healthcare system and will therefore be a focus of the discussion on these two inputs.[13]

1. *"General hospital" beds.*[14] In 2015, there were forty-four general hospitals in Israel, the vast majority of which are publicly owned with only 3 percent under private ownership.

   The number of general beds per capita in 2015 was 1.83 per thousand population and over the years this figure has declined (by about 38 percent during the period 1990–2015). The number of general hospital beds in Israel is one of the lowest among the OECD countries (Israel is ranked 30th among the 35 members). The ratio is expected to continue declining during the coming decade.

   Alongside the downward trend in general hospital beds, there has been a long-term decline in the average length of stay: from five days in the 1990s to four in recent years. The occupancy rate of beds has been high during this entire period, in the vicinity of 90 percent – one of the highest among the OECD countries.

---

[13] All of the figures in this section are taken from publications of the Ministry of Health: *Manpower in the Health Professions, 2015*; *Hospitals and Outpatient Clinics in Israel, 2015*.

[14] In 2014, the OECD changed its definition of "general beds," which now also includes psychiatric beds; nonetheless, this part of the chapter will consider general hospital beds without this component.

The long-term decline in the number of hospital beds per capita in Israel is one of the main explanations for the stability in national health expenditure, but at the same time it made a major contribution to the decline in the quality of medical care (overburdened medical staff, beds in the corridors, hospital-acquired infections, an increase in errors, early release, etc.) and less respect for patients and concern for their welfare. This situation is exacerbated in the winter which is characterized by full occupancy and hospitalization in the corridors.

2. *Manpower.* According to the Manpower Survey carried out by the CBS, the employees in the healthcare system reached in 2016, about 5.5 percent of the total labor force. Employees in the medical professions (physicians, nurses, and other health professions) account for 59 percent of the total. The number of employees in the health professions in Israel (14.8 per thousand population) is lower than the OECD average (22 per thousand population).

- *Physicians.* The number of physicians per capita in Israel (3.4) is similar to the OECD average, although in most of the industrialized countries this number is characterized by an upward trend, while in Israel the opposite is the case. The reasons for the downward trend in Israel include the low number of graduates from medical schools, the reduced number of arriving immigrant physicians, and the high rate of physicians reaching retirement (physicians aged 65 or older accounted for 14 percent of the total in 2016, in contrast to only 7 percent in the previous decade). In order to deal with this phenomenon, the medical schools have been expanded and a new medical school was opened in Tsefat (in 2011). An analysis of the sources of new physicians reveals something unique about Israel, namely that the graduates of medical schools constitute only a small proportion of new physicians each year. Thus, in the 1980s, the proportion of Israeli graduates among those receiving a medical license was about 43 percent; and in the 1990s the figure dropped to 22 percent, due primarily to the arrival of a large number of physicians as part of the huge wave of immigration from the Former Soviet Union.[15] The annual number

---

[15] In the early 1990s, the wave of immigration from the former Soviet Union reached its peak. This wave of immigration was characterized by a particularly high

of new physicians is currently lower than the number of retiring physicians. As a result, and due to the drop in the arrival of immigrant physicians, the number of physicians per capita is liable to continue to decline, even after the opening of the new medical school and the increase in the number of students enrolled in existing medical schools.

- *Nurses*. During the years 2013–2015, there were about 4.9 nurses per thousand population and they accounted for about 20 percent of total employees in the healthcare system. In contrast, the number of nurses per capita in the OECD is almost double that (9.4 per thousand), and there are only three OECD countries (out of 35) in which the rate is lower (Latvia, Greece, and Mexico).

In sum, the review of the main inputs into the healthcare system indicate a general downward trend per thousand population.[16] This decline (hospital beds and manpower), together with the erosion in the cost of the basket and reduced public financing, apparently constitutes the main reason that the State of Israel is an outlier relative to the

Table 15.4 *Manpower and hospital beds, 1990–2015*

| | Number of general hospital beds, physicians and nurses per 1000 population | | | | | |
	1990	1995	2000	2005	2010	2015
General hospital beds	2.53	2.33	2.22	2.09	1.91	1.83
Employed physicians	2.5	3.4	3.5	3.3	3.3	3.4
Employed nurses	5.7	5.4	5.2	4.9	4.7	4.9

Sources: Ministry of Health (2016), Information and Computer Branch, *Hospitals and Outpatient Clinics in Israel, 2015*; Manpower Survey of the CBS.

[16] proportion of physicians. Thus, in 1992, 2,468 immigrant physicians received medical licenses, about five times the annual average for the 1990s as a whole. It is also worth mentioning that with respect to other expensive factors of production, Israel also has a low ranking relative to the OECD countries. Thus, for example, the average number of CT (computerized tomography) machines per million population in the OECD countries is four times that in Israel and in the case of MRI machines it is 2.5 times higher.

OECD countries with respect to the trend in national health expenditure. In the OECD countries, national health expenditure as a percentage of GDP is growing, while in Israel it has remained stable during the last twenty years (Figure 15.1).

15.5.2 The System's Outputs: The Population's Health Situation

The main indexes used to evaluate a population's level of health are life expectancy and infant mortality at birth per thousand live births.[17] In the case of Israel, these indexes show long-term improvement. Life expectancy in 2015 was 80.1 for men and 84.1 for women. During the past decade, the life expectancy of men rose by 2.5 years and that of women by 2.1 years. In comparison to the OECD average, the life expectancy of men in Israel is two years higher and that of women is one year higher.

The situation for infant mortality is similar: During the past two decades, there has been a sharp decline in infant mortality, from 7.4 per thousand live births in 1994 to 3.1 in 2015. This is the lowest rate among the OECD countries.

Table 15.5 *Outputs of the healthcare system: life expectancy and infant mortality, 1990–2015*

	Life expectancy (in years) and infant mortality (per 1,000 live births)					
	1990	1995	2000	2005	2010	2015
Life expectancy						
Men	74.9	75.5	76.7	78.2	79.7	80.1
Women	78.4	79.5	80.9	82.2	83.6	84.1
Infant mortality	9.7	6.7	5.5	4.3	3.8	3.0

Source: Central Bureau of Statistics (2016b)

---

[17] Other indexes of health outputs for which international comparison is possible include standardized mortality according to age group, maternal mortality, deaths from accidents, deaths of children from infectious diseases, the proportion of newborns under 2,500 grams, vaccination coverage, the incidence of sexually transmitted diseases, health behavior patterns, and others.

The table shows that the population's level of health (the system's "output") has risen according to these indexes and is high relative to the OECD, despite the fact that the healthcare system's inputs (manpower and hospital beds) and the percentage of national health expenditure within GDP are among the lowest of the OECD countries.

Is it possible to draw conclusions about the efficiency of the healthcare system in Israel from the ratio of input to outputs? Not necessarily. It is well known that the health level of the population is influenced by factors outside the healthcare system, and their weight in achieving health outcomes is even greater than that of the inputs into the system. The population's level of health is influenced by a host of variables, including biological-genetic factors (which can be controlled to only a limited extent), environmental factors (sewage, drinking water, and air pollution), lifestyle (smoking, physical activity, and nutrition) and socioeconomic factors (employment, income, education, housing conditions and employment). Only a small number of these factors are under the direct responsibility of the healthcare system, and therefore care must be taken in attributing achievements in output (according to the aforementioned indexes) exclusively to the healthcare system. Furthermore, the indexes of life expectancy and infant mortality do not reflect the quality of health services and their availability to the population). Similarly, it should be recalled that these indexes reflect the population's average health situation and conceal the distribution of health among the various population groups.

15.6 Health Equality

According to the commonly held view in Western countries (apart from the United States), health services should be provided – to whatever extent possible – on the basis of medical need rather than the ability or willingness to pay. Although this view is widespread, there exist major health disparities and inequality between various populations, including demographic, social, geographic, and other types of inequality.[18]

Health equality is measured by the appropriate dispersal of services and delinking between ability to pay and usage of health services. In

[18] See also Ministry of Health (2016), *Inequality in Health and the Effort to Reduce It*, Jerusalem; The Israel National Institute for Health Policy Research (2013), *Disparities and Inequality in Health: Economic Aspects*, Jerusalem. [Hebrew]

Table 15.6 *Healthcare equality: selected data*

Private expenditure (percent)	1995	2000	2005	2010	2015
Proportion of private financing within total national health expenditure	31.5	35.6	37.1	36.6	36.1
Proportion of household expenditure on health services and private health insurance within total household expenditure	3.7	4.6	5.1	5.2	5.7

Access and availability (2015)	South	North	National
Manpower (per 1,000 population)	3.1	2.3	3.5
Physicians	3.3	4.4	4.9
Nurses	4.2	3.1	4.7
Medical support professions (elderly caregiver, technicians, etc.)	2.6	2.8	4.1
Other medical professions (pharmacists, physiotherapists, etc.)			

Hospital beds (per 1,000 population)			
Total general hospital beds	1.34	1.49	1.83
Of this: Intensive care beds	0.065	0.067	0.086
Rehabilitation beds	0.043	0.043	0.101
Mental health beds	0.28	0.29	0.42

Health indexes	South	North	National
Infant mortality (per 1000 live births, average for 2013–15)	2.8	2.8	2.2
Jews and others	11.0	4.8	6.2
Arabs			

	Men	Women
Life expectancy (in 2015)	80.7	84.5
Jews and others	76.9	81.1
Arabs		

The figures for manpower are the average for the years 2013–2015. *Source:* Ministry of Health, Information Branch (2015), *Manpower in the Health Professions in 2015*, Jerusalem. The figures for hospital beds are as of the end of 2015. *Source:* Ministry of Health, Information Branch (2016, *Hospitals and Outpatient Clinics in Israel in 2015*, Jerusalem. The figures for life expectancy and infant mortality are from the *Statistical Abstract of Israel 2016* (Central Bureau of Statistics, 2016b).

a broader sense, health equality also includes preventing discrimination against patients who have difficulty in fully exploiting their rights and the ability of users to understand and internalize the existing body of medical and healthcare information.

A review of the principles included in the National Health Insurance Law shows that these principles indeed support the values of justice, equality, and solidarity. The combination of these principles held great promise for the egalitarian nature of the healthcare system and the law was perceived – not unjustifiably – as one of the most important social reforms in the Israeli society.

However, the aforementioned contribution of the law to achieving the goals of equality have been eroded over the years due to two factors: (a) amendments to the law – over the years about 470 amendments have been made to the law, some of which were intended to eliminate lacunae or to apply lessons learned from experience although others tended to undermine the principles of the law; (b) the reduction in public financing of the system and the growth of private financing, a trend that has reduced both horizontal equality (access and availability) and vertical equality (fairness of financing).

The uniform geographic dispersal of healthcare infrastructure (physicians, nurses, hospital beds, etc.) is, as mentioned, an important component in the achievement of health equality. An examination of the dispersal of these infrastructures indicates that there are still major disparities between various regions of the country. Thus, for example, the number of intensive care beds per capita in the north of the country is 78 percent of the national average; the number of rehabilitation beds per capita in the south is about one-half of the national average and the number of physicians per capita in the north is only 65 percent of the national average.[19]

During the entire period, life expectancy in the Arab sector has been significantly lower than in the Jewish sector, among both men and women. Nonetheless, the difference in life expectancy between the two populations for women has remained unchanged at about 3.3 years, while that of men has grown during the period being surveyed from 3 years to 4.3 years. Infant mortality in the northern and southern

---

[19] The expansion of supplementary health insurance and the possibility it provides of shortening the wait in queues for service by resorting to the private healthcare system have also contributed to inequality, since the Periphery is characterized by low availability of specialists.

peripheries is 30 percent higher than the national average, both among Arabs and among Jews. The rate of infant mortality among the Arab population is three times that of the Jewish population. These disparities in life expectancy and infant mortality between Jews and non-Jews and between various regions of the country have not diminished over the years.

Self-diagnosis, risky behavior, incidence of cardiovascular disease, high blood pressure, cancer, asthma, and dental problems are all more common among the disadvantaged sectors of the population. The trends over time are not showing any narrowing of these gaps in Israel.

The main cause of health disparities and inequality is to be found outside the healthcare system. Thus, there is a high correlation between income, level of education, and occupation on the one hand and health disparities on the other. Age-adjusted death rates are higher among populations with a low level of education, while health disparities are less pronounced among populations where income is more equally distributed. Thus, the connection between socioeconomic inequality and health transform social disparities into a health risk factor no less important than blood pressure or cholesterol level.

The disparities in the healthcare system are, as mentioned, dependent only partially on the way in which the system is organized and financed, but there is nonetheless plenty of room to improve the situation. The healthcare system can reorganize the public financing arrangements while reducing economic barriers and weakening the link between the usage of health services and the payment for them; it can improve the situation of manpower, hospital beds, and other infrastructures in the periphery; it can implement focused intervention programs to reduce disparities between the various population groups; etc. Cooperation between all of the players in the system (the Ministry of Health, the health funds, and other service providers), as well as between government ministries and between sectors, is a necessary condition for reducing disparities and achieving health equality.

15.7 Conclusion

The National Health Insurance Law (1995) is one of the main milestones in the development of the healthcare system in Israel. It introduced universal eligibility for health insurance, complete freedom of choice between health funds, definition of a basket of services that would be provided to the entire population, progressive health insurance premiums, and a mechanism for a fair and more efficient allocation of financing, all of which changed the face of the healthcare system and strengthened to a large extent the equality and efficiency of the system. Nonetheless, there were a series of amendments and government decisions since the law's enactment which led to an undermining of the law's fundamental principles, the most important of which have been presented in this chapter.

Over the years, the only partial mechanism in the law for updating the cost of the basket has been one of the main factors behind the erosion of the real value of the health funds' sources of financing. This erosion has resulted in permanent deficits among the health funds and has constituted a means for constraining expenditure and for monitoring and controlling the health funds.

The erosion of the sources of financing provided by the law and the system's infrastructures (manpower and hospital beds) is the main reason that the level of national health expenditure as a percentage of GDP has remained unchanged during the last twenty years. The stability in health expenditure in Israel stands in contrast to the upward trends observed in most of the OECD countries. The share of public health expenditure in Israel is among the lowest of the OECD countries, while the level of private financing of healthcare is among the highest, a situation that undermines both the equality and the efficiency of the system.

During the years surveyed, efforts have been made to find an allocation formula ("capitation") that would more accurately represent the population's health needs, but up till now, no new variables, such as socioeconomic status, which would reflect existing difference among the members of the health funds in need and consumption of health services, have been added to the demographic variables (i.e., age and gender).

The healthcare system in Israel suffers from a number of problems, some of which have been described in this chapter. Alongside localized shortages of medical infrastructure, there are also duplications in the system; the rate of private financing of the healthcare system is among the highest in the Western world; there are long queues for surgery and diagnostic procedures; and there are health disparities between various population groups.

Nonetheless, it is worth pointing to the significant achievements of the healthcare system in Israel over the years. These include a broad dispersal of health services throughout the country and their availability to all; there is a high rate of vaccination coverage in the population; medical care and the use of drugs and medical technologies are among the most advanced in the Western world; and there is overall a high level of satisfaction with the healthcare system among the public.

With a view to the future, there appear to be a number of major challenges facing the healthcare system:

a. The aging of the population: This is the main challenge facing the healthcare system. Although Israel's population is younger than those of the OECD countries (the 65+ age group constitutes 11 percent of the population as opposed to an average of 17 percent in the OECD), the rate of increase in the aging of the population is among the highest in the world and within thirty years, the 75+ age group is expected to double in size. The system is, as mentioned, facing demographic change that will impact numerous domains (the labor market, pensions, etc.) and will directly affect the healthcare system. It will in the future have to deal with an increase in the incidence of chronic disease and in the consumption of health services. In addition, the system is facing a serious shortage in health infrastructure. These are challenges on a major scale.

b. The challenge of technological innovation: The healthcare system is facing the need to adjust to an accelerated pace of progress in medical technology and to contain the costs of those technologies. The accelerated pace of technological improvements and their high cost constitute a major challenge to the system which will require it to correctly choose from among the technological innovations to be included in the public basket, in the knowledge that it is impossible to provide the entire population with all that technological progress can offer.

c. Greater national priority for the healthcare system in Israel: As mentioned, the level of public expenditure on healthcare in Israel is lower by about two percent of GDP than the OECD average. Notwithstanding the country's defense burden, the gap in spending on healthcare between Israel and other developed countries should be narrowed.

References

Bin Nun, G. (2011). *Disparities and Inequality in Healthcare: Economic Aspects*. Tel Hashomer: The Israel National Institute for Health Policy Research. [Hebrew]

Bin Nun, G., Berlovitz, Y., and M. Shani. (2010). *The Healthcare System in Israel*. Tel Aviv: Am Oved. [Hebrew]

Bin Nun, G., and Ofer, G. (2011). The Law, Health and the Healthcare System. In G. Bin Nun and G. Ofer (eds.), *A Decade Since the National Health Insurance Law 1995–2005*. Tel Hashomer: The Israel National Institute for Health Policy Research, 13–59. [Hebrew]

Carmeli-Greenberg, S., and Keidar, N. (2012). Private Health Insurance. Paper presented at the 13th Annual Dead Sea Conference: Health Insurance in Israel: Developments, Mutual Relations, Problems and Directions for a Solution. Tel Hashomer: The Israel National Institute for Health Policy Research. [Hebrew]

Carmeli-Greenberg, S., and Gross, R. (2011). The Private Health Insurance Market: Discussion of Policy Issues. In G. Bin Nun and G. Ofer (eds.), *A Decade Since the National Health Insurance Law 1995–2005*. Tel Hashomer: The Israel National Institute for Health Policy Research, 340–376. [Hebrew]

Carmeli-Greenberg, S., and Medina-Hartum, T. (2015). *Public Opinion on the Level of Service and Functioning of the Healthcare System in 2014 and Comparison to 2012*. Jerusalem: Myers–JDC–Brookdale Institute. [Hebrew]

Central Bureau of Statistics (2016a). *National Expenditure on Health, 1962–2015*, Publication 1316 and press release, 2016. Jerusalem. [Hebrew]

Central Bureau of Statistics (2016b). *Statistical Abstract of Israel 2016*. No. 67. Jerusalem. 2017. [Hebrew]

Central Bureau of Statistics. *Household Survey*, 1992–2015. Jerusalem. [Hebrew]

Central Bureau of Statistics. *Manpower Survey*, 1990–2015. Jerusalem. [Hebrew]

Einthoven, A. C. (1993). The History and Principles of Managed Competition. *Health Affairs*, 12 (suppl. 1).

Ministry of Finance, Capital Market, Insurance and Saving Branch (2017). *Report of the Director for 2015*. Jerusalem: Ministry of Finance. [Hebrew]

Ministry of Health, Strategic Planning Authority (2016, 2017). *Health Inequality and Its Solution*. Jerusalem: Ministry of Health. [Hebrew]

Ministry of Health, Information Branch and Health Department (2016). *Manpower in the Health Professions in 2015*. Jerusalem: Ministry of Health. [Hebrew]

Ministry of Health, Information Branch, Authority for Medical Technology and Infrastructure (2017). *Hospitals and Outpatient Clinics in Israel 2016*, Jerusalem: Ministry of Health.

Ministry of Health, Ministry Comptrollership (2017). *Financial Report 2015*. Jerusalem: Government Medical Centers. [Hebrew]

National Insurance Institute (2017). Research and Planning Authority (1995–2015), *Membership in the Health Funds*. Jerusalem: National Insurance Institute. [Hebrew]

OECD (2015). *Health at a Glance 2015: OECD Indicators*. Paris: OECD Publishing.

OECD (2017). *Health at a Glance 2017: OECD indicators*. Paris: OECD Publishing.

Plotnik, R., and Keidar, N. (2017). *National Health Insurance Law: Collection of Statistical Data, 1995–2016*. Jerusalem: Ministry of Health, Strategic Economic Planning Authority. [Hebrew]

Plotnik, R., and Keidar, N. (2017).*The Healthcare System in Israel in the OECD Mirror for 2015*. Jerusalem: Ministry of Health, Strategic Economic Planning Authority. [Hebrew]

Shmueli, A. (2011).*The Illnesses of the Healthcare System in Israel: Diagnosis and Prescription for Treatment and Rehabilitation*. Tel Aviv: The Yosef Sapir Institute for the Study of Society and the Economy. [Hebrew]

State of Israel (1990). *State Investigation Committee to Examine the Functioning and Efficiency of the Healthcare System (Netanyahu Committee): Report*. Jerusalem: Government Publisher. [Hebrew]

(2014). *Advisory Committee for the Strengthening of the Public Healthcare System (German Committee): Report*. Jerusalem: Government Publisher. [Hebrew]

Topper Hever, Tov, R., and Bartov, S. (2016). *Final Public Report on the Plans for Additional Health Services of the Health Funds for 2015*. Jerusalem: Ministry of Health. [Hebrew]

16 | *The Arab Economy in Israel*

NITSA (KALINER) KASIR AND ERAN YASHIV

16.1 Introduction

This chapter deals with the state of the economy of Israeli Arabs. All indicators of this economy point to inferior outcomes. These imply a significant loss of output relative to potential. This situation has negative effects on the standard of living in the economy, engendering lower than potential tax revenues, and higher fiscal transfer payments. It exacerbates the inherent problems of Arab society, a big minority within Israel. The relatively low level of economic development has a negative impact on the relations between Jews and Arabs and hinders the creation of an integrated society.

This chapter presents key data of this economy and a dynamic model of barriers facing Arabs in Israel. We have chosen to undertake the analysis from two perspectives: (1) human capital acquisition and related barriers; and (2) the labor market and related barriers.

The gaps between the Arab and Jewish populations are the result of these barriers, as well as low-quality transportation infrastructure and the weakness of Arab local authorities. The chapter also examines the various differences between Arabs and Jews by gender, all the while distinguishing between human capital barriers and labor market barriers.

The data on the Arabs in Israel do point to an improvement over time in most of the aforementioned issues; however, they also point to the continued existence of major gaps relative to Jewish society. The dynamic empirical analysis, which is based on a model of optimal economic decision-making within a general equilibrium framework,

* The authors are grateful to Chad Jones, Pete Klenow, and Chang-Tai Hsieh for useful conversations and the use of their computer code, to Amer Abu Kern and the editors for useful comments, and to David Eliezer, Nadav Kunievsky, Alon Rieger, and Assaf Tsachor-Shai for excellent research assistance.

shows an increase over time in barriers to the acquisition of human capital in highly skilled occupations, and, in parallel, a reduction in labor market barriers in all occupations.

This chapter proceeds as follows. Section 16.2 presents data on Arab society. Section 16.3 describes the current situation in the acquisition of human capital, including a discussion of barriers. Section 16.4 surveys the labor market and its barriers. Section 16.5 presents a model based on Hsieh, Hurst, Jones, and Klenow (2019) which makes it possible to break down and quantify the barriers and the levels of discrimination, both in the acquisition of human capital and in the labor market. The chapter ends with a brief concluding section.

16.2 Arab Society and the Arab Economy: Background

In this section we outline some key facts on Arab society and its economy within Israel. We focus on the issues we deem central for our analysis.

16.2.1 Characteristics of the Arab Population in Israel

The Arabs are a sizable minority in Israel. In what follows we focus on some salient features.

16.2.1.1 Demographic Structure

As of the end of 2018, the Arab population in Israel numbered about 1.88 million, which represents 20.9 percent of the total population of 8.97 million.[1] According to the forecast of the Central Bureau of Statistics (CBS), this rate is expected to decline after 2035, reaching about 19.3 percent in 2065 (Halihal, 2017).

The Arab population in Israel is composed of more than 1.6 million Muslims, 18 percent of Israel's population, about 134,000 Christians, which constitutes about 1.6 percent of the population, and about 143,000 Druse, which constitutes about 1.6 percent.[2] The Muslim population's rate of growth has declined over the past two decades, reaching 2.3 percent per annum in 2018. Nonetheless, it is still higher

---

[1] Press release of the Central Bureau of Statistics (CBS), December 31, 2018b.
[2] Press releases of the CBS: April 17, 2019a, August 12, 2019b, and November 24, 2018a.

than the Jewish growth rate (1.7 percent per annum), the Druse growth rate (1.4 percent per annum), and the Christian growth rate (1.5 percent per annum).

The total rate of fertility (average number of children that a woman is expected to bear during her lifetime) of the Muslim population was 3.20 in 2018. It has fallen in recent years but is still higher than that of Christian women (2.06 children), Druse women (2.16 children), and Jewish women (3.17 children).

The Muslim population in Israel was composed of about 316,000 households (12 percent of the total in Israel) in 2018. These are relatively large households: about 4.7 individuals on average as compared to 3.9 individuals in a Druse household, 3.1 individuals in a Jewish household, and 3.0 individuals in a Christian household. There are six or more members in about 32 percent of Muslim households, as compared to only 9 percent of Jewish households and 6 percent of Christian households.

16.2.1.2 Geographical Dispersion

The Arab population is concentrated primarily in the north of Israel. As of 2018, about one-half of the Muslim population in Israel live in the north (35.3 percent in the northern district and 13.7 percent in the Haifa region); 21.9 percent live in the Jerusalem region, 11.0 percent in the center, 16.9 percent in the southern region, and 1.2 percent in the Tel Aviv area. The city with the largest Muslim concentration is Jerusalem with about 337,000 Muslims, which account for 21.1 percent of the Muslim population in Israel and 36.6 percent of Jerusalem's total population. There is also a large concentration in the towns of Rahat (68,900), Nazareth (55,000), and Umm el Fahm (55,100).[3] The Druse in Israel live in two main regions: about 81 percent in the north and about 19 percent in Haifa.[4] Of the Arab Christian population in Israel, 70.6 percent live in the north, 13.3 percent in the Haifa region, and 9.6 percent in the Jerusalem region.[5]

16.2.2 Arabs Living in Mixed Towns versus Arab Towns

Most of the Arab population live in separate towns, while only about 1 percent live in Jewish towns. An examination of the population

---

[3] CBS, press release, August 12, 2019b.   [4] CBS, press release, April 17, 2019a.
[5] CBS, press release, November 24, 2018a.

distribution points to differences according to type of town (Bank of Israel, 2017 using data from the 2008 census). With respect to economic indicators, the situation of Arabs living in Jewish neighborhoods is superior to that of Arabs living in Arab neighborhoods in mixed towns and to that of Arabs living in Arab towns.

Arabs who live in Jewish towns or in Jewish neighborhoods in mixed towns enjoy higher socioeconomic-demographic outcomes. Thus, their rates of employment are relatively high and so are their annual incomes. The neighborhood socioeconomic ranking (which ranges from 1 to 20, where 20 represents the highest ranking) is 8.9 in Jewish neighborhoods in mixed towns and 10.1 in Jewish towns. By contrast, the ranking in mixed towns is 6.3 and in Arab towns it is only 4.7.

The total annual income per standardized individual (aged 25 or older) in Arab households located in Arab neighborhoods in mixed towns is more than 20 percent higher than among Arab households in Arab towns. But the rate of home ownership is higher in Arab towns (86 percent as compared to 59 percent).

With respect to the age distribution, Arab families are relatively young, but the distribution varies across locations. The median age of the head of the Arab household in a Jewish neighborhood in a mixed town is 36 and in a Jewish town is 31, as compared to 41 and 44 in Arab towns and in Arab neighborhoods in mixed towns, respectively. It is 48 among Jews.

16.2.3 The Housing Shortage

Housing density is higher in Arab society than among the Jewish population, though it has declined over the years. According to the Bank of Israel (2017), the main reasons for the housing shortage in the Arab sector are as follows: Arab towns have limited areas of jurisdiction; they have no approved and detailed zoning plans; there are no records of land rights, and therefore builders find it difficult to obtain credit from the banks and households find it difficult to get a mortgage; there are not many private reserves of land; and, until recently, the State marketed very little land in Arab local authorities, construction tended to be low-rise, residents refrained from building new neighborhoods, and population growth was relatively high (Bank of Israel, 2017).

16.3 Human Capital

Education is one of the most important factors in determining the quality of human capital, labor productivity, and economic outcomes. The results produced by the education system over the years provide evidence of significant gaps between Arab and Jewish students, which are reflected in lower attendance rates and scholastic achievement. This is due to the insufficient allocation of resources to the Arab sector and low teaching quality in the Arab education system.

The difference in outcomes of students is already evident at a young age. There are high dropout rates in middle and high school, the substantial decline over the years notwithstanding. There are significant gaps in achievement between Arabs and Jews, as measured by the international PISA test (Figure 16.1). The achievements of Arab speakers on these tests has improved over the past decade, but gaps remain substantial and in some cases have even widened.

The significant gaps in achievement between the two populations can also be seen in the TIMSS (Trends in International Mathematics and Science Study) test, which looks at the proportions of high and low achievers in science and math. The scores indicate that the proportion of high achievers in math and science among Hebrew speakers is higher than the median of all the participating countries, while the proportion

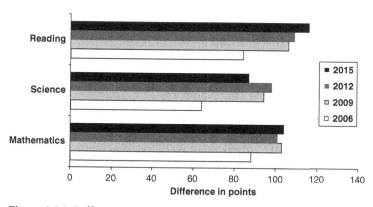

Figure 16.1 Differences in PISA test achievements between Hebrew-speaking and Arab-speaking students by field of study, 2006–2015.
Source: National Authority for Measurement and Evaluation in Education (RAMA), Ministry of Education.

of low achievers in these two subjects is lower than the median; in contrast, among Arab-speaking students, the proportion of high achievers is similar to the international median, but the proportion of low achievers is double the median (Ministry of Education, 2016).

Among high school graduates in the Arab sector, the rate of matriculation, which is the basis for continuing on to higher education, is relatively low. Although the difference has narrowed by about one-quarter relative to 2009, it remains substantial.

With respect to high school graduation, the situation of women is better than that of men and the rate of improvement among women has been higher. The proportion of Grade 12 students who meet the entrance requirements of universities in Israel rose among males from 25.7 percent in 2007 to 30.6 percent in 2014 and among females from 33.7 percent to 46.8 percent (see Gharrah, 2018).

An examination of the achievements of Arabs and Jews on the matriculation exams and on the psychometric exam shows that the achievements of Arabs are lower in quantitative thinking, verbal ability, and English.

The data show that the difference in psychometric exam scores is larger than in the matriculation exam scores, and the difference is also evident in the test of basic skills, which is part of the PIAAC (Programme for the International Assessment of Adult Competencies) survey of adult skills. According to the most recent CBS data (2014–2015), the average scores of Jews were similar to the OECD average: 264 in reading, 262 in mathematics and 280 in problem solving in a computerized environment. The scores for Arabs were about 40 to 50 points lower (up to about a full standard deviation): 225, 212, and 238, respectively. Similarly, 34 percent of the Arabs were found to lack basic computer skills, as opposed to only 9 percent of Jews (CBS, 2016).

The proportion of Arab students in higher education has risen over the years, primarily as a result of the opening of academic tracks under the auspices of the universities and also the increased accessibility to higher education by means of academic teachers colleges in the periphery, where the Arab population is concentrated. Nonetheless, the proportion of Arabs in higher education is still lower than their proportion of the population, and these gaps are higher for the more advanced degrees. Similarly, the duration of studies for Arab students is about 33 percent longer than that of Jewish students and the dropout rate is higher by about 50 percent.[6]

Another indication of the limited accessibility of higher education for the Arab population can be found in the data of the Planning and Budget Committee and the Council for Higher Education regarding the distribution of Arabs among the institutions of higher learning (Council for Higher Education, 2019). Most of the Arab students in an undergraduate program in Israel are studying in a college rather than in a university. Thus, in the 2017–2018 academic year only 15.7 percent of Arab undergraduate students were studying in one of the main campuses of the universities (as compared to 24.1 percent in teacher's colleges and 31.2 percent in colleges under the auspices of the universities). Although the proportion of Arab students studying in a university has grown over the years (from 8.1 percent in 2000 to 15.7 percent in 2018), the rate of growth in colleges was higher. Thus, the proportion of Arab students studying in colleges that are under the auspices of the universities rose sharply during the same period from 16.6 to 31.2 percent.

Furthermore, there is a relatively high proportion of Arab students studying abroad. According to the Knesset Center for Research and Information, 9,260 Arab-Israeli students were studying abroad in 2012, with about 60 percent of them in Jordan and the Palestinian Authority.[7] Moreover, in 2012 the proportion of Arab students in all institutions of higher education in Israel (apart from the Open University) was only 11.5 percent, while their proportion of all Israeli students studying abroad was 38–47 percent (46–55 percent if the students studying in the Palestinian Authority are taken into account).

There is also a significant difference between the genders with respect to the integration of Arabs in the higher education system, with women integrating more successfully than men. The proportion of Muslim women receiving a bachelor's or master's degree is substantially higher than that of Muslim men, but somewhat lower in the case of a Ph.D. Furthermore, there has been a significant upward trend in the proportion of Arab women in the higher education system over the years. The proportion of Arab women aged 20–64 with thirteen years or more of

[6] See the Ministry of Finance, the Ministry for Social Equality, and the Prime Minister's Office (2016).

[7] Letter to Member of Knesset Yaakov Margi, Chairman of the Education, Culture and Sports Committee, January 16, 2019.

schooling rose from 14.5 percent in 2001 to 32.3 percent in 2014, as compared to a much more moderate increase among men from 20.6 percent to 27.9 percent (see Gharrah, 2018).

Among those graduating with a bachelor's degree, the proportion of Arab students is particularly high in the fields of education and teaching and in paramedical fields. In these occupations there is an oversupply in the labor market, and therefore they are characterized by low potential income. There is a relatively low proportion of Arabs in hi-tech and the exact sciences, fields that are in high demand in the labor market, although the proportion has increased in recent years. There has also been a significant increase in the proportion of Arab students studying engineering at the Technion, Israel's leading technology institute, in recent years.

A significant portion of the aforementioned gaps between Jews and Arabs stems from disparities in budget allocation within the education system in the pre-academic stage. Figure 16.2 presents the Ministry of Education budget per Arab student relative to that per Jewish student.

The budget per Arab student was 2.4 percent less in 2018 than that per Jewish student, a difference that has narrowed from 7.1 percent in 2015. It is also worth noting that households in the Arab sector allocate a smaller sum to the education of their children than Jewish households, due to, *inter alia*, their lower level of income (Ministry of Education, 2019).

The difference in the average cost of Jewish and Arab students widens as we move from kindergarten to high school and as the socioeconomic situation worsens.

In conclusion, the Arab sector faces numerous barriers in the development of human capital, due to under-budgeting and the low quality of the Arab education system. As a result, the dropout rate among Arab students is much higher, the grades of those who stay in school are lower, and their matriculation rates and psychometric scores are lower. There is lower participation in higher education in the Arab sector, dropout rates of Arab students are higher, the duration of studies to attain a degree is longer, and there is a high concentration of Arabs in fields of study with low potential earnings.

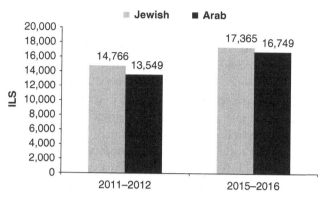

Figure 16.2 Budget per student in the education system, by sector.
Notes: Not including the Circassians, and other unclassified populations.
Source: Education transparency site, Ministry of Education (http://ic.educa
tion.gov.il)

16.4 The Labor Market

The labor market is a focal point of our analysis. In this section we describe its key features. In the next section we study the dynamics of barriers related to it.

16.4.1 The Current Situation

Israeli Arabs are not fully integrated in the labor market, which is manifested in low rates of employment, low wages, and a relatively high proportion of workers in jobs for which they are overqualified.[8]

The rates of employment among Israeli Arabs are lower than those among Jews. This is particularly the case among women, where about 38 percent of Arab women of working age (25–65) are employed as compared to about 82 percent of Jewish women. The relatively low rates of employment among Arab women are the result of many factors, including a relatively low level of education (though it has risen in recent years); traditional cultural norms with respect to the role of women and whether a woman should work outside the home; a limited geographical distribution and the resulting distance from places of employment; the high cost of commuting; and discrimination (Kasir

---

[8] This section is partly based on Kasir (Kaliner) and Tsachor-Shai (2016).

(Kaliner) and Yashiv, 2013). There is a high level of variation in labor force participation rates among Arab women, such that women with little education (and who, therefore, lack the skills demanded by the labor market) and who hold traditional views with respect to the role of women do not choose to work, while women with a higher level of education and a more modern approach do tend to join the labor force.

The most prevalent phenomenon in the labor market with respect to Arab men is relatively early retirement (Kasir (Kaliner) and Peled-Levi, 2015). The phenomenon of early retirement is in contrast to labor force participation among Jews in Israel, among Palestinians, and among men in Western economies, and even relative to the patterns in Muslim and Arab countries. Kasir (Kaliner) and Yashiv (2011) found that the most important fact in explaining the drop in the participation rates of Arab men at a young age is the high proportion employed in jobs requiring physical ability, which diminishes with age. Moreover, they can be replaced by foreign workers once they become less physically fit. The option of receiving various forms of government benefits makes it possible for them to leave the labor market when they become less physically able. This early retirement is also related to the cultural characteristics of Arab society, in which there is a widespread practice of children supporting their parents from a very young age.

Most Arab men are employed in occupations that require low levels of education (Figure 16.3).

An analysis by industry, shows a high concentration of Arab workers in industries that are intensive in unskilled labor, such as construction, wholesale and retail commerce, repair of cars, motorcycles, motorbikes and appliances, and traditional manufacturing. There is also a relatively high concentration in education. Arab men are employed at lower rates than Jewish men in occupations requiring a high level of education, such as managers, academic occupations, engineers and technicians, and some of those with higher education are employed in occupations for which they are overqualified (Lazarus and Miaari, 2015). Others from the start avoid a field of study in which their chances of finding employment are low. Most of those with a high level of education are employed in community-oriented jobs in the public sector and only a small minority of the university graduates are employed in the hi-tech sector. An examination of the distribution of occupations among Jews and Arabs by level of education shows that the gaps in level of education explain much of the gaps in occupations between Jews and Arabs.

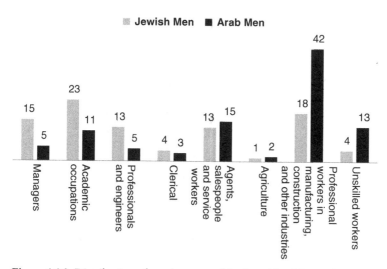

Figure 16.3 Distribution of employment of Arab and Jewish men by occupation, 2016 (%).
Notes: Unknown occupations were omitted.
Source: CBS Labor Force Survey (2016)

In the case of Arab women, about 35 percent of those in the labor market are employed in an academic occupation, as compared to only 31 percent among Jewish women (Figure 16.4).

Nonetheless, the proportion of Arab women who are working in unskilled jobs (about 11 percent) is substantially higher than that of Jewish women (5 percent). It can be seen that there is a high concentration of Arab women working in sales and services (about 30 percent) and also in education and health services (see also Kasir (Kaliner) and Yashiv, 2014). The concentration of Arab women in these occupations is partly the result of a lack of jobs in other occupations in Arab towns. The lack of variety of workplaces in Arab towns, together with their preferences to work in their own locality – due both to the traditional character of Arab society and to the high cost of commuting (Caesarea Forum, 2010) – has an impact on the field of study chosen by Arab women.

16.4.2 Employment and Wages

Apart from the level of human capital, there are other factors that influence the low rates of employment among the Arab population

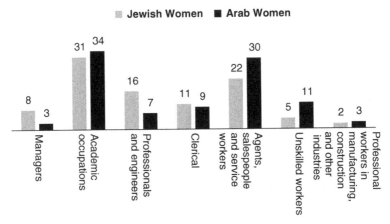

Figure 16.4 Distribution of employment of Arab and Jewish women by occupation, 2016 (%)
Notes: Occupations in which less than 2 percent of Arab and Jewish women are employed and unknown occupations were omitted.
Source: CBS Labor Force Survey (2016)

and their productivity and wages, including discrimination in the labor market; the shortage of daycare centers and the lower subsidization of daycare; the low level of transportation infrastructure; the lack of accessible places of employment; and the economic situation and functioning of Arab local authorities.

The Arab population in Israel suffers from discrimination and labor law violations, due to both their status as a minority group and the fact that most of them are part of a weak group of workers (who have a relatively low level of education and earn a low wage). Discrimination in hiring and in wages is a barrier to suitable employment for many Arabs (Caesarea Forum, 2010). Violations of labor laws in the case of Israeli Arabs are more common in the case of women, skilled workers, and unskilled agricultural workers, who have low negotiating power.

One of the sources of discrimination in the labor market is, according to Becker (1957), discrimination by customers who prefer to purchase goods and services from places of employment where most of the employees belong to the majority group. Bar and Zussman (2017) found evidence of discrimination in the (online) market for services, such as renovations, painting, electricity repairs, cleaning, and transportation, which is consistent with a model of customer discrimination against Arabs. They found that a significant proportion of Jewish customers preferred to obtain services from suppliers that employed mainly Jewish workers and that these preferences were strongly related to concerns about personal security. It was also found that these customer preferences affect hiring decisions and that the price of services in firms who employ Arab workers is lower than among firms that employ only Jews.

The wage difference between Jews and Arabs exists at all levels of education, among both men and women (Table 16.1). Interestingly, it is among individuals with only a matriculation certificate that wage gaps are narrower.

Bank of Israel (2016) used a Mincerian wage equation to examine the causes for the disparity in hourly wages among men and found that differences in skill levels explain most of the disparity in hourly wages (about 80 percent) between Arab and Jewish men.

Asali (2006) examined wage discrimination, studying wage differences between Jewish and Arab men in the period 1990–2003. The observable factors that explain the wage differences are divided into three categories: human capital differences, hiring discrimination, and wage discrimination. The findings point to the existence of wage discrimination and that it worsened over the sample period. Thus, wage discrimination in 1991–1992 was found to account for 5–10 percent of the wage difference and during the period 1999–2003 for 20–30 percent. Cohen and Haberfeld (2007) investigated the effect of the increase in income inequality in the Israeli labor market during the period 1975–2001 on income differences. They found that discrimination against Arab workers did not lessen from 1992 onward and perhaps even intensified. Miaari, Navuoni and Hattab (2011) found significant wage discrimination throughout the period 1997–2009, with varying intensity according to economic events, such as the large wave of immigration, the Intifada, and fluctuations in the number of foreign workers.

Daycare is an important factor in a woman's decision to work outside the home (Shahar, 2012). The subsidization of daycare encourages labor force participation among women whose earning potential is diminished by the high cost of daycare. Over the past decade, the proportion of working mothers who make use of daycare among the Arab population has increased more rapidly than among the Jewish population. The proportion of working Arab women whose children are in daycare reached 64.2 percent in 2013 as compared to 49.3

Table 16.1 *Average labor income – Arabs vs. Jews (in NIS)*

	Men			Women		
	Jews	Arabs	Difference (%)	Jews	Arabs	Difference (%)
Completed elementary school or middle school	8,529	6,974	–18	4,648	3,805	–18
High school diploma (without matriculation)	10,077	7,025	–30	5,665	3,812	–33
Matriculation certificate	8,749	7,163	–18	6,255	3,930	–37
Nonacademic post-high-school certificate	12,137	11,058	–9	7,771	4,598	–41
Bachelor's degree	17,721	10,909	–38	10,462	7,778	–26

Source: CBS, Household Expenditure Survey (2017)

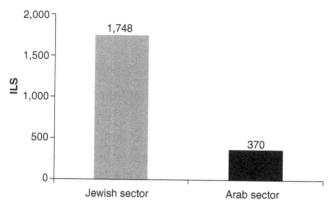

Figure 16.5 Budget for daycare centers subsidies, average per child aged 0–3, 2013.
Notes: Computed for all children in the relevant age range, not only for those in daycare.
Source: Ministry of Finance (2015)

percent in 2004 (Pichtelberg-Bermatz and Greenstein, 2015). The main reason for this change is apparently the greater access to government daycare services for preschoolers in the Arab sector. Nonetheless, the proportion of working Arab women who use this service remains about 20 percentage points lower than for Jewish women.

The proportion of Arab children in recognized daycare is 4.5 percent, even though their proportion of the population is about 23.5 percent (The State Comptroller, 2016). Moreover, according to Ministry of Finance (2015) figures, there is a difference of about 80 percent between the budget for subsidization of daycare in the Arab sector and the corresponding budget for the Jewish sector (Figure 16.5).

Up until 2011, there were almost no daycare centers built in the Arab sector and since then the supply of public daycare centers has been expanded from 39 to about 80 (of about 1,800 daycare centers in Israel) in 2016; however, these constitute only about 4.4 percent of all daycare centers in Israel. Since 2014, 20 percent of the budget for the construction of daycare centers has been earmarked for the Arab sector. However, this allocation is not sufficient to eliminate existing differences due to the cumulative under-budgeting over the years (see Ministry for Social Equality, 2016). Similarly, there has been only partial usage of the construction and subsidization budget in the

Arab sector, due to, among other things, bureaucratic barriers and the limited amount of land allocated for construction. Thus, there is still a lag in the construction of new daycare centers.

16.5 A Model of Occupational Selection and the Occupational Distribution

A prominent characteristic of the population of Arab men is, as mentioned above, high concentration in low-skilled and low-earning occupations, while in the case of Arab women it is a low rate of labor force participation (Kasir (Kaliner) and Yashiv, 2011). The key questions therefore concern the relative roles of pre-labor-market barriers to the acquisition of human capital, barriers in the labor market after the acquisition of human capital, and workers' preferences for occupations. Answers to these questions require an explicit discussion of the worker's decision to acquire education and to participate in the labor force.

We present a model of occupational choice proposed by Hsieh et al. (2019) and apply the model to data on the Israeli economy, with the goal of understanding the situation of Israeli Arabs. The model is based on an enhanced version of the Roy (1951) occupational choice model, in a general equilibrium framework, which can be used to examine differences in occupational outcomes between various groups in the population. Specifically, the model takes into account decisions regarding the acquisition of education, barriers to investment in human capital, various barriers related to the labor market, such as discrimination, and occupational preferences.

In what follows, we briefly describe the model, including the relevant optimization decisions. The full presentation of the model can be found in Hsieh et al. (2019).

16.5.1 The Model

Workers. The economy is composed of a continuum of workers, each of whom is either in the labor market in a given occupation or is in the household sector. We assume three types of occupations: those requiring a high level of skill, those requiring a mid-level, and those requiring a low level. We divide the population into four groups: Arab men, Arab women, Jewish men, and Jewish women. We will look at three periods of a worker's life cycle.

Each worker has a level of skill in each of these occupations and in the household sector. Workers have preferences for working in a particular occupation and preferences vary across groups.

Workers invest in human capital and choose an occupation in an initial "pre-period," and following that they work for three periods (young, middle, and old age). The investment in human capital and the chosen occupation are fixed at the end of the "pre-period." In each of the three periods, the workers choose between working in the occupation they chose and informally working in the household sector.

Accumulation of Human Capital. Workers use time and goods in order to acquire human capital during the "pre-period." This human capital remains fixed throughout their lifetime. There is no accumulation of additional human capital after the end of the "pre-period," apart from specific human capital, i.e., a return on accumulated on-the-job experience.

Forces that Affect the Allocation. It is assumed that discrimination exists in the labor market, as well as barriers to investment in human capital. Discrimination in the labor market can be viewed as kind of "tax" on wages. It is assumed that firm owners discriminate against all the workers in a particular group, such that the "tax" affects all of the members of the group equally and at every point in time. This idea is based on Becker (1957) who assumed that firm owners discriminate against workers belonging to particular groups due to taste discrimination, whereby firms owners get lower utility when employing workers from groups for which they have a lower preference.

The barriers to investment in human capital are manifested in the higher monetary cost of acquiring specific skills for a particular occupation. Examples include discrimination in favor of certain groups in the development of certain skills; the allocation of fewer resources; restrictions on acceptance to higher education or to training programs; differences in the quality of schools between communities; and social norms that prevent the members of a certain group from entering a particular occupation.

Occupational Choice. When individuals decide to invest in human capital, they assume that they will be working in that occupation. The choice of whether or not to work is made at a later stage. The occupational choice is essentially the choice of an occupation during the initial period of an individual's working life in order to maximize his lifetime utility subject to his budget constraint. The individual's utility is positively affected by his level of consumption, negatively affected by the time he invests in human capital, and positively affected by the utility gained from working in each of the occupations.

Labor Force Participation. After choosing an occupation, the individual decides whether to work in it or in the household. If the individual chooses to work in the household, his consumption will consist of income from household production less the payments for the investment in human capital (repayment of loans obtained to finance the investment in human capital).

Firms Producing a Consumption Good. Firms produce the consumption good using workers in the three occupations. Following Becker (1957), firm owners (in the final goods sector) discriminate against workers in certain groups. This is manifested in lower utility from employing workers who belong to those groups. The utility of each firm owner is the firm's basic level of profit, which is affected by the firm's discrimination policy and the extent of the owner's prejudice. Thus, when the firm owners hire a worker from a group they favor less, they compensate themselves for the aforementioned loss in utility by paying a lower wage to that worker. Since it is assumed that these are the preferences of all firm owners (an homogeneity assumption), there is a full offset. In other words, the lower wage exactly compensates for the owners' loss of utility from employing workers whom they favor less.

Firms Producing Education (Schools). These firms sell education to workers, who use it as an input to acquire human capital. As in the case of firms that produce the consumption good, the firms that produce education also discriminate against various groups.

Equilibrium. Competitive equilibrium in this economy is composed of individuals' choices of consumption and the investment of time and goods in human capital over their lifetimes; their choice of occupation during the "pre-period"; the decision to participate in the labor force in each subsequent period; the total effective units of labor from each group in each occupation; the total output of the economy; and the wages in each of the occupations.

16.5.2 Empirical Testing of the Model

The model is tested using census data and the calibration of its key parameters. We start by briefly describing the data used.

16.5.2.1 The Data
All data are from the CBS. The employment data are taken from the censuses of 1972, 1983, 1995, and 2008; the wage and schooling data for 1972 and 1983 are also taken from the censuses, while for 1995 and 2008 the data are taken from the Income Survey.

The analysis includes four groups: Jewish men, Arab men, Jewish women, and Arab women, all aged 25–69. We do not include the unemployed, since the model does not explain unemployment; rather, only workers and individuals not participating in the labor force are included. We define three age groups: young (25–34), middle aged (35–49), and old (50–69).[9]

We thus obtain a panel of six cohorts over six years – the first consists of the young in 2008 and the sixth consists of the old in 1972. There is information on the following cohorts: for cohorts 3 and 4 we have all three life-cycle points; for cohorts 2 and 5 there are two points, and for cohorts 1 and 6 only one point.

The division into occupations is based on the CBS occupation classification at the level of one digit. We divide occupations according to skill level (low, mid, and high) as follows:

1. In the 1995 and 2008 censuses, the division is based on the 1994 CBS uniform classification of occupations:

   - *Highly skilled occupations* – academic occupations (0), professionals and engineers (1), and managers (2).
   - *Middle-skilled occupations* – clerical (3) and agents, salespeople, and service workers (4).

---

[9] The minimal working age is 25, such that the differences due to military service and the use of time at an early age do not have a direct effect on the analysis.

   - *Low-skilled occupations* – agriculture (5), professional workers
     in manufacturing, construction, and other industries (6–8), and
     unskilled workers (9).[10]

2. In the 1972 and 1985 censuses, the division is based on the 1972
   occupation classification:

   - *Highly skilled occupations* – scientific and academic (0), profes-
     sionals, engineers, and similar occupations (1), and managers (2).
   - *Middle-skilled occupations* – service workers (5), agriculture
     (6), professional workers in manufacturing, construction and
     transportation, and other professional laborers (7–8), and
     other workers in manufacturing and transportation and
     unskilled laborers (9).

16.5.2.2 Results

As mentioned above, the goal of the analysis is to identify the
forces determining the occupational allocation of the various
groups and their rate of labor force participation. The model
makes it possible to identify three such forces: barriers in the
labor market, pre-labor-market barriers (human capital barriers),
and occupational preferences.

The model predicts that for each group, the rate of labor force
participation will be higher among individuals who choose to
work in higher-earning occupations. The model also implies that
the differences between the groups with respect to occupation are
the result of the operation of two factors: skills and barriers in
the labor market. When barriers rise in the labor market the
proportion of individuals choosing to work declines. In groups
characterized by high participation rates, the model suggests that
the proportion of individuals choosing high-earning occupations
is high, or the barriers they face in the labor market are low.

After calibrating the model using census data, we get the following
results. Table 16.2 and Figure 16.6 show occupational preferences and
the total barriers facing the cohorts that were young in the census years
for Arab men and women.

---

[10] It should be emphasized that we are dividing occupations according to skill level
      rather than income level.

Table 16.2 *Occupational preferences and total barriers facing the young cohorts*

A. *Occupational preferences of the young cohorts*

	Arab women			Arab men		
Year	Low-skill level	Mid-skill level	High-skill Level	Low-skill level	Mid-skill level	High-skill level
1972	1.00	0.92	0.84	1.00	0.94	0.92
1983	1.00	1.42	1.37	1.00	1.00	1.00
1995	1.00	1.05	0.51	1.00	0.98	1.07
2008	1.00	0.91	0.67	1.00	1.06	1.07

B. *Total barriers facing the young cohorts*

	Arab women			Arab men		
Year	Low-skill level	Mid-skill level	High-skill level	Low-skill level	Mid-skill level	High-skill level
1972	24.54	16.09	7.74	1.05	2.19	2.42
1983	11.43	8.02	5.21	1.16	2.21	2.34
1995	6.13	4.84	3.67	0.77	1.57	2.54
2008	4.74	2.83	3.27	0.64	1.81	2.80

Consider first the occupational preferences of the Arab population. The low-skill occupations in each group are normalized to 1, and occupations with values greater than 1 indicate a preference for the occupation relative to the base occupation. It can be seen that Arab men have no clear pattern of preference for an occupational level over time. This result indicates that the high concentration of Arab men in low-skill occupations is not the result of individuals' preferences but rather the barriers they face. In contrast, the various occupational preferences among Arab women changed significantly over time.

Next, consider total barriers facing individuals in each group in the occupational choice stage relative to those facing Jewish men. The value of the barriers for the latter is normalized to 1. To the extent that the value is greater than 1, the barrier facing the group will be higher and vice versa.

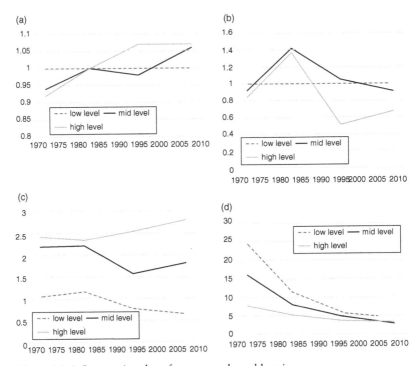

Figure 16.6 Occupational preferences and total barriers
a Occupational preferences, Arab men
b Occupational preferences, Arab women
c Total barriers by occupation, Arab men
d Total barriers by occupation, Arab women

Table 16.2 shows a downward trend in the barriers facing young Arab men in low- and mid-skill occupations. On the other hand, and in contrast to conventional wisdom, the results point to the opposite trend in the high-skill occupations. Thus, Arab men have an incentive not to choose these occupations. From 1995 onward, Arab men have an incentive to choose low-skill occupations and therefore it appears that the market "prefers" Arab workers in low-skill occupations. These results, in addition to the model's results regarding preferences, indicate that the high concentration of Arab men in low-skill occupations is the result of barriers they face in other occupations, rather the result of their preferences.

With respect to the barriers faced by Arab women in choosing an occupation, convergence can be seen in the barriers in all occupations. Thus, barriers were very high relative to Jewish men in the 1970s, but they decreased significantly up until 2008. Nonetheless, it appears that the barriers facing Arab women are still high relative to Arab and Jewish men, which apparently reflects the fact that they are members of a minority group and a group that has more traditional views. Interestingly, the highest barrier is in the low-skill occupations. The high volatility in the values of preferences for an occupation make it impossible to draw any conclusions with regard to the tendency of Arab women in their choice of occupation. However, it can be said that the effect of the various barriers on the occupational choice of Arab women is declining over time.

It should be recalled that barriers consist of barriers in the labor market and barriers to human capital accumulation. The model makes it possible to separate the barriers into these two components and to understand what drives the trends in total barriers. Table 16.3 and Figure 16.7 show the results with respect to labor market barriers and human capital barriers and their combination, for the three occupation levels.

Table 16.3 *Labor market and human capital barriers*
A. *Labor market barriers*

Year	Arab women			Arab men		
	Low-skill level	Mid-skill Level	High-skill level	Low-skill level	Mid-skill Level	High-skill level
1972	10.19	13.96	7.74	1.05	2.19	7.74
1983	3.88	6.54	3.00	1.16	2.21	1.65
1995	3.67	4.55	1.59	0.93	1.57	1.18
2008	2.49	2.83	1.49	0.77	1.81	1.07

B. *Human capital barriers facing cohorts that were young in 2008*

Year	Arab women			Arab men		
	Low-skill level	Mid-skill level	High-skill level	Low-skill level	Mid-skill level	High-skill level
1972	2.41	1.15	1.56	1.00	1.00	1.18
1983	2.95	1.23	1.73	1.00	1.00	1.42
1995	1.67	1.06	2.31	0.83	1.00	2.15
2008	1.90	1.00	2.19	0.83	1.00	2.61

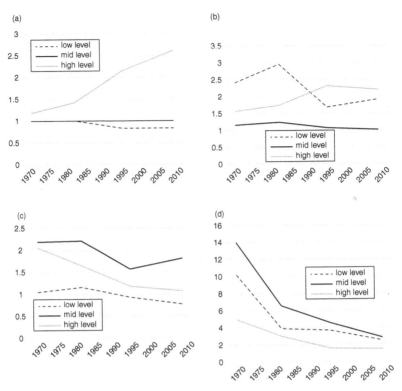

Figure 16.7 Human capital and labor market barriers:
a Human capital barriers, Arab men
b Human capital barriers, Arab women
c Labor market barriers, Arab men
d Labor market barriers, Arab women

Arab Men

A downward trend can be seen in *labor market barriers* across all
occupation levels. In the high-skill occupations, barriers have been
lowered substantially, and in 2008 the barriers to Arab men in the
labor market, relative to those facing Jewish men, were quite low. In
contrast, in the mid-skill occupations there was a more moderate
decline and significant barriers persist. In the low-skill occupations, it
appears that Arab men did not face any barriers in the labor market,
and since the 1990s they have been lower than the normalized zero

"tax" level. Thus, it appears that the market is "encouraging" Arab men to work in occupations which require only a low skill level.

A different picture emerges with respect to the *human capital barriers* facing Arab men. While in the low- and mid-skill occupations, there have been no significant changes, there appears to have been a major increase in the barriers facing Arab men who choose high-skill occupations.

Therefore, there appears to have been a downward trend in *total barriers* facing Arab men in low- and mid-skill occupations, which is the result of the decline in labor market barriers, while the increase in barriers in the high-skill occupations is the result of human capital barriers, offset only partially by lower labor market barriers.

The model predicts two opposing effects as a result of these trends in labor market barriers. On the one hand, the lowering of *labor market barriers* is expected to raise the wages of Arab men and thus to increase their incentive to work. On the other hand, the increase in *total barriers* in the high-skill occupations "pushes" more men to choose mid- and low-skill occupations, which have lower wages, and therefore there will be a higher concentration of Arab men in those occupations. Thus, as a result of the repeated choice in each period between the labor market and working in the household, and given relatively low wages, Arab men will have a lower rate of labor force participation.

Arab Women

An examination of *labor market barriers* shows a downward trend at all skill levels. The largest decrease was in the low-skill occupations and the most moderate was in the high-skill occupations. In 2008, labor market barriers facing Arab women in the high-skill occupations were lower than in the other two occupation levels.[11]

When we look at *human capital barriers* facing young Arab women, it can be seen that here as well there was a decrease in the low- and mid-skill occupations and that the relatively high barriers that prevailed in the 1970s declined during subsequent decades, with the most dramatic decrease in the low-skill occupations. In contrast, and as in the case of

---

[11] Note that the model assumes that the distribution of ability is identical in all the occupations and therefore it may be that high barriers to women in the labor market in the low-skilled occupations, which sometimes require physical labor, is related to the relative disadvantage of women in this respect.

Arab men, there was a moderate increase in barriers facing Arab women in high-skill occupations. In 2008, the biggest barrier was in the high-skill occupations, which is in contrast to the 1970s when the biggest barrier was in the low-skill occupations.

In summary, the downward trend in *total barriers* facing young Arab women in low- and mid-skill jobs is a result of declines in both human capital barriers and labor market barriers. However, it should be recalled that the barriers facing Arab women in these occupations were very high in the past, relative to both Jewish men and Arab men. Therefore, it appears that the process of convergence is not yet complete and in 2008 Arab women still faced high barriers in these occupations relative to the other groups. As in the case of Arab men, we also see two opposing trends among Arab women in high-skill occupations: a decrease in labor market barriers and an increase in human capital barriers. However, and in contrast to Arab men, the net effect of the two trends is a decrease in the barriers in these occupations.

An examination of the trends in the barriers faced by Arab women indicates that the significant decrease in labor market barriers is what led to greater integration of Arab women in the labor force.[12]

16.6 Conclusions

We have presented socioeconomic data and the empirical results of a dynamic model catering for occupational choice in the presence of barriers facing the Arab population in Israel. The overall picture is a complex one and cannot be briefly summarized. Nonetheless, it can be stated that despite the progress made in many areas, including education and employment, the socioeconomic outcomes of the Arab population are inferior to those of the Jewish population. In view of the continued existence of substantial disparities, there is a need for greater

---

[12] In a more detailed analysis, it can be seen that the decrease in total barriers was primarily concentrated in the low and intermediate-skilled occupations. Therefore, according to the model one would expect an increase in the proportion of women that choose low- or intermediate-skilled occupations, in which wages are relatively low. The higher the proportion of Arab women who choose relatively low-skilled occupations, the lower relative overall labor force participation rate we would expect. This is because their incentive to work rather than choose the household sector is relatively low. Therefore, this is apparently the source of the moderating effect on the increase in the participation rate of Arab women.

policy effort on the part of the government. This pertains mostly to investment in human capital and in physical infrastructure capital.[13]

References

Asali, M. (2006). *Why Do Arabs Earn Less than Jews in Israel?* Discussion Paper No. 06.03. Jerusalem: Maurice Falk Institute of Economic Research in Israel.

Bank of Israel (2016). Survey of Adult Skills: General Background. *Annual Fiscal Survey and Collection of Research Analyses*, 142, 16–20. [Hebrew]

(2017). *Bank of Israel Annual Report 2016*. Chapter 8, Welfare Issues. Jerusalem: Bank of Israel.

Bar, R., and Zussman, A. (2017). Customer Discrimination: Evidence from Israel. *Journal of Labor Economics*, 35(4), 1031–1059.

Becker, G. (1957). *The Economics of Discrimination*. Chicago: University of Chicago Press.

Caesarea Forum (2010). *Arab Employment in Israel: The Challenge of the Israeli Economy*. Jerusalem: Israel Democracy Institute. [Hebrew]

Central Bureau of Statistics (1994). Key for Transition from the 1972 *Classification to the 1994 Classification*. Jerusalem. [Hebrew]

Central Bureau of Statistics (1994). *The Uniform Classification of Occupations 1994*, technical publication no. 64. Jerusalem. [Hebrew]

(2016). *Adult Skills in Israel, 2014–15*. Special Publication 1640. Jerusalem. [Hebrew]

(2018a). *The Christian Population in Israel: Data to Mark the Christmas Holiday*. Press release, November 24, 2018. [Hebrew]

(2018b). *As We Approach 2019 – about 9.0 million residents in the State of Israel*. Press release, December 31, 2018. [Hebrew]

(2019a). *The Druse Population of Israel*. Press release, April 17, 2019. [Hebrew]

(2019b). *The Muslim Population in Israel: Data to Mark the Festival of the Sacrifice*. Press release, August 12, 2019. [Hebrew]

Cohen, Y., and Haberfeld, Y. (2007). Development of Gender, Ethnic, and National Earnings Differences in Israel: The Role of Rising Inequality. *Social Science Research*, 36(2), 654–672.

Council for Higher Education, Planning and Budgeting Committee (2019, September 15). *Table 14: Arab Students for Bachelor's*

---

[13] For some ideas of such policy solutions, see Kasir (Kaliner) and Yashiv (2014).

Degree, by Institution type (2000–2018). https://che.org.il/
הג-ההשכלה-אודות-סטטיסטיים-נתונים-קצבי/ [Hebrew]

Gharrah, R. ed. (2018). *Arab Society in Israel: Population, Society, Economy.* Jerusalem: Van Leer Jersusalem Institute.

Halihal, A. (2017). The Population of Israel at the Start of 2017 and Scenarios for Future Population Growth. Paper presented at the Central Bureau of Statistics. [Hebrew]

Hsieh, C., Hurst, E., Jones, C. I., and Klenow, P. J. (2019). The Allocation of Talent and U.S. Economic Growth. *Econometrica,* 87(5), 1439–1474.

Kasir (Kaliner), N., and Peled-Levi, O. (2015). *To Search or Not to Search, That Is the Question: On Giving Up Job Search in Israel.* Jerusalem: Bank of Israel. [Hebrew]

Kasir (Kaliner), N., and Tsachor-Shai, A. (2016). *The Current Situation: Economic Development in the Arab, Druse and Circassian Sectors.* Givat Haviva: Center for a Shared Society, Givat Haviva. [Hebrew]

Kasir (Kaliner), N., and Yashiv E. (2011). Patterns of Labor Force Participation Among Israeli Arabs. *The Israel Economic Review,* 9(1), 53–101.

(2013). Arab Women in the Labor Market in Israel: Characteristics and Policy Measures. *The Israel Economic Review,* 10(2), 1–41.

(2014). *The Labor Market of Israeli Arabs: Key Features and Policy Solutions.* Tel-Aviv University.

Lazarus, A., and Miaari, S. (2015). *Does Higher Education Make a Contribution? Mismatch Between Education and Employment in Creating Wage Inequality.* Jerusalem: Israel Democracy Institute. [Hebrew]

Letter to MK Yaakov Margi, Chairman of the Education, Culture and Sport Committee, January 19, 2016. [Hebrew]

Miaari, S., Navuoni, O., and Hattab, N. (2011). *Trends in Wage Differences Between Arabs and Jews 1997–2009.* Jerusalem: Israel Democracy Institute. [Hebrew]

Ministry of Education (2016). *Main Findings of the 2015 TIMSS International Research.* Jerusalem. [Hebrew]

(2019, July 18). *Shkifut Reports.* Retrieved from https://shkifut.education .gov.il/national. [Hebrew]

Ministry of Finance (2015). Proposed Budget for the Fiscal Year 2015–16 and Introduction, submitted to the 20th Knesset – Higher Education. Jerusalem. [Hebrew]

Ministry of Finance, Ministry for Social Equality and the Prime Minister's Office (2016). *Systemic Plan for the Economic Integration of Arab Society by Means of Eliminating Distortions in the Government Allocation Mechanisms.* Jerusalem. [Hebrew]

Ministry for Social Equality (2016). *Report of the Systemic Plan for the Economic Integration of Arab Society.* Jerusalem. [Hebrew]

Pichtelberg-Bermatz, O., and Greenstein, M. (2015). Daycare Frameworks: Current Trends and Changes over the Past Decade. *Research and Economics*, Ministry of the Economy. [Hebrew]

Roy, A. D. (1951). Some Thoughts on the Distribution of Earnings. *Oxford Economic Papers*, 3, 135–146.

Shahar, E., (2012). *The Effect of Child Care Cost on the Labor Supply of Mothers with Young Children.* Discussion Paper 2012.12. Jerusalem: Bank of Israel Research Department.

The State Comptroller (2016). State Measures to Encourage the Integration of the Arab Population in Employment. In *Annual Report 66c for 2015 and for the 2014 Fiscal Year.* Jerusalem. [Hebrew]

PART IV

Key Issues in Various Sectors

17 | *The High-Tech Sector*

NEIL GANDAL, STEFANIA ROCCAS GANDAL,
AND NADAV KUNIEVSKY

17.1 Introduction

Israel is recognized as one of the most innovative countries in the world. According to the Bloomberg Index of Innovation, Israel stands at number five,[1] while according to the Global Competitive Index, Israel ranks third in the innovation category.[2] The country is now recognized around the world for its excellence in technology and as a center for high-tech entrepreneurship.

There are approximately 100 Israeli companies listed on the NASDAQ stock exchange.[3] Leading players in high tech, such as Intel, IBM, Google, Motorola, Microsoft, Facebook, and many others have set up research centers in Israel, hoping to harvest local talent and knowledge. In 2015 alone, there were ninety-five mergers and acquisitions of Israeli high-tech companies.[4] In 2017, Intel's acquisition of Israeli computer vision firm Mobileye for $15.3 billion set a financial record; Mobileye will become the global center of Intel's efforts to develop new technology for the worldwide automobile industry.

Israeli companies today play a key role in shaping the global high-tech industry – from semiconductors to the end user applications. Israel

[*] We especially thank the Maurice Falk Institute for Economic Research in Israel for the funding for this project. We are also grateful to Reuben Gronau for helpful comments and suggestions that significantly improved the chapter. We also thank Avi Be-Bassat, Eugene Kandel, Niron HaShai, and Asaf Zussman for helpful comments and suggestions.

[1] "The Bloomberg Innovation Index", www.bloomberg.com/graphics/2015-innovative-countries/ (accessed 17/12/2016).

[2] "Global Competitiveness Report 2015–2016 – Reports – World Economic Forum", http://reports.weforum.org/global-competitiveness-report-2015–2016/economies/#economy=ISR (accessed 17/12/2016).

[3] "Companies in Israel – Nasdaq.com", www.nasdaq.com/screening/companies-by-region.aspx?region=Middle+East&country=Israel (accessed 17/12/2016).

[4] IVC Research Centre (2016).

is a world leader in information and communications technology (ICT), which is the largest component of high tech in Israel. In particular, Israel is the world leader in information security, which is one of the largest and fastest-growing subsectors of ICT.

In 2000, near the peak of the worldwide high-tech boom (or "dotcom" bubble), there were already more than 2,000 high-tech firms in Israel. By 2015, there were more than 4,400 high-tech firms in the Israeli information and communication technology sector alone![5] Most of the high-tech companies are concentrated in the so-called Silicon Wadi,[6] in the coastal plain in Israel. Additional companies are located in Haifa and Jerusalem. In 2015, Israeli firms raised a staggering $4.43 billion in venture capital, much of it from abroad.[7] Clearly, venture capital abounds in Israel.

The degree to which Israel stands out – even when compared to other nations that are emerging as global R&D centers – is revealed in work by Branstetter, Glennon, and Jensen (2018). They use data on US multinational affiliates to measure the productivity of R&D investment around the world. They associate US affiliates abroad with the patents these affiliates generate, using the addresses of individual inventors listed on the patent documents. Then they regress these patents on affiliate-level measures of R&D spending and other control variables. They find that US affiliates in Israel are approximately six times more productive than the baseline destination (outside the United States) in terms of turning R&D dollars into US patents.

17.1.1 Road Map

An article or a chapter about high tech can be very different, depending on the type of analysis the researcher wishes to conduct. The goal of this chapter is to provide some background, summary, and trend data, as well as examine key problems facing Israeli high tech.

The chapter proceeds as follows: In section 17.2, we provide background, summary, and trend data regarding high tech in Israel. In this section, we provide a brief historical perspective as well as an

---

5 Getz and Goldberg (2016).   6 De Fontenay and Carmel (2004).

7 Inbal Orpaz, "Israeli Tech Companies Raise Record Capital in 2015 but Outlook Growing Dimmer." *Haaretz*, January 25, 2016. https://www.haaretz.com/israel-news/business/.premium-israeli-tech-companies-raise-record-capital-in-2015-1.5395519.

examination of key trends over the last twenty years. At the end of the section, we focus on promising new frontiers for Israeli high-tech. We believe the patterns and empirical regularities we highlight here are likely to be applicable to other domains in information technology (like digital health and the digital automotive revolution) where Israel has found success.

Section 17.3 addresses key problems facing the high-tech sector, in particular a shortage of skilled engineers and computer scientists. In this section, we discuss the potential sources to increase the supply of high-tech professionals in Israel.

Section 17.4 provides very brief conclusions.

17.2 Background, Summary Data, and Trends

17.2.1 What Is High Tech?

Despise the widespread use of "high tech," the term remains relatively amorphous. Contrary to other economic activities, which are traditionally defined according to the end product (health, education, real-estate, etc.), industries which are classified as high tech are usually defined by innovation in the production method, innovation in the final product, and the share of engineers, scientists, and academic scholars in the labor force. As a result, the high-tech sector includes activities associated with the manufacturing sector (pharmaceutical products, computer manufacturing, etc.), and activities associated with the services sector (computer programming, etc.)[8]

Despite, the difficulty in defining innovative, and hence which firms fall under the high-tech umbrella, high-tech firms are usually firms that invest heavily in research and development, and employ R&D personnel, regardless of whether they produce a high-tech product or service. Fortunately, the Israeli Central Bureau of Statistics (CBS) defines the "boundaries" of high tech – and we will use their definition in our analysis.

The goal of this section (Section 17.2) is to survey the development of the Israeli high-tech sector in the past thirty years, as well as to explore its various facets. The rest of section 17.2 proceeds as follows: We first briefly discuss the early days of Israeli innovative activities. We then

---

[8] Hence, it is difficult to measure productivity in high tech.

describe trends in the high-tech sector. As mentioned, firms in the high-tech sector rely heavily on R&D; hence, we follow by delving deeper into the R&D sector in Israel. Next, we turn to describe government policies which helped nurture the current high-tech sector. We then examine Israeli "startups," a unique character of the Israeli high-tech sector. We close the section by discussing up-and-coming high-tech fields that play to Israel's strengths.

17.2.2 A Brief Selective History of the Foundations of High Tech in Israel

A famous English proverb (source unknown) states, "Necessity is the mother of invention." Clearly, necessity was a driving force in innovation in Israel. Israel is primarily a desert with limited water resources, so early on the country needed to find innovative ways to make its land productive. The solution was drip irrigation. It enabled Israel to turn arid land into a productive industry. In 1965, the company Netafim was founded on Kibbutz Hatzerim and Israel's irrigation technology took off both locally and all over the world. Today, Netafirm is a global company operating in more than 100 countries. Drip irrigation technology was the beginning of what became a large Israeli agricultural technology industry.

Similarly, the defense needs of the new state required innovation in military technologies. From the very beginning, military R&D was a necessity. In 1948, Israel founded the Science Corps, which was responsible for the development of arms and electronic appliances for the Israeli Defense Forces (IDF). Ten years later, the IDF Science Corps were reorganized as Rafael – the Authority for the Development of Armaments. Rafael is still known today for high-quality weaponry and other elite technologies used by the IDF. The defense technology developed in Israel runs the gamut from antimissile systems to cybersecurity. Many of the military innovations led to breakthroughs in products for nonmilitary use.

The French Government's arms embargo on Israel in 1967 forced Israel to start developing its own advanced weapons. It also incentivized the Israeli government to invest heavily in these developments. It did not take long for Israel to become an innovative and creative player in advanced weaponry. One of the embargo's effects was the subsequent decision of the Israeli government to develop new weapons systems.[9] The development of these systems helped the local labor force to specialize in creating and developing chips and advance sensors. As these weapons programs were scaled back (in favor of partial reliance on weapons systems from the United States), highly skilled engineering talent was released into Israel's civilian economy and many top engineers found civilian applications for the skills they acquired in the military.

In addition to investing in military and agricultural technologies, the government invested in universities that, from the beginning, made cutting-edge contributions in basic research in a wide range of fields. Hebrew University and the Israel Institute of Technology (the Technion) were established in 1925, more than twenty years before Israel came into existence. The Weizmann Institute for Science was also founded before Israel achieved its independence.

Knowledge from the universities quickly spilled over to the private sector. The University R&D foundations – the first of which was established in 1952 by the Technion – were primarily responsible for jumpstarting the interaction between university researchers and industry which has grown significantly over time.

Elron, the first nongovernmental Israeli company in the high-tech industry, was formed in the 1962. It was the first electronics company in Israel and its early products were measurement tools for medical applications. Shortly thereafter, Elron established a new joint venture (Elbit) which created mini-computers for the IDF. New companies such as Elscint and Tadiran joined the small industry and started to specialize in communications, medical equipment, and printing. One of Israel's earliest successful Telecom companies, ECI Telecom, was initially a producer of technology for military applications.

Israel's initial success in military and agricultural innovations attracted international firms. In 1964, Motorola established its first non-US subsidiary in Israel. Motorola was followed by IBM (1972) and Intel (1974). Both of the tech giants established R&D centers in Israel when highly regarded Israeli engineers in these companies moved back to Israel after years of experience in the US high-tech sector. This was the beginning of "two-way" flows of top scientific and engineering talent between Israel and technology centers in the United States. This flow played an extremely important role in the subsequent

---

[9] www.calcalist.co.il/articles/0,7340,L-3720135,00.html.

development of the Israeli high-tech industry – and it continues to be important today. Flows of knowledge and venture capital from the United States have often been initiated by direct, personal connections between Israeli scientists and entrepreneurs and key investors in the United States.

Despite the early foreign direct investments, both banks and the government were initially skeptical about whether Israeli companies would be able to become important players in the global high-tech industry. A turning point came in 1972 when Elscint had a successful initial public offering (IPO) in the United States on the NASDAQ stock exchange. This drew the interest of banks, other investors, and the Israeli government.

Before the potential shown by Elscint's successful IPO could be realized, the Israeli economy needed to undergo some significant changes. From independence through the early 1980s, the Israeli economy operated under a quasi-socialist model with heavy state intervention, intrusive regulation, and widespread inefficiency in the allocation of resources across sectors and firms. Persistent macroeconomic policy errors eventually led to hyperinflation in the mid-1980s. The resulting economic crisis turned out to be an opportunity and the "centralized" model of economic activity was effectively abandoned. This enabled flows of talent and capital out of the bureaucratized organizations that had dominated the Israeli economy in prior decades.

At the same time when Israel's economy was shifting to a more market-driven model, the Soviet Union was collapsing. The unexpected and rapid unraveling of the Soviet Union provided an opportunity for hundreds of thousands of Soviet Jews to immigrate to Israel. Many of the Russian immigrants were highly skilled engineers and scientists. The flows of engineering talent out of the indigenous weapons programs described above, combined with flows of highly educated Soviet emigres, led to a significantly larger engineering labor market that could be mobilized for civilian technological development.

This pool of engineering talent emerged at an ideal time. The personal computer revolution of the 1980s and 1990s drove massive growth in the demand for increasingly sophisticated software to run on the rapidly growing installed base of smart machines. The rise of the Internet in the 1990s created demand for (increasingly wireless) communications to link computers, more sophisticated cybersecurity systems, and new internet business models. These global technological shifts created unprecedented opportunities for R&D-intensive firms that did not require large fabrication facilities or other extensive manufacturing capabilities. As nations like Japan struggled in the internet era, Israel's emerging high-tech industry benefitted from the new software technologies that played to its strengths.

Foreign firms realized the potential in Israel in information technology and began to increase investments. During the 1980s, more large international technology companies followed in the footsteps of the early pioneers, Motorola, IBM, and Intel, forming R&D centers in Israel in order to harvest local talent. During the 1990s, this flow became a flood, as Israel was inundated with foreign investments made by leading players in the global high-tech industry. The increasing number of R&D centers and general growth in venture capital led to the formation of hundreds of startups.

Currently, most major high-tech firms in the world have R&D centers in Israel. Intel itself has four R&D facilities, as well as two manufacturing centers in Israel, and employs more than 7,000 people in Israel. Google opened two R&D centers in Israel, and Facebook established its first R&D venture outside the United States in Israel. Strongly connected networks that originate in the IDF continue to infuse the Israeli high-tech industry with high-quality and well-connected engineers and computer scientists.[10] In part because of its defense needs, Israel has a comparative advantage in ICT/information security. It is considered by many to be the top country for innovation and R&D in this field. Many local firms (like Checkpoint) are world leaders. The digitalization of "health services" and "automotive mobility" are upcoming fields that also play to Israel's strengths.

17.2.3 The High-Tech Sector: Trends from 1990 to Today

Following the Israeli CBS, we divide the high-tech sector into its two main components – manufacturing and services. For high-tech manufacturing, we use the CBS definition of "high-tech manufacturing activities." This includes the manufacture of pharmaceutical products,

---

[10] Ellis et al. (2013) argue that the development of high tech in Israel was in part driven by successful Israeli "serial entrepreneurs," i.e., those who established more than one startup each. They follow Israeli "serial entrepreneurs."

office and accounting machinery and computers, electronic components, electronic and communication equipment, industrial equipment for control and supervision, and medical/scientific equipment. For high-tech services, we use the CBS definition of information and communication technology (ICT), which consists mostly of services activities, and includes all of the high-tech services in Israel.[11] This category includes all software services: data processing, computer programming, telecommunication services, and cybersecurity.

In 2012, the CBS adopted the OECD definition for ICT. The main differences between the new definition of ICT and the definition previously used in CBS publications are the removal of (1) research and development[12] and (2) the manufacture of industrial equipment for control and supervision, as well as (3) the addition of ICT wholesale. The key change was the removal of R&D, since the manufacture of industrial equipment for control and supervision and the wholesale categories are relatively small. These changes make it hard to track continuous trends in the ICT sector from 1990 and 2015. To avoid comparing apples and oranges, we focus on the changes before 2012 and then discuss the ICT sector today.

The ICT service sector experienced significant growth during the 1990s and the early 2000s. Between 1990 and 2001, the ICT services sector's real GDP rose by 500 percent. At the same time, the ICT manufacturing sector grew by 135 percent. Because of the extremely fast growth rate in services, the service sector part of ICT grew from less than 40 percent in 1990 to 70 percent by 2001.

The rapid growth during this period earned the sector the title "the growth engine of Israel." For comparison, during the same (1990–2001) period, the Israeli business sector grew by 34 percent. Without the ICT sector services and the high-tech manufacturing sectors, the growth rate would have been 26 percent. This illustrates the critical importance of the high-tech sector to Israel's economy, which, short on labor and natural resources, relies heavily on innovation as its growth engine. Although the focus is primarily on services, manufacturing industries with "high technological intensity" have grown much faster than manufacturing industries with "low technological

[11] www.cbs.gov.il/www/publications/hitech/hi_class_heb.pdf. For the iCBS high-tech definition, see www.cbs.gov.il/shnaton67/st12_00.pdf.
[12] R&D, which directly relates to ICT, is still part of the ICT sector.

intensity." After 2001, and the burst of the "dot-com" bubble, the growth rate of the ICT sector slowed and during the 2001–2012 period, the sector grew at an average rate of approximately 5.5 percent in both services and manufacturing.

The greater importance of services over time also can be seen in venture capital investment. Semiconductor venture capital investment accounted for approximately 19 percent of the venture capital invested in Israel in 2007, but only 4 percent of the venture capital in 2015. Software venture capital on the other hand accounted for 49 percent of the venture capital invested in Israel in 2007 and shot up to 69 percent in 2015.

This rapid growth in the Israeli high-tech sector during the 1990s and first decade of the twenty-first century in Israel was a part of a global trend of growth in high-tech industries in general and in the ICT sector in particular. In some sense, Israel was lucky to ride this wave. The increase in the supply of skilled workers in Israel, primarily from immigration from the former Soviet Union (FSU), coincided with a huge increase in demand worldwide for ICT products and services.

Between 1990 and 2000, immigrants from FSU totaled a million people. Many of the immigrants from the FSU were highly educated and highly skilled, with a large number having advanced degrees and technical training. This influx of immigrants increased Israel population by a fifth and reinforced its general educational level. Among the immigrants, there were approximately 100,000 scientists and engineers. With the influx of these skilled workers, Israel had the highest number of engineers per capita in the world, by far – 140 per 10,000 employees.[13] This was twice the per capita level of the United States and Japan, the second- and third-ranked countries in this category. This massive increase in skilled labor helped to answer rising demand for workers in the ICT sector.

Another boost to the sector in those years came from the increase in investments during the 1990s. During this period, according to Lach et al. (2008), the share of ICT investment (as a percentage of GDP) nearly doubled. While Israel started the 1990s with a relatively low level of investment in the ICT sector, by the end of the decade it had eclipsed many other Western economies.

During the 1990s, investment was primarily provided by public funds. A report for the Ministry of Economics and Industry found

---

[13] Getz and Goldberg (2016).

that between 1990 and 2007, every million NIS (new Israeli shekels) subsidized by the government in R&D, resulted in an addition of 1.28 million NIS to R&D.[14] This large support by the Israeli government led to even larger investments by the business sector in R&D and helped "jump-start" the high-tech sector in Israel.

17.2.4 Employment, Productivity, and Wages

By 2013, the share of high-tech jobs[15] reached 9 percent of the total number of jobs in the Israeli economy. Using OECD data, we can compare the share of the ICT sector to other OECD countries. This comparison shows that the share of ICT jobs in the economy is relatively large in Israel, accounting for nearly 5 percent of employment as of 2015. This is larger than other OCED countries, where the average was 3.7 percent.[16]

The average wage in the sector is one of the highest in Israel and in 2015 was approximately 20,000 NIS, while the overall average wage in Israel was less than 10,000 NIS. The difference in wages between the high-tech sector and other sectors in the economy has increased in recent years. The rise in wages in high tech contributes to Israel's high level of income inequality. (As of 2015, Israel was #7 among OECD countries in the (Gini) inequality index.[17])

The wage gap between high tech and other sectors is unlikely to diminish because productivity in the high-tech sector is relatively high compared to other sectors. One of the reasons for the high productivity is the skilled workforce.

Another reason for the high level of productivity in the sector stems from high-tech firms in Israel selling their products and services in international markets. Various studies have highlighted the connection between international trade and productivity (Melitz, 2003). Gallo (2011) examines the effect of trade on productivity in Israel and finds that Israeli firms which rely more on exports are much more product-

---

[14] Applied Economics (2008).
[15] High-tech jobs refer to positions in the ICT sector and in the high-tech manufacturing sector.
[16] From OECD data, see https://data.oecd.org/ict/ict-employment.htm#indicator-chart.
[17] www.oecd.org/social/income-distribution-database.htm (accessed 20/10/2017).

ive. Gallo (2011) also points out that although the exporting firms have high levels of productivity before they start exporting, these firms become even more productive after they start exporting, implying that exporting might increase the level of productivity.

The sector's high level of productivity raises the question whether there are positive spillovers to other sectors in the Israeli economy. These spillovers may occur through multiple channels. For example, it is possible that workers who are working in high tech would use the knowledge they gain and use it when they move into other sectors. Another channel might be that innovative products developed in high tech would be used in other sectors to improve their productivity.

Unfortunately, this does not seem to be the case in Israel. Brand and Regev (2015) show that between 1995–2009, the productivity gap in high-tech between leading OECD countries and Israel fell. In all other sectors, the gaps have stayed the same, or worsened.

One possible reason for the low spillovers between the sectors might be that Israeli high tech is mainly focused on creating new knowledge and selling it abroad and not in developing the final product. As a result, there is not much interaction between traditional local firms and high-tech firms in Israel. Brand and Regev (2015) also show that mobility of workers between sectors declined between 1996 and 2011, implying that workers are less likely to spread the knowledge acquired in the high-tech sector to other sectors.

17.2.5 *Investment in Research and Development (R&D)*

Israel invests a large amount of capital in R&D. In 2014, the national expenditure on civilian R&D stood at 12.4 billion USD[18] and constituted 4.3 percent of GDP, which is the highest rate per capita in the world. This reflects a rise of 235 percent in R&D expenditure since 1990.

In Israel, in 2014, the private/business sector accounted for 84 percent of the civilian expenditure on R&D. A further 13 percent of the expenditure took place in institutes of higher education (primarily universities.) Private nonprofit organizations and the government

---

[18] CBS Annual Report, table 26.1, www.cbs.gov.il/reader/shnaton/templ_shnaton .html?num_tab=st26_01&CYear=2016.

conducted the remaining 3 percent of R&D expenditure.[19] The share of R&D expenditure by the business sector is higher than in any other OECD country.[20]

The share of R&D performed by the business sector significantly increased during the 1991–2013 period. During this period, research and development shifted from the government/public sector to the private sector. The changes over time are dramatic. Currently the government conducts a very small share, while the share of R&D conducted by institutes of higher education has declined by about 50 percent in the period from 1991–2013.

The main source of financing for Civilian R&D in Israel now comes from abroad.[21] In 2013, investment from abroad made up nearly 50 percent of Civilian R&D, while the local business sector financed another 37 percent. The government financed 12 percent, while higher education institutions and nonprofit organizations financed the remaining 2 percent. Note that through the period private sector financing has replaced the large share of government finance.

The very large share of R&D financing from abroad is unique to Israel. Financing from abroad soared during the 1991–2012 period. Israel receives a higher percent of foreign R&D "venture capital" than any other OECD member country, and large numbers of multinational firms have R&D centers in Israel.[22]

17.2.6 Government Support and Incentives

The importance placed on R&D in Israel can be traced back to one of the initial meetings of the Israeli Parliament, the Knesset, in 1948. In that meeting, Israel's first Prime Minister, David Ben Gurion, made the following statement:

We cannot match other nations in strength, wealth, size or material, but we are also not inferior to any other nation in our intellectual and moral

---

[19] CBS Annual Report, table 26.1, www.cbs.gov.il/reader/shnaton/templ_shnaton .html?num_tab=st26_01&CYear=2016.

[20] OECD (2016).

[21] CBS Annual Report, table 26.2, www.cbs.gov.il/reader/shnaton/templ_shnaton .html?num_tab=st26_02&CYear=2016.

[22] OECD (2016).

abilities ... we must take scientific research, be it basic or applied, to its highest peak..[23]

In the spirit of Ben Gurion's words, Israel invests heavily in innovation, R&D, and scientific research through different channels. We discuss the main government/public channels for investment in R&D below.

A key institution in Israel's support of R&D is the Innovation Authority,[24] which operates under the Ministry of Economics. In 2015, the Innovation Authority (IA) replaced the Office of the Chief Scientist (OCS). The IA is responsible for all governmental support to R&D and entrepreneurship. It supports hundreds of projects in different ways, from pre-seed initiatives to startup companies.

The IA provides matching grants for commercial R&D projects. Grants from the IA are especially important for startup firms. In the past decade, IA/OCS grants have declined both in scale and in their share of the state budget. This is in large part because the private venture capital industry has attracted so much capital in recent years. The government is still important, however, for targeted projects (i.e., support for integrating Israeli Arabs into high tech.)

Legislation has also been enacted in support of R&D and high tech. In 1984, Israel legislated the establishment of the Law for the Encouragement of Industrial Research and Development (the R&D law). The goal was to create new jobs and to absorb skilled workers and increase growth while exploiting the technological infrastructure and the existing human resources in the state. The law offers funds for R&D initiatives and export-targeted products that meet certain criteria of eligibility. Funds are supplied through the IA.[25]

Another important channel in which the government affects R&D in Israel is investment in military R&D. In 1982, MAFAT, the Administration for the Development of Weapons and Technological Infrastructure, was established under the Ministry of Defense and the Israeli Defense Force, replacing the former R&D department in the Ministry of Defense. MAFAT controls all defense R&D programs in Israel and coordinates between the Ministry of Defense, the Israeli

---

[23] Lemarchand et al. (2016).
[24] The Innovation Authority, www.economy.gov.il/RnD/pages/default.aspx [Hebrew].
[25] www.economy.gov.il/RnD/InnovationStrategy/Pages/GovernmentSupport.aspx.

Defense Force, Israel Military Industries, Israel Aerospace Industries, Rafael Advanced Defense Systems, the Institute for Biological Research, and the Space Agency. Tabansky and Ben-Israel (2015) estimate that Israel's expenditures on defense R&D is between 1 percent and 1.5 percent of GDP. This is in addition to the 4.3 percent of GDP spent on civilian R&D.

Higher education, of course, plays a key role as well and the government provides much of the funding for Israel's top universities. Nearly 50 percent of Israelis[26] between the ages 25–64 have completed some higher education. This rate is one of the highest among OECD countries. In addition to supplying the high-tech industry with highly skilled and educated workers, 13 percent of R&D expenditure takes place in the universities and other research institutions funded by the government.[27]

17.2.7 Venture Capital

The rise in private sector financing of civilian R&D in Israel was due in part to the creation of a robust venture capital industry. Although it was not always the case, Israel now has a very sophisticated and mature venture capital industry.

During the mid-1990s, government money (80 million USD) created ten "Yozma" (initiative) funds, which were privately managed. An additional 20 million USD were directly managed by a government-owned fund. A further 150 million USD came from financial institutions and corporations from abroad and from Israel. This "seed money" was invested in nearly 200 startups.[28] Yozma was created, in part, because of an increase in the supply of high-tech personnel in Israel. As discussed, the increase in supply was due to two key events: (1) In the late 1980s, the Israeli military industries laid off many engineers and scientists, and (2) The massive immigration of more than 1 million Jews from the FSU in the early 1990s included a nontrivial number of engineers and scientists.

---

[26] From the OECD data, https://data.oecd.org/eduatt/adult-education-level.htm.

[27] Additional government support includes bi-national programs for Israeli R&D, such as Binational Industrial Research and Development Foundation (BIRD), the Canada-Israel Industrial R&D foundation (CIIRDF), the Binational (US-Israel) Science Foundation (BSF), and many others, providing additional funding.

[28] Avnimelech and Teubal (2006.)

Between 2013 and 2015, venture capital raised by Israeli startups and other entities nearly doubled. According to Israel Venture Capital (IVC), Israeli firms and startups raised about $2.3 billion in 2013. In 2015, as noted, Israel's high-tech sector attracted a staggering $4.43 billion in investment, much of it from abroad.[29]

17.2.8 Startups

A key aspect of Israeli innovation is its startup industry. There are more startups per capita in Israel than in any other country in the world,[30] and many of these startups are in the ICT field. Most of the financing for startups comes from "venture capital."

17.2.9 Foreign R&D Centers

The impressive growth of the high-tech sector, and especially the development of the Israeli ICT sector, was accompanied by a large increase in the number of foreign R&D. Leading companies such as Google, Apple, Intel, and Facebook all have R&D centers in Israel, and they are part of 307 such companies in 2007. According to a report by Dun and Bradstreet,[31] these international R&D companies, which total 5.4 percent of Israeli R&D companies, are responsible for 63 percent of the total business R&D expenditure, in 2015. Today most of the internationally held R&D centers are focused in IT & Enterprise software and Medical devices and come from the United States.

Since the 1960s, 380 foreign R&D centers were opened in Israel.[32] The first R&D centers were relatively small, with 7–10 employees. During the 1990s, as part of globalization and the information revolution, more companies started to open R&D centers around the world, and especially in Israel.[33] Two main factors typically drive global expansions in foreign R&D. The first is lower costs overseas.

---

[29] Inbal Orpaz, "Israeli Tech Companies Raise Record Capital in 2015 but Outlook Growing Dimmer." *Haaretz*, January 25, 2016. https://www.haaretz.com/israel-news/business/.premium-israeli-tech-companies-raise-record-capital-in-2015-1.5395519. For more on the development of the venture capital industry, see Avnimelech and Teubal (2006).

[30] Senor and Singer (2009) and the sources cited within.

[31] www.iati.co.il/files/files/R&D%20Centers%20of%20Int.%20Corporates%20in%20Israel.pdf.

[32] See Slonim (2013).   [33] http://unctad.org/en/Docs/wir2005_en.pdf.

The second is the use of foreign R&D as enhancer of innovation and the use of foreign knowledge as unique inputs for international corporations. Wages in high-tech Israel are competitive with the United States. Hence, improved innovation rather than lower costs is the primary reason for the increase in the number and size of foreign R&D centers in Israel.

Benefits from foreign R&D centers flow to Israel as well. Additionally, a report for the IA[34] examined the effect of foreign firms on the local industry and found that an increase in R&D expenditures of foreign firms is positively correlated with the expansion of local firms, implying that there might be spillovers. The report notes that a relatively large number of workers who worked in foreign firms become entrepreneurs and started their own companies, suggesting an additional channel of potential knowledge spillover.

Although multinational R&D centers show great advantages, some fear that they might have some negative effects on local firms. The main issue is that these multinational companies increase the demand for local engineers and raise wages, therefore, making it harder for local firms to compete in international markets. The same Ministry of Economics report from 2014 also found that wage increases in foreign centers correlate with wage increases in local firms. Further, a large portion of the workers who were working in foreign firms had previously worked in Israeli firms, implying that foreign and local firms compete for the same labor force.

17.2.10 New Frontiers in Israeli High Tech: Automotive Industry + Digital Health

Before closing this section, we very briefly discuss other emerging high-tech sectors: (1) the automotive industry and (2) health IT + digital health. These relatively new sectors require skills similar to those needed in ICT. Hence, Israel is well positioned to be an important player in these fields.

There were two large acquisitions of Israeli firms in the automotive sector recently. The huge acquisition of the Israeli firm "Mobileye" in 2017 by the semiconductor giant Intel for a staggering 15.3 billion USD was the largest acquisition in Israeli high tech ever. The goal for Intel is

---

[34] Applied Economics (2008).

to team up with BMW to produce autonomous (driverless) vehicles. This acquisition followed the 2013 acquisition of Waze by Google for 1.3 billion USD. Other firms are increasing investments in Israel as well. In 2016, GM announced the doubling of its workforce at its Israeli research center.[35]

In general, technological changes in the automotive industry mean that consumers will be increasingly "consuming mobility" rather than purchasing automobiles. The digitalization of mobility (for "object recognition" and advanced driver systems, for example) play to the strengths of Israel's tightly networked high-tech workforce, namely ICT.[36]

The Israel life sciences industry has seen rapid growth in recent years.[37] Two especially promising subsectors of the life sciences industry in Israel are health IT and digital health. Like the "digitalization of mobility" in the automobile industry, there have been significant advances in the digitation of health in recent years. These two subsectors are thus very similar to the ICT industry and draw upon the skilled ICT workforce in Israel. Unlike clinical trials that require significant upfront investments, health IT and digital health, similar to ICT in general, require relatively modest amounts of investment.

As noted in the IATI (2015) report, the health IT market is potentially huge, since (due to regulation among other reasons) healthcare organizations traditionally used little IT. This, of course, has changed in recent years, and the Israeli ICT strengths mean that Israel is extremely well-positioned in health IT. Not surprisingly, there has been a large increase in the number of Israeli firms in health IT. As the IATI (2015) report notes, half of the nearly 300 Israeli companies active in 2015 were formed during the 2011–2014 period.

17.3 The Future of High Tech in Israel

In recent years, the growth rate of the ICT sector has slowed down considerably. Between 2011 and 2015, the real growth rate of the ICT

---

[35] "General Motors to double size of Israel R&D center," *Globes Online*, Tali Tsipori, April 19, 2016, available at www.globes.co.il/en/article-in-the-future-we-might-team-up-with-apple-or-google-1001118610.

[36] See Bernhard et al. (2016).

[37] See Israel's life sciences industry report, Israel Advanced Technology Industry (IATI, 2015). IATI is "Israel's largest umbrella organization for the High-Tech and Life Sciences Industry."

sector (under the new definition of the CBS) was approximately 3 percent per year.

17.3.1 Shortage of Skilled Workers

Until recently, the high-tech industry benefited from (1) academics and employees of the public sector (including the military industries) moving into the private sector and (2) the immigration of tens of thousands of Jewish engineers from the FSU. These sources have been all but exhausted. Further, the success itself of high tech in Israel has led to an increase in venture capital funding and an associated demand from firms for skilled labor. The demand currently exceeds the supply of skilled labor. Hence, a critical question is will the high-tech sector in Israel be able to continue its remarkable success going forward.

Despite the success of Israeli high tech, there has been stagnation in the high-tech sector in Israel during the last few years. Between 1998 and 2012, the tech industry grew on average more than double the rate of Israel's GDP. In recent years, the tech sector has expanded at a slower rate than the overall economy. This slowdown is often blamed on a growing shortage of skilled workers. According to sources quoted by *The Economist* magazine,[38] there is a significant lack of engineers and computer scientists in Israel. Three main causes for the lack of supply of skilled personnel in the high-tech sector are: (1) a decreasing stream of graduates, (2) the lower quality of engineers and computer scientists who study at nonuniversity institutions, and (3) inefficient use of the existing workforce.

According to the report, the first reason is due to the relatively low number of "mathematical oriented" high school graduates. According to the reports, and to voices within the industry,[39] the second reason is that the quality of a nontrivial percentage of students who graduate with degrees in relevant fields from "colleges" is not sufficiently high to meet the market needs.[40]

---

[38] "The 'Startup Nation' is running out of steam," *The Economist*, July 9, 2016. "High-tech boom may be over, Israel's chief scientist warns," Shoshana Salomon, *The Times of Israel*, June 30, 2016.

[39] www.ynet.co.il/articles/0,7340,L-4865128,00.html.

[40] Perhaps more than other fields, there is a large variation in the productivity of programmers. Indeed, research shows that there are "order-of-magnitude" differences among programmers." This mean that high quality makes a big difference. See https://softwareengineering.stackexchange.com/questions/1796

Other voices argue that there is no real shortage in skilled workforce. Specifically, Bentel and Peled (2016) argue there is no shortage in the number of STEM (science, technology, engineering, and mathematics) graduates. They point out that currently, each year, there are 10,000 bachelor students who major in STEM subjects, and an additional 4,000 who graduate from advanced STEM degrees. According to Bentel and Peled, these numbers correspond to approximately 10 percent of the skilled labor force in the high-tech sector and are enough to compensate for the natural retirement from the sector. They also argue that during the last fifteen years in the high-tech sector, there was no substantial real increase in wages, implying, again, that there is no shortage of skilled labor.

The inefficient usage of the existing workforce is primarily due to the norm in which engineers and computer scientists often leave technical fields at relatively young ages. However, this has changed in recent years – and it is not unusual for high-tech workers to continue working into their 50s and even 60s.

17.3.2 Future Labor Supply

Israeli Arabs and the ultra-Orthodox are currently underrepresented in high-tech. Here we examine a very important trend: the entry of Israeli Arabs and the ultra-Orthodox into the Israeli high-tech sector. A nontrivial increase in future supply of high-tech workers may come from sectors of the population underrepresented today in high tech: Israeli Arabs and the ultra-Orthodox. These sectors together make up around 30 percent of the population, but less than 4 percent of high-tech workers. Currently, out of the current estimate of 250,000–300,000 high-tech employees, only about 6,000 (4,000 women and 2,000 men) are ultra-Orthodox,[41] while there are approximately 2,700 Israeli Arab high-tech professionals.[42]

There is a quiet "high-tech" movement in the Israeli Arab sector. In the case of Israeli Arabs, only 350 worked in high tech in 2008. Hence, the increase is 670 percent since 2008. While the actual numbers may be small, the percentage changes are large. Additionally, there is

---

16/a-good-programmer-can-be-as-10x-times-more-productive-than-a-medi ocre-one.

[41] Raz and Tzruya (2018).

[42] The estimate is from the Tsofen High Technology Center in Nazareth.

a significant increase in the number of Arab students in high-tech disciplines.

More Israeli Arab students are studying at universities in Israel than ever before. In the 1989–1990 academic year, there were 46,519 students studying for bachelor's degrees in the arts and sciences in "universities" in Israel (Tel Aviv University, Hebrew University, Bar-Ilan, Ben Gurion, the Technion, the Weizman Institute, and the University of Haifa.) Only 2,950 or 6.3 percent of the students were Israeli Arabs.[43]

Twenty-five years later, the picture is very different. Overall, the undergraduate student population at top universities increased by 52 percent from 1989–1990 to 2014–2015 when it reached 70,785 students. The Arab student population increased by 296 percent during the same time period. The percentage of Arab students studying for bachelor's degrees at the top universities increased to 16.5 percent (11,672 out of 70,785) in the 2014–2015 academic year.

The change is even more dramatic when we examine the changes between 1999–2000 and 2014–2015. During that fifteen-year period, the overall number of BA/BS students studying at Israeli universities actually decreased by 5 percent.[44] During that period, on the other hand, the number of Arab students studying for bachelor's degrees at Israeli universities increased by 84 percent.

More importantly for the future of high tech in Israel, there has been a large percentage increase in Israeli Arab students of engineering and other technical disciplines in universities. During the fifteen-year period from 1999–2000 to 2014–2015, Arab students of engineering (which includes all subdisciplines plus architecture) increased by 86 percent, while non-Arab students of engineering increased by 22 percent. In the case of mathematics and science, Arab undergraduate students increased by 114 percent, while non-Arab undergraduate students decreased by 14 percent.

When we look at more detailed data (which is only available from 2011–2012 to 2015–2016), we find that the number of Arab students of electrical engineering increased by 81 percent, which represents an actual increase of 300 students (from 372 to 672), while non-Arab students of electrical engineering increased from 4,528 to 5,572 (a 23 percent increase.) In the case of mathematics and computer science,

---

[43] All data on university students is from the Council of Higher Education.

[44] The decline is due, in part, to the large increase in students studying in colleges.

Arab undergraduate students in universities increased by 62 percent from 670 to 1,084 over the same period, while Jewish undergraduates increased from 4,279 to 5,329 (or 25 percent).

In the case of colleges, the total number of students studying engineering increased from 14,649 in 2007–2008 to 19,552 in 2014–2015 (the delineated data do not go back further than that). Of the engineering students in colleges, 5.1 percent or 747 were Arabs in 2007–2008, while in 2014–2015, 1,401 or 8.6 percent of the engineering students in colleges were Arabs.

Gains in employment have also been significant in recent years. As noted, in 2008, there were only 350 Arab engineers and computer scientists working in high tech. By the end of 2015, the number had increased to 2,700, according to the Tsofen High Technology Center in Nazareth, which works to integrate Arabs into Israel's high-tech sector.

The number of high-tech firms based in Nazareth has grown from (essentially) zero in 2006 to more than seventy today. One particularly bright success story is Galil Software, which is based in Nazareth and was founded in 2007. Galil Software currently employs about 150 high-tech personnel. The management team as well as the workers include both Jews and Arabs.

17.3.3 *The Ultra-Orthodox Sector in High Tech*

By the end of 2015, the ultra-Orthodox community numbered approximately 950,000 people, meaning one in every nine Israelis is Ultra-Orthodox (11% of the population). Some 18% of the total population of children and youth (ages 0–19) are Ultra-Orthodox, and they make up 8% of the working-age population (20–46). The annual growth rate of the ultra-Orthodox population is 4% as opposed to 1% among non-ultra-Orthodox Jews. The share of ultra-Orthodox as a percentage of Israel's total population is predicted to be 14% in 2024, 19% in 2039, and 27% in 2059.[45]

While it is hard to pin down precisely, in 2000, the participation rate of ultra-Orthodox women in the work force was 48%–49%, while the participation rate of ultra-Orthodox men was 38%–43%. In 2015, the numbers increased to 75%–77% and 50%–53% respectively. Although a change in measurement methodology makes it difficult to

[45] Malach et al. (2016).

make exact comparisons before and after 2011, the trend is clear: many more ultra-Orthodox women are working and there has been little change in the percentage of Orthodox men in the workforce.[46]

Only 10% of ultra-Orthodox students earn a high school matriculation certificate, compared with 70% of their non-ultra-Orthodox peers. Only 2% of ultra-Orthodox men earn a matriculation certificates; in contrast, roughly 17% of ultra-Orthodox women earn a matriculation certificate.

In a Central Bureau of Statistics (CBS) survey, in 2013–2014, 19% of the ultra-Orthodox population reported that it was pursuing, or had pursued, an academic degree. This is an increase over 2007–2008, when the overall figure was 15%.

The share of women engaged in academic study (23%) was much greater than that of men (15%).[47] In terms of actual numbers, over 6,000 ultra-Orthodox students were enrolled in colleges and academic institutions where they were acquiring a profession.

Some higher educational institutions (for example, the Open University) provide a science and engineering curriculum for ultra-Orthodox women and men (in separate programs). Overall, there has been a 45 percent increase in the number of ultra-Orthodox students in the past five years.[48]

The main path, however, to employment in high tech for the ultra-orthodox women is not via universities and colleges. The most popular option for ultra-Orthodox women is a two-year extension of high school that grants a technical diploma as a "practical" software engineer, i.e., a computer programmer.

Based on current estimates,[49] there are about 600 ultra-Orthodox women graduating each year with at least two years of higher education in high tech (primarily software programming) via the two-year extension of high school. About ten companies tap into this ultra-Orthodox trained workforce and offer the mainstream Israeli high-tech companies an outsourcing option, which is an alternative to an offshore model for high-quality/low-cost labor.

Some companies provide separate working environments for ultra-Orthodox women: The "separate" offices are located within proximity

[46] Moshe (2016).   [47] Malach et al. (2016).
[48] *Globes*, January 13, 2016. www.globes.co.il/news/article.aspx?did=1001094800.
[49] Discussions with Rachip and calculations of the authors.

to ultra-Orthodox neighborhoods; there are children-friendly working hours, suitable eating facilities, maternity rooms, etc. The pioneer in this model of employment is Matrix, a leading IT company in Israel, which employs about 8,000 professionals. In 2004, Matrix opened a site tailored for ultra-Orthodox women. Today they employ about 800 women in this model.[50]

Another company is Rachip, which employed more than 100 ultra-Orthodox women in 2016. I-ROX and SW outsourcing services employs about 100 women software engineers and takes pride in having the "best orthodox female programmers from Israel's leading educational institutions."[51]

Barriers to entry still exist, especially for ultra-Orthodox men. In general, there is a very big educational gap between ultra-Orthodox men and women. While all ultra-Orthodox women study mathematics and English, these subjects are not part of the curriculum for ultra-Orthodox men.

17.3.4 *Skilled Workers from the Palestinian Territories*

Another possible source of supply of skilled workers is the Palestinian territories. In part, because of its proximity to Israel, by 2013, approximately 4,500 Palestinians worked in the ICT sector, specializing primarily in software. Most of the Palestinian ICT firms are located in Ramallah. According to *Globes* (April 17, 2012,) the Palestinian ICT sector grew from less than 1 percent of GDP in 2008 to 5 percent in 2010. In 2014, according to *The Economist*, ICT outsourcing accounted for 10 percent of the West Bank's GDP.[52] At that time, there were more than 300 ICT firms in the West Bank. A nontrivial amount of the outsourcing work comes from Israeli subsidiaries of Cisco, Microsoft, HP, and Intel. Two relatively successful firms are Asal Technologies and Exalt Technologies, which had 120 and 80 employees respectively in 2014.[53]

---

[50] See Matrix at www.matrix.co.il/About/Pages/givun.aspx.
[51] See http://i-rox.co.il/en/excellence-model/.
[52] "IT in the West Bank: Palestinian Connection," *The Economist*, February 26, 2014. www.economist.com/schumpeter/2014/02/26/palestinian-connection.
[53] Ibid.

17.3.5 Reasons to Be Concerned About the Future

Despite the (1) impressive increase in the number of Israeli Arabs studying engineering and computer science and (2) the entry of ultra-Orthodox women in the sector, it is not clear that these two trends can overcome the shortage of engineers and computer scientists in Israel. First, although the percentage increase of high-tech workers from these sectors is relatively large, the absolute numbers are currently relatively small. Further, as discussed above, the increase in the number of Jewish students in computer science and engineering at Israeli universities has been relatively modest.

17.3.6 Limit to Network Benefits

Entry into high tech is difficult for Arab students primarily for two reasons: (1) Arab Israeli engineers live on average quite a big distance from high-tech hubs in the center of the country and (2) there is a lack of professional network connections with Jewish Israeli engineers because they are not subject to military service. Spillovers from the military to the civilian sector are considered a prominent aspect of the high-tech industry in Israel – and those who do not serve with elite technical units are at a disadvantage.

17.3.7 Brain Drain

An additional concern for the future of high tech in Israel is the brain drain. Some of the benefits have spilled over to multinationals who collectively invested billions acquiring Israeli startups and expanding their Israel-based R&D units. Further, these acquisitions have made it relatively easy for Israeli scientists to migrate, in particular to the United States. Statistics compiled by Ben David (2008) reveal the following: (1) In computer science, the number of Israelis in top-40 American universities is equal to about one-third of computer scientists in Israeli research universities. (2) The number of Israeli physicists in top-40 American universities is equal to 10 percent of physicists in Israeli research universities. The numbers of Israelis at top US universities are also large for other high-tech disciplines. While the brain drain in academia does not directly translate to high tech, a nontrivial brain drain (primarily to the Silicon Valley) has occurred in high tech as well.

17.3.8 Reasons to Be Optimistic About the Future

17.3.8.1 Future Labor Supply

Despite the discussion above about the limit to network benefits, the government and private foundations are helping to make it easier for Israeli Arabs to enter high tech. For example, the Nazareth Business Incubator Center was launched in 2014. The goal of this center is to enable experienced high-tech entrepreneurs to connect with Israeli Arab engineers.[54]

Several governmental ministries have produced initiatives to encourage high-tech firms to hire or retain older qualified workers and to help the integration of Arabs in high tech. There is also targeted funding available from the IA. One program called the "Early Stage Fund" helps minority entrepreneurs overcome the difficulties of raising venture capital in the private sector. For qualifying firms, financing can reach 85 percent (versus 50 percent for other startups).[55]

17.3.8.2 Brain Gain

While the brain drain has harmed the Israeli economy in many ways, it is not a cut and dried issue. Recent research by Lobel (2015) suggests that a country's international connectedness has positive benefits from skilled emigration. For example, Lobel (2015) notes that skilled emigration is correlated with the amount of foreign investment in the country of departure. Further, recent numbers suggest that the drain has mitigated.

17.3.9 Closing Thoughts: Women in High Tech

By far the best hope for increasing the supply of hi-tech workers is women. In Israel, women make up approximately 47% of the workforce and 55% of the students studying law and medicine. However, female engineers and computer scientists are relatively rare, and the absolute number is declining.[56] In 2009/2010, women accounted for 31% of all applicants to universities in engineering. This percentage

---

[54] "Israel Seeks to Share High-tech Success with Arab Sector," March 11, 2016, by Robert Swift, *The Media Line*, at www.themedialine.org/top-stories/nazareth-israels-next-high-tech-hub/.

[55] The Innovation Authority, www.economy.gov.il/RnD/pages/default.aspx.

[56] See "Ahead of International Women's Day, Israel sees decline in number of women in hi-tech," by Chelsea Mosery Birnbaum, Jerusalem Post, March 7,

rose to nearly 33% in 2012/2013. However, this percentage fell back to 29% in 2014/2015.

While the lack of women in high-tech is a universal phenomenon,[57] it is more critical in Israel, since the country relies on "home-grown" talent much more than countries like the United States. In order to significantly increase the supply of university-trained engineers and computer scientists in Israel, an effort has to be made to encourage women to study these fields. Reversing the trend can only be done by increasing the number of female high school students graduating with a high-quality diploma and positive early exposure to the world of science and engineering. Some steps have been taken, but more are needed.

17.4 Brief Conclusion

In this chapter, we first provided historical background on high tech in Israel. We then showed that the rapid growth of the high-tech sector in Israel during the 1990s and first decade of the twenty-first century was a part of a global trend of growth in information and communications technology (ICT). Timing was also critical for the success in Israeli high tech. The huge increase in the supply of skilled workers from immigration from the FSU in the 1990s coincided with a huge increase in demand worldwide for ICT products and services, an area in which Israel has a comparative advantage.

We discussed the challenges facing high tech in Israel today. The excess demand for high-tech workers is an opportunity, but a huge concern as well. While recent increases in skilled workers from sectors that have not traditionally participated in high tech is encouraging, it is not clear that the future supply is large enough without activist government programs. The most important step involves increasing the number of high school students graduating with high-quality "math and science" diplomas and providing these students with "early positive exposure" to the world of science and engineering. Hopefully, the country will be up to the task.

2017, www.jerusalemonline.com/high-tech/alarming-decline-in-the-number-of -women-in-israels-hi-tech-industry-27093.
[57] See, for example, Ashcraft et al. (2016.)

References

Applied Economics Consulting (2008). The Effect of Government Support for Industrial R&D on the Israeli Economy. http://economy.gov.il/RnD/Documents/GovSupportFinalPaper.pdf. [Hebrew].

Ashcraft, C., McLain, B., and Eger, E. (2016.) Women in High Tech: The Facts. NCWIT Workforce Alliance. www.ncwit.org/sites/default/files/resources/womenintech_facts_fullreport_05132016.pdf.

Avnimelech, G., and Teubal, M. (2006). Creating Venture Capital Industries that Co-evolve with High Tech: Insights from an Extended Industry Life Cycle Perspective of the Israeli Experience. *Research Policy*, 35, 1477–1498.

Ben-David, D. (2008). Brain Drained: A Tale of Two Countries. CEPR Discussion Paper 6717. www.tau.ac.il/~danib/econ-rankings/BrainDrained.pdf.

Bental, B., and Peled, D. (2016). *Is There a Shortage of Academic Degree Holders in Science and Technology?* Haifa: Samuel Neaman Institute.

Bernhard, W., Leutiger, P., and Ernst, C. (2016). Israel's Automotive & Smart Mobility Industry. www.rolandberger.com/publications/publication_pdf/roland_berger_israel_automotive_and_smart_mobility_final_131216.pdf.

Brand, G., and Regev, E. (2015). The Dual Labor Market: Trends in Productivity, Wages and Human Capital in the Economy. In *A Macroeconomic Perspective on Economy and Society in Israel*. http://taubcenter.org.il/wp-content/files_mf/theduallabormarketenglish.pdf.

Branstetter, L., Glennon, B., and Jensen, J. (2018). The IT Revolution and the Globalisation of R&D. Mimeo. https://voxeu.org/article/it-revolution-and-globalisation-rd.

Central Bureau of Statistics. (Various years). Statistical Abstract of Israel. Available at www.cbs.gov.il/en/Pages/default.aspx.

De Fontenay, C., and Carmel, E. (2004). Israel's Silicon Wadi: The Forces Behind Cluster Formation. In T. Bresnahan and A. Gambardella (eds.), *Building High-Tech Clusters: Silicon Valley and Beyond*. Cambridge University Press, 40–77.

Ellis, S. Drori, I, Shapira, Z., and Aharonson, B. (2013). Imprinting, Inheritance, and Entrepreneurial Inclinations: A Genealogical Approach to the Study of Founding New Firms. https://coller.tau.ac.il/sites/nihul.tau.ac.il/files/media_server/Recanati/management/hurvitz/forms/articles/SmuelEllis/ASQ%20G%20paper%20June%204%20Final.pdf.

Gallo, L. (2011). *Export and Productivity: Evidence from Israel*. Discussion Paper 2011.08. Jerusalem: Bank of Israel Research Department.

Getz, D., and Goldberg, I. (2016). Best Practices and Lessons Learned in ICT Sector Innovation: A Case Study of Israel. Background paper for *World Development Report 2016 Digital Dividends.*

Israel Advanced Technology Industries (IATI) (2015). *Summary Report.* www .iati.co.il/.

Lach, S., Shiff, G., and Trajtenbergy, M. (2008). Together But Apart: ICT and Productivity Growth in Israel. *CEPR Discussion Paper*, No. DP6732.

Lemarchand, G. A., Leck, E., and Tash, A. (2016). *Mapping Research and Innovation in the State of Israel.* GO-SPIN Country Profiles in Science, Technology and Innovation Policy, volume 5. Paris: UNESCO Publishing.

Lobel, O. (2015.) *Networks for Prosperity: Connecting Development Knowledge Beyond 2015.* Report. Vienna: United Nations Industrial Development Organization (UNIDO). www.mdgfund.org/sites/default/ files/Networks%20for%20Prosperity%20Connecting%20Beyond%2 02015.pdf.

Malach, G., Choshen, M., and Cahaner, L. (2016). *Statistical Report on Ultra-Orthodox Society in Israel.* Israel Democracy Institute. https://en .idi.org.il/publications/4282.

Melitz, M. (2003). The Impact of Trade on Intra-Industry Reallocations and Aggregate Industry Productivity. *Econometrica*, 71(6), 1695–1725.

Moshe, N., (2016). Data on Ultra-Orthodox Employment. The Knesset Center of Research and Information. https://main.knesset.gov.il/Activi ty/Info/mmm/pages/document.aspx?docid=4e572e2a-f5ce-e511-80d6-00155d0204d4&businesstype=1. [In Hebrew]

Raz, A., and Tzruya, G. (2018). Doing Gender in Segregated and Assimilative Organizations: Ultra-Orthodox Jewish Women in the Israeli High-Tech Labour Market. *Gender Work & Organization*, 25, 4, 361–378.

OECD (2014). *Science, Technology and Industry Outlook.* Paris: OECD Publishing.

OECD (2016). *Main Science and Technology Indicators.* (Edition 2016/1). Paris: OECD Publishing.

Senor, D., and Singer, S. (2009). *Start-Up Nation: The Story of Israel's Economic Miracle.* Toronto: McClelland & Stewart,

Slonim, O. (2013). Foreign Owned Research Centers. [In Hebrew]. www .idc.ac.il/he/research/ips/Documents/HC2012/R_D2013A.pdf.

Tabansky, L., and Israel, I. (2015). *Cybersecurity in Israel.* Springer Press.

18 | The Israeli Housing Market: Structure, Boom, and Policy Response

DAVID GENESOVE

18.1 Introduction

After the 1985 stabilization, the government retreated from heavy intervention in the Israeli housing market, cutting back on subsidized housing and mortgages, and residential construction. In the early 1990s it returned, responding to immigration from the former Soviet Union by providing hundreds of thousands of additional apartments and cheap mortgages. Once immigration declined, the government retreated again.

Large housing price growth from 2009 drew the government in yet again. In planning, it first tried bypassing local authorities, before incentivizing them through greater planning autonomy and infrastructure funding to accept development. In fiscal policy, it attempted to dampen investor demand through taxes, and worked to alter the extent and ownership structure of the rental market. In macroprudential policy, the central bank limited both individual and bank portfolio mortgage loan to value ratios, and adjustable rate mortgages.

The most unorthodox policy upended the price mechanism for new housing on government-owned land.[1] Land and associated development rights were no longer auctioned to the highest bidder, but to the firm offering to sell apartments at the lowest price. Inevitably, this policy entailed government determination of new homes' attributes, and their residents.

After characterizing the spatial structure of the housing market, we focus on the takeoff of housing prices and rents since 2008. We consider three competing explanations – the post-crisis fall in interest rates, a continual increase in the gap between demand and supply, and a bubble – and the policy response. The analysis employs the perfect

---

[1] This chapter deems land owned by the Jewish National Fund as land owned by the government.

asset and monocentric city housing models, along with accepted income and price elasticity estimates and "back of the envelope" calculations. Transparency and ease of understanding privilege such calculations over a fully dynamic analysis.

18.2 Basic Facts

Tel Aviv is the business and cultural center, and housing prices, land prices, and structural density reflect that, with all falling off with increasing distance from the city (see Figure 18.1 for prices). At a one-hour commute away, quality-adjusted prices are a third lower, land prices 75 percent lower, and average building height nearly two floors lower (Table 18.1, columns 1–3).[2] These patterns strongly support viewing Israel as a single monocentric housing market (Alonso, 1964; Mills, 1967, and Muth, 1969).[3] An additional feature is that poorer households live further out, with wages 20 percent lower an hour outside of Tel Aviv (Table 18.1, column 4).

We assume a competitive construction industry with costs constant countrywide. As of 2017, costs were about 4,000 NIS/m^2 for low rises, rising to about 5000 NIS for tall buildings.[4] The ten largest contractors were supplying less than 15 percent of new apartments in the country (Ministry of Finance, 2017). Conditions are especially competitive in Tel Aviv with the difference between the high and the next highest bid in the Israel Land Authority (ILA) residential land auctions an (insignificant) 4 percent, but it is about 22 percent higher an hour out (Table 18.1, column 5). The bid difference ("money left on the table") reflects competitive factors such as the effective number of competitors and firm cost heterogeneity.

About two-thirds of all homes are owner-occupied, and one-quarter rentals, the vast majority private.[5] This is similar to other OECD

---

[2] Price differences are estimated locality dummy coefficients from a 1998–2016 log price regression with 228 month dummies, number of rooms dummies, log square meters, and a socioeconomic indicator, using the property transaction database. Time is measured at weekday afternoon rush hour via Google Maps.

[3] Eckstein et. al. (2012) models localities on a north–south axis mostly along the Mediterranean, and an east–west axis connecting Tel Aviv to Jerusalem. The estimates ignore the country south of Beer-Sheva.

[4] Thanks to Avichai Snir for this information.

[5] About 6 percent of households live in "special arrangements," such as nursing homes.

Table 18.1 *Price, wage, height, and "money left on the table" gradients*

	Log housing price	Log land price	Building height	Log wage	Log (high / 2nd highest bid)
	(1)	(2)	(3)	(4)	(5)
Travel time	−0.44	−1.44	−1.92	−0.20	0.20
(in hours)	(0.04)	(0.17)	(0.04)	(0.05)	(0.03)
Constant	−0.25	−0.51	7.74	8.91	0.04
	(0.06)	(0.21)	(0.51)	(0.07)	(0.04)
R-squared	0.63	0.55	0.30	0.15	0.27
Number of localities	57	62	58	106	139

Standard errors in parentheses. The regression in Column 5 is weighted by the number of planned units in each tender.

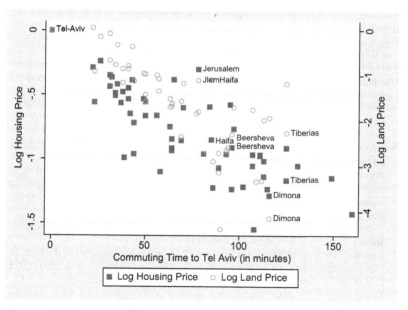

Figure 18.1 Housing and land prices, relative to Tel Aviv

countries, especially richer, older EU members, the United States, and Canada.[6] Unlike the last two, but like European cities, the owner-occupied stock is physically similar to the rental, with both mostly located in multi-unit buildings, but with rentals smaller.[7] About a fifth of renter-households own a unit they are not living in.[8] These two facts justify assuming perfect substitutability between owner-occupancy and renting, however inappropriate it may be for other markets (Glaeser and Gyourko, 2009).

Owner-occupiers' housing consumption is untaxed, their purchases generally taxed at lower rates than investors', but their mortgage payments are not tax deductible; so the tax system favors owner-occupancy, but less so than in the United States. Household ownership of rental properties is favored, as household rental income is untaxed below 5,030 NIS/month, and at only 10 percent above that. Consequently, most rental housing is owned by small landlords: 22 percent of all housing units are owned by individuals who own two units, and 11 percent by those with 3–9 units.[9] The share of households owning two or more homes has been rising, however, from 3.2 percent in 2003 to 9.9 percent in 2016.[10]

Housing investment is a significant part of the economy, unsurprisingly given Israel's high population and income growth. In 2015, gross investment in residential dwelling was 76.8 billion NIS compared to 635.5 billion NIS of private consumption.

---

[6] Switzerland and Germany are the main outliers, with rental shares of about 60 percent (Scanlon, 2011).

[7] According to the transaction database, since 1998, three-quarters of new apartments have been in multi-unit buildings with three or more floors. The share has exceeded 90 percent since 2013. Since 2016, more than half of the stock is in five plus storey buildings (Government Authority for Urban Renewal, 2017).

[8] Central Bureau of Statistics (2016). Almost no renters in the American Housing Survey report rental income (Chambers et al., 2009).

[9] Very few are second homes for own use. Vacant homes reported in the Labour Force Survey increased from 91,000 to 151,000, over the period 2001–2011 (Table 18.3, column 1), but only about a quarter are "for occasional use." The Trajtenberg Committee found only some 47,000 apartments with minimal electricity consumption.

[10] Israel Tax Authority figures for 2016 (personal correspondence, 2016). The number of apartments owned by an individual is top-coded at 10 units. Assuming no owner with more than 10 units, the figures account for only 1.88 million units. This serves as the denominator for calculating the percentages above.

18.3 The Evolution of Market Conditions

Figure 18.2 shows the Central Bureau of Statistics (CBS) hedonic housing price index, along with various rent indices, all but one deflated by the nonhousing Consumer Price Index (CPI), from 1995 to 2017.[11] Prices peaked in 1997, and then declined steadily at 2.8 percent annually until bottoming out in 2007. In 2009, real price growth jumped to 13 percent. Rates stayed high for a couple more years and then moderated; still, annual real housing price growth averaged 7.5 percent between 2009 and 2016. Ben-Tovim et al.'s (2014) repeat sales index behaves similarly, as do regional indices after 2000, with the exception of the South, where many army training bases were transferred. Along with section 18.2's evidence of an integrated market, the mostly common price movements justify our all-country analysis.

The CBS housing rent index behaves similarly to price, although it is more muted. It increased over the 1990s, peaking in 1997, and then remained more or less steady before declining

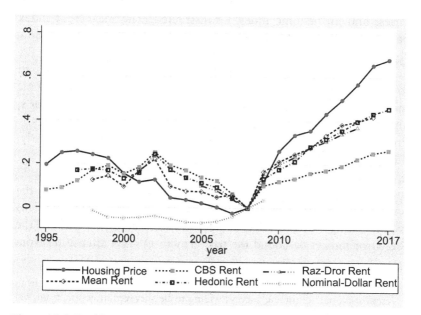

Figure 18.2 Real house price and real rent indices

---

[11] The exception is the "nominal dollar" index of section 18.4.3.

in the period 2002–2007. Like price, it increased in 2008–2016, but at only 3 percent. A full percent of that is due to the 10 percent growth in 2008–2009, the result of residual dollar rent-setting and exceptionally sharp swings in the shekel–dollar exchange rate (see section 18.4.3). After 2009, real annual growth in the CPI rent index was 2 percent.

The rent index, however, is heavily biased downward. Based on a panel of renters,[12] with growth measured by the average change in log rent among continuing tenants only, it "differences out" unit characteristics, thus controlling for compositional changes, but missing rent changes upon tenant turnover. These are likely to be large (Guasch and Marshall, 1987; Genesove, 2003; and Raz-Dror, 2018).

Raz-Dror's (2018) alternative index properly averages the CBS index with a new, hedonic index for turnover units. Its average growth rate is much greater: 5.3 percent after 2008, and 3.6 after 2009. As this index begins only in 2005, we add two more series to Figure 18.2: the CBS (unadjusted for unit attributes) mean rent series, and an hedonic index I constructed. The mean rent index behaves much like Raz-Dror's after 2008. This is due to the slow change of the rental housing stock composition coupled with the fact that rental transactions occur essentially ever year, compared to the constantly changing set of sales transactions. My hedonic index grows faster than the CBS's, but slower than Raz-Dror's, after 2008, likely due to underrepresentation of first year tenants.[13] Pre-2008, all four real rent indices in Figure 18.2 behave similarly, mimicking the dollar–shekel exchange rate.

With the rental share increasing slightly, from 24.3 percent in 1997 to 26.7 percent in 2015, and richer households more likely to own, the unobserved quality of rentals is likely to have increased over time. This would bias upward growth in hedonic indices, leading the CBS and the Raz-Dror indices to bound the true growth in rents after 2008 from

[12] More precisely, a panel of telephone numbers of self-identified renters from cross-sectional continuing surveys willing to be surveyed at contract renewal time. With land lines, attempts (usually unsuccessful) were made to continue with the incoming tenant. Landline mobility and then cellphones made this infeasible. The methodology also undersamples new tenants.

[13] As the rental sample data initially failed to identify turnover, Raz-Dror's index does not cover those years, and mine weights new and existing tenants equally.

either side. Although the true growth is probably closer to the Raz-Dror index, we consider both indices below, partly because previous work relies on the CBS index.

Non-land building cost is unimportant. It increased before 2008 by an average real 1.5 percent per year and declined annually by half a percent since. Thus it trends opposite to prices and rents.[14] The location premia in Figure 18.2 makes clear that non-land cost is a small share of overall costs in high-demand areas.

18.4 Explaining Market Changes Since 2008

18.4.1 *Interest Rates and Credit Restrictions*

The leading explanation for the initial price rise is the interest rate cut in the first quarter of 2009 (Figure 18.3). Part of the general cut in rates

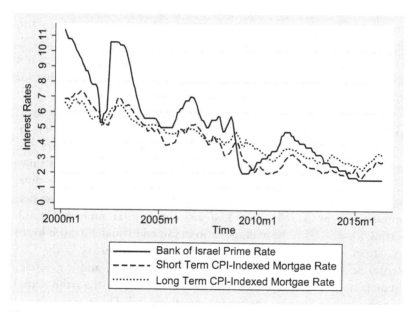

Figure 18.3 Interest rates

---

[14] The failure of costs to increase with construction activity suggests little specialized labor used in the industry, consistent with the view that construction in Israel is technologically backward.

engineered worldwide by central banks responding to the 2008 financial crisis, the Bank of Israel rate fell from 4.25 percent in September 2008 (when Lehman Brothers went bankrupt) to 0.50 percent in April 2009, where it remained before increasing slightly in August. In real terms, the rate fell by 4.05 percentage points.[15]

The timing of the rate cut lines up well with the price takeoff. The sequence of events that preceded the cut, the relative stability of the housing market up to the end of 2008 and Israeli's small open capital market, establishes its exogeneity. Quantitatively, though, 405 basis points widely overstates the effect on current and future interest rates faced by home buyers. The Bank of Israel rate cut would not have been considered permanent. Interest rates generally mean revert (Glaeser et al., 2013),[16] and with the rate bordering on the nominal lower bound, future increases were expected, as the change in the yield curve, implicit in Figure 18.3, shows. Indeed, short-term (up to five years) CPI-linked mortgage rates fell only by half as much, and with a lag, from a high of 4.09 in January 2009 to a low of 2.11 in the same year. Long-term (17–20 year) CPI-indexed rates fell less: 100 basis points over the year from December 2008, from 4.76 to 3.76. This is a fair approximation of the long-term interest rate change not only for those financing home purchases with long-term loans, but for those relying on short-term instruments as well.

According to basic asset pricing, housing prices are inversely related to the interest rate. Ignoring bubbles, price is the discounted sum of future rents, or housing services. For a constant real growth rate g of rents, depreciation rate d, and real interest r, price equals rent times $1/(d + r - g)$. With $\frac{R}{P}|_0$ the initial rent to price ratio, a one time, permanent interest rate decrease Δr should lead price to increase percentage-wise by $\Delta r/\left(\frac{R}{P}|_0 - \Delta r\right)$, *all else constant* (Himmleberg et al.). Setting $\frac{R}{P}|_0 = 0.055$, the average ratio obtained by matching (on locality, street name, year, and number of rooms) properties in the CBS Rental Survey to the property transaction database, and $\Delta r = 0.01$ predicts a 22 percent price increase. This is higher than the actual 15 percent increase over the twelve-month period. The overestimation

---

[15] Calculated by subtracting off the one-year expected inflation rate (inferred by comparing indexed and non-indexed government bonds), which fell from 2.1 to 0.3 over the first month of the decline. Recovering over the succeeding months, it returned to 2.1 by May.

[16] Mortgage rates prior to 2008 were mean reverting.

may be explained by both mean reversion beyond the 17–20 year horizon and residential construction induced by the higher prices (Poterba, 1984). This reduces the marginal value of housing services, over time, lowering g and mitigating the increase in price.

Although the perfect asset model does a fair job of explaining the 2009 price takeoff, it succeeds less at explaining co-movements of interest rates and housing prices at other times. Equally great changes in interest rates pre-2008 were unaccompanied by comparable changes in housing prices. The relatively muted price decline coincident with the one point increase in indexed mortgage rates over 2002 is consistent with the convexity of log price in the interest rate (Himmelberg et al., 2005) and higher contemporary rates. More problematic is the failure of prices to rise as interest rates declined over the next four and a half years.

Likewise, after the initial interest rate cuts of 2009, price failed to match three large gyrations in interest rates, although continuing to trend upwards as interest rates fell. Figure 18.4 compares the real housing price index with two predicted price series (normalized to September 2008 prices), both constructed under the perfect asset

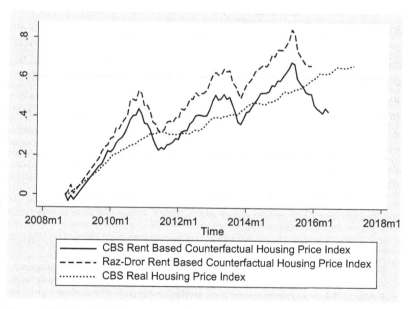

Figure 18.4 Real housing price and two counterfactuals

model according to the long-term mortgage rate at each date, assuming an unchanged g, but conditioning on the CBS or Raz-Dror rent index. The counterfactual prices increase over time, while, by construction, following the medium-term movements of the interest rate; the CBS-based counterfactual keeps up with price, while the Raz-Dror-based counterfactual trends faster. In other words, medium-term movements in the actual price-rent ratio fail to follow changes in interest rates as predicted by theory, while the long-term trend in prices falls short of that predicted by our preferred rent index, and only matches it for a rent index whose growth is clearly biased downwards.[17]

Why did the price-rent ratio continue to rise even when interest rates increased sharply? Household response may have been sluggish: it takes time to accumulate funds for housing purchases, and to change schools and jobs. Yet each of the three interest rate increases, and the two decreases, extended over about a year. Adaptive expectations is another explanation: experiencing rising prices may lead households to expect further price growth, leading in turn to higher prices (Mayer and Sinai, 2000).[18] Yet although such a mechanism can perpetuate an initial fundamental-based price increase, it need not imply insensitivity to further, contrary, shocks.[19] It does hinder inference, though.

Interest rates alone need not fully capture credit conditions. Macroprudential concerns led the Bank of Israel in October 2010 to require greater capital set asides for mortgages exceeding 60 percent of home value and in November 2012 to set hard limitations, forbidding loan-to-value beyond 50 percent for investors, 75 percent for first-home buyers, and 70 percent for other owner occupiers. It also limited variable rate mortgages. These steps constituted a reversal of the liberalization in the mortgage market over the previous decades. Nevertheless, Tzur-Ilan (2019) presents evidence that the effect of the October 2010 intervention was felt through higher interest rates, not credit rationing, justifying the sole reliance on the former in the analysis above.

---

[17] Assuming that g increases after September 2008, in line with the increase in the subsequent growth of rents, would predict even higher price-rent ratios.

[18] Burnside et al. (2016) offer a similar mechanism based on social interactions.

[19] Asset pricing models predict a relationship between price and interest rate. Gruber (2014) documents a strong correlation between the interest rate and a ten-month moving average of housing price *changes*. Possibly this stems from self-perpetuating expectations set off by interest rate changes.

18.4.2 The Count Gap

Much of the lay discussion, as well as governmental exegesis, blames the price rise on a deficit in the number of newly constructed apartments relative to population increases. Figure 18.5 shows housing starts tracking the increase in normalized population (population divided by 3.5)[20] nearly exactly in the early years of immigration from the former Soviet Union. After that, excessively optimistic expectations of further net immigration (Borukhov, 1993) led starts to exceed population growth – by some 75 percent in 1995. Although starts subsequently fell, they remained substantially above population growth until 1998. For the next few years, the two aligned, but in 2001–2009, starts fell short of population increase. At 2010, the two series cross; thereafter, starts exceeded the population increase.

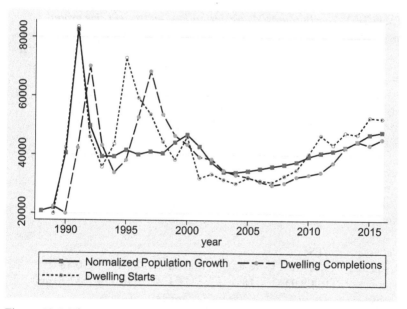

Figure 18.5 The count gaps: starts, completions, and normalized population growth

---

[20] This is the average size after 2008. It fell steadily by 0.3 persons over the previous two decades, mostly because of a decline in adults per household. A higher number before 2008 would not change our results materially.

Completions, shown in the same figure, mostly act similarly. They lagged starts by about one year at the beginning of the mass immigration from the former Soviet Union, but otherwise by the usual two to two and half years it takes to build, so that excess completions is largest in 1997, and the deficit opens up in in 2004. The completion count gap closes briefly in 2013, but then turns negative again, contrary to what would be predicted from starts.

18.4.3 Rent and the Gap

How do we expect the co-movements of construction and population growth in Figure 18.5 to translate into price and rent changes? Although public debate focused on prices, understanding rents

Table 18.2 *Yearly trends: depreciation and apartment size growth*

	Transaction price	Square meters of transacted units (new and existing)			Square meters (new units)
	(1)	(2)	(3)	(4)	(5)
Year		0.0046	0.0047	0.0047	2.64
		(0.0012)	(0.0002)	(0.0002)	(0.21)
Age of unit	−0.00492				
	(0.00002)				
Locality fixed effects	YES			YES	NO
Number of rooms	YES				NO
Net area	YES				NO
R-squared	0.81	0.48	0.003	0.010	0.88
Number of obs.	1,009,034 (units)	18 (years)	216,174 (units)	216,174 (units)	22 (years)

Standard errors in parentheses. The dependent variable in Column 2 is the estimated year fixed effect in the regression of log square meters on year and locality fixed effects. The sample for columns 3 and 4 are repeat sale pairs; the dependent variables is the difference in the log of square meters, while Year is the difference in years across the two transactions. The data for column 5 appear in column 2 of Table 18.3.

theoretically is more straightforward. Rent is determined by the intersection of the housing services demand curve and the housing stock (Poterba, 1984). Completions is the relevant series here, as only finished units produce housing services. Ignoring other demand determinants, Figure 18.5 predicts rent to decrease over the second half of the 1990s, stay constant over the turn of the century, and increase from 2004 on, perhaps flattening out from 2013 on. Actual growth does not always line up with what is predicted: rents did not fall in the second half of the 1990s, and rents fell from 2004 to 2008.

However, simple counts do not account for all relevant aspects of demand and supply. Begin with supply. Over time, units both deteriorate and are renovated. Regressing log price on age (controlling for transaction year, locality, and physical attributes) provides an estimate of net yearly depreciation of half a percent (Table 18.2, column 1).[21]

Since we control for size, this estimate misses enlargements – building out on ground level, digging into hillsides, enclosing balconies, or building up. Whether with controls for building year and attributes, or repeat sales,[22] regressing unit area on transaction year shows existing units increasing by half a percent a year (Table 18.2, columns 2–4).[23] Also, newly constructed homes are typically larger than existing ones. Column 2 of Table 18.3 shows a steady absolute increase of 2.6 square meters a year from 1995 to 2015 (the regression is shown in Table 18.2, column 5), or 1.6 percent at the mean 170 square meters. Yet the growth of new construction is only a second order effect, and so negligible.

Changing land quality, especially its location, affects effective supply. In August 2008, the government decreed a halt to development in the center, consistent with attempts to increase Jewish population in the Negev and the Galilee (State Comptroller, 2015, p. 71). This showed up

---

[21] Expenditure on maintenance or renovation (that do not alter apartment dimensions) amount to 8,227 million NIS in 2015. Per apartment, this is about 3,900 NIS per apartment per year, or about a quarter of 1 percent of average apartment value, implying a gross depreciation of about 0.75 percent.

[22] The matching procedure may bias repeat sales downwards (Ben-Tovim et al., 2014). Hedonic estimates are biased upwards if smaller units trade less as average unit size increases over time.

[23] Underreporting of enlargements biases the estimate downwards, but selection of enlarged units into the transaction database through the complementarity of renovations and transfer of ownership-occupancy, as well as the failure to account for demolitions, biases it upward.

in ILA auctions only in 2010, when, after a steady seven- year decline, the average travel time to Tel Aviv of tendered planned apartments jumped up by about 20 minutes (Table 18.3, column 3). In June 2011, the government reversed itself, yet only in 2017 did travel time fall back

Table 18.3 *Trends in vacancy, size of new apartments, and travel time*

Year	Vacant apartments (thousands)	Average size of new units (square meters)	Travel time (minutes)
	(1)	(2)	(3)
1995		155	
1996		141	
1997		139	
1998		144	64
1999		144	56
2000		151	66
2001	93	158	80
2002	100	160	82
2003	107	162	74
2004	111	164	68
2005	110	165	65
2006	108	167	68
2007	119	173	59
2008	134	177	56
2009	141	183	52
2010	141	187	72
2011	150	193	77
2012	137	196	75
2013	151	187	79
2014		191	76
2015		185	73
2016		186	73
2017		–	56

Vacant apartment figures are the estimates from the CBS's Labour Force Survey. The survey frequency changed to monthly in 2012, so pre-2012 and 2012 and post-2012 figures are not comparable. Average size of new units is from the CBS's New Construction Series. Travel time is the average commuting time to Tel Aviv (see footnote 3) of ILA land auctions, weighted by the number of units in the planned project.

to near 2009 levels. The temporary shift to the periphery moderates the effective increase in housing supply over those years, yet by an amount too small to affect our conclusions. Travel time for tendered apartment five years after 2008 is 8 minutes greater than for the five years before. Table 18.1, column 1, then implies that the value of the construction on ILA land auctioned off before and after 2008 differed by only 6 percent, which again is negligible, when calculating the yearly change in supply.

Thus, taking into account net quality depreciation, increases in apartment size, and the location of new construction (on government land), overall yearly growth in the stock apart from new construction is about zero. Construction counts capture the growth in the effective stock of housing fairly well.

In contrast, demand growth is not well proxied by a simple population count. Real per capita GNP has increased over time; its annual growth is positive in every year since 1995 apart from the Second Intifada recession (late 2001–2003) and 2009, in the wake of the global financial crisis. On average, the annual real per capita growth rate has been 1.9 since 1995 and 1.6 since 2008.

How much per capita income growth leads to increased housing demand depends on the income elasticity of demand for housing services. Recent US cross-city estimates for it are 0.67 (Albouy et al., 2016) and 1.0 (Davis and Ortalo-Magné, 2011).[24] Cross-sectional estimates of the log-linear regression of monthly rental payments on income for renters in the Israeli Household Expenditure Survey are similar (Table 18.4). Minimally conditioned, the estimate is around 1.0; adding demographic variables reduces it to a robust 0.91. We use that value.

On net, then, real income growth should increase housing demand annually by 0.91*1.9 = 1.73 percent. With a 2.1 million apartment stock,[25] this is equivalent to an additional annual inflow of 2,100,000 X .0173 = 36,330 normalized households. This overwhelms the simple count gap between normalized population growth and completions, which, after 2008, never exceeded 6,500.

---

[24] Income elasticities estimates rarely exceed one (Albouy et al., 2016).

[25] 2016 Registry of Apartments. The 2013 figure for Haifa replaces its missing 2016 number. The CBS's 2016 report of 2.4 million households, along with 0.15 million vacancies, implies 0.45 million more households than occupied units. More than one household can live in a unit.

Table 18.4 *Income elasticity of demand for housing services*

Variable	(1)	(1)	(2)	(4)	(5)
Log income	0.98	1.01	0.91	0.91	0.91
	(0.02)	(0.02)	(0.03)	(0.03)	(0.03)
Fixed effects:					
Survey year	YES	YES	YES	YES	YES
# of household members	NO	YES	YES	YES	YES
# of household earners	NO	NO	YES	YES	YES
Religion	NO	NO	NO	YES	YES
# of adult men & women	NO	NO	NO	NO	YES
# of observations	12,650	12,650	12,650	12,650	12,650
R-squared	0.18	0.18	0.19	0.19	0.19

Standard errors in parentheses. The dependent variable is the log of rent. All variables other than the log of income are mutually exclusive and exhaustive sets of categories. Data source: Family micro dataset of CBS Household Expenditure Survey for survey years 2003–2010. Renters only.

The next step translates the combined gap into a predicted rent increase. This requires a price elasticity of housing demand. Albouy et al. (2016) suggests 0.67 while Davis and Ortalo-Magné (2011) offers 1.0 – identical to the income elasticities. Lacking Israeli estimates, we consider both. Let housing (services) demand be $POP \times I^{0.9} \times D(R)$, where POP is normalized population, in millions, I per capita income, $D(R)$ per capita housing demand at baseline income and R is rent. Demand equals supply (the housing stock S) implies $dlnD(R) = dlnS - 0.9dlnI - dlnPOP$, where dln denotes yearly growth. Thus $dlnR = e^{-1}(0.91 \times dlnI + [dPOP - dS]/2.1)$, where e is the price elasticity of demand.

Per capita income growth explains much of post-2008 rents. At 1.6, per capita income growth predicts rent growth of 1.46 for $e = 1$, and 2.17 for $e = 0.67$. The latter is about right to explain the CBS rent index growth, although not quite enough for our preferred Raz-Dror index. Per capita growth can also explain why rents did not fall when completions exceeded normalized population growth in 1992 and 1996–1998.[26]

---

[26] Shoddy, rushed building in the low-demand South for immigrant demand may have played some role.

Income growth explains the behaviour of rents before 2008, as well, but with a twist. The fall in rents from 2002 through 2004 lines up qualitatively with the fall in income during the Second Intifada. However, neither the very large extent of the fall in rents nor the continued decrease over the subsequent years, when income was increasing again, accord with our expectations. Here we need to turn to the contemporary use of the dollar in setting rents, a remnant of hyperinflation two decades earlier. Rents were not merely indexed to the exchange rate; quotes and initial monthly levels were set in dollars. This strongly suggests that rents were thought of in dollar terms, and that dollar amounts were conceived as real, not nominal (Genesove 2019). Indeed, Figure 18.2's "nominal dollar" rent index, which uses only dollar denominated rents (nearly every rent in 2002 but less than 10 percent by 2010) and is not corrected for inflation, increases after 2004. It also declines more gradually in 2002–2004.

18.4.4 Price and the Gap

The public uproar was mostly about prices, not rents, and much blame was placed on a failure to construct adequate numbers of new housing units. Can the simple count gap explain any substantial part of the continued rise in prices after 2009?

Price differs from rent. First, price incorporates the stream of future, not only current, housing services. At low interest rates, it should not reflect current demand and supply determinants, including the count gap, substantially more than future ones. Second, apart from changing interest rates, and especially at a low interest rate, price changes reflect essentially only unanticipated changes, in the gap or other factors. Third, price can include a bubble.

Since price should respond to a gap when market participants first become aware of it, starts measure changes in known supply better than completions, especially as time to build has been fairly constant, exempting the speeded-up government- promoted construction at the start of the mass immigration from the former Soviet Union. Raz-Dror (2018) goes further back in the process, documenting very low permit numbers in the early 2000s. However, even most developers are likely to have only a partial picture at that stage. Accurate information on planning is locality-specific and, at least until the improvements of the last few years, fairly dispersed.

If the price response to the current count gap reflects only the effect on current rent, then, as for rents, the response must be small, as the start gap opened up already in 2001. Qualitatively, an increasing sensitivity to the gap can be rationalized by market participants' growing awareness of its persistence, with each year's gap portending future ones. Yet, even if viewed as permanent, the count gap was clearly too small to drive real annual price increases of 7.5 percent.

18.4.5 Long-Run Supply

Up to now, the analysis has taken investment as given. Taking it as exogenous is useful for assessing the government's response, but a full, positive analysis of the market must incorporate investment and endogenous policy.

New housing supply in Israel is generally viewed as very inelastic. Inelastic demand accentuates the effect of any initial price shock, wherever it originates, and, conversely, restrains quantity growth. Bubbles may also develop more readily under inelastic supply.[27]

The institutional basis for claiming a small supply elasticity is the substantial government control over the development process. Common everywhere (Werceberger, 1997), Israel nevertheless stands out for government ownership of nearly all undeveloped land.[28] The release of this land is therefore not automatically subject to market forces. Indeed, the ILA, responsible for managing undeveloped government-owned land, disproportionately offers land in low-demand areas. Where demand does not justify current construction, auctioning off land will not add supply: contractors will bid for land but will not build. The tenders' standard two to three years construction deadline is generally unenforced (Wercberger and Borukhov, 1999).

Yet it is important not to overstate the role of the ILA in housing investment. Government-owned land targeted to development is offered for sale only after an average 7.5 years of planning, two-thirds of which is spent obtaining approval at the district level, rather than in actual professional planning (Bank of Israel, 2011).

---

[27] Thus concludes Glaeser et al. (2008), theoretically, for adaptive expectations-based bubbles, and, empirically, for the 1980s US housing price cycle.

[28] Other countries with sole government ownership, or right of purchase, of undeveloped land are Singapore, Hong Kong, and South Korea.

Furthermore, although 94 percent of undeveloped land is government owned, its share in high demand areas is much lower: about half of undeveloped Tel Aviv land is privately held, and half of floor space constructed since 2005 has been on private land (Rubin and Felsenstein, 2017). Additionally, building up on existing building requires no new land. Even in 2008, more than three-quarters of transacted apartments in three-floor or higher buildings in Tel Aviv had per meters prices above 8,700 NIS, which corresponds to building costs of 5,000 NIS;[29] by 2016, that fraction was 96.5 percent. For such development, and for that on the substantial amount (Wercberger and Borukhov, 1999) of sold but still undeveloped land, regional and local planning committees' and local governments' decisions determine development.[30]

Local resistance significantly hinders residential development. Differential property tax rates[31] incentivize localities to attract commercial rather than residential users (Eckstein et al., 2014 and Snir, 2015). Tel Aviv receives, per square meter, four times as much from commercial properties as from residential. Lower construction rates in localities with higher number of legal appeals of its local planning commission decisions hint at the effectiveness of local authorities' resistance (Yeshurun, 2015).

Nonuniformity in rules across local committees further hinders development, as it leads developers to specialize in particular localities, thus reducing competition (Snir, 2015). This might be related to the falloff in competition away from Tel Aviv (Table 18.1, column 5). Policy uncertainty within a given locality is also important (Rubin and Felsenstein, 2017). Contractors' lobbying of local planning committees for greater building rights adds to the lag in construction's response to increased prices. There are also simple bureaucratic delays: the time to obtain

---

[29] Calculated with a 1.6 multiplier for common areas (Glaeser et al., 2005), plus legal fees (10,000 NIS), assessor (25,000), architect (50,000), and overseer (20,000), using Houdi's (2014) higher estimates and an 85 m^2 unit. All but the first are fixed at the building level; we assume twelve existing units. Even with bargaining costs among unit owners, it is reasonable to expect that absent regulation, building would be profitable.

[30] The central government also has a role in built-up areas in funding improved infrastructure.

[31] These are determined locally but are subject to central government restrictions which cap residential and commercial rates differently.

a permit for simple construction exceeds 200 days, double that of the highly regulated UK and eight times the United States (Snir, 2015).

This picture of government sclerosis is misleading, however. The full effect of government on the elasticity of supply includes its tendency to take substantive legislative and administrative acts (often ad hoc) in response to higher prices. Both during the immigration from the former Soviet Union and more recently, the government took extraordinary measures to increase supply. Econometric estimates will reflect those actions no less than the fixed institutions described above, and positive analyses of the housing market must incorporate endogenous governmental responses.

Figure 18.6 shows apartment starts against the real housing price, after 2008. The relationship is interpretable as the policy-endogenous housing investment function, assuming it stable relative to demand. This is appropriate, given the large demand variation – the large changes in interest rates, the continual increase in per capita income and population – and the essential constancy of building costs. The implied investment elasticity is 0.77 (se=0.07).

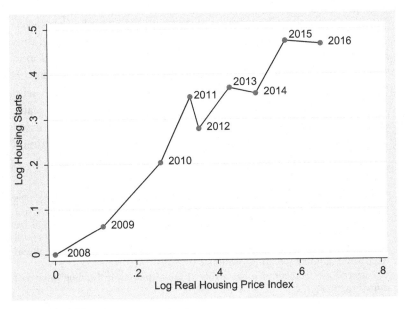

Figure 18.6 Housing starts and prices

This estimate is an upper bound for the investment function elasticity, when conditioned on the tax and regulation policy in place pre-takeoff, assuming that subsequent policy changes were, on net, not counterproductive.[32] An upward-shifting conditional investment function will lead price to increase less and starts to increase more than had it been stable. Nonetheless, the estimated elasticity increases as one truncates the sample earlier and earlier, at least back to 2011, although it is never significantly different from 0.77.

By comparison, Caldera and Johansson's (2013) error-correction estimate of Israel's long-run investment elasticity is 0.38 (s.e. = 0.185), for 1995q2:2009q1.[33] Their estimate (insignificantly different from ours) fits right in place in the cross-country negative relationship between population density and investment elasticity they document. Israel is no outlier: with 300 persons per square kilometer, its elasticity is somewhat larger than Belgium's, which has 50 more people, and twice as large as that of the Netherlands, which has nearly 150 more.

18.4.6 Bubbles

A bubble is the excess of price over fundamental value, the expected net present value of current and future rents, or housing service values, conditional on current information. Bubbles have a number of consequences. Since they can end suddenly, a bubble today means uncertainty over the future and a threat to macro stability. Bubble-induced construction is excessive; once the bubble bursts, its overhang can impart much lower prices than before it developed (Glaeser et al., 2008). Appropriate government policy depends on whether or not there is a bubble. Decreasing regulatory hindrances to development may exacerbate bubble-induced construction and so the extent of the bust. Altering subjective perceptions of prices becomes attractive when there is a bubble, since, unanchored in fundamentals, it is more susceptible to shifts in expectations. Also, knowing whether previous price

---

[32] Uncertainty over future policy might have made waiting optimal, shifting in the investment function.

[33] They estimate a long-run elasticity between price and income of 0.80 (s.e. = 0.17). Since it is conditional on both interest and the stock of housing, this corresponds to the relationship for rent above. Setting $e^{-1}0.9 = 0.8$ implies a price elasticity of demand of $e = 1.125$. Also, see Bar-Nathan et al. (1998) who estimate a long-run investment (of square meters) elasticity of 0.35 for Israel over the period 1974–1990.

booms were bubble driven is crucial to understanding the price formation process.

Dovman et al. (2012) employ three different methodologies to determine whether price includes a bubble. They first construct a fundamental price by substituting, for expected rents, realized rents at pre-2012 dates, and predicted values from an assumed stable stochastic process at later dates. Comparing constructed with actual, they find no post-takeoff bubble. The second approach is a Kalman filter estimation of the asset model. This yields a 5 percent bubble at sample end. Updating the analysis, Caspi (2015) finds the bubble increasing over time, exceeding 20 percent by mid-2013. Nonetheless, the overall results are odd, as they include a 10 percent *negative* bubble over the period 2003–2009.[34] The third approach compares recent prices to predictions from an econometric estimation of the relationship between housing prices and fundamentals. A stable relationship need not accord with the perfect asset model, nor preclude systematic bubbles. This approach merely asks whether the present differs from the past, conditioned on economically relevant variables. They find a rent to price ratio about 8 percent (insignificantly) lower than predicted, at a level seen in the early 2000s.

Caspi (2015) follows Phillips and Yu (2011) in testing for explosive housing prices.[35] Since rents and interest rates are nonexplosive, so must be the fundamental value. Explosive prices would imply a bubble. (Rational bubbles, i.e., those precluding temporal arbitrage, are explosive.) Evidence for a bubble, although never sufficient to reject the no bubble null hypothesis, grows stronger as one approaches the mid-2013 sample end. Updated to early 2017, though, the test does reject the no bubble null (personal correspondence).

International Monetary Fund studies put prices substantially above long-run values, based on estimated co-integrating relationships between housing prices and the population to stock ratio, rent, wage income, and GNP share of mortgage debt: 26 percent above in February 2014, 30 percent by September 2015 (International Monetary Fund, 2014, 2015). (Earlier work by Nagar and Segel [2011] came to similar, but unsurprisingly given the date, more

---

[34] Negative bubbles are impossible under weak assumptions (Blanchard and Watson, 1982).

[35] An explosive series has a growth rate that increases with the value of the variable.

moderate, conclusions.) This does not indicate a bubble, only deviations from long-run trends. All four studies use the CBS rent index, which surely is biased toward finding excessive prices, given the downwardly biased of growth in this index.

18.5 Policy Response

Housing price increases have large distributive effects that tend to swamp allocative effects. For the given stock, net sellers' gains balance the harm to net buyers (Bajari et al., 2008). Likewise, the increased prices of infra-marginal new construction, while a loss to buyers, is offset by the corresponding increase in land value for households, whether as owners of private land or, for construction on government land, taxpayers and beneficiaries of government services. The only allocative effect is increased construction due to the higher prices. Yet even were all post-2008 starts in excess of that year's starts induced by the price rise, their value would be small with respect to the 1.4 trillion increase in the value of housing over that period.[36]

Harm and benefit did not offset each other politically. The price rise led to street protests, "tent cities," and relentless media coverage and public discussion. Although the first tent was raised in response to rental conditions (Granot, 2011), the overall focus quickly shifted to price, since it had increased much more (especially as measured) than rent, and the most sought-after part of the electorate, that which would give its support to the *Yesh Atid* and *Kulanu* centrist parties, was middle-class, young renters who aspired to own.

The government responded in a myriad of ways. One was institutional, aimed at reducing regulatory burden and delays. The National Housing Committee was established to bypass regional planning committees for large projects, although it proved ineffective (Bank of Israel, 2014). Land expropriation for residential purposes was permitted (Bank of Israel Report, 2015). Better performing (i.e., with fewer delays, greater transparency, and more professional members) local planning committees were to be granted greater authority, although only at the minister's discretion (Snir, 2015). The amendment also

---

[36] This ignores macroprudential concerns. Also, the price increase was accompanied by mortgage rate declines, which benefited net buyers (Friedman and Ribon, 2014).

replaced some permit requirements with general regulations. Of course, speeding up the regulatory process risks degrading neighbors' protection from negative externalities and insufficient infrastructure.

With local resistance to the government's efforts, the latter found itself negotiating with localities for their assent to development. The Ministry of Construction and Housing negotiated individual encompassing agreements between it and the local authority for infrastructure funding, in return for cooperation. Nahariya's agreement, for example, ran to seventy-nine pages and detailed funding timing, planned ritual baths, expenditures on watering public gardens, etc., as well as promised support from the ministry in negotiations with the Ministry of Education. Another concession set aside a share of *Mehir l'Mishtaken* units (see below) for local residents.

Ministerial appointments and responsibilities were taken in response to the housing market conditions. After the 2015 election, the Finance and Construction and Housing ministries were purposely assigned to the same party, and the ILA and planning committees put under the aegis of the Finance Ministry.

The government took significant fiscal actions. Transaction taxes were increased for investors and owner-occupied high-end properties. Incidence theory predicts that tax increases decrease the pre-tax (which is the headline) price but increase the tax-inclusive price. Transaction taxes also reduce transactions. Expectations of their remaining in place in the future further reduce price, whether due to capitalization of future tax payments, or reduction in liquidity from avoiding them.

The government also imposed a property tax on a household's third or more apartment and permitted municipalities to double tax vacant properties, although the first was struck down by the courts on procedural grounds, and not reintroduced, while the second rule has been barely used (Alemu, 2019). Similar policies have been enacted elsewhere (Segu and Vignolles, 2016, and Hilber and Schoni, 2018).

One reason for differential treatment of investors was a desire to increase home ownership, secularly decreasing but viewed as superior to renting. Another was the view that speculative investor demand was driving the price increase, as Haughwout et al. (2011) and Barlevy and Fisher (2010) have argued for the United States. Steady at 25 percent since 2004, the investor share of transactions increased 3 percentage points at the time of the interest rate cuts, remaining there until a first increase in the transaction tax for investors drove the share down to

23 percent for two years. Only from 2013:II to 2015:I did the share climb, by about 5 percentage points; after a second transaction tax increase, it fell to 20 percent (Ministry of Finance, 2017). Thus, the investor share tended to move with price (as one might expect if a significant fraction of households are credit constrained) but not lead it.

Mostly, the anti-investor taxation reflected an overriding concern for price over rent. As noted, price was more politically salient. Policymakers failed to understand that restraining investor demand limits renting opportunities, thereby increasing the demand for owner-occupancy, and so leaving price much less affected than a narrow focus on investor demand suggests.

18.5.1 *Mehir l'Mishtaken*

The most exceptional policy was provision of below market price housing via the *Mehir l'Mishtaken* program: land auctions in which developers compete in the per-meter price offered to selected consumers.[37] The winning bidder paid a stipulated assessed land value less a subsidy of 120,000 NIS per unit (in high-value areas) or 20 percent of assessed value (low-value areas), plus the usual infrastructure costs. Assessment was based on past standard land auction results. Relative to new construction, this was on a very large scale, eventually replacing traditional ILA land sales. The aim was to drive down prices of not only new but also existing homes. With a stock more than forty times construction, this hope seems misplaced.

Setting price before production may lead to low-quality construction.[38] The first units constructed under the scheme cut back on certain unspecified attributes, such as the number of interior walls (Bank of Israel, 2013, 2014). Subsequent tenders were much more detailed, specifying not only the number of rooms, but also, e.g., electrical outlets and cabinet space. Yet it remains to see whether ex-ante pricing with contractual commitment can induce the same level of quality as ex-post market pricing.

---

[37] Nonowner couples and singles over 35 were eligible. Lotteries were held for excess enrollments.

[38] Similar issues arise in franchise bidding for a regulated monopoly (Williamson, 1976).

The new program should lower the prices among the auctioned apartments by the subsidy amount. When developers compete in offering a payment to the ILA, bidding increases to the point at which the total developer cost equals the market price, i.e., the payment equals the difference between market price and cost (production cost plus stipulated payments). This difference is location rents. When developers compete in offering the lowest price to final buyers, price falls to cost. Thus, the new mechanism shifts surplus in the amount of the subsidy from the government, to the households.

Thorough research on the new auctions has yet to be done. Winning per-meter prices have been about half those of other transactions in the locality (Bank of Israel, 2016) – much greater than the subsidy – but the true quality-controlled price reduction is surely much less. Many lottery winners have turned down the opportunity, suggesting no great bargains; projects are typically built on previously undeveloped land on the unattractive periphery of a locality; as noted, quality may be low; sales are "on paper," before final construction; units are illiquid: they may be rented out but may not be sold for five years.

Why such a complicated scheme? By basic economics, lump sum grants to the targeted groups would have been superior. But public discourse defined harm not as decreased consumer welfare, but as price increases and, to a lesser extent, falls in home ownership, especially among the young.[39] That determined the political objective. Unconditional lump sum grants to targeted households would have improved their welfare but would have no obvious, negative effect on price or the rental share; house price subsidies would have increased the pre-subsidy price.

To be fair, redistribution is inevitably inefficient. It leads to anticipation of more, which, if progressive, dulls work incentives. In practise, most major redistributions, whether Iran's 1963 White Revolution (Katouzian, 2013), or the 1862 US Homestead Act (Luce, 2017), have been land based. Housing subsidies may be the modern equivalent of such policies.

---

[39] Although the rental share was relatively stable, that of young households increased more than 10 percentage points over the period 2002–2012 (Bank of Israel, 2014). Most of the increase occurred before the takeoff in prices and rents, yet the takeoff was widely seen as driving ownership rates down.

18.5.2 Rental Housing

Along with tilting the field against rentals via taxes, the government also promoted alternative contractual and governance structures. These aimed at ensuring greater tenure security and limiting exposure to rental price risk, by both increasing contract duration and "corporatizing" the landlord function. The *Dira l'Haskir* program provided developers with subsidized land in return for renting out a share of the units with ten- or twenty-year contracts (the standard in Israel is one year) at 20 percent below market value. The government also encouraged real estate investment trusts to enter the rental market. These policies were driven by a perception that landlords in advanced economies tend to be firms, thought to provide greater tenancy security. In fact, most rentals in most housing markets are owned by households.[40]

Policymakers also apparently believed that improved rental conditions would reduce prices by reducing demand for owner-occupied housing. They failed to appreciate that the one-for-one pass-through of rental housing services demand to landlords' derived demand for property leaves overall demand for property generally invariant to the relative conditions in the two sectors.

18.6 Conclusion

This chapter has explored the Israeli housing market, with a focus on the determinants of the dramatic increase in prices and rents since 2008. The spatial-structural nature of prices justifies a single, all-Israel conception of the market. The chapter has combined a careful accounting of demand and supply changes with generally accepted estimates of income and price elasticities to explain the evolution of housing rents over this period. We found it mostly attributable to the continual increase in per capita income. The gap between the population increase and the number of new homes constructed each year, on which much of the debate focused, pales in comparison. The chapter

---

[40] France, Ireland, Denmark, Australia, Belgium, Spain, and the United States have corporate rates below 15 percent, and Norway, the United Kingdom, Switzerland, and Germany below 25 percent (Scanlon, 2011). Only in Austria and Sweden are most rentals corporate owned. See also Chambers et al. (2008 and Lawrence (1996, p. 38).

has also shown that the sudden increase in housing prices in early 2009, and the subsequent general trend of prices relative to rents, is broadly reconcilable with the perfect asset model of housing, given the dramatic long-term mortgage rate cuts in early 2009 and the subsequent trend of further rate decreases, although not at more intermediate frequencies. There is thus no need to resort to bubbles, the statistical case for which, if any, is based on a flawed rent index.

The large price increase, whose consequences were mostly distributive, led to a public uproar. The government responded with political, administrative, and legal actions aimed at reducing price. Construction increased substantially. How much was due to the government and how much simply to contractors' responses to higher prices is difficult to tell; together, the pattern of construction and prices is consistent with a policy-endogenous housing investment function elasticity of about 0.8. Government also acted through a heterodox program to reduce infra-marginal price per se by forgoing its land profits from the sale of construction on government-owned land. Other policies disadvantaged investor purchases, and thus the rental market. These policies were determined in large measure by how harm was defined in public discourse.

References

Alonso, W. (1964). *Location and Land Use: Toward a General Theory of Land Rent*. Cambridge, MA: Harvard University Press.

Albouy, D., Erlich, G., and Liu, Y. (2016). Housing Demand, Cost-of-Living Inequality, and the Affordability Crisis. NBER Working Paper 22816. https://www.nber.org/papers/w22816.pdf.

Alemu, Jerusalem. (2019). *Double Property Tax on Ghost Apartments*. Center for Research and Information, Knesset. [In Hebrew]

Bajari, P., Benkard, C. Lanier, and Krainer, J. (2005). House Prices and Consumer Welfare. *Journal of Urban Economics*, 58, 474–487. www.elsevier.com/locate/jue.

Bank of Israel (2011). *Bank of Israel Annual Report*. Jerusalem.
    (2013). *Bank of Israel Annual Report*. Jerusalem.
    (2014). *Bank of Israel Annual Report*. Jerusalem.
    (2015). *Bank of Israel Annual Report*. Jerusalem.
    (2016). *Bank of Israel Annual Report*. Jerusalem.

Barlevy, G., and Fisher, J. (2010). *Mortgage Choice and Housing Speculation*. Working Paper Series WP-2010–12. Federal Reserve Bank of Chicago.

Bar-Nathan, M., Beenstock, M., and Haitovsky, Y. (1998). The Market for Housing in Israel. *Regional Science and Urban Economics*, 28, 21–49.

Ben-Tovim, N., Yakin, Y., and Zussman, N. (2014). *Measuring Home Price Variation Using Repeated Sales Methodology*. Occasional Paper 2014.01. Jerusalem: Bank of Israel Research Department. [In Hebrew]

Blanchard, O. J., and Watson, M. W. (1982). Bubbles, Rational Expectations and Financial Markets. In P. Wachtel (ed.), *Crises in the Economic and Financial Structure*. Lexington, MA: D.C. Heath and Company, 295–316.

Borukhov, E. (1993). Housing Policy in Light of the Large Immigration: A Two-Year View. *The Economic Quarterly*, 40(3), 325–333. [In Hebrew]

Burnside, C., Eichenbaum, M., and Rebelo, S. (2016). Understanding Booms and Busts in Housing Markets. *Journal of Political Economy*, 124(4), 1088–1147.

Caldera, A., and Johansson, A. (2013). The Price Responsiveness of Housing Supply in OECD Countries. *The Journal of Housing Economics*, 22, 231–249.

Caspi, I. (2015). *Testing for a Housing Bubble at the National and Regional Level: The Case of Israel*. Discussion Paper No. 2015.05. Jerusalem: Bank of Israel Research Department.

Central Bureau of Statistics. (2016). *Dwelling in Israel: Findings from the Household Expenditure Survey 2016*, December. [In Hebrew]

Chambers, M., Garriga, C., and Schlagenhauf, D. E. (2008). *The Tax Treatment of Homeowners and Landlords and the Progressivity of Income Taxation*. FRB Atlanta Working Paper 2008–06. Federal Reserve Bank of Atlanta.

(2009). Accounting for Changes in the Home Ownership Rate. *International Economic Review*, 50(3), 677–726.

Davis, M., and Ortalo-Magné, F. (2011). Household Expenditures, Wages, Rents. *Review of Economic Dynamics*, 14, 248–261.

Dovman, P., Ribon, S., and Yakhin, Y. (2012). The Housing Market in Israel 2008–2010: Are House Prices a "Bubble"? *Israel Economic Review*, 10 (1), 1–38. [In Hebrew]

Eckstein, Z., Tolkovsky, E., and Tsur, N. (2012). *Are Housing Prices in Israel High because of a Small Planning Stock?* Gazit-Globe Institute for the Study of Real Estate, Interdisciplinary Center Herzliya. [In Hebrew]

Eckstein, Z., Tolkovsky, E., Eizenberg Be-Lulu, A., and Sherman, Y. (2014). *Do Local Authorities Face a Negative Incentive to Increase the*

Population Under their Jurisdiction? Policy Paper – GGA/2014, Gazit-Globe Institute for the Study of Real Estate, Interdisciplinary Center Herzliya.

Friedman, Y., and Ribon, S. (2014). *Whence the Money? Home Purchases and Their Financing: An Analysis Using Household Expenditures Survey Data.* Occasional Paper 2014–05. [In Hebrew]

Genesove, D. (2003). Nominal Rigidity in Apartment Rents. *Review of Economics and Statistics,* 85(4), 844–853.

(2019). *Currency as an Economic Norm.* Falk Working Papers.

Glaeser, E. L., Gottlieb, J. D., and Gyourko, J. (2013). Can Cheap Credit Explain the Housing Boom? In E. Glaeser and T. Sinai (eds.), *Housing and the Financial Crisis.* Chicago, IL: University of Chicago Press, 301–360.

Glaeser, E. L., and J. Gyourko, J. (2009). Arbitrage in Housing Markets. In E. Glaeser and J. Quigley (eds.), *Housing Markets and the Economy: Risks, Regulation and Policy.* Cambridge, MA: Lincoln Institute of Land Policy, 113–148.

Glaeser, E. L., Gyourko, J. and Saiz, A. (2008). Housing Supply and Housing Bubbles. *Journal of Urban Economics,* 64, 198–217.

Glaeser, E. L., Gyourko, J. and Saks, R. (2005). Why Is Manhattan so Expensive? Regulation and the Rise in Housing Prices. *Journal of Law and Economics,* 48, 331–369.

Gruber, N. (2014). The Israeli Housing Market. In D. Ben-David (ed.), *State of the Nation Report: Society, Economy and Policy in Israel.* Jerusalem: Taub Center for Social Policy Studies in Israel, 91–168.

Guasch, J. L., and Marshall, R. C. (1987). A Theoretical and Empirical Analysis of the Length of Residency Discount in the Rental Housing Market. *Journal of Urban Economics,* 22(3), 291–311.

Government Authority for Urban Renewal, Ministry of Construction and Housing, Maintenance Towers (2017). *The Maintenance of Governmental Towers.* [In Hebrew]

Granot, R. (2011) Dividends: Who Evicted Daphni Leef from Her Rented Apartment in Tel Aviv – and Set Off a Protest? *Calcalist,* August 3. [In Hebrew]

Haughwout, A., Lee, D., Tracy, J., and van der Klaauw, Wilbert. (2011). *Real Estate Investors, the Leverage Cycle, and the Housing Market Crisis.* Staff Report no. 514. Federal Reserve Bank of New York.

Hilber, C., and Schoni, O. (2018). *The Economic Impacts of Constraining Home Investments.* Centre for Economic Performance, LSE, CEP Discussion Papers.

Himmelberg, C., Mayer, C., and Sinai, T. (2005). Assessing High House Prices: Bubbles, Fundamentals and Misperceptions. *Journal of Economic Perspectives*, 19(4), 67–92.

Houdi, Uri. (2014) Considering Tama 38 for the Building? Prepare to Spend a Lot More Money. *Calcalist*, October 21. [In Hebrew]

International Monetary Fund (2014). *IMF Country Report No. 14/48.* Washington, DC: IMF.

International Monetary Fund (2015). *IMF Country Report No. 15/261.* Washington, DC: IMF.

Kahn, M., and Ribon, S. (2013). *The Effect of Home and Rental Prices on Private Consumption in Israel: A Micro Data Analysis.* Occasional Paper 2013.06. Jerusalem: Bank of Israel. [In Hebrew]

Katouzian, H. (2013). Iran: A Long History and Short-Term Society. In P. Furtado (ed.), *Histories of Nations: How Their Identities were Forged.* London: Thames and Hudson, 31–38.

Lawrence, R. (1996). Switzerland. In Paul Balchin (ed.), *Housing Policy in Europe*, London, New York: Routledge, 36–50.

Luce, E. (2017). *The Retreat of Western Liberalism.* London: Little Brown.

Mayer, C., and Sinai, T. (2000). U.S. House Price Dynamics and Behavorial Finance. In C. Foote, L. Goette, and S Meier (eds.), *Policymaking Insights from Behavorial Economics.* Federal Reserve Bank of Boston, 261–308.

Mills, E. S. (1967). An Aggregative Model of Resource Allocation in a Metropolitan Area. *American Economic Review (Papers and Proceedings)*, 57(2), 197–210.

Ministry of Finance, Chief Economist Branch. (2017). *Survey of the Residential Real Estate Industry for the Second Quarter, 2017.* [In Hebrew]

Muth, R. F. (1969). *Cities and Housing.* Chicago, IL: University of Chicago Press.

Nagar, W., and Segel, G. (2011). *What Explains the Development of Housing Prices and Rents in Israel 1999–2010.* Bank of Israel Survey, 85. [in Hebrew]

Phillips, P. C. B., and Yu, J. (2011). Dating the Timeline of Financial Bubbles During the Subprime Crisis. *Quantitative Economics*, 2(3), 455–491.

Poterba, J. M. (1984). Tax Subsidies to Owner-Occupied Housing: An Asset-Market Approach. *The Quarterly Journal of Economics*, 99(4), 729–752.

Raz-Dror, O. (2018). Issues in the Housing Market. Doctoral Dissertation, Hebrew University of Jerusalem. [In Hebrew]

Rubin, Z., and Felsenstein, D. (2017). Supply Side Constraints in the Israeli Housing Market: The Impact of State-Owned Land. *Land Use Policy*, 65, 266–276.

(2019). Is Planning Delay Really a Constraint in the Provision of Housing? Some Evidence from Israel. *Papers in Regional Science*, 1–22.

Scanlon, K. (2011). Private Renting in Other Countries. In K. Scanlon and B. Kochan (eds.), *Towards a Sustainable Private Rented Sector: The Lessons from Other Countries*. London: LSE London, 15–44.

Snir, A. (2015). *Breaking Barriers to Housing, Part C: Building Permits*. Kohelet Policy Forum.

State Comptroller. (2015). *Audit Report on the Housing Crisis*. [In Hebrew]

Tzur-Ilan, N. (2019). *The Effect of Credit Constraints on Housing Choices: The Case of LTV Limits*. Discussion Paper 2017.03. http://dx.doi.org /10.2139/ssrn.2927783.

Segu, M., and Vignolles, B. (2016). *Taxing Vacant Apartments: Can Fiscal Policy Reduce Vacancy?* Working Papers 2016.02, International Network for Economic Research.

Wercberger, E. (1997). Public Ownership of Land: A Vital Element in Land Policy or an Anachronistic Remnant? *Economic Quarterly*, 44(4), 558–573. [In Hebrew]

Wercberger, E., and Borukhov, E. (1999). The Israel Land Authority: Relic or Necessity? *Land Use Policy*, 16, 129–138.

Williamson, O. (1976). Franchise Bidding for Natural Monopoly: In General and with Respect to CATV. *Bell Journal of Economics*, 7, 73–104.

Yeshurun, G. (2015). Local Housing Supply Regulation and Domestic Migration in Israel. MA thesis, Hebrew University of Jerusalem.

19 | Policy Tools to Promote Environmental Quality in Israel: A Comparison of Economic Tools with Direct Regulation

DORON LAVEE

19.1 Introduction

Since the end of the 1960s, policymakers around the world have been looking for tools to achieve their environmental goals. The two main environmental policy instruments are direct regulation and market-based economic tools.

19.1.1 Direct Regulation

Direct regulation includes a set of measures that define what is permitted and what is not. Environmental regulation generally establishes a threshold for pollution/emission. The polluter who passes the threshold is liable to fines and even criminal penalties, the purpose of which is to deter the continuation of the deviation (Zito et al., 2011). Traditionally, the regulatory tools implemented in most developed countries were based on direct regulation of command and control (CAC), contrary to marketable permits (Hepburn, 2006). One of the central arguments against environmental regulation is the need to rely on government enforcement, whose effectiveness, applicability, and its ability to bring about the required environmental improvement is not apparent (Karsin, 2009).

19.1.2 Economic Tools

Economic tools are a set of tools that rely on market mechanisms to internalize external environmental costs and to incentivize the players to move towards optimal equilibrium without explicit guidance or guidance regarding the level of that equilibrium. Economic tools do not limit the level of pollution but demand payment for each unit of pollution (Seroa Da Motta et al., 2004).

Over the past four decades, Israel has developed a broad and varied policy aimed at protecting and protecting the environment, a policy based mainly on regulatory tools and CAC mechanisms, similar to the trend in most OECD countries. Over the past decades, however, the use of economic tools has been extended in many OECD countries, as it has become apparent that a policy of CAC regulation often leads to unnecessarily expensive solutions (Bailey, 2007). In Israel, the implementation of economic tools in environmental policy began only in the late 1990s, but it is rapidly gaining momentum and is becoming a legitimate and leading tool in the country's environmental legislation (Bank of Israel, 2009).

19.2 Mythology

The comparison between CAC regulation and economic tools will be based on a number of criteria:

a. *Implementation ability and cost*: With which tool the compliance is higher and the government administrative costs in achieving the reduction targets are lower (Lavee and Joseph-Ezra, 2015).
b. *Efficiency*: In a cost–benefit analysis to the economy. Which tool achieves an optimal equilibrium for the economy. Meaning, with which tool the net benefit is the highest (marginal cost of reducing the pollution is equal to the marginal benefit of its removal).
c. *Morality*: The polluter pays principle – In the use of each tool, who bears the cost of pollution? The polluter or the population exposed to pollution.
d. *Harm to competitiveness and market forces*: With which tool the effects on economic competitiveness and trade are minimal.

In this chapter I Intend to examine case studies according to these criteria. The analysis will look at each criterion separately without specifying a quantitative score and weight for each criterion. The goal is to give a general indication of the priority given to the use of each tool.

19.2.1 Examining the Use of Economic Tools in Environmental Policy Compared to Direct Regulation

Case studies are divided according to central areas of pollution – air, waste, water, and effluents (Lavee, 2019). Case studies were selected according to the importance of the field of activity, the level of existing data, and the cases where regulation and economic tools were both used.

19.2.1.1 Plans to Reduce Air Pollution

Air pollution in Israel is one of the most severe environmental hazards affecting public health and quality of life. Most of the air pollution is caused by human-made anthropogenic emissions, mainly from energy, transportation, and industrial plants. Scientific studies point to the negative health effects – premature death, lung cancer, asthma, and more (Lavee et al., 2015). In recent years, the Clean Air Law has been enacted, which includes, among other things, a multi-year government plan to improve air quality in Israel (Lavee et al., 2018). I included two case studies from the field of air pollution. The two cases are from the transportation sector.

Green Taxation

After many attempts to impose restrictions on the pollution of older vehicles, including the obligation to install a catalytic converter in old vehicles, an environmental reform was introduced in 2009 in the taxation of private vehicles, which changed the tax rates imposed on the purchase of vehicles to reflect the pollution they create. The share of purchase tax increased from 72 percent to 90 percent. However, after the tax benefit corresponding to the pollution level of each model, the adjusted tax rates ranged from 30 percent to 90 percent. This policy resulted in a reduced price for less polluting vehicles and an increased price for more polluting vehicles. A report by the OECD (2016) recommends that other countries learn from Israel and adopt similar programs for the taxation of vehicles.

Although the rise in fuel prices in Israel has affected pollutant emissions and the motivation to purchase cost-effective vehicles, changes in the average engine size of new vehicles since 2000 indicate that the average engine capacity increased between 2000 and 2008 despite the rise in price, while at the end of 2008 (with the 2009 models entering the market), the average engine volume declined consistently (Figure 19.1). Therefore, it seems likely that the environmental reform rather than the rise in fuel prices is the reason for the change in the composition of the new vehicles being purchased. An analysis I conducted showed that the economic benefit from "green taxation" is estimated at NIS 314 million a year (Lavee 2019).

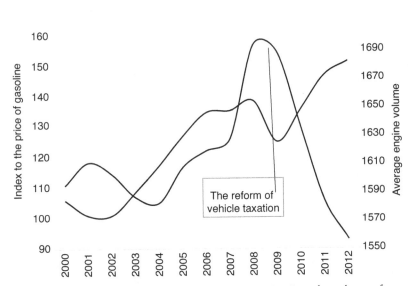

Figure 19.1 The effect of the reform in "green taxation" on the volume of cars purchased in Israel

Implementation Ability and Cost. The tax led to a decrease in average engine capacity, reduced emissions, and a 7 percent reduction in emissions relative to the state of origin

Efficiency. The incremental benefit of the economic tool compared to regulation benefit from "green taxation" is estimated at NIS 314 million a year (Lavee 2019).

Morality. The polluter pays principle – The cost Is imposed on the pollutant according to the degree of pollution emitted by the vehicle.

Harm to Competitiveness and Market Forces: Not relevant to Israel. In Israel, all vehicles are imported and therefore have no effect on competitiveness.

Program for Early Scrapping of Old Cars

The program for early scrapping of old cars was operated in Israel in 2010–2013. The program was based on economic research that examined both its utility and the optimal amount payable to the owners of the vehicle (Lavee and Becker, 2009). The purpose of the plan was to remove vehicles of twenty years or older from the road because they emit twenty times more pollutants than new vehicles. The study was able to predict exactly the number of vehicles that were cut in the first program, and as a result of the success, two additional programs were approved. In the general plan, about 28,000 old cars were scrapped and their owners received a grant of NIS 3,000. As can be seen from Figure 19.2, the percentage of old vehicles has decreased considerably during the years of operation of the grating plans.

Implementation Ability and Cost. The economic incentive led to a massive reduction in the number of old vehicles – 28,000 (the percentage of old vehicles dropped drastically from 9 percent to 2 percent – see Figure 19.2) and a 5.8 percent reduction in air pollution from this group of vehicles.

Efficiency. The incremental benefit of the economic tool compared to regulation benefit is estimated to be $127 million a year, while the cost of the plan amounted to $27 million. NB Ratio of 5.3.

Morality. The polluter pays principle – No, the cost of the program is on the entire population. The cost is on the government budget.

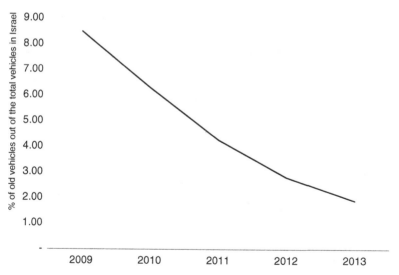

Figure 19.2 The proportion of old passenger cars (20 years) from the total number of cars in the economy, 2009–2013

Harm to Competitiveness and Market Forces. Not relevant to Israel. In Israel, all vehicles are imported and therefore have no effect on competitiveness.

19.2.1.2 Change in Waste Treatment Policy

The waste sector was chosen because over the years extensive use has been made of CAC regulation, and since the beginning of the 2000s, economic tools have commonly been used. Therefore, the effectiveness of each tool can be compared more easily according to the methodology mentioned above.

In Israel, 5.4 million tons of municipal and commercial waste are produced each year, and the annual growth rate is 1.8 percent. In the past, the waste treatment policy was based mainly on its assimilation, but this solution has broad environmental implications – air pollution and greenhouse gas emissions, soil and groundwater pollution, land seizure, public health implications, and more. Ayalon et al. (2001) have shown that the waste sector in Israel accounts for 13 percent of greenhouse gas emissions. In another study, Eshet et al. (2007) showed that the external effects of waste transit stations scattered around the country close to residential areas affect the nearby population up to a range of 2.3–3.3 km from the transit station.

The Transition from Pirate Dumps to Regulated Landfill

At the end of the 1980s, about 96 percent of the municipal waste in Israel was transferred to landfills in pirate dumps, which were located in some 500 waste disposal sites and constituted a severe environmental hazard. The landfills operated without regulation, causing pollution of groundwater, soil and air, and odor hazards, and they constituted a safety risk for flights (Nissim et al., 2005). At the beginning of the 1990s, significant actions were taken to close the landfills, primarily National Outline Plan 16, which set the standards required from waste sites and was supposed to close most of the unplanned landfills in Israel and establish some central and regulated burial sites. The plan aroused the opposition of municipalities whose territory was planned to establish a central burial site (NIMBY). On the other hand, remote municipalities were more concerned about an increase in the cost of transporting waste to these sites (Feinerman et al., 2004). Following the fierce opposition of the local municipalities, the closure of landfills was postponed despite some government decisions on the issue.

To deal with these objections, the state established an economic incentive: "hosting fees" – an ongoing payment to the municipalities in whose area central landfills were created and subsidizing transportation to landfills farther away. The subsidy mechanism for transport costs is set for five years. Initially, 100 percent of the difference between the cost of transportation and the local garbage dump (which was closed) and the cost of transportation to the landfill site was subsidized. Each year the subsidy is reduced by 20 percent so that at the end of the program, the municipality pays the full cost of transportation. At the height of the program, 107 municipalities participated in the program, and all the large garbage dumps (77) operating in Israel close to major cities and more than 250 local dumps were closed. It was the transition to the use of economic incentives that enabled the implementation of this plan. Subsidies of transportation costs to local municipalities increased by $82 million for all closed sites, while the benefit of transfer of the central site in Israel (Hiriya site), responsible for 29 percent of the waste produced by the municipalities in Israel was estimated at $285 million (Ayalon et al., 2006).

Implementation Ability and Cost. The subsidy of transit costs led to the closure of more than 50 percent of the unregulated sites.

Efficiency. In Hiriya, about a quarter of the waste produced in Israel was buried, and therefore, if the benefits of the other landfills are similar, it can be extrapolated, according to the extent of the landfilling, that the benefit of closing all the landfills is about $1 billion a year. A cost–benefit ratio of twelve times.

Morality. The polluter pays principle – Yes in the long run (after five years) the polluter (municipalities) pays for the transportation to the landfill site. In the short run the government partially subsidizes the program.

Harm to Competitiveness and Market Forces. Not relevant, the municipalities do not have a competitive market.

Reduction of Waste Disposal to Landfill

To reduce the rates of buried waste, the 1998 Recycling Regulations stipulate that the municipalities must recycle at least 25 percent of the waste. The transition to recycling was usually accompanied by direct incremental cost, so most of the municipalities did not meet the target and used various excuses to avoid compliance. In the early 2000s, however, the trend changed and its rates declined. One of the main reasons for this was the low cost of landfilling, which did not include the external costs and therefore did not reflect all the costs to society. Studies from the same period indicated the need for a change in the treatment policy of waste (Ayalon et al., 2000). The levy was supposed to reflect the external costs of the landfill, which will force the waste producer to internalize these costs and change the patterns of waste production.

(1) *Landfilling levy*. This was implemented gradually. In 2007 it was $2.5 per ton, and each year it rose so that it was up to $30 per ton in 2016. The gradual increase in the levy in 2012 led to a 5 percent reduction in the amount of waste landfill in 2011. However, the price of landfilling in Israel is still very low compared to the accepted practice in the world and in relation to other waste treatment methods. In comparison, the average landfill levy in European countries in 2016 was about $100 per ton and more (CEWEP, 2016).

(2) *Encouraging separation at the source of different waste streams*: To reach high rates of reduction of landfilling and recycling of waste, it is necessary – in addition to imposing a landfill levy – to separate waste at source (Ayalon and Schechter, 1997). In 2008, the Ministry of the Environment began a program of extensive assistance to the local municipalities to promote the establishment of infrastructures for separating waste at source into two streams (wet and dry). In addition to subsidizing the required investments (purchasing garbage cans and trucks and setting up infrastructures), it was decided to grant each municipality that makes the separation a grant of $800 for each household that separated waste at source. After many years of refusing to collaborate, forty-four municipalities (35 percent of the population) submitted the applications (Lavee et al., 2013). A study that examined the life cycle of solid waste showed that when external costs are priced and internalized in the direct costs of the waste management system, the efficient solution for the waste management system is the separation of the source into two streams (Ayalon et al., 2010). Kan et al. (2010) showed

that the economy loses about $102 million each year as a result of the lack of separation at the source of the various waste streams.

Implementation Ability and Cost. From the beginning of the use of economic tools there is a decrease in landfills.

Efficiency. The economy will gain about $102 million each year as a result of separation at source of the various waste streams.

Morality. The polluter pays principle – Yes in the long run the polluter (municipalities) pays for the source separation. In the short run the government partially subsidizes the program.

Harm to Competitiveness and Market Forces. Not relevant, as the municipalities do not participate in a competitive market.

Recycling Market of Beverage Containers and Deposit Refund Law on Beverage Containers

The importance of the deposit law stems from the significant volume of plastic from the total waste (41 percent), most of which comes from beverage containers. Increasing the volume of recycling of the beverage containers will significantly reduce the volume of landfill. To encourage the public to refinance beverage containers, the Deposit Law on beverage containers was enacted and came into force at the end of 2001. The law imposed the obligation to collect a deposit for beverage containers with a capacity of less than 1.5 liters. In 2010, the law was amended so that it placed the responsibility for collecting the large containers and recycling them on the manufacturers and importers, and set a target for the collection and recycling of these containers (Ayalon et al., 2000a). The objectives of the Deposit Law (from small and large beverage containers) include, among others, raising the level of cleanliness in the public space and reducing the amount of waste buried (Lavee, 2010). Although the purpose of the law is the same for both types of beverage containers, due to pressure from stakeholders, the legislator used two different policy tools to induce consumers to return the containers. For the small containers, an economic tool was used. For the large containers, a regulatory action was used in the form of a voluntary collection target that beverage manufacturers and importers must meet.

The use of two different policy tools allows us to compare the economic incentive with the regulatory obligation. According to the ELA Recycling Corporation, the rate of return of the small beverage containers that require a deposit is about 80 percent. While the voluntary return rate of the large beverage containers is only 55 percent. But if we examine the volume of voluntary recycling, and do not consider containers collected from sorting stations, which also contain other plastic containers thrown into the recycling cages, the rate of voluntary recycling in Israel is estimated at only 11 to 30 percent, similar to other countries (Lavee, 2018). A study conducted in the United States in 2014 found that the rate of return of beverage containers in countries where there is a deposit law is about 80 percent, compared to 23 percent in countries where there is no such law (MSC, 2014). The net benefit per container is $0.03 or $44 million per year for the total containers (Lavee, 2010). Thus, the economic viability of implementing the Deposit Law is clear: the economic tool is the means by which it can bring the economy to optimum levels.

Implementation Ability and Cost. Collecting about 80 percent of the tanks under the deposit refund law, compared to 30 percent under the voluntary collection target.

Efficiency. Benefit of $44 million per year from deposit refund law.

Morality. The polluter pays principle – Since the beverage manufacturers are the polluters and the law is imposed on them, the cost is borne by the polluter.

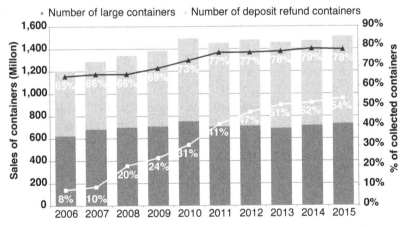

Figure 19.3 Collection of containers with deposit refund and voluntary collection

The black line is the rate of return (%) of deposit refund containers, the white line is the rate of return (%) of large containers.

Harm to Competitiveness and Market Forces. There is some damage to competition, but since the law applies uniformly to all beverage manufacturers, there is no harm to specific manufacturers.

19.2.1.3 Change in Environmental Policy in the Water Sector
From the mid-1990s until the end of the first decade of the 2000s, with the entry into operation of the desalination plants, Israel's water sector suffered from an ongoing shortage of water. In the next section, we will describe one of the actions taken to encourage agriculture to switch from the use of fresh water to effluents.

Economic Incentive Programs to Encourage Agricultural to Switch to Effluents
The irrigation of treated wastewater for agricultural use has additional external benefits: agricultural irrigation water accounts for about 36 percent of the annual recharge of the Coastal Aquifer, and the treated wastewater contributes significantly to the enrichment of the aquifer (Haruvy, 1998). Other positive effects are the reduction in demand for fresh water for agriculture, and therefore the decrease in the need for new drilling or the construction of desalination plants (Friedler, 2001).

The government ministries decided to incentivize the agriculture sector to switch to effluents. To encourage the farmers to switch to effluents, the government used quota policy from the year 1992. The price of water under the quota was subsidized. Any deviation from the quota was accompanied by fines and administrative enforcement (Becker et al., 2002). The policy did not achieve its goals (that is, for 50 percent of the water used for agriculture to be based on treated wastewater – see Figure 19.4), as the farmers did not switch to significant use of treated wastewater (Finkelshtain and Kislev, 1997).

In the early 2000s, the government decided to combine two economic measures simultaneously: (1) To subsidize the reclamation of effluents for agriculture. The state funded 60 percent of the cost of the investment, on condition that the farmers would undertake to waive the quotas for fresh water they received under the previous policy of quotas. (2) To stop subsidizing the price of fresh water for agriculture. This has been implemented since 2006 (Lavee, 2011). Thanks to these government policy measures, the

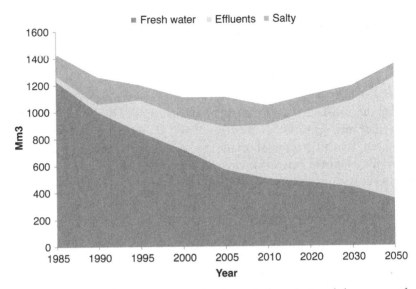

Figure 19.4 Annual water consumption in agriculture in Israel, by source of water, 1985–2050.
Source: Water Authority (2010)

consumption of fresh water in agriculture declined by about 60 percent between 1985 and 2010, and the consumption of treated wastewater in agriculture increased by nearly 900 percent (Figure 19.4). According to the government forecast, by 2025 90 percent of effluents will be in agricultural use and the economic benefit will amount to $212 million a year (Lavee, 2014).

As a result of government policy, Israel is the world leader in the use of treated wastewater – see Figure 19.5.

Implementation Ability and Cost. The consumption of fresh water in agriculture declined by about 60 percent between 1985 and 2010, and the consumption of treated wastewater in agriculture increased by nearly 900 percent.

Efficiency. The economic benefit will amount to $212 million a year.

Morality. The polluter pays principle – Not relevant.

Harm to Competitiveness and Market Forces. No, the cost of treated wastewater is lower than the cost of fresh water even compared to the cost of fresh water before the reform. The government

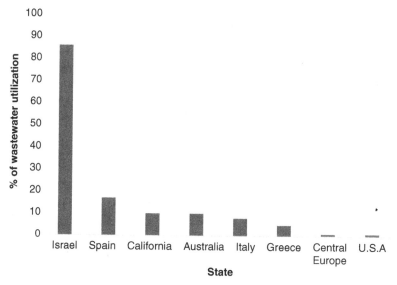

Figure 19.5 Comparison of the percentage of treated wastewater, 2014. Source: Water Authority (2015). Source of California data: Olivieri et al. (2014)

assistance in the transition from fresh water to effluents has reduced the costs for farmers and therefore their competitiveness has increased.

19.3 Comparison Between the Application of Direct Regulation and the Operation of Economic Instruments

In the last two decades, a growing proportion of environmental policy in Israel has been based on the use of economic tools rather than regulation. This change is the result of policymakers' understanding that a market approach should be applied, that positive and negative incentives can motivate individuals to internalize the external and social effects of their actions more effectively (Lavee, 2019).

Table 19.1 presents a comparison between six policy processes in Israel that use tools based on CAC regulation and the use of economic tools. The table contains a reference to policy objectives and a comparison of the results of both approaches, accompanied by quantification in monetary terms where possible. In all six of the cases presented, the use of the economic tool was made after policymakers tried to achieve results through regulation. The increased use of economic tools led to a change in consumption and production patterns, accompanied by external influences, while avoiding harm to the proper functioning of the economy and minimizing costs to the state.

The use of economic tools has led to a reduction in air pollution from transportation due to the "green taxation" policy and the car-scapping plan. The economic incentive for taxation created a link between the level of pollution and the price of the vehicle and led to the internalization of the external influences from traveling in a polluting vehicle, and as a result, a decrease in engine volume. The car-scrapping program helped reduce the number of older vehicles on the roads to a greater extent than the differential vehicle licensing fee for older vehicles, which did not quantify the benefit of taking them off the road.

In the field of waste treatment, the regulation, which prohibited the use of unregulated waste sites, was unsuccessful, and achievement of goals was achieved only when policymakers adopted an economic model that enabled the various elements in the field to adapt to the change and internalize the external influences caused by their actions. Also, the reduction in the amount of waste was effected through the imposition of a landfill levy and subsidization of recycling activity, which increased turnover and reduced the amount of landfill waste.

In the case of the collection of the beverage containers, the collection rate under the regulation requirement is significantly lower, and it takes a long time to reach the collection point. Also, an expensive enforcement system is required by the supervisory body to examine compliance with the recycling targets. On the other hand, the market forces led to about 80 percent of the small containers being recycled due to the economic value attached to each empty container.

The environmental policy in the field of water presented an example where significant change occurred in the use of effluents because of the transition from the use of administrative quotas to the use of economic tools. As a result, Israel became a world leader in the use of effluents.

On the basis of the criteria presented in the chapter on methodology, it seems that economic tools have an advantage both in their ability to motivate processes and achieve the goals of government policy and in meeting the moral principle of the polluter pays. On the other hand, there may be instances of harm to competitiveness and even an increase in the cost of living. Regulation sets environmental objectives. If the

Table 19.1 *Comparison between the use of regulatory tools and the use of economic tools*

Field of activity	Policy target	CAC regulation	Economic tool	Implementation ability and cost gap of the economic tool compared to regulation	Efficiency: the incremental benefit of the economic tool compared to regulation	Morality	Harm to competitiveness and market forces
Air pollution	Reducing air pollution from transportation	Limitation on Pollutant Emissions from Vehicles (1963)	Green taxation – creating a link between the pollution and the cost of the vehicle	The tax led to a decrease in average engine capacity, reduced emissions, and a 7% reduction in emissions relative to the state of origin	314 million NIS	The cost Is imposed on the pollutant according to the degree of pollution emitted by the vehicle	Not relevant to Israel. In Israel, all vehicles are imported and therefore have no effect on competitiveness
	Reducing air pollution and reducing the dangers of old vehicles	The obligation to perform two annual licensing tests	A plan to encourage car scrapping	The economic incentive led to a massive reduction in the number of old vehicles and a 5.8% reduction in air pollution from this group of vehicles.	NB of $100 million; Cost–benefit ratio of 5.3	The cost of the program is on the entire pollution.	Not relevant to Israel. In Israel, all vehicles are imported and therefore have no effect on competitiveness
MSW	Reducing unregulated landfills	Regulations prohibiting the use of landfills	Subsidization of the cost of transferring to organized landfills	The subsidy of transit costs led to the closure of more than 50% of the unregulated sites.	during the period of the plan, benefit of $ 1 billion; Cost–benefit ratio of 12.3	In the long run the polluter (municipalities) pays for the transportation to the landfill site.	Not relevant, the municipalities do not Competitive market.
	Reduction of waste transferred for landfilling	Regulations of Recycling 1998	Waste disposal levy Encouraging source separation	From the beginning of the use of economic tools, there is a decrease in landfills.	Savings of $102 million per year from source separation	In the long run the polluter (municipalities) pays for the source separation.	Not relevant, the municipalities do not **Competitive market.

Table 19.1 (*cont.*)

Field of activity	Policy target	CAC regulation	Economic tool	Implementation ability and cost gap of the economic tool compared to regulation	Efficiency: the incremental benefit of the economic tool compared to regulation	Morality	Harm to competitiveness and market forces
	Increasing public cleanliness and reducing landfilling	A voluntary collection destination for large drink containers	Deposit on small beverage containers	Collecting about 80% of the tanks under the deposit, compared to 30% under the voluntary collection target	Benefit of $44 million per year from deposit refund law	Since the beverage manufacturers are the polluters and the law is imposed on them, the cost is borne by the polluter.	Since the law applies uniformly to all beverage manufacturers, there is no harm to specific manufacturers.
Water	Reducing the use of fresh water and encouraging the transfer of effluents	Allowance of quantities of fresh water	Subsidize the reclamation of effluents for agriculture, stop subsidizing the price of fresh water for agriculture	The consumption of fresh water in agriculture declined by about 60%, and the consumption of treated wastewater in agriculture increased by 900%	The economic benefit will amount to $212 million a year	Not relevant	No, the cost of treated wastewater is lower than the cost of fresh water.

pollutant meets the same goals, he is not required to pay for the pollution he produces (i.e., the remaining pollution permitted under the same regulation). On the other hand, the economic tools operate according to the principle of the polluter pays, and therefore a manufacturer that meets optimal environmental objectives will continue to pay for the balance of the pollutant it creates (the assumption is that even at optimum, pollution will be created). This situation, even if it is moral and correct, still generates incremental cost (beyond the cost of production and the cost of investment by means of reducing pollution). The cost of the additive both damages the manufacturer's competitiveness and increases the cost of living because the producer will pass on part of the cost to the consumer. If the cost falls on all producers in an equal and symmetrical manner, harmful competitiveness is not expected. However, in many cases, the local producer deals with manufacturers in other countries (whether he is an exporter or provides products to the local market, but there are imports from other countries).

In addition, in any case, the consumer is expected to see an increase in the price of the product. Although the increase in price is correct in terms of economic optimality, there are sometimes additional considerations that the government must consider. Such as harm to weak population and inequality. In order to deal with such broad effects, the government must examine all the implications of the policy and address those undesirable effects. These issues are beyond the scope of analysis in this chapter, but they deserve further examination.

19.4 Summary

Economic tools are assuming an important role in environmental policy as effective instruments for managing a wide range of environmental issues. In the past, the use of economic tools was a tiny part of environmental policy tools, as opposed to the widespread use of direct regulation in Israel. In recent years, Israel has undergone significant developments and is at the beginning of a revolution in the implementation of an extensive public environmental policy, which relates to the external influences of actions that harm the environment and the quality of life of the residents. Israel is working to expand the use of environmental taxes and other economic incentives, in part because of the process of joining the OECD.

Behind these developments was a change in approach, not only by the Ministry of the Environment but also by other government ministries, such as the Ministry of Finance, the water authority, and the Ministry of Transportation. Direct regulation and economic tools require enforcement, since both rely on traditional enforcement mechanisms. In the test, it appears that economic tools are more conducive to internalization of the external effects of the market than direct regulation. The reason for the success of the economic tools is probably because an economic system based on a market economy adopts economic tools more easily. Also, the transition to economic tools and the reduction in direct regulation is in line with the process of deregulation that the Israeli government has adopted in recent years.

References

Ayalon, A., and Schechter M. (1997). *Economic Incentives in Solid Urban Waste Policy: Research Report for 1995–1996.* Technion City, Haifa: Samuel Neaman Institute. [In Hebrew]

Ayalon, O., Avnimelech Y., and Shechter M. (2000). Application of a Comparative Multidimensional Life Cycle Analysis in Solid Waste Managemen Policy: The Case of Soft Drink Containers. *Environmental Science & Policy,* 3, 135–144.

(2001). Solid Waste Treatment as a High-Priority and Low-Cost Alternative for Greenhouse Gas Mitigation. *Environmental Management,* 27(5), 697–704.

Ayalon, O., Becker, N., and Shani, E. (2006). Economic Aspects of the Rehabilitation of the Hiriya Landfill. *Waste Management,* 26(11), 1313–1323.

Ayalon, A., Kun, E., and Segev, T. (2010). *Life Cycle Analysis of Solid Urban Waste Treatment.* Research 7321 for the Ministry of the Environment. Technion City, Haifa.

Bailey, I. (2007). Market Environmentalism: New Environmental Policy Instruments, and Climate Policy in the United Kingdom and Germany. *Annals of the Association of American Geographers,* 97 (3), 530–550.

Bank of Israel (2009). *Environmental Policy Issues, 2008 Report.* www .bankisrael.gov.il/deptdata/mehkar/doch09/eng/pe_9.pdf]]g.

Becker, N., and Lavee, D. (2002). The Effect and Reform of Water Pricing: The Israeli Experience. *International journal of Water Resource Development,* 18(2), 353–366.

CEWEP (2016). Landfill Tax & Bans: Confederation of European Waste-to-Energy Plants. http://cewep.eu/media/cewep.eu/org/med_557/1529_2016–10-10_cewep-landfill_inctaxesbans.pdf.

Eshet, T., Baron, M. G., Shechter, M., and Ayalon O. (2007). Measuring Externalities of Waste Transfer Stations in Israel Using Hedonic Pricing. *Waste Management*, 27(5), 614–625.

EU (2016). *EU Energy in Figures Statistical Pocketbook*. Luxembourg: Publications Office of the European Union. https://ec.europa.eu/energy/sites/ener/files/documents/pocketbook_energy-2016_web-final_final.pdf.

Feinerman, E., Finkelshtain, I., and Kan, I. (2004). On a Political Solution to the NIMBY Conflict. *The American Economic Review*, 94(1), 369–381.

Finkelshtain, I., and Kislev, Y. (1997). Prices versus Quantities: The Political Perspective. *Journal of Political Economy*, 105(1), 83–100.

Friedler E. (2001). Water Reuse: An Integral Part of Water Resources Management: Israel as a Case Study. *Water Policy*, 3, 29–39.

Haruvy, N. (1998). Wastewater Reuse: Regional and Economic Considerations, Resources. *Conservation and Recycling*, 23, 57–66.

Hepburn, C. (2006). Regulation by Prices, Quantities or Both: A Review of Instrument Choice. *Oxford Review of Economic Policy*, 22(2), 226–247.

Kan, I., Ayalon, O., and Federman, R. (2010). On the Efficiency of Composting Organic Wastes. *Agricultural Economics*, 41(2), 151–163.

Karsin, A. (2009). *Effective Implementation of Environmental Policy: Encouraging Compliance and Streamlining Enforcement*. Jerusalem: Jerusalem Institute for Israel Studies, Center for Environmental Policy. [In Hebrew]

Lavee, D. (2010). A Cost–Benefit Analysis of a Deposit-Refund Program for Beverage containers in Israel. *Waste Management*, 30(2), 338–345.

(2011). A Cost–Benefit Analysis of Alternative Wastewater Treatment Standards: A Case Study in Israel. *Water and Environment Journal*, 25 (4), 504–512.

(2014). Is the Upgrading of Wastewater Treatment Facilities to Meet More Stringent Standards Economically Justified? The Case of Israel. *Water Resources*, 41(5), 564–573.

Lavee, D., and Becker N. (2009). A Cost–Benefit Analysis of Accelerated Vehicle Retirement. *Journal of Environmental Planning and Management*, 52(6), 777–795.

Lavee, D., and Joseph-Ezra, H. (2015). The Development and Use of Economic Instruments in Environmental Policy: The Case of Israel. *Journal of Environmental Assessment Policy and Management*, 17(2), 1–23.

Lavee, D., and Menachem, O. (2018). Identifying Policy Measures for Reducing Expected Air Pollution Across Israel and Analyzing Their Expected Effects. *Journal of Environmental Assessment Policy and Management*, 20(1), 1850001.

Lavee, D., and Nardiya, S. (2013). A Cost Evaluation Method for Transferring Municipalities to Solid Waste Source-Separated System. *Waste Management*, 33(5), 1064–1072.

Lavee, D., Moshe, A., Menachem, O., Hubner, V., and Tenanzap, K. (2015). Analyzing Current and Expected Air Quality and Pollutant Emissions Across Israel. *Water, Air, & Soil Pollution*, 226(12), Article number 416.

MSC (2014). *An Analysis of the Effects of Passage of S.379 on Litter, Recycling, Employment, and State and Local Financing.* Boston: MSC (Massachusetts Siera Club).

Nissim, I., Shohat T., and Inbar Y. (2005). From Dumping to Sanitary Landfills: Solid Waste Management in Israel. *Waste Management*, 25 (3), 323–327.

OECD (2016). Car Purchase Tax: Green Tax Reform in Israel. Working Party on Integrating Environmental and Economic Policies, June 30, 2016.

Olivieri, A., Seto, E., Cooper, R., Cahn, M., Colford, J., Crook, J., Debroux, J., Mandrell, R., Suslow, T., Tchobanoglous, G., Hultquist, R., Spath, D., and Mosher, J. (2014). Risk-Based Review of California's Water-Recycling Criteria for Agricultural Irrigation. *Journal of Environmental Engineering*, 140(6). DOI: 10.1061/(ASCE)EE.1943-7870.0000833. http://ucanr.edu/datastoreFiles/234–2791.pdf.

Seroa Da Motta, R., Alban T., Saade Hazin L., Feres J. G., Nauges X. C., and Saade, Hazin A., eds. (2004). *Economic Instruments for Water Management: The Cases of France, Mexico, and Brazil.* Cheltenham, UK: Edward Elgar Publishing.

Water Authority (2010). *National Long-Term Master Plan for the Water Sector, Policy Paper.* 2nd edn. Tel Aviv: Water Authority, Planning Division. [Hebrew]

(2015). *Government Water and Sewage Municipality, Activity Report for 2014.* Tel Aviv: Water Authority, Planning Division.

Zito, A. R., Jordan, A. J., and Wurzelx, R. (2011). Escaping the Regulatory State? Issues of Policy Instruments in the EU Environmental Policy Context. Paper prepared for the Sixth ECPR Annual Conference in Reykavik, Iceland 2011.

Index